Gleim®

CPA REVIEW

FAR | Financial Accounting and Reporting

2024 EDITION

by

Irvin N. Gleim, Ph.D., CPA, CIA, CMA, CFM

and

Michael Kustanovich, CPA

with the assistance of
Grady M. Irwin, J.D.

Gleim Publications, Inc.
PO Box 12848
Gainesville, Florida 32604
(800) 87-GLEIM or (800) 874-5346
(352) 375-0772
www.gleim.com/cpa
CPA@gleim.com

For updates to this 2024 edition of
CPA Review: Financial Accounting and Reporting

Go To: www.gleim.com/CPAupdate

Or: Email update@gleim.com with **CPA FAR 2024** in the subject line. You will receive our current update as a reply.

Updates are available until the next edition is published.

ISSN: 1547-8025

ISBN: 978-1-61854-607-4   *CPA Review: Auditing and Attestation*
ISBN: 978-1-61854-605-0   *CPA Review: Financial Accounting and Reporting*
ISBN: 978-1-61854-606-7   *CPA Review: Taxation and Regulation*
ISBN: 978-1-61854-608-1   *CPA Review: Business Analysis and Reporting*
ISBN: 978-1-61854-610-4   *CPA Review: Information Systems and Controls*
ISBN: 978-1-61854-609-8   *CPA Review: Tax Compliance and Planning*
ISBN: 978-1-61854-611-1   *CPA Exam Guide: A System for Success*

First Printing: June 2023

Acknowledgments

Material from *Uniform CPA Examination, Selected Questions and Unofficial Answers*, Copyright © 1974-2023 by the American Institute of Certified Public Accountants, Inc., is reprinted and/or adapted with permission. Visit the AICPA's website at www.aicpa.org for more information.

The authors are indebted to the Institute of Certified Management Accountants for permission to use problem materials from past CMA Examinations. Questions and unofficial answers from the Certified Management Accountant Examinations, copyright by the Institute of Certified Management Accountants, are reprinted and/or adapted with permission.

The authors are grateful for permission to reproduce Certified Internal Auditor Examination Questions, Copyright © 1991-2023 by The Institute of Internal Auditors, Inc.

About the Authors

Irvin N. Gleim, who authored the first edition of the Gleim CPA Review over 40 years ago, was Professor Emeritus in the Fisher School of Accounting at the University of Florida and a member of the American Accounting Association, Academy of Legal Studies in Business, American Institute of Certified Public Accountants, Association of Government Accountants, Florida Institute of Certified Public Accountants, The Institute of Internal Auditors, and the Institute of Management Accountants. The late Dr. Gleim published articles in the *Journal of Accountancy*, *The Accounting Review*, and the *American Business Law Journal* and authored numerous accounting books, aviation books, and CPE courses.

Michael Kustanovich, M.A., CPA, is a Clinical Assistant Professor in the Department of Accountancy at the University of Illinois at Urbana-Champaign. He teaches advanced financial accounting courses at both the undergraduate and graduate levels, and he is the instructor of the CPA Exam Review Course there. He is an editor of accounting books, the author of many CPE courses, and a member of the American Accounting Association. Previously, Mr. Kustanovich worked in the assurance departments of KPMG and PwC.

A Personal Thanks

This edition would not have been possible without the extraordinary effort and dedication of Sophia Arnold, Jacob Bennett, Julie Cutlip, Fernanda Martinez, Bryce Owen, Bobbie Stanley, Joanne Strong, Elmer Tucker, Ryan Van Tress, and Lau Wood, who typed the entire manuscript and all revisions and drafted and laid out the diagrams, illustrations, and cover for this book.

We also appreciate the production and editorial assistance of Brianna Barnett, Rayne Chance, Abigail Curtis, Doug Green, Jessica Hatker, Sonora Hospital-Medina, David Sox, and Alyssa Thomas.

We are also thankful for the critical reading assistance of Ryan Guard, Paul Harris, Jess Joyson, Michael Nagarathinam, Andrew Schreiber, Valerie Wendt, and Sydney White.

We are also grateful for the video production expertise of Gary Brook, Philip Brubaker, and Matthew Church, who helped produce and edit our Gleim Instruct Video Series.

Finally, we appreciate the encouragement, support, and tolerance of our families throughout this project.

Reviewers and Contributors

Garrett W. Gleim, CPA, CIA, CGMA, leads production of the Gleim CPA, CMA, CIA, and EA exam review systems. He is a member of the American Institute of Certified Public Accountants and the Florida Institute of Certified Public Accountants and holds a Bachelor of Science in Economics with a Concentration in Accounting from The Wharton School, University of Pennsylvania. Mr. Gleim is coauthor of numerous accounting and aviation books and the inventor of multiple patents with educational applications. He is also an avid pilot who holds a commercial pilot rating and is a flight instructor. In addition, as an active supporter of the local business community, Mr. Gleim serves as an advisor to several start-ups with ties to the University of Florida.

Amy Ford, CPA, CMA, is a senior instructor of accounting at Western Illinois University. She has more than 15 years' experience teaching business and accounting students with a specialty in managerial and cost accounting. Prior to teaching, she worked in public accounting. Professor Ford is one of the CPA Gleim Instruct lecturers.

Grady M. Irwin, J.D., is a graduate of the University of Florida College of Law, and he has taught in the University of Florida College of Business. Mr. Irwin provided substantial editorial assistance throughout the project.

LouAnn M. Lutter, M.S. Acc., CPA, received a Master of Science in Accounting from the University of Colorado, Boulder. Previously, she was an Accounting Manager in Corporate Accounting and Shared Business Services at Caesars Entertainment. Ms. Lutter provided substantial editorial assistance throughout the project.

Dwayne McSwain, Ph.D., CPA, is a professor of accounting at Appalachian State University. He received his Ph.D. in accounting from the University of Texas at Arlington. He worked in public accounting for 15 years and has been teaching accounting for 25 years. Dr. McSwain provided substantial editorial assistance throughout the project.

Mark S. Modas, M.S.T., CPA, holds a Bachelor of Arts in Accounting from Florida Atlantic University and a Master of Science in Taxation from Nova Southeastern University. He is currently an Assistant Professor of Accounting at Santa Fe College and was formerly the head of the Internal Audit department of Perry Ellis International and the Director of Accounting and Financial Reporting for the School Board of Broward County, Florida. Additionally, he worked as the corporate tax compliance supervisor for Ryder Systems, Inc., and has worked as a tax practitioner for more than 25 years. Mr. Modas provided substantial editorial assistance throughout the project.

Gleim

Accounting Titles from Gleim Publications

CPA Review:

- Auditing and Attestation (AUD)
- Financial Accounting and Reporting (FAR)
- Taxation and Regulation (REG)
- Business Analysis and Reporting (BAR)
- Information Systems and Controls (ISC)
- Tax Compliance and Planning (TCP)

CIA Review:

- Part 1: Essentials of Internal Auditing
- Part 2: Practice of Internal Auditing
- Part 3: Business Knowledge for Internal Auditing
- CIA Challenge Exam

CMA Review:

- Part 1: Financial Planning, Performance, and Analytics
- Part 2: Strategic Financial Management

EA Review:

- Part 1: Individuals
- Part 2: Businesses
- Part 3: Representation, Practices and Procedures

Exam Questions and Explanations (EQE) Series:

- Auditing & Systems
- Business Law & Legal Studies
- Cost/Managerial Accounting
- Federal Tax
- Financial Accounting

Gleim also publishes aviation training materials. Go to www.GleimAviation.com for a complete listing of our aviation titles.

TABLE OF CONTENTS

DETAILED TABLE OF CONTENTS

A Message from Our Authors

Welcome to the 2024 Edition of Gleim CPA Review! The purpose of this book is to facilitate your preparation to pass the Financial Accounting and Reporting (FAR) section of the CPA Exam.

The CPA Exam is continuously changed in order to maintain its relevance and prestige in the world of accounting. As technology develops, accountants and auditors face new and increasingly complex challenges, which are reflected in the AICPA Blueprints. Our team of accounting experts ensures our materials are always up-to-date, so regardless of when you're preparing for the CPA Exam with Gleim, you have everything you need to succeed.

Our goal is to provide a comprehensive, effective, affordable, and easy-to-use study program. Our course

- ✓ Explains how to maximize your score through learning strategies and exam-taking techniques.

- ✓ Outlines all of the content topics described in the AICPA FAR Blueprint and tested on the FAR section of the exam in 15 easy-to-use study units.

- ✓ Presents multiple-choice questions taken or modeled from CPA Examinations to prepare you for the types of questions you will find on your CPA Exam.

  - In our book, the answer explanations are presented to the immediate right of each multiple-choice question for your convenience. Use a piece of paper to cover our detailed explanations as you answer the question and then review all answer choices to learn why the correct one is correct and why the other choices are incorrect.

  - You also should practice answering these questions through our online platform, which mimics Prometric's user interface, so you are comfortable answering questions online like you will do on test day. Our adaptive course will focus and target your weak areas.

The outline format, spacing, and question and answer formats in this book are designed to increase readability, learning, understanding, and success on the CPA Exam. Our most successful candidates use the Gleim Premium CPA Review System, which includes Gleim Instruct videos; our Access Until You Pass Guarantee; our innovative SmartAdapt technology; expertly authored books; the largest test bank of multiple-choice questions and simulations; audio lectures; flashcards; and the support of our team of accounting experts.

Since the release of our first CPA Review book in 1974, Gleim has helped candidates pass more than 1 million CPA Exams with our study materials and recommended learning techniques. With our cutting-edge adaptive technology creating personalized learning paths, we will help candidates pass millions more. Candidates' success is based on the Gleim system of teaching not only the topics tested, but also what you can expect on exam day. We want you to feel confident and in control when you sit for the exam.

We want your feedback immediately after you take the exam and receive your exam score. Please go to www.gleim.com/feedbackFAR to share suggestions on how we can improve this edition. The CPA Exam is a **nondisclosed** exam, which means you must maintain the confidentiality of the exam by not divulging the nature or content of any CPA question or answer under any circumstances. We ask only for information about our materials and any improvements that can be made regarding topics that need to be added or expanded or need more emphasis. Our approach has AICPA approval.

Good Luck on the Exam,

Irvin N. Gleim
Michael Kustanovich

Optimizing Your Financial Accounting and Reporting Score

Uniform CPA Examination

CPA Exam Section	Auditing and Attestation	Financial Accounting and Reporting	Taxation and Regulation	Business Analysis and Reporting	Information Systems and Controls	Tax Compliance and Planning
Acronym	AUD	**FAR**	REG	BAR	ISC	TCP
Exam Length	4 hours	**4 hours**	4 hours	4 hours	4 hours	4 hours
Testlet 1: Multiple-Choice	39 questions	**25 questions**	36 questions	25 questions	41 questions	34 questions
Testlet 2: Multiple-Choice	39 questions	**25 questions**	36 questions	25 questions	41 questions	34 questions
Testlet 3: Task-Based Simulations	2 tasks	**2 tasks**	2 tasks	2 tasks	1 task	2 tasks
Standardized Break	Clock stops for 15 minutes					
Testlet 4: Task-Based Simulations	3 tasks	**3 tasks**	3 tasks	3 tasks	3 tasks	3 tasks
Testlet 5: Task-Based Simulations	2 tasks	**2 tasks**	3 tasks	2 tasks	2 tasks	2 tasks

Passing the CPA Exam is a serious undertaking. Begin by becoming an expert in the content, formatting, and functionality of the FAR exam before you take it. The objective is no surprises on exam day. Also, you will save time and money, decrease frustration, and increase your probability of success by learning all you can about how to prepare for and take FAR.

2024 CPA Exam Changes

Effective January 2024, the CPA Exam will undergo the most significant exam change since becoming a computerized exam in 2004. The new exam–CPA Evolution–will consist of three Core exams: Auditing and Attestation (AUD), Financial Accounting and Reporting (FAR), and Taxation and Regulation (REG). Every exam candidate must take and pass the three core exams. Candidates will choose one of three Discipline exams as their fourth required exam section: Business Analysis and Reporting (BAR), Information Systems and Controls (ISC), or Tax Compliance and Planning (TCP).

If you are studying with this edition, you are more than likely preparing to take your exams after December 2023. If you have already started your exam journey and find yourself "transitioning" to the new exam, NASBA has published a CPA Evolution Transition Policy that will allow candidates to retain credit for exam sections passed before the new exam launches. CPA Exam candidates who have already passed the AUD, FAR, or REG sections when CPA Evolution launches will be given credit for the corresponding AUD, FAR, or REG Core sections. Candidates who have already passed the BEC section will be given credit for the Discipline exam.

All of this is good news for current exam candidates! But it is highly recommended that you have an exam plan in place before you start scheduling your exams. Knowing how exam credit will transition to the new exam, you should be very strategic in planning which order to sit for your exams.

Review *CPA Exam Guide: A System for Success* at www.gleim.com/PassCPA for a complete explanation of how to prepare for and take each section of the CPA Exam. This free guide includes all of the basic information, test-taking techniques, and time management strategies you need.

More exam tactics and information, as well as breaking news and updates from the AICPA and NASBA, are available in our Resource Center at www.gleim.com/CPAresources and on our blog at www.gleim.com/CPAblog. Follow us on all your favorite social media networks for blog updates and other critical information.

CPA Exam Pass Rates

The implication of these pass rates for you as a CPA candidate is that you have to be, on average, in the top 50% of all candidates to pass. The major difference between CPA candidates who pass and those who do not is their preparation program. You have access to the best CPA review material; it is up to you to use it. Even if you are enrolled in a review course that uses other materials, you will benefit with the Gleim Premium CPA Review System.

Percentage of Candidates			
	2020	2021	2022*
AUD	53	48	48
BEC	66	62	60
FAR	50	45	45
REG	62	60	61

*2022 scores for Q1-Q3 only

Gleim Premium CPA Review with SmartAdapt

Gleim Premium CPA Review features the most comprehensive coverage of exam content and employs the most efficient learning techniques to help you study smarter and more effectively. The Gleim Premium CPA Review System is powered by SmartAdapt technology, an innovative platform that continually zeros in on areas you should focus on when you move through the following steps for optimized CPA review:

Step 1:

Complete a diagnostic exam. Your results set a baseline that our SmartAdapt technology will use to create a custom learning track.

Step 2:

Solidify your knowledge by reading the suggested digital text material or watching the suggested Gleim Instruct video(s).

Step 3:

Focus on weak areas and perfect your question-answering techniques by taking the adaptive quizzes and simulations that SmartAdapt directs you to.

Final Review:

After completing all study units, take the first Mock Exam. Then, SmartAdapt will walk you through a Final Review based on your results. Finally, a few days before your exam date, take the second Mock Exam so you feel confident that you are ready to pass.

To facilitate your studies, the Gleim Premium CPA Review System uses the most comprehensive test bank of exam-quality CPA questions on the market. Our system's content and presentation are the most realistic representation of the whole exam environment so you feel completely at ease on test day.

Learning from Your Mistakes

One of the main building blocks of the Gleim studying system is that learning from questions you answer incorrectly is very important. Each question you answer incorrectly is an **opportunity** to avoid missing actual test questions on your CPA Exam. Thus, you should carefully study the answer explanations provided so you understand why the original answer you chose is wrong as well as why the correct answer indicated is correct. This learning technique is the difference between passing and failing for many CPA candidates.

The Gleim Premium CPA Review System has built-in functionality for this step. After each quiz and simulation you complete, the Gleim system directs you to study why you answered questions incorrectly so you can learn how to avoid making the same errors in the future. Reasons for answering questions incorrectly include

- ⊘ Misreading the requirement (stem)
- ⊘ Not understanding what is required
- ⊘ Making a math error
- ⊘ Applying the wrong rule or concept
- ⊘ Being distracted by one or more of the answers
- ⊘ Incorrectly eliminating answers from consideration
- ⊘ Not having any knowledge of the topic tested
- ⊘ Using a poor educated-guessing strategy

Subject Matter for Financial Accounting and Reporting

Below, we have provided the AICPA's major content areas from the Blueprint for Financial Accounting and Reporting (FAR). The averaged percentage of coverage for each topic is indicated.

> I.   (35%) Financial Reporting
> II. (35%) Select Balance Sheet Accounts
> III. (30%) Select Transactions

Appendix A contains the AICPA's Blueprint for FAR with cross-references to the subunits in our materials where topics are covered. Remember that we have studied and restudied the Blueprint and explain the subject matter thoroughly in our CPA Review. Accordingly, you do not need to spend time with Appendix A. Rather, it should give you confidence that Gleim CPA Review is the best review available to help you PASS the CPA Exam.

Candidates are expected to demonstrate knowledge and skills related to the financial accounting and reporting frameworks used by business entities (public and nonpublic), not-for-profit entities, and state and local government entities. The FAR section will test standards and regulations issued by the Financial Accounting Standards Board (FASB), the U.S. Securities and Exchange Commission (U.S. SEC), the American Institute of Certified Public Accountants (AICPA), and the Governmental Accounting Standards Board (GASB).

To demonstrate the knowledge and skills associated with financial accounting and reporting, the following general topics will be tested:

- FASB

  - Accounting Standards Codification

    - General-purpose financial statements applicable to for-profit entities, not-for-profit entities, and employee benefit plans

    - Disclosures specific to public companies

    - Select financial statement accounts: for-profit and not-for-profit

    - Select transactions: for-profit and not-for-profit

- U.S. SEC

  - Interim, annual, and periodic filing requirements for U.S. registrants

- AICPA Codification of Statements on Auditing Standards

  - Financial statements prepared under special purpose frameworks

- GASB

  - Conceptual framework
  - Requirements for state and local governments

Which Laws, Rules, and Pronouncements Are Tested?

The following is the AICPA's pronouncement policy:

Changes in accounting and auditing pronouncements are eligible to be tested on the Uniform CPA Examination in the later of: (1) the first calendar quarter beginning after the pronouncement's earliest mandatory effective date, regardless of entity type or (2) the first calendar quarter beginning six (6) months after the pronouncement's issuance date.

Changes in the Internal Revenue Code, and federal taxation regulations are eligible to be tested in the calendar quarter beginning six (6) months after the change's effective date or enactment date, whichever is later.

Changes in federal laws outside the area of federal taxation are eligible to be tested in the calendar quarter beginning six (6) months after their effective date.

Changes in uniform acts are eligible to be tested in the calendar quarter beginning one (1) year after their adoption by a simple majority of the jurisdictions.

For all other subjects covered in the Uniform CPA Examination, changes are eligible to be tested in the later of: (1) the first calendar quarter beginning after the earliest mandatory effective date, regardless of entity type or (2) six (6) months after the issuance date.

Once a change becomes eligible for testing in the Uniform CPA Examination, previous content impacted by the change is removed. [This simply means that once a new pronouncement is testable, you will no longer be tested on the old pronouncement.]

AICPA's Nondisclosure Agreement

As part of the AICPA's nondisclosure policy and to prove each candidate's willingness to adhere to this policy, a confidentiality and break policy statement must be accepted by each candidate during the introductory screens at the beginning of each exam. Nonacceptance of this policy means the exam will be terminated and the test fees will be forfeited.

The AICPA's nondisclosure policy contains three main tenets. By agreeing to it, you are stating that

- You agree to maintain the confidentiality of the Uniform CPA Exam.

- You will not divulge or remove unauthorized information from outside of the testing space, nor will you refer to any unauthorized materials during testing.

- You understand the liability and repercussions of violating any terms of the agreement.

You can find the nondisclosure policy in its entirety on the AICPA's website at www.aicpa-cima.com/news/download/uniform-cpa-examination-conduct-and-non-disclosure-agreement.

Gleim CPA Review Essentials

Gleim CPA Review has the following features to make studying easier:

Backgrounds

In certain instances, we have provided historical background or supplemental information. This information is intended to illuminate the topic under discussion and is set off in bordered boxes with shaded headings. This material does not need to be memorized for the exam.

Background 1-1   Temporary vs. Permanent Accounts
The accounts presented on the balance sheet are real or permanent accounts. They report an entity's resources and financing elements that exist from period to period. The accounts presented on the income statement are nominal or temporary accounts. They are reported for a period of time, closed at the end of the period, and reopened at the beginning of the next period with zero balances.

Examples

Illustrative examples, both hypothetical and those drawn from actual events, are set off in shaded, bordered boxes.

Example 2-17   Output Method -- Practical Expedient
A law firm enters into a contract to provide consulting services to a customer for a 1-year period for a fixed amount per hour of service provided. Because the customer simultaneously receives and consumes the benefits provided by the law firm's performance as it performs, revenue is recognized over time. Under the practical expedient, the law firm may recognize revenue that it has a right to bill to the customer.

Gleim Success Tips

These tips supplement the core exam material by suggesting how certain topics might be presented on the exam or how you should prepare for an issue.

Success Tip

The AICPA has previously tested candidates on their knowledge of what the classification of current liabilities entails. Potentially, candidates could see a list of fixed accounts with a question on the amount of current liabilities of the firm.

Detailed Table of Contents

This information at the beginning of the book is a complete listing of all study units and subunits in this Gleim CPA Review program. Use this list as a study aid to mark off your progress and to provide jumping-off points for review.

Blueprint with Gleim Cross-References

Appendix A contains a reprint of the AICPA Blueprint for FAR along with cross-references to the corresponding Gleim study units.

Rapid Review

We have also provided additional study materials to supplement the Knowledge Transfer Outlines in the digital Gleim CPA Review Course. The Rapid Reviews, for example, are consolidated documents providing an overview of the key points of each subunit that serve as the foundation for learning. As part of your review, you should make sure that you understand each of them.

Time Budgeting and Question-Answering Techniques for FAR

To begin the exam, you will enter your Launch Code on the Welcome screen. If you do not enter the correct code within 5 minutes of the screen appearing, the exam session will end.

Next, you will have an additional 5 minutes to view a brief exam introduction containing two screens: the nondisclosure policy and a section information screen. Accept the policy and then review the information screen, but be sure to click the Begin Exam button on the bottom right of the screen within the allotted 5 minutes. If you fail to do so, the exam will be terminated and you will not have the option to restart your exam.

These 10 minutes, along with the 5 minutes you may spend on a post-exam survey, are not included in the 240 minutes of exam time.

Once you complete the introductory screens and begin your exam, expect two testlets of 25 multiple-choice questions (MCQs) each and three testlets of Task-Based Simulations (TBSs) (two with 2 TBSs each and one with 3 TBSs). You will have 240 minutes to complete the five testlets.

- **Budget your time so you can finish before time expires.**

  - Here is our suggested time allocation for Financial Accounting and Reporting:

Testlet	Minutes	Start Time	
Testlet 1 (MCQ)	37*	4 hours	00 minutes
Testlet 2 (MCQ)	37*	3 hours	23 minutes
Testlet 3 (TBS)	40	2 hours	46 minutes
Break	15	Clock stops	
Testlet 4 (TBS)	60	2 hours	06 minutes
Testlet 5 (TBS)	40	1 hour	06 minutes
**Extra time	26	0 hours	26 minutes

  - Before beginning your first MCQ testlet, prepare a Gleim Time Management plan as recommended in *CPA Exam Guide: A System for Success*.

  - As you work through the individual questions, monitor your time. In FAR, we suggest 37 minutes (1.25 minutes per question) for each testlet of 25 MCQs. If you answer five items in 7 minutes, you are fine, but if you spend 10 minutes on five items, you need to speed up. In the TBS testlets, spend no more than 20 minutes on each TBS.

* Rounded down.

**Remember to allocate your budgeted extra time, as needed, to each testlet. Your goal is to answer all of the items and achieve the maximum score possible. As you practice answering TBSs in the Gleim Premium CPA Review System, you will be practicing your time management.

- **Answer the questions in consecutive order.**

  - Do not agonize over any one question. **Stay within your time budget.**

  - Never leave an MCQ unanswered. Your score is based on the number of correct responses. You will not be penalized for answering incorrectly. If you are unsure about a question,

    - Make an educated guess.

    - Flag it for review by clicking on the flag icon at the bottom of the screen.

    - Return to it before you submit the testlet as time allows. Remember, once you have selected the Submit Testlet option, you will no longer be able to review or change any answers in the completed testlet.

- **Read the question carefully to discover exactly what is being asked.**

  - Ignore the answer choices so they do not affect your precise reading of the question.

  - Focusing on what is required allows you to

    - Reject extraneous information

    - Concentrate on relevant facts

    - Proceed directly to determining the best answer

  - **Careful!** The requirement may be an exception that features negative words.

  - Decide the correct answer before looking at the answer choices.

- **Read the answer choices, paying attention to small details.**

  - Even if an answer choice appears to be correct, do not skip the remaining choices. Each choice requires consideration because you are looking for the best answer provided.

  - **Only one answer option is the best.** In the MCQs, four answer choices are presented, and you know one of them is correct. The remaining choices are distractors and are meant to appear correct at first glance. Eliminate them as quickly as you can.

  - Treat each answer choice like a true/false question as you analyze it.

  - In computational MCQs, the distractor answers are carefully calculated to be the result of common mistakes. Be careful, and double-check your computations if time permits.

    - There will be a mix of conceptual and calculation questions. When you take the exam, it may appear that more of the questions are calculation-type because they take longer and are more difficult.

- **Click on the best answer.**

  - You have a 25% chance of answering correctly by guessing blindly, but you can improve your odds with an educated guess.

  - For many MCQs, you can **eliminate two answer choices with minimal effort** and increase your educated guess to a 50/50 proposition.

    - Rule out answers that you think are incorrect.

    - Speculate what the AICPA is looking for and/or why the question is being asked.

    - Select the best answer or guess between equally appealing answers. Your first guess is usually the most intuitive.

- **Do not click the Submit Testlet button until you have consulted the question status list at the bottom of each MCQ screen.**

    - Return to flagged questions to finalize your answer choices if you have time.
    - Verify that you have answered every question.
    - Stay on schedule because time management is critical to exam success.

How to Be in Control

Remember, you must be in control to be successful during exam preparation and execution. Perhaps more importantly, control can also contribute greatly to your personal and other professional goals. Control is the process whereby you

- Develop expectations, standards, budgets, and plans
- Undertake activity, production, study, and learning
- Measure the activity, production, output, and knowledge
- Compare actual activity with expected and budgeted activity
- Modify the activity, behavior, or study to better achieve the expected or desired outcome
- Revise expectations and standards in light of actual experience
- Continue the process or restart the process in the future

Exercising control will ultimately develop the confidence you need to outperform most other CPA candidates and PASS the CPA Exam!

Questions about Gleim Materials

Gleim has an efficient and effective way for candidates who have purchased the Gleim Premium CPA Review System to submit an inquiry and receive a response regarding Gleim materials **directly through their course**. This system also allows you to view your Q&A session online in your Gleim Personal Classroom.

Questions regarding the information in this **introduction and/or the Gleim *CPA Exam Guide*** (study suggestions, study plans, exam specifics) may be emailed to personalcounselor@gleim.com.

Questions concerning **orders, prices, shipments, or payments** should be sent via email to customerservice@gleim.com and will be promptly handled by our competent and courteous customer service staff.

For **technical support**, you may use our automated technical support service at www.gleim.com/support, email us at support@gleim.com, or call us at (800) 874-5346.

Citations to Authoritative Pronouncements

Throughout the book, we refer to certain authoritative accounting pronouncements by the following abbreviations:

GAAP – The sources of authoritative U.S. generally accepted accounting principles (GAAP) recognized by the FASB as applicable by nongovernmental entities are (1) the FASB's Accounting Standards Codification (ASC) and (2) (for SEC registrants only) pronouncements of the SEC. All guidance in the Codification is equally authoritative. SEC pronouncements must be followed by registrants regardless of whether they are reflected in the codification.

ASC – The FASB's Accounting Standards Codification is "the single source of authoritative nongovernmental U.S. generally accepted accounting principles" for entities that are not SEC registrants. The Codification organizes the many pronouncements that constitute U.S. GAAP into a consistent, searchable format accessible through the Internet.

Feedback

Please fill out our online feedback form (www.gleim.com/feedbackFAR) IMMEDIATELY after you take the CPA Financial section so we can adapt our material based on where candidates say we need to increase or decrease coverage. Our approach has been approved by the AICPA.

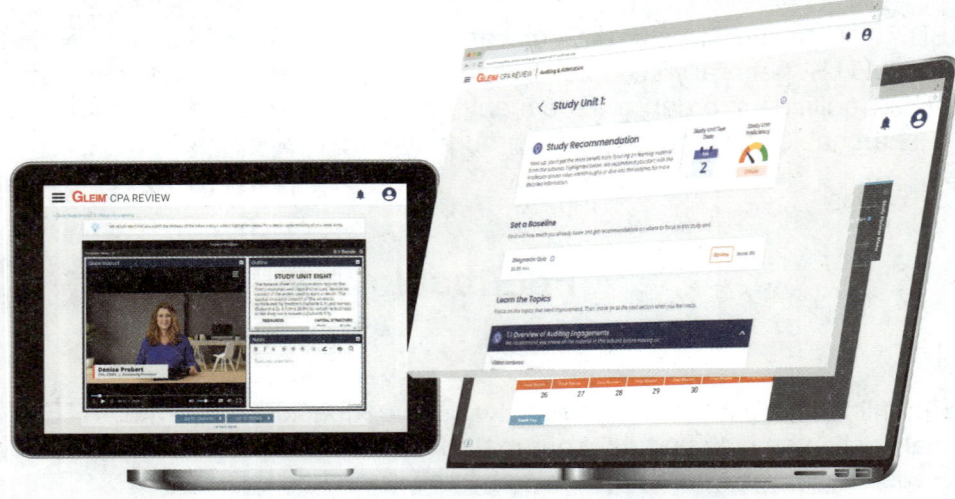

Study Unit One

Financial Statements

(17 pages of outline)

1.1 Balance Sheet (Statement of Financial Position)

General purpose financial reporting includes the full set of financial statements, the notes to the financial statements, and required supplemental information.

A **full set of financial statements** presents the elements of financial statements and their related recognition and measurement. It reports the following:

- Financial position at the end of the period, including assets, liabilities, and equity
- Comprehensive income, including revenue, expenses, gains, and losses for the period
- Investment by and distributions to owners (changes in owners' equity) during the period
- Cash flows during the period

Notes to the financial statements supplement or further explain information on the face of the financial statements.

- Examples of such information are descriptions of the accounting policies used and other disclosures required by generally accepted accounting principles (GAAP).

- Notes may **not** be used (1) to correct an improper presentation in the statements or (2) as a substitute for recognition in the statements.

- The notes should contain information about

  - Financial statement line items
  - The reporting entity
  - Unrecognized past events and current circumstances that can affect cash flows

Supplemental information, such as management's discussion and analysis (MD&A), provides information in addition to that in the statements and notes.

Basic Accounting Equation

The balance sheet (statement of financial position) reports assets, liabilities, equity, and their relationships at a moment in time. It helps users to assess liquidity, financial flexibility, and risk.

The balance sheet is a detailed presentation of the basic accounting equation:

$$\text{Assets} = \text{Liabilities} + \text{Equity}$$

- The left side of this equation depicts the entity's resource structure. The right side depicts the financing structure.

Assets are generally reported in order of liquidity.

- Some variation of the following classifications is used by most entities:

Example 1-1   Comparative Statement of Financial Position

CURRENT ASSETS:	Current Year End	Prior Year End	CURRENT LIABILITIES:	Current Year End	Prior Year End
Cash and equivalents	$ 325,000	$ 275,000	Accounts payable	$ 200,000	$ 125,000
Available-for-sale debt securities	165,000	145,000	Accrued interest on note	5,000	5,000
Accounts receivable	120,000	115,000	Current maturities of L.T. debt	100,000	100,000
Notes receivable	55,000	40,000	Accrued salaries and wages	15,000	10,000
Inventories	85,000	55,000	Income taxes payable	70,000	35,000
Prepaid expenses	10,000	5,000			
Total current assets	$ 760,000	$ 635,000	Total current liabilities	$ 390,000	$ 275,000
NONCURRENT ASSETS:			NONCURRENT LIABILITIES:		
Equity-method investments	$ 120,000	$ 115,000	Bonds payable	$ 500,000	$ 600,000
Property, plant, and equipment	1,000,000	900,000	Long-term notes payable	90,000	60,000
Minus: Accum. depreciation	(85,000)	(55,000)	Employee-related obligations	15,000	10,000
Goodwill	5,000	5,000	Deferred income taxes	5,000	5,000
Total noncurrent assets	$1,040,000	$ 965,000	Total noncurrent liabilities	$ 610,000	$ 675,000
			Total liabilities	$1,000,000	$ 950,000
			EQUITY:		
			Common stock $1 par	$ 500,000	$ 500,000
			Additional paid-in capital	200,000	80,000
			Accumulated OCI	30,000	20,000
			Retained earnings	70,000	50,000
			Total equity	$ 800,000	$ 650,000
Total assets	$1,800,000	$1,600,000	Total liabilities and equity	$1,800,000	$1,600,000

Current Assets

Current assets consist of "cash and other assets or resources commonly identified as reasonably expected to be realized in cash or sold or consumed **during the normal operating cycle** of the business."

The operating cycle is the average time between the acquisition of resources and the final receipt of cash from their sale as the culmination of revenue generating activities. If the cycle is less than a year, **1 year** is the period used for segregating current from noncurrent assets.

- Thus, an asset is classified as current on the statement of financial position if it is expected to be realized within the entity's **operating cycle or 1 year**, whichever is **longer**.

Current assets include

- Cash and cash equivalents;
- Certain individual investments in trading, available-for-sale, and held-to-maturity debt securities;
- Receivables;
- Inventories;
- Prepaid expenses; and
- Certain individual investments in equity securities.

Noncurrent Assets

Noncurrent assets are those not qualifying as current.

Investments and funds include nonoperating items intended to be held beyond the longer of 1 year or the operating cycle. The following assets are typically included:

- Investments in equity securities made to control or influence another entity

- Other noncurrent equity securities

    - Certain individual investments in available-for-sale and held-to-maturity debt securities may be noncurrent.

- Funds restricted as to withdrawal or use for other than current operations, for example, to

    - Retire long-term debt,
    - Satisfy pension obligations, or
    - Pay for the acquisition or construction of noncurrent assets

- Capital assets not used in current operations, such as

    - Idle facilities or
    - Land held for a future plant site

Property, plant, and equipment (PPE) are tangible operating items recorded at cost and reported net of any accumulated depreciation. They include

- Land and natural resources subject to depletion, e.g., oil and gas

- Buildings, equipment, furniture, fixtures, leasehold improvements, land improvements, noncurrent assets under construction, and other depreciable assets

Intangible assets are nonfinancial assets without physical substance. Examples are patents and goodwill.

Other noncurrent assets include noncurrent assets not readily classifiable elsewhere. Examples are deferred tax assets and long-term receivables.

The category **deferred charges** (long-term prepayments) appears on some balance sheets.

Success Tip

The AICPA has previously tested candidates on their knowledge of what the classification of current liabilities entails. Potentially, candidates could see a list of fixed accounts with a question on the amount of current liabilities of the firm.

Current Liabilities

Current liabilities are "obligations whose liquidation is reasonably expected to require the use of existing resources properly classifiable as current assets, or the creation of other current liabilities."

- Current liabilities generally are expected to be settled or liquidated in the ordinary course of business during the longer of 1 year or the operating cycle.

Current liabilities include

- **Trade payables** for items entering into the operating cycle, e.g., for materials and supplies used in producing goods or services for sale.

- **Other payables** arising from operations, such as accrued wages, salaries, rentals, royalties, and taxes.

- **Unearned revenues** (contract liabilities) arising from collections in advance of delivering goods or performing services, e.g., ticket sales revenue.

Other current liabilities include

- Short-term notes given to acquire capital assets
- Payments on the current portion of serial bonds or other noncurrent debt

Noncurrent obligations callable by the creditor because of the debtor's violation of the debt agreement (e.g., covenant violation) at the balance sheet date are classified as current.

Current liabilities **do not include**

- Current obligations if an entity (1) intends to refinance them on a noncurrent basis and (2) demonstrates an ability to do so. *← Intent+Ability*
  - The ability to refinance may be demonstrated by
    - ▸ Entering into a financing agreement meeting all conditions before the balance sheet is issued.
    - ▸ Issuing a noncurrent obligation or equity securities after the end of the reporting period but before issuance of the balance sheet.
  - The amount excluded from current liabilities must not exceed the proceeds from the new obligation or equity securities issued.
- Debts to be paid from funds accumulated in noncurrent asset accounts. Thus, a liability for bonds payable in the next period will not be classified as current if payment is to be from a noncurrent fund.

The difference between current assets and current liabilities is working capital.

Noncurrent Liabilities

Noncurrent liabilities are those not qualifying as current. The noncurrent portions of the following items are reported in this section of the balance sheet:

- Noncurrent notes and bonds
- Lease liabilities
- Most postretirement benefit obligations
- Obligations under product or service warranty agreements
- Advances for noncurrent commitments to provide goods or services
- Deferred revenue

Deferred tax liabilities arising from interperiod tax allocation are classified as noncurrent.

Equity

Equity is the residual after total liabilities are subtracted from total assets.

- Equity consists of the following:
  - Capital contributed by owners (par value of common and preferred stock issued and additional paid-in capital)
  - Retained earnings (income reinvested)
  - Accumulated other comprehensive income (all comprehensive income items not included in net income)
  - The noncontrolling interest in a consolidated entity
- Treasury stock is the entity's own common stock that it has repurchased. Treasury stock is presented as a reduction of total equity (discussed in Study Unit 12).

Stop & Review

You have completed the outline for this subunit.
Study multiple-choice questions 1 through 4 beginning on page 33.

1.2 Statement of Income

Background 1-1	Temporary vs. Permanent Accounts

The accounts presented on the balance sheet are real or permanent accounts. They report an entity's resources and financing elements that exist from period to period. The accounts presented on the income statement are nominal or temporary accounts. They are reported for a period of time, closed at the end of the period, and reopened at the beginning of the next period with zero balances.

Nature of the Income Statement

The results of operations are reported in the income statement (statement of earnings) on the **accrual basis** using an approach oriented to historical transactions.

- The traditional income statement reports **revenues** from, and **expenses** of, the entity's major activities and **gains** and **losses** from other activities.

- The sum of these income statement elements is net income (loss) for an interval of time.

Revenues − Expenses + Gains − Losses = Net income or loss

Income statement elements are reported in temporary **(nominal)** accounts that are periodically closed to permanent **(real)** accounts. The accountant need not close each transaction directly to equity.

- Net income or loss for the period is **closed to retained earnings** at the end of the period.

Any recognized amounts not included in continuing operations are reported in a separate section for **discontinued operations**.

- The term "continuing operations" is used only when a discontinued operation is reported.

The **transactions not included** in net income are

- Transactions with owners,
- Error corrections,
- Items reported initially in other comprehensive income,
- Transfers to and from appropriated retained earnings, and
- Effects on prior periods of accounting changes.

Income Statement Format

Three formats are commonly used for presentation of recurring items:

1. The **single-step income statement** provides one grouping for revenues and gains and one for expenses and losses. The single step is the one subtraction necessary to arrive at net income.

Example 1-2	Single-Step Income Statement

Bouffie Company
Income Statement
For Year Ended December 31, Year 1

Revenues and gains:		
Net sales	$1,050,000	
Other revenues	580,000	
Gains	495,000	
Total revenues and gains		$ 2,125,000
Expenses and losses:		
Costs of goods sold	$ 820,000	
Selling expenses	70,000	
General and administrative expenses	78,000	
Interest expense	124,000	
Losses	198,000	
Income tax expense	85,000	
Total expenses and losses		(1,375,000)
Net income		$ 750,000
Earnings per common share (simple capital structure) -- assuming 20,000 shares issued and outstanding		$37.50

2. The **multiple-step income statement** reports operating revenues and expenses in a section separate from nonoperating items. It enhances disclosure by presenting subtotals.

Example 1-3	Multiple-Step Income Statement

Bouffie Company
Income Statement
For Year Ended December 31, Year 1

Revenues:			
Gross sales			$1,600,000
Minus: Sales discounts		$ (350,000)	
Sales returns and allowances		(200,000)	(550,000)
Net sales			$1,050,000
Cost of goods sold:			
Beginning inventory		$1,200,000	
Purchases	$ 500,000		
Minus: Purchase returns and discounts	(100,000)		
Net purchases	$ 400,000		
Transportation-in	50,000	450,000	
Goods available for sale		$1,650,000	
Minus: Ending inventory		(830,000)	
Cost of goods sold			(820,000)
Gross profit			$ 230,000
Operating expenses:			
Selling expenses:			
Sales salaries and commissions	$18,000		
Freight-out	5,000		
Travel	25,000		
Advertising	10,000		
Office supplies	12,000	$ 70,000	
General and administrative expenses:			
Executive salaries	$40,000		
Professional salaries	7,000		
Wages of office staff	19,000		
Depreciation	7,000		
Office supplies	5,000	78,000	
Total operating expenses			(148,000)
Income from operations			$ 82,000
Other revenues and gains:			
Gain on investments		$495,000	
Dividend revenue		580,000	1,075,000
Other expenses and losses:			
Interest expense		$124,000	
Loss on disposal of equipment		198,000	(322,000)
Income before taxes*			$ 835,000
Income tax expense			(85,000)
Net income*			$ 750,000
Earnings per common share (simple capital structure) -- assuming 20,000 shares issued and outstanding			$37.50

* If a discontinued operation is reported, these line items are "Income from continuing operations before taxes" and "Income from continuing operations," respectively.

3. The **condensed income statement** is the most common method of presentation. It includes only the section totals of the **multiple-step format**. The enhanced disclosure of each line item is presented in the notes to the financial statements.

Example 1-4   Condensed Income Statement

Bouffie Company
Income Statement
For Year Ended December 31, Year 1

Net sales	$1,050,000
Cost of goods sold	(820,000)
Gross profit	$ 230,000
Selling expenses	(70,000)
General and administrative expenses	(78,000)
Income from operations	$ 82,000
Other revenues and gains	1,075,000
Interest expense	(124,000)
Other expenses and losses	(198,000)
Income before taxes*	$ 835,000
Income tax expense	(85,000)
Net income*	$ 750,000
Earnings per common share (simple capital structure) -- assuming 20,000 shares issued and outstanding	$37.50

* If a discontinued operation is reported, these line items are "Income from continuing operations before taxes" and "Income from continuing operations," respectively.

Income Statement Sections

Success Tip

> Previous CPA Exams have included questions with cost and inventory information that require candidates to calculate cost of goods sold or cost of goods manufactured.

Cost of goods sold equals purchases for a retailer or cost of goods manufactured (COGM) for a manufacturer, adjusted for the change in finished goods (FG) in inventory.

	Beginning FG inventory
+	**Purchases or COGM**
	Goods available for sale
−	**Ending FG inventory**
	Cost of goods sold

Cost of goods manufactured equals the period's manufacturing costs adjusted for the change in work-in-process. It also may be stated as cost of goods sold adjusted for the change in finished goods inventory.

Beginning work in process	Ending FG inventory
+ Sum of periodic manufacturing costs	+ Cost of goods sold
− Ending work-in-process	− Beginning FG inventory
Cost of goods manufactured	Cost of goods manufactured

NOTE: Study Unit 6, Subunit 1, contains a more detailed explanation of this topic.

Selling expenses are incurred in selling or marketing.

- Examples include

    - Sales representatives' salaries, commissions, and traveling expenses;
    - Sales department rent, salaries, and depreciation; and
    - Communications (e.g., Internet) costs.

- Shipping costs also may be classified as selling costs.

- Advertising costs should be expensed either as incurred or when advertising first occurs.

    - Sellers may agree to reimburse customers for the customers' advertising costs (cooperative advertising). The revenues related to the transactions that created such obligations generally are recognized before reimbursement. Accordingly, the obligations must be accrued and the advertising costs expensed when the related revenues are recognized.

General and administrative expenses are incurred for the direction of the entity as a whole and are not related entirely to a specific function, e.g., selling or manufacturing. They include

- Accounting, legal, and other fees for professional services;
- Officers' salaries;
- Insurance;
- Wages of office staff;
- Miscellaneous supplies; and
- Office occupancy costs.

Interest expense is recognized based on the passage of time. In the case of bonds, notes, and finance leases, the effective interest method is used.

Material items that are **unusual in nature, infrequent in occurrence, or both** are reported as a separate component of income from **continuing operations**.

- These items must **not** be reported net of taxes.

- Gains or losses of a similar nature that are not individually material must be aggregated.

- The nature and financial effect of each item is disclosed in the notes to the financial statements or reported in the income statement.

- The effects of such items on earnings per share must **not** be presented on the income statement.

Discontinued Operation

The operating results of a **discontinued operation** are reported **separately net of tax** in the income statement. This section is presented **after the results of continuing operations**.

- If a component of an entity (discontinued operation) is disposed of during the period, any **gain or loss on disposal** must be disclosed on the face of the income statement or in the notes.

- If a component of an entity (discontinued operation) is classified as **held for sale**, it is measured at the **lower** of its **carrying amount** or **fair value minus cost to sell** (discussed in Study Unit 7, Subunit 8).

  - Operating results reported in discontinued operations include any **income** earned or **loss** incurred during the **entire** reporting period (i.e., before and after the component was classified as held for sale).

  - Operating results also include any loss for a write-down to fair value minus cost to sell recognized on the initial classification as held for sale and subsequently.

- **Intraperiod tax allocation** is required. Thus, income tax expense or benefit is allocated to

  - Continuing operations,
  - Discontinued operations,
  - Other comprehensive income, and
  - Items debited or credited directly to other components of equity.

    ▸ The operating results of a discontinued operation also must be reported in the comparative financial statements.

- The discontinued operations section presents separately the (1) income or loss from operations of the component and (2) income tax expense or benefit.

- If a discontinued operation is reported, basic and diluted earnings per share amounts for the discontinued operation are presented on the face of the income statement or in the notes (discussed in Study Unit 2, Subunit 2).

Example 1-5	Income Statement Presentation of Discontinued Operations

On July 1, Year 1, Emkay Co. approved a plan to dispose of Segment X on October 1, Year 1. As a result, Segment X (a component of the entity) was properly classified as a discontinued operation. It was sold on October 1, Year 1, for $480,000. Emkay's income tax rate is 40%. The following data pertain to Segment X:

- Operating losses were $110,000 for the period January 1 to June 30, Year 1.
- Operating losses were $100,000 for the period July 1 to October 1, Year 1.
- The operating losses presented above do not include a loss on disposal or a write-down to fair value minus cost to sell.
- The carrying amount on July 1, Year 1, was $600,000.
- Fair value minus cost to sell on July 1, Year 1, was $450,000.

-- Continued on next page --

Example 1-5 -- Continued

The following are Emkay's Year 1 income statement items excluding Segment X's operating results:

Revenues	$950,000
Cost of goods sold	380,000
General and administrative expenses	90,000
Interest expense	50,000

Year 1 operating results of Segment X are reported in discontinued operations. The loss from discontinued operations for the year ended December 31, Year 1, includes all of the following:

- Operating losses incurred during the entire reporting period were $210,000 ($110,000 + $100,000).
- The loss on write-down to fair value minus cost to sell on July 1 was $150,000 ($600,000 carrying amount – $450,000 fair value minus cost to sell).
- The gain on disposal of the segment on October 1 was $30,000 ($480,000 – $450,000).

The total Year 1 loss from discontinued operations before tax is $330,000 ($210,000 + $150,000 – $30,000). The loss on discontinued operations (net of tax) reported in the income statement is $198,000 [$330,000 × (1 – 40%)].

The following format may be used by Emkay to present its Year 1 income statement:

Emkay Co.
Income Statement
For the Year Ended 12/31/Yr 1

Revenues		$950,000
Cost of goods sold		(380,000)
Gross profit		$570,000
General and administrative expenses	$ 90,000	
Interest expense	50,000	(140,000)
Income from continuing operations before income taxes		$430,000
Income tax expense		(172,000)
Income from continuing operations		**$258,000**
Discontinued operations		
Loss from operations of component unit – Segment X		
(including gain on disposal of $30,000)	$(330,000)	
Income tax benefit	132,000	
Loss from discontinued operations		**(198,000)**
Net income		**$ 60,000**
Earnings (loss) per common share (simple capital structure):		
Continuing operations		$ 12.90
Discontinued operations		(9.90)
Net earnings -- assuming 20,000 shares outstanding		$ 3.00

Stop & Review

You have completed the outline for this subunit.

Study multiple-choice questions 5 through 10 beginning on page 35.

1.3 Comprehensive Income

Comprehensive income includes all changes in equity of a business during a period except those from investments by and distributions to owners. It includes all components of

- **Net income** and
- **Other comprehensive income (OCI).**

OCI includes all items of comprehensive income not included in net income. Under existing accounting standards, items of OCI include, among others,

- Unrealized holding gains and losses on **available-for-sale debt securities** (Study Unit 4).
- Gains and losses on **derivatives** designated and qualifying as **cash flow hedges**.
- Foreign currency translation adjustments for a foreign operation (translation gains and losses).
- Changes in fair value attributable to instrument-specific credit risk of financial liabilities for which the fair value option is elected (Study Unit 4).

Each component of OCI must be presented **net of tax**, or one amount must be presented for the aggregate tax effect on the total of OCI. In either case, the tax effect on each component must be disclosed.

[handwritten notes:]
CI → NI + OCI
OCI → AFS, CF Hedge,
   Foriegn curr Δ,
   Δ in FV → credit risk
→ must be pres. Net of tax
1 or 2 statement
OCI ↑ A°CI
OCL ↓ A°Cl
(1.3)

Reporting

An entity that presents a full *[obscured]* of OCI need not report OCI or comprehensive income. O *[obscured]* comprehensive income recognized for the period eith *[obscured]*

- In one continuous financia *[obscured]*
- In two separate but conse *[obscured]*

One continuous statement *[obscured]* I. It must include

- A total of net income with *[obscured]*
- A total of OCI with its com *[obscured]*
- A total of comprehensive income.

Separate but consecutive statements must be presented as follows:

- The first statement (the income statement) presents the components of net income and total net income.
- The second statement (the statement of OCI) is presented immediately after the first. It presents
    - The components of OCI,
    - The total of OCI, and
    - A total of comprehensive income.
- The entity must begin the second statement with net income.

The following is an example of the **single-statement** presentation for reporting comprehensive income:

Example 1-6	Single-Statement Presentation

CI Company
Statement of
Comprehensive Income (in millions)
Year Ended December 31, Year 1

	Revenues and gains:		
	Net revenues	$250	
	Gain on sale of available-for-sale debt securities	10	
	Gains reclassified from AOCI	14	$274
Statement of Income	Expenses and losses:		
	Expenses	$122	
	Losses	12	(134)
	Income from continuing operations		$140
	Income tax expense		(30)
	Net income		**$110**
	OCI, net of tax:		
	Foreign currency translation adjustments		20
	Unrealized holding gains	40	
	Minus: Reclassification of gains from AOCI	(14)	26
Statement of OCI	Loss on hedging instrument designated as cash flow hedge		(21)
	OCI		$ 25
	Comprehensive income		**$135**

A **two-statement** presentation is easily derived from the example above.

- The final component of the **statement of net income** is net income.

- The first component of the **statement of OCI** is net income, and the final component is comprehensive income.

The **components of OCI** are recorded initially in a temporary (nominal) account. At the end of each reporting period, the total OCI for a period is **closed to accumulated OCI**, a permanent account that is reported in the equity section of the balance sheet. (AOCI)

- Other comprehensive income for the period increases accumulated OCI. OCI ↑ Acc OCI
- Other comprehensive loss for the period decreases accumulated OCI. OC LOSS ↓ Acc OCI
  AOCI

Stop & Review

You have completed the outline for this subunit.

Study multiple-choice questions 11 through 15 beginning on page 37.

1.4 Statement of Changes in Equity

A statement of changes in equity is presented as part of a full set of financial statements. This statement provides disclosure of changes during the accounting period in the separate equity accounts. These are retained earnings, accumulated OCI, common stock, preferred stock, additional paid-in capital, and noncontrolling interest.

Example 1-7   Statement of Changes in Equity

CI Company
For the Year Ended December 31, Year 1

	Total Equity	Retained Earnings	Accumulated Other Comprehensive Income	Common Stock	Additional Paid-in Capital	Treasury Stock
Beginning balance	$500	$350	$100	$40	$ 30	$(20)
Net income for the period	110	110				
OCI for the period	25		25			
Common stock issued	90			10	80	
Dividends declared	(60)	(60)				
Repurchase of common stock	(15)					(15)
Ending balance	$650	$400	$125	$50	$110	$(35)

Statement of Retained Earnings

A statement of retained earnings reconciles the beginning and ending balances of the account. This statement is not separately reported. Instead, it is reported as part of the statement of changes in equity in a separate column.

The changes in retained earnings can result from the following adjustments:

- Net income (loss) for the period;

- Any prior-period adjustments, net of tax (discussed in Study Unit 3);

- Dividends declared; and

- Certain other rare items, e.g., reissuance of treasury stock under the cost method (discussed in Study Unit 12).

 Retained earnings are sometimes appropriated (restricted) to a special account to disclose that earnings retained in the business (not paid out in dividends) are being used for special purposes (discussed in Study Unit 12).

Stop & Review

You have completed the outline for this subunit.

Study multiple-choice questions 16 and 17 on page 40.

1.5 Special Purpose Frameworks

Other Bases of Accounting

Financial statements may be prepared using a comprehensive basis of accounting that is not in accordance with GAAP.

Common examples are the following:

- The cash basis or modified cash basis
- A basis used for tax purposes
- A basis used to comply with the requirements of a regulator

Statements using a basis other than GAAP should include a summary of significant accounting policies that discusses the basis used and how it differs from GAAP.

Cash Basis

Under the strict cash basis of accounting, revenues and expenses are recognized when cash is received or paid, respectively, regardless of when goods are delivered or received or when services are rendered.

- The cash basis ignores the revenue and expense recognition principles that are fundamental to the accrual basis.

- This method may be appropriate for small businesses operated as sole proprietorships.

Success Tip

The following equations will help you to convert the accrual-basis amounts in the income statement to the cash basis amount and the opposite:

Beginning accounts receivable	$XXX	Beginning accounts payable	$XXX
Sales (accrual basis)	XXX	Purchases (accrual basis)	XXX
Ending accounts receivable	(XXX)	Ending accounts payable	(XXX)
Cash collected from customers	$XXX	Cash paid to suppliers	$XXX
Beginning interest payable	$XXX	Ending prepaid expenses	$XXX
Interest expense (accrual basis)	XXX	Current-period expense (accrual basis)	XXX
Ending interest payable	(XXX)	Beginning prepaid expenses	(XXX)
Interest paid during the period	$XXX	Expenses paid during the period	$XXX

Modified Cash Basis

The modified cash basis uses the cash basis for typical operating activities with modifications to the accrual basis for activities having substantial support, for example, reporting inventory, accruing income taxes, and capitalizing and depreciating fixed assets.

This method often is used by professional services firms, such as physicians, realtors, and architects.

Income Tax Basis

This basis must be applied to calculate income tax liability.

Certain doctrines underlying the federal tax code differ significantly from those in the conceptual framework. For example, the code requires use of the modified accelerated cost recovery system (MACRS), a depreciation method not recognized under GAAP.

Stop & Review

You have completed the outline for this subunit.
Study multiple-choice questions 18 through 20 beginning on page 41.

Questions

1.1 Balance Sheet (Statement of Financial Position)

1. Brite Corp. had the following liabilities at December 31, Year 6:

Accounts payable	$ 55,000
Unsecured notes, 8%, due 7/1/Yr 7	400,000
Accrued expenses	35,000
Contingent liability	450,000
Deferred income tax liability	25,000
Senior bonds, 7%, due 3/31/Yr 7	1,000,000

The contingent liability is an accrual for possible losses on a $1 million lawsuit filed against Brite. Brite's legal counsel expects the suit to be settled in Year 8 and has estimated that Brite will be liable for damages in the range of $450,000 to $750,000. The deferred income tax liability is not related to an asset for financial reporting and is expected to reverse in Year 8. What amount should Brite report in its December 31, Year 6, balance sheet for current liabilities?

A. $515,000

B. $940,000

C. $1,490,000

D. $1,515,000

✔ **Answer (C) is correct.**
Required: The amount reported for current liabilities.
Discussion: The following are current liabilities: (1) Obligations that, by their terms, are or will be due on demand within 1 year (or the operating cycle if longer) and (2) obligations that are or will be callable by the creditor within 1 year because of a violation of a debt covenant. Deferred tax assets and liabilities are classified as noncurrent. Thus, current liabilities are calculated as

Accounts payable	$ 55,000
Unsecured notes, 8%, due 7/1/Yr 7	400,000
Accrued expenses	35,000
Senior bonds, 7%, due 3/31/Yr 7	1,000,000
Current liabilities	$1,490,000

✘ **Answer (A) is incorrect.** The amount of $515,000 excludes the senior bonds due within 1 year and includes the deferred income tax liability that will not reverse within 1 year. Deferred tax assets and liabilities are classified as noncurrent amounts.

✘ **Answer (B) is incorrect.** The amount of $940,000 includes the contingent liability not expected to be settled until Year 8 and excludes the senior bonds.

✘ **Answer (D) is incorrect.** The amount of $1,515,000 includes the deferred income tax liability that should be classified as noncurrent.

2. A company has outstanding accounts payable of $30,000 and a short-term construction loan in the amount of $100,000 at year end. The loan was refinanced through issuance of long-term bonds after year end but before issuance of financial statements. How should these liabilities be recorded in the balance sheet?

A. Noncurrent liabilities of $130,000.

B. Current liabilities of $130,000.

C. Current liabilities of $30,000, noncurrent liabilities of $100,000.

D. Current liabilities of $130,000, with required footnote disclosure of the refinancing of the loan.

✔ **Answer (C) is correct.**
Required: The classification of liabilities.
Discussion: Accounts payable are properly classified as current liabilities because they are for items entering into the operating cycle. Short-term debt that is refinanced by a post-balance-sheet-date issuance of long-term debt should be classified as noncurrent. (The ability to refinance on a long-term basis has been demonstrated.) Thus, the short-term construction loan is classified as noncurrent. Accordingly, the entity records current liabilities of $30,000 and noncurrent liabilities of $100,000.

✘ **Answer (A) is incorrect.** Outstanding accounts payable are normally classified as current liabilities.

✘ **Answer (B) is incorrect.** The $100,000 that is to be refinanced on a long-term basis should be reclassified as noncurrent.

✘ **Answer (D) is incorrect.** The $100,000 that is to be refinanced on a long-term basis should be reclassified as noncurrent.

Questions 3 and 4 are based on the following information.

The trial balance of Trey Co. at December 31, Year 6, has been adjusted except for income tax expense.

	Dr.	Cr.
Cash	$ 550,000	
Accounts receivable	1,650,000	
Prepaid taxes	300,000	
Accounts payable		$ 120,000
Common stock		500,000
Additional paid-in capital		680,000
Retained earnings		630,000
Foreign currency translation adjustment	430,000	
Revenues		3,600,000
Expenses	2,600,000	
	$5,530,000	$5,530,000

Additional Information
- During Year 6, estimated tax payments of $300,000 were charged to prepaid taxes. Trey has not yet recorded income tax expense. There were no differences between financial statement and income tax income, and Trey's tax rate is 30%.
- Included in accounts receivable is $500,000 due from a customer. Special terms granted to this customer require payment in equal semiannual installments of $125,000 every April 1 and October 1.

3. In Trey's December 31, Year 6, balance sheet, what amount should be reported as total current assets?

A. $1,950,000

B. $2,200,000

C. $2,250,000

D. $2,500,000

✔ **Answer (A) is correct.**
Required: The total current assets.
Discussion: Trey's current assets include cash, accounts receivable, and prepaid taxes. However, income tax expense is $300,000 [($3,600,000 revenues – $2,600,000 expenses) × 30%]. After recording income tax expense, prepaid taxes equal $0. Moreover, $250,000 of the receivables is due in Year 8 and is therefore noncurrent. Thus, total current assets equal $1,950,000 [$550,000 cash + ($1,650,000 – $250,000 noncurrent A/R)].

✘ **Answer (B) is incorrect.** The amount of $2,200,000 includes the noncurrent accounts receivable.

✘ **Answer (C) is incorrect.** The amount of $2,250,000 includes $300,000 of prepaid taxes.

✘ **Answer (D) is incorrect.** The amount of $2,500,000 includes $300,000 of prepaid taxes and the noncurrent accounts receivable.

4. In Trey's December 31, Year 6, balance sheet, what amount should be reported as total retained earnings?

A. $1,029,000

B. $1,200,000

C. $1,330,000

D. $1,630,000

✔ **Answer (C) is correct.**
Required: The total retained earnings.
Discussion: Retained earnings equal $1,330,000 {$630,000 beginning retained earnings + [($3,600,000 revenues – $2,600,000 expenses) × (1.0 – .30 tax rate)]}.

✘ **Answer (A) is incorrect.** The amount of $1,029,000 results from subtracting the $430,000 foreign currency translation adjustment from retained earnings and subtracting $171,000 of taxes [($1,000,000 – $430,000) × 30%].

✘ **Answer (B) is incorrect.** The amount of $1,200,000 results from subtracting the $430,000 foreign currency translation adjustment and from not subtracting the $300,000 in taxes.

✘ **Answer (D) is incorrect.** The amount of $1,630,000 results from not subtracting the $300,000 in taxes.

1.2 Statement of Income

5. Pak Co.'s professional fees expense account had a balance of $82,000 at December 31, Year 1, before considering year-end adjustments relating to the following:

   - Consultants were hired for a special project at a total fee not to exceed $65,000. Pak has recorded $55,000 of this fee based on billings for work performed in Year 1.

   - The attorney's letter requested by the auditors dated January 28, Year 2, indicated that legal fees of $6,000 were billed on January 15, Year 2, for work performed in November Year 1, and unbilled fees for December Year 1 were $7,000.

   What amount should Pak report for professional fees expense for the year ended December 31, Year 1?

   A. $105,000

   B. $95,000

   C. $88,000

   D. $82,000

✔ **Answer (B) is correct.**
Required: The professional fees expense for the year.
Discussion: Pak should recognize an expense only for the work done by the attorneys in Year 1. Thus, no adjustment is necessary for the consulting fees, but the legal fees, billed and unbilled, for November and December Year 1 should be debited to the account. The professional fees expense for the year is therefore $95,000 ($82,000 + $6,000 + $7,000).

✘ **Answer (A) is incorrect.** The amount of $105,000 includes the maximum fee that may be payable to the consultants.

✘ **Answer (C) is incorrect.** The amount of $88,000 excludes the attorneys' fees for December.

✘ **Answer (D) is incorrect.** The amount of $82,000 excludes the attorneys' fees for November and December.

6. The changes in account balances of the Vel Corporation during Year 6 are presented below:

	Increase
Assets	$356,000
Liabilities	108,000
Capital stock	240,000
Additional paid-in capital	24,000

   Vel has **no** items of other comprehensive income (OCI), and the only charge to retained earnings was for a dividend payment of $52,000. Thus, the net income for Year 6 is

   A. $16,000

   B. $36,000

   C. $52,000

   D. $68,000

✔ **Answer (B) is correct.**
Required: The net income for the year given the increase in assets, liabilities, and paid-in capital.
Discussion: Assets equal the sum of liabilities and equity (contributed capital, retained earnings, and accumulated OCI). The total increase in equity must be $248,000 ($356,000 increase in assets – $108,000 increase in liabilities). Dividends paid decrease retained earnings, and net income increases retained earnings. The increase in equity disregarding the net income component is $212,000 ($240,000 increase in capital stock + $24,000 increase in additional paid-in capital – $52,000 dividends paid). Given no items of OCI, the Year 6 net income is $36,000 ($248,000 – $212,000).

✘ **Answer (A) is incorrect.** The amount of $16,000 is the excess of the sum of the increases in the capital accounts other than retained earnings over the increase in net assets.

✘ **Answer (C) is incorrect.** The amount of $52,000 is the dividend.

✘ **Answer (D) is incorrect.** The amount of $68,000 equals the sum of the dividend and the excess of the sum of the increases in the capital accounts other than retained earnings over the increase in net assets.

7. On September 30, Year 1, a component that represents a major line of an entity's business was properly classified as held for sale. This transaction is probable and is expected to qualify for recognition as a completed sale within 1 year. The component's operating loss for the period October 1 through December 31, Year 1, should be included in the Year 1 income statement as part of

A. Gain or loss on disposal of the discontinued component.

B. Operating gain or loss of the discontinued component.

C. Income or loss from continuing operations.

D. Other comprehensive income.

✓ **Answer (B) is correct.**
Required: The treatment of the segment operating loss for the period from the measurement date to the balance sheet date.
Discussion: A component of an entity, e.g., an operating segment, reporting unit, subsidiary, or asset group, may be disposed of or classified as held for sale. In these circumstances, the component's results of operations are reported in discontinued operations if the component has a major effect on an entity's operations and financial results (e.g., major line of business, major geographical area, major equity method investment, or other major part of an entity). The income statement reports the component's results of operations, including (1) any gain or loss from measuring the component at fair value minus cost to sell or (2) any gain or loss on disposal in discontinued operations in the period(s) when they occur. Accordingly, the operating loss of the component for the last quarter of Year 1 should be included in the operating gain or loss of the discontinued component reported in the discontinued operations section of the income statement.

8. On January 1, Year 4, Dart, Inc., entered into an agreement to sell the assets and product line of its Jay Division, which met the criteria for classification as an operating segment. The sale was consummated on December 31, Year 4, and resulted in a gain on disposal of $400,000. The division's operations resulted in losses before income tax of $225,000 in Year 4 and $125,000 in Year 3. For both years, Dart's income tax rate is 30%, and the criteria for reporting a discontinued operation have been met. In a comparative statement of income for Year 4 and Year 3, under the caption discontinued operations, Dart should report a gain (loss) of

	Year 4	Year 3
A.	$122,500	$(87,500)
B.	$122,500	$0
C.	$(157,500)	$(87,500)
D.	$(157,500)	$0

✓ **Answer (A) is correct.**
Required: The amounts reported for discontinued operations in comparative statements.
Discussion: When a component (e.g., an operating segment) has been disposed of or is classified as held for sale, and the criteria for reporting a discontinued operation have been met, the income statements for current and prior periods (in this case, Year 3 and Year 4) must report its operating results in discontinued operations. The gain from operations of the component for Year 4 is the net of the $225,000 operating loss for Year 4 and the $400,000 gain on disposal. The pretax gain is therefore $175,000 ($400,000 – $225,000), and the after-tax amount is $122,500 [$175,000 × (1.0 – .30)]. The $125,000 pretax loss for Year 3 should be reported in the comparative statements for Years 3 and 4 as an $87,500 [$125,000 × (1.0 – .30)] loss from discontinued operations.

✗ **Answer (B) is incorrect.** The comparative statement of income for Year 4 and Year 3 should report a loss on discontinued operations for Year 3.

✗ **Answer (C) is incorrect.** An after-tax loss of $157,500 for Year 4 does not consider the gain on disposal.

✗ **Answer (D) is incorrect.** The comparative statement of income for Year 4 and Year 3 should report a loss on discontinued operations for Year 3, and an after-tax loss of $157,500 for Year 4 does not consider the gain on disposal.

9. The following items were among those that were reported on Lee Co.'s income statement for the year ended December 31, Year 1:

Legal and audit fees	$170,000
Rent for office space	240,000
Interest on inventory floor plan	210,000
Loss on abandoned data processing equipment used in operations	35,000

The office space is used equally by Lee's sales and accounting departments. What amount of the above-listed items should be classified as general and administrative expenses in Lee's multiple-step income statement?

A. $290,000

B. $325,000

C. $410,000

D. $500,000

✔ **Answer (A) is correct.**
Required: The general and administrative expenses for the year.
Discussion: The interest expense and the loss on the abandoned data processing equipment should be classified as other expenses. The legal and audit fees and one-half of the rent for the office space should be classified as general and administrative expenses. The total is $290,000 [$170,000 + ($240,000 × 50%)].

✘ **Answer (B) is incorrect.** The amount of $325,000 includes the loss.

✘ **Answer (C) is incorrect.** The amount of $410,000 includes the legal and audit fees as well as the total rent for the office space.

✘ **Answer (D) is incorrect.** The amount of $500,000 includes the interest.

10. The following data were available from Mith Co.'s records on December 31:

Finished goods inventory, 1/1	$120,000
Finished goods inventory, 12/31	110,000
Cost of goods manufactured	520,000
Loss on sale of plant equipment	50,000

The cost of goods sold for the year was

A. $510,000

B. $520,000

C. $530,000

D. $580,000

✔ **Answer (C) is correct.**
Required: The cost of goods sold.
Discussion: Cost of goods sold equals cost of goods manufactured (or purchases for a retailer) adjusted for the change in finished goods inventory. The loss on sale of equipment is not an inventoriable cost. Thus, cost of goods sold is $530,000 ($520,000 COGM + $120,000 BI – $110,000 EI).

✘ **Answer (A) is incorrect.** The amount of $510,000 results from subtracting, rather than adding, the inventory decrease.

✘ **Answer (B) is incorrect.** The amount of $520,000 equals the cost of goods manufactured.

✘ **Answer (D) is incorrect.** The amount of $580,000 includes the loss.

1.3 Comprehensive Income

11. Comprehensive income includes

	Net Income	Unrealized Holding Gains and Losses on Available-for-Sale Debt Securities
A.	Yes	No
B.	Yes	Yes
C.	No	Yes
D.	No	No

✔ **Answer (B) is correct.**
Required: The item(s), if any, included in comprehensive income.
Discussion: The components of comprehensive income are net income and other comprehensive income (OCI). Under existing accounting standards, items of OCI include, among others, (1) unrealized holding gains and losses on available-for-sale debt securities; (2) certain foreign currency items; and (3) gains or losses on a derivative designated and qualifying as a cash flow hedge.

12. When a full set of general-purpose financial statements is presented, comprehensive income and its components

  A. Appear as a part of discontinued operations.

  B. Must be reported net of related income tax effects in total and individually.

  C. Appear only in a supplemental schedule in the notes to the financial statements.

  D. Must be reported in a presentation that includes the components of other comprehensive income and their total.

✔ **Answer (D) is correct.**
Required: The presentation of comprehensive income and its components.
Discussion: If an entity that reports a full set of financial statements has items of other comprehensive income (OCI), it must report comprehensive income in one continuous statement or in two separate but consecutive statements. One continuous statement has two sections: net income and OCI. It must include (1) a total of net income with its components, (2) a total of OCI with its components, and (3) a total of comprehensive income. In separate but consecutive statements, the first statement (the income statement) must present the components of net income and total net income. The second statement (the statement of OCI) must be presented immediately after the first. It presents (1) the components of OCI, (2) the total of OCI, and (3) a total of comprehensive income. The entity must begin the second statement with net income.

✘ **Answer (A) is incorrect.** Discontinued operations is a component of net income, a component of comprehensive income.

✘ **Answer (B) is incorrect.** The components of OCI must be presented either (1) net of related tax effects or (2) pretax, with one amount shown for the aggregate tax effect related to the total of OCI. No amount is displayed for the tax effect related to total comprehensive income.

✘ **Answer (C) is incorrect.** Comprehensive income must be reported in one continuous statement or in two separate but consecutive statements.

13. A company reports the following information as of December 31:

Sales revenue	$800,000
Cost of goods sold	600,000
Operating expenses	90,000
Unrealized holding gain on available-for-sale debt securities, net of tax	30,000

What amount should the company report as comprehensive income as of December 31?

  A. $30,000

  B. $110,000

  C. $140,000

  D. $200,000

✔ **Answer (C) is correct.**
Required: The amount to report as comprehensive income.
Discussion: Comprehensive income includes net income and other comprehensive income. Net income equals $110,000 ($800,000 sales revenue – $600,000 COGS – $90,000 operating expenses). Unrealized holding gains on available-for-sale debt securities ($30,000) are included in other comprehensive income. Thus, comprehensive income is $140,000 ($110,000 + $30,000).

✘ **Answer (A) is incorrect.** The amount of other comprehensive income is $30,000. Comprehensive income includes net income and other comprehensive income.

✘ **Answer (B) is incorrect.** The amount of net income is $110,000. Comprehensive income includes net income and other comprehensive income.

✘ **Answer (D) is incorrect.** The excess of sales revenue over cost of goods sold is $200,000.

14. Rock Co.'s financial statements had the following balances at December 31:

Infrequently occurring gain	$ 50,000
Foreign currency translation gain	100,000
Net income	400,000
Unrealized holding gain on available-for-sale debt securities	20,000

What amount should Rock report as comprehensive income for the year ended December 31?

A. $400,000

B. $420,000

C. $520,000

D. $570,000

✓ **Answer (C) is correct.**
Required: The amount to report as comprehensive income.
Discussion: Comprehensive income includes all changes in equity of a business entity except those changes resulting from investments by owners and distributions to owners. Comprehensive income includes two major categories: net income and other comprehensive income (OCI). Net income includes the results of continuing and discontinued operations. Components of comprehensive income not included in the determination of net income are included in OCI. These include unrealized holding gains and losses on available-for-sale debt securities and certain foreign currency items, such as a translation adjustment. The infrequently occurring gain of $50,000 has already been included in the determination of net income. Thus, comprehensive income equals $520,000 ($400,000 net income + $100,000 translation gain + $20,000 unrealized holding gain on available-for-sale securities)

✗ **Answer (A) is incorrect.** Certain foreign currency items and unrealized holding gains on available-for-sale debt securities are components of OCI.

✗ **Answer (B) is incorrect.** A foreign currency translation gain is a component of OCI.

✗ **Answer (D) is incorrect.** The infrequently occurring gain already is included in the net income amount of $400,000.

15. Which of the following describes how comprehensive income is reported?

A. **No** specific format is required.

B. It should be disclosed in the notes but not reported in the financial statements.

C. It may be reported in a statement of equity.

D. It must be reported in two separate but consecutive statements or in one continuous statement.

✓ **Answer (D) is correct.**
Required: The reporting of comprehensive income.
Discussion: Two reporting formats for comprehensive income are allowed: (1) two separate but consecutive statements and (2) one continuous statement. One continuous statement must have two sections: net income and other comprehensive income (OCI). It must include (1) a total of net income with its components, (2) a total of OCI with its components, and (3) a total of comprehensive income. If separate but consecutive statements are presented, the first statement (the income statement) presents the components of net income and total net income. The second statement (the statement of OCI) is presented immediately after the first. It presents (1) the components of OCI, (2) the total of OCI, and (3) a total of comprehensive income. The entity must begin the second statement with net income.

✗ **Answer (A) is incorrect.** Comprehensive income must be reported in (1) one continuous financial statement or (2) two separate but consecutive financial statements.

✗ **Answer (B) is incorrect.** Comprehensive income and its components must be presented in a financial statement.

✗ **Answer (C) is incorrect.** Reporting in a statement of equity is prohibited under U.S. GAAP.

1.4 Statement of Changes in Equity

16. Zinc Co.'s adjusted trial balance at December 31, Year 6, includes the following account balances:

Common stock, $3 par	$600,000
Additional paid-in capital	800,000
Treasury stock, at cost	50,000
Net unrealized holding loss on available-for-sale securities	20,000
Retained earnings: Appropriated for uninsured earthquake losses	150,000
Retained earnings: Unappropriated	200,000

What amount should Zinc report as total equity in its December 31, Year 6, balance sheet?

   A. $1,680,000

   B. $1,720,000

   C. $1,780,000

   D. $1,820,000

✔ **Answer (A) is correct.**
Required: The total equity.
Discussion: Total credits to equity equal $1,750,000 ($600,000 common stock at par + $800,000 additional paid-in capital + $350,000 retained earnings). The treasury stock recorded at cost is subtracted from (debited to) total equity, and the unrealized holding loss on available-for-sale securities is debited to other comprehensive income, a component of equity. Because total debits equal $70,000 ($50,000 cost of treasury stock + $20,000 unrealized loss on available-for-sale securities), total equity equals $1,680,000 ($1,750,000 – $70,000).

✘ **Answer (B) is incorrect.** The amount of $1,720,000 treats the unrealized loss as a credit.

✘ **Answer (C) is incorrect.** The amount of $1,780,000 treats the treasury stock as a credit.

✘ **Answer (D) is incorrect.** The amount of $1,820,000 treats the treasury stock and the unrealized loss as credits.

17. Data regarding Ball Corp.'s investment in available-for-sale debt securities follow:

	Cost	Fair Value
December 31, Year 3	$150,000	$130,000
December 31, Year 4	150,000	160,000

Differences between cost and fair values are not due to credit losses. The decline in fair value was properly accounted for at December 31, Year 3. Ball's Year 4 statement of changes in equity should report an increase of

   A. $30,000

   B. $20,000

   C. $10,000

   D. $0

✔ **Answer (A) is correct.**
Required: The increase reported in the statement of changes in equity because of a change in the fair value of available-for-sale securities.
Discussion: Available-for-sale debt securities are measured at fair value in the financial statements. Unrealized holding gains or losses on their remeasurement to fair value, that are not related to credit losses, are reported in OCI. On 12/31/Year 3, the amount reported was $130,000. The increase in the fair value in Year 4 of $30,000 ($160,000 – $130,000) is recognized as an unrealized holding gain in Year 4 OCI. The OCI for the period (a temporary account) is closed to accumulated OCI (a permanent account) that is reported in the equity section of the balance sheet. Thus, the unrealized holding gain of $30,000 increases the accumulated OCI in Year 4. The statement of changes in equity reports the changes in all the equity accounts, including accumulated OCI.

✘ **Answer (B) is incorrect.** The amount of $20,000 is the excess of cost over fair value on 12/31/Year 3.

✘ **Answer (C) is incorrect.** The amount of $10,000 is the excess of fair value over cost on 12/31/Year 4.

✘ **Answer (D) is incorrect.** Equity increases when the unrealized holding gain is reported in other comprehensive income.

1.5 Special Purpose Frameworks

18. Which of the following is **not** a comprehensive basis of accounting other than generally accepted accounting principles?

    A. Cash receipts and disbursements basis of accounting.

    B. Basis of accounting used by an entity to file its income tax returns.

    C. Basis of accounting used by an entity to comply with the financial reporting requirements of a government regulatory agency.

    D. Basis of accounting used by an entity to comply with the financial reporting requirements of a lending institution.

✔ **Answer (D) is correct.**
Required: The item not a comprehensive basis of accounting other than GAAP.
Discussion: A comprehensive basis of accounting other than GAAP may be (1) a basis that the reporting entity uses to comply with the requirements or financial reporting provisions of a regulatory agency; (2) a basis used for tax purposes; (3) the cash basis, and modifications of the cash basis having substantial support, such as recording depreciation on fixed assets or accruing income taxes; or (4) a definite set of criteria having substantial support that is applied to all material items, for example, the price-level basis. However, a basis of accounting used by an entity to comply with the financial reporting requirements of a lending institution does not qualify as governmentally mandated or as having substantial support.

19. On April 1, Julie began operating a service proprietorship with an initial cash investment of $1,000. The proprietorship provided $3,200 of services in April and received a payment of $2,500 in May. The proprietorship incurred expenses of $1,500 in April that were paid in June. During May, Julie drew $500 from her capital account. What was the proprietorship's income for the 2 months ended May 31 under the following methods of accounting?

	Cash-Basis	Accrual-Basis
A.	$500	$1,200
B.	$1,000	$1,700
C.	$2,000	$1,200
D.	$2,500	$1,700

✔ **Answer (D) is correct.**
Required: The income for a proprietorship under the cash basis and accrual basis.
Discussion: Under the cash basis, $2,500 of income is recognized for the payments received in May for the services rendered in April. The $1,500 of expenses is not recognized until June. Under the accrual basis, the $3,200 of income and the $1,500 of expenses incurred in April but not paid until June are recognized. The net income is $1,700 under the accrual basis. The cash investment and capital withdrawal are ignored because they do not affect net income.

✖ **Answer (A) is incorrect.** The $500 withdrawal should not be recognized in the computation of net income under either method, and the $1,500 of expenses should not be recognized under the cash basis.

✖ **Answer (B) is incorrect.** The cash basis does not recognize the $1,500 in expenses until June.

✖ **Answer (C) is incorrect.** The $500 withdrawal should not be recognized in the computation of net income under either method.

20. Hahn Co. prepared financial statements on the cash basis of accounting. The cash basis was modified so that an accrual of income taxes was reported. Are these financial statements in accordance with the modified cash basis of accounting?

A. Yes.

B. No, because the modifications are illogical.

C. No, because there is **no** substantial support for recording income taxes.

D. No, because the modifications result in financial statements equivalent to those prepared under the accrual basis of accounting.

✔ **Answer (A) is correct.**
Required: The true statement about whether cash-basis statements may be modified for income tax accrual.
Discussion: A comprehensive basis of accounting other than GAAP includes the cash basis. Modifications of the cash basis having substantial support, such as accruing income taxes or recording depreciation on fixed assets, may be made when preparing financial statements on the cash basis (AU-C 800).

✘ **Answer (B) is incorrect.** Accrual of quarterly income taxes is a logical modification of the cash basis of accounting.

✘ **Answer (C) is incorrect.** Substantial support exists for accrual of a reasonably estimable expense such as income taxes.

✘ **Answer (D) is incorrect.** A modification of the cash basis that accrues income taxes but incorporates no other accruals or deferrals will not result in financial statements equivalent to those prepared under the accrual basis.

Go to Online Course

Access the **Gleim CPA Premium Review System** featuring our SmartAdapt technology from your Gleim Personal Classroom to continue your studies.

You will experience a personalized study environment with exam-emulating multiple-choice questions.

Study Unit Two

Income Statement Items

(26 pages of outline)

2.1 Foreign Currency Transaction Gains and Losses

Definitions

The **functional currency** is the currency of the primary economic environment in which the entity operates. Normally, that environment is the one in which it primarily generates and expends cash.

A **foreign currency** is any currency other than the entity's functional currency.

The current exchange rate is the rate used for currency conversion.

Foreign currency transaction terms are stated in a currency different from an entity's functional currency.

- For example, if an entity whose functional currency is the U.S. dollar purchases inventory on credit from a German entity, payment is to be in euros.

Initial Measurement

The initial measurement of the transaction must be in the reporting entity's functional currency.

- The exchange rate used is the rate in effect on the date the transaction was initially recognized.

Example 2-1	Foreign Currency Transaction -- Initial Measurement

On November 15, Year 1, JRF Corporation, a U.S. entity, purchases and receives inventory from Paris Corporation, a French entity. The transaction is fixed in euros and calls for JRF to pay Paris €500,000 on January 15, Year 2. On November 15, Year 1, the euro-dollar exchange rate is $1.2 to €1.

November 15, Year 1:

Inventory	$600,000	
Accounts payable (€500,000 × 1.2 exchange rate)		$600,000

Subsequent Measurement

A foreign currency transaction gain or loss results from a change in the exchange rate between the date the transaction was recognized, the date of the financial statements, and the date the transaction is settled.

- This gain or loss is included in the income statement in the period the exchange rate changes.

- If the monetary aspect of the transaction has not yet occurred at the end of the reporting period, monetary items (accounts payable and accounts receivable) are measured at the period-end exchange rate.

Example 2-2	Foreign Currency Transaction -- Gain or Loss

In continuation of Example 2-1, the euro-dollar exchange rate was $1.4 to €1 on December 31, Year 1, and $1.55 to €1 on January 15, Year 2.

December 31, Year 1 (financial statements day):

Loss on foreign currency transactions	$100,000	
Accounts payable [$600,000 − (€500,000 × 1.4 year-end exchange rate)]		$100,000

For the period between the initial recognition of the transaction (November 15, Year 1) and the date of the financial statements (December 31, Year 1), the dollar has depreciated against the euro. At that date, €500,000 euros cost $700,000 (€500,000 × 1.4). On December 31, Year 1, accounts payable is reported at $700,000, and the loss on foreign currency transactions is reported at $100,000.

January 15, Year 2 (transaction settlement day):

Accounts payable	$700,000	
Loss on foreign currency transactions [€500,000 × (1.55 − 1.4)]	75,000	
Cash (€500,000 × 1.55 settlement date exchange rate)		$775,000

The loss of $75,000 on foreign currency transactions is included in the Year 2 income statement.

NOTE: The total loss recognized on the exchange rate difference is $175,000 [€500,000 × (1.2 − 1.55)].

Stop & Review

You have completed the outline for this subunit.
Study multiple-choice questions 1 through 4 beginning on page 70.

2.2 Earnings per Share (EPS)

Earnings per share (EPS) is the amount of current-period earnings that can be associated with a single share of a corporation's common stock.

- The guidance regarding calculation and presentation of EPS must be followed by **public entities** and by other entities that choose to report EPS.

- EPS is calculated only for common stock.

Success Tip

> The topic of earnings per share has been tested continually on CPA Exams, often through calculations. Several questions testing earnings per share will likely appear on the exam.

Basic Earnings per Share (BEPS)

All corporations must report two BEPS amounts on the face of the income statement. Their numerators are **income from continuing operations** and **net income**, respectively.

$$\text{BEPS} = \frac{\text{Income available to common shareholders}}{\text{Weighted-average number of common shares outstanding}}$$

Example 2-3	Basic Earnings per Share (BEPS)

At year end, an entity's capital structure consisted of 10,000,000 shares of $1 par-value common stock. The entity issued no new shares during the year. Its income from continuing operations and net income for the year were $1,278,000 and $1,141,000, respectively.

BEPS calculations:
Income from continuing operations: $1,278,000 ÷ 10,000,000 = $0.128
Net income: $1,141,000 ÷ 10,000,000 = $0.114

If an entity has no discontinued operations, the income from continuing operations equals net income. Thus, one amount of BEPS for net income available to common shareholders is presented on the face of the income statement.

If a discontinued operation is reported, basic and diluted EPS amounts for the discontinued operation are presented on the face of the income statement or in the notes.

Calculation of the BEPS Numerator

Income available to common shareholders is the BEPS numerator.

- Thus, neither BEPS amount (income from continuing operations or net income) is calculated directly from the amount reported for that line item on the income statement.

  - Income in the BEPS numerator is reduced by dividends

    ▸ **Declared in the current period on preferred stock (whether or not paid)** and

    ▸ **Accumulated for the current period on cumulative preferred stock (whether or not declared).**

  - Dividends paid in the current period for undistributed accumulated preferred dividends for prior years do not affect the calculation. They were included in BEPS of prior years.

- The following calculation is performed for net income and income from continuing operations (or other number):

> Income statement amount
> − Dividends on preferred stock for the current period
>   (cumulative or declared noncumulative)
> _____
> Income available to common shareholders

Example 2-4   BEPS Numerator

An entity has two classes of preferred stock. It declared a 4% dividend on its $100,000 of noncumulative preferred stock. The entity did not declare a dividend on its $200,000 of 6% cumulative preferred stock. Undistributed dividends for the past 4 years have accumulated on this stock. The following is an excerpt from the entity's condensed income statement for the year:

Income from continuing operations before income taxes		$1,666,667
Income taxes		(666,667)
Income from continuing operations		**$1,000,000**
Discontinued operations:		
Loss from operations of component unit --		
Pipeline Division (including gain on disposal of $30,000)	$(216,667)	
Income tax benefit	86,667	
Loss on discontinued operations		(130,000)
Net income		**$ 870,000**

The numerators for income from continuing operations and for net income are calculated as follows:

	Income from Continuing Operations	Net Income
Income statement amounts	$1,000,000	$870,000
Declared or accumulated preferred dividends:		
Dividends declared on noncumulative preferred stock in the current period	(4,000)	(4,000)
Dividends accumulated on cumulative preferred stock in the current period	(12,000)	(12,000)
Income available to common shareholders	**$ 984,000**	**$854,000**

Calculation of the BEPS Denominator

The **weighted-average number of common shares outstanding** is determined by relating the portion of the period that the shares were outstanding to the total time in the period.

- Weighting is necessary because some shares may have been issued or reacquired during the period.

Example 2-5	BEPS Denominator

Using the data from Example 2-4, assume the following common stock transactions during the year just ended:

Date	Stock Transactions	Common Shares Outstanding		Portion of Year		Weighted Average
Jan 1	Beginning balance	240,000	×	2 ÷ 12	=	40,000
Mar 1	Issued 60,000 shares	300,000	×	5 ÷ 12	=	125,000
Aug 1	Repurchased 20,000 shares	280,000	×	3 ÷ 12	=	70,000
Nov 1	Issued 80,000 shares	360,000	×	2 ÷ 12	=	60,000
	Total					**295,000**

The **BEPS** amounts for income from continuing operations and net income are **$3.335** ($984,000 ÷ 295,000) and **$2.895** ($854,000 ÷ 295,000), respectively. Basic loss per share (negative BEPS) from discontinued operations of $0.44 ($130,000 ÷ 295,000) is reported on the face of the income statement or in the notes.

Stock dividends and **stock splits** require an adjustment to the weighted-average of common shares outstanding.

- EPS amounts for all periods presented are adjusted **retroactively** to reflect the change in capital structure as if it had occurred at the **beginning** of the **first period** presented.

- Adjustments are made for such changes even if they occur after the end of the current reporting period but before issuance (or the availability for issuance) of the financial statements.

Example 2-6	Effect of Stock Dividend and Stock Split on BEPS Denominator

Using the data from Example 2-4, assume declaration of a 50% common stock dividend on June 1 and a 2-for-1 common stock split on October 1:

Date	Stock Transactions	Common Shares Outstanding		Restate for Stock Div.		Restate for Stock Split		Portion of Year		Weighted Average
Jan 1	Beginning balance	240,000	×	1.5	×	2	×	2 ÷ 12	=	120,000
Mar 1	Issued 60,000 shares	300,000	×	1.5	×	2	×	5 ÷ 12	=	375,000
Jun 1	Distrib. 50% stock dividend	450,000								
Aug 1	Repurchased 20,000 shares	430,000			×	2	×	3 ÷ 12	=	215,000
Oct 1	Distrib. 2-for-1 stock split	860,000								
Nov 1	Issued 80,000 shares	940,000					×	2 ÷ 12	=	156,667
	Total									866,667

The **BEPS** amounts for income from continuing operations and net income are **$1.135** ($984,000 ÷ 866,667) and **$0.985** ($854,000 ÷ 866,667), respectively. Basic loss per share (negative BEPS) from discontinued operations of $0.15 ($130,000 ÷ 866,667) is reported in the income statement or in the notes.

Contingently issuable shares are shares issuable for little or no cash consideration upon satisfaction of certain conditions.

- Contingently issuable common shares are treated as outstanding and included in the calculation of the BEPS denominator from the date when the conditions for contingent issuance have been met.

Diluted Earnings per Share (DEPS)

An entity with **only common stock** outstanding (a simple capital structure) must report only BEPS amounts but not DEPS.

- An entity that does not have a simple capital structure must report DEPS as well as BEPS. Thus, the DEPS calculation includes the effects of **dilutive potential common shares (PCS)**.

  - PCS are securities or other contracts that may entitle the holder to obtain common stock.
  - PCS are included in the DEPS calculation only if they are dilutive.

Dilution is a reduction in BEPS (or an increase in loss per share) resulting from the assumption that

- **Convertible** securities (preferred stock or debt) were converted
- **Stock options** were exercised

Calculation of DEPS

DEPS measures performance after considering the effect on the numerator and denominator of dilutive PCS. DEPS is calculated as follows:

- **The BEPS denominator is increased** to include the weighted-average number of additional shares of common stock that would have been outstanding if dilutive PCS had been issued.

- **The BEPS numerator** is adjusted to **add back** any dividends on convertible preferred stock and the after-tax interest expense (an amount that includes amortization of discount or premium) related to any convertible debt.

$$\text{DEPS} = \frac{\text{BEPS numerator} + \text{Effect of dilutive PCS}}{\text{BEPS denominator} + \text{Effect of dilutive PCS}}$$

Example 2-7	Calculation of DEPS

Green Company's current year BEPS is $40 ($400,000 income available to common shareholders ÷ 10,000 weighted-average number of common shares outstanding). No dividend was declared this year, and the company's effective tax rate is 30%. The following PCS were outstanding during the year:

- $500,000 face amount, 10-year, 6%, convertible bonds. The bonds were originally issued at par, and each $5,000 bond is convertible into 10 of Green's common shares.

- 10,000 shares of $20 par, 10%, cumulative, convertible preferred stock. The conversion ratio is 5 shares of preferred stock to 2 shares of common stock.

-- Continued on next page --

Example 2-7 -- Continued

Assuming that the bonds and the preferred stock are dilutive securities, the DEPS for the period is calculated as follows:

Adjustment of BEPS Numerator

Convertible bonds: The BEPS numerator is adjusted to add back the after-tax amount of interest expense recognized in the current period associated with the convertible bonds. Because the bonds were issued at par, interest expense is calculated using the bonds' stated rate. Thus, the amount added back is calculated as follows:

$$\$500,000 \text{ face amount} \times 6\% \times (1.0 - .30) = \$21,000$$

Cumulative convertible preferred stock: The BEPS numerator is adjusted to add back any convertible preferred dividends that were declared or accumulated. No dividends were declared. However, the income available to common shareholders of $400,000 reflected the dividends accumulated for the current period on cumulative convertible preferred stock. Thus, the amount added back is calculated as follows:

$$10,000 \text{ preferred shares} \times \$20 \text{ par} \times 10\% = \$20,000$$

Adjustment of BEPS Denominator

Convertible bonds: The BEPS denominator is increased to include the weighted-average number of additional shares of common stock that would have been outstanding if the dilutive convertible bonds (PCS) had been converted. Thus, the increase is calculated as follows:

$$(\$500,000 \text{ face amount} \div \$5,000 \text{ par}) \times 10 = 1,000 \text{ common shares}$$

Cumulative convertible preferred stock: The BEPS denominator is increased to include the weighted-average number of additional shares of common stock that would have been outstanding if the dilutive convertible preferred stock (PCS) had been converted. Thus, the increase is calculated as follows:

$$10,000 \text{ preferred shares} \div (5 \div 2) \text{ conversion ratio} = 4,000 \text{ common shares}$$

The DEPS for the year is $29.40 $= \dfrac{\$400,000 + \$21,000 + \$20,000}{10,000 + 1,000 + 4,000}$

- The calculation of DEPS does not assume the conversion or exercise of antidilutive securities, i.e., securities that increase EPS or decrease loss per share.

- Dilutive PCS issued during a period are included in the DEPS denominator for the period they were outstanding.

  - Moreover, dilutive convertible securities that were actually converted are included for the period **before** conversion. Common shares actually issued are included for the period **after** conversion.

- Previously reported DEPS is not retroactively adjusted for subsequent conversions or changes in the market price of the common stock.

Three methods are used to determine the **dilutive effect** of PCS:

1. The if-converted method for convertible securities,
2. The treasury stock method for call options, and
3. The reverse treasury stock method for put options.

The If-Converted Method

The if-converted method calculates DEPS assuming the conversion of all dilutive convertible securities at the **beginning** of the period or at the **time of issue, if later**.

- The conversion of **antidilutive** securities (those whose conversion increase EPS or decrease loss per share) is **not assumed**. Thus, convertible PCS are antidilutive if the current dividend or after-tax interest per common share issuable exceeds BEPS.

In determining whether PCS are dilutive, each issue or series of issues of PCS are considered separately (rather than in the aggregate) and in sequence from the most dilutive to the least dilutive. The goal of this process is to maximize the dilution of BEPS (lowest possible DEPS).

- The **control number** to establish whether PCS are dilutive or antidilutive is the BEPS for the period.
  - If a discontinued operation is reported, the control number is BEPS from continuing operations.
- The issue with the lowest earnings per incremental share is included in DEPS before issues with higher earnings per incremental share. If the issue with the lowest earnings per incremental share is found to be dilutive with respect to BEPS, it is included in a trial calculation of DEPS.
- If the issue with the next lowest earnings per incremental share is dilutive with respect to the first trial calculation of DEPS, it is included in a new DEPS calculation that adjusts the numerator and denominator from the prior calculation.
- This process continues until all issues of PCS have been tested.

Example 2-8	The If-Converted Method for DEPS

Using the data from Example 2-7 on the previous pages, assume that Green's current-year BEPS is $23.20 ($232,000 income available to common shareholders ÷ 10,000 weighted-average number of common shares outstanding). The DEPS for the period is calculated as follows:

The earnings per incremental share of the convertible bonds is $21 ($21,000 ÷ 1,000). The earnings per incremental share of the cumulative convertible preferred stock is $5 ($20,000 ÷ 4,000).

Because the preferred stock's earnings per incremental share ($5) is lower than bond's earnings per incremental share ($21), it is more dilutive. Thus, it is compared first with the BEPS for the period (the control number). Because $5 is lower than $23.20, the cumulative convertible preferred stock is dilutive. Accordingly, it is included in the trial calculation of DEPS.

$$\text{The result is } \$18 = \frac{\$232,000 + \$20,000}{10,000 + 4,000}$$

The next step is to compare the earnings per incremental share of the convertible bonds ($21) with the new control number ($18). Because it is higher than the control number, the convertible bonds are antidilutive and must not be included in the calculation of DEPS. Thus, the DEPS for the period is **$18**.

NOTE: The inclusion of convertible bonds and preferred stock in the calculation of DEPS results in DEPS of $18.20 [($232,000 + $20,000 + $21,000) ÷ (10,000 + 4,000 + 1,000)]. This amount ($18.20) is not the lowest possible DEPS ($18).

NOTE: The inclusion of only convertible bonds in the calculation of DEPS results in DEPS of $23 [($232,000 + $21,000) ÷ (10,000 + 1,000)]. This amount also is not the lowest DEPS possible ($18).

If a discontinued operation is reported, the same number of shares used to adjust the denominator for income from continuing operations is used to adjust the DEPS denominator for income from discontinued operations. This rule applies even if the effect on the other amounts is antidilutive.

Treasury Stock Method

The second method used to determine the dilutive effect of PCS is the treasury stock method. It is used to determine the dilutive effect of outstanding **call options**.

- Call options are **dilutive** only if the **average market price** for the period of the common shares is **greater** than the **exercise price** of the options (they are in the money).

The treasury stock method assumes that

- The options are exercised at the beginning of the period (or time of issuance, if later),
- Common shares are issued, and
- The proceeds of exercise are used to purchase common stock at the period's average market price.

If the options are dilutive, their exercise affects only the denominator in the computation of DEPS. Any additional number of common shares outstanding (incremental shares) is added as an adjustment of the BEPS denominator.

- Because the numerator in the computation of DEPS is not affected, the earnings per incremental share is $0. Thus, options are generally the most dilutive PCS. They should be included first (before other series of PCS) in the trial calculation of DEPS.

The number of incremental shares from dilutive call options that must be included in the denominator of the DEPS computation is calculated as follows:

- Proceeds from exercising the options (Number outstanding × Exercise price).
- Number of shares assumed purchased (Proceeds from exercise ÷ Average market price for the period of common shares).
- Number of incremental shares (Number of common shares assumed issued – Number of common shares assumed purchased).
  - The number of common shares assumed issued is the amount of common shares that would have been issued assuming all the options were exercised.

Example 2-9   The Effect of Call Options on DEPS

Troupe Company's current-year BEPS is $11 ($440,000 net income ÷ 40,000 weighted-average number of common shares outstanding). Unexercised call options to purchase 20,000 shares of Troupe's common stock at $20 per share were outstanding at the beginning and end of the year. For the year, the average market price per share of Troupe's common stock was $25. The DEPS for the current year is calculated as follows:

- The call options are dilutive because the exercise price ($20) is less than the average market price ($25).
- The proceeds from exercising the options are $400,000 (20,000 number of call options outstanding × $20 exercise price of the options).
- The number of shares assumed purchased is 16,000 ($400,000 proceeds from exercising the options ÷ $25 average market price).
- The number of incremental shares is **4,000** (20,000 number of common shares assumed issued – 16,000 number of common shares assumed purchased).
- The number of incremental shares is added to the BEPS denominator in the computation of DEPS.

Thus, DEPS for the current year is $10 $= \dfrac{\$440,000}{40,000 + 4,000}$

Reverse Treasury Stock Method

The third method used to determine the dilutive effect of PCS is the reverse treasury stock method. It is used when the entity has entered into contracts to repurchase its own stock, for example, when it has **written put options** held by other parties.

- When the contracts are **in the money** (the exercise price exceeds the average market price), the potential dilutive effect on EPS is calculated by

    - Assuming the issuance at the beginning of the period of sufficient shares to raise the proceeds needed to satisfy the contracts,

    - Assuming those proceeds are used to repurchase shares, and

    - Including the excess of shares assumed to be issued over those assumed to be repurchased in the calculation of the DEPS denominator.

Stop & Review

You have completed the outline for this subunit.

Study multiple-choice questions 5 through 9 beginning on page 72.

2.3 Revenue from Contracts with Customers

The guidance for recognition of revenue from contracts with customers (ASC 606) provides a **single, principles-based** model for all contracts with customers regardless of the industry-specific or transaction-specific fact pattern.

The **core principle** is that an entity recognizes revenue for the transfer of promised goods or services to customers in an amount that reflects the consideration to which the entity expects to be entitled in the exchange.

This guidance applies to all contracts with customers **except** the following:

- Leases

- Financial instruments

- Contractual rights and obligations within the scope of specific topics, such as receivables, derivatives and hedging, insurance, and guarantees (other than product or service warranties)

- Nonmonetary exchanges between entities in the same line of business to facilitate sales to customers or potential customers

Below is the **five-step model** for recognizing revenue from contracts with customers.

- Step 1: Identify the contract(s) with a customer.
- Step 2: Identify the performance obligations in the contract.
- Step 3: Determine the transaction price.
- Step 4: Allocate the transaction price to the performance obligations in the contract.
- Step 5: Recognize revenue when (or as) a performance obligation is satisfied.

Step 1: Identify the Contract with a Customer

A contract is an agreement between two or more parties that creates enforceable rights and obligations.

A contract is accounted for under ASC 606 if **all** of the following criteria are met:

- The contract was approved by the parties.

- The contract has commercial substance.

- Each party's rights can be identified regarding

  - Goods or services to be transferred and
  - The payment terms.

- It is probable that the entity will collect substantially all of the consideration to which it is entitled according to the contract.

  - **Probable** means the future event is likely to occur.

If the criteria described above are not met (e.g., if collectibility cannot be reliably estimated), the consideration received is recognized as a liability, and **no revenue is recognized** until the criteria are met.

- However, even when the criteria described above are not met, revenue in the amount of **nonrefundable consideration** received from the customer is recognized if at least one of the following has occurred:

  - The contract has been terminated.

  - Control over the goods or services was transferred to the customer and the entity has stopped transferring (and has no obligation to transfer) additional goods or services to the customer.

  - The entity (1) has no obligation to transfer goods or services and (2) has received substantially all consideration from the customer.

A **contract modification** exists when the parties approve a change in the scope or price of a contract.

- It is accounted for as a **separate contract** if the following conditions are met:

  - The scope of the contract increases because of the addition of promised goods or services that are distinct, and

  - The price of the contract increases by an amount of consideration that reflects the entity's standalone selling prices of the additional promised goods or services.

Step 2: Identify the Performance Obligations in the Contract

A **performance obligation** is a promise in a contract with a customer to transfer to the customer

- A good or service that is distinct or

- A series of distinct goods or services that are substantially the same and have the same pattern of transfer to the customer.

Promised goods or services are **distinct** if

- The customer can benefit from them either on their own or together with other resources that are readily available **(capable of being distinct)** and

- The entity's promise to transfer them to the customer is separately identifiable from other promises in the contract **(distinct within the context of the contract)**. A **separately identifiable good or service**

  - Does not significantly modify or customize another good or service promised in the contract and

  - Is not highly dependent on, or highly interrelated with, other goods or services promised in the contract.

Customer options to acquire **additional goods or services for free or at a discount** have many forms, such as sales incentives, coupons, customer award points, or other discounts on future goods or services.

- When the option to acquire additional goods or services (e.g., a coupon or discount voucher) provides a material right to the customer, it results in a separate performance obligation in the contract.

  - A material right is an option that the customer would not receive without entering into that contract. An example is a discount in addition to the range of discounts typically given for those goods or services.

  - But an option to acquire an additional good or service at a price that reflects its standalone selling price does **not** provide a material right.

Step 3: Determine the Transaction Price

The **transaction price** is the amount of consideration to which an entity expects to be entitled in exchange for transferring promised goods or services to a customer.

- It excludes amounts collected on behalf of third parties (e.g., sales taxes).

- Any consideration payable to the customer, such as coupons, credits, or vouchers, reduces the transaction price.

- To determine the transaction price, an entity should consider the effects of the **time value of money** and **variable consideration**.

The revenue recognized must reflect the price that a customer would have paid for the promised goods or services if the cash payment had been made when they were transferred to the customer (i.e., the cash selling price).

- Thus, the transaction price is adjusted for the effect of the time value of money when the contract includes a **significant financing component**.

- The following factors should be considered in assessing whether a contract includes a significant financing component:

  - The difference between

    - The cash selling price of the promised goods or services and
    - The amount of consideration to be received

  - The combined effect of

    - The expected time between the payment and the delivery of the promised goods or services and
    - Market interest rates

The transaction price should **not** be adjusted for the effect of the time value of money if

- The time between the payment and the delivery of the promised goods or services to the customer is **1 year or less**

- The customer paid in advance and the transfer of goods or services is at the discretion of the customer

  - An example is a bill-and-hold contract in which the seller provides storage services for goods it sold to the buyer.

- A substantial amount of the consideration promised is **variable** and its amount or timing varies with future circumstances that are **not** within the control of the entity or the customer

  - An example is consideration in the form of a sales-based royalty.

Interest income or expense is recognized using the **effective interest method**.

- It must be presented in the income statement **separately** from revenue from contracts with customers.

Example 2-10   Significant Financing Component

On January 1, Year 1, BIF Co. sold and transferred a machine to a customer for $583,200 that is payable on December 31, Year 2. Other customers pay $500,000 upon delivery of the same machine at contract inception. The cost of the machine to BIF is $400,000. BIF determined that the contract includes a significant financing component because of the difference between the consideration ($583,200) and the cash selling price ($500,000). The contract includes an implicit interest rate of 8%. The following entries are recorded by BIF:

January 1, Year 1

Accounts receivable	$500,000		Cost of goods sold	$400,000
Revenue		$500,000	Machine inventory		$400,000

December 31, Year 1

Accounts receivable ($500,000 × 8%)	$40,000
Interest income	$40,000

December 31, Year 2

Accounts receivable ($540,000 × 8%)	$43,200		Cash	$583,200
Interest income		$43,200	Accounts receivable		$583,200

Example 2-11   Significant Financing Component -- Advance Payment

On January 1, Year 1, Eva Co. received a payment of $100,000 for delivering a machine to a customer at the end of Year 2. The cost of the machine to Eva is $70,000. Eva determined that (1) the contract includes a significant financing component and (2) a financing rate of 10% is an appropriate discount rate. The following entries are recorded by Eva:

January 1, Year 1

Cash	$100,000
Contract liability	$100,000

December 31, Year 1

Interest expense ($100,000 × 10%)	$10,000
Contract liability	$10,000

December 31, Year 2

Interest expense ($110,000 × 10%)	$11,000
Contract liability	$11,000

Cost of goods sold	70,000
Machine inventory	70,000

Contract liability	$121,000
Revenue	$121,000

Variable Consideration

If a contract includes a variable amount, an entity must estimate the consideration to which it will be entitled in exchange for transferring the promised goods or services to a **customer**. For example, the contract price may vary because of the following:

- Refunds due to a right of return provided to customers (Study Unit 6, Subunit 1)

- Prompt payment discounts (Study Unit 5, Subunit 1)

- Volume discounts

- Other uncertainties in contract price based on the occurrence or nonoccurrence of some future event

Variable consideration is **estimated** using one of the following methods:

- The **expected value** is the sum of probability-weighted amounts in the range of possible consideration amounts. This method may provide an appropriate estimate if an entity has many contracts with similar characteristics.

- The **most likely amount** is the single most likely amount in a range of possible consideration amounts. This method may provide an appropriate estimate if the contract has only two possible outcomes. For example, a construction entity either will receive a performance bonus for finishing construction on time or will not.

The estimated transaction price must be updated at the **end** of each reporting period.

Constraint. Revenue from variable consideration is recognized only to the extent that it is **probable** that a **significant reversal** will **not** occur when the uncertainty associated with the variable consideration is subsequently resolved.

A **volume discount** offered as an incentive to increase future sales requires the customer to purchase a specified quantity of goods or services to receive a discount. The discount may be applied (1) **prospectively** on additional goods purchased in the future or (2) **retrospectively** on all goods purchased to date.

- A **prospective volume discount** that provides a **material right** to the customer is accounted for as a separate performance obligation in the contract (Study Unit 9, Subunit 4).

- **Retrospective volume discounts** are accounted for as **variable consideration**. The uncertainty of the contract price for current goods sold is based on the occurrence or nonoccurence of some future event (i.e., whether the customer completes the specified volume of purchase).

Example 2-12   Retrospective Volume Discount

Barashka Co. manufactures wool coats. On October 1, Year 1, Barashka entered into a 3-year contract with a customer to sell coats for $200 per unit. Based on the contract, if the customer purchased more than 3,000 coats over the contract period, the contract price per coat would be retroactively reduced to $150. The cost per coat to Barashka is $80. Barashka determined that the contract has no significant financing component.

The retrospective volume discount is variable consideration. In Year 1, the customer purchased with cash 100 coats, and Barashka estimated that the customer's purchases would not exceed 3,000 during the contract period. Thus, based on the most likely amount method, the contract price per coat was $200.

The following entries were recorded by Barashka in Year 1:

Cash (100 × $200)	$20,000	Cost of goods sold (100 × $80)	$8,000
Sales revenue	$20,000	Inventory of coats	$8,000

The winter in Year 2 was colder than expected. The customer purchased an additional 2,200 coats. Accordingly, Barashka estimated that the customer would purchase more than 3,000 coats over the contract period. The price per coat therefore was retrospectively reduced to $150, and Year 2 revenue is calculated as a cumulative catch up adjustment. Year 2 revenue of $325,000 was the difference between total revenue that should be recognized for Year 1 and Year 2 of $345,000 [(2,200 + 100) × $150)] minus revenue recognized in Year 1 of $20,000. A contract liability is recognized for the excess of consideration received over the amount of revenue recognized. It equals the future amount of goods to be transferred to the customer for which the consideration was already received.

The following entries were recorded by Barashka in Year 2:

Cash (2,200 × $200)	$440,000	Cost of goods sold (2,200 × $80)	$176,000
Sales revenue	$325,000	Inventory of coats	$176,000
Contract liability	115,000		

As expected, the customer purchased an additional 1,100 coats in Year 3. Accordingly, 3,400 (100 + 2,200 + 1,100) coats were purchased during the contract period. In Year 3, the customer retroactively received the discount on all the coats previously purchased, paying cash of $50,000 [(3,400 × $150) − ($440,000 + $20,000)].

The following entries were recorded by Barashka in Year 3:

Cash	$ 50,000	Cost of goods sold (1,100 × $80)	$88,000
Contract liability	115,000	Inventory of coats	$88,000
Sales revenue (1,100 × $150)	$165,000		

Consideration payable to a customer includes cash amounts that an entity pays, or expects to pay, to the customer (or to other parties that purchase the entity's goods or services from the customer).

- Consideration payable to a customer is recognized as a **reduction** of the **transaction price** and therefore of revenue.

Example 2-13   Consideration Paid to a Customer

Haf Company is a manufacturer of printing machines, and Gary Company is a large electronics retail store. On January 1, Year 1, Haf entered into a 1-year contract with Gary to sell 5,000 printing machines for $400 each. The contract also required Haf to make a nonrefundable payment of $150,000 to Gary at the inception of the contract. The $150,000 payment compensates Gary for needed changes in shelving to accommodate the new printing machines.

The consideration payable to Gary of $150,000 is accounted for as a reduction of the transaction price. Accordingly, (1) the total transaction price is $1,850,000 [(5,000 × $400) – $150,000], and (2) the revenue recognized on the sale of each printing machine is $370 ($1,850,000 ÷ 5,000).

- Revenue is reduced for consideration payable to a customer at the **later** of when the entity

  - Recognizes revenue for the transfer of the related goods or services to the customer or
  - Promises to pay the consideration to the customer.

Step 4: Allocate the Transaction Price to the Performance Obligations in the Contract

After separate performance obligations are identified and the total transaction price is determined, the transaction price is allocated to performance obligations on the basis of relative standalone selling prices.

A **standalone selling price** is the price at which an entity would sell a promised good or service separately to a customer.

- The best evidence of a standalone selling price is the **observable price** of a good or service when it is (1) sold separately (2) in similar circumstances and (3) to similar customers (e.g., the list price of a good or service).

If the standalone price is **not directly observable**, it must be estimated. The following are suitable approaches:

- **Adjusted market assessment.** An entity evaluates the market in which it sells goods or services and estimates the price that a customer in that market would be willing to pay for them.

    - For example, the prices of competitors for similar goods or services adjusted for the entity's costs and margins are estimates of standalone selling prices.

- **Expected cost plus an appropriate margin.** An entity forecasts its expected costs of satisfying a performance obligation and adds an appropriate margin for that cost.

- **Residual.** An entity estimates the standalone selling price by reference to the total transaction price minus the sum of the observable standalone selling prices of other goods or services promised in the contract. The residual approach may be used only in limited circumstances.

Example 2-14   Allocation of Contract Price

A company entered into a contract with a customer to sell a machine and provide 3 years of maintenance services for the machine. The total consideration is $200,000. The company determined that the machine and the maintenance services are distinct performance obligations. The company regularly sells machines separately at a directly observable standalone selling price of $160,000. But it does not sell maintenance services on a standalone basis. Based on the expected cost plus an appropriate margin approach, the estimated standalone selling price for 3 years of maintenance services was $90,000. The transaction price is allocated to each performance obligation in the contract using relative standalone selling prices.

Performance Obligation	Standalone Selling Price	Allocation of the Contract Price
Machine	$160,000	$128,000 = ($160,000 ÷ $250,000) × $200,000
Maintenance services	90,000	72,000 = ($90,000 ÷ $250,000) × $200,000
Total	$250,000	$200,000

Step 5: Recognize Revenue when (or as) a Performance Obligation Is Satisfied

An entity recognizes revenue when (or as) it satisfies a performance obligation by transferring a promised good or service (an asset) to a **customer**.

- An **asset** is transferred when (or as) the customer obtains control of that asset.

Control of an asset is transferred when the customer

- Has the ability to direct the use of the asset and
- Obtains substantially all of the remaining benefits (potential cash flows) from the asset.

A performance obligation can be satisfied either over time or at a point in time.

- Recognizing revenue **over time** requires transfer of the control of goods or services to a customer over time and therefore satisfaction of a performance obligation over time. **One** of the following criteria must be met:

  - The customer **simultaneously** receives and consumes the benefits provided by the entity's performance as the entity performs. For example, cleaning services are provided to a customer's offices every day throughout the accounting period.

  - The entity's performance **creates or enhances an asset** that the customer controls as the asset is created or enhanced. For example, a construction company erects a building on the customer's land.

  - The asset created has **no alternative use** to the entity, and the entity has an enforceable **right** to payment for the performance completed to date. For example, an aerospace company contracts to build a satellite designed for the unique needs of a specific customer.

    ▸ An entity does not have an alternative use for an asset if the entity is restricted contractually or limited practically from directing the asset for another use.

- The accounting for contracts in which revenue is recognized over time is described in Subunit 2.4.

- If a performance obligation is **not satisfied over time**, an entity satisfies the performance obligation **at a point in time**.

  - Revenue is recognized at a point in time when the customer obtains **control** over the promised asset. The following indicators of the transfer of control should be considered:

    ▸ The entity has a present right to payment for the asset.
    ▸ The customer has legal title to the asset.
    ▸ The entity has transferred physical possession of the asset.
    ▸ The customer has the significant risks and rewards of ownership of the asset.
    ▸ The customer has accepted the asset.

Balance Sheet Presentation

A **contract liability** is recognized for an entity's obligation to transfer goods or services to a customer for which the entity has received consideration from the customer.

- Deposits and other advance payments by the customer, such as sales of gift certificates, are recognized as contract liabilities (Study Unit 9, Subunit 4).

A **contract asset** is recognized for an entity's right to consideration in exchange for goods or services that the entity has transferred to a customer.

- However, the entity must have an **unconditional** right to the consideration to recognize a **receivable**.
- A right to consideration is unconditional if only the passage of time is required before payment of that consideration is due.

Contract assets and contract liabilities resulting from different contracts must not be presented net in the statement of financial position.

Incremental Costs of Obtaining a Contract

The incremental costs of obtaining a contract with a customer must be capitalized **(recognized as an asset)** if the entity expects to recover them.

- The asset recognized must be **amortized** on a systematic basis consistent with the transfer to the customer of the goods or services to which the asset relates.

The cost of obtaining a contract may be **expensed as incurred** if its amortization period is **1 year or less**.

Costs to obtain a contract that would have been incurred **regardless** of whether the contract was obtained must be **expensed as incurred**.

- But costs explicitly chargeable to the customer regardless of whether the contract is obtained are capitalized.

Example 2-15	Costs of Obtaining a Contract

A company wins a bid to provide consulting services for 5 years to a new customer. The following costs were incurred to obtain the contract:

External legal fees for due diligence	$30,000
Commissions to sales employees	20,000
Total costs incurred to obtain the contract	$50,000

The commissions to sales employees of $20,000 are incremental costs of obtaining the contract. Because the company expects to recover those costs through future fees for consulting services, they must be capitalized. The costs capitalized are amortized over 5 years as the services are delivered to the customer. The external legal fees for due diligence of $30,000 must be expensed as incurred. Such costs are not incremental costs of obtaining the contract. They would have been incurred regardless of whether the contract was obtained.

Costs Incurred to Fulfill a Contract

Costs incurred to fulfill a contract must be capitalized (recognized as an asset) only if they meet all of the following criteria:

- The costs relate directly to a current or anticipated contract.

- The costs generate or enhance resources of the entity that will be used in satisfying performance obligations **in the future**.

- The costs are expected to be recovered.

The asset recognized must be **amortized** on a systematic basis consistent with the transfer to the customer of the goods or services to which the asset relates.

Stop & Review

You have completed the outline for this subunit.
Study multiple-choice questions 10 through 14 beginning on page 75.

2.4 Recognition of Revenue over Time

For each performance obligation satisfied over time, an entity must recognize revenue over time. For this purpose, the entity measures the **progress toward complete satisfaction** using the **output method** or the **input method**.

- To determine the appropriate method, an entity must consider the nature of the good or service that it promised to transfer to the customer.

- The chosen method should describe the entity's performance in transferring control of the promised asset to the customer.

At the end of each reporting period, the progress toward complete satisfaction of the performance obligation must be **remeasured** and updated for any changes in the outcome of the performance obligation.

- Such changes must be accounted for prospectively as a **change in accounting estimate**.

The **input method** recognizes revenue on the basis of (1) the entity's inputs to the satisfaction of the performance obligation relative to (2) the total expected inputs to the satisfaction of that performance obligation.

- Examples of input include

  - Costs incurred,
  - Labor hours expended,
  - Resources consumed,
  - Time elapsed, or
  - Machine hours used.

- In long-term construction contracts, **costs incurred relative to total estimated costs** often are used to measure the progress toward completion. This method is the **cost-to-cost** method.

  - Only costs that contribute to progress in satisfying the performance obligation are used in the cost-to-cost method. Thus, the following costs must not be included in measuring the progress:

    - Costs incurred that relate to significant inefficiencies in the entity's performance (e.g., abnormal amounts of wasted materials or labor) that were not chargeable to the customer under the contract

    - General and administrative costs not directly related to the contract

    - Selling and marketing costs

Example 2-16   Cost-to-Cost Method

On January 1, Year 1, a contractor agrees to build on the customer's land a bridge that is expected to be completed at the end of Year 3. The promised bridge is a single performance obligation to be satisfied over time. The contractor determines that the progress toward completion of the bridge is reasonably measurable using the input method based on costs incurred. The contract price is $2,000,000, and expected total costs of the project are $1,200,000.

	Year 1	Year 2	Year 3
Costs incurred during each year	$300,000	$600,000	$550,000
Costs expected in the future	900,000	600,000	

Year 1

By the end of Year 1, 25% [$300,000 ÷ ($300,000 + $900,000)] of the total expected costs have been incurred. Using the input method based on costs incurred, the contractor recognizes 25% of the total expected revenue ($2,000,000 contract price × 25% = $500,000).

Revenue	$500,000
Construction costs	(300,000)
Gross profit -- Year 1	$200,000*

* The gross profit in Year 1 of $200,000 also may be calculated as total expected gross profit from the project of $800,000 ($2,000,000 contract price – $1,200,000 total expected construction costs) times the progress toward completion of the contract of 25%.

Year 2

By the end of Year 2, total costs incurred are $900,000 ($300,000 + $600,000). Given that $600,000 is expected to be incurred in the future, the total expected cost is $1,500,000 ($900,000 + $600,000). The change in the total cost of the contract must be accounted for prospectively. By the end of Year 2, 60% ($900,000 ÷ $1,500,000) of expected costs have been incurred. Thus, $1,200,000 ($2,000,000 × 60%) of cumulative revenue should be recognized for Years 1 and 2. Because $500,000 of revenue was recognized in Year 1, revenue of $700,000 ($1,200,000 cumulative revenue – $500,000) is recognized in Year 2.

Revenue	$700,000
Construction costs	(600,000)
Gross profit -- Year 2	$100,000*

* The gross profit in Year 2 of $100,000 also may be calculated as the cumulative gross profit for Years 1 and 2 of $300,000 [($2,000,000 – $1,500,000) × 60%] minus the gross profit recognized in Year 1 of $200,000.

Year 3

At the end of Year 3, the project is completed, and the total costs incurred for the contract are $1,450,000 ($300,000 + $600,000 + $550,000). Given $1,200,000 of cumulative revenue for Years 1 and 2, $800,000 ($2,000,000 contract price – $1,200,000) of revenue is recognized in Year 3.

Revenue	$800,000
Construction costs	(550,000)
Gross profit -- Year 3	$250,000

NOTE: The total gross profit from the project of $550,000 ($200,000 + $100,000 + $250,000) equals the contract price of $2,000,000 minus the total costs incurred of $1,450,000.

- When an entity's inputs are incurred evenly over time, recognition of revenue on a straight-line basis may be appropriate.

The **output method** recognizes revenue based on direct measurement of (1) the value of goods or services transferred to the customer to date relative to (2) the remaining goods or services promised under the contract.

- Examples of output methods include (1) appraisals of results achieved, (2) milestones reached, (3) units produced, and (4) units delivered.

- An entity may have a right to consideration from a customer in an amount corresponding directly with the value to the customer of performance to date. Using a practical expedient, revenue may be recognized at the amounts to which the entity has a **right to invoice the customer**.

Example 2-17	Output Method -- Practical Expedient

A law firm enters into a contract to provide consulting services to a customer for a 1-year period for a fixed amount per hour of service provided. Because the customer simultaneously receives and consumes the benefits provided by the law firm's performance as it performs, revenue is recognized over time. Under the practical expedient, the law firm may recognize revenue that it has a right to bill to the customer.

An entity recognizes revenue for a performance obligation satisfied over time only if progress toward complete satisfaction of the performance obligation can be reasonably measured.

- However, revenue can be recognized to the **extent of the cost incurred** (zero profit margin) when an entity

  - Is not able to reasonably measure the outcome of a performance obligation or its progress toward satisfaction of that obligation but
  - Expects to recover the costs incurred in satisfying the performance obligation.

Example 2-18	Revenue Recognition to the Extent of the Costs Incurred

On January 1, Year 1, Sadik Co. agrees to build on the customer's land a bridge that is expected to be completed at the end of Year 3. The contract price is $2 million. The promised bridge is a single performance obligation to be satisfied over time. Because Sadik has no experience with this type of contract, it cannot reasonably determine the total expected costs of the project. Accordingly, by the end of Year 1, progress toward completion of the bridge is not reasonably determinable. In Year 1, $300,000 of costs were incurred and paid by Sadik. However, the contract specified that Sadik has an enforceable right to payment of the costs incurred. Sadik therefore expects to recover these costs.

In Year 1, revenue is recognized at the amount of costs incurred of $300,000, and no gross profit is recognized. The following entries are recorded by Sadik in Year 1:

Accounts receivable	$300,000		Construction costs	$300,000	
Revenue		$300,000	Cash		$300,000

As soon as an **estimated loss** on any project becomes apparent, it must be **recognized in full**, regardless of the methods used.

Stop & Review

You have completed the outline for this subunit.

Study multiple-choice questions 15 through 18 beginning on page 78.

Questions

2.1 Foreign Currency Transaction Gains and Losses

1. Which of the following statements regarding foreign exchange gains and losses is true (where the exchange rate is the ratio of units of the functional currency to units of the foreign currency)?

A. An exchange gain occurs when the exchange rate increases between the date a payable is recorded and the date of cash payment.

B. An exchange gain occurs when the exchange rate increases between the date a receivable is recorded and the date of cash receipt.

C. An exchange loss occurs when the exchange rate decreases between the date a payable is recorded and the date of the cash payment.

D. An exchange loss occurs when the exchange rate increases between the date a receivable is recorded and the date of the cash receipt.

✔ **Answer (B) is correct.**
Required: The true statement about foreign exchange gains and losses.
Discussion: A foreign currency transaction gain or loss (commonly known as a foreign exchange gain or loss) is recorded in earnings. When the amount of the functional currency exchangeable for a unit of the currency in which the transaction is fixed increases, a transaction gain or loss is recognized on a receivable or payable, respectively. The opposite occurs when the exchange rate (functional currency to foreign currency) decreases.

✘ **Answer (A) is incorrect.** The payable will become more expensive in the functional currency, resulting in a loss.

✘ **Answer (C) is incorrect.** The payable will become less expensive in the functional currency, resulting in a gain.

✘ **Answer (D) is incorrect.** An exchange gain occurs.

2. Fogg Co., a U.S. company, contracted to purchase foreign goods. Payment in foreign currency was due 1 month after the goods were received at Fogg's warehouse. Between the receipt of goods and the time of payment, the exchange rates changed in Fogg's favor. The resulting gain should be included in Fogg's financial statements as a(n)

A. Component of income from continuing operations.

B. Decrease in the carrying amount of the goods.

C. Deferred credit.

D. Item of other comprehensive income.

✔ **Answer (A) is correct.**
Required: The accounting treatment of a foreign currency transaction gain.
Discussion: This foreign currency transaction resulted in a payable stated in a foreign currency. The favorable change in the exchange rate between the functional currency and the currency in which the transaction was stated should be included in determining net income for the period in which the exchange rate changed. It should be classified as a component of income from continuing operations.

✘ **Answer (B) is incorrect.** The historical cost of the goods is based on the exchange rate on the date the goods were purchased and received. The change in the payables between that date and the payment date is recognized in the income statement.

✘ **Answer (C) is incorrect.** The gain should not be deferred but should be recognized in the period in which the exchange rate changed.

✘ **Answer (D) is incorrect.** Translation adjustments, not transaction gains and losses, are included in OCI.

3. Toigo Co. purchased merchandise from a vendor in England on November 20 for 500,000 British pounds. Payment was due in British pounds on January 20. The spot rates to purchase 1 pound were as follows:

November 20 $1.25
December 31   1.20
January 20   1.17

How should the foreign currency transaction gain be reported on Toigo's financial statements at December 31?

A. A gain of $40,000 as a separate component of stockholders' equity.

B. A gain of $40,000 in the income statement.

C. A gain of $25,000 as a separate component of stockholders' equity.

D. A gain of $25,000 in the income statement.

✔ **Answer (D) is correct.**
Required: The reporting of a foreign currency transaction gain.
Discussion: Foreign currency transactions are recorded at the spot rate in effect at the transaction date. Transaction gains and losses are included in the income statement in the period the exchange rate changes. On November 20, the entity made the following entry:

Inventory (500,000 lbs. × $1.25) $625,000
    Accounts payable $625,000

On December 31, the entity made the following entry:

Accounts payable [500,000 lbs. ×
   ($1.25 – $1.20)] $25,000
    Foreign currency transaction gain $25,000

✘ **Answer (A) is incorrect.** The entity recognizes a gain in earnings of $15,000 [500,000 pounds × ($1.20 – $1.17)] on January 20.

✘ **Answer (B) is incorrect.** The only effect of the change in the spot rate during the period is recognized at the balance sheet date.

✘ **Answer (C) is incorrect.** The gain is recognized in earnings. Translation adjustments are recognized in OCI.

4. On September 22, Year 2, Yumi Corp. purchased merchandise from an unaffiliated foreign company for 10,000 units of the foreign company's local currency. On that date, the spot rate was $.55. Yumi paid the bill in full on March 20, Year 3, when the spot rate was $.65. The spot rate was $.70 on December 31, Year 2. What amount should Yumi report as a foreign currency transaction loss in its income statement for the year ended December 31, Year 2?

A. $0

B. $500

C. $1,000

D. $1,500

✔ **Answer (D) is correct.**
Required: The amount of foreign currency transaction loss to be reported in the income statement.
Discussion: A receivable or payable stated in a foreign currency is adjusted to its current exchange rate at each balance sheet date. The resulting gain or loss should ordinarily be included in determining net income. It is the difference between the spot rate on the date the transaction originates and the spot rate at year end. Thus, the Year 2 transaction loss for Yumi Corp. is $1,500 [10,000 units × ($0.55 – $0.70)].

✘ **Answer (A) is incorrect.** A loss resulted when the spot rate increased.

✘ **Answer (B) is incorrect.** The amount of $500 results from using the spot rates at December 31, Year 2, and March 20, Year 3.

✘ **Answer (C) is incorrect.** The amount of $1,000 results from using the spot rates at September 22, Year 2, and March 20, Year 3.

2.2 Earnings per Share (EPS)

5. A firm has basic earnings per share of $1.29. If the tax rate is 30%, which of the following securities would be dilutive?

   A. Cumulative 8%, $50 par preferred stock.

   B. Ten percent convertible bonds, issued at par, with each $1,000 bond convertible into 20 shares of common stock.

   C. Seven percent convertible bonds, issued at par, with each $1,000 bond convertible into 40 shares of common stock.

   D. Six percent, $100 par cumulative convertible preferred stock, issued at par, with each preferred share convertible into four shares of common stock.

✔ **Answer (C) is correct.**
Required: The dilutive securities given BEPS and the tax rate.
Discussion: The calculation of dilutive EPS (DEPS) gives effect to dilutive potential common shares (e.g., options and convertible securities). Dilution is a reduction in basic EPS (BEPS) resulting from the assumption that (1) convertible securities were converted, (2) options were exercised, or (3) contingently issuable shares were issued. The conversion of the bonds would eliminate after-tax interest expense per bond of $49 [($1,000 par × 7%) × (1.0 − 30% tax rate)]. (The bonds were issued at par, so amortization of premium or discount does not affect the calculation.) The per-share effect is $1.225 ($49 ÷ 40 shares per bond). Thus, the convertible debt is dilutive ($1.225 < $1.29 BEPS).

✘ **Answer (A) is incorrect.** Unless the preferred stock is convertible, it is not dilutive. Nonconvertible preferred shares are not potential common stock and therefore are not considered in the calculation of DEPS.

✘ **Answer (B) is incorrect.** The conversion of the bonds would eliminate after-tax interest expense per bond of $70 [($1,000 par × 10%) × (1.0 − 30% tax rate)]. (The bonds were issued at par, so amortization of premium or discount does not affect the calculation.) The per-share effect is $3.50 ($70 ÷ 20 shares per bond). Thus, the convertible debt is antidilutive ($3.50 > $1.29 BEPS).

✘ **Answer (D) is incorrect.** If the preferred stock is converted, the EPS numerator increases by the dividend savings of $6 ($100 par × 6%) per share of preferred stock (the additional income available to common shareholders). The per-share effect is $1.50 ($6 ÷ 4 common shares per share of preferred stock). Thus, the preferred stock is antidilutive ($1.50 > $1.29 BEPS).

6. During the current year, Comma Co. had outstanding: 25,000 shares of common stock; 8,000 shares of $20 par, 10% cumulative preferred stock; and 3,000 bonds that are $1,000 par and 9% convertible. The bonds were originally issued at par, and each bond was convertible into 10 shares of common stock. During the year, net income was $200,000, **no** dividends were declared, and the tax rate was 30%. What amount was Comma's basic earnings per share for the current year?

A. $6.78

B. $7.36

C. $7.07

D. $8.00

✔ **Answer (B) is correct.**
Required: The basic earnings per share.
Discussion: The numerator of the basic earnings per share (BEPS) ratio is income available to common shareholders. Declared dividends and accumulated dividends on preferred stock are removed from net income for the period to arrive at this amount. The undeclared but cumulative dividends on preferred stock equal $16,000 (8,000 shares × $20 par × 10%). Thus, given no dividends declared, the income available to common shareholders is $184,000 ($200,000 − $16,000). This amount is divided by the weighted-average common shares outstanding. All 25,000 of the common shares were outstanding during the entire period. Accordingly, BEPS equals $7.36 ($184,000 ÷ 25,000 shares).

✘ **Answer (A) is incorrect.** The amount of $6.78 is diluted EPS [(BEPS numerator + $189,000 after-tax bond interest saved by a hypothetical bond conversion) ÷ (BEPS denominator + 30,000 common shares assumed to have been issued at the beginning of the period after the conversion of the bonds)].

✘ **Answer (C) is incorrect.** The amount of $7.07 is the diluted EPS amount if the preferred stock were not cumulative.

✘ **Answer (D) is incorrect.** The amount of $8.00 ignores the undeclared cumulative preferred dividends.

7. At December 31, Year 1, Lex, Inc., had 600,000 shares of common stock outstanding. On April 1, Year 2, an additional 180,000 shares of common stock were issued for cash. Lex also had $5 million of 8% convertible bonds outstanding at December 31, Year 2, which are convertible into 150,000 shares of common stock. The bonds were dilutive in the Year 2 DEPS computation. **No** bonds were issued or converted into common stock during Year 2. What is the number of shares that should be used in computing DEPS for Year 2?

A. 735,000

B. 780,000

C. 885,000

D. 930,000

✔ **Answer (C) is correct.**
Required: The number of shares to be used in computing DEPS.
Discussion: DEPS should be based on the weighted-average number of (1) shares of common stock outstanding and (2) the shares of common stock assumed to have been issued to reflect the conversion of the bonds. The weighted-average number of shares for Year 2 should therefore be 885,000, based on 750,000 shares outstanding for the entire year (600,000 beginning balance + 150,000 from the hypothetical conversion of bonds) and 180,000 additional shares issued on April 1.

$$
\begin{array}{rcl}
750{,}000 \times (3 \div 12) &=& 187{,}500 \\
930{,}000 \times (9 \div 12) &=& \underline{697{,}500} \\
&& \underline{\underline{885{,}000}}
\end{array}
$$

✘ **Answer (A) is incorrect.** The figure of 735,000 results from not assuming conversion of the convertible bonds as of the beginning of the year.

✘ **Answer (B) is incorrect.** The figure of 780,000 results from not assuming conversion of the convertible bonds as of the beginning of the year and treating the additional issue of stock as occurring at the beginning of the year.

✘ **Answer (D) is incorrect.** The figure of 930,000 results from treating the additional issue of stock as occurring at the beginning of the year.

8. Deck Co. had 120,000 shares of common stock outstanding at January 1. On July 1, it issued 40,000 additional shares of common stock. Outstanding all year were 10,000 shares of nonconvertible cumulative preferred stock. What is the number of shares that Deck should use to calculate basic earnings per share?

A. 140,000

B. 150,000

C. 160,000

D. 170,000

✓ **Answer (A) is correct.**
Required: The weighted-average number of shares used to calculate BEPS.
Discussion: Basic earnings per share (BEPS) is used to measure earnings performance based on common stock outstanding during the period. BEPS equals income available to common shareholders divided by the weighted-average number of common shares outstanding. The weighted-average number of common shares outstanding relates the portion of the period that the shares were outstanding to the total time in the period. Consequently, the number of shares used to calculate BEPS is 140,000 {120,000 shares outstanding throughout the period + [40,000 shares × (6 months ÷ 12 months)]}.

✗ **Answer (B) is incorrect.** The figure of 150,000 includes the preferred shares.

✗ **Answer (C) is incorrect.** The figure of 160,000 includes the unweighted number of additional shares.

✗ **Answer (D) is incorrect.** The figure of 170,000 includes the preferred shares and does not weight the additional common shares.

9. The following information pertains to Ceil Co., a company whose common stock trades in a public market:

Shares outstanding at 1/1	100,000
Stock dividend at 3/31	24,000
Stock issuance at 6/30	5,000

What is the weighted-average number of shares Ceil should use to calculate its basic earnings per share (BEPS) for the year ended December 31?

A. 120,500

B. 123,000

C. 126,500

D. 129,000

✓ **Answer (C) is correct.**
Required: The weighted-average number of shares used to calculate BEPS.
Discussion: BEPS measures earnings performance based on common stock outstanding during all or part of the period. BEPS equals income available to common shareholders divided by the weighted-average number of shares of common stock outstanding. The weighted-average number of common shares outstanding is determined by relating the portion of the reporting period that the shares were outstanding to the total time in the period. Weighting is necessary because some shares may have been issued or reacquired during the period. The stock dividend is assumed to have occurred at the beginning of the period. The BEPS denominator is 126,500, based on 124,000 shares outstanding for the entire year (100,000 beginning balance + 24,000 stock dividend) and 5,000 additional shares issued on 6/30.

$$124,000 \times (6 \div 12) = 62,000$$
$$129,000 \times (6 \div 12) = \underline{64,500}$$
$$\overline{126,500}$$

✗ **Answer (A) is incorrect.** The figure of 120,500 is based on the assumption that the stock dividend was outstanding for 9 months.

✗ **Answer (B) is incorrect.** The figure of 123,000 is based on the assumption that (1) the stock dividend was outstanding for 9 months and (2) the 6/30 issuance was outstanding for 12 months.

✗ **Answer (D) is incorrect.** The figure of 129,000 is the number outstanding at year end.

2.3 Revenue from Contracts with Customers

10. On January 1, Year 1, an entity receives a payment of $20,000 for delivering a product to a customer at the end of Year 3. Based on the contract's terms, the performance obligation will be satisfied at a point in time (upon delivery of the product). The entity determined that (1) the contract includes a significant financing component and (2) a financing rate of 6% is an appropriate discount rate. What amount of interest expense and contract liability will be recognized in the entity's December 31, Year 2, financial statements?

	Year 2 Interest Expense	Contract Liability on December 31, Year 2
A.	$1,200	$21,200
B.	$2,400	$22,400
C.	$1,272	$22,472
D.	$1,348	$0

✓ **Answer (C) is correct.**
Required: The interest expense and contract liability recognized for a performance obligation satisfied at a point in time.
Discussion: Until the product is delivered to the customer, all payments received are recognized as a contract liability. Because the contract includes a significant financing component, interest expense is recognized using the effective interest method. The contract liability at the beginning of Year 2 equals $21,200 ($20,000 × 1.06). Thus, Year 2 interest expense equals $1,272 ($21,200 × 6%), and the contract liability at the end of Year 2 equals $22,472 ($21,200 × 1.06).

✗ **Answer (A) is incorrect.** The amounts of $1,200 and $21,200 are the Year 1 interest expense and the December 31, Year 1, contract liability, respectively.

✗ **Answer (B) is incorrect.** The contract includes a significant financing component, so interest expense is recognized using the effective interest method, not a simple interest method.

✗ **Answer (D) is incorrect.** The amounts of $1,348 and $0 are the Year 3 interest expense and December 31, Year 3, contract liability, respectively.

11. A promised asset is transferred in full satisfaction of a performance obligation in a contract when the customer

A. Obtains control of the asset.

B. Can direct use of the product.

C. Has physical possession of the asset.

D. Pays for the asset in full.

✓ **Answer (A) is correct.**
Required: The time when an asset transfer fully satisfies a performance obligation.
Discussion: Revenue is recognized when a performance obligation is satisfied by transferring a promised good or service to a customer. It happens when the customer obtains control of the good or service (i.e., an asset). Control of an asset is transferred to the customer when the customer (1) has the ability to direct the use of the asset and (2) obtains substantially all of the remaining benefits (potential cash flows) from the asset.

✗ **Answer (B) is incorrect.** Control of the asset is not transferred to the customer unless the customer also obtains substantially all of the remaining benefits from the asset.

✗ **Answer (C) is incorrect.** Transfer of a physical possession is only one of the indicators for transfer of control. However, according to the terms of some contracts, the control of an asset may be transferred to a customer even when the product is still physically in the seller's warehouse. An example is a bill-and-hold contract in which the transfer of goods or services is at the discretion of the customer.

✗ **Answer (D) is incorrect.** Control of an asset is transferred to the customer when the customer (1) has the ability to direct the use of the asset and (2) obtains substantially all of the remaining benefits (potential cash flows) from the asset. Control can be transferred to a customer before (installment sale contract) or after (prepaid contract) the full payment is made.

12. The transaction price from contracts with customers generally should **not** be adjusted for the effect of the time value of money when

    A. The transfer of goods is at the discretion of the seller.

    B. A substantial amount of the consideration is contingent on a future event that is not within the control of the seller.

    C. The time between the payment and the delivery of the promised goods in the contract to the customer is 18 months.

    D. The selling price of the product and the consideration promised in the contract differ significantly.

✔ **Answer (B) is correct.**
Required: The reason not to adjust the transaction price for the time value of money.
Discussion: The transaction price should not be adjusted for the effect of the time value of money if

- The time between the payment and the delivery of the promised good or service to the customer is 1 year or less.
- The transfer of goods or services is at the discretion of the customer (e.g., a bill-and-hold contract in which the seller provides storage services for goods it sold to the buyer).
- A substantial amount of the consideration promised is variable, and its amount or timing varies on the basis of future circumstances that are not within the control of the entity or the customer. An example is a sales-based royalty contract in which the amount of consideration depends on sales by the customer to third parties.

✘ **Answer (A) is incorrect.** The transaction price should not be adjusted when the transfer of goods or services is at the discretion of the customer.

✘ **Answer (C) is incorrect.** The transaction price should not be adjusted for the effect of the time value of money if the time between the payment and the delivery of the promised good or service to the customer is 1 year or less.

✘ **Answer (D) is incorrect.** The transaction price should be adjusted for the effect of the time value of money when the contract includes a significant financing component. A significant difference between (1) the selling price of the product and (2) the consideration promised in the contract may indicate that the financing component is significant.

13. According to the guidance for recognition of revenue from contracts with customers (ASC 606), the incremental costs of obtaining a contract with a customer that are expected to be recovered must be

    A. Reported as an item of other comprehensive income.

    B. Recognized as an item of equity.

    C. Recognized as an asset and amortized in subsequent periods.

    D. Recognized directly in the income statement.

✔ **Answer (C) is correct.**
Required: The accounting for incremental costs of obtaining a contract with a customer.
Discussion: The incremental costs of obtaining a contract with a customer must be capitalized (recognized as an asset) if the entity expects to recover them. These costs would not have been incurred if the contract had not been obtained. The cost capitalized (asset recognized) must be amortized on a systematic basis that is consistent with the transfer to the customer of the goods or services to which the asset relates.

✘ **Answer (A) is incorrect.** The incremental costs of obtaining a contract with a customer must be capitalized if the entity expects to recover them.

✘ **Answer (B) is incorrect.** The incremental costs of obtaining a contract with a customer are not an item of equity. These costs must be capitalized if they are expected to be recovered.

✘ **Answer (D) is incorrect.** The incremental costs of obtaining a contract with a customer must be capitalized (recognized as an asset) if those costs are expected to be recovered.

14. Which of the following can be used to estimate the standalone selling price of a performance obligation in a contract with customers when that price is **not** directly observable?

	Adjusted Market Assessment	Expected Cost Plus an Appropriate Margin
A.	Yes	No
B.	Yes	Yes
C.	No	No
D.	No	Yes

✔ **Answer (B) is correct.**

Required: The method(s), if any, of estimating the standalone selling price when the price is not directly observable.

Discussion: The transaction price is allocated to performance obligations in the contract based on their standalone selling prices. The best evidence of a standalone selling price is the observable price of a good or service when it is sold separately in similar circumstances and to similar customers. The adjusted market assessment and the expected cost plus an appropriate margin are acceptable estimates of the standalone selling price of a performance obligation when that price is not directly observable. Using the adjusted market assessment approach, an entity evaluates the market in which it sells goods or services and estimates the price that a customer in that market would be willing to pay for them. Using the expected cost plus an appropriate margin approach, an entity forecasts its expected costs of satisfying a performance obligation and adds an appropriate margin for that cost.

✘ **Answer (A) is incorrect.** The expected cost plus an appropriate margin approach also is an acceptable estimate of the standalone selling price of a performance obligation when that price is not directly observable.

✘ **Answer (C) is incorrect.** If the standalone price of a performance obligation is not directly observable, it can be estimated by the following approaches: (1) adjusted market assessment, (2) expected cost plus an appropriate margin, and (3) residual.

✘ **Answer (D) is incorrect.** The adjusted market assessment also is an acceptable estimate of the standalone selling price of a performance obligation when that price is not directly observable.

2.4 Recognition of Revenue over Time

15. An entity is calculating the income recognized in the third year of a 5-year construction contract. It uses the input method based on costs incurred to measure the progress toward completion. The ratio used in calculating income is

    A. Costs incurred in Year 3 to total billings.

    B. Costs incurred in Year 3 to total estimated costs.

    C. Total costs incurred to date to total billings.

    D. Total costs incurred to date to total estimated costs.

✔ **Answer (D) is correct.**
Required: The ratio used in calculating income under the input method based on costs incurred to measure the progress toward completion.
Discussion: The entity is using a cost-to-cost accounting method. The input method based on costs incurred to measure the progress toward completion recognizes gross profit or revenue based on the ratio of costs to date to estimated total costs.

✘ **Answer (A) is incorrect.** The estimate of progress may be based on various methods, e.g., units delivered, units of work performed, efforts expended, or cost incurred. However, billings do not necessarily measure progress. Also, the elements of the ratio should be measured on the same basis, but billings are not measured in terms of costs. Moreover, the gross profit or revenue recognized to date should be based on a cumulative calculation that reflects changes in estimates.

✘ **Answer (B) is incorrect.** The ratio of costs in one year to total costs does not estimate progress.

✘ **Answer (C) is incorrect.** Billings do not necessarily measure progress, and the elements of the ratio should be measured on the same basis.

16. An entity recognizes revenue from a long-term contract over time. However, early in the performance of the contract, it cannot reasonably measure the outcome, but it expects to recover the costs incurred. Revenue should be recognized based on

    A. The output method.

    B. A straight-line calculation.

    C. A zero profit margin.

    D. The completed-contract method.

✔ **Answer (C) is correct.**
Required: The basis for recognizing revenue for a performance obligation satisfied over time if the outcome cannot be reasonably measured but cost recovery is expected.
Discussion: When the outcome of the contract is not reasonably measurable but the costs incurred in satisfying the performance obligation are expected to be recovered, revenue must be recognized only to the extent of the costs incurred. Revenue recognized is based on a zero profit margin until the entity can reasonably measure the outcome of the performance obligation.

✘ **Answer (A) is incorrect.** When the outcome of the contract is not reasonably measurable but the costs incurred in satisfying the performance obligation are expected to be recovered, revenue must be recognized only to the extent of the costs incurred. Thus, neither the input nor the output method is used until the entity can reasonably measure the outcome of the performance obligation.

✘ **Answer (B) is incorrect.** When the outcome of the contract is not reasonably measurable but the costs incurred in satisfying the performance obligation are expected to be recovered, revenue must be recognized only to the extent of the costs incurred.

✘ **Answer (D) is incorrect.** When the outcome of the contract is not reasonably measurable but the costs incurred in satisfying the performance obligation are expected to be recovered, revenue is recognized to the extent of the costs incurred.

17. Haft Construction Co. has consistently used the input method based on costs incurred to measure progress toward completion of the project. On January 10, Year 3, Haft began work on a $3 million construction contract. At the inception date, the estimated cost of construction was $2,250,000. The following data relate to the progress of the contract:

Gross profit recognized at
12/31/Yr 3 .... $ 300,000
Costs incurred 1/10/Yr 3
through 12/31/Yr 4 1,800,000
Estimated cost to complete
at 12/31/Yr 4 600,000

In its income statement for the year ended December 31, Year 4, what amount of gross profit should Haft report?

A. $450,000

B. $300,000

C. $262,500

D. $150,000

✔ **Answer (D) is correct.**
Required: The gross profit reported using the input method.
Discussion: The input method based on costs incurred recognizes gross profit based on the relationship between costs incurred to date and estimated total costs. The total anticipated gross profit is multiplied by the ratio of the costs incurred to date to the total estimated costs, and the product is reduced by previously recognized gross profit. The percentage-of-completion at 12/31/Yr 4 is 75% [$1,800,000 ÷ ($1,800,000 + $600,000)]. The total anticipated gross profit is $600,000 ($3,000,000 contract price − $2,400,000 expected total costs). Consequently, a gross profit of $150,000 [($600,000 total gross profit × 75%) − $300,000 previously recognized gross profit] is recognized for Year 4.

✗ **Answer (A) is incorrect.** The current year's profit equals the cumulative income minus the previously recognized gross profit.

✗ **Answer (B) is incorrect.** The amount of $300,000 is the previously recognized gross profit.

✗ **Answer (C) is incorrect.** The amount of $262,500 assumes the total estimated gross profit is $750,000 ($3,000,000 price − $2,250,000 originally estimated total cost).

18. Frame Construction Company's contract requires the construction of a bridge in 3 years. The expected total cost of the bridge is $2,000,000, and Frame will receive $2,500,000 for the project. The actual costs incurred to complete the project were $500,000, $900,000, and $600,000, respectively, during each of the 3 years. Progress payments received were $600,000, $1,200,000, and $700,000, respectively. Frame uses the input method based on costs incurred to recognize revenue from a performance obligation satisfied over time. What amount of gross profit should Frame report during the last year of the project?

A. $120,000

B. $125,000

C. $140,000

D. $150,000

✔ **Answer (D) is correct.**
Required: The recognized gross profit during the last year of the project.
Discussion: The expected gross profit is $500,000 ($2,500,000 price − $2,000,000 expected cost). Cumulative recognized gross profit in Year 2 is $350,000 {$500,000 × [($500,000 + $900,000) ÷ $2,000,000]}. Recognized gross profit in Year 3 is $150,000 [($2,500,000 price − $500,000 − $900,000 − $600,000) actual gross profit − $350,000 previously recognized].

✗ **Answer (A) is incorrect.** The amount of $120,000 is the recognized gross profit in the first year based on the percentage of the price paid ($600,000 ÷ $2,500,000).

✗ **Answer (B) is incorrect.** The amount of $125,000 is the amount recognized in the first year.

✗ **Answer (C) is incorrect.** The amount of $140,000 is the recognized gross profit in the third year based on the percentage of the price paid ($700,000 ÷ $2,500,000).

Study Unit Three

SEC Reporting and Other Accounting Topics

(22 pages of outline)

3.1 SEC Reporting

The Securities and Exchange Commission (SEC) was created by the Securities Exchange Act of 1934 to regulate the trading of securities and otherwise to enforce securities legislation.

- The basic purposes of the securities laws are to prevent fraud and misrepresentation and to require full and fair disclosure so investors can evaluate investments.

Under the Securities Exchange Act of 1934, all regulated, publicly held companies must register with the SEC. Registration is required of all securities listed on a national exchange.

- Under the 1934 act, disclosures about subsequent trading of securities are made by filing periodic reports using the Electronic Data Gathering, Analysis, and Retrieval (EDGAR) system that are available to the public for review.

Regulation S-X describes the form and content of, and requirements for, financial statements filed with the SEC. It applies to the reporting of **interim** and **annual financial statements**, including notes and schedules.

- The following are examples of information that must be provided in addition to the financial statements:

    - **Management's discussion and analysis (MD&A)** of financial condition and results of operations

        ▸ This information includes the entity's outlook and significant effects of known trends, events, and uncertainties. It addresses such matters as (1) liquidity, (2) capital resources, (3) results of operations, and (4) the effect of changing prices.

    - Management and general data for each director and officer

    - Compensation of the five highest-paid directors and officers

    - Security holdings of directors, officers, and those owning 5% or more of the security

    - Matters submitted to shareholders for approval

    - Pending litigation, e.g., principal parties, allegations, and relief sought

Periodic Reporting

After registration with the SEC and the initial issuance of the securities under the Securities Act of 1933, the SEC requires the issuer to file many different forms (reports).

The following forms filed with the SEC may be tested on the CPA Exam:

- **Form 10-K** is the **annual report** to the SEC. It must be **audited** by an independent public accountant.

    - Annual financial statements include

        ▸ Balance sheets for the 2 most recent fiscal year ends

        ▸ Statements of income, cash flows, and changes in equity for the 3 most recent fiscal years

    - The annual report must be filed within

        ▸ 60 days of the last day of the fiscal year by **large accelerated filers** [companies with a public float (the market value of shares held by the public) of $700 million or more]

        ▸ 75 days by **accelerated filers** (public float of $75 million to $700 million and annual revenues of $100 million or more)

        ▸ 90 days by **nonaccelerated filers** [(1) public float of less than $75 million or (2) public float of $75 million to $700 million and annual revenues of less than $100 million]

- **Form 10-Q** is the **quarterly report** of operations and financial condition filed with the SEC. It must be **reviewed** by an independent public accountant. A review offers a lower level of assurance than an audit regarding financial condition and the results of operations.

    - An entity required to file Form 10-K also must file Form 10-Q for each of the first three quarters. No filing for the fourth quarter is required; Form 10-K is filed instead.

- The quarterly report must be filed within
    - 40 days of the last day of the fiscal quarter by large accelerated filers and accelerated filers
    - 45 days by nonaccelerated filers

Status	Public Float	Annual Revenues	10-K Is Filed within	10-Q Is Filed within
Large accelerated filer	$700 million or more	Any	60 days	40 days
Accelerated filer	$75 million to $700 million	$100 million or more	75 days	40 days
Nonaccelerated filer	$75 million to $700 million	Less than $100 million	90 days	45 days
	Less than $75 million	Any		

Form 8-K is a **current report** to disclose material events.

- It must be filed within **4 business days** after the material event occurs.
- The following are some examples of material events:
    - A change in control of the registrant
    - Acquisition or disposition of a significant amount of assets not in the ordinary course of business
    - Bankruptcy or receivership
    - Resignation of a director
    - A change in the registrant's certifying accountant

Form 20-F is the annual report to the SEC filed by **foreign** private issuers. It is similar to Form 10-K. The financial statements in Form 20-F may be prepared in accordance with U.S. GAAP or IFRS (International Financial Reporting Standards).

Periodic Issuer Reporting to SEC under the 1934 Act

Report	Form	Content	Timing
Annual (certified by CEO and CFO)	10-K	Audited financial statements and many other matters	60, 75, or 90 days after fiscal year end
Quarterly (certified by CEO and CFO)	10-Q	Reviewed quarterly financial information and changes during quarter	40 or 45 days after fiscal quarter end
Current	8-K	Material events	Within 4 business days of event

Stop & Review

You have completed the outline for this subunit.
Study multiple-choice questions 1 through 4 beginning on page 103.

3.2 Interim Financial Reporting

GAAP do not require reporting of interim financial information. But GAAP must be applied when entities report such information, including when **publicly traded companies** issue summarized interim information. Moreover, federal securities law requires certain entities that meet the definition of an **issuer** to report interim quarterly information on Form 10-Q.

- For many reasons, the usefulness of interim financial information is limited. Thus, its best qualitative characteristic is **timeliness**.

Each interim period is treated primarily as an **integral part** of an annual period. Ordinarily, the results for an interim period should be based on the **same accounting principles** the entity uses in preparing annual statements, but certain principles may require modification at interim dates.

Revenue and Associated Costs

Revenue should be recognized as earned during an interim period on the same basis as followed for the full year.

Costs associated with revenue are treated similarly for annual and interim reporting. However, some exceptions are appropriate for inventory accounting at interim dates.

- The gross profit method may be used for estimating cost of goods sold and inventory because a physical count at the interim date may not be feasible (described in Study Unit 6, Subunit 7).

- An inventory loss from a write-down below cost may be deferred if no loss is reasonably anticipated for the year.

    - But inventory losses from nontemporary declines below cost must be recognized at the interim date. If the loss is recovered during the year (in another quarter), it is treated as a change in estimate. The amount recovered is limited to the losses previously recognized. (Study Unit 6, Subunit 6, contains the relevant outlines.)

All Other Costs and Expenses

Costs and expenses other than product costs are either charged to income in interim periods as incurred or allocated among interim periods.

The **allocation** is based on the (1) benefits received, (2) estimates of time expired, or (3) activities associated with the period. If an item expensed for annual reporting benefits more than one interim period, it should be allocated.

- **Gains and losses** that are similar to gains and losses that would not be deferred at year end are not deferred to later interim periods.

    - For example, an unusual or infrequently occurring item and a gain or loss on the disposal of an asset are **recognized in full** in the quarter in which they occur. They **must not** be prorated over the fiscal year.

- Some items expensed in annual statements should be allocated to the interim periods that are clearly benefited.

- **Quantity discounts** based on annual sales volume should be charged to interim periods based on periodic sales.

- **Interest, rent, and property taxes** may be accrued or deferred at interim dates to assign an appropriate cost to each period.

Example 3-1	Interim Reporting -- Costs and Expenses

On March 15 of the current year, Chen Company paid property taxes of $120,000 on its factory building for the current calendar year. On April 1, Chen made $240,000 in unanticipated repairs to its equipment. The repairs will benefit operations for the remainder of the calendar year.

The benefit from the payment of the property taxes relates to all four quarters of the current year and should be prorated at $30,000 ($120,000 ÷ 4) per quarter. The benefit from the unanticipated repairs to plant equipment relates to the second, third, and fourth quarters. It should be spread evenly over these quarters at $80,000 ($240,000 ÷ 3) per quarter.

- **Advertising costs** may be deferred within a fiscal year if the benefits clearly extend beyond the interim period of the expenditure.

- Certain costs and expenses, such as (1) inventory shrinkage, (2) allowance for credit losses, and (3) discretionary bonuses, are subject to **year-end adjustment**. To the extent possible, these adjustments should be estimated and assigned to interim periods.

Seasonality

If interim information is issued, certain disclosures are mandatory for businesses that have material seasonal fluctuations. These fluctuations cannot be smoothed in interim information.

Accordingly, reporting entities must disclose the seasonal nature of their activities. They also should consider supplementing interim reports with information for the 12-month period that ended at the interim date for the current and preceding years.

Interim Period Tax Expense (Benefit)

At the end of each interim period, the entity should estimate the annual effective tax rate.

Interim period tax expense (benefit) equals the **estimated annual effective tax rate**, times year-to-date ordinary income (loss) before income taxes, minus the tax expense (benefit) recognized in previous interim periods.

- Ordinary in this context means excluding unusual or infrequently occurring items and results of discontinued operations.

The **estimated annual effective tax rate** is based on the statutory rate adjusted for the current year's expected conditions. These include (1) anticipated tax credits, (2) foreign tax rates, (3) capital gains rates, and (4) other tax planning alternatives.

- The rate also includes the effect of any expected valuation allowance at year end for deferred tax assets related to deductible temporary differences and carryforwards arising during the year.

- The rate is determined without regard to (1) significant unusual or infrequently occurring items to be reported separately or (2) items reported net of tax effect. However, such items are recognized in the interim period when they occur. The method of intraperiod tax allocation described in Study Unit 9, Subunit 5, is used.

A **tax benefit** is recognized for a loss early in the year if the benefits are expected to be realized during the year or recognizable as a deferred tax asset at year end.

- A valuation allowance must be recognized if it is more likely than not that a deferred tax asset will not be fully realized. Accordingly, the tax benefit of an ordinary loss early in the year is not recognized to the extent that this criterion is met.

  - However, no income tax expense is recognized for subsequent ordinary income until the earlier unrecognized tax benefit is used.

- The foregoing principles are applied in determining the estimated tax benefit of an ordinary loss for the fiscal year used to calculate (1) the annual effective tax rate and (2) the year-to-date tax benefit of a loss.

Example 3-2	Interim Reporting – Income Tax Expense

The information below was used in preparing quarterly income statements during the first half of the current year.

Quarter	Income before Income Taxes	Estimated Effective Annual Income Tax Rate
1	$80,000	45%
2	70,000	45%
3	50,000	40%

The tax expense for the third quarter equals the estimated annual effective tax rate determined at the end of the third quarter, times the cumulative year-to-date ordinary income (loss), minus the cumulative tax expense for the first two quarters. At the end of the third quarter, the year-to-date ordinary income is $200,000 ($80,000 + $70,000 + $50,000), and the cumulative tax expense is $80,000 ($200,000 × 40%). Because the cumulative tax expense at the end of the second quarter was $67,500 [($80,000 + $70,000) × 45%], $12,500 ($80,000 − $67,500) should be reported as income tax expense in the income statement for the third quarter.

Interim Period Accounting Changes

In interim as well as annual periods, a change in accounting principle is **retrospectively** applied unless it is impracticable to determine the cumulative or period-specific effects of the change.

The **cumulative effect** of the change on periods prior to those presented is reflected in the carrying amounts of assets, liabilities, and retained earnings at the beginning of the first period presented.

- All periods presented must be adjusted for **period-specific effects**.

A **change in an accounting estimate**, including a change in the estimated effective annual tax rate, is accounted for **prospectively** in the interim period in which the change is made and in future periods. Prior-period information is not retrospectively adjusted.

Prior Interim Period Adjustments

The following items apply to adjustment or settlement of (1) litigation, (2) income taxes (except for the effects of retroactive tax legislation), or (3) renegotiation proceedings.

- All or part of the adjustment or settlement must relate specifically to a prior interim period of the current year.

  - Moreover, its effect must be material, and the amount must have become reasonably estimable only in the current interim period.

- If an **item of profit or loss** occurs in other than the first interim period and meets the criteria for an adjustment, the portion of the item allocable to the current interim period is included in net income for that period.

  - The financial statements for the **prior interim periods are restated** to include their allocable portions of the adjustment.

  - The portion of the adjustment directly related to prior fiscal years is included in net income of the first interim period of the current fiscal year.

Example 3-3	Prior Interim Period Adjustments

On June 1, Year 5, a calendar-year entity settled a patent infringement lawsuit. The court awarded it $3,000,000 in damages. Of this amount, $1,000,000 related to Year 3, $1,000,000 to Year 4, and $500,000 to each of the first two quarters in Year 5. The applicable tax rate is 40%. Prior interim periods should be restated to include their allocable portions of the adjustment. Accordingly, $2,500,000 of the settlement is included in earnings for the first quarter and $500,000 of the settlement should be included in earnings for the second quarter. Given a tax rate of 40%, the settlement increases net income of the first and second quarter by $1,500,000 and $300,000, respectively.

Success Tip

Expect to possibly be tested on interim financial reporting, as the AICPA has traditionally tested candidates' knowledge of this topic. Candidates could see either a conceptual question or a calculation question.

Stop & Review

You have completed the outline for this subunit.

Study multiple-choice questions 5 through 10 beginning on page 105.

3.3 Accounting Changes and Error Corrections

Success Tip

The AICPA tests candidates' knowledge of how to account for the effects of (1) a change in accounting principle, (2) a change in accounting estimate, and (3) the correction of errors. Be prepared for questions that ask for (1) a description of the accounting, (2) calculation of amounts, or (3) the journal entries.

Accounting Changes

If financial information is to be comparable and consistent, entities must not make voluntary changes in accounting principles unless they can be justified as **preferable**.

- Thus, the assumption is that an adopted **principle must be applied consistently** in preparing financial statements.

The three types of accounting changes are

- A change in accounting principle,
- A change in accounting estimate, and
- A change in the reporting entity.

Change in Accounting Principle (Retrospective Application)

A change in accounting principle occurs when an entity (1) adopts a generally accepted principle different from the one previously used, (2) changes the **method** of applying a generally accepted principle, or (3) changes to a generally accepted principle when the principle previously used is no longer generally accepted.

- A change in principle does **not** include the initial adoption of a principle because of an event or transaction occurring for the first time.

Retrospective application is required for all direct effects and the related income tax effects of a change in principle.

- An example of a direct effect is an adjustment of an inventory balance to implement a change in the method of measurement.

- Retrospective application must **not include indirect effects**. These are changes in current or future cash flows from a change in principle applied retrospectively.

  - An example of an indirect effect is a required profit-sharing payment based on a reported amount that was directly affected (e.g., revenue).

  - Indirect effects are recognized and reported in the period of change.

Retrospective application requires the carrying amounts of (1) assets, (2) liabilities, and (3) retained earnings at the beginning of the first period reported to be adjusted for the **cumulative effect (CE)** of the new principle on the prior periods.

- All periods presented must be individually adjusted for the **period-specific effects (PSE)** of the new principle.

It may be **impracticable** to determine the CE of a new principle on any prior period.

- The new principle then must be applied as if the change had been made prospectively at the earliest date practicable.

It may be **practicable** to determine the CE of applying the new principle to all prior periods but **not** the PSE.

- In these circumstances, CE adjustments must be made to the beginning balances for the first period to which the new principle can be applied.

IMPRACTICABILITY EXCEPTIONS

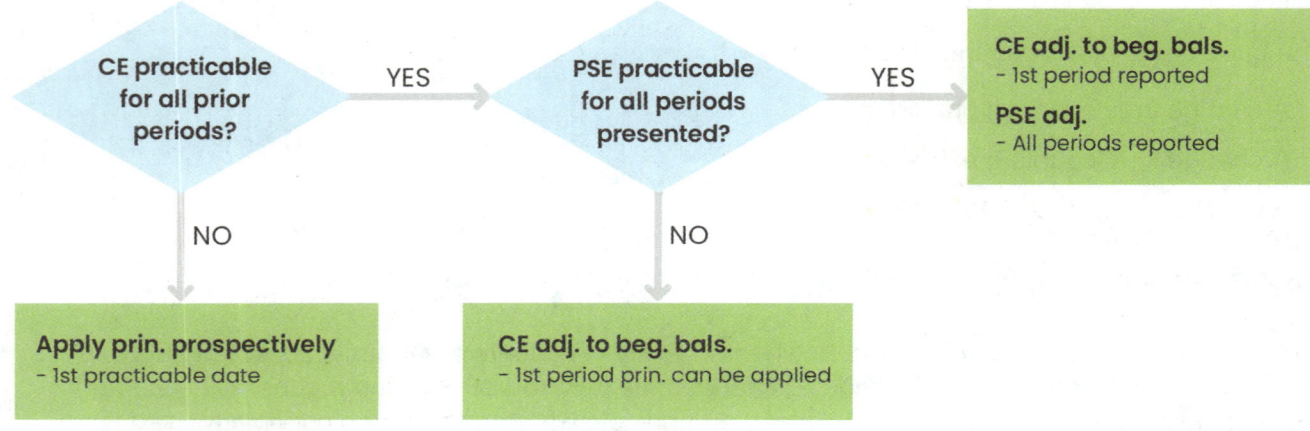

Figure 3-1

Change in Accounting Estimate (Prospective Application)

A change in accounting estimate results from new information. It is a reassessment of the future status, benefits, and obligations of assets and liabilities. Its effects must be accounted for only in (1) the period of change and (2) any future periods affected **(prospectively)**.

- The prospective application must be applied from the **beginning of the accounting period** in which the accounting estimate was changed.

- For a change in estimate, the entity **must not**

  - Restate or retrospectively adjust prior-period statements or
  - Report pro forma amounts for prior periods.

Example 3-4	Change in Accounting Estimate

On January 1, Year 1, Entity D purchased a machine for $98,000. Depreciation is based on the straight-line method using an estimated useful life of 10 years with a salvage value of $8,000. During Year 3, Entity D determined that the machine has a useful life of 8 years from the date of acquisition and that its salvage value is $2,000. Entity D reports only annual financial statements.

Annual depreciation on the machine in Years 1 and 2 is $9,000 [($98,000 historical cost – $8,000 salvage value) ÷ 10 years]. On December 31, Year 2, the carrying amount of the machine is $80,000 [$98,000 historical cost – ($9,000 annual depreciation × 2 years elapsed)].

The annual depreciation of the machine from the beginning of Year 3 is based on revised estimates of the machine's useful life (8 years) and salvage value ($2,000). The carrying amount of the machine ($80,000) at the beginning of the accounting period in which the change in estimates occurred is used in the new calculation.

- The new depreciable base of the machine is **$78,000** ($80,000 – $2,000).
- The remaining useful life of the machine from the beginning of the accounting period in which the change in estimates occurred (January 1, Year 3) is **6** years (8 – 2).
- Annual depreciation on the machine in Years 3 through 8 is **$13,000** ($78,000 ÷ 6).
- The carrying amount of the machine on December 31, Year 3, is **$67,000** ($80,000 January 1, Year 3, carrying amount – $13,000 depreciation expense in Year 3).

A **change in estimate inseparable from a change in principle** is accounted for as a **change in estimate**, i.e., prospective application.

- An example is a change in a method of depreciation, amortization, or depletion of long-lived, nonfinancial assets.

Change in the Reporting Entity

A change in the reporting entity results in statements that are effectively those of a different entity.

- Most such changes occur when

  - Consolidated or combined statements replace those of individual entities,
  - Consolidated statements include different subsidiaries, or
  - Combined statements include different entities.

- A business combination or consolidation of a variable interest entity is not a change in the reporting entity.

A change in the reporting entity is retrospectively applied to interim and annual statements.

Error Correction

An error in prior statements results from

- A mathematical mistake,
- A mistake in the application of GAAP, or
- An oversight or misuse of facts existing when the statements were prepared.

A change to a generally accepted accounting principle from one that is not generally accepted is an error correction, **not an accounting change**.

- Any error related to a prior period discovered after the statements are, or are available to be, used must be reported as an error correction by restating the prior-period statements. In addition to the revision of the previously issued financial statements, **restatement** requires the same adjustments as **retrospective application** of a new principle.

  - The carrying amounts of (1) assets, (2) liabilities, and (3) retained earnings **at the beginning of the first period reported** are adjusted for the cumulative effect of the error on the prior periods.

  - Corrections of prior-period errors **must not** be included in current period net income.

Example 3-5   Error Correction

On January 1, Year 1, Entity E acquired a machine at a cost of $240,000. The freight-in and site preparation costs for the machine of $30,000 were mistakenly expensed as incurred by the bookkeeper. The machine was depreciated on the straight-line basis over a 6-year period with no residual value. During Year 3, Entity E's controller discovered the error made by the bookkeeper in Year 1.

All the costs necessarily incurred to bring the machine to the condition and location necessary for its intended use ($30,000) must be capitalized as part of the historical cost of the machine and depreciated in future periods. Ignoring the tax effect, the following error correction should be made by Entity E in Year 3:

- The incorrect carrying amount of the machine on January 1, Year 3, is **$160,000** [$240,000 historical cost – ($40,000 annual depreciation × 2 years)].

- The correct carrying amount of the machine on January 1, Year 3, is **$180,000** [$270,000 historical cost – ($45,000 annual depreciation × 2 years)].

- The cumulative effect of the error for the two prior periods on the carrying amount of retained earnings is **$20,000**. This amount is the difference between (1) cumulative expenses actually recognized for Years 1 and 2 of $110,000 ($30,000 freight-in and site preparation costs + $80,000 depreciation expense in the first 2 years) and (2) cumulative expenses that should have been recognized of $90,000 (depreciation expense in Years 1 and 2). The carrying amount of retained earnings should be credited (i.e., increased) for the cumulative effect. The correct expense in Years 1 and 2 is $20,000 lower. Thus, the correct net income (ignoring tax effect) for these years is $20,000 greater, and the beginning balance of retained earnings on 1/1/Year 3 also should be $20,000 greater.

- The error correction journal entry in Year 3 is

Machine -- cost ($270,000 – $240,000)	$30,000	
Retained earnings January 1, Year 3		$20,000
Accumulated depreciation ($90,000 – $80,000)		10,000

- The annual depreciation expense recognized in Years 3 to 6 is **$45,000** ($270,000 historical cost ÷ 6 years of useful life).

- Error corrections must be reported in **single-period** statements as adjustments of the opening balance of retained earnings.

  - If comparative statements are presented, corresponding adjustments must be made to net income (and its components) and retained earnings (and other affected balances) for all periods reported.

Error Analysis

A correcting journal entry combines the reversal of the error with the correct entry. Thus, it requires a determination of the

- Journal entry originally recorded,
- Event or transaction that occurred, and
- Correct journal entry.

Example 3-6   Correcting Journal Entry

If the purchase of a fixed asset on account had been debited to purchases:

Incorrect Entry	Correct Entry	Correcting Entry
Purchases	Fixed asset	Fixed asset
Payables	Payables	Purchases

If cash had been incorrectly credited:

Incorrect Entry	Correct Entry	Correcting Entry
Purchases	Fixed asset	Fixed Asset
Cash	Payables	Cash
		Purchases
		Payables

Error analysis addresses

- Whether an error affects prior-period statements,
- The timing of error detection,
- Whether comparative statements are presented, and
- Whether the error is counterbalancing.

An error affecting **prior-period statements** may or may not affect prior-period net income. For example, misclassifying an item as a gain rather than a revenue does not affect income and is readily correctable. No prior-period adjustment to retained earnings is required.

An error that affects prior-period net income is **counterbalancing** if it self-corrects over two periods. Figures 6-2 and 6-3 in Study Unit 6, Subunit 7, illustrate self-correction of inventory errors. However, despite the self-correction, the financial statements remain misstated. They should be restated if presented comparatively in later periods.

An example of a **noncounterbalancing** error is a misstatement of depreciation. Such an error does not self-correct over two periods. Thus, a prior-period adjustment will be necessary.

Stop & Review

You have completed the outline for this subunit.
Study multiple-choice questions 11 through 14 beginning on page 107.

3.4 Subsequent Events

Subsequent events are events or transactions that occur **after the balance sheet date** and **prior to the issuance or availability for issuance of the financial statements**.

- An SEC filer evaluates subsequent events through the date the statements are issued (become widely available for general use).

- Other entities evaluate subsequent events through the date statements are available for issuance (are complete in accordance with GAAP and approved).

  - The entity must disclose the date through which subsequent events have been evaluated.

Recognized Subsequent Events

One type of subsequent event provides additional evidence about **conditions that existed at the date of the balance sheet**, including the estimates inherent in statement preparation.

- This type of event **must be recognized** in the financial statements.

- Subsequent events affecting the realization of assets (such as receivables and inventories) or the settlement of estimated liabilities ordinarily require recognition.

  - They usually reflect the resolution of conditions that existed over a relatively long period. Examples are

    - The settlement of litigation for an amount differing from the liability recorded in the statements,

    - A loss on a receivable resulting from a customer's bankruptcy, and

    - Changes in the data used in inventory valuation at the lower of cost or NRV.

- Adjustments to earnings per share (EPS) are made as a result of stock dividends and stock splits that occurred after the balance sheet date but prior to the issuance of the financial statements (discussed in Study Unit 2, Subunit 2).

Unrecognized Subsequent Events

The second type of subsequent event provides evidence about **conditions that did not exist at the date of the balance sheet**. These events **do not require recognition**, but some of them do require disclosure.

- Examples of nonrecognized subsequent events requiring **disclosure only** include

  - Sale of a bond or capital stock issue

  - A business combination

  - Settlement of litigation when the event resulting in the claim occurred after the balance sheet date

  - Loss of plant or inventories as a result of a fire or natural disaster

  - Losses on receivables resulting from conditions (e.g., a customer's major casualty) occurring after the balance sheet date

  - Classification of long-lived assets as held for sale

  - Extinguishment of debt after the balance sheet date

- Some events of the second type may be so significant that the most appropriate disclosure is to supplement the historical statements with pro forma financial data.

Stop & Review

You have completed the outline for this subunit.
Study multiple-choice questions 15 and 16 on page 109.

3.5 Significant Accounting Policies and Credit Risk

Accounting Policies

Accounting policies are the specific principles and the methods of applying them used by the reporting entity. Management selects these policies as the most appropriate for fair presentation of financial statements.

Business and not-for-profit entities **must disclose** all significant accounting policies as an **integral part** of the financial statements.

- Disclosure of accounting policies in unaudited interim financial statements is not required when the reporting entity has not changed its policies since the end of the preceding fiscal year.

Disclosure of Accounting Policies

The preferred presentation is a **summary of accounting policies** in a separate section preceding the notes or in the initial note.

The disclosure should include accounting principles adopted and the methods of applying them that materially affect the financial statements. Disclosure extends to accounting policies that involve

- A selection from existing acceptable alternatives,

- Policies unique to the industry in which the entity operates, even if they are predominantly followed in that industry, and

- GAAP applied in an unusual or innovative way.

Certain disclosures about policies of business entities are commonly required. These items include the following:

- Basis of consolidation
- Depreciation methods
- Amortization of intangibles
- Inventory pricing
- Recognition of revenue from contracts with customers
- Recognition of revenue from leasing operations

Disclosure of accounting policies should **not duplicate details** presented elsewhere.

- For example, the summary of significant policies should not contain the composition of plant assets or inventories or the maturity dates of noncurrent debt.

Concentration of Credit Risk

Credit risk is the risk of accounting loss from a financial instrument because of the possible failure of another party to perform.

- With certain exceptions, for example, (1) instruments of pension plans, (2) certain insurance contracts, (3) warranty obligations and rights, and (4) unconditional purchase obligations, an entity must disclose significant **concentrations of credit risk** arising from financial instruments, whether from one counterparty or groups.

  - Group concentrations arise when multiple counterparties have similar activities and economic characteristics that cause their ability to meet obligations to be similarly affected by changes in conditions.

- **Disclosures** (in the body of the statements or the notes) should include

  - Information about the shared activity, region, or economic characteristic that identifies the concentration.

  - The **maximum loss** due to credit risk if parties failed completely to perform and the security, if any, proved to be of no value.

  - The **policy of requiring collateral** or other security, information about access to that security, and the nature and a brief description of the security.

Market Risk

An entity is encouraged, but not required, to disclose quantitative information about the **market risks** of instruments that is consistent with the way the entity manages those risks.

Stop & Review

You have completed the outline for this subunit.
Study multiple-choice questions 17 through 20 beginning on page 110.

3.6 Fair Value Measurements

GAAP establish a framework for fair value measurements (FVMs) required by other pronouncements. But they do not determine when FVMs are required. Accordingly, they

- Define **fair value**,
- Discuss **valuation** techniques,
- Establish a **fair value hierarchy** of inputs to valuation techniques, and
- Require expanded **disclosures** about FVMs.

Definitions

Fair value is the **price** that would be **received** to sell an asset or paid to transfer a liability in an **orderly transaction between market participants** at the measurement date.

The FVM is for a particular asset or liability that may stand alone (e.g., a financial instrument) or constitute a group (e.g., a business). The definition also applies to instruments measured at fair value that are classified as equity.

The price is an **exit price** paid or received in a hypothetical transaction considered from the perspective of a market participant.

Market participants are not related parties. They are independent of the reporting entity.

- They are knowledgeable (i.e., they have a reasonable understanding based on all available information).
- They are willing and able (but not compelled) to engage in transactions involving the asset or liability.
- The FVM is market-based, not entity-specific.

An **orderly transaction** is not forced, and time is assumed to be sufficient to allow for customary marketing activities.

- The transaction is assumed to occur in the reporting entity's **principal market** for the asset or liability.
- In the absence of such a market, it is assumed to occur in the most advantageous market. This market is the one in which the specific reporting entity can
  - Maximize the amount received for selling the asset or
  - Minimize the amount paid for transferring the liability, after considering transaction costs.
- Given a principal (or most advantageous) market, the FVM is the price in that market **without adjustment for transaction costs**.

Example 3-7   Fair Value Measurement

On January 1, Year 1, Brooke Co. acquired 50 shares of common stock of John Co. In its December 31, Year 1, balance sheet, Brooke must report the investment in shares of John at fair value. (The accounting for an investment in equity securities is discussed in detail in Study Unit 4, Subunit 3.) John's shares are actively traded on two different stock exchanges (London and Madrid). Below is the information for the stock price and transaction costs of John's stock on the two stock exchanges on December 31, Year 1:

12/31/Year 1	Quoted Stock Price	Transaction Costs	Net Proceeds
London	$100	$4	$96
Madrid	102	7	95

- If one of the two stock exchanges is a principal market, the **quoted stock price** on this stock exchange is the fair value.

- If neither of the two stock exchanges is a principal market, the most advantageous market is the market in which Brooke can receive the maximum proceeds from selling the shares (quoted stock price – transaction costs). Consequently, London is the most advantageous market, and the **quoted stock price** of $100 on the London stock exchange is the fair value measurement of John's shares.

On December 31, Year 1, Brooke reports the investment in shares of John Co. at $5,000 (50 shares × $100 fair value per share).

Assets

The FVM is based on the **highest and best use (HBU)** by market participants.

- The HBU is in-use if the value-maximizing use is in combination with other assets in a group. An example is machinery in a factory.

- The HBU is in-exchange if the value-maximizing use is as a stand-alone asset. An example is a financial asset.

Liabilities

The FVM assumes transfer, not settlement.

Valuation Techniques

The following valuation techniques (approaches) are used to measure fair value:

- The **market approach** is based on information, such as multiples of prices, from market transactions involving identical or comparable items.

  market = x of Prices

- The **income approach** uses valuation methods based on current market expectations about future amounts, e.g., earnings or cash flows.

  Income → cashflows / mkt expect.

  - It converts future amounts to one present discounted amount.
  - Examples are present value methods and option-pricing models.

- The **cost approach** is based on current replacement cost. It is the cost to buy or build a comparable asset.

  Cost ap. = replace cost

Inputs to valuation techniques are the pricing assumptions of market participants.

- **Observable inputs** are based on market data obtained from independent sources.

  Observe = Market data

- **Unobservable inputs** are based on the entity's own assumptions about the assumptions of market participants that reflect the best available information.

  - An entity should maximize the use of relevant observable inputs and minimize the use of unobservable inputs.

The Fair Value Hierarchy

Level 1 inputs are the **most reliable**. They are unadjusted quoted prices in active markets for identical assets or liabilities that the entity can access at the measurement date.

- EXAMPLE: If the entity has an investment in securities that are traded in an active market, the investment is measured within Level 1. The FVM equals the quantity of securities held times the securities' quoted price.

Level 2 inputs are **observable**. But they exclude quoted prices included within Level 1. The following are examples:

- Quoted prices for similar items in active markets,
- Quoted prices in markets that are not active, and
- Observable inputs that are not quoted prices.

Level 3 inputs are the **least reliable**. They are **unobservable** inputs that are used given no observable inputs. They should be based on the best available information in the circumstances. An example of a Level 3 input is the reporting entity's own data (e.g., present value of future cash flows).

Unobs. 3
Observ. 2
most rel. 1

Disclosures

Quantitative disclosures in a tabular format are made for **each class** of assets and liabilities measured at fair value in the balance sheet after initial recognition. The following are examples:

- Fair value measurement at the end of the reporting period

- The level of the fair value hierarchy within which the fair value measurements are categorized (Level 1, 2, or 3)

- A description of the valuation technique(s) and the inputs used in the fair value measurements categorized within Level 2 and Level 3

- Quantitative information about the significant unobservable inputs used in the fair value measurements categorized within Level 3

The appropriate classes of assets and liabilities are determined on the basis of the following:

- The nature, characteristics, and risks of the asset or liability
- The level of the fair value hierarchy within which the fair value measurement is categorized

Stop & Review

You have completed the outline for this subunit.

Study multiple-choice questions 21 through 23 beginning on page 111.

Questions

3.1 SEC Reporting

1. The management's discussion and analysis (MD&A) section of an annual report (Form 10-K)

    A. Includes earnings per share information.

    B. Covers three financial aspects of a firm's business: liquidity, capital resources, and results of operations.

    C. Is a technical analysis of past results and a defense of those results by management.

    D. Covers marketing and product line issues.

✔ **Answer (B) is correct.**
Required: The item that is an aspect of MD&A.
Discussion: The MD&A section is included in SEC filings. It addresses in a nonquantified manner the prospects of a filer. The SEC examines it to determine that management has disclosed material information affecting future results. Disclosures about commitments and events that may affect operations or liquidity are mandatory. Thus, the MD&A section pertains to liquidity, capital resources, and results of operations.

✘ **Answer (A) is incorrect.** Earnings per share information is reported in the income statement, not in the MD&A section of the annual report.

✘ **Answer (C) is incorrect.** A technical analysis and a defense are not required in the MD&A section because it is primarily forward-looking.

✘ **Answer (D) is incorrect.** The MD&A section need not address marketing and product line issues.

2. Each of the following events is required to be reported to the United States Securities and Exchange Commission on Form 8-K, **except**

    A. The creation of an obligation under an off-balance sheet arrangement of a registrant.

    B. The unregistered sale of equity securities.

    C. A change in a registrant's certifying accountant.

    D. The quarterly results of operations and financial condition of a registrant.

✔ **Answer (D) is correct.**
Required: The event not reported on Form 8-K.
Discussion: Form 8-K is a current report to disclose material events within 4 business days after such an event occurs. However, the quarterly results of operations and financial condition of a registrant (interim financial information) must be reported not on Form 8-K but on Form 10-Q, the quarterly report to the SEC.

✘ **Answer (A) is incorrect.** Disclosure on Form 8-K is required when the registrant becomes (1) obligated on a material direct financial obligation or (2) liable for a material obligation arising from an off-balance sheet arrangement.

✘ **Answer (B) is incorrect.** The unregistered sale of equity securities must be disclosed on Form 8-K.

✘ **Answer (C) is incorrect.** The registrant's principal auditor (or an auditor of a significant subsidiary whose report was relied upon) may (1) decline to be reappointed after completion of the audit or (2) resign or be dismissed. These events must be disclosed on Form 8-K.

3. U.S. Securities and Exchange Commission (SEC) regulations for the financial statement presentation and disclosure requirements of SEC filings can be found in

   A. Regulation S-B.

   B. Regulation S-K.

   C. Regulation S-T.

   D. Regulation S-X.

✔ **Answer (D) is correct.**
Required: The source of SEC regulations for financial statement presentation and disclosure.
Discussion: Regulation S-X applies to the reporting of financial statements, including notes and schedules.

✘ **Answer (A) is incorrect.** Regulation S-B applies to smaller reporting companies (small business issuers and nonaccelerated filers).

✘ **Answer (B) is incorrect.** Regulation S-K provides integrated disclosure standards, many of which are nonfinancial. It does not state requirements for financial statements.

✘ **Answer (C) is incorrect.** Regulation S-T governs the types of documents the SEC requires to be filed electronically.

4. Which of the following is the annual report that is filed with the United States Securities and Exchange Commission?

   A. Form 8-K.

   B. Form 10-K.

   C. Form S-1.

   D. Form 10-Q.

✔ **Answer (B) is correct.**
Required: The annual report filed with SEC.
Discussion: Form 10-K is the annual report filed with the SEC. It must be reported within (1) 60 days of the last day of the fiscal year by large accelerated filers (with $700 million or more in publicly held stock), (2) 75 days by accelerated filers (with $75 million to $700 million in public stock and annual revenues of $100 million or more), and (3) 90 days by non-accelerated filers.

✘ **Answer (A) is incorrect.** Form 8-K is a current report used to disclose material events. It must be filed within 4 business days after the material event occurs.

✘ **Answer (C) is incorrect.** Form S-1 is filed by (1) nonreporting issuers or (2) unseasoned issuers.

✘ **Answer (D) is incorrect.** Form 10-Q is the quarterly report of operations and financial condition to the SEC.

3.2 Interim Financial Reporting

5. On January 16, Tree Co. paid $60,000 in property taxes on its factory for the current calendar year. On April 2, Tree paid $240,000 for unanticipated major repairs to its factory equipment. The repairs will benefit operations for the remainder of the calendar year. What amount of these expenses should Tree include in its third quarter interim financial statements for the 3 months ended September 30?

A. $0

B. $15,000

C. $75,000

D. $95,000

✓ **Answer (D) is correct.**
Required: The expenses included in the interim statements.
Discussion: Property taxes are accrued or deferred at interim dates to assign an appropriate cost to each period. Moreover, annual major repairs are allocated to the periods benefited. Thus, the benefit from the payment of the property taxes relates to all four quarters of the current year. It should be prorated at $15,000 ($60,000 ÷ 4) per quarter. The benefit from the unanticipated repairs relates to the second, third, and fourth quarters. It should be allocated to these quarters at $80,000 ($240,000 ÷ 3) per quarter. Thus, the amount of these expenses recognized in the third quarter is $95,000 ($15,000 + $80,000).

✗ **Answer (A) is incorrect.** The property tax payments and repairs benefited the third quarter.

✗ **Answer (B) is incorrect.** An allocation of repairs expense should be made to the third quarter.

✗ **Answer (C) is incorrect.** The amount of $75,000 includes an allocation of repairs expense of only $60,000, implying an assignment to all four quarters instead of the three benefited.

6. Because of a decline in market price in the second quarter, Petal Co. incurred an inventory loss, but the market price was expected to return to previous levels by the end of the year. At the end of the year, the decline had not reversed. Petal accounts for its inventory using the LIFO method. When should the loss be reported in Petal's interim income statements?

A. Ratably over the second, third, and fourth quarters.

B. Ratably over the third and fourth quarters.

C. In the second quarter only.

D. In the fourth quarter only.

✓ **Answer (D) is correct.**
Required: The true statement about reporting inventory at interim dates when a market decline is expected to reverse by year end but does not.
Discussion: A decline below cost reasonably expected to be restored within the fiscal year may be deferred at an interim reporting date because no loss is anticipated for the year. (Inventory losses from nontemporary market declines must be recognized at the interim reporting date.) Consequently, Petal would not have reported the market decline until it determined at the end of the fourth quarter that the expected reversal would not occur.

7. Conceptually, interim financial statements can be described as emphasizing

A. Timeliness over reliability.

B. Reliability over relevance.

C. Relevance over comparability.

D. Comparability over neutrality.

✓ **Answer (A) is correct.**
Required: The emphasis of interim statements.
Discussion: Interim financial statements cover periods of less than 1 year. Because of (1) the seasonality of some businesses, (2) the need for increased use of estimates, (3) the need for allocations of costs and expenses among interim periods, and (4) other factors, the usefulness of the information provided by interim financial statements may be limited. Hence, they emphasize timeliness over reliability.

8. In general, an enterprise preparing interim financial statements should

    A. Defer recognition of seasonal revenue.

    B. Disregard permanent decreases in the market value of its inventory.

    C. Allocate revenues and expenses evenly over the quarters, regardless of when they actually occurred.

    D. Use the same accounting principles followed in preparing its latest annual financial statements.

✔ **Answer (D) is correct.**
Required: The method of preparing interim financial statements.
Discussion: Each interim period is an integral part of an annual period. Ordinarily, interim results are based on the same principles applied in annual statements. Certain principles and practices used for annual reporting, however, may require modification so that interim reports may relate more closely to the results of operations for the annual period.

✘ **Answer (A) is incorrect.** Seasonal revenue is not deferred. However, an entity with material seasonal fluctuations must disclose the seasonal nature of its activities and should consider making additional disclosures.

✘ **Answer (B) is incorrect.** Inventory losses from nontemporary market declines must be recognized at the interim date. Recovery during the fiscal year is treated as a change in estimate.

✘ **Answer (C) is incorrect.** Revenue is recognized as earned during an interim period on the same basis followed for the annual period.

9. A loss from a market price decline on inventory accounted for under the LIFO method occurred in the first quarter. The loss was not expected to be restored in the fiscal year. However, in the third quarter the inventory had a market price recovery that exceeded the market decline that occurred in the first quarter. For interim financial reporting, the dollar amount of net inventory should

    A. Decrease in the first quarter by the amount of the market price decline and increase in the third quarter by the amount of the market price recovery.

    B. Decrease in the first quarter by the amount of the market price decline and increase in the third quarter by the amount of decrease in the first quarter.

    C. Decrease in the first quarter by the amount of the market price decline and not be affected in the third quarter.

    D. Not be affected in either the first quarter or the third quarter.

✔ **Answer (B) is correct.**
Required: The proper interim financial reporting of a market decline and a market price recovery.
Discussion: A market price decline in inventory must be recognized in the interim period in which it occurs unless it is expected to be temporary, i.e., unless the decline is expected to be restored by the end of the fiscal year. This loss was not expected to be restored in the fiscal year, and the company should report the dollar amount of the market price decline as a loss in the first quarter. Inventory may never be written up to an amount above its original cost. Accordingly, the market price recovery recognized in the third quarter is limited to the extent of losses previously recognized in a prior interim period.

✘ **Answer (A) is incorrect.** The recovery recognized in the third quarter is limited to the amount of the losses previously recognized.

✘ **Answer (C) is incorrect.** Assuming no market price decline had been recognized prior to the current year, the first quarter loss and the third quarter recovery would be offsetting. The recognized third quarter gain is limited to the amount of the first quarter loss, and the year-end results would not be affected.

✘ **Answer (D) is incorrect.** The inventory amount is affected in both the first and third quarters.

10. During the first quarter of Year 4, Tech Co. had income before taxes of $200,000, and its effective income tax rate was 15%. Tech's Year 3 effective annual income tax rate was 30%, but Tech expects its Year 4 effective annual income tax rate to be 25%. In its first quarter interim income statement, what amount of income tax expense should Tech report?

A. $0

B. $30,000

C. $50,000

D. $60,000

✓ **Answer (C) is correct.**
Required: The provision for income taxes for the first interim period.
Discussion: At the end of each interim period, the entity should estimate the annual effective tax rate. This rate is used in providing for income taxes on a current year-to-date basis. Tech's income before taxes for the first quarter is $200,000, and the estimated annual effective tax rate for Year 4 is 25%. The provision for income taxes for the first interim period is therefore $50,000 ($200,000 × 25%).

✗ **Answer (A) is incorrect.** Zero excludes any income tax expense.

✗ **Answer (B) is incorrect.** The amount of $30,000 uses Tech's quarterly effective income tax rate.

✗ **Answer (D) is incorrect.** The amount of $60,000 uses Tech's Year 3 effective annual income tax rate.

3.3 Accounting Changes and Error Corrections

11. On January 2, Year 1, Air, Inc., agreed to pay its former president $300,000 under a deferred compensation arrangement. Air should have recorded this expense in Year 1 but did not do so. Air's reported income tax expense would have been $70,000 lower in Year 1 had it properly accrued this deferred compensation. In its December 31, Year 2, financial statements, Air should adjust the beginning balance of its retained earnings by a

A. $230,000 credit.

B. $230,000 debit.

C. $300,000 credit.

D. $370,000 debit.

✓ **Answer (B) is correct.**
Required: The adjustment to the beginning balance of retained earnings.
Discussion: Error corrections in single-period statements are reflected net of applicable income taxes as changes in the opening balance in the statement of retained earnings of the current period. The net effect of the error on Year 1 after-tax income was to understate expenses and overstate income by $230,000 ($300,000 expense – $70,000 tax savings). Consequently, beginning retained earnings should be debited (decreased) by $230,000.

12. How should the effect of a change in accounting estimate be accounted for?

A. By retrospectively applying the change to amounts reported in financial statements of prior periods.

B. By reporting pro forma amounts for prior periods.

C. As a prior-period adjustment to beginning retained earnings.

D. By prospectively applying the change to current and future periods.

✓ **Answer (D) is correct.**
Required: The accounting for the effect of a change in accounting estimate.
Discussion: The effect of a change in accounting estimate is accounted for in the period of change, if the change affects that period only, or in the period of change and future periods, if the change affects both. For a change in accounting estimate, the entity may not (1) restate or retrospectively adjust prior-period statements or (2) report pro forma amounts for prior periods.

13. Volga Co. included a foreign subsidiary in its Year 6 consolidated financial statements. The subsidiary was acquired in Year 4 and was excluded from previous consolidations. The change was caused by the elimination of foreign currency controls. Including the subsidiary in the Year 6 consolidated financial statements results in an accounting change that should be reported

    A. By note disclosure only.

    B. Currently and prospectively.

    C. Currently with note disclosure of pro forma effects of retrospective application.

    D. By retrospective application to the financial statements of all prior periods presented.

✔ **Answer (D) is correct.**
Required: The reporting of the change in the subsidiaries included in consolidated financial statements.
Discussion: A change in the reporting entity requires retrospective application to all prior periods presented to report information for the new entity. The following are changes in the reporting entity: (1) presenting consolidated or combined statements in place of statements of individual entities, (2) changing the specific subsidiaries included in the group for which consolidated statements are presented, and (3) changing the entities included in combined statements.

✘ **Answer (A) is incorrect.** The change requires recognition in the financial statements.
✘ **Answer (B) is incorrect.** A change in reporting entity requires retrospective application.
✘ **Answer (C) is incorrect.** The change must apply to the financial statements for all periods presented.

14. On January 2, Year 4, Raft Corp. discovered that it had incorrectly expensed a $210,000 machine purchased on January 2, Year 1. Raft estimated the machine's original useful life to be 10 years and its salvage value at $10,000. Raft uses the straight-line method of depreciation and is subject to a 30% tax rate. In its December 31, Year 4, financial statements, what amount should Raft report as a prior period adjustment?

    A. $102,900

    B. $105,000

    C. $165,900

    D. $168,000

✔ **Answer (B) is correct.**
Required: The prior period adjustment to correct the expensing of an asset purchase.
Discussion: Expensing the machine in Year 1 resulted in an after-tax understatement of net income equal to $147,000 [$210,000 × (1.0 − .30 tax rate)]. Not recognizing annual depreciation of $20,000 [($210,000 − $10,000 salvage value) ÷ 10 years] in Years 1-3 resulted in an after-tax overstatement of net income equal to $42,000 [($20,000 × 3 years) × (1.0 − .30 tax rate)]. Thus, the prior period adjustment is for a net understatement of $105,000 ($147,000 − $42,000).

✘ **Answer (A) is incorrect.** The amount of $102,900 assumes no salvage value.
✘ **Answer (C) is incorrect.** The amount of $165,900 equals $102,900 plus $63,000 (total pre-tax effect of omitting depreciation for three years and assuming no salvage value).
✘ **Answer (D) is incorrect.** The amount of $168,000 equals $105,000 plus $63,000 (total pre-tax effect of omitting depreciation for three years and assuming no salvage value).

3.4 Subsequent Events

15. On January 15, Year 2, before the Mapleview Co. released its financial statements for the year ended December 31, Year 1, it settled a long-standing lawsuit. A material loss resulted and **no** prior liability had been recorded. How should this loss be disclosed or recognized in the Year 1 financial statements?

   A. The loss should be disclosed, but the financial statements themselves need not be adjusted.

   B. The loss should be disclosed in an explanatory paragraph in the auditor's report.

   C. **No** disclosure or recognition is required.

   D. The loss must be recognized in the financial statements.

✔ **Answer (D) is correct.**
Required: The proper treatment of a material loss on an existing lawsuit after year end.
Discussion: Subsequent events that provide additional evidence with the respect to conditions that existed at the balance sheet date, including the estimates inherent in preparing the financial statements, must be recognized in the financial statements of the year affected by the subsequent event. Settlement of a lawsuit is indicative of conditions existing at year end and calls for recognition in the statements.

✘ **Answer (A) is incorrect.** The loss must be recognized in the financial statements.

✘ **Answer (B) is incorrect.** The audit report need not be modified.

✘ **Answer (C) is incorrect.** Failure to recognize a material loss on an asset that existed at year end is a departure from GAAP.

16. Zero Corp. suffered a loss that would have a material effect on its financial statements on an uncollectible trade account receivable due to a customer's bankruptcy. This occurred suddenly due to a natural disaster 10 days after Zero's balance sheet date but 1 month before the issuance of the financial statements. Under these circumstances,

	The Loss Must Be Recognized in the Financial Statements	The Event Requires Financial Statement Disclosure Only
A.	Yes	Yes
B.	Yes	No
C.	No	No
D.	No	Yes

✔ **Answer (D) is correct.**
Required: The effect on the financial statements of a customer's bankruptcy after the balance sheet date but before the issuance of the statements.
Discussion: Certain subsequent events may provide additional evidence about conditions at the date of the balance sheet, including estimates inherent in the preparation of statements. These events require recognition in the statements at year end. Other subsequent events provide evidence about conditions not existing at the date of the balance sheet but arising subsequent to that date and before the issuance of the statements or their availability for issuance. These events may require disclosure but not recognition in the statements. Thus, the loss must not be recognized in Zero's statements, but disclosure must be made.

3.5 Significant Accounting Policies and Credit Risk

17. Which of the following must be included in a summary of significant accounting policies in the notes to the financial statements?

    A. Description of current year equity transactions.

    B. Summary of long-term debt outstanding.

    C. Schedule of fixed assets.

    D. Revenue recognition policies.

✔ **Answer (D) is correct.**
Required: The item in the summary of significant accounting policies.
Discussion: Disclosure should include "important judgments as to appropriateness of principles related to recognition of revenue and allocation of asset costs to current and future periods."

18. Which of the following information should be included in Melay, Inc.'s current-year summary of significant accounting policies?

    A. Property, plant, and equipment is recorded at cost with depreciation computed principally by the straight-line method.

    B. During the current year, the consulting services operating segment was sold.

    C. Operating segment current-year sales are $2 million for the software segment, $4 million for the book production segment, and $6 million for the technical services segment.

    D. Future common share dividends are expected to approximate 60% of earnings.

✔ **Answer (A) is correct.**
Required: The item properly disclosed in the summary of significant accounting policies.
Discussion: The commonly required disclosures in a summary of significant accounting policies include (1) the basis of consolidation, (2) depreciation methods, (3) amortization of intangible assets, (4) inventory pricing, (5) recognition of profit on long-term construction-type contracts, (6) recognition of revenue from franchising and leasing operations, and (7) the policy for defining cash equivalents. Hence, the summary of significant accounting policies should include information about property, plant, and equipment depreciated by the straight-line method.

✘ **Answer (B) is incorrect.** The sale of an operating segment is a transaction, not an accounting principle. It is reflected in the discontinued operations section of the income statement.

✘ **Answer (C) is incorrect.** Specific operating segment information does not constitute an accounting policy. An accounting policy is a specific principle or a method of applying it.

✘ **Answer (D) is incorrect.** Future dividend policy is not an accounting policy.

19. Disclosure of information about significant concentrations of credit risk is required for

    A. Most financial instruments.

    B. Financial instruments with off-balance-sheet credit risk only.

    C. Financial instruments with off-balance-sheet market risk only.

    D. Financial instruments with off-balance-sheet risk of accounting loss only.

✔ **Answer (A) is correct.**
Required: The financial instruments for which disclosure of significant concentrations of credit risk is required.
Discussion: GAAP require the disclosure of information about the fair value of financial instruments, whether recognized or not (certain nonpublic entities and certain instruments, such as leases and insurance contracts, are exempt from the disclosure requirements). GAAP also require disclosure of all significant concentrations of credit risk for most financial instruments (except for obligations for deferred compensation, certain instruments of a pension plan, insurance contracts, warranty obligations and rights, and unconditional purchase obligations).

20. Where in its financial statements should a company disclose information about its concentration of credit risks?

    A. **No** disclosure is required.

    B. The notes to the financial statements.

    C. Supplementary information to the financial statements.

    D. Management's report to shareholders.

✔ **Answer (B) is correct.**
Required: The method of disclosure about concentration of credit risk.
Discussion: An entity must disclose significant concentrations of risk arising from most instruments. These disclosures should be made in the basic financial statements, either in the body of the statements or in the notes.

✘ **Answer (A) is incorrect.** Disclosure in the basic statements is required.

✘ **Answer (C) is incorrect.** Disclosure in supplementary information is normally done when certain entities are excluded from the scope of the requirements. However, the required disclosures are to be made by all entities.

✘ **Answer (D) is incorrect.** Management's report to shareholders is not part of the basic statements.

3.6 Fair Value Measurements

21. Fair value measurement (FVM) of an asset or liability is based on a fair value hierarchy that establishes priorities among inputs to valuation techniques. According to the hierarchy,

    A. Observable inputs are on Level 1.

    B. Unobservable inputs are on Level 2.

    C. Quoted prices for items similar to the asset or liability are on Level 3.

    D. Unadjusted quoted prices for an identical asset or liability are on Level 1.

✔ **Answer (D) is correct.**
Required: The appropriate level of the fair value hierarchy for inputs to valuation techniques.
Discussion: The level of the FVM depends on the lowest level input significant to the entire FVM. Level 1 inputs are unadjusted quoted prices in active markets for identical assets (liabilities) that the entity can access at the measurement date. An adjustment for new information results in a lower level FVM.

✘ **Answer (A) is incorrect.** Observable inputs that are not Level 1 quoted prices are on Level 2. Examples are quoted prices for similar items in active markets and quoted prices in markets that are not active.

✘ **Answer (B) is incorrect.** Level 3 inputs are unobservable. They are used in the absence of observable inputs and should be based on the best available information in the circumstances.

✘ **Answer (C) is incorrect.** Quoted prices for items similar (not identical) to the asset or liability are on Level 2.

22. For the purpose of a fair value measurement (FVM) of an asset or liability, a transaction is assumed to occur in the

    A. Principal market if one exists.

    B. Most advantageous market.

    C. Market in which the result is optimized.

    D. Principal market or most advantageous market at the election of the reporting entity.

✔ **Answer (A) is correct.**
Required: The market in which a transaction is assumed to occur.
Discussion: For FVM purposes, a transaction is assumed to occur in the principal market for an asset or liability if one exists. The principal market has the greatest volume or level of activity. If no such market exists, the transaction is assumed to occur in the most advantageous market.

23. Each of the following would be considered a Level 2 observable input that could be used to determine an asset or liability's fair value **except**

    A. Quoted prices for identical assets and liabilities in markets that are not active.

    B. Quoted prices for similar assets and liabilities in markets that are active.

    C. Internally generated cash flow projections for a related asset or liability.

    D. Interest rates that are observable at commonly quoted intervals.

✔ **Answer (C) is correct.**
Required: The Level 2 observable inputs.
Discussion: Internally generated cash flow projections are not observable and would be considered a Level 3 input. Level 3 inputs are unobservable inputs that are used in the absence of observable inputs. They should be based on the best available information in the circumstances.

✘ **Answer (A) is incorrect.** Quoted prices for identical assets and liabilities in markets that are not active is an example of a Level 2 input. Level 2 inputs are observable.

✘ **Answer (B) is incorrect.** Quoted prices for similar assets and liabilities in markets that are active is an example of a Level 2 input. Level 2 inputs are observable.

✘ **Answer (D) is incorrect.** Interest rates that are observable at commonly quoted intervals are an example of a Level 2 input. Level 2 inputs are observable.

GLEIM

Go to Online Course

Access the **Gleim CPA Premium Review System** featuring our SmartAdapt technology from your Gleim Personal Classroom to continue your studies.

You will experience a personalized study environment with exam-emulating multiple-choice questions.

Study Unit Four

~~C~~ ~~ash~~ and Investments

4.1 Cash

Nature of Cash

Cash is the **most liquid of assets**. Because of that liquidity and the ability to transfer it electronically, internal control of cash must be strong.

As the customary **medium of exchange**, it also provides the **standard of value** (the unit of measurement) of the transactions that are reported in the financial statements.

Cash is classified as a **current asset** unless its use is restricted to such purposes as payments to sinking funds.

- In this case, cash is reported as a noncurrent asset with an account title such as bond sinking fund.

Readily Available

To be classified as current, cash must be readily available for use. The cash account on the balance sheet should consist of

- Coin and currency on hand, including petty cash and change funds
- Demand deposits (checking accounts)
- Time deposits (savings accounts)
- Near-cash assets

  - They include many negotiable instruments, such as money orders, bank drafts, certified checks, cashiers' checks, and personal checks.

  - They are usually in the process of being deposited (deposits in transit).

  - They must be depositable (excluding unsigned and postdated checks).

  - Checks written to creditors but not mailed or delivered at the balance sheet date should be included in the payor's cash account (not considered cash payments at year end).

Restricted Cash

Restricted cash is not actually set aside in special accounts. However, it is designated for special uses and should be separately presented and disclosed in the notes.

- Examples are bond sinking funds, new building funds, and restricted compensating balances.

- The nature of the use determines whether cash is current or noncurrent.

  - A bond sinking fund used to redeem noncurrent bond debt is noncurrent, but a fund to be used to redeem bonds currently redeemable is a current asset.

Compensating Balances

As part of an agreement regarding either an existing loan or the provision of future credit, a borrower may keep an average or minimum amount on deposit with the lender. This compensating balance increases the effective rate of interest paid by the borrower.

It also creates a disclosure issue because the full amount reported as cash might not be available to meet general obligations.

Cash Equivalents

Cash equivalents are short-term, highly liquid investments. Common examples are Treasury bills, money market funds, and commercial paper.

Cash equivalents are

- Readily convertible to known amounts of cash and
- So near maturity that interest rate risk is insignificant.

  - Only investments with an **original maturity to the holder of 3 months or less** qualify.

Example 4-1	Cash Equivalents

Debtor issues a note with a 2-year maturity to Creditor. After 1 year and 10 months, Creditor sells the note to Holder. The original maturity to Holder is 2 months. If the note is highly liquid, it may be a cash equivalent. The note would not have been a cash equivalent to Creditor at the date of sale.

Noncash Items

Nonsufficient funds (NSF) checks and postdated checks should be treated as receivables. Advances for expenses to employees may be classified as receivables (if expected to be paid by employees) or as prepaid expenses.

An **overdraft** is a current liability unless the entity has sufficient funds in another account at the same bank to cover it.

Noncash short-term investments are usually substantially restricted and thus not readily available for use by the entity. They should be classified as current or temporary investments, not cash. However, they may qualify as cash equivalents.

- Money market funds are essentially mutual funds that have portfolios of commercial paper and Treasury bills. However, a money market fund with a usable checking feature might be better classified as cash.

- Commercial paper (also known as negotiable instruments) consists of short-term (no more than 270 days) corporate obligations.

- Treasury bills are short-term, guaranteed U.S. government obligations.

- Certificates of deposit are formal debt instruments issued by a bank or other financial institution and are subject to penalties for withdrawal before maturity.

Recording Cash

Cash may be recorded in a general ledger control account, with a subsidiary ledger for each bank account. An alternative is a series of general ledger accounts.

- On the balance sheet, one account is presented. It reflects all unrestricted cash.

- Each transfer of cash from one account to another requires an entry.

- At the end of each period, a schedule of transfers should be prepared and reviewed to make certain all cash transfers are counted only once.

Bank Reconciliation

Success Tip

The AICPA has released bank reconciliation problems that test cash reporting on the exam. CPA candidates may see a bank reconciliation problem on the CPA Exam.

A bank reconciliation is a schedule comparing the cash balance per books with the balance per bank statement (usually received monthly). The common approach is to reconcile the bank balance to the book balance to reach the true balance.

- The bank and book balances usually vary. Thus, the reconciliation permits the entity to determine whether the difference is attributable to normal conditions, error, or fraud. It is also a basis for entries to adjust the books to reflect unrecorded items.

- The bank and the entity inevitably record many transactions at different times. Both also may make errors.

Items Known to Entity but Not Known to Bank

Outstanding checks. The books may reflect checks written by the entity that have not yet cleared the bank. These amounts are subtracted from the bank balance to arrive at the true balance.

Deposits in transit. A time lag may occur between deposit of receipts and the bank's recording of the transaction. Thus, receipts placed in a night depository on the last day of the month are reflected only in the next month's bank statement. These receipts are added to the bank balance to arrive at the true balance.

Errors. If the bank has wrongly charged or credited the entity's account (or failed to record a transaction at all), the error will be detected in the process of preparing the reconciliation.

Items Known to Bank but Not Known to Entity

Amounts added by the bank. Interest income added to an account may not be included in the book balance. Banks may act as collection agents, for example, for notes on which the depositor is the payee. If the depositor has not learned of a collection, it will not be reflected in its records.

- These amounts are added to the book balance to arrive at the true balance.
- They should be recorded on the entity's books, after which they are no longer reconciling items.

Amounts subtracted (or not added) by the bank. These amounts generally include service charges and customer checks returned for insufficient funds (NSF checks). Service charges cannot be recorded in the books until the bank statement is received. Customer checks returned for insufficient funds are not added to the bank balance but are still included in the book balance.

- These amounts are subtracted from the book balance to get the true balance.
- They should be recorded on the entity's books, after which they are no longer reconciling items.

Errors. Bookkeeping errors made by the entity will likewise be discovered.

4.2 Fair Value Option (FVO)

Scope

The FVO allows entities to measure most recognized financial assets and liabilities at **fair value**.

An entity **may elect** the **FVO** for most recognized financial assets and liabilities.

The FVO **may not be elected** for the following:

- An investment that must be consolidated

    - The FVO is not an alternative to consolidation.
    - Consolidation is required for subsidiaries. Study Unit 13 addresses this topic.

- Postretirement employee benefit obligations, employee stock option and purchase plans, and deferred compensation obligations

- Most financial assets and liabilities under leases

- Demand deposit liabilities

- Financial instruments at least partly classified in equity

Election of the FVO

The decision whether to elect the FVO is **made irrevocably at an election date** (unless a new election date occurs).

- With certain exceptions, the decision is made **instrument by instrument** and only for an **entire instrument**.

- Thus, the FVO generally need **not** be applied to all instruments in a single transaction.

    - For example, it might be applied only to some of the shares or bonds issued or acquired in a transaction.

The election may be made only on the date of one of the following:

- Initial recognition of an eligible item

- Making an eligible firm commitment

- A change in accounting for an investment in another entity because it becomes subject to the **equity method**

- Deconsolidation of a subsidiary

FVO – Presentation of Financial Assets and Liabilities

Balance Sheet

Under the FVO, financial assets and liabilities are measured at **fair value** each balance sheet date.

Assets and liabilities measured using the FVO are reported by separating their reported fair values from the carrying amounts of similar items measured using another attribute, such as amortized cost or present value.

Income Statement

Transaction costs related to the acquisition of an item for which the FVO was elected must be expensed as incurred. They must not be capitalized at the initial cost of the item.

Dividends received from an investment that is accounted for using the FVO are recognized as dividend income.

Changes in the Fair Value of Financial Assets

Under the FVO, **unrealized holding gains and losses** on the remeasurement to fair value of financial assets are recognized in the **income statement** (net income) at each subsequent reporting date.

Example 4-3	FVO for Financial Asset

On October 1, Year 1, Mill Co. purchased 5,000 shares of Floss Co.'s common stock, out of a total of 20,000 outstanding, for their fair value. Mill elected the fair value option for its investment in the common stock of Floss. The following are the fair values per share of Floss common stock:

Date	Fair Value
October 1, Year 1	$15
December 31, Year 1	13
December 31, Year 2	20

October 1, Year 1

Investment – FVO (5,000 × $15)	$75,000	
Cash		$75,000

December 31, Year 1
At each balance sheet date, an investment accounted for using the FVO is remeasured at fair value. Unrealized holding gains and losses are reported in earnings.

Unrealized holding loss on FVO investment [5,000 × ($15 – $13)]	$10,000	
Investment – FVO		$10,000

In Mill's December 31, Year 1, balance sheet, the investment in Floss is measured at year-end fair value of $65,000 (5,000 × $13).

December 31, Year 2

Investment – FVO [5,000 × ($20 – $13)]	$35,000	
Unrealized holding gain on FVO investment		$35,000

In Mill's December 31, Year 2, balance sheet, the investment in Floss is measured at year-end fair value of $100,000 (5,000 × $20).

Changes in the Fair Value of Financial Liabilities

Under the FVO, unrealized gains and losses on the remeasurement to fair value of **financial liabilities** are recognized in the statement of comprehensive income.

- The portion of the total change in the fair value attributable to the **change in instrument-specific credit risk** is recognized as an item of **other comprehensive income** (OCI).

    ■ This amount is the difference between

        ▸ The total change in the fair value of the financial liability and

        ▸ The amount that results from a change in a base market risk, such as a risk-free interest rate.

- The **remaining change in fair value** (total change in fair value – change attributable to instrument-specific credit risk) is recognized directly in the **income statement**.

- When the financial liability is derecognized, the accumulated gains or losses due to changes in instrument-specific credit risk are reclassified from OCI to the income statement.

Example 4-4   FVO for Financial Liability

The following amounts are for a financial liability accounted for using the fair value option:

Fair value on January 1, Year 1	$ 9,000
Fair value on December 31, Year 1	15,000
Change in fair value attributable to instrument-specific credit risk	2,000

Year 1 total unrealized loss on the financial liability is $6,000 ($15,000 – $9,000). The $2,000 change in fair value attributable to instrument-specific credit risk is recognized in OCI. The remaining $4,000 change in fair value ($6,000 – $2,000) is recognized in the income statement.

Unrealized loss – OCI	$2,000	
Unrealized loss – Income statement	4,000	
Financial liability – FVO		$6,000

Stop & Review

You have completed the outline for this subunit.

Study multiple-choice questions 4 and 5 on page 144.

4.3 Investments in Equity Securities

An **equity security** is an **ownership** interest in an entity (e.g., common stock or preferred stock) or a right to acquire or dispose of such an interest (e.g., warrants or call options).

- Convertible debt securities are not equity interests in the issuer.

This subunit applies to all investments in equity securities **except** for investments

- Accounted for under the equity method
- In consolidated subsidiaries
- For which the entity has elected the FVO

The accounting method for an investment in voting stock depends on the presumed influence the investor has over the investee.

- The presumed influence usually is determined based on the ownership interest held.
- The following table depicts the three possibilities:

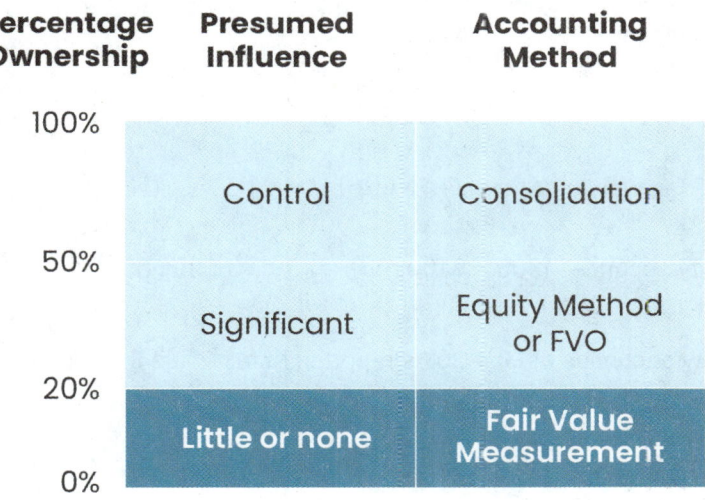

Percentage Ownership	Presumed Influence	Accounting Method
100% – 50%	Control	Consolidation
50% – 20%	Significant	Equity Method or FVO
20% – 0%	Little or none	Fair Value Measurement

Figure 4-1

Fair Value Through Net Income Method

When there is little or no influence, the investment in equity securities is measured at **fair value** at each balance sheet date.

Unrealized holding gains and losses on the remeasurement of the investment to fair value are reported in the **income statement** (net income) at each subsequent reporting date.

Dividends received from investments in equity securities are reported as dividend income in the income statement.

Cash flows from purchases and sales of equity securities are classified in the statement of cash flows based on the nature and purpose for which the securities were acquired.

Example 4-5	Fair Value through Net Income Approach

On November 1, Year 1, Abi Co. purchased 200 shares of Gail Co.'s common stock at fair value. This investment is less than 1% of the ownership interests in Gail Co. The following are the fair values per share of Gail common stock at the relevant dates:

Date	Fair Value
November 1, Year 1	$100
December 31, Year 1	90
December 31, Year 2	115

November 1, Year 1

Investment in equity securities (200 × $100)	$20,000	
Cash		$20,000

This investment in equity securities of Gail Co. is reported at fair value through net income on each balance sheet date.

December 31, Year 1

Unrealized holding loss [200 × ($90 − $100)]	$2,000	
Investment in equity securities		$2,000

In Abi's December 31, Year 1, balance sheet, the investment in equity securities of Gail Co. is reported at its fair value of $18,000 (200 × $90). In the Year 1 income statement, a loss of $2,000 is recognized.

December 31, Year 2

Investment in equity securities [200 × ($115 − $90)]	$5,000	
Unrealized holding gain		$5,000

In Abi's December 31, Year 2, balance sheet, the investment in equity securities of Gail Co. is reported at its fair value of $23,000 (200 × $115). In the Year 2 income statement, a gain of $5,000 is recognized.

Measurement Alternative for Investment in Equity Securities without a Readily Determinable Fair Value

Measurement Alternative

An entity may elect a measurement alternative for an investment in equity securities without a readily determinable fair value.

- This alternative is **cost minus impairment** (if any), **plus or minus** changes resulting from observable price changes for the identical or a similar investment of the same issuer.

If the measurement alternative is selected, it must be applied until the investment has a readily determinable fair value.

- The entity must reassess at each reporting period whether the fair value of an equity investment is readily determinable.

- When the fair value of an equity investment is readily determinable, the investment is measured at fair value through net income.

Impairment Test

A qualitative assessment of whether an investment is impaired must be performed at each reporting date. An investment is impaired if the fair value of the investment is lower than its carrying amount.

- A **qualitative** assessment may consider many impairment indicators, such as significant deterioration in earnings performance, credit rating, or asset quality.

If the qualitative assessment indicates potential impairment, the entity must estimate the fair value of the investment and perform a **quantitative** impairment test.

- The carrying amount of the investment is compared with its fair value. An impairment loss is recognized in the income statement (net income) for the excess of the carrying amount over the fair value.

Impairment loss = Carrying amount – Fair value

Observable Price Changes

To identify observable price changes, a reasonable effort should be made to identify relevant transactions by the same issuer that occurred on or before the balance sheet date. Accordingly, an entity does not need to make an exhaustive search for all observable price changes.

Similar Investment of the Same Issuer

Different rights and obligations of the securities should be considered when identifying whether a security issued by the same issuer is similar to the equity investment.

Decision Tree: Classification and Measurement of an Investment in Equity Securities

Does the investment in equity securities result in control or significant influence over the investee?

YES

NO

Control = Consolidation

Significant influence = Equity method or FVO

Is the fair value of the investment in equity securities readily determinable?

YES

NO

The investment is measured at fair value. Changes in fair value are recognized in the income statement (net income).

NO

Was the measurement alternative elected?

YES

The investment is measured as follows:

Cost – Impairment ± Observable price changes of the identical or a similar investment of the same issuer

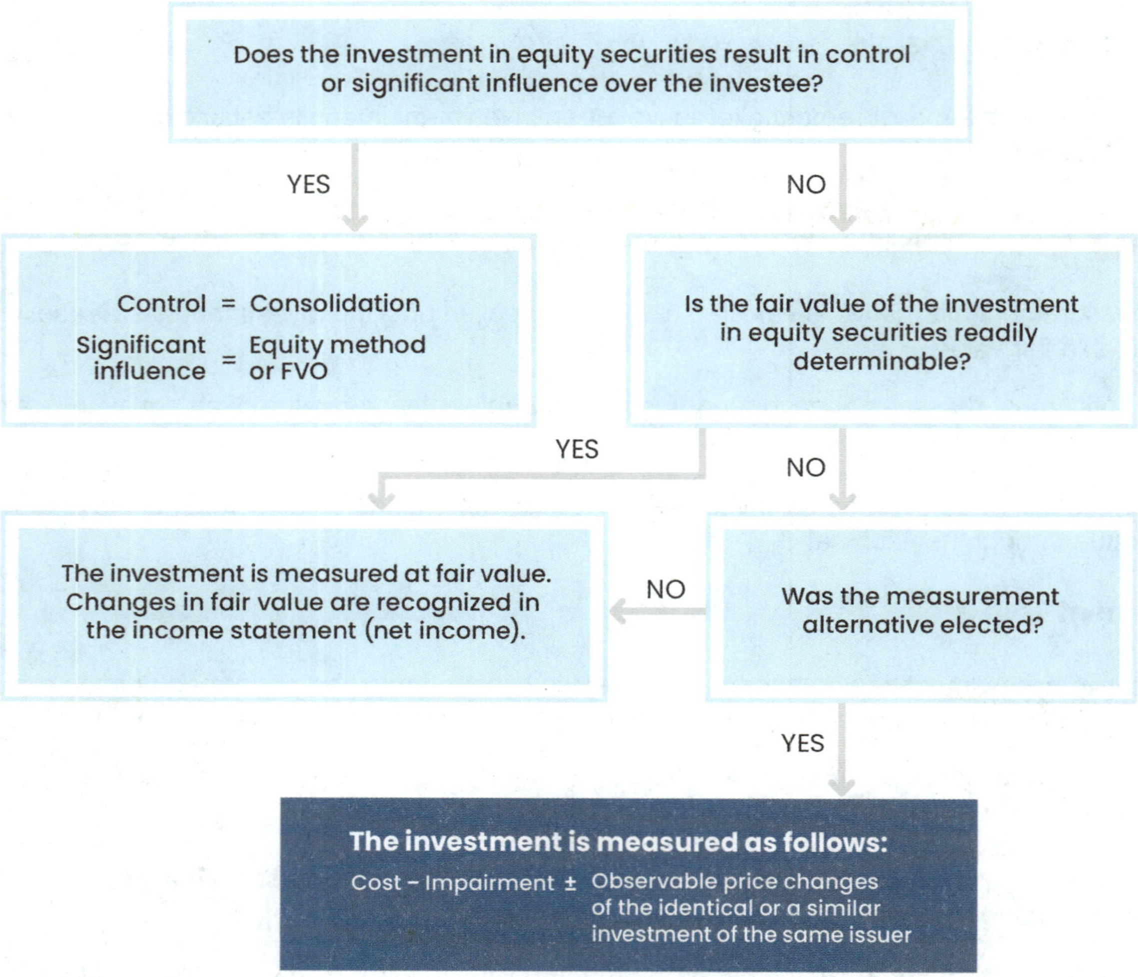

Figure 4-2

Stop & Review

You have completed the outline for this subunit.
Study multiple-choice questions 6 through 8 beginning on page 145.

4.4 Equity Method

Significant Influence

An investment in voting stock that enables the investor to exercise significant influence over the investee should be accounted for by the equity method (assuming no FVO election).

The accounting method used by the investor depends on its presumed influence based on the ownership interest held. The following table depicts the three possibilities:

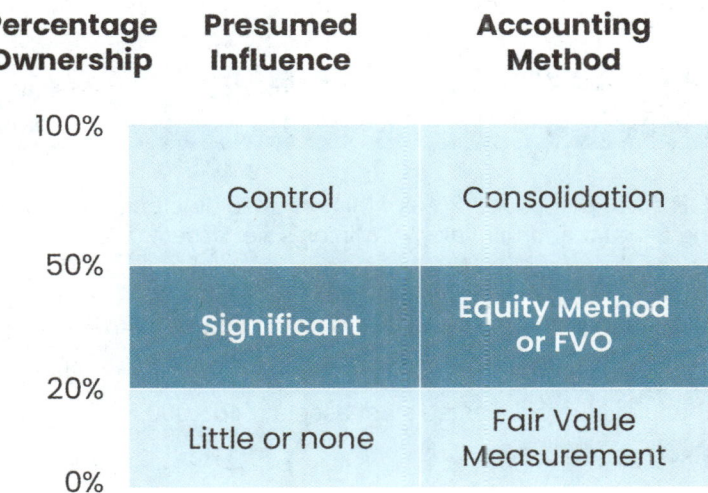

Figure 4-3

- The **FVO**, which may be elected when the investor does not have control, is covered in Subunit 4.2.

- The **equity method**, used when the investor has significant influence and has not elected the FVO, is covered in this subunit.

- An investment of 20% or more (but not more than 50%) in the voting stock of the investee generally results in significant influence over an investee.

- **Consolidation**, which is required when the investor owns more than 50% of the outstanding voting interests, is covered in Study Unit 13.

Success Tip

CPA candidates should expect to see questions on applying the equity method to investments. Past exam questions most often have required calculations to test candidates' understanding of this topic.

Applying the Equity Method at the Acquisition Date

An equity method investment is initially recognized at cost. The difference between the cost of the investment and the underlying equity in the investee's net assets may consist of the following:

- **Equity method goodwill.** Goodwill resulting from the acquisition is the difference between the consideration transferred (cost of the investment) and the investor's equity in the fair value of the investee's net assets.

    - Equity method goodwill is **not** a separately identifiable asset. Accordingly, it is **not recognized and presented separately** in the investor's financial statements. Instead, it is included in the carrying amount of the equity method investment.

Example 4-6	Equity Method Investment and Goodwill

On January 1, Year 1, GRV Co. purchased 25% of Minion Co.'s outstanding common stock for $130,000. On that date, the carrying amount and fair value of Minion's net assets (assets minus liabilities) was $400,000.

Equity method goodwill resulting from the acquisition is calculated as follows:

Cost of the investment	$130,000
Equity in the fair value of investee's net assets ($400,000 × 25%)	(100,000)
Equity method goodwill	$ 30,000

Investment in Minion Co.	$130,000	
Cash		$130,000

- On the acquisition date, the fair values of the investee's assets and liabilities may differ from their carrying amounts.

Example 4-7	Equity Method Investment and Goodwill -- Plant Asset

Using the data from Example 4-6, assume that on January 1, Year 1, the fair values and the carrying amounts of Minion's net assets were the same for all items except for a plant asset. The fair value of this asset exceeded the carrying amount by $40,000.

Cost of the investment	$130,000	
Equity in the carrying amount of investee's net assets ($400,000 × 25%)	(100,000)	Equity in fair value
Equity in the excess of plant's fair value over its carrying amt. ($40,000 × 25%)	(10,000)	of net assets
Equity method goodwill	$ 20,000	

Investment in Minion Co.	$130,000	
Cash		$130,000

Private Companies Accounting

A **private company** is any entity that is not (1) a public business entity, (2) a not-for-profit entity, or (3) an employee benefit plan.

In accounting for subsequent measurement of **equity method goodwill**, a private company may

- Use the general FASB codification guidance that applies to all entities or
- May elect to apply the **goodwill accounting alternative**.

Under the goodwill accounting alternative, goodwill recognized must be **amortized on a straight-line basis over 10 years**. The amortization expense is recognized in the income statement.

- A private company may amortize goodwill over a period shorter than 10 years if it can demonstrate that this useful life is more appropriate.

NOTE: Unless specifically stated otherwise, all questions and simulations are based on the FASB codification guidance applied to all entities. The guidance for private companies should be used only when the facts of a question or simulation state that (1) a company has elected the accounting alternative and (2) the company is private.

Applying the Equity Method after the Acquisition Date

Under the equity method, the investor recognizes in income its **share of the investee's earnings or losses** in the periods for which they are reported by the investee. The journal entry is as follows:

Investee reported net income for the period			Investee reported net loss for the period		
Investment in X Co.	$XXX		Equity method loss --		
Equity method income --			Share of X Co. losses	$XXX	
Share of X Co. earnings		$XXX	Investment in X Co.		$XXX

- The investor's share of the investee's earnings or losses is recognized only for the portion of the year that the investment was held under the equity method.

- The investor's share of the investee's earnings or losses is adjusted to eliminate intraentity profits and losses not realized in third-party transactions.

Dividends from the investee are treated as a return of an investment. They **decrease the investment balance** but have no effect on the investor's income. The journal entry is

Cash or dividend receivable	$XXX	
Investment in X Co.		$XXX

Example 4-8 — Equity Method Subsequent to Initial Recognition

On March 1, H.E. Bird Company purchased, at the market price, 40% of the outstanding common stock of Dowland Corporation. On March 1, Dowland had 50,000 shares of $1 par value common stock outstanding, and the market price was $12 per share.

Investment in Dowland Corp. (50,000 × $12 × 40%)	$240,000	
Cash		$240,000

On September 13, Dowland declared and paid a $15,000 cash dividend.

Cash ($15,000 × 40%)	$6,000	
Investment in Dowland Corp.		$6,000

For the year ending December 31, Dowland reported net income of $60,000, earned at a constant rate throughout the year. Bird held its equity-method investment in Dowland for 10 months of the year.

Investment in Dowland Corp. [$60,000 × 40% × (10 ÷ 12)]	$20,000	
Equity method income		$20,000

Presentation in Bird's year-end financial statements:

Balance sheet: Investment in Dowland Corp. ($240,000 + $20,000 − $6,000)	$254,000
Income statement: Equity method income from Dowland Corp.	20,000

The equity method requires the investor's share of the investee's earnings or losses to be adjusted for its share in the difference at the acquisition date between the fair value and the carrying amount of the investee's net assets. This adjustment is made as the assets are sold or consumed in operations (e.g., depreciated).

- For example, the investee's depreciable assets may be understated at the acquisition date. Thus, subsequent amortization of the excess of the fair value over the carrying amount decreases equity method income. It is recognized by the following entry:

Equity method loss	$XXX	
Investment in X Co.		$XXX

- No adjustment is made for assets with an indefinite useful life (e.g., land) because they are not depreciated.

Example 4-9	Equity Method Subsequent to Initial Recognition -- Plant Asset

Using the data from Example 4-7, assume that

- On January 1, Year 1, the remaining useful life of the plant asset is 5 years.
- Minion depreciates its assets using the straight-line depreciation method.
- In Year 1, Minion reported net income of $60,000.

The following journal entries are recorded by GRV on December 31, Year 1:

GRV's share in Minion's Year 1 net income
Investment in Minion Co. $15,000
    Equity method income ($60,000 × 25%) $15,000

GNV's share in Year 1 amortization of the excess of plant asset's fair value over the carrying amount
Equity method income [($40,000 ÷ 5 years) × 25%] $2,000
    Investment in Minion Co. $2,000

The total Year 1 equity method income recognized by GNV is $13,000 ($15,000 – $2,000).

Use of the equity method is discontinued when the investment is reduced to zero by investee losses unless the investor has committed to providing additional financial support to the investee.

Change from the Equity Method

If an investor can **no longer be presumed** to exercise significant influence (for example, due to a decrease in the level of ownership), it ceases to account for the investment using the equity method.

- Any retained investment is measured based on the carrying amount of the investment on the date significant influence is lost.

Stop & Review

You have completed the outline for this subunit.
Study multiple-choice questions 9 through 11 beginning on page 146.

4.5 Investments in Debt Securities

A **debt security** represents a **creditor** relationship with the issuer.

- In addition to the common forms of debt, this category includes (1) mandatorily redeemable preferred stock (stock that must be redeemed by the issuer), (2) preferred stock redeemable at the investor's option, and (3) collateralized mortgage obligations.

- Leases, options, financial futures contracts, and forward contracts are not debt securities.

This subunit applies to all investments in debt securities.

Debt securities are classified at acquisition into one of **three categories**. The classification is reassessed at each reporting date.

Category	Criteria
Held-to-maturity	Debt securities that the reporting entity has the positive intent and ability to hold to maturity
Trading	Debt securities intended to be sold in the near term
Available-for-sale	Debt securities not classified as held-to-maturity or trading

Held-to-Maturity Securities -- Amortized Cost

An investment in a debt security is classified as held-to-maturity when the holder has both the **positive intent** and the **ability** to hold the security until its maturity date.

- The investor may intend to hold the security for an indefinite period. Also, the possibility may exist that it will be sold before maturity to supply needed cash, avoid interest rate risk, etc. In these cases, the security cannot be classified as held-to-maturity.

- If a sale before maturity takes place, the security still can be deemed to have been held-to-maturity if

  - Sale is near enough to the maturity or call date (e.g., within 3 months) so that interest rate risk (change in the market rate) does not have a significant effect on fair value, or

  - Sale is after collection of 85% or more of the principal.

Held-to-maturity securities are measured at **amortized cost**.

- Amortized cost is the amount at which an investment in debt securities was recognized, adjusted for accrued interest, collection of cash, and amortization of premium or discount.

- The purchase of held-to-maturity securities is recorded as follows:

Held-to-maturity securities	$XXX	
Cash		$XXX

An **allowance for credit losses** is a valuation account that is deducted from the amortized cost basis of held-to-maturity debt securities to present the net amount expected to be collected.

- Initial recognition of the allowance for credit losses and subsequent changes in the allowance balance are recognized immediately in the income statement in the credit loss expense account.

- The allowance for credit losses represents the portion of an amortized cost basis that an entity does not expect to collect over the security's contractual life.

  ▸ It is estimated based on the entity's past experience considering current and forecasted economic conditions.

  ▸ The discounted cash flow method can be used to measure the allowance.

An impairment for credit losses is recognized when the present value of the cash flows (interest and principal) expected to be collected from the security is less than its amortized cost basis. The following is the journal entry:

Credit loss expense	$XXX	*PVCF < Amort.*
Allowance for credit losses		$XXX

Presentation -- balance sheet. On the face of the balance sheet, held-to-maturity securities are presented net of any unamortized premium or discount. (This topic is addressed in Subunit 4.6.)

- Amortization of any discount (premium) is reported by a debit (credit) to held-to-maturity securities and a credit (debit) to interest income.

- Individual securities are presented as current or noncurrent.

- The allowance for credit losses must be separately presented as a deduction from the held-to-maturity securities' balance.

Balance sheet:	
Debt securities held-to-maturity	$X,XXX
(Allowance for credit losses)	(X,XXX)
Debt securities held-to-maturity, net of allowance for credit losses	$X,XXX

Success Tip

Unless the question indicates that a portion of the investment in debt securities is not expected to be collected, you can ignore the recognition of the allowance for credit losses.

Presentation -- income statement. Realized gains and losses and interest income (including amortization of premium or discount) are included in earnings.

Presentation -- cash flow statement. Cash flows are from investing activities.

Trading Securities -- Fair Value through Net Income

Trading securities are bought and held primarily for sale in the near term. They are purchased and sold frequently.

- Each trading security is initially recorded at **cost** (including brokerage commissions and taxes).

Trading securities	$XXX	
Cash		$XXX

- At each balance sheet date, trading securities are **remeasured at fair value**. (The fair value measurement framework is covered in Study Unit 3, Subunit 6.)

Unrealized holding gains and losses on trading securities are reported in the **income statement** (net income). A holding gain or loss is the net change in fair value during the period, not including recognized dividends or interest not received.

- To retain historical cost in the accounts while reporting changes in the carrying amount from changes in fair value, a valuation allowance may be established.

  - For example, the entry below debits an allowance for an increase in the fair value of trading securities.

Securities fair value adjustment (trading)	$XXX	
Unrealized holding gain		$XXX

Presentation -- balance sheet. The balances of the securities and valuation allowances are netted. One amount is displayed for fair value.

- Trading securities are current assets.

Presentation -- income statement. Unrealized and realized holding gains and losses, dividends, and interest income (including premium or discount amortization) are included in earnings (income statement).

Presentation -- cash flow statement. Classification of cash flows depends on the nature of the securities and the purpose of their acquisition. They are typically considered to be from operating activities.

The accounting for (1) trading securities and (2) financial assets under the fair value option is similar. Under both methods, the investment is measured in the balance sheet at fair value. Unrealized holding gains or losses on the remeasurement to fair value then are recognized in earnings (income statement).

Example 4-10   Trading Debt Securities

On October 1, Year 1, Maverick Co. purchased 1,000 shares of Larson Co. mandatorily redeemable preferred stock (i.e., debt securities) at fair value. Maverick classified this investment as trading securities. On March 1, Year 2, Maverick sold all of its investment at fair value. The following are the fair values per share of Larson mandatorily redeemable preferred stock at the relevant dates:

Date	Fair Value
October 1, Year 1	$15
December 31, Year 1	14
March 1, Year 2	21

October 1, Year 1

Trading securities (1,000 × $15)	$15,000	
Cash		$15,000

December 31, Year 1

At each balance sheet date, trading securities are remeasured at fair value. Unrealized holding gains and losses are reported in earnings.

Unrealized holding loss [1,000 × ($15 – $14)]	$1,000	
Securities fair value adjustment (trading)		$1,000

In Maverick's December 31, Year 1, balance sheet, the investment in Larson is reported in the current assets section as trading securities. It is measured at year-end fair value of $14,000 (1,000 × $14).

March 1, Year 2

Cash (1,000 × $21)	$21,000	
Trading securities		$14,000
Gain on disposal of trading securities		7,000

Available-for-Sale Securities -- Fair Value through OCI

An investment in debt securities that are not classified as held-to-maturity or trading is considered available-for-sale. The initial acquisition is recorded at **cost** by a debit to available-for-sale securities and a credit to cash.

Available-for-sale securities	$XXX	
Cash		$XXX

At each balance sheet date, available-for-sale securities are **remeasured at fair value**.

Unrealized holding gains and losses resulting from the remeasurement to fair value are reported in **other comprehensive income** (OCI).

Unrealized holding loss -- OCI	$XXX	
Securities fair value adjustment		
(available-for-sale)		$XXX

- Tax effects are debited or credited directly to OCI.

- Amortization of any discount (premium) is reported by a debit (credit) to available-for-sale securities and a credit (debit) to interest income.

Presentation -- balance sheet. On the face of the balance sheet, available-for-sale securities are reported at **fair value**. The amounts of the allowance for credit losses and amortized cost basis should be indicated within the text (presented parenthetically).

- Individual securities are presented as current or noncurrent.

- In the equity section, unrealized holding gains and losses are reported in accumulated OCI (the real account to which OCI is closed).

Presentation -- income statement. Realized gains and losses, dividends, and interest income (including premium or discount amortization) are included in earnings.

Presentation -- statement of comprehensive income. Unrealized holding gains and losses for the period are included in comprehensive income.

- Reclassification adjustments also must be made for each component of OCI. Their purpose is to avoid double counting when an item included in net income also was included in OCI for the same or a prior period. For example, if a gain on available-for-sale securities is realized in the current period, the prior-period recognition of an unrealized holding gain must be eliminated by debiting OCI and crediting a gain.

Presentation -- cash flow statement. Cash flows are from investing activities.

Example 4-11   Available-for-Sale Debt Securities

On April 1, Year 1, Maverick Co. purchased 1,000 shares of White Co. mandatorily redeemable preferred stock at fair value. Maverick classified this investment as available-for-sale securities. On May 1, Year 3, Maverick sold all of its investment at fair value. The following are the fair values per share of White mandatorily redeemable preferred stock at the relevant dates:

Date	Fair Value
April 1, Year 1	$25
December 31, Year 1	32
December 31, Year 2	27
May 1, Year 3	31

The changes in the fair value of White preferred shares are not due to credit losses.

<u>April 1, Year 1, Journal Entry</u>

Available-for-sale securities (1,000 × $25)	$25,000	
Cash		$25,000

<u>December 31, Year 1, Journal Entry</u>
At each balance sheet date, available-for-sale securities are remeasured at fair value. Unrealized holding gains and losses are included in OCI.

Available-for-sale securities fair value adjustment [1,000 × ($32 – $25)]	$7,000	
Unrealized holding gain (OCI item)		$7,000

Presentation in Maverick's December 31, Year 1, financial statements:

Balance sheet: Assets section -- Available-for-sale securities (1,000 × $32)	$32,000	($25,000 + $7,000)
Equity section -- Accumulated OCI	7,000	
Statement of comprehensive income -- Unrealized holding gain (OCI)	7,000	

<u>December 31, Year 2, Journal Entry</u>

Unrealized holding loss (OCI item) [1,000 × ($27 – $32)]	$5,000	
Available-for-sale securities fair value adjustment		$5,000

Presentation in Maverick's December 31, Year 2, financial statements:

Balance sheet: Assets section -- Available-for-sale securities (1,000 × $27)	$27,000	($25,000 + $2,000)
Equity section -- Accumulated OCI ($7,000 – $5,000)	2,000	
Statement of comprehensive income -- Unrealized holding loss (OCI)	5,000	

<u>May 1, Year 3, Journal Entry</u>

Cash (1,000 × $31)	$31,000	
Available-for-sale securities		$25,000
Available-for-sale securities fair value adjustment		2,000
Realized gain on AFS securities		4,000
Reclassification of holding gains from AOCI (OCI item)	$2,000	
Realized gain on AFS securities		$2,000

Presentation in Maverick's December 31, Year 3, financial statements:

Income statement: Realized gain on AFS securities	$6,000	($4,000 + $2,000)
Statement of OCI: Reclassification of holding gains from accumulated OCI	(2,000)	
Total comprehensive income for Year 3 ($31,000 – $27,000)	$4,000	

Impairment of Available-for-Sale (AFS) Securities

An available-for-sale debt security is impaired only if its fair value is less than its amortized cost basis.

The accounting question is to determine the portion of the impairment that relates to credit losses (recognized in net income) and the noncredit losses portion (unrealized holding loss recognized in OCI).

The debt security's fair value often may be lower than its amortized cost due to factors that are not related to credit losses (the issuer's ability to pay). For example, the fair value of the security may decline solely due to an increase in market interest rates.

- In these cases, the entire decline in the fair value of the security is recognized as an unrealized holding loss in OCI.

A credit loss exists if the present value of cash flows expected to be collected from the security is less than its amortized cost basis.

Amortized cost basis > Present value of cash flows = Credit loss exists

- The impairment for credit losses recognized is limited by the amount that the fair value of the security is less than the security's amortized cost basis.

Amortized cost basis – Fair value = Maximum amount of impairment for credit losses

The impairment for credit losses is recognized in the **income statement** and recorded through an allowance for credit losses. The following is the journal entry:

Credit loss expense	$XXX	
Allowance for credit losses		$XXX

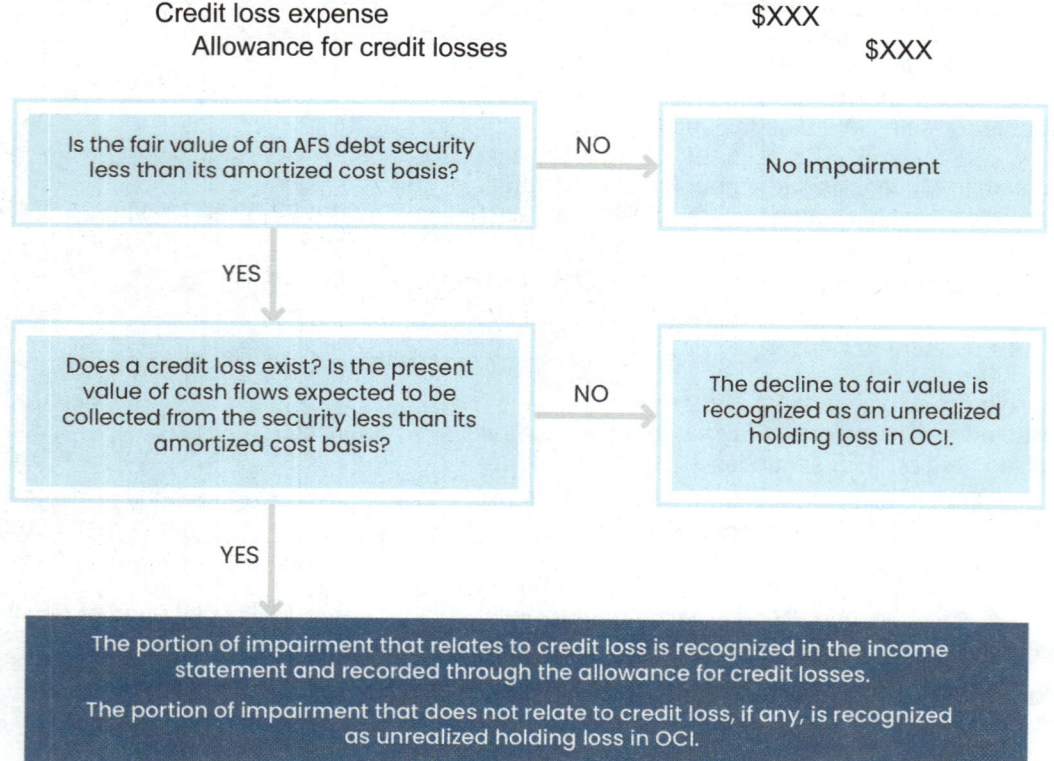

Figure 4-4

Example 4-12   Impairment of AFS Debt Securities

The following year-end information pertains to Ariel Co's investment in available-for-sale debt securities:

Amortized cost basis	$100,000
Fair value	90,000
Discounted cash flows expected to be collected from the securities	88,000

The fair value is lower than amortized cost. Thus, the securities are impaired by $10,000 ($100,000 – $90,000). This entire amount is an impairment for credit losses that is recognized in the income statement. The journal entry is

Credit loss expense	$10,000	
Allowance for credit losses		$10,000

Balance sheet presentation:
Available-for-sale debt securities (amortized cost $100,000; allowance for credit losses $10,000) $90,000

Example 4-13   Impairment of AFS Debt Securities

Using the data from Example 4-12, assume that the fair value of the securities is $85,000. The securities are impaired by $15,000 ($100,000 amortized cost basis – $85,000 fair value). The impairment for credit losses of $12,000 ($100,000 amortized cost – $88,000 discounted cash flows expected from the securities) is recognized in the income statement. The remaining decline in the securities' fair value of $3,000 ($15,000 – $12,000) is recognized in OCI. The following are the journal entries:

Credit loss expense	$12,000	
Allowance for credit losses		$12,000
Unrealized holding loss – OCI	$3,000	
AFS securities fair value adjustment		$3,000

Balance sheet presentation:
Available-for-sale debt securities (amortized cost $100,000; allowance for credit losses $12,000) $85,000

Example 4-14   Impairment of AFS Debt Securities

Using the data from Example 4-12, assume that the discounted cash flows expected to be collected from the securities are $100,000. The securities are impaired by $10,000 ($100,000 – $90,000). Given that the discounted cash flows expected to be collected from the securities are not less than the amortized cost, no impairment for credit losses is recognized. The entire decline in the fair value of $10,000 is recognized in OCI. The journal entry is

Unrealized holding loss – OCI	$10,000	
AFS securities fair value adjustment		$10,000

The allowance for credit losses is reassessed each reporting period. Subsequent changes in the allowance for credit losses on available-for-sale debt securities are recognized in the income statement. The previously recorded allowance cannot be reversed below zero.

Success Tip

If the change in the fair value of the security is **not due to credit losses**, you can (1) ignore the recognition of the allowance for credit losses and (2) recognize the entire change in the fair value of the AFS security in OCI.

Transfers between Categories

Transfers between categories are accounted for at **transfer-date fair value**. The following describes the treatment of **unrealized holding gains and losses** at that date:

- **From trading to any category.** Amounts already recognized in earnings are not reversed.

- **To trading from any category.** Amounts not already recognized in earnings are recognized in earnings.

- **To available-for-sale from held-to-maturity.** Amounts are recognized in OCI.

- **To held-to-maturity from available-for-sale.** Amounts recognized in OCI are not reversed but are amortized in the same way as a premium or discount.

- Transfers **from held-to-maturity** or **into or from trading** should be rare.

Summary of Transfers		
From	**To**	**Earnings Recognition**
Trading	Any category	Already recognized, not reversed
Any category	Trading	If not already recognized
Held-to-maturity	Available-for-sale	Unrealized gain (loss) recognized in OCI
Available-for-sale	Held-to-maturity	Amounts in OCI not reversed but are amortized in same way as premium (discount)

Stop & Review

You have completed the outline for this subunit.
Study multiple-choice questions 12 through 15 beginning on page 148.

4.6 Investments in Bonds

Definition and Classification

A bond is a formal contractual agreement by an issuer to pay an amount of money (face amount) at the maturity date plus interest at the stated rate at specific intervals. All terms are stated in a document called an indenture.

- An investment in a bond is a financial asset. Thus, the investor may elect the FVO.

- Absent this election (or proper classification as a trading security), a bond is classified as held-to-maturity or available-for-sale.

- Study Unit 10, Subunit 1, contains a description of the various types of bonds.

Purchase Price

An investment in a bond is recorded on the purchaser's books at the present value of the bond's two cash flows, discounted at the interest rate prevailing in the market at the time of the purchase. (Study Unit 10, Subunit 2, has a thorough outline of the time value of money.)

- The **face amount** (also called the maturity amount) is received on the bond's maturity date, e.g., 20 years after the initial purchase.

- The annual **cash interest** equals the bond's face amount times the stated (or coupon) rate, e.g., $1,000 face amount × 4% stated rate = $40 annual cash interest.

If the bond's stated (coupon) rate differs from the market rate at the time of the purchase, the price paid will not equal the face amount.

Stated rate > MR = ↑ = prem.

- If the bond's stated rate is greater than the current market rate, the purchase price is higher than the face amount and the bond is purchased at a premium.

  - An investor in bonds rarely uses a separate premium or discount account, instead recording the investment at historical cost.

Example 4-15   Bond Purchased at Premium

An investor purchases an 8%, 5-year, $5,000 bond when the prevailing interest rate in the market is 6%. The present value of $1 at 6% for 5 periods is 0.747, and the present value of an ordinary annuity of $1 at 6% for 5 periods is 4.213. The present value of the face amount is $3,735 ($5,000 × 0.747), and the present value of the annual cash interest is $1,686 ($5,000 face amount × 8% stated rate × 4.213 PV of ordinary annuity). Thus, the amount paid for the bond is $5,421 ($3,735 + $1,686). The premium on the bond is $421 ($5,421 cost − $5,000 face amount). The investor records the following entry:

Investment in bond	$5,421	
Cash		$5,421

Stated rate < M ⇒ Discount.

- If the bond's stated rate is less than the current market rate, the purchase price is lower than the face amount and the bond is purchased at a discount.

Example 4-16	Bond Purchased at Discount

An investor purchases a 6%, 5-year, $5,000 bond at 92 (meaning 92% of par). The cost of the bond (the present value of the face amount and annual cash interest) is $4,600 ($5,000 × .92). The cost reflects a market rate of 8%. The discount at the date of purchase is $400 ($5,000 face amount – $4,600 present value). The investor records the following entry:

Investment in bond	$4,600	
Cash		$4,600

When a bond is purchased between interest dates, the investor generally pays to the issuer the amount of interest that has accrued since the last interest payment. On the next payment date, the investor receives a full interest payment.

- The purchaser of the bond, in effect, "buys" the amount of interest that has accrued since the last payment.

Amortizing a Premium or Discount

Any premium or discount is amortized over the life of the bond using the effective-interest method.

- The effective rate is the interest rate prevailing in the market at the time of the initial purchase (also called the yield).

- The essence of the effective rate method is application of a constant interest rate. The total amount of interest revenue recognized changes every period.

- Amortization results in the carrying amount of the asset (liability) being adjusted over time, reaching the face amount at maturity.

- The straight-line method is used only if its results are not materially different from those of the effective-interest method.

Example 4-17	Amortization of Premium and Discount on Bonds

The following are bond premium and discount amortization schedules:

Year	Beginning Carrying Amount	Times: Effective Rate	Equals: Interest Revenue	Minus: Interest Received	Equals: Premium Amortized	Ending Carrying Amount
1	$5,421	6%	$325	$400	$ (75)	$5,346
2	5,346	6%	321	400	(79)	5,267
3	5,267	6%	316	400	(84)	5,183
4	5,183	6%	311	400	(89)	5,094
5	5,094	6%	306	400	(94)	5,000
					$(421)	

-- Continued on next page --

Example 4-17 -- Continued

Year	Beginning Carrying Amount	Times: Effective Rate	Equals: Interest Revenue	Minus: Interest Received	Equals: Discount Amortized	Ending Carrying Amount
1	$4,600	8%	$368	$300	$ 68	$4,668
2	4,668	8%	374	300	74	4,742
3	4,742	8%	379	300	79	4,821
4	4,821	8%	386	300	86	4,907
5	4,907	8%	393	300	93	5,000
					$400	

The entries recorded by the two investors in Examples 4-15 and 4-16 are shown here:

Amortization of Premium			Amortization of Discount		

End of Year 1:

Amortization of Premium			Amortization of Discount		
Cash	$400		Cash	$300	
Investment in bond		$ 75	Investment in bond	68	
Interest revenue		325	Interest revenue		$368

End of Year 2:

Amortization of Premium			Amortization of Discount		
Cash	$400		Cash	$300	
Investment in bond		$ 79	Investment in bond	74	
Interest revenue		321	Interest revenue		$374

End of Year 3:

Amortization of Premium			Amortization of Discount		
Cash	$400		Cash	$300	
Investment in bond		$ 84	Investment in bond	79	
Interest revenue		316	Interest revenue		$379

End of Year 4:

Amortization of Premium			Amortization of Discount		
Cash	$400		Cash	$300	
Investment in bond		$ 89	Investment in bond	86	
Interest revenue		311	Interest revenue		$386

End of Year 5:

Amortization of Premium			Amortization of Discount		
Cash	$400		Cash	$300	
Investment in bond		$ 94	Investment in bond	93	
Interest revenue		306	Interest revenue		$393

The bond's carrying amount at the maturity date equals its face amount.

End of Year 5:

Cash	$5,000		Cash	$5,000	
Investment in bond		$5,000	Investment in bond		$5,000

Stop & Review

You have completed the outline for this subunit.

Study multiple-choice questions 16 through 19 beginning on page 110.

Questions

4.1 Cash

1. Burr Company had the following account balances at December 31, Year 1:

Cash in banks	$2,250,000
Cash on hand	125,000
Cash legally restricted for additions to plant (expected to be disbursed in Year 2)	1,600,000

Cash in banks includes $600,000 of compensating balances related to short-term borrowing arrangements. The compensating balances are not legally restricted as to withdrawal by Burr. In the current assets section of Burr's December 31, Year 1, balance sheet, total cash should be reported at

A. $1,775,000

B. $2,250,000

C. $2,375,000

D. $3,975,000

✓ **Answer (C) is correct.**
Required: The total cash reported in current assets given legal restrictions and compensating balance requirements.
Discussion: Legally restricted amounts related to long-term arrangements should be classified separately as noncurrent. Thus, the amount restricted for additions should be classified as noncurrent because it relates to a plant asset. Compensating balances against short-term borrowing arrangements that are legally restricted should be reported separately among the cash and cash equivalents in the current assets section. Total cash reported as current assets therefore equals $2,375,000 ($2,250,000 + $125,000).

✗ **Answer (A) is incorrect.** The amount of $1,775,000 results from subtracting the $600,000 of compensating balances from cash in banks.

✗ **Answer (B) is incorrect.** Cash on hand should be included in total cash.

✗ **Answer (D) is incorrect.** The legally restricted cash related to a long-term arrangement should be classified as noncurrent.

2. The following information pertains to Grey Co. at December 31, Year 4:

Checkbook balance	$12,000
Bank statement balance	16,000
Check drawn on Grey's account, payable to a vendor, dated and recorded 12/31/Yr 4 but not mailed until 1/10/Yr 5	1,800

On Grey's December 31, Year 4, balance sheet, what amount should be reported as cash?

A. $12,000

B. $13,800

C. $14,200

D. $16,000

✓ **Answer (B) is correct.**
Required: The amount of cash that should be reported on the balance sheet.
Discussion: The cash account on the balance sheet should consist of (1) coin and currency on hand, (2) demand deposits (checking accounts), (3) time deposits (savings accounts), and (4) near-cash assets (e.g., deposits in transit or checks written to creditors but not yet mailed). Thus, the cash balance should be $13,800 ($12,000 checkbook balance + $1,800 check drawn but not mailed). The checkbook balance is used instead of the bank balance in the calculation. It more closely reflects the amount of cash that is unrestricted at the balance sheet date.

✗ **Answer (A) is incorrect.** The amount of $12,000 excludes the check that was recorded but not mailed.

✗ **Answer (C) is incorrect.** The amount of $14,200 equals the bank statement balance minus the check not mailed.

✗ **Answer (D) is incorrect.** The amount of $16,000 is the bank statement balance.

3. Ral Corp.'s checkbook balance on December 31, Year 7, was $5,000. In addition, Ral held the following items in its safe on that date:

Check payable to Ral Corp., dated January 2, Year 8, in payment of a sale made in December Year 7, not included in December 31 checkbook balance $2,000

Check payable to Ral Corp., deposited December 15 and included in December 31 checkbook balance but returned by Bank on December 30 stamped "NSF." The check was redeposited on January 2, Year 8, and cleared on January 9   500

Check drawn on Ral Corp.'s account, payable to a vendor, dated and recorded in Ral's books on December 31, but not mailed until January 10, Year 8   300

The proper amount to be shown as cash on Ral's balance sheet at December 31, Year 7, is

A. $4,800

B. $5,300

C. $6,500

D. $6,800

✔ **Answer (A) is correct.**
Required: The amount to be recorded as cash on the year-end balance sheet.
Discussion: The December 31 checkbook balance is $5,000. The $2,000 check dated January 2, Year 8, is properly not included in this balance because it is not negotiable at year end. The $500 NSF check should not be included in cash because it is a receivable. The $300 check that was not mailed until January 10 should be added to the balance. This predated check is still within the control of the company and should not decrease the cash account. Consequently, the cash balance to be reported on the December 31, Year 7, balance sheet is $4,800.

Balance per checkbook	$5,000
Add: Predated check	300
Deduct: NSF check	(500)
Cash balance 12/31/Year 7	$4,800

✘ **Answer (B) is incorrect.** The amount of $5,300 does not include the NSF check.

✘ **Answer (C) is incorrect.** The amount of $6,500 includes the postdated check but not the predated check.

✘ **Answer (D) is incorrect.** The amount of $6,800 includes the postdated check.

4.2 Fair Value Option (FVO)

4. During Year 3, Gilman Co. purchased 5,000 shares of the 500,000 outstanding shares of Meteor Corp.'s common stock for $35,000. During Year 3, Gilman received $1,800 of dividends from its investment in Meteor's stock. The fair value of Gilman's investment on December 31, Year 3, is $32,000. Gilman has elected the fair value option for this investment. What amount of income or loss that is attributable to the Meteor stock investment should be reflected in Gilman's earnings for Year 3?

A. Income of $4,800.

B. Income of $1,800.

C. Loss of $1,200.

D. Loss of $3,000.

✔ **Answer (C) is correct.**
Required: The income or loss reflected in current-year earnings when the FVO for measuring investments is used.
Discussion: Under the fair value option, dividends received and unrealized gains and losses on remeasurement of financial assets to fair value are reported in earnings. Thus, the $1,800 of dividend income received and the $3,000 ($35,000 – $32,000) of unrealized loss are reflected in Gilman's earnings for Year 3. This results in a total loss of $1,200 ($1,800 – $3,000) attributable to the Meteor stock investment.

✘ **Answer (A) is incorrect.** Income of $4,800 is calculated by treating the change in fair value of the Meteor stock investment as a gain. However, the fair value has declined from $35,000 to $32,000, resulting in an unrealized loss of $3,000, not a gain.

✘ **Answer (B) is incorrect.** Income of $1,800 is calculated by excluding the unrealized loss from the Meteor stock investment from earnings. However, under the fair value option, unrealized gains and losses are reported in earnings.

✘ **Answer (D) is incorrect.** A loss of $3,000 is calculated by excluding the $1,800 of dividend income from Gilman's earnings for Year 3. However, under the fair value option, dividends received are treated as income and included in earnings for the year.

5. The reporting entity may elect the fair value option (FVO) for

A. An investment consisting of more than 50% of the outstanding voting interests of another entity.

B. An interest in a variable interest entity (VIE) if the reporting entity is the primary beneficiary.

C. Its obligation for pension and other postretirement employee benefits.

D. Most financial assets and liabilities.

✔ **Answer (D) is correct.**
Required: The item eligible for the FVO election.
Discussion: An entity may elect the FVO for most recognized financial assets and liabilities.

✘ **Answer (A) is incorrect.** An investment in a subsidiary required to be consolidated is not an eligible item.

✘ **Answer (B) is incorrect.** The primary beneficiary must consolidate the VIE. Thus, the interest in the VIE is not an eligible item.

✘ **Answer (C) is incorrect.** Items eligible for the FVO election do not include employers' and plans' obligations for (1) employee pension benefits, (2) other postretirement employee benefits, (3) postemployment benefits, (4) employee stock option and stock purchase plans, or (5) other deferred compensation.

4.3 Investments in Equity Securities

6. On December 31, Ott Co. had investments in equity securities as follows:

	Cost	Fair Value
Man Co.	$10,000	$ 8,000
Kemo, Inc.	9,000	11,000
Fenn Corp.	11,000	9,000
	$30,000	$28,000

Ott's December 31 balance sheet should report the equity securities as

A. $26,000

B. $28,000

C. $29,000

D. $30,000

✔ **Answer (B) is correct.**
Required: The amount at which the trading securities should be reported.
Discussion: An investment in equity securities that does not result in significant influence or control over the investee is reported at fair value, and unrealized holding gains and losses are included in earnings. Consequently, the securities should be reported as $28,000.

✘ **Answer (A) is incorrect.** The amount of $26,000 is the lower of cost or fair value determined on an individual security basis.

✘ **Answer (C) is incorrect.** The amount of $29,000 is the average of the aggregate cost and aggregate fair value.

✘ **Answer (D) is incorrect.** The aggregate cost is $30,000.

7. Plack Co. purchased 10,000 shares (2% ownership) of Ty Corp. on February 14 and did not elect the fair value option. Plack received a stock dividend of 2,000 shares on April 30, when the market value per share was $35. Ty paid a cash dividend of $2 per share on December 15. In its income statement for the year, what amount should Plack report as dividend income?

A. $20,000

B. $24,000

C. $90,000

D. $94,000

✔ **Answer (B) is correct.**
Required: The amount of dividend income to be reported.
Discussion: Plack Co. owns 2% of the stock of Ty Corp. Accordingly, this investment should be accounted for using the fair value method. If the fair value of the stock is not readily determinable, the measurement alternative may be selected. This alternative is cost minus any impairment, plus or minus changes resulting from observable price changes for the identical or a similar investment of the same issuer. Under either method, dividends from an investee are accounted for by the investor as dividend income unless a liquidating dividend is received. The recipient of a stock dividend does not recognize income. Thus, Plack should report dividend income of $24,000 [(10,000 shares + 2,000 shares received as a stock dividend on April 30) × $2 per share dividend].

✘ **Answer (A) is incorrect.** The amount of $20,000 does not include the dividends received on the 2,000 shares from the April 30 stock dividend.

✘ **Answer (C) is incorrect.** The amount of $90,000 equals the sum of the $2 per share cash dividend on 10,000 shares and the April 30 market value of the 2,000-share stock dividend. However, the recipient of a stock dividend does not recognize income.

✘ **Answer (D) is incorrect.** The amount of $94,000 equals the sum of the $2 per share cash dividend on 12,000 shares and the April 30 market value of the 2,000-share stock dividend. However, the recipient of a stock dividend does not recognize income.

8. During Year 6, Wall Co. purchased 2,000 shares of Hemp Corp. common stock for $31,500. They represent 2% of ownership in Hemp Corp. The fair value of this investment was $29,500 at December 31, Year 6. Wall sold all of the Hemp common stock for $14 per share on December 15, Year 7, incurring $1,400 in brokerage commissions and taxes. In its income statement for the year ended December 31, Year 7, Wall should report a recognized loss of

A. $4,900

B. $3,500

C. $2,900

D. $1,500

✔ **Answer (C) is correct.**
Required: The realized loss on the sale of equity securities.
Discussion: A realized loss or gain is recognized when an individual equity security is sold or otherwise disposed of. Wall would have included the $2,000 ($31,500 – $29,500) decline in the fair value of the equity securities (an unrealized holding loss) in earnings at 12/31/Yr 6. Consequently, the realized loss on disposal at 12/15/Yr 7 is $2,900 [(2,000 shares × $14) – $29,500 carrying amount – $1,400].

✘ **Answer (A) is incorrect.** The sum of the recognized losses for Year 6 and Year 7 is $4,900.

✘ **Answer (B) is incorrect.** The sum of the recognized losses for Year 6 and Year 7 without regard to the commissions and taxes is $3,500.

✘ **Answer (D) is incorrect.** Ignoring the commissions and taxes results in $1,500.

4.4 Equity Method

9. Birk Co. purchased 30% of Sled Co.'s outstanding common stock on December 31 for $200,000. On that date, Sled's equity was $500,000, and the fair value of its net assets was $600,000. On December 31, what amount of equity method goodwill results from this acquisition?

A. $0

B. $20,000

C. $30,000

D. $50,000

✔ **Answer (B) is correct.**
Required: The amount of goodwill attributable to a purchase of 30% of the investee's common stock.
Discussion: The equity method of accounting is used when the investor has significant influence over the investee (investment is at least 20% but not more than 50% of the voting interests) and the FVO was not elected. Equity method goodwill is the difference between the cost of the $200,000 investment and the investor's equity in the fair value of the investee's net assets of $180,000 (30% × $600,000). Accordingly, equity method goodwill equals $20,000 ($200,000 – $180,000).

✘ **Answer (A) is incorrect.** Equity method goodwill exists if the cost of the investment exceeds the fair value of the underlying equity in net assets acquired.

✘ **Answer (C) is incorrect.** The amount of $30,000 equals 30% of the difference between the carrying amount of the investee's equity and the fair value of the underlying equity in net assets.

✘ **Answer (D) is incorrect.** The amount of $50,000 is the difference between 30% of the equity and the investment cost.

Questions 10 and 11 are based on the following information.

Grant, Inc., acquired 30% of South Co.'s voting stock for $200,000 on January 2. Year 1, and did not elect the fair value option. The price equaled the carrying amount and the fair value of the interest purchased in South's net assets. Grant's 30% interest in South gave Grant the ability to exercise significant influence over South's operating and financial policies. During Year 1, South earned $80,000 and paid dividends of $50,000. South reported earnings of $100,000 for the 6 months ended June 30, Year 2, and $200,000 for the year ended December 31, Year 2. On July 1, Year 2, Grant sold half of its stock in South for $150,000 cash. South paid dividends of $60,000 on October 1, Year 2.

10. Before income taxes, what amount should Grant include in its Year 1 income statement as a result of the investment?

   A. $15,000

   B. $24,000

   C. $50,000

   D. $80,000

Answer (B) is correct.
Required: The income statement amount derived from an equity-based investment.
Discussion: Under the equity method, Grant's share of South's revenue reported in the income statement is $24,000 ($80,000 × 30%). The cash dividends received are recorded as a decrease in the investment's carrying amount.

✗ **Answer (A) is incorrect.** Grant's share of the cash dividends equals $15,000.

✗ **Answer (C) is incorrect.** The amount of cash dividends South paid is $50,000.

✗ **Answer (D) is incorrect.** The amount of South's Year 1 earnings is $80,000.

11. In its Year 2 income statement, what amount should Grant report as gain from the sale of half of its investment?

   A. $24,500

   B. $30,500

   C. $35,000

   D. $45,500

Answer (B) is correct.
Required: The gain reported from the sale of half of the investment.
Discussion: At December 31, Year 1, the carrying amount of the investment is $209,000 ($200,000 original investment + $24,000 share of Year 1 earnings − $15,000 share of Year 1 dividends). At June 30, Year 2, the investment is increased to $239,000 by the $30,000 share of South's earnings. Half of the new carrying amount is $119,500. Grant received $150,000, so the gain is $30,500 ($150,000 − $119,500).

✗ **Answer (A) is incorrect.** The amount of $24,500 is based on a carrying amount of $251,000.

✗ **Answer (C) is incorrect.** The amount of $35,000 is based on a carrying amount of $230,000.

✗ **Answer (D) is incorrect.** The amount of $45,500 is based on a carrying amount of $209,000, which does not include the $30,000 of Year 2 income.

4.5 Investments in Debt Securities

12. Kale Co. purchased bonds at a discount on the open market as an investment and has the intent and ability to hold these bonds to maturity. Absent an election of the fair value option, Kale should account for these bonds at

   A. Cost.

   B. Amortized cost.

   C. Fair value.

   D. Lower of cost or market.

✔ **Answer (B) is correct.**
Required: The recording of held-to-maturity securities.
Discussion: Without an election of the fair value option, investments in debt securities that the investor has the ability and positive intent to hold until maturity must be classified as held-to-maturity and measured at amortized cost.
✗ **Answer (A) is incorrect.** The discount is amortized over the term of the bonds.
✗ **Answer (C) is incorrect.** Trading and available-for-sale debt securities are accounted for at fair value.
✗ **Answer (D) is incorrect.** LIFO or retail inventory is measured at lower of cost or market.

13. The following information pertains to Lark Corp.'s available-for-sale debt securities:

	December 31	
	Year 2	Year 3
Cost	$100,000	$100,000
Fair value	90,000	120,000

Differences between cost and fair values are not due to credit losses. The decline in fair value was properly accounted for at December 31, Year 2. Ignoring tax effects, by what amount should other comprehensive income (OCI) be credited at December 31, Year 3?

   A. $0

   B. $10,000

   C. $20,000

   D. $30,000

✔ **Answer (D) is correct.**
Required: The credit to OCI if fair value exceeds cost.
Discussion: Unrealized holding gains and losses on available-for-sale debt securities not related to credit losses are not included in earnings but ordinarily are reported in OCI, net of tax effects (ignored in this question). At December 31, Year 2, OCI should have been debited for $10,000 for the excess of cost over fair value to reflect an unrealized holding loss. At December 31, Year 3, OCI should be credited to reflect a $30,000 unrealized holding gain ($120,000 fair value at 12/31/Year 3 – $90,000 fair value at 12/31/Year 2).
✗ **Answer (A) is incorrect.** Unrealized holding gains on available-for-sale securities are recognized.
✗ **Answer (B) is incorrect.** The amount of $10,000 is the recovery of the previously recognized unrealized holding loss. The recognition of gain is not limited to that amount.
✗ **Answer (C) is incorrect.** The excess of fair value over cost is $20,000.

14. When the fair value of an investment in debt securities exceeds its amortized cost, how should each of the following debt securities be measured at the end of the year, given **no** election of the fair value option?

Debt Securities Classified As	
Held-to-Maturity	Available-for-Sale
A. Amortized cost	Amortized cost
B. Amortized cost	Fair value
C. Fair value	Fair value
D. Fair value	Amortized cost

✔ **Answer (B) is correct.**
Required: The measurement of debt securities classified as held-to-maturity and available-for-sale.
Discussion: Investments in debt securities must be classified as held-to-maturity and measured at amortized cost in the balance sheet if the reporting entity has the positive intent and ability to hold them to maturity. Debt securities that are not expected to be sold in the near term and that are not held-to-maturity should be classified as available-for-sale. Available-for-sale debt securities should be reported at fair value, with unrealized holding gains and losses (excess of fair value over amortized cost).

15. The following information was extracted from Gil Co.'s December 31 balance sheet:

Noncurrent assets:
  Available-for-sale debt
    securities (carried at fair value) $96,450
Equity:
  Accumulated other
    comprehensive income (OCI)
    Unrealized holding gains and
    losses on available-for-sale
    debt securities   (19,800)

Historical cost of the available-for-sale debt securities was

A. $63,595
B. $76,650
C. $96,450
D. $116,250

✔ **Answer (D) is correct.**
Required: The historical cost of the available-for-sale debt securities.
Discussion: The existence of an equity account with a debit balance signifies that the available-for-sale debt securities are reported at fair value that is less than historical cost. The difference is the net unrealized holding loss balance. Thus, historical cost must have been $116,250 ($96,450 available-for-sale securities at fair value + $19,800 net unrealized loss).
✘ **Answer (A) is incorrect.** The amount of $63,595 is a nonsense figure.
✘ **Answer (B) is incorrect.** The amount of $76,650 results from subtracting the unrealized loss instead of adding.
✘ **Answer (C) is incorrect.** The amount of $96,450 ignores the unrealized loss balance.

4.6 Investments in Bonds

16. An investor purchased a bond as a long-term investment between interest dates at a premium. At the purchase date, the cash paid to the seller is

A. The same as the face amount of the bond.
B. The same as the face amount of the bond plus accrued interest.
C. More than the face amount of the bond.
D. Less than the face amount of the bond.

✔ **Answer (C) is correct.**
Required: The cash paid for a bond issued at a premium.
Discussion: At the date of purchase, the cash paid to the seller is equal to interest accrued since the last interest date, plus the face amount of the bonds, plus the premium. The carrying amount of the bonds (face amount plus the premium) is equal to the present value of the cash flows associated with the bond discounted at the market rate of interest (yield).

17. An investor purchased a bond classified as a long-term investment between interest dates at a discount. At the purchase date, the carrying amount of the bond is more than the

	Cash Paid to Seller	Face Amount of Bond
A.	No	Yes
B.	No	No
C.	Yes	No
D.	Yes	Yes

✔ **Answer (B) is correct.**
Required: The carrying amount of a bond purchased at a discount between interest dates.
Discussion: At the date of purchase, the carrying amount of the bond equals its face amount minus the discount. The cash paid equals the initial carrying amount plus accrued interest. Hence, the initial carrying amount is less than the cash paid by the amount of the accrued interest.

18. Jent Corp. purchased bonds at a discount of $10,000. Subsequently, Jent sold these bonds at a premium of $14,000. During the period that Jent held this investment, amortization of the discount amounted to $2,000. What amount should Jent report as gain on the sale of bonds?

A. $12,000

B. $22,000

C. $24,000

D. $26,000

✔ **Answer (B) is correct.**
Required: The amount reported as gain on the sale of bonds.
Discussion: The gain equals the sale price (Face amount + $14,000 premium) minus the carrying amount [Face amount – ($10,000 original discount – $2,000 amortization)]. Consequently, the gain is $22,000 [(Face amount + $14,000) – (Face amount – $8,000)].

✘ **Answer (A) is incorrect.** The amount of $12,000 assumes a carrying amount equal to face amount plus the amortization.

✘ **Answer (C) is incorrect.** The amount of $24,000 ignores the amortization.

✘ **Answer (D) is incorrect.** The amount of $26,000 results from increasing the discount by the amortization.

19. On July 1, Year 4, Pell Co. purchased Green Corp. 10-year, 8% bonds with a face amount of $500,000 for $420,000. The bonds are classified as held-to-maturity, mature on June 30, Year 14, and pay interest semiannually on June 30 and December 31. Using the interest method, Pell recorded bond discount amortization of $1,800 for the 6 months ended December 31, Year 4. From this long-term investment, Pell should report Year 4 revenue of

A. $16,800

B. $18,200

C. $20,000

D. $21,800

✔ **Answer (D) is correct.**
Required: The interest revenue when amortization of bond discount is known.
Discussion: Interest income for a bond issued at a discount is equal to the sum of the periodic cash flows and the amount of bond discount amortized during the interest period. The periodic cash flows are equal to $20,000 ($500,000 face amount × 8% coupon rate × 1/2 year). The discount amortization is given as $1,800. Thus, revenue for the 6-month period from July 1 to December 31, Year 4, is $21,800 ($20,000 + $1,800).

✘ **Answer (A) is incorrect.** The amount of $16,800 is 50% of 8% of $420,000.

✘ **Answer (B) is incorrect.** The amount of $18,200 equals the cash flow minus discount amortization.

✘ **Answer (C) is incorrect.** The amount of $20,000 equals the cash flow.

Go to Online Course

Access the **Gleim CPA Premium Review System** featuring our SmartAdapt technology from your Gleim Personal Classroom to continue your studies.

You will experience a personalized study environment with exam-emulating multiple-choice questions.

Study Unit Five

Receivables

(16 pages of outline)

5.1 Accounts Receivable -- Fundamentals

Definition

A receivable is an asset recognized to reflect a claim against another party for the receipt of money, goods, or services. For most accounting purposes, the claim is expected to be settled in cash.

The recording of a receivable, which often coincides with revenue recognition, is consistent with accrual accounting.

Current vs. Noncurrent Receivables

A receivable is a **current** asset if it is reasonably expected to be collected within the longer of 1 year or the entity's normal operating cycle.

- Otherwise, it should be classified as **noncurrent**. Noncurrent receivables are measured at the present value of expected cash flows.

Trade vs. Nontrade Receivables

Trade receivables, the majority of receivables, are current assets resulting from credit sales to customers in the normal course of business and due in customary trade terms.

- They are normally unsecured and noninterest-bearing.
- They represent unconditional rights to consideration from contracts with customers.

Nontrade receivables are all other receivables. They include among others

- Lease receivables
- Interest, dividends, rent, or royalties accrued

Trade Discounts

Trade discounts adjust the **gross (list) price** for different buyers, quantities, and costs. **Net price after the trade discount** is the basis for recognition.

Example 5-1	Trade Discount

An item with a list price of $1,000 may be subject to a 40% trade discount in sales to wholesalers. Thus, $400 is subtracted from the list price in arriving at the actual selling price of $600. Only the $600 is recorded. The accounts do not reflect trade discounts.

Some sellers offer **chain-trade discounts** such as 40%, 10%, which means certain buyers receive both a 40% discount and a 10% discount.

Example 5-2	Chain-Trade Discount

In Example 5-1, an additional discount of $60 reduces the actual selling price to $540. All journal entries by the buyer and seller are for $540, with no recognition of the list price or the discount. The two discounts are not added but are calculated sequentially.

Trade discounts are solely a means of calculating the sales price. They are not recorded.

Cash Discounts

Cash discounts (prompt payment discounts) accelerate cash collection by rewarding customers for early payment.

- A common example of prompt payment discount is 2/10, n/30. It means a 2% discount if the invoice is paid within 10 days, or the entire balance is due in 30 days.

Because of the uncertainty as to whether customers will pay during the discount period and receive the discount, the consideration in this type of contract is variable.

- At contract inception, an entity should estimate the number of customers that are expected to receive the discount and recognize revenue based on the expected amount of consideration to which it will be entitled.

Measurement

Accounts receivable are presented at the net amount expected to be collected. They are measured using the amortized cost basis and reported minus the allowance for credit losses (previously called the allowance for uncollectible accounts).

The amortized cost basis is the amount at which an account receivable is originated or acquired, adjusted for applicable accrued interest and amortization of premium or discount (in the case of noncurrent receivables), cash and trade discounts, collection of cash, and write-offs.

The **allowance for credit losses** on accounts receivable must be recorded at the reporting date. It represents the portion of accounts receivable that the entity does not expect to collect.

- The allowance for credit losses is a valuation account that is deducted from the accounts receivable balance.

Initial recognition of the allowance for credit losses and subsequent changes in the allowance balance are recognized immediately in the income statement in the **credit loss expense** (previously called bad debt expense) account.

- An increase in the balance of the allowance for credit losses is recognized as a credit loss expense.

Credit loss expense	$XXX	
Allowance for credit losses		$XXX

- A decrease in the balance of the allowance for credit losses is recognized as a reversal of credit loss expense.

Allowance for credit losses	$XXX	
Credit loss expense		$XXX

The allowance for credit losses should be estimated based on entity's past experience taking into account current and forecasted economic conditions.

Balance Sheet Presentation

On the face of the balance sheet, the carrying amount of accounts receivable is presented net of any allowance for credit losses.

The allowance for credit losses must be separately presented as a deduction from the balance of accounts receivable.

Balance sheet:	
Accounts receivable	$X,XXX
(Allowance for credit losses)	(X,XXX)
Accounts receivable, net	$X,XXX

Material receivables should be segregated. Among the usual categories are

- Notes receivable (with disclosure of the effective interest rates)
- Trade receivables
- Nontrade receivables

Receivables should be separated into **current and noncurrent** portions.

Discount or premium resulting from a present value measurement directly decreases or increases the face amount of a note.

Disclosure should be made of

- Related party receivables, e.g., those arising from loans to employees or affiliates
- Pledged or assigned receivables
- Concentrations of credit risk

Stop & Review

You have completed the outline for this subunit.
Study multiple-choice question 1 on page 166.

5.2 Trade Receivables

Trade receivables are current, noninterest-bearing accounts receivable that are reported at the net amount expected to be collected, i.e., net of an allowance for credit losses.

- Interest recognition (except for late payment) and present value calculations are not relevant.

The principal measurement issue for accounts receivable is the estimation of the **allowance for credit losses** and calculation of **credit loss expenses** for the period.

- The two approaches to accounting for credit losses are the direct write-off method and the allowance method. However, only the allowance method is acceptable under GAAP.

Direct Write-Off Method (not allowed under GAAP)

The direct write-off method expenses bad debts when they are determined to be uncollectible. It is **not acceptable under GAAP** because

- It does not match revenue and expense when the receivable and the write-off are recorded in different periods.

- It does not state receivables at the net amount expected to be collected.

This method is acceptable for tax purposes.

Allowance Method (required under GAAP)

The allowance method attempts to match credit loss expense with the related revenue. This method is **required under GAAP**.

- The periodic journal entry to record credit loss expense is

Credit loss expense	$XXX	
Allowance for credit losses		$XXX

- As specific accounts receivable are written off, they are charged to the allowance account.

Allowance for credit losses	$XXX	
Accounts receivable		$XXX

- Thus, the **write-off** of a particular account has no effect on expenses.

  - Write-offs do not affect the carrying amount of the net accounts receivable balance because the reductions of gross accounts receivable and the allowance are the same.

- In the balance sheet, the carrying amount of accounts receivable is reported at the net amount expected to be collected.

Gross accounts receivable	–	Allowance for credit losses	=	Carrying amount of accounts receivable

Measurement of the Allowance for Credit Losses

The ending balance of the allowance for credit losses is a percentage of the ending balance of accounts receivable.

- Credit loss expense reflects the adjustment of the allowance to its correct ending balance.

Example 5-3	Allowance for Credit Losses

Midburg Co. has the following unadjusted account balances at year end:

Cash	$ 85,000 Dr.
Accounts receivable	100,000 Dr.
Allowance for credit losses	2,000 Cr.
Sales on credit	500,000 Cr.

Based on Midburg's experience, 6% of accounts receivable are determined to be uncollectible. Thus, the ending balance of the allowance for credit losses is $6,000 ($100,000 × 6%). Because the allowance currently has a balance of $2,000, the following journal entry is required:

Credit loss expense ($6,000 – $2,000) $4,000	
Allowance for credit losses	$4,000

Balance sheet presentation

Accounts receivable	$100,000
Minus: Allowance for credit losses	(6,000)
Accounts receivable, net	$ 94,000

An entity rarely experiences a single rate of uncollectibility on all its accounts. For this reason, entities generally prepare an **aging schedule** for accounts receivable.

Example 5-4	Aging Schedule for Accounts Receivable

Midburg prepares the following aging schedule for its accounts receivable:

Balance Range	Less than 30 Days	31-60 Days	61-90 Days	Over 90 Days	Total Balances
$0 - $100	$ 5,000	$ 200	$ 100	$ 100	$ 5,400
$100 - $1,000	8,000	3,800			11,800
$1,000 - $5,000	20,000	2,000	1,900		23,900
$5,000 - $10,000	38,000		8,000	900	46,900
Over $10,000		12,000			12,000
Totals	$71,000	$18,000	$10,000	$1,000	$100,000

Midburg then applies an appropriate percentage to each stratum based on experience.

Aging Intervals	Balance	Estimated Uncollectible	Ending Allowance
Less than 30 days	$ 71,000	2%	$1,420
30-60 days	18,000	12%	2,160
61-90 days	10,000	15%	1,500
Over 90 days	1,000	20%	200
Total	$100,000		$5,280

Because the allowance currently has a balance of $2,000, the following journal entry is required to establish the proper measurement:

Credit loss expense ($5,280 – $2,000)	$3,280	
Allowance for credit losses		$3,280

Balance sheet presentation

Accounts receivable	$100,000
Minus: Allowance for credit losses	(5,280)
Accounts receivable, net	$ 94,720

Collection of Accounts Previously Written Off

Occasionally, a customer pays an account that was previously written off and was not expected to be recovered. The journal entry is

Cash	$XXX	
Allowance for credit losses		$XXX

Success Tip

The following equation illustrates the reconciliation of the beginning and ending balances of the allowance for credit losses:

Beginning allowance for credit losses	$XXX
Credit loss expense recognized for the period	XXX
Minus: Accounts receivable written off	(XXX)
Collection of accounts receivable previously written off	XXX
Ending allowance for credit losses	$XXX

The ending balance of the allowance is a percentage of the ending balance of accounts receivable, and credit loss expense is calculated using the equation above.

Example 5-5   Collection of Written-Off Accounts

A retailer had the following account balances on January 1, Year 1:

Accounts receivable	145,000 Dr.
Allowance for credit losses	8,000 Cr.

The following information pertains to the retailer's accounts receivable in Year 1:

Credit sales for the year	$400,000
Collections of current-year credit sales	240,000
Accounts written off on 7/1/Year 1	5,000
Collection of accounts that were written off last year that the retailer did not expect to collect	6,000

Based on past experience and considering current and forecasted economic conditions, the retailer estimates that 4% of year-end accounts receivable are expected to be uncollectible. The retailer recorded the following journal entries in Year 1:

Sales on credit:

(A)	Accounts receivable	$400,000	
	Sales		$400,000

Collections on credit sales:

(B)	Cash	$240,000	
	Accounts receivable		$240,000

Accounts considered uncollectible written off:

(C)	Allowance for credit losses	$5,000	
	Accounts receivable		$5,000

Account previously written off collected:

(D)	Cash	$6,000	
	Allowance for credit losses		$6,000

-- Continued on next page --

Example 5-5 -- Continued

After the Year 1 activity is recorded, the year-end balance of accounts receivable is calculated as follows:

Accounts Receivable

1/1/Year 1	$145,000		
(A)	400,000	$240,000	(B)
		5,000	(C)
12/31/Year 1	$300,000		

The year-end balance of the allowance for credit losses is **$12,000** ($300,000 × 4%). The credit loss expense for Year 1 is calculated below as an adjustment of the allowance to its ending balance.

Allowance for Credit Losses

(C) $5,000	$ 8,000	1/1/Year 1	
	6,000	(D)	
	3,000	**Credit loss expense** (E)	
	$12,000	12/31/Year 1	

Year-end adjustment of the allowance and credit loss expense recognition:

(E)	Credit loss expense	$3,000	
	Allowance for credit losses		$3,000

On the balance sheet, the carrying amount of accounts receivable is reported as follows:

12/31/Year 1 balance sheet:

Accounts receivable	$300,000
Minus: Allowance for credit losses	(12,000)
Accounts receivable, net	$288,000

In practice, the collection of accounts previously written off also may be recorded directly as a reduction of credit loss expense. However, both methods result in the same amounts of allowance for credit losses and credit loss expense for the period.

Account previously written off collected and recorded in the credit loss expense account:

(D)	Cash	$6,000	
	Credit loss expense		$6,000

The year-end allowance is still $12,000 ($300,000 × 4%), and its ending balance adjustment is $9,000.

Allowance for Credit Losses

(C) $5,000	$ 8,000	1/1/Year 1	
	9,000	**Credit loss expense** (E)	
	$12,000	12/31/Year 1	

Year-end adjustment of the allowance and credit loss expense recognition:

(E)	Credit loss expense	$9,000	
	Allowance for credit losses		$9,000

Thus, the credit loss expense for Year 1 is $3,000 ($9,000 E – $6,000 D).

Stop & Review

You have completed the outline for this subunit.

Study multiple-choice questions 2 through 6 beginning on page 167.

5.3 Transfers of Receivables and Other Financial Assets

Factoring

Factoring is a transfer of receivables to a third party (a factor) who assumes the responsibility of collection.

Factoring discounts receivables on a **nonrecourse, notification basis**. Thus, payments by the debtors on the transferred assets are made to the factor. If the transferor (seller) surrenders control, the transaction is a sale of accounts receivable.

- If a sale is **with recourse**, the transferor (seller) may be required to make payments to the transferee or to buy back receivables in specified circumstances. For example, the seller may become liable for defaults up to a given percentage of the transferred receivables.

  - The sale proceeds are reduced by the fair value of the recourse obligation.

  - If the transfer with recourse does not qualify as a sale, the parties account for the transaction as a secured borrowing with a pledge of noncash collateral.

- If a sale is **without recourse**, the transferee (credit agency) assumes the risks and receives the rewards of collection. This sale is final, and the seller has no further liabilities to the transferee.

A factor usually receives a high financing fee plus a fee for collection. Furthermore, the factor often operates more efficiently than its clients because of the specialized nature of its services.

Example 5-6   Transfer of Accounts Receivable

A factor charges a 2% fee plus an interest rate of 18% on all cash advanced to a transferor of accounts receivable. Monthly sales are $100,000, and the factor advances 90% of the receivables submitted after deducting the 2% fee and the interest. Credit terms are net 60 days. What is the cost to the transferor of this arrangement?

Amount of receivables submitted	$100,000	
Minus: 10% reserve	(10,000)	
Minus: 2% factor's fee	(2,000)	
Amount accruing to the transferor	$ 88,000	
Minus: 18% interest for 60 days	(2,640)	[$88,000 × 18% × (60 ÷ 360)]
Amount to be received immediately	$ 85,360	

The transferor also will receive the $10,000 reserve at the end of the 60-day period if it has not been absorbed by sales returns and allowances. Thus, the total cost to the transferor to factor the receivables for the month is $4,640 ($2,000 factor fee + interest of $2,640). Assuming that the factor has approved the customers' credit in advance (the sale is without recourse), the transferor will not absorb any bad debts.

The journal entry to record the preceding transaction is

Cash	$85,360	
Due from factor	10,000	
Loss on sale of receivables	2,000	
Prepaid interest/interest expense	2,640	
Accounts receivable		$100,000

Credit card sales are a common form of factoring. The retailer benefits by prompt receipt of cash and avoidance of credit losses and other costs. In return, the credit card company charges a fee.

- Two methods of accounting for credit card sales may be necessary depending upon the reimbursement method used.

  - If payment is after submission of credit card receipts, the retailer initially records a sale and a receivable. After payment, the entry is

Cash	$XXX	
Service charge expense	XXX	
Receivable		$XXX

  - If the retailer's checking account is increased by the direct deposit of credit card receipts, no receivable is recognized. The entry is to credit sales instead of a receivable.

Cash	$XXX	
Service charge expense	XXX	
Sales		$XXX

Pledging

A pledge (a general assignment) is the use of receivables as collateral (security) for a loan. The borrower agrees to use collections of receivables to repay the loan.

- Upon default, the lender can sell the receivables to recover the loan proceeds.

Because a pledge is a relatively informal arrangement, it is not reflected in the accounts. A transfer of financial assets is a sale only when the transferor relinquishes control.

- If the transfer (e.g., a pledge) of accounts receivable is not a sale, the transaction is a secured borrowing. The transferor becomes a debtor, and the transferee becomes a creditor in possession of collateral.

    - However, absent default, the collateral remains an asset of the transferor.

Transfers of Financial Assets -- Objectives and Control

The accounting for transfers of financial assets is based on a **financial-components approach** focused on control.

The objective is for each party to

- Recognize the assets it controls and the liabilities it has incurred,
- Derecognize assets when control has been given up, and
- Derecognize liabilities when they have been extinguished.

Whether **control** exists depends, among other things, on the transferor's continuing involvement. **Continuing involvement** is the right to receive benefits from the assets or an obligation to provide additional assets to a party related to the transfer.

Transfers of Financial Assets -- Sales

Transfers of financial assets include transfers of (1) an entire financial asset, (2) a group of entire financial assets, and (3) a participating interest in an entire financial asset.

- The holder of a **participating interest** receives cash in proportion to the share of ownership, and all holders have the same priority.

A transfer of financial assets is a **sale** when the transferor **relinquishes control**. The transferor relinquishes control only if certain conditions are met:

- The transferred assets are beyond the reach of the transferor and its creditors;
- Transferees may pledge or exchange the assets or interests received; and
- The transferor does not maintain effective control through, for example,

    - An agreement to reacquire the assets before maturity or
    - An agreement making it probable that the transferee will require repurchase.

If the transfer of an **entire financial asset** (or a group) qualifies as a sale, the financial components approach is applied. The transferor

- Derecognizes the financial assets transferred
- Recognizes and initially measures at fair value the assets obtained and liabilities incurred
- Recognizes any gain or loss in earnings

Example 5-7	Transfer of a Financial Asset

A company transfers its entire financial interest in its notes receivable for $60,000. The receivable has a carrying amount of $62,500. The journal entry to record this transfer is

Cash	$60,000	
Loss on transfer	2,500	
Notes receivable		$62,500

Transfers of Financial Assets -- Secured Borrowings

If the transfer is not a sale, the transaction is a secured borrowing. The transferor becomes a debtor, and the transferee becomes a creditor in possession of collateral.

A secured borrowing is a formal borrowing arrangement. The borrower signs a promissory note and financing agreement, and specific receivables are pledged as **collateral**.

- The loan is at a specified percentage of the face amount of the collateral, and interest and service fees are charged to the borrower.

The collateral may be segregated from other receivables on the balance sheet.

Accounts receivable assigned	$XXX	
Accounts receivable		$XXX

- The note payable is reported as a **liability**.

Cash	$XXX	
Notes payable		$XXX

Stop & Review

You have completed the outline for this subunit.

Study multiple-choice questions 7 through 9 beginning on page 169.

5.4 Notes Receivable

Definition

A note receivable is a debt evidenced by a two-party writing (a **promissory note**). Notes are more formal promises to pay than accounts receivable.

Most notes bear interest (explicitly or implicitly) because they represent longer-term borrowings than accounts receivable.

Notes with original maturities to the holder of **3 months or less** are treated as cash equivalents and accounted for at **net realizable value**.

- Because the interest implicit in the maturity amount is immaterial, no interest revenue is recognized.

Notes classified as **current assets** are usually recorded at face amount and reported minus an allowance for credit losses.

Notes classified as **noncurrent assets** are recorded at the **present value of the expected future cash flows** and reported minus an allowance for credit losses.

- Any difference between the proceeds and the face amount must be recognized as a premium or discount and amortized.

When the note's stated interest rate is a reasonable rate (e.g., the market rate), the note is issued at its face amount, and no discount or premium is recognized.

Noninterest-Bearing Notes

Sometimes notes are issued with no stated rate and an **unknown effective rate**. In these cases, the rate must be **imputed** from other facts surrounding the transaction. Such facts include the marketability of the note and the debtor's creditworthiness.

- Thus, the interest is **implicit**.

A note may bear no explicit interest because interest is included in the amount to be paid at maturity. The accounting treatment is to debit notes receivable for its face (maturity) amount, credit cash (or other appropriate account), and credit discount. The discount is amortized to interest revenue.

- The entry for initial recognition is

Notes receivable	$XXX	
Cash		$XXX
Discount on note		XXX

- Notes receivable are reported in the financial statements at their face amount minus any unamortized discount.

- At the end of the period, the discount is amortized to interest revenue using the effective-interest method explained in Study Unit 4, Subunit 6.

  - The entry for recognition of interest is

Discount on note	$XXX	
Interest revenue		$XXX

- When the note arises in the ordinary course of business and is "due in customary trade terms not exceeding approximately 1 year," the interest element need not be recognized.

Unreasonable Interest

The term "noninterest-bearing" is confusing. It is used not only (1) when a note bears implicit interest but also (2) when no actual interest is charged (the cash proceeds equal the face amount).

- When a note is noninterest-bearing in the second scenario above or bears interest at a rate that is unreasonable in the circumstances, interest must be **imputed (estimated)**. A note with imputed interest also results in amortization of discount or premium.

When a **note is exchanged solely for cash**, and no other right or privilege is exchanged, the proceeds are assumed to reflect the present value of the note. The effective interest rate is therefore the interest rate implicit in that present value.

When a **note is exchanged for property, goods, or services**, the interest rate determined by the parties in an arm's-length transaction is presumed to be fair.

- That presumption is overcome when (1) no interest is stated, (2) the stated rate is unreasonable, or (3) the nominal amount of the note materially differs from the cash sales price of the item or the market value of the note.

  - In these circumstances, the transaction should be recorded at the more clearly determinable of

    ▸ The fair value of the property, goods, or services or
    ▸ The market value of the note.

  - Absent established exchange prices or evidence of the note's market value, the present value of a note with no stated rate or an unreasonable rate should be determined by discounting future payments using an imputed rate. The prevailing rate for similar instruments of issuers with similar credit ratings normally helps determine the appropriate rate.

The stated interest rate may be less than the effective rate applicable in the circumstances because the lender has received **other stated (or unstated) rights and privileges** as part of the bargain.

- The difference between the respective present values of the note computed at the stated rate and at the effective rate should be accounted for as the cost of the rights or privileges obtained.

Discounting of Notes Receivable

When a note receivable is discounted (sold, usually at a bank), the gain or loss on disposition of the note must be calculated.

The holder of the note receives the maturity amount (Principal + Interest at maturity) of the note minus the bank's discount. The bank usually collects the maturity amount from the maker of the note.

Stop & Review

You have completed the outline for this subunit.

Study multiple-choice questions 10 through 18 beginning on page 170.

Questions

5.1 Accounts Receivable -- Fundamentals

1. The following information relates to Jay Co.'s accounts receivable for the year just ended:

Accounts receivable, 1/1	$ 650,000
Credit sales for the year	2,700,000
Sales returns for the year	75,000
Accounts written off during the year	40,000
Collections from customers during the year	2,150,000
Estimated uncollectible accounts at 12/31	110,000

What amount should Jay report for accounts receivable, before allowance for credit losses, at December 31?

A. $1,200,000

B. $1,125,000

C. $1,085,000

D. $1,165,000

✓ **Answer (C) is correct.**

Required: The year-end balance in accounts receivable.

Discussion: The ending balance in accounts receivable consists of the $650,000 beginning debit balance, plus debits for $2,700,000 of credit sales, minus credits for $2,150,000 of collections, $40,000 of accounts written off, and $75,000 of sales returns.

Accounts Receivable (in 000s)			
1/1	$ 650	$ 75	Sales returns
Credit sales	2,700	2,150	Collections
		40	Write-offs
12/31	$1,085		

The $110,000 of estimated uncollectible receivables is not relevant because it affects the allowance account but not gross accounts receivable.

✗ **Answer (A) is incorrect.** The amount of $1,200,000 does not subtract write-offs and sales returns from accounts receivable.

✗ **Answer (B) is incorrect.** The amount of $1,125,000 does not subtract write-offs during the year.

✗ **Answer (D) is incorrect.** The accounts written off during the year decrease, not increase, the gross balance of accounts receivable.

5.2 Trade Receivables

2. Rue Co.'s allowance for credit losses had a credit balance of $12,000 at December 31, Year 1. During Year 2, Rue wrote off uncollectible accounts of $48,000. The aging of accounts receivable indicated that a $50,000 allowance for credit losses was required at December 31, Year 2. What amount of credit loss expense should Rue report for Year 2?

A. $48,000

B. $50,000

C. $60,000

D. $86,000

✔ **Answer (D) is correct.**
Required: The amount of credit loss expense for Year 2.
Discussion: The beginning balance of the allowance for credit losses was a credit of $12,000. The account was debited for $48,000 when the uncollectible accounts were written off. Thus, the credit for credit loss expense must be $86,000 if the ending balance is $50,000.

Allowance for Credit Losses		
	$12,000	1/1/Year 2
Write-offs $48,000	86,000	Expense
	$50,000	12/3/Year 2

✘ **Answer (A) is incorrect.** The amount of uncollectible accounts written off in Year 2 is $48,000.

✘ **Answer (B) is incorrect.** The ending balance is $50,000.

✘ **Answer (C) is incorrect.** The sum of the beginning balance and the amount written off is $60,000.

3. In its December 31, Year 3, balance sheet, Fleet Co. reported accounts receivable of $100,000 before allowance for credit losses of $10,000. Credit sales during Year 4 were $611,000, and collections from customers, excluding recoveries, totaled $591,000. During Year 4, accounts receivable of $45,000 were written off and $17,000 were recovered. Fleet estimated that $15,000 of the accounts receivable at December 31, Year 4, were uncollectible. In its December 31, Year 4, balance sheet, what amount should Fleet report as accounts receivable before allowance for credit losses?

A. $58,000

B. $67,000

C. $75,000

D. $82,000

✔ **Answer (C) is correct.**
Required: The balance of accounts receivable.
Discussion: The ending balance in accounts receivable consists of the beginning balance, plus credit sales, minus collections, and minus write-offs. The recovery of accounts that were previously written off does not affect the accounts receivable balance.

Accounts Receivable (in 000s)		
1/1/Yr 4	$100	$591 Collections
Sales	611	45 Write-offs
12/31/Yr 4	$ 75	

✘ **Answer (A) is incorrect.** Subtracting the recovered accounts results in $58,000. The collection of written-off accounts has no effect on the ending balance of accounts receivable.

✘ **Answer (B) is incorrect.** The amount of $67,000 equals the ending accounts receivable balance, plus the amount recovered, minus the beginning balance of the allowance for credit losses, minus the estimated uncollectible accounts at year end.

✘ **Answer (D) is incorrect.** The amount of $82,000 is calculated by adding the recovered accounts and subtracting the allowance for credit losses from Year 3.

4. For the year ended December 31, Beal Co. estimated its allowance for credit losses using the year-end aging of accounts receivable. The following data are available:

Allowance for credit losses, 1/1	$42,000
Uncollectible accounts written off, 11/30	46,000
Estimated uncollectible accounts per aging, 12/31	52,000

After year-end adjustment, the credit loss expense should be

A. $46,000

B. $48,000

C. $52,000

D. $56,000

✔ **Answer (D) is correct.**
Required: The adjusted credit loss expense for the year.
Discussion: As indicated in the T-account analysis presented below, the credit loss expense is calculated as follows:

Allowance		
	$42,000	1/1
Write-offs $46,000	56,000	Credit loss expense
	$52,000	12/31

✘ **Answer (A) is incorrect.** The amount written off is $46,000.

✘ **Answer (B) is incorrect.** The amount of $48,000 would result if the beginning balance in the allowance account had been $46,000 and the write-offs had equaled $42,000.

✘ **Answer (C) is incorrect.** The estimate of uncollectible accounts at year end is $52,000.

5. An internal auditor is deriving cash flow data based on an incomplete set of facts. Credit loss expense was $2,000. Additional data for this period follows:

Credit sales	$100,000
Gross accounts receivable -- beginning balance	5,000
Allowance for credit losses -- beginning balance	(500)
Accounts receivable written off	1,000
Increase in net accounts receivable (after subtraction of allowance for credit losses)	30,000

How much cash was collected this period on credit sales?

A. $64,000

B. $68,000

C. $68,500

D. $70,000

✔ **Answer (B) is correct.**
Required: The cash collected on credit sales.
Discussion: The beginning balance of gross accounts receivable (A/R) was $5,000 (debit). Thus, net beginning A/R was $4,500 ($5,000 – $500 credit in the allowance for credit losses). The allowance was credited for the $2,000 credit loss expense. Accordingly, the ending allowance (credit) was $1,500 ($500 – $1,000 write-off + $2,000). Given a $30,000 increase in net A/R, ending net A/R must have been $34,500 ($4,500 beginning net A/R + $30,000), with ending gross A/R of $36,000 ($34,500 + $1,500). Collections were therefore $68,000 ($5,000 beginning gross A/R – $1,000 write-off + $100,000 credit sales – $36,000 ending gross A/R).

Gross A/R		
$ 5,000 Beg. Bal.	$ 1,000	Write-off
100,000 Cr. Sales	68,000	Collections
$ 36,000 End. Bal.		

✘ **Answer (A) is incorrect.** Credit sales minus the ending gross accounts receivable equals $64,000.

✘ **Answer (C) is incorrect.** The amount of $68,500 equals credit sales, minus the increase in net accounts receivable, minus the ending allowance.

✘ **Answer (D) is incorrect.** Credit sales minus the increase in net accounts receivable equals $70,000.

6. Foster Co. adjusted its allowance for credit losses at year end. The general ledger balances for the accounts receivable and the related allowance account were $1,000,000 and $40,000, respectively. Foster uses the percentage-of-receivables method to estimate its allowance for credit losses. Accounts receivable were estimated to be 5% uncollectible. What amount should Foster record as an adjustment to its allowance for credit losses at year end?

A. $10,000 decrease.

B. $10,000 increase.

C. $50,000 decrease.

D. $50,000 increase.

✓ **Answer (B) is correct.**
Required: The adjustment of the allowance for credit losses.
Discussion: Because the percentage of accounts receivable method is used, the accounts receivable balance must be multiplied by 5%. Thus, the allowance for credit losses should be $50,000 ($1,000,000 × 5%). Given that the pre-adjustment allowance for credit losses is $40,000, the year-end adjustment must increase the allowance by $10,000 (debit credit loss expense, credit the allowance).

✗ **Answer (A) is incorrect.** The adjustment should be a $10,000 increase, not a decrease.

✗ **Answer (C) is incorrect.** The year-end allowance for credit losses is $50,000.

✗ **Answer (D) is incorrect.** The year-end allowance for credit losses is $50,000.

5.3 Transfers of Receivables and Other Financial Assets

7. Red Co. had $3 million in accounts receivable recorded on its books. Red wanted to convert the $3 million in receivables to cash in a more timely manner than waiting the 45 days for payment as indicated on its invoices. Which of the following would alter the timing of Red's cash flows for the $3 million in receivables already recorded on its books?

A. Change the due date of the invoice.

B. Factor the receivables outstanding.

C. Discount the receivables outstanding.

D. Demand payment from customers before the due date.

✓ **Answer (B) is correct.**
Required: The action that alters the timing of cash flows from receivables.
Discussion: Factoring transfers accounts receivable to a finance company or bank (the factor) on a nonrecourse, notification (to debtors) basis. The arrangement is an outright sale. If it meets certain criteria, it is accounted for as a sale of financial assets. The seller therefore accelerates cash inflows in exchange for the factor's fee.

✗ **Answer (A) is incorrect.** Red and its customers have entered into contracts that establish the due date. It cannot be changed without a new agreement.

✗ **Answer (C) is incorrect.** Calculating the present value of the future amounts to be received does not result in cash flows.

✗ **Answer (D) is incorrect.** Customers are not contractually obligated to pay before the due date.

8. Gar Co. factored its receivables without recourse with Ross Bank. Gar received cash as a result of this transaction, which is best described as a

A. Loan from Ross collateralized by Gar's accounts receivable.

B. Loan from Ross to be repaid by the proceeds from Gar's accounts receivable.

C. Sale of Gar's accounts receivable to Ross, with the risk of uncollectible accounts retained by Gar.

D. Sale of Gar's accounts receivable to Ross, with the risk of uncollectible accounts transferred to Ross.

✓ **Answer (D) is correct.**
Required: The effect of factoring receivables without recourse.
Discussion: When receivables are factored without recourse, the transaction is treated as a sale and the buyer accepts the risk of collectibility. The seller bears no responsibility for credit losses. A sale without recourse is not a loan. In a sale without recourse, the buyer assumes the risk of uncollectible accounts.

9. Which of the following is a method to generate cash from accounts receivable?

	Assignment	Factoring
A.	Yes	No
B.	Yes	Yes
C.	No	Yes
D.	No	No

✔ **Answer (B) is correct.**
Required: The method(s) of generating cash from accounts receivable.
Discussion: Methods of generating cash from accounts receivable include both assignment and factoring. Assignment occurs when specifically named accounts receivable are pledged as collateral for a loan. The accounts receivable remain those of the assignor. However, when cash is collected from these accounts receivable, the cash must be remitted to the assignee. Accounts receivable are factored when they are sold outright to a third party. This sale may be with or without recourse.

✘ **Answer (A) is incorrect.** Factoring is a way to generate cash from accounts receivable.

✘ **Answer (C) is incorrect.** Assignment is a way to generate cash from accounts receivable.

✘ **Answer (D) is incorrect.** Both assignment and factoring are ways to generate cash from accounts receivable.

5.4 Notes Receivable

10. On January 1, Year 3, Mill Co. exchanged equipment for a $200,000, noninterest-bearing note due on January 1, Year 6. The prevailing rate of interest for a note of this type at January 1, Year 3, was 10%. The present value of $1 at 10% for three periods is 0.75. What amount of interest revenue should be included in Mill's Year 4 income statement?

A. $0

B. $15,000

C. $16,500

D. $20,000

✔ **Answer (C) is correct.**
Required: The interest income from a noninterest-bearing note received for property.
Discussion: When a noninterest-bearing note is exchanged for property, and neither the note nor the property has a clearly determinable exchange price, the present value of the note should be determined by discounting all future payments using an appropriately imputed interest rate. Mill Company will receive $200,000 cash in 3 years. Assuming that 10% is the appropriate imputed rate of interest, the present value (initial carrying amount) of the note at January 1, Year 3, was $150,000 ($200,000 × 0.75). Interest revenue for Year 3 was $15,000 ($150,000 × 10%), and the entry was to debit the discount and credit interest revenue for that amount. Thus, the carrying amount of the note at January 1, Year 4, was $165,000 ($200,000 face amount – $35,000 unamortized discount). Interest revenue for Year 4 is therefore $16,500 ($165,000 carrying amount × 10% interest rate).

✘ **Answer (A) is incorrect.** Interest should be recognized equal to the imputed rate times the carrying amount of the note.

✘ **Answer (B) is incorrect.** Interest income for Year 3 was $15,000.

✘ **Answer (D) is incorrect.** The amount of $20,000 is 10% of the face amount of the note.

11. A note payable was issued in payment for services received. The services had a fair value less than the face amount of the note payable. The note payable has **no** stated interest rate. How should the note payable be presented in the statement of financial position?

    A. At the face amount.

    B. At the face amount with a separate deferred asset for the discount calculated at the imputed interest rate.

    C. At the face amount with a separate deferred credit for the discount calculated at the imputed interest rate.

    D. At the face amount minus a discount calculated at the imputed interest rate.

✔ **Answer (D) is correct.**
Required: The presentation of a noninterest bearing note on the statement of financial position.
Discussion: When a note is exchanged for property, goods, or services, the interest rate determined by the parties in an arm's-length transaction is presumed to be fair. But when the note is issued with no stated rate, the transaction should be recorded at the more clearly determinable of (1) the fair value of goods or services received or (2) the market value of the note. Assuming that the market value of the note cannot be reliably determined, the transaction is recorded at the fair value of services received, if known. Because the fair value of services received is lower than the note's face amount, a discount on the note is recognized. The imputed interest rate on this note is the one that equates the present value of future payments on the note with the fair value of services received.

✘ **Answer (A) is incorrect.** When a note exchanged for services has no stated rate, the transaction should be recorded at the more clearly determinable of (1) the fair value of services received or (2) the market value of the note. Thus, the note cannot be presented at its face amount.

✘ **Answer (B) is incorrect.** Issuance of a note for services received does not result in recognition of a deferred asset.

✘ **Answer (C) is incorrect.** Issuance of a note for services received does not result in recognition of a deferred credit.

12. On August 15, Benet Co. sold goods for which it received a note bearing the market rate of interest on that date. The 4-month note was dated July 15. Note principal, together with all interest, is due November 15. When the note was recorded on August 15, which of the following accounts increased?

    A. Unearned discount.

    B. Interest receivable.

    C. Prepaid interest.

    D. Interest revenue.

✔ **Answer (B) is correct.**
Required: The account that increased when the note was recorded.
Discussion: Because the note bears interest at a reasonable rate (in this case, the market rate), its present value at the date of issuance is the face amount. Accordingly, the note should be recorded at this amount. Interest receivable also may be debited, and unearned interest revenue may be credited. The simple alternative is to debit cash and credit interest revenue when payment is received. If the reporting period ends prior to November 15, the period-end entry is to debit interest receivable and credit accrued interest revenue.

✘ **Answer (A) is incorrect.** The note bears interest at the market rate. Thus, no discount from its face amount s recorded.

✘ **Answer (C) is incorrect.** No prepayment of interest has been made.

✘ **Answer (D) is incorrect.** Interest revenue has not yet been earned.

13. On December 1, Year 4, Tigg Mortgage Co. gave Pod Corp. a $200,000, 12% loan. Pod received proceeds of $194,000 after the deduction of a $6,000 nonrefundable loan origination fee. Principal and interest are due in 60 monthly installments of $4,450, beginning January 1, Year 5. The repayments yield an effective interest rate of 12% at a present value of $200,000 and 13.4% at a present value of $194,000. What amount of accrued interest receivable should Tigg include in its December 31, Year 4, balance sheet?

A. $4,450

B. $2,166

C. $2,000

D. $0

✔ **Answer (C) is correct.**
Required: The accrued interest receivable at year end.
Discussion: Accrued interest receivable is always equal to the face amount times the nominal rate for the period of the accrual. Thus, the accrued interest receivable is $2,000 [$200,000 × 12% × (1 ÷ 12)].

✘ **Answer (A) is incorrect.** The monthly installment is $4,450. It includes principal as well as interest.

✘ **Answer (B) is incorrect.** The amount of $2,166 is based on a present value of $194,000 and an effective rate of 13.4%. It is the interest revenue from the loan.

✘ **Answer (D) is incorrect.** One month's interest should be accrued.

14. On Merf's April 30, Year 4, balance sheet, a note receivable was reported as a noncurrent asset, and its accrued interest for 8 months was reported as a current asset. Which of the following terms would fit Merf's note receivable?

A. Both principal and interest amounts are payable on August 31, Year 4, and August 31, Year 5.

B. Principal and interest are due December 31, Year 4.

C. Both principal and interest amounts are payable on December 31, Year 4, and December 31, Year 5.

D. Principal is due August 31, Year 5. Interest is due August 31, Year 4, and August 31, Year 5.

✔ **Answer (D) is correct.**
Required: The terms explaining classification of a note receivable as a noncurrent asset and its accrued interest as a current asset.
Discussion: A noncurrent note receivable is one that is not expected to be converted into cash within 1 year or one operating cycle, whichever is longer. Because the principal is due more than 1 year from the balance sheet date, it must be regarded as noncurrent. However, the accrued interest is a current asset because it is due in 4 months.

Questions 15 and 16 are based on the following information.

On January 2, Year 3, Emme Co. sold equipment with a carrying amount of $480,000 in exchange for a $600,000 noninterest-bearing note due January 2, Year 6. There was no established exchange price for the equipment, and the market value of the note cannot be reasonably approximated. The prevailing rate of interest for a note of this type at January 2, Year 3, was 10%. The present value of 1 at 10% for three periods is 0.75.

15. In Emme's Year 3 income statement, what amount should be reported as interest income?

A. $15,000

B. $45,000

C. $48,000

D. $60,000

✔ **Answer (B) is correct.**
Required: The interest income from a noninterest-bearing note received for property.
Discussion: When a noninterest-bearing note is exchanged for property, and neither the note nor the property has a clearly determinable exchange price, the present value of the note should be the basis for recording the transaction. The present value is determined by discounting all future payments using an appropriately imputed interest rate. Emme Co. will receive $600,000 cash in 3 years. Assuming that 10% is the appropriate imputed rate of interest, the present value (initial carrying amount) of the note at January 2, Year 3, was $450,000 ($600,000 × 0.75). Under the interest method, interest income for Year 3 was $45,000 ($450,000 × 10%), and the entry is to debit the discount and credit interest income for that amount.

✘ **Answer (A) is incorrect.** The amount of $15,000 is the difference between 10% of the face amount and 10% of the carrying amount.

✘ **Answer (C) is incorrect.** Interest income is based on the present value of the note, not the carrying amount of the equipment.

✘ **Answer (D) is incorrect.** Interest income is based on the carrying amount of the note, not the face amount.

16. In Emme's Year 3 income statement, what amount should be reported as gain (loss) on sale of equipment?

A. $(30,000)

B. $30,000

C. $120,000

D. $150,000

✔ **Answer (A) is correct.**
Required: The amount reported as gain (loss) on the sale of machinery.
Discussion: Emme Co. sold equipment with a carrying amount of $480,000 and received a note with a present value of $450,000 ($600,000 × .75). Thus, Emme should report a $30,000 loss ($480,000 − $450,000).

✘ **Answer (B) is incorrect.** The present value of the note is $30,000 less than the carrying amount surrendered.

✘ **Answer (C) is incorrect.** The amount of $120,000 is the difference between the face amount of the note and the carrying amount of the equipment.

✘ **Answer (D) is incorrect.** The amount of $150,000 is the discount (Face amount − Present value).

17. On December 1, Year 4, Money Co. gave Home Co. a $200,000, 11% loan. Money paid proceeds of $194,000 after the deduction of a $6,000 nonrefundable loan origination fee. Principal and interest are due in 60 monthly installments of $4,310, beginning January 1, Year 5. The repayments yield an effective interest rate of 11% at a present value of $200,000 and 12.4% at a present value of $194,000. What amount of income from this loan should Money report in its Year 4 income statement?

A. $0

B. $1,833

C. $2,005

D. $7,833

✔ **Answer (C) is correct.**
Required: The amount of income from the loan at year end.
Discussion: Under the effective-interest method, the effective rate of interest is applied to the net carrying amount of the receivable to determine periodic interest revenue. Thus, interest revenue from the loan for the month of December equals $2,005 [$194,000 × 12.4% × (1 ÷ 12)].

✘ **Answer (A) is incorrect.** One month's interest should be accrued.

✘ **Answer (B) is incorrect.** The amount of $1,833 is the accrued interest receivable, which equals the face amount times the nominal rate for the period [$200,000 × 11% × (1 ÷ 12)].

✘ **Answer (D) is incorrect.** The amount of $7,833 equals the $6,000 origination fee plus the accrued interest receivable of $1,833.

18. Leaf Co. purchased from Oak Co. a $20,000, 8%, 5-year note that required five equal, annual year-end payments of $5,009. The note was discounted to yield a 9% rate to Leaf. At the date of purchase, Leaf recorded the note at its present value of $19,485. What should be the total interest revenue earned by Leaf over the life of this note?

A. $5,045

B. $5,560

C. $8,000

D. $9,000

✔ **Answer (B) is correct.**
Required: The total interest revenue earned on a discounted note receivable.
Discussion: Leaf Co. will receive cash of $25,045 ($5,009 × 5). Thus, interest revenue is $5,560 ($25,045 – $19,485 present value).

✘ **Answer (A) is incorrect.** The amount of $5,045 does not include the discount amortization.

✘ **Answer (C) is incorrect.** The amount of $8,000 equals $20,000 times 8% nominal interest for 5 years.

✘ **Answer (D) is incorrect.** The amount of $9,000 equals $20,000 times the 9% yield rate for 5 years.

GLEIM

Go to Online Course

Access the **Gleim CPA Premium Review System** featuring our SmartAdapt technology from your Gleim Personal Classroom to continue your studies.

You will experience a personalized study environment with exam-emulating multiple-choice questions.

Study Unit Six

Inventories

(29 pages of outline)

6.1 Inventory Fundamentals

Definition

Inventory is the total of tangible personal property

- Held for sale in the ordinary course of business,
- In the form of work-in-process to be completed and sold in the ordinary course of business, or
- To be used up currently in producing goods or services for sale.

Inventory does not include long-term assets subject to depreciation.

Sources of Inventories

Retailing

A trading (retailing) entity purchases merchandise to be resold without substantial modification. Such entities may also have supplies inventories.

For a retailer, **cost of goods sold** essentially equals beginning merchandise inventory, plus purchases for the period, minus ending merchandise inventory (purchases adjusted for the change in inventory).

Cost of Goods Sold for a Retailer

Beginning inventory		$ XXX,XXX
Purchases	$X,XXX,XXX	
Purchase returns and discounts	(XX,XXX)	
Freight-in	XX,XXX	
Net purchases		X,XXX,XXX
Goods available for sale		$X,XXX,XXX
Ending inventory		**(XXX,XXX)**
Cost of goods sold		$X,XXX,XXX

Manufacturing

An entity that acquires goods for conversion into substantially different products has inventories of goods consumed directly or indirectly in production (direct materials and supplies), goods in the course of production (work-in-process), and goods awaiting sale (finished goods).

For a manufacturer, **cost of goods sold** essentially equals beginning finished goods inventory, plus the cost of goods manufactured, minus ending finished goods inventory.

Cost of goods manufactured equals beginning work-in-process, plus current manufacturing costs (Direct materials + Direct labor + Production overhead), minus ending work-in-process (current manufacturing costs adjusted for the change in work-in-process).

Cost of Goods Sold for a Manufacturer

Beginning materials inventory		$ XXX,XXX
Purchases	$X,XXX,XXX	
Purchase returns and discounts	(XX,XXX)	
Freight-in	XX,XXX	
Net purchases		X,XXX,XXX
Materials available for use		$X,XXX,XXX
Ending materials inventory		**(XXX,XXX)**
Direct materials used in production		$X,XXX,XXX
Direct labor costs		X,XXX,XXX
Manufacturing overhead costs		XXX,XXX
Total manufacturing costs for the period		$X,XXX,XXX
Beginning work-in-process inventory		XXX,XXX
Ending work-in-process inventory		**(XXX,XXX)**
Cost of goods manufactured		$X,XXX,XXX
Beginning finished goods inventory		XXX,XXX
Goods available for sale		$X,XXX,XXX
Ending finished goods inventory		**(XXX,XXX)**
Cost of goods sold		$X,XXX,XXX

Inventory Accounting Systems

Entities that require continuous monitoring of inventory use a perpetual system. Entities that have no need to monitor continuously use a periodic system.

Perpetual System

In a perpetual system, purchases, purchase returns and allowances, purchase discounts, and freight-in (transportation in) are charged directly to inventory.

- Inventory and cost of goods sold are adjusted as sales occur.

- A physical count is needed to detect material misstatements in the records.

- The amount of inventory on hand and the cost of goods sold can be determined at any moment in time.

- Inventory over-and-short is debited (credited) when the physical count is less (greater) than the balance in the perpetual records.

  - This account is either closed to cost of goods sold or reported separately under (1) other revenues and gains or (2) other expenses and losses.

Journal Entries in a Perpetual Inventory System

Acquisition and Returns		
Inventory	$XXX	
Accounts payable		$XXX
Sale		
Accounts receivable	$XXX	
Sales		$XXX
Cost of goods sold	XXX	
Inventory		XXX

Periodic System

In a periodic system, the inventory and cost of goods sold accounts are updated at specific intervals, such as quarterly or annually, based on the results of a **physical count**.

- The beginning inventory balance remains unchanged during the accounting period.

- Goods bought from suppliers, freight-in, and adjustments usually are tracked in a separate temporary account (i.e., **purchases**).

- Changes in inventory and cost of goods sold are recorded only at the end of the period, based on the physical count.

- After the physical count,

  - The inventory balance is adjusted to match the physical count and
  - Cost of goods sold is calculated.

Journal Entries in a Periodic Inventory System

Acquisition and Returns

Purchases	$XXX	
Accounts payable		$XXX
Accounts payable	XXX	
Purchase returns		XXX

Sale

Accounts receivable	$XXX	
Sales		$XXX

Closing

Inventory (physical count)	$XXX	
Cost of goods sold (difference)	XXX	
Purchases (total amount for period)		$XXX
Inventory (beginning balance)		XXX

Example 6-1	Perpetual vs. Periodic Inventory System

Entity A's January 1, Year 1, inventory consists of 1,000 units with a cost of $5 per unit. The following are Entity A's Year 2 transactions:

April 1: Sold 600 inventory units for $4,800 in cash.

May 1: Purchased 250 inventory units for $5 in cash per unit.

The year-end result of the physical count was 650 inventory units. The following are Entity A's journal entries under the perpetual and periodic systems:

Perpetual System			Periodic System		
Inventory sale April 1:					
Cash	$4,800		Cash	$4,800	
Sales		$4,800	Sales		$4,800
Cost of goods sold (600 × $5)	$3,000				
Inventory		$3,000			
Inventory purchase May 1:					
Inventory (250 × $5)	$1,250		Purchases	$1,250	
Cash		$1,250	Cash		$1,250
After the physical count on December 31:					
No journal entry is needed because the physical count equals the amount of inventory on the books (1,000 − 600 + 250 = 650).			Inventory (year-end) (650 × $5)	$3,250	
			Cost of goods sold (difference)	3,000	
			Inventory (beginning)		$5,000
			Purchases		1,250

Beginning inventory	$5,000
Purchases of inventory during the period	1,250
Ending inventory	(3,250)
Cost of goods sold	**$3,000**

The perpetual and periodic systems have the same result. However, under the periodic system, the amounts of inventory and cost of goods sold are updated only at the end of the period after the physical count.

Items Counted in Inventory

Items in Transit

Not all inventory is on hand. Most sales are recorded by the seller at the time of shipment and by the buyer at the time of receipt.

- However, this procedure may misstate inventory, receivables, payables, and earnings at the end of the period.

Proper cut-off is observed by determining when control has passed under the FOB (free on board) terms of the contract.

- **FOB shipping point** means control over goods passes to the buyer when the seller makes a proper tender of delivery of the goods to the carrier. The buyer then includes the goods in inventory.

- **FOB destination** means control over goods passes to the buyer when the seller makes a proper tender of delivery of the goods at the destination. The seller should include the goods in inventory until that time.

Shipping services performed before control over the goods is transferred to the customer are activities to fulfill the contract. Thus, revenue from shipping activities is recognized when control over the goods transfers to the customer.

- Shipping services performed after control over the goods is transferred to the customers may be accounted for as either of the following:

  - An additional promised service. In this case, revenue from shipping activities is recognized when shipping services occur.

  - A contract fulfillment activity. In this case, revenue from shipping activities is recognized when control over the goods transfers to the customer.

Right of Return

When sales are made with the understanding that unsatisfactory goods may be returned, the consideration in the contract is **variable**. Sales revenue then is recognized only to the extent that it is **probable** that a significant reversal will not occur when the uncertainty is resolved. To account for the transfer of products with a right of return at the time of the sale, an entity should recognize all of the following:

- **Sales** revenue is recognized only for the amount of consideration to which an entity expects to be entitled. Thus, no sales are recognized for the products expected to be returned.

- A **refund liability** is recognized for the amount of consideration expected to be returned to customers. The refund liability is estimated at each reporting period to reflect the changes in the expectations about the refund amount. The adjustments to the refund liability are recognized as revenue (or reductions of revenue).

- A **return asset** is recognized for the entity's right to recover products from customers. The return asset is measured initially at the former carrying amount of the products expected to be returned minus any expected costs to recover those products. The return asset is presented separately from (1) the refund liability and (2) inventory.

- **Cost of goods sold** is measured at the carrying amount of the products sold minus the return asset recognized.

Some entities differentiate between the gross sales amount and the sales amount that probably will be returned. In this situation, sales are recorded at their gross amount and **sales returns**, a contra sales revenue account, is recognized.

Example 6-2   Sales with Right of Return

Zaya Company is a producer of printing machines. On January 1, Year 1, Zaya sold 20 machines for $500 in cash each. The cost of each machine is $400. Zaya allows customers to return any unused machine within 2 months and receive a full refund. Because the contract allows customers a **right of return**, the consideration received is variable. Zaya uses the expected value method to estimate the variable consideration. Based on its past experience, Zaya estimates that four machines will be returned. Only three machines were returned by the customers during the return period.

Because revenue is recognized for the products not expected to be returned, sales of $8,000 [(20 − 4) × $500] are recognized on the transaction date. The following journal entries were recorded by Zaya:

January 1, Year 1

Cash (20 × $500)	$10,000		Cost of goods sold (16 × $400)	$6,400	
Sales (16 × $500)		$8,000	Return asset (4 × $400)	1,600	
Refund liability (4 × $500)		2,000	Inventory (20 × $400)		$8,000

Return of three machines

| Refund liability (3 × $500) | $1,500 | | Inventory (3 × $400) | $1,200 | |
| Cash | | $1,500 | Return asset | | $1,200 |

March 1, Year 1 – End of the return period

| Refund liability | $500 | | Cost of goods sold | $400 | |
| Sales | | $500 | Return asset | | $400 |

NOTE: If sales were recorded at their gross amount and sales returns were recognized, the following entries would be made on 1/1/Year 1:

Cash (20 × $500)	$10,000		Cost of goods sold (16 × $400)	$6,400	
Sales returns (contra revenue)	2,000		Return asset (4 × $400)	1,600	
Sales		$10,000	Inventory (20 × $400)		$8,000
Refund liability (4 × $500)		2,000			

- The entity may not be able to make a reasonable estimate of the probability and the amount of a refund. If the entity also cannot conclude that a significant reversal of revenue recognized is not probable, no revenue or cost of goods sold is recognized until the right of return expires.

  - The entire consideration received is recognized as a contract liability.

  - The decrease in inventory is recognized as a contract asset to reflect the right to recover products from customers on settling the refund liability.

Goods Out on Consignment (discussed in detail in the next subunit)

Example 6-3	Items Counted in Inventory

Entity A's December 31, Year 1, physical count of inventory results in a measurement of $50,000. The following is additional information about year-end inventory:

- During the year, Entity A (the consignor) consigned goods with a total cost of $60,000 to Entity B (the consignee). The annual statement sent by Entity B to Entity A indicates that 60% of the goods were sold for $42,000.

- Goods costing $40,000 were shipped FOB shipping point by a vendor on December 29, Year 1. They were received by Entity A on January 4, Year 2.

- Goods costing $70,000 were shipped FOB destination by a vendor on December 30, Year 1. They were received by Entity A on January 5, Year 2.

- Goods costing $25,000 were billed to a customer FOB destination on December 27, Year 1. They were shipped by Entity A on December 28, Year 1, and received by the customer on January 3, Year 2.

In Entity A's December 31, Year 1, financial statements, the inventory balance is $139,000. This amount consists of

Physical inventory count	$ 50,000
Goods out on consignment ($60,000 × 40%)	24,000
Goods shipped FOB shipping point (title and risk of loss passed to Entity A on December 29, Year 1, at the time of shipment)	40,000
Goods shipped FOB destination to customer (title and the risk of loss will pass to the customer only on January 3, Year 2)	25,000
December 31, Year 1, inventory balance	**$139,000**

Success Tip

CPA candidates have been asked to calculate amounts for inventory and cost of goods sold using information given in the question, such as shipping terms and consignment sales.

Cost Basis of Inventory – Initial Measurement

The **cost of inventories** includes all costs incurred in bringing them to their existing condition and location.

The **cost of purchased inventories** includes

- The price paid or consideration given to acquire the inventory, net of trade discounts, rebates, and other similar items;

- Import duties and other unrecoverable taxes; and

- Handling, insurance, freight-in, and other costs directly attributable to (1) acquiring finished goods and materials and (2) bringing them to their present location and condition (salable or usable condition).

The **cost of manufactured inventories** (work-in-process and finished goods inventories) includes the cost of direct materials used, direct labor costs, and production overhead.

- Abnormal production costs are not inventoriable costs. They are expensed as incurred.

Period costs, such as (1) general and administrative expenses or (2) selling expenses, should be expensed as incurred. They are not inventoriable costs.

Purchases, Freight Costs, and Discounts

Purchased inventory is measured at invoice cost net of any discounts taken.

- **Trade discounts** are usually subtracted prior to invoicing.

  - A chain discount applies more than one trade discount. The first discount is applied to the list price, the second is applied to the resulting amount, etc.

- Cash discounts are offered to induce early payment and improve cash flow.

The buyer's **transportation (freight) costs** for purchased goods are inventoried.

- In a perpetual system, these costs can be assigned to specified purchases.
- In a periodic system, transportation costs are usually debited to purchases.

Stop & Review

You have completed the outline for this subunit.
Study multiple-choice questions 1 and 2 on page 204.

6.2 Consignment Accounting

A consignment sale is an arrangement between the owner of goods and a sales agent. Consigned goods are not sold but rather transferred to an agent for possible sale.

- The consignor (owner) records sales only when the goods are sold to third parties by the consignee (agent).

- Goods out on consignment are **included in inventory** at cost. Costs of transporting the goods to the consignee are inventoriable costs, not selling expenses.

The following are examples of indicators that the contract with an agent is a consignment arrangement:

- The product is controlled by the entity until a specified event occurs, such as the sale of the product to a third party, or until a specified period expires.

- The entity is able to require the return of the product or transfer the product to a third party.

- The dealer does not have an unconditional obligation to pay for the product.

Consignor's Accounting

The **consignor** records the initial shipment by a debit to **consigned goods out** (a separate inventory account) and a credit to inventory at cost.

Consigned goods out is used in a perpetual or periodic inventory system when consignments are recorded in separate accounts.

- If the consignor uses a perpetual system, the credit on shipment is to inventory.

- If a periodic system is used, the credit is to consignment shipments, a contra cost of goods sold account. Its balance is then closed at the end of the period when the inventory adjustments are made.

Consignee's Accounting

The **consignee** never records the consigned goods as an asset.

- The basic account used in consignee accounting is **consignment-in**, a receivable (payable). Its balance is the amount payable to the consignor (a credit) or the amount receivable from the consignor (a debit).

  - Before consigned goods are sold, expenses chargeable to the consignor (e.g., freight-in or service costs) are recorded in the consignment-in account as a receivable. After the consigned goods are sold, the credit balance reflects the consignee's net liability to the consignor.

  - Sales are recorded with a debit to cash (or accounts receivable) and credits to consignment-in (a payable) and commission income.

  - Payments to the consignor result in a debit to consignment-in and a credit to cash.

Comparative Journal Entries

Example 6-4	Consignment Accounting

The consignor ships 100 units, costing $50 each, to the consignee.

Consignor		**Consignee**
Consigned goods out	$5,000	Only a memorandum entry
Inventory	$5,000	

The consignee pays $120 for freight-in.

Consignor		**Consignee**		
No entry at this time		Consignment-in	$120	
		Cash		$120

The consignee sells 80 units at $80 each. The consignee is to receive a 15% commission on all sales.

Consignor	**Consignee**		
No entry at this time	Cash (80 × $80)	$6,400	
	Consignment-in		$5,440
	Commission income		
	($6,400 × 15%)		960

The consignee sends a monthly statement to the consignor with the balance owed. The cost of shipping goods to the consignee, including the $120 payment by the consignee, is debited as a cost of consigned inventory.

Consignor		**Consignee**	
Cash	$5,320	Consignment-in	$5,320 ($5,440 – $120)
Commission expense	960	Cash	$5,320
Consigned goods out	120		
Cost of goods sold	4,096 [($5,000 + $120) × 80%]		
Sales	$6,400		
Consigned goods out	4,096		

Stop & Review

You have completed the outline for this subunit.

Study multiple-choice questions 3 and 4 on page 205.

6.3 Cost Flow Methods -- Application

Success Tip

The AICPA has asked candidates to solve calculation questions concerning average-cost, FIFO, and LIFO inventory. Candidates may also see questions that ask for adjusting year-end entries.

Specific Identification

Specific identification requires determining which specific items are sold and therefore reflects the actual physical flow of goods. It can be used for special inventory items, such as automobiles or heavy equipment.

A practical weakness of specific identification is the need for detailed records.

Average Cost

The assumption in an average cost system is that goods are indistinguishable and are therefore measured at an average of the costs incurred.

The **moving-average** method requires determination of a new weighted-average cost after each purchase and thus is used only in a **perpetual system**.

Example 6-5	Moving-Average Method

The following data relate to Entity A's Year 1 activities:

Date	Transaction	Number of units	Purchase price per unit ($)	Sale price per unit ($)
January 1	Beginning balance	100	20	
March 1	Purchase	20	32	
April 1	Sale	70		40
June 1	Purchase	30	14	
October 1	Sale	40		24

-- Continued on next page --

Example 6-5 -- Continued

Under the **moving-average method**, the year-end inventory and Year 1 cost of goods sold are calculated as follows:

Date	Activity	Units	Price	Cost of inventory purchased (sold)	Inventory total balance	On-hand units	Cost per unit
Jan. 1	Beg. bal.	100	$20		$2,000 (100 × 20)	100	**$20**
Mar. 1	Purchase	20	$32	$640 = 20 × $32	$2,640 (2,000 + 640)	120	**$22** ($2,640 ÷ 120)
Apr. 1	Sale	70	**$22**	($1,540) = 70 × $22	$1,100 (2,640 − 1,540)	50	**$22** ($1,100 ÷ 50)
Jun. 1	Purchase	30	$14	$420 = 30 × $14	$1,520 (1,100 + 420)	80	**$19** ($1,520 ÷ 80)
Oct. 1	Sale	40	**$19**	($760) = 40 × $19	**$760** (1,520 − 760)	40	**$19** ($760 ÷ 40)

The cost of **inventory** on December 31, Year 1, is **$760**. The Year 1 **cost of goods sold** is **$2,300**.

Beginning inventory	$2,000
Purchases ($640 + $420)	1,060
Ending inventory	(760)
Cost of goods sold ($1,540 + $760)	**$2,300**

The **weighted-average method** is used under the **periodic** inventory accounting system. The average cost is determined only at the end of the period. The weighted-average cost per unit is used to determine the ending inventory and the cost of goods sold for the period. It is calculated as follows:

$$\frac{\text{Cost of beginning inventory (\$) + Cost of purchases during the period (\$)}}{\text{Units in beginning inventory + Number of units purchased during the period}}$$

Example 6-6   Weighted-Average Method

Under the **weighted-average method**, Entity A's ending inventory and Year 1 cost of goods sold are determined as follows:

First, the weighted-average cost per unit is calculated.

$$\frac{\text{Cost of beginning inventory + Cost of purchases during the period}}{\text{Units in beginning inventory + Number of units purchased}} = \frac{\$2,000 + \$1,060}{100 + 20 + 30} = \$20.40$$

Second, the ending inventory and Year 1 cost of goods sold are calculated using the weighted-average cost per unit (WACPU):

Beginning inventory	$2,000	
Purchases	1,060	
Ending inventory	(816)	(40 × $20.40) = (WACPU × Units in ending inventory)
Cost of goods sold	$2,244	(110 × $20.40) = (WACPU × Units sold during the period)

First-in, First-out (FIFO)

This method assumes that the first goods purchased are the first sold. Thus, ending inventory consists of the latest purchases.

Cost of goods sold includes the earliest goods purchased.

Under the FIFO method, year-end inventory and cost of goods sold for the period are **the same** regardless of whether the perpetual or the periodic inventory accounting system is used.

Example 6-7	FIFO Method

The number of units in Entity A's ending inventory is 40. Under the FIFO method, the cost of these units is the cost of the **latest purchases ($740)**.

Date of purchase	Units	Price per unit	Total cost
June 1, Year 1	30	$14	$420
March 1, Year 1	10	32	320
Ending inventory	40		$740

The Year 1 cost of goods sold is $2,320.

Beginning inventory	$2,000
Purchases ($640 + $420)	1,060
Ending inventory	(740)
Cost of goods sold	$2,320

NOTE: The results are the same under the periodic and perpetual systems.

Last-in, First-out (LIFO)

This method assumes that the newest items of inventory are sold first. Thus, the items remaining in inventory are recognized as if they were the oldest.

- Under the LIFO method, the perpetual and the periodic inventory accounting systems may result in different amounts for the cost of year-end inventory and cost of goods sold.

- Increasing inventory results in the creation of **LIFO layers**.

LIFO Periodic

In a periodic system, a purchases account is used. Cost of goods sold and ending inventory are determined only at the end of the period.

Example 6-8	LIFO Method in a Periodic Inventory System

The number of units in Entity A's ending inventory is 40. Under the LIFO method, the cost of those units is the cost of the **earliest purchases** (beginning inventory) of **$800** (40 units × $20). The Year 1 cost of goods sold is **$2,260**.

Beginning inventory	$2,000
Purchases ($640 + $420)	1,060
Ending inventory	(800)
Cost of goods sold	**$2,260**

LIFO Perpetual

In a perpetual system, purchases are directly recorded in inventory. Cost of goods sold is calculated when a sale occurs and consists of the latest purchases.

Example 6-9	LIFO Method in a Perpetual Inventory System

Date	Activity	Units	Cost per unit	Cost of inventory purchased/sold	Inventory total balance		Number of units
Jan. 1	Beg. bal.	100	$20			100 × $20 = $2,000	100
Mar. 1	Purchase	20	$32	20 × $32 = $640	January 1 layer March 1 layer	100 × $20 = $2,000 20 × $32 = 640 $2,640	120
Apr. 1	Sale	70		20 × $32 = $ 640 50 × $20 = 1,000 $(1,640)	January 1 layer	50 × $20 = $1,000	50
Jun. 1	Purchase	30	$14	30 × $14 = $420	January 1 layer June 1 layer	50 × $20 = $1,000 30 × $14 = 420 $1,420	80
Oct. 1	Sale	40		30 × $14 = $ 420 10 × $20 = 200 $(620)	January 1 layer	40 × $20 = **$800**	40

Entity A's cost of ending **inventory** is **$800** and the Year 1 **cost of goods sold** is **$2,260** ($1,640 + $620).

NOTE: The results of the LIFO method under the perpetual and periodic systems are the same in this example but may differ in other situations.

LIFO Conformity Rule

An IRS regulation requires LIFO to be used for financial reporting if it is used in the tax return.

LIFO Valuation Allowance

Entities that use a different inventory costing method for internal purposes must convert to LIFO for reporting purposes if they use LIFO for tax purposes.

To adjust the inventory to LIFO, an allowance, sometimes called the **LIFO reserve**, is created. This account is reported as a contra to inventory account.

At period end, this allowance is adjusted to reflect the difference between LIFO and the internal costing method.

Cost of goods sold	$XXX	
Allowance to reduce inventory to LIFO		$XXX

Stop & Review

You have completed the outline for this subunit.
Study multiple-choice questions 5 through 7 beginning on page 206.

6.4 Cost Flow Methods -- Comparison

Varying Results under the Five Methods

Example 6-10	Comparison of Cost Flow Methods

The following are Entity A's varying results under each of the five cost flow methods:

	Ending Inventory	Cost of Goods Sold
Moving average	$760	$2,300
Weighted average	816	2,244
FIFO	740	2,320
LIFO periodic	800	2,260
LIFO perpetual	800	2,260

The cost flow model selected should be the one that most clearly reflects periodic income.

FIFO vs. LIFO

An advantage of FIFO is that ending inventory approximates the market value.

- A disadvantage is that current revenues are matched with older costs.

Under LIFO, management can affect net income with an end-of-period purchase that immediately alters cost of goods sold.

- An end-of-period FIFO purchase has no such effect.

In a time of **rising prices** (inflation), use of the **LIFO** method results in the lowest year-end inventory, the highest cost of goods sold, and the lowest gross profit.

- LIFO assumes that

  - The earliest (and therefore the lowest-priced) goods purchased are in ending inventory and
  - Cost of goods sold consists of the latest (and therefore the highest-priced) goods purchased.

- The results for the **FIFO** method are opposite of those for the LIFO method.

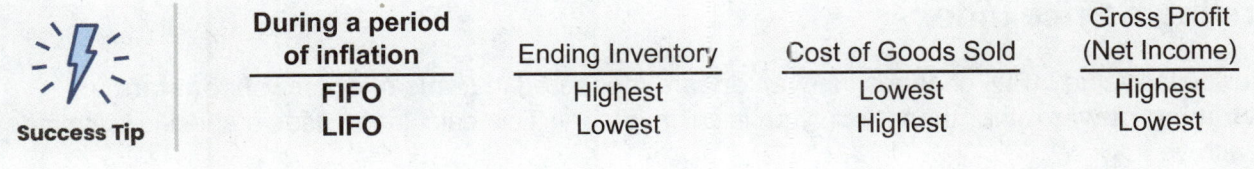

During a period of inflation	Ending Inventory	Cost of Goods Sold	Gross Profit (Net Income)
FIFO	Highest	Lowest	Highest
LIFO	Lowest	Highest	Lowest

Success Tip

Stop & Review

You have completed the outline for this subunit.

Study multiple-choice questions 8 and 9 on page 208.

6.5   Dollar-Value LIFO

Success Tip

In recent years, dollar-value LIFO has been less tested on the CPA Exam.

Pools of Specific Goods

The previous discussion of LIFO has assumed that the method is applied to specific units of inventory with specific unit costs. Dollar-value LIFO is applied to groups (pools) of inventory items that are substantially identical.

Recordkeeping is simplified because all goods in a beginning inventory pool are presumed to have been acquired on the same date and at the same cost.

- Using the pooling method, beginning inventory is costed at a weighted-average unit price (Total cost ÷ Unit quantity).

- Usually, purchases of goods in a pool also are recorded at a weighted-average cost (Total cost ÷ Unit quantity). If the quantity of units in the pool increases during the year, a new LIFO layer will be formed at the new weighted-average cost.

Each period's inventory layer equals the total change in inventory during that period. The example below illustrates this concept.

Example 6-11   Dollar-Value LIFO -- Inventory Layers
Beginning inventory has a base-year cost and an end-of-year cost of $100,000. Ending inventory has a base-year cost and an end-of-year cost of $120,000 and $150,000, respectively. The year's inventory layer at base-year cost is $20,000 ($120,000 – $100,000). This layer at current-year cost is $50,000 ($150,000 – $100,000).

Deriving a Price Index

Under dollar-value LIFO, changes in inventory are measured in terms of dollars of **constant purchasing power** rather than units of physical inventory. This calculation uses a specific price index for each year.

Selecting an appropriate price index is crucial to dollar-value LIFO accounting.

- An entity may choose to use published indexes. Examples are the Consumer Price Index for All Urban Consumers (CPI-U) and indexes published by trade associations.

- Most often, an index is generated internally for each year.

The **double-extension method** is the most common technique for internally generating a price index.

- Extending inventory is the process of multiplying the quantity of each good on hand by the unit cost to arrive at a total amount for inventory.

- To enable the calculation of price indexes, this operation must be performed twice: once using current-year cost and once using base-year cost.

Example 6-12	Dollar-Value LIFO -- Data

Retailer B has the following extended inventory cost data. Note that LIFO liquidation occurred in Year 3.

	At Base-Year Cost	At Current-Year Cost
1/1/Year 1	$250,000	$250,000
Year 1 layer	50,000	50,000
Year 2 layer	40,000	74,000
Year 3 layer	(20,000)	10,000
Year 4 layer	30,000	71,000

A price index can be computed for each year with the following ratio:

$$\text{Price index} = \frac{\textbf{Ending inventory at current-year cost}}{\textbf{Ending inventory at base-year cost}}$$

Example 6-13	Dollar-Value LIFO -- Calculation of Price Indexes

Using the values provided in Example 6-12, the price indexes for computing Retailer B's dollar-value LIFO inventory are calculated as follows:

Year 1 price index = ($250,000 + $50,000) ÷ ($250,000 + $50,000)
           = $300,000 ÷ $300,000
           = 1.00

Year 2 price index = ($250,000 + $50,000 + $74,000) ÷ ($250,000 + $50,000 + $40,000)
           = $374,000 ÷ $340,000
           = 1.10

Year 3 price index = ($250,000 + $50,000 + $74,000 + $10,000) ÷ ($250,000 + $50,000 + $40,000 – $20,000)
           = $384,000 ÷ $320,000
           = 1.20

Year 4 price index = ($250,000 + $50,000 + $74,000 + $10,000 + $71,000) ÷
           ($250,000 + $50,000 + $40,000 – $20,000 + $30,000)
           = $455,000 ÷ $350,000
           = 1.30

Dollar-Value LIFO Calculations

To arrive at dollar-value LIFO ending inventory, **each layer** must be inflated by the relevant price index.

Example 6-14   Dollar-Value LIFO -- Year 1 and Year 2 Ending Inventory

The following example uses Retailer B's information from Examples 6-12 and 6-13:

Year 1 Calculation:	At Base-Year Cost		Price Index		At Dollar-Value LIFO Cost
1/1/Year 1	$250,000	×	1.00	=	$250,000
Year 1 layer	50,000	×	1.00	=	50,000
12/31/Year 1	$300,000				$300,000

Year 2 Calculation:	At Base-Year Cost		Price Index		At Dollar-Value LIFO Cost
1/1/Year 1	$250,000	×	1.00	=	$250,000
Year 1 layer	50,000	×	1.00	=	50,000
Year 2 layer	40,000	×	1.10	=	44,000
12/31/Year 2	$340,000				$344,000

In any year when the balance declines, a portion of the most recent year's layer must be removed.

Example 6-15   Dollar-Value LIFO -- Year 3 Ending Inventory

The following example uses Retailer B's information from Examples 6-12 and 6-13:

Year 3 Calculation:	At Base-Year Cost		Price Index		At Dollar-Value LIFO Cost
1/1/Year 1	$250,000	×	1.00	=	$250,000
Year 1 layer	50,000	×	1.00	=	50,000
Year 2 layer	40,000	×	1.10	=	44,000
Year 2 liquidation	(20,000)	×	1.10	=	(22,000)
12/31/Year 3	$320,000				$322,000

Once liquidated, layers cannot be replaced.

Example 6-16	Dollar-Value LIFO -- Year 4 Ending Inventory

The following example uses Retailer B's information from Examples 6-12 and 6-13:

Year 4 Calculation:	At Base-Year Cost		Price Index		At Dollar-Value LIFO Cost
1/1/Year 1	$250,000	×	1.00	=	$250,000
Year 1 layer	50,000	×	1.00	=	50,000
Year 2 layer	40,000	×	1.10	=	44,000
Year 2 liquidation	(20,000)	×	1.10	=	(22,000)
Year 4 layer	30,000	×	1.30	=	39,000
12/31/Year 4	$350,000				$361,000

Stop & Review

You have completed the outline for this subunit.

Study multiple-choice questions 10 and 11 on page 209.

6.6 Measurement of Inventory Subsequent to Initial Recognition

Statement of Rule

The subsequent measurement of inventory depends on the cost method used.

- Inventory accounted for using LIFO or the retail inventory method is measured at the **lower of cost or market (LCM)**.

- Inventory accounted for using any other cost method (e.g., **FIFO or average cost**) is measured at the **lower of cost or net realizable value**.

The **loss on write-down** of inventory to market or net realizable value (NRV) generally is presented as a component of cost of goods sold. However, if the amount of loss is material, it should be presented as a separate line item in the current-period income statement.

- A write-down of inventory below its cost may result from damage, deterioration, obsolescence, changes in price levels, changes in demand, etc.

A reversal of a write-down of inventory recognized in the annual financial statements is **prohibited** in subsequent periods.

- Once inventory is written down below cost, the reduced amount is the new cost basis.

Depending on the nature of the inventory, the rules for write-down below cost may be applied either directly to each item or to the total of the inventory (or in some cases, to the total of each major category). The method should be the one that most clearly reflects periodic income.

Measurement of Inventory at the Lower of Cost or Market (LCM)

Inventory accounted for using the **LIFO or retail inventory method** must be written down to **market** if its utility is no longer as great as its cost.

- The excess of cost over market is recognized as a loss on write-down in the income statement.

Market is the current cost to replace inventory, subject to certain limitations. Market should not (1) exceed a **ceiling** equal to **net realizable value (NRV)** or (2) be less than a **floor** equal to NRV reduced by an allowance for an approximately **normal profit margin**.

- NRV is the estimated selling price in the ordinary course of business minus reasonably predictable costs of completion, disposal, and transportation.

- Thus, **current replacement cost** (CRC) is not to be greater than NRV or less than NRV minus a normal profit (NRV − P).

Market (M)	
CRC 1	M = NRV
CRC 2	M = (> NRV − P and < NRV)
CRC 3	M = NRV − P

Example 6-17   Measurement of Inventory at LCM

The following information is related to a company's year-end inventories:

Cost per inventory unit	Item A		Item B		Item C	
Estimated selling price	$80		$70		$44	
Minus: Cost of completion	(20)		--		(3)	
Minus: Cost of disposal	(6)		(5)		(2)	
NRV **(ceiling)**	$54		$65		$39	
Minus: Normal profit margin	(3)		(7)		(4)	
NRV − NPM **(floor)**	$51		$58		$35	
Current replacement cost **(CRC)**	53		55		40	
(a) Market	53	Ceiling > CRC > Floor	58	Floor > CRC	39	CRC > Ceiling
(b) Historical cost per unit	50		60		45	
Lower of cost (b) or market (a)	50	Cost < Market	58	Market < Cost	39	Market < Cost

LCM by item always will be equal to or less than the other LCM measurements, and LCM in total always will be equal to or greater than the other LCM measurements.

- Most entities use LCM by item. This method is required for **tax purposes**.

  - If **dollar-value LIFO** is used, LCM should be applied to pools of items.
  - An entity may not use LCM with LIFO for tax purposes.

Example 6-18   Lower of Cost or Market

Lala Co. accounts for its inventory using the **LIFO** cost method. The following is its inventory information at the end of the fiscal year:

Historical cost	$100,000
Current replacement cost	82,000
Net realizable value (NRV)	90,000
Normal profit margin	5,000

Under the LIFO method, inventory is measured at the lower of cost or market (current replacement cost subject to certain limitations). Market cannot be higher than NRV ($90,000) or lower than NRV reduced by a normal profit margin ($90,000 – $5,000 = $85,000). Thus, market is $85,000. (The current replacement cost of $82,000 is below the floor.) Because market is lower than cost, the inventory is reported in the balance sheet at market of $85,000. The write-down of inventory of $15,000 ($100,000 – $85,000) is recognized as a loss in the income statement. The journal entry is as follows:

Loss from inventory write-down	$15,000	
Inventory		$15,000

Measurement of Inventory at the Lower of Cost or NRV

Inventory measured using any method other than LIFO or retail (e.g., **FIFO or average cost**) must be measured at the **lower of cost or net realizable value**.

- **Net realizable value (NRV)** is the estimated selling price in the ordinary course of business minus reasonably predictable costs of completion, disposal, and transportation.

- The excess of cost over NRV is recognized as a loss on write-down in the income statement.

Example 6-19   Measurement of Inventory at Lower of Cost or NRV

Using the data from Example 6-18, assume that Lala Co. accounts for its inventory using the **FIFO** cost method.

Under the FIFO method (or any other method except for LIFO or retail), inventory is measured at the **lower of cost or net realizable value**. NRV of $90,000 is lower than cost of $100,000. Thus, a loss on write-down to NRV of $10,000 is recognized. The journal entry is as follows:

Loss from inventory write-down	$10,000	
Inventory		$10,000

Inventory Measurement at Interim Dates

A write-down of inventory below cost (to market for LIFO and retail and to NRV for all other methods) may be **deferred in the interim financial statements** if no loss is reasonably anticipated for the year.

- But inventory losses from a **nontemporary** decline below cost must be recognized at the interim date.

- If the loss is recovered in another quarter, it is recognized as a gain and treated as a change in estimate. The amount recovered is limited to the losses previously recognized.

Example 6-20	Interim LCM Measurement -- Loss Expected

A company accounts for its inventory using the LIFO cost method. The following is its inventory information for the interim period ending March 31, Year 1:

Historical cost	$93,000
Current replacement cost	87,000
Net realizable value (NRV)	90,000
Normal profit margin	5,000

Under LIFO, inventory is measured at LCM. Additional information: (1) This inventory was sold on January 5, Year 2. (2) On March 31, Year 1, the company expects no changes during the year regarding inventory information determined. (3) On June 30, Year 1, as a result of an increase in the demand for the company's products, the company determines the following data:

Current replacement cost	$95,000
Net realizable value (NRV)	99,000
Normal profit margin	5,000

March 31, Year 1

The current replacement cost ($87,000) is below the ceiling of NRV ($90,000) and above the floor of NRV minus normal profit margin ($85,000). Thus, **market** is equal to the current replacement cost of **$87,000**. Because market is lower than cost, the inventory is reported in the balance sheet at market of $87,000. The loss is not expected to be restored in the fiscal year, and the write-down of inventory of $6,000 ($93,000 – $87,000) is recognized as a loss in the income statement. The journal entry is as follows:

Loss from inventory write-down	$6,000	
Inventory		$6,000

June 30, Year 1

The current replacement cost ($95,000) is below the ceiling of NRV ($99,000) and above the floor of NRV minus normal profit margin ($94,000). Thus, **market** is equal to current replacement cost of **$95,000**. The loss is recovered in the second quarter ($95,000 > $87,000). The amount of reversal of the write-down recognized in the first quarter is limited to the losses previously recognized. The inventory must not be reported above its cost. The journal entry is as follows:

Inventory	$6,000	
Loss from inventory write-down		$6,000

Example 6-21   Interim LCM Measurement -- No Loss Expected

Tal Co. accounts for its inventory using the LIFO cost method. The following is its inventory information at the end of the interim period on March 31, Year 1:

Historical cost	$100,000
Current replacement cost	82,000
Net realizable value (NRV)	90,000
Normal profit margin	5,000

Tal expects that on December 31, Year 1, the inventory's NRV reduced by a normal profit margin will be at least $100,000.

No write-down of inventory is recognized in the interim financial statements on March 31, Year 1, because no loss is reasonably anticipated for the year.

Stop & Review

You have completed the outline for this subunit.
Study multiple-choice questions 12 through 15 beginning on page 210.

6.7   Special Topics in Inventory Accounting

Estimating Inventory

The estimated **gross profit method** is used to determine inventory for **interim statements**.

Because of its imprecision, GAAP and federal tax law **do not permit** use of the gross profit method **at year end**. But other applications are possible.

- If inventory is destroyed, the method may be used to estimate the loss.

- External auditors apply the gross profit method as an analytical procedure to determine the fairness of the ending inventory balance.

- The method may be used internally to generate estimates of inventory throughout the year, e.g., as a verification of perpetual records.

The gross profit method calculates ending inventory at a given time by subtracting an estimated cost of goods sold from the sum of beginning inventory and purchases (or cost of goods manufactured).

- The estimated cost of goods sold equals sales minus the gross profit.

- The gross profit equals sales multiplied by the gross profit percentage, an amount ordinarily computed on a historical basis.

$$\text{Gross profit percentage} = \frac{\text{Gross profit}}{\text{Sales}}$$

Example 6-22   Gross Profit Method

Beginning inventory		$60,000
Purchases		20,000
Goods available for sale		$80,000
Sales (at selling price)	$50,000	
Gross profit (20% of sales)	(10,000)	
Cost of goods sold		(40,000)
Estimated ending inventory		**$40,000**

Purchase Commitments

A commitment to acquire goods in the future is **not** recorded at the time of the agreement, e.g., by debiting an asset and crediting a liability.

- But a **loss** is recognized on a firm, noncancelable purchase commitment (unconditional purchase obligation) if the market price of the goods is less than the commitment price.

- The reason for current loss recognition is the same as that for inventory. A decrease (not an increase) in future benefits should be recognized when it occurs even if the contract is unperformed on both sides.

- Material losses expected on purchase commitments are measured in the same way as inventory losses, recognized, and separately disclosed.

The entry is

Unrealized holding loss -- earnings	$XXX	
Liability -- purchase commitment		$XXX

Example 6-23   Purchase Commitment

During the year, the Lisbon Company signed a noncancelable contract to purchase 2,000 pounds of materials at $64 per pound during the forthcoming year. On December 31, the market price of the materials is $52 per pound, and the selling price of the finished product is expected to decline accordingly. A loss of $24,000 [2,000 × ($64 − $52)] should be reported in the annual income statement.

GAAP require recognition in the income statement of a material loss on a purchase commitment as if the inventory were already owned. Losses on firm purchase commitments are measured in the same way as inventory losses. If the cost is $128,000 and the market price is $104,000, a $24,000 loss should be recognized.

Disclosure of commitments to transfer funds for fixed or minimum amounts of goods or services at fixed or minimum prices is required.

- A **take-or-pay contract** requires one party to purchase a certain number of goods from the other party or else pay a penalty.

- **Sinking-fund requirements** for the retirement of noncurrent debt also are affected by the provisions of this pronouncement.

- Disclosure of the aggregate amount of **payments** for unconditional purchase obligations is required for recorded obligations for each of the 5 years following the date of the latest balance sheet presented.

Retail Method

Some entities, such as major retailers, have a high volume of transactions in relatively low-cost merchandise. They often use the retail method because it is applied to the dollar amounts of goods, not quantities. The result is **easier and less expensive estimates** of ending inventory and cost of goods sold.

Records of the beginning inventory and net purchases are maintained at both cost and retail. Sales at retail and any other appropriate items are subtracted from goods available for sale at retail (the sum of beginning inventory and net purchases at retail) to provide ending inventory at retail.

NOTE: The retail method is rarely tested on the CPA Exam.

Inventory Errors

These errors may have a material effect on current assets, working capital (Current assets – Current liabilities), cost of goods sold, net income, and equity. A common error is inappropriate timing of the recognition of transactions.

If a purchase on account is not recorded and the goods are not included in ending inventory, cost of goods sold (BI + Purchases – EI) and net income are unaffected. But current assets and current liabilities are understated.

If purchases and beginning inventory are properly recorded but items are excluded from ending inventory, cost of goods sold is overstated. Net income, inventory, retained earnings, working capital, and the current ratio are understated.

If the goods are properly included in ending inventory but the purchase is not recorded, net income is overstated because cost of goods sold is understated. Also, current liabilities are understated and working capital overstated.

Errors arising from recording transactions in the wrong period may reverse in the subsequent period.

- If ending inventory is overstated, the overstatement of net income will be offset by the understatement in the following year that results from the overstatement of beginning inventory.

An **overstatement error in year-end inventory** of the current year affects the financial statements of 2 different years.

- The **first year's** effects may be depicted as follows:

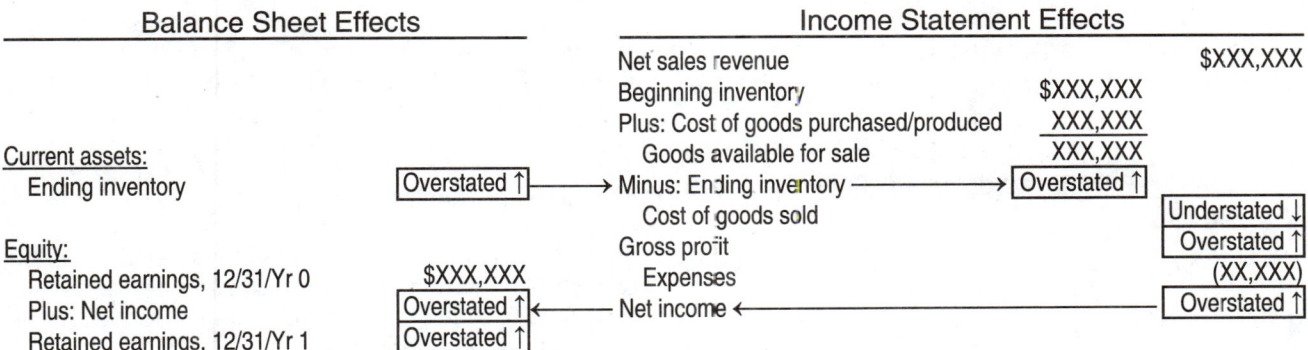

Figure 6-1

- At the end of the **second year**, retained earnings is correctly stated:

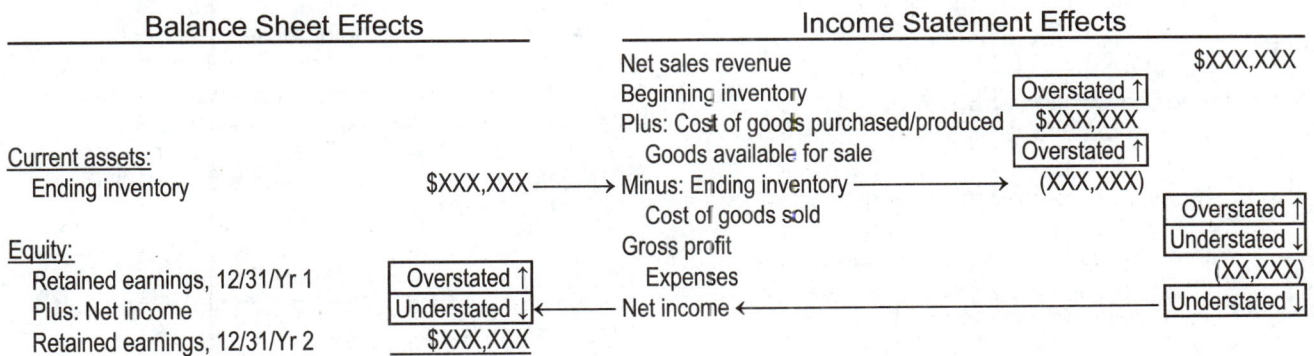

Figure 6-2

Stop & Review

You have completed the outline for this subunit.

Study multiple-choice questions 16 through 20 beginning on page 212.

Questions

6.1 Inventory Fundamentals

1. How should the following costs affect a retailer's inventory?

	Freight-in	Interest on Inventory Loan
A.	Increase	No Effect
B.	Increase	Increase
C.	No effect	Increase
D.	No effect	No effect

Answer (A) is correct.
Required: The effect of certain costs on inventory.
Discussion: Cost is "the sum of the applicable expenditures and charges directly or indirectly incurred in bringing an article to its existing condition and location." Freight costs are therefore an inventoriable cost to the extent they are not abnormal. However, interest cost for inventories is not capitalized. Interest cost is capitalized only for assets produced for an enterprise's own use or for sale or lease as discrete projects.

2. Herc Co.'s inventory at December 31, Year 1, was $1.5 million based on a physical count priced at cost, and before any necessary adjustment for the following:

- Merchandise costing $90,000 was shipped FOB shipping point from a vendor on December 30, Year 1, and was received and recorded on January 5, Year 2.

- Goods in the shipping area were excluded from inventory although shipment was not made until January 4, Year 2. The goods, billed to the customer FOB shipping point on December 30, Year 1, had a cost of $120,000.

What amount should Herc report as inventory in its December 31, Year 1, balance sheet?

A. $1,500,000

B. $1,590,000

C. $1,620,000

D. $1,710,000

Answer (D) is correct.
Required: The year-end inventory.
Discussion: The inventory balance prior to adjustments was $1.5 million. The merchandise shipped FOB shipping point to Herc should be included because title passed when the goods were shipped. The goods in the shipping area should be included because title did not pass until the goods were shipped in Year 2. Thus, inventory reported at December 31, Year 1, should be $1,710,000 ($1,500,000 + $90,000 + $120,000).

Answer (A) is incorrect. The amount of $1,500,000 excludes the $90,000 of goods shipped by a vendor and the $120,000 of goods not shipped until January 4.

Answer (B) is incorrect. The amount of $1,590,000 results from failing to include the $120,000 of goods not shipped until January 4.

Answer (C) is incorrect. The amount of $1,620,000 does not include the $90,000 of goods shipped by a vendor FOB shipping point.

6.2 Consignment Accounting

3. The following items were included in Opal Co.'s inventory account at December 31:

Merchandise out on consignment, at
  sales price, including 40% markup
  on selling price $40,000
Goods purchased, in transit,
  shipped FOB shipping point   36,000
Goods held on consignment by Opal   27,000

By what amount should Opal's inventory balance at December 31 be reduced?

A. $103,000

B. $67,000

C. $51,000

D. $43,000

✓ **Answer (D) is correct.**
Required: The recognition of inventory for consignment sales and goods in transit.
Discussion: Consigned goods are in the possession of the consignee but remain the property of the consignor and are included in the consignor's inventory count at cost, not selling price. Thus, Opal should reduce inventory by $16,000 ($40,000 selling price × 40%). Opal should also reduce inventory by $27,000 for the goods held on consignment. The goods in transit are properly included in inventory because title and risk of loss pass to the buyer at the shipping point when the shipping term is FOB shipping point. Consequently, inventory should be reduced by a total of $43,000 ($16,000 + $27,000).

✗ **Answer (A) is incorrect.** The cost of goods on consignment and the cost of the goods in transit are included in inventory.

✗ **Answer (B) is incorrect.** The cost of goods on consignment is included in inventory.

✗ **Answer (C) is incorrect.** The amount of $51,000 is the result of deducting the cost, not the markup, of the goods on consignment.

4. On October 20, Grimm Co. consigned 40 freezers to Holden Co. for sale at $1,000 each and paid $800 in transportation costs. On December 30, Holden reported the sale of 10 freezers and remitted $8,500. The remittance was net of the agreed 15% commission. What amount should Grimm recognize as consignment sales revenue for the year?

A. $7,700

B. $8,500

C. $9,800

D. $10,000

✓ **Answer (D) is correct.**
Required: The amount of consignment sales revenue to be recognized.
Discussion: Under a consignment sales agreement, the consignor ships merchandise to the consignee, who acts as agent for the consignor in selling the goods. The goods are in the physical possession of the consignee but remain the property of the consignor and are included in the consignor's inventory account. Accordingly, sales revenue from these consigned goods should be recognized by the consignor when the merchandise is sold (delivered to the ultimate customer). Grimm should recognize sales revenue of $10,000 ($1,000 sales price × 10 units). Transportation costs and commissions are consignor inventory costs and selling expenses, respectively, and are not used to compute sales revenue.

✗ **Answer (A) is incorrect.** The amount of $7,700 is the amount received from the consignee minus $800 of transportation costs.

✗ **Answer (B) is incorrect.** The amount of $8,500 is the amount received from the consignee.

✗ **Answer (C) is incorrect.** The amount of $9,800 equals the sales price of 10 freezers minus 25% (10 ÷ 40) of the transportation costs.

6.3 Cost Flow Methods -- Application

During January, Metro Co., which maintains a perpetual inventory system, recorded the following information pertaining to its inventory:

	Units	Unit Cost	Total Cost	Units On Hand
Balance on 1/1	1,000	$1	$1,000	1,000
Purchased on 1/7	600	3	1,800	1,600
Sold on 1/20	900			700
Purchased on 1/25	400	5	2,000	1,100

5. Under the moving-average method, what amount should Metro report as inventory at January 31?

A. $2,640

B. $3,225

C. $3,300

D. $3,900

✔ **Answer (B) is correct.**
Required: The ending inventory using the moving-average method.
Discussion: The moving-average system is only applicable to perpetual inventories. It requires that a new weighted average be computed after every purchase. This moving average is based on remaining inventory held and the new inventory purchased. Based on the calculations below, the moving-average cost per unit for the 1/20 sale is $1.75, and the cost of goods sold (COGS) for January is $1,575 (900 units sold × $1.75). Thus, ending inventory is $3,225 ($1,000 beginning balance + $1,800 purchase on 1/7 − $1,575 COGS on 1/20 + $2,000 purchase on 1/25).

	Units	Moving-Average Cost/Unit	Total Cost
Balance 1/1	1,000	$1.00	$1,000
Purchase 1/7	600	3.00	1,800
	1,600	$1.75	$2,800

✘ **Answer (A) is incorrect.** The amount of $2,640 is based on the weighted-average method.

✘ **Answer (C) is incorrect.** The amount of $3,300 is based on a cost of $3 being assigned to each unit in ending inventory.

✘ **Answer (D) is incorrect.** The amount of $3,900 is based on the FIFO method.

6. Under the LIFO method, what amount should Metro report as inventory at January 31?

A. $1,300

B. $2,700

C. $3,900

D. $4,100

✔ **Answer (B) is correct.**

Required: The ending inventory using a perpetual LIFO system.

Discussion: In a perpetual inventory system, purchases are directly recorded in the inventory account, and cost of goods sold (COGS) is determined as the goods are sold. Under LIFO, the latest goods purchased are assumed to be the first to be sold. Using LIFO perpetual, 600 of the 900 units sold on 1/20 are assumed to have come from the last purchase. Their cost was $1,800 (600 × $3). The remaining 300 came from the beginning balance at a cost of $300 (300 × $1). Hence, the total COGS for January was $2,100, and ending inventory must equal $2,700 ($1,000 beginning inventory + $1,800 purchase on 1/7 + $2,000 purchase on 1/25 − $2,100 COGS).

✘ **Answer (A) is incorrect.** The amount of $1,300 is based on the periodic LIFO method.

✘ **Answer (C) is incorrect.** The amount of $3,900 is based on the periodic FIFO method.

✘ **Answer (D) is incorrect.** The amount of $4,100 is based on an ending inventory of 400 units at $5 per unit and 700 units at $3 per unit.

7. Flex Co. uses a periodic inventory system. The following are inventory transactions for the month of January:

1/1	Beginning inventory	10,000 units at $3
1/5	Purchase	5,000 units at $4
1/15	Purchase	5,000 units at $5
1/20	Sales at $10 per unit	10,000 units

Flex uses the average pricing method to determine the value of its inventory. What amount should Flex report as cost of goods sold on its income statement for the month of January?

A. $30,000

B. $37,500

C. $40,000

D. $100,000

✔ **Answer (B) is correct.**

Required: The cost of goods sold using the average pricing method.

Discussion: The total cost of beginning inventory and purchases is $75,000 ($30,000 + $20,000 + $25,000), and the total number units of beginning inventory and purchases is 20,000. The average price of the beginning inventory and purchases is $3.75 ($75,000 cost ÷ 20,000 units). The total cost of goods sold equals $37,500 (10,000 units sold × $3.75).

✘ **Answer (A) is incorrect.** The amount of $30,000 is based on FIFO (10,000 units in beginning inventory × $3).

✘ **Answer (C) is incorrect.** The amount of $40,000 is based on the January 5 price.

✘ **Answer (D) is incorrect.** The amount of $100,000 is based on the selling price of the 10,000 units.

6.4 Cost Flow Methods -- Comparison

8. The UNO Company was formed on January 2, Year 1, to sell a single product. Over a 2-year period, UNO's costs increased steadily. Inventory quantities equaled 3 months' sales at December 31, Year 1, and zero at December 31, Year 2. Assuming the periodic system and **no** accounting changes, the inventory cost method that reports the highest amount for each of the following is

	Inventory 12/31/Year 1	Cost of Sales Year 2
A.	LIFO	FIFO
B.	LIFO	LIFO
C.	FIFO	FIFO
D.	FIFO	LIFO

✔ **Answer (C) is correct.**
Required: The method resulting in the highest beginning inventory and cost of sales given zero ending inventory.
Discussion: In a period of rising prices, FIFO inventory is higher than LIFO inventory. FIFO assumes that the latest and therefore the highest priced goods purchased are in inventory. But LIFO assumes that these goods were the first to be sold. Accordingly, the inventory at December 31, Year 1 (beginning inventory for Year 2), is higher for FIFO than LIFO. Given zero inventory at December 31, Year 2, the units sold in Year 2 must have equaled the sum of Year 2 purchases and beginning inventory. Because beginning inventory for Year 2 is reported at a higher amount under FIFO than LIFO, the result is a higher cost of goods sold under FIFO.

9. The Hastings Company began operations on January 1, Year 1, and uses the FIFO method in costing its raw material inventory. Management is contemplating a change to the LIFO method and is interested in determining what effect such a change will have on net income. Accordingly, the following information has been developed:

Final Inventory	Year 1	Year 2
FIFO	$240,000	$270,000
LIFO	200,000	210,000
Net income per FIFO	$120,000	$170,000

Based upon the above information, a change to the LIFO method in Year 2 results in net income for Year 2 of

A. $110,000

B. $150,000

C. $170,000

D. $230,000

✔ **Answer (B) is correct.**
Required: The second-year net income after a change from FIFO to LIFO in the second year of operations.
Discussion: A change in accounting principle requires retrospective application. All periods reported must be individually adjusted for the period-specific effects of applying the new principle. The difference in income in the second year is equal to the $20,000 difference between the FIFO inventory change and the LIFO inventory change (FIFO: $270,000 – $240,000 = $30,000 change; LIFO: $210,000 – $200,000 = $10,000 change; $30,000 – $10,000 = $20,000 difference). The $170,000 FIFO net income will decrease by $20,000. Net LIFO income will therefore be $150,000 ($170,000 – $20,000).

✘ **Answer (A) is incorrect.** The amount of $110,000 incorrectly subtracts the difference from Year 1 from the net income under LIFO for Year 2.

✘ **Answer (C) is incorrect.** The amount of $170,000 is the income for Year 2 under FIFO.

✘ **Answer (D) is incorrect.** The amount of $230,000 incorrectly adds the cumulative difference between LIFO and FIFO to FIFO net income instead of subtracting the difference from FIFO net income.

6.5 Dollar-Value LIFO

10. Bach Co. adopted the dollar-value LIFO inventory method as of January 1, Year 4. A single inventory pool and an internally computed price index are used to compute Bach's LIFO inventory layers. Information about Bach's dollar-value inventory follows:

	Inventory:	
Date	At Base-Year Cost	At Current-Year Cost
1/1/Year 4	$90,000	$90,000
Year 4 layer	20,000	30,000
Year 5 layer	40,000	80,000

What was the price index used to compute Bach's Year 5 dollar-value LIFO inventory layer?

A. 1.09

B. 1.25

C. 1.33

D. 2.00

✔ **Answer (C) is correct.**
Required: The price index used to compute the current year dollar-value LIFO inventory layer.
Discussion: To compute the ending inventory under dollar-value LIFO, the ending inventory stated in year-end or current-year cost must be restated at base-year cost. The layers at base-year cost are computed using a LIFO flow assumption and then weighted (multiplied) by the relevant indexes to price the ending inventory. A price index for the current year may be calculated by dividing the ending inventory at current-year cost by the ending inventory at base-year cost. This index is then applied to the current-year inventory layer stated at base-year cost. Thus, the Year 5 index (rounded) is 1.33 {[($90,000 + $30,000 + $80,000) EI at current-year cost] ÷ [($90,000 + $20,000 + $40,000) EI at base-year cost]}.

✘ **Answer (A) is incorrect.** The figure of 1.09 is the price index for Year 4.

✘ **Answer (B) is incorrect.** The figure of 1.25 is calculated by dividing the difference in the current-year cost of inventory layers for Year 4 and Year 5 by the Year 5 base-year cost.

✘ **Answer (D) is incorrect.** The figure of 2.00 equals the current year cost of the Year 5 layer divided by its base-year.

11. Walt Co. adopted the dollar-value LIFO inventory method as of January 1, when its inventory was valued at $500,000. Walt's entire inventory constitutes a single pool. Using a relevant price index of 1.10, Walt determined that its December 31 inventory was $577,500 at current-year cost and $525,000 at base-year cost. What was Walt's dollar-value LIFO inventory at December 31?

A. $525,000

B. $527,500

C. $552,500

D. $577,500

✔ **Answer (B) is correct.**
Required: The dollar-value LIFO inventory cost reported in the balance sheet.
Discussion: A price index for the current year may be calculated by dividing the ending inventory at current-year cost by the ending inventory at base-year cost. This index is then applied to the current-year inventory layer stated at base-year cost. Consequently, the index is 1.10 ($577,500 ÷ $525,000), and the dollar-value LIFO cost at December 31 is $527,500 {$500,000 base layer + [($525,000 – $500,000) × 1.10]}.

✘ **Answer (A) is incorrect.** The base-year cost is $525,000.

✘ **Answer (C) is incorrect.** The amount of $552,500 results from using $525,000 as the base layer.

✘ **Answer (D) is incorrect.** The amount of $577,500 is the year-end inventory at current cost.

6.6 Measurement of Inventory Subsequent to Initial Recognition

12. Lialia Co. has determined the cost of its fiscal year-end unfinished FIFO inventory to be $300,000. Information pertaining to that inventory at year-end is as follows:

Estimated selling price	$330,000
Estimated cost of disposal	20,000
Normal profit margin	15%
Current replacement cost	280,000
Estimated completion costs	15,000

What amount should Lialia report as inventory on its year-end balance sheet?

A. $295,000

B. $280,000

C. $300,000

D. $330,000

✔ **Answer (A) is correct.**
Required: The ending balance of inventory measured using FIFO.
Discussion: Inventory accounted for using the FIFO method (or any cost method other than LIFO or retail) is measured at the lower of cost or net realizable value (NRV). NRV is the estimated selling price in the ordinary course of business, minus reasonably predictable costs of completion, disposal, and transportation. At year-end, the NRV of the inventory of $295,000 ($330,000 estimated selling price – $15,000 estimated completion costs – $20,000 estimated costs of disposal) is lower than its cost of $300,000. Thus, the inventory is reported at its NRV of $295,000.

✘ **Answer (B) is incorrect.** If the inventory were accounted for under the LIFO or the retail inventory method, it would have been reported at its current replacement cost of $280,000.

✘ **Answer (C) is incorrect.** Inventory accounted for using the FIFO method is measured at the lower of cost or net realizable value (NRV). The NRV is lower than cost, so the inventory must be reported at its NRV.

✘ **Answer (D) is incorrect.** Inventory should not be reported at an amount greater than its historical cost.

13. Rose Co. sells one product and uses the last-in, first-out method to determine inventory cost. Information for the month of January follows:

	Total Units	Unit Cost
Beginning inventory, 1/1	8,000	$8.20
Purchases, 1/5	12,000	7.90
Sales	10,000	

Rose has determined that at January 31, the replacement cost of its inventory was $8 per unit, and the net realizable value was $8.80 per unit. Rose's normal profit margin is $1 per unit. Rose applies the lower-of-cost-or-market rule to total inventory and records any resulting loss. At January 31, what should be the net carrying amount of Rose's inventory?

A. $79,000

B. $78,000

C. $80,000

D. $81,400

✔ **Answer (C) is correct.**
Required: The net carrying amount of LIFO-based inventory.
Discussion: Subject to certain restrictions, inventory is valued at the lower of cost or market. Because Rose uses the LIFO method to determine inventory cost, the 10,000 units sold are treated as coming from the purchases made on 1/5. Thus, 2,000 units remain from the purchase, and 8,000 units remain from beginning inventory. The average cost of the remaining 10,000 units is $8.14 {[(8,000 × $8.20) + (2,000 × $7.90)] ÷ 10,000}. The replacement cost of $8, which exceeds NRV minus a normal profit ($8.80 – $1.00 = $7.80) but is lower than NRV ($8.80), is lower than the average cost of $8.14. Consequently, ending inventory on a LIFO-LCM basis is $80,000 (10,000 units × $8 replacement cost).

✘ **Answer (A) is incorrect.** The amount of $79,000 assumes that LCM was applied using the FIFO method.

✘ **Answer (B) is incorrect.** The amount of $78,000 equals 10,000 units times $7.80 (NRV – a normal profit).

✘ **Answer (D) is incorrect.** The amount of $81,400 is based on the assumption that average unit cost is below the unit replacement cost.

14. Based on a physical inventory taken on December 31, Chewy Co. determined its chocolate inventory on a LIFO basis at $26,000 with a replacement cost of $20,000. Chewy estimated that, after further processing costs of $12,000, the chocolate could be sold as finished candy bars for $40,000. Chewy's normal profit margin is 10% of sales. Under the lower-of-cost-or-market rule, what amount should Chewy report as chocolate inventory in its December 31 balance sheet?

A. $28,000

B. $26,000

C. $24,000

D. $20,000

✔ **Answer (C) is correct.**
Required: The LCM value of inventory.
Discussion: Under LIFO, inventory is measured at the lower of cost or market (LCM). Market equals current replacement cost subject to maximum and minimum values. The maximum is NRV, and the minimum is NRV minus normal profit. When replacement cost is within this range, it is used as market. Cost is given as $26,000. NRV is $28,000 ($40,000 selling price – $12,000 additional processing costs), and NRV minus a normal profit equals $24,000 [$28,000 – ($40,000 × 10%)]. Because the lowest amount in the range ($24,000) exceeds replacement cost ($20,000), it is used as market. Because market value ($24,000) is less than cost ($26,000), it is also the inventory amount.

✘ **Answer (A) is incorrect.** The NRV is $28,000.

✘ **Answer (B) is incorrect.** The cost is $26,000.

✘ **Answer (D) is incorrect.** The replacement cost is $20,000.

15. The original cost of an inventory item is above the replacement cost. The inventory item's replacement cost is above the net realizable value. Under the lower-of-cost-or-market method, the inventory item accounted for using the retail inventory method should be valued at

A. Original cost.

B. Replacement cost.

C. Net realizable value.

D. Net realizable value less normal profit margin.

✔ **Answer (C) is correct.**
Required: The measurement of an inventory item under the LCM method given that cost exceeds replacement cost and replacement cost exceeds NRV.
Discussion: Inventory accounted for using LIFO or the retail inventory method is measured at the lower of cost or market. Market is the current cost to replace inventory, subject to certain limitations. Market should not exceed a ceiling equal to net realizable value (NRV) or be less than a floor equal to NRV minus a normal profit margin. Because replacement cost exceeds NRV, the ceiling is NRV.

✘ **Answer (A) is incorrect.** The inventory item should be written down to market if its utility is no longer as great as its cost.

✘ **Answer (B) is incorrect.** Market should not exceed a ceiling equal to NRV.

✘ **Answer (D) is incorrect.** Net realizable value minus a normal profit margin is the minimum amount (the floor) for market.

6.7 Special Topics in Inventory Accounting

16. On December 30, Year 1, Astor Corp. sold merchandise for $75,000 to Day Co. The terms of the sale were net 30, FOB shipping point. The merchandise was shipped on December 31, Year 1, and arrived at Day on January 5, Year 2. Due to a clerical error, the sale was not recorded until January Year 2, and the merchandise, sold at a 25% markup, was included in Astor's inventory at December 31, Year 1. As a result, Astor's cost of goods sold for the year ended December 31, Year 1, was

   A. Understated by $75,000.

   B. Understated by $60,000.

   C. Understated by $15,000.

   D. Correctly stated.

✓ **Answer (B) is correct.**
Required: The cost of goods sold given delayed recording of a sale.
Discussion: Astor should have debited a receivable and credited sales for $75,000, the net amount, on the date of shipment. Astor also should have debited cost of sales and credited inventory at cost on the same date. Under the shipping terms, the sale should have been recognized on December 31, Year 1, because title and risk of loss passed to the buyer on that date; that is, an earning process was complete. The error therefore understated cost sales by $60,000 ($75,000 sales price ÷ 125% of cost).

✗ **Answer (A) is incorrect.** The selling price is $75,000.

✗ **Answer (C) is incorrect.** The amount of the markup is $15,000.

✗ **Answer (D) is incorrect.** Cost of goods was understated by $60,000.

17. Bren Co.'s beginning inventory at January 1 was understated by $26,000, and its ending inventory was overstated by $52,000. As a result, Bren's cost of goods sold for the year was

   A. Understated by $26,000.

   B. Overstated by $26,000.

   C. Understated by $78,000.

   D. Overstated by $78,000.

✓ **Answer (C) is correct.**
Required: The misstatement of cost of goods sold.
Discussion: When beginning inventory is understated, cost of goods sold will be understated. When ending inventory is overstated, cost of goods sold will be understated. Thus, Bren Co.'s cost of goods sold is understated by $78,000 ($26,000 + $52,000).

✗ **Answer (A) is incorrect.** The overstatement of ending inventory also understates cost of goods sold.

✗ **Answer (B) is incorrect.** COGS was understated in the current year by the amounts of both the beginning inventory error and the ending inventory error.

✗ **Answer (D) is incorrect.** Both errors understate cost of goods sold.

18. The following information was obtained from Smith Co.:

Sales	$275,000
Beginning inventory	30,000
Ending inventory	18,000

Smith's gross margin is 20%. What amount represents Smith purchases?

   A. $202,000

   B. $208,000

   C. $220,000

   D. $232,000

✓ **Answer (B) is correct.**
Required: The amount of purchases given the gross margin.
Discussion: Gross margin equals sales minus cost of goods sold. If it is 20% of sales, cost of goods sold equals $220,000 [$275,000 × (1.0 – .20)]. Cost of goods sold equals beginning inventory, plus purchases, minus ending inventory. Thus, purchases equals $208,000 ($220,000 COGS – $30,000 BI + $18,000 EI).

✗ **Answer (A) is incorrect.** Cost of goods sold minus ending inventory equals $202,000.

✗ **Answer (C) is incorrect.** Cost of goods sold equals $220,000.

✗ **Answer (D) is incorrect.** The amount of $232,000 equals cost of goods sold plus beginning inventory, minus ending inventory.

19. On January 1, Year 4, Card Corp. signed a 3-year, noncancelable purchase contract that allows Card to purchase up to 500,000 units of a computer part annually from Hart Supply Co. The price is $.10 per unit, and the contract guarantees a minimum annual purchase of 100,000 units. During Year 4, the part unexpectedly became obsolete. Card had 250,000 units of this inventory at December 31, Year 4, and believes these parts can be sold as scrap for $.02 per unit. What amount of probable loss from the purchase commitment should Card report in its Year 4 income statement?

A. $24,000

B. $20,000

C. $16,000

D. $8,000

✓ **Answer (C) is correct.**
Required: The amount of probable loss from the purchase commitment.
Discussion: The entity must accrue a loss in the current year on goods subject to a firm purchase commitment if their market price declines below the commitment price. This loss should be measured in the same manner as inventory losses. Disclosure of the loss also is required. Consequently, given that 200,000 units must be purchased over the next 2 years for $20,000 (200,000 × $.10), and the parts can be sold as scrap for $4,000 (200,000 × $.02), the amount of probable loss for Year 4 is $16,000 ($20,000 – $4,000).

✗ **Answer (A) is incorrect.** The amount of $24,000 includes the purchase commitment for the current year.

✗ **Answer (B) is incorrect.** The amount of $20,000 excludes the net realizable value of the parts from the calculation.

✗ **Answer (D) is incorrect.** The amount of $8,000 excludes the probable loss expected in the last year of the purchase commitment.

20. Fireworks, Inc., had an explosion in its plant that destroyed most of its inventory. Its records show that beginning inventory was $40,000. Fireworks made purchases of $480,000 and sales of $620,000 during the year. Its normal gross profit percentage is 25%. It can sell some of its damaged inventory for $5,000. The insurance company will reimburse Fireworks for 70% of its loss. What amount should Fireworks report as loss from the explosion?

A. $50,000

B. $35,000

C. $18,000

D. $15,000

✓ **Answer (D) is correct.**
Required: The loss from destruction of inventory.
Discussion: The loss from the destruction of inventory equals the cost of the damaged inventory minus any sales of the damaged inventory and insurance proceeds.

Beginning inventory	$ 40,000
Purchases	480,000
Cost of goods sold [$620,000 × (1.0 – .25)]	(465,000)
Estimated inventory	$ 55,000
NRV	(5,000)
Loss before insurance proceeds	$ 50,000
Insurance ($50,000 × 70%)	(35,000)
Reported loss	$ 15,000

✗ **Answer (A) is incorrect.** The loss without regard to the insurance proceeds equals $50,000.

✗ **Answer (B) is incorrect.** The insurance proceeds equal $35,000.

✗ **Answer (C) is incorrect.** The estimated selling price of damaged inventory should be included in the calculation of a loss.

Study Unit Seven

Property, Plant, Equipment, and Depletable Resources

(27 pages of outline)

7.1 Initial Measurement of Property, Plant, and Equipment (PPE)

Definition

These assets are called property, plant, and equipment; fixed assets; or plant assets. They provide benefits from their use in the production of goods and services, not from their consumption.

- PPE are tangible. They have physical existence.

- PPE may be either **personal property** (something movable, e.g., equipment) or **real property** (such as land or a building).

- PPE are used in the **ordinary operations** of an entity and are not held primarily for investment, resale, or inclusion in another product. But they are often sold.

- PPE are **noncurrent**. They are not expected to be used up within 1 year or the normal operating cycle of the business, whichever is longer.

Carrying Amount

The carrying amount of an item of PPE is the amount at which it is presented in the financial statements. This amount is equal to the historical cost minus accumulated depreciation and impairment losses.

Historical or initial cost	$XXX
Accumulated depreciation	(XXX)
Impairment losses	(XXX)
Asset's carrying amount	$XXX

Types of PPE

Types of PPE include the following:

- **Land**

- **Buildings**

- **Land improvements**, such as landscaping, drainage, streets, street lighting, sewers, sidewalks, parking lots, driveways, and fences

- **Machinery and equipment**, such as furniture, fixtures (personal property permanently attached to real property, such as a central heating system), and vehicles

- **Leasehold improvements**, such as buildings constructed on, and other modifications made to, the leased property by a lessee

- **Internally constructed assets**

- **Miscellaneous items**, such as tools, patterns and dies, and returnable containers

Relevant Accounting Principles

PPE are initially measured at **historical cost**, which consists of

- The amount paid to acquire the asset and

- The costs needed to bring the asset to the condition and location necessary for its intended use.

  - The initial measurement embraces all other costs to acquire PPE, transport them to the sites of their intended use, and prepare them for operations.

  - Freight-in (transportation-in), installation costs, renovation or reconditioning costs, expenses of tests or trial runs, and insurance and taxes during the preoperations period are capitalized to the initial cost of the asset.

Historical cost is adjusted for changes in utility over the life of the asset, e.g., depreciation and impairment.

- In general, expenses should be recognized at the time related revenues are earned.

- However, no direct relationship ordinarily exists between the consumption of service potential and specific revenues. Thus, the **depreciation expense** must be **systematically and rationally allocated** to periods expected to be benefited.

Depreciation does not start until PPE are placed in operation and begin to contribute economic benefits.

Under GAAP, PPE are not revalued upward to reflect appraisal, market, current, or fair values that are above historical cost (or carrying amount) of PPE.

Success Tip

The AICPA often tests candidates' knowledge of the initial measurement of PPE with both conceptual and calculation questions. A common format for calculation questions gives information about the noncurrent asset and asks for the amount at which the asset should be initially recorded.

Initial Costs -- Land

The costs of acquiring and preparing land for its expected use are capitalized.

The price should include not only the cash price but also any **encumbrances assumed** (such as mortgages or tax liens).

The cost of land also includes **transaction costs**, e.g., surveying costs, legal fees, brokers' commissions, title insurance, and escrow fees.

Site preparation costs [clearing, draining, filling, leveling the property, and razing existing buildings, minus any proceeds (such as timber sales)] are costs of the land, not of the building to be constructed on the land.

Certain **permanent improvements** of the land made by the entity that have **indefinite lives** are debited to the land account.

Land has an indefinite useful life and therefore is **not depreciated**.

Initial Costs -- Land Improvements

Land improvements with **finite useful lives** that are maintained and replaced by the reporting entity are capitalized separately from land and depreciated.

Initial Costs -- Buildings

The costs that are necessary to the purchase or construction of a building and that will result in future economic benefits should be capitalized. These include

- The **purchase price**, including any liens assumed by the purchaser, etc.

- Costs of **renovating and preparing the structure** for its expected use.

- The expenses of **excavating the site** to build the foundation (but not site preparation costs).

  - The **costs of razing an old building** are either debited to the land account or treated as an adjustment of a gain or loss on disposal. The accounting depends on whether the land was purchased as a site for the new structure or the old building was previously used in the entity's operations.

  - The **carrying amount of an existing building** previously used in the entity's operations is not included in the cost of the new structure. It will not produce future benefits.

- The materials, labor, and overhead **costs of construction**

- Interest costs incurred during construction of a building for an entity's own use should be capitalized. (The outline for capitalization of interest is in Subunit 7.2.)

Initial Costs -- Machinery and Equipment

Costs include

- Purchase price (including sales taxes)
- Freight-in, handling, insurance, and storage until use begins
- Preparation, installation, and start-up costs, such as testing and trial runs

Example 7-1	Initial Cost of Equipment

On January 1, Year 1, an entity purchased a machine to be used in production. The machine was installed and ready for its intended use on July 1, Year 1. The following costs were incurred during Year 1:

Purchase price	$100,000
Year 1 insurance costs incurred evenly throughout year	10,000
Shipping costs	3,000
Installation costs	4,000
Testing costs	2,500

The historical (initial) cost of the machine is **$114,500** [$100,000 + ($10,000 × 0.5) + $3,000 + $4,000 + $2,500]. The $5,000 of insurance costs for the 6 months after the machine is ready for its intended use (after July 1, Year 1) should be expensed, not capitalized, as part of the machine's initial cost.

Initial Costs -- Leasehold Improvements

Leasehold improvements, such as buildings constructed on leased land, are accounted for by the lessee in the same way as property to which title is held. However, the term of the lease may limit the depreciation period.

If the useful life of the asset extends beyond the lease term and lease renewal is reasonably certain, the amortization period may include all or part of the renewal period. If renewal is uncertain, the useful life is the remaining term of the lease.

Other Factors Affecting Initial Measurement

Acquisition in exchange for a noncurrent obligation. If an item of PPE is acquired in exchange for a noncurrent note, its cost is the present value of the consideration paid (the note). But the note's interest rate may be unstated or unreasonable, or the face amount may differ materially from the cash price of the PPE or the market value of the note. In these cases, the cost of the PPE should be the more clearly determinable of the cash price of the PPE or the market value of the note.

Donated assets. In general, contributions received should be recognized as (1) revenues or gains in the period of receipt and (2) assets, or decreases in liabilities or expenses. They are measured at fair value.

PPE	$XXX	
Contribution revenue		$XXX

Acquisition of a Group of Assets (Lump-Sum Purchase)

When two or more assets are acquired for a single price, the cost must be allocated to the individual assets in the group.

- Allocation is based on the **relative fair values** of the assets acquired.

Example 7-2   Acquisition of a Group of Assets

Mike Co. paid a lump-sum purchase price of $100,000 to acquire the following assets:

Assets Acquired	Fair Value
Building	$ 72,000
Machine	36,000
Inventory	12,000
	$120,000

The lump-sum cost of the assets of $100,000 is allocated to the individual assets acquired based on their relative fair values.

Assets Acquired	Fair Value	Relative % of the Total Fair Value	Allocated Cost
Building	$ 72,000	60%	$ 60,000 = $100,000 × 60%
Machine	36,000	30%	30,000 = $100,000 × 30%
Inventory	12,000	10%	10,000 = $100,000 × 10%
	$120,000	100%	$100,000

Stop & Review

You have completed the outline for this subunit.

Study multiple-choice questions 1 through 3 beginning on page 242.

7.2 Internally Constructed Assets (ICAs) -- Capitalization of Interest

Capitalization of Interest

The costs necessary to bring an asset to the condition and location of its intended use are part of the historical cost. **Interest incurred during construction** is such a cost and must be capitalized as part of an asset's initial cost. An imputed cost of equity capital is not recognized.

Qualifying Assets

Qualifying assets are assets for which interest must be capitalized. The following are qualifying assets:

- Assets that are constructed or produced by the entity for its own use

- Assets that are constructed or produced for the entity by others for which deposits or progress payments have been made

- Assets that are constructed or produced for sale or lease as separate projects, such as real estate developments or ships

Nonqualifying Assets

The following are assets for which interest must not be capitalized (nonqualifying assets):

- Inventories routinely produced in large quantities on a repetitive basis

- Assets in use or ready for their intended use in earning activities

- Assets not being used in earning activities that are not undergoing the activities necessary to ready them for use

Capitalization Period for Interest Costs

This period is the time required to carry out the activities necessary to bring a qualifying asset to the condition and location necessary for its intended use.

The period begins and continues as long as

- Expenditures for a qualifying asset are being made,

- Activities necessary to make the asset ready for its intended use (i.e., construction) are in progress, and

- Interest cost is being incurred.

Capitalization ends when the asset is substantially complete and ready for its intended use. Also, interest capitalization must cease if substantially all asset-related activities are suspended.

Limitation on Capitalized Interest

Interest cost includes interest (1) on obligations with explicit interest rates (including amortization of issue costs and discount or premium), (2) imputed on certain payables, and (3) on a finance lease.

Capitalizable interest is limited to the **amount theoretically avoidable** if expenditures for ICAs had not been made. For example, if the entity had not incurred costs for ICAs, it might have used the funds to repay debt or to avoid issuing new debts.

Interest capitalized may not exceed the actual total interest cost incurred during the period.

Interest earned on borrowed funds is ordinarily not offset against interest cost to determine either capitalization rates or limitations on interest costs to be capitalized.

Amount of Interest to be Capitalized

Capitalized interest equals the weighted **average accumulated expenditures (AAE)** for the qualifying asset during the capitalization period times the interest rate(s). The weighting is based on the time expenditures incurred interest.

If a specific new borrowing outstanding during the period can be identified with the asset, the rate on that obligation may be applied to the extent that the AAE do not exceed the amount borrowed.

To the extent that AAE exceed the amount of specific new borrowings, a weighted-average rate must be applied that is based on other (not the specific) borrowings outstanding during the period.

Example 7-3	Capitalization of Interest

Lyssa Co. constructed a building for its own use. The capitalization period began on 1/1/Year 1 and ended on 12/31/Year 1. The AAE are based on the following construction-related expenditures and the amounts of time they incurred interest:

	Quarter Beginning			AAE
1/1/Year 1:	$500,000 ×	(12 ÷ 12)	=	$ 500,000
4/1/Year 1:	$400,000 ×	(9 ÷ 12)	=	300,000
7/1/Year 1:	$600,000 ×	(6 ÷ 12)	=	300,000
10/1/Year 1:	$400,000 ×	(3 ÷ 12)	=	100,000
12/31/Year 1:	$900,000 ×	(0 ÷ 12)	=	0
				$1,200,000

On 1/1/Year 1, Lyssa specifically borrowed $1,000,000 at a rate of 10% to finance the construction. Its other borrowings outstanding during the entire construction period consisted of a $2,000,000 bond issue bearing 8% interest and a $6,000,000 bond issue bearing 9%. All interest is paid at fiscal year end. Accordingly, the weighted-average rate on other borrowings is 8.75%.

		Interest	Principal	Rate
$2,000,000 × 8%	=	$160,000	$2,000,000	
$6,000,000 × 9%	=	540,000	6,000,000	
		$700,000 ÷	$8,000,000	= 8.75%

Total actual interest cost for the fiscal year is $800,000.

$1,000,000 × 10%	=	$100,000
$2,000,000 × 8%	=	160,000
$6,000,000 × 9%	=	540,000
		$800,000

The AAE for the qualifying asset ($1,200,000) exceed the amount of specific borrowing associated with that asset ($1,000,000). The capitalization rate to be applied to this excess ($1,200,000 – $1,000,000 = $200,000) must be the weighted average of rates applicable to other borrowings of Lyssa (8.75%). Thus, the amount of avoidable interest is $117,500.

$1,000,000 × 10%		=	$100,000
($1,200,000 – $1,000,000) × 8.75%		=	17,500
			$117,500

The amount of $117,500 is capitalized as part of the initial cost of the building because it is less than actual interest.

Interest expense recognized in Year 1 is $682,500 ($800,000 – $117,500).

Disclosures

If no interest cost is capitalized, the amount incurred and expensed during the period should be reported. If some interest cost is capitalized, the total incurred and the amount capitalized should be disclosed.

Stop & Review

You have completed the outline for this subunit.

Study multiple-choice questions 4 and 5 beginning on page 243.

7.3   Subsequent Expenditures for PPE

Accounting Issues

The issues are to determine whether subsequent expenditures should be capitalized or expensed and to determine the accounting methods to be used.

Capital expenditures are capitalized. They provide additional benefits by improving the quality of services rendered by the asset, extending its useful life, or increasing its output.

Revenue expenditures (expenses) maintain an asset's normal service capacity.

- These costs are recurring, are not expected to benefit future periods, and are expensed when incurred.

- An entity usually specifies a materiality threshold below which all costs are expensed, thereby avoiding the burden of depreciating immaterial amounts.

Additions

Substantial expenditures for extensions or expansions of existing assets are **capitalized**. An example is an additional floor for a building.

If the addition is essentially a separate asset, it is recorded in a separate account and depreciated over its own useful life. Otherwise, the addition should be debited to the original asset account and depreciated over the life of that asset.

The basic entry is

Asset (new or old)	$XXX	
Cash, etc.		$XXX

Replacements and Improvements (Betterments)

A **replacement** substitutes a new component of an asset for a similar one, for example, a tile roof for a tile roof. But an **improvement** substitutes a better component, such as a more efficient heating system.

Substitution method. If the old component was recorded separately, e.g., recording a central air conditioning system separately from the building, the procedure is to remove it from the ledger, along with accumulated depreciation, and to **substitute the cost of the new component**. A loss may be recognized.

- The new component will be depreciated over the shorter of its useful life or that of the entire asset.

- The basic entry is

New asset	$XXX	
Accumulated depreciation of old asset	XXX	
Loss	XXX	
Old asset		$XXX
Cash, etc.		XXX

If (1) the component replaced or improved has not been separately accounted for or (2) the old component has been modified, the substitution method is not used.

- If the replacement or improvement increases the asset's service potential but does not extend its estimated useful life, the asset is debited. The carrying amount of the old component is not removed.

- If the replacement or improvement primarily extends the useful life without enhancing service potential, the entry is to debit accumulated depreciation. The expenditure is a recovery of depreciation, not an increase in the quality of service.

Accumulated depreciation	$XXX	
Cash, etc.		$XXX

Rearrangements, Reinstallations, Relocations

Rearranging the configuration of plant assets, reinstalling such assets, or relocating operations may require material outlays that are separable from recurring expenses and provide probable future benefits.

The **substitution method** of accounting for these costs may be used if the original installation costs and accumulated depreciation **are known**.

Otherwise, if these costs are material, they should be debited to a new account and amortized over the period benefited.

Relocation (moving) costs often are expensed as incurred.

Repairs and Maintenance

Routine, **minor expenditures** made to maintain the operating efficiency of PPE are **ordinarily expensed as incurred**. However, as the amounts involved become more significant and the benefits to future periods increase, treatment of a **major repair as an addition, etc.**, may be more appropriate.

Although a repair or maintenance cost ordinarily should be allocated to a single annual period only, its full recognition at the interim date when incurred may distort the interim statements.

- Accordingly, an anticipated repair or maintenance cost may be allocated to the interim periods that will benefit.

Summary

Action	Accounting Treatment	
Additions	Debit separate asset or debit old asset	
Replacements/Improvements – Carrying Amount Known	Substitution method	
Replacements/Improvements – Carrying Amount Not Known	Increase service potential only: debit asset	Extend useful life only: debit accumulated depreciation
Rearrangements/Reinstallations	Cost known: substitution method	Otherwise, material costs debited to new asset
Repairs	Minor: expense	Major: treatment as addition, etc.

Stop & Review

You have completed the outline for this subunit.
Study multiple-choice questions 6 and 7 beginning on page 244.

7.4 Depreciation Methods -- Calculations

Success Tip

CPA candidates can expect to answer questions that test depreciation concepts. CPA Exam questions often ask for depreciation calculations but not in the manner of simply calculating the depreciation amount using a depreciation method. The question may state that the useful life of the asset has increased/decreased and ask for the amount of accumulated depreciation.

Definition

Depreciation is the process of systematically and rationally **allocating the depreciable base** of a tangible capital asset over its expected useful life.

- It is not a process of valuation.

The periodic depreciation expense is recognized in the income statement. Accumulated depreciation is a contra-asset account. The journal entry is

Depreciation expense	$XXX	
Accumulated depreciation		$XXX

An asset's **depreciable base** is the total amount that is to be systematically and rationally allocated.

Depreciable base = Historical cost – Salvage value – Recognized impairment loss

- **The estimated useful life** is an estimated period over which services (economic benefits) are expected to be obtained from the use of the asset.

- **Salvage value** is the amount that an entity expects to obtain from disposal of the asset at the end of the asset's useful life.

Example 7-4	Depreciable Base of an Asset

Jayhawk Co. recently acquired a robot to be used in its fully automated factory for a purchase price of $850,000. Jayhawk spent another $150,000 installing and testing the robot. The company estimates that the robot will have a 5-year useful life and can be sold at the end of that time for $100,000.

The depreciable base for this asset is calculated as follows:

Purchase price	$ 850,000
Installation and testing	150,000
Historical cost	$1,000,000
Estimated salvage value	(100,000)
Depreciable base	$ 900,000

The depreciation method chosen should reflect the pattern in which economic benefits (services) from the assets are expected to be received. The chosen method allocates the cost of the asset as equitably as possible to the periods during which services (economic benefits) are obtained from the use of the asset.

Depreciation Methods -- Straight-Line

Straight-line depreciation is the simplest method because an equal amount of depreciation is charged to each period of the asset's useful life.

- The easiest way to calculate straight-line depreciation is to divide the depreciable base by the estimated useful life.

Periodic expense = Depreciable base ÷ Estimated useful life

- The straight-line percentage is 100% divided by the number of years in the asset's estimated useful life.

Example 7-5   Straight-Line Depreciation Method

If Jayhawk applies the straight-line method, depreciation expense over the life of the asset will be calculated as follows:

	Depreciable Base	Divided by: Estimated Useful Life	Equals: Depreciation Expense	Accumulated Depreciation	Carrying Amount, End of Year
Year 1:	$900,000	5	$180,000	$180,000	$820,000
Year 2:	900,000	5	180,000	360,000	640,000
Year 3:	900,000	5	180,000	540,000	460,000
Year 4:	900,000	5	180,000	720,000	280,000
Year 5:	900,000	5	180,000	900,000	100,000
Total			$900,000		

The straight-line percentage for Jayhawk's new robot is 20% (100% ÷ 5-year estimated useful life).

Depreciation Methods -- Declining Balance

Accelerated methods were popularized when they became allowable on tax returns. But the same method need not be used for tax and financial statement purposes.

- Accelerated methods are time-based. They result in decreasing depreciation charges over the life of the asset. The two major time-based methods are declining balance and sum-of-the-years'-digits.

Declining balance determines depreciation expense by multiplying the carrying amount (not the depreciable base equal to cost minus salvage value) at the beginning of each period by some percentage (e.g., 200% or 150%) of the straight-line rate of depreciation.

Periodic expense = Carrying amount × Declining-balance percentage

- The carrying amount decreases by the depreciation recognized. The result is the use of a constant rate against a declining balance.

- Salvage value is ignored in determining the carrying amount, but the asset is not depreciated below salvage value.

Example 7-6	Declining-Balance Depreciation Method

If Jayhawk applies double-declining-balance (DDB) depreciation to the robot, the declining-balance percentage will be 40% (20% straight-line rate × 2). Depreciation expense over the life of the asset will be calculated as follows:

	Carrying Amount, First of Year	Times: DDB Rate	Equals: Depreciation Expense	Accumulated Depreciation	Carrying Amount, End of Year
Year 1:	$1,000,000	40%	$400,000	$400,000	$600,000
Year 2:	600,000	40%	240,000	640,000	360,000
Year 3:	360,000	40%	144,000	784,000	216,000
Year 4:	216,000	40%	86,400	870,400	129,600
Year 5:	129,600	40%	29,600*	900,000	100,000
			$900,000		

*Year 5 depreciation expense is $29,600 because the carrying amount cannot be less than salvage value.

Depreciation Methods -- Sum-of-the-Years'-Digits

Sum-of-the-years'-digits (SYD) multiplies not the carrying amount but the constant depreciable base (cost minus salvage value) by a declining fraction. It is a declining-rate, declining-charge method.

$$\text{Periodic expense} = \text{Depreciable base} \times \frac{\text{Remaining years in useful life}}{\text{Sum of all years in useful life}}$$

Example 7-7	Sum-of-the-Years'-Digits Depreciation Method

If Jayhawk applies sum-of-the-years'-digits depreciation, the denominator of the SYD fraction is 15 (1 + 2 + 3 + 4 + 5). Depreciation expense over the life of the asset will be calculated as follows:

	Depreciable Base	SYD Fraction	Depreciation Expense	Accumulated Depreciation	Carrying Amount, Year End
Year 1:	$900,000	(5 ÷ 15)	$300,000	$300,000	$700,000
Year 2:	900,000	(4 ÷ 15)	240,000	540,000	460,000
Year 3:	900,000	(3 ÷ 15)	180,000	720,000	280,000
Year 4:	900,000	(2 ÷ 15)	120,000	840,000	160,000
Year 5:	900,000	(1 ÷ 15)	60,000	900,000	100,000
			$900,000		

Depreciation Methods -- Usage-Centered

Usage-centered activity methods calculate depreciation as a function of an asset's use rather than the time it has been held.

The **units-of-output method** allocates cost based on production. As production varies, so will the depreciation expense.

$$\text{Periodic depreciation expense} = \text{Depreciable base} \times \frac{\text{Units produced during current period}}{\text{Estimated total lifetime units}}$$

Example 7-8   Units-of-Production Depreciation Method

On the date of purchase, Jayhawk anticipated that the robot would produce 8,000 units of product over its 5-year life. In actuality, the robot produced the following:

Year 1	Year 2	Year 3	Year 4	Year 5	Total
2,300 units	2,000 units	1,800 units	1,200 units	700 units	8,000 units

Depreciation expense over the life of the asset will be calculated as follows:

	Depreciable Base	Times: Units-of-Production Fraction	Equals: Depreciation Expense	Accumulated Depreciation	Carrying Amount, Year End
Year 1:	$900,000	(2,300 ÷ 8,000)	$258,750	$258,750	$741,250
Year 2:	900,000	(2,000 ÷ 8,000)	225,000	483,750	516,250
Year 3:	900,000	(1,800 ÷ 8,000)	202,500	686,250	313,750
Year 4:	900,000	(1,200 ÷ 8,000)	135,000	821,250	178,750
Year 5:	900,000	(700 ÷ 8,000)	78,750	900,000	100,000
Total			$900,000		

Group and Composite Depreciation

These methods apply **straight-line** accounting to a collection of assets depreciated as if they were a single asset. The composite method applies to groups of **dissimilar assets** with varying useful lives, and the group method applies to **similar assets**. They provide an efficient way to account for large numbers of depreciable assets. They also result in the offsetting of under- and overstated depreciation estimates.

Each method calculates (1) the total depreciable cost (Total acquisition cost – Salvage value) for all the assets debited to a control account, (2) the weighted-average estimated useful life (Total depreciable cost ÷ Total annual straight-line depreciation), and (3) the weighted-average depreciation rate based on cost (Total annual straight-line depreciation ÷ Total acquisition cost). One accumulated depreciation account also is maintained.

Early and late retirements are expected to offset each other. Thus, gains and losses on retirements of single assets are not recognized but are treated as adjustments of accumulated depreciation. The entry is

Cash (proceeds)	$XXX	
Asset (cost)		$XXX
Accumulated depreciation (dr. or cr.)		XXX

Periodic depreciation equals the weighted-average rate times the beginning balance of the asset account for the period. Thus, depreciation is calculated based on the cost of assets in use during the period. Prior-period retirements are reflected in this balance.

Example 7-9   Composite Depreciation Method

For its first year of operations, Argent Co. used the composite method of depreciation and prepared the following schedule of machinery owned:

	Total Cost	Estimated Salvage Value	Estimated Life in Years
Machine X	$320,000	$40,000	20
Machine Y	180,000	20,000	10
Machine Z	80,000	--	8

Argent computes depreciation using the straight-line method. The composite or average useful life of the assets is essentially a weighted average. As illustrated below, the annual straight-line depreciation for each asset should be calculated. The total cost, estimated salvage value, and depreciable base of the assets should then be computed. Dividing the composite depreciable base ($520,000) by the total annual straight-line depreciation ($40,000) gives the composite life (13 years) of these assets.

	Total Cost	Estimated Salvage Value	Depreciable Base	Est. Life	Annual S-L Dep.
Machine X	$320,000	$40,000	$280,000	20	$14,000
Machine Y	180,000	20,000	160,000	10	16,000
Machine Z	80,000	0	80,000	8	10,000
	$580,000	$60,000	$520,000		$40,000

The average composite rate is 6.9% ($40,000 total annual straight-line depreciation ÷ $580,000 total cost).

Depreciation for a Fractional Period

An asset is most likely to be acquired or disposed of at a time other than the beginning or end of a fiscal year. Thus, depreciation may need to be calculated for a fraction of a period. Time-based methods most often compute depreciation to the nearest month of a partial year, but other conventions also are permitted.

Example 7-10	Depreciation for a Fractional Period

Using the data from Example 7-4, assume that Jayhawk purchased the robot on October 1, Year 1. Using the straight-line depreciation method, the annual depreciation expense is $180,000 ($900,000 ÷ 5 years). Thus, the depreciation expense recognized in Year 1 is $45,000 [$180,000 × (3 months ÷ 12 months)]. Annual depreciation expense recognized in Years 2 through 5 is $180,000. Depreciation expense recognized in Year 6 is $135,000 [$180,000 × (9 months ÷ 12 months)].

Each entity might have different policies for depreciation of a fractional period. For example,

- A full year's depreciation may be recognized in the year of acquisition and none in the year of disposal or vice versa.

- Depreciation may be recognized to the nearest full year or the nearest half-year.

- A half-year's depreciation may be recognized in both the year of acquisition and the year of disposal.

Disclosure

Full disclosure should be made of depreciation methods and practices, including

- Depreciation expense for the period
- Balances of major classes of depreciable assets by nature or function
- Accumulated depreciation either by major class or in total
- Description of depreciation methods for each major class of assets

Stop & Review

You have completed the outline for this subunit.
Study multiple-choice questions 8 and 9 beginning on page 245.

7.5 Depreciation Methods -- Changes and Comparison

Effects on Net Income

Because the accelerated methods charge higher amounts to depreciation expense in the earlier years of an asset's economic life, those methods result in lower net income than the straight-line method in those years.

Effects of Accounting Changes

A change in the estimates for depreciation is accounted for prospectively (from the beginning of the period in which the change in estimate was made). The new estimates are used in the year of the change, and no "catch-up" amounts are recorded.

Example 7-11	Change in Estimates for Depreciation

On January 2, Year 1, a company purchased a machine for $500,000 and depreciated it by the straight-line method using an estimated useful life of 10 years with no salvage value. On January 2, Year 4, the company determined that the machine had a useful life of 6 years from the date of acquisition and will have a salvage value of $20,000. An accounting change was made in Year 4 to reflect the additional data.

For Years 1 through 3, the amount of depreciation was $50,000 per year ($500,000 depreciable base ÷ 10 years estimated useful life), resulting in a balance of accumulated depreciation at December 31, Year 3, of $150,000 ($50,000 × 3 years). The company calculates the new depreciable base as follows:

Historical cost	$500,000
Revised salvage value	(20,000)
Revised depreciable base	$480,000
Balance of accumulated depreciation, 1/1/Year 4	(150,000)
Remaining depreciable base, 1/1/Year 4	$330,000

Annual depreciation for the remaining years of the machine's estimated life is $110,000 ($330,000 depreciable base ÷ 3 years estimated remaining useful life).

Stop & Review

You have completed the outline for this subunit.

Study multiple-choice questions 10 and 11 beginning on page 246.

7.6 Disposals of PPE

Procedures

Depreciation is recorded up to the time of disposal so that periodic depreciation expense is not understated and the carrying amount of the asset is not overstated.

The asset's carrying amount is removed from the accounts by eliminating the asset, its accumulated depreciation, and any other valuation account.

Any consideration (proceeds) received is debited appropriately.

Gain or loss is recognized for the difference between the proceeds received and the carrying amount of an asset.

Sale

Accounting for a cash sale of PPE (including a scrap sale) is straightforward.

- Depreciation, if any, is recognized to the date of sale, the carrying amount is removed from the books, the proceeds are recorded, and any gain or loss is recognized.

Example 7-12	Disposal of an Item of PPE

A company sold a machine with a carrying amount of $100,000 ($180,000 historical cost − $80,000 accumulated depreciation) for $135,000 in cash. The gain on disposal recognized is $35,000 ($135,000 − $100,000). The journal entry is

Cash	$135,000	
Accumulated depreciation	80,000	
Machine		$180,000
Gain on disposal		35,000

If the machine were sold for $90,000 in cash, the loss on disposal recognized would be $10,000 ($90,000 − $100,000). The journal entry would be

Cash	$90,000	
Accumulated depreciation	80,000	
Loss on disposal	10,000	
Machine		$180,000

Abandonment

An asset to be abandoned is disposed of when it is no longer used.

If the asset to be abandoned is still in use, it is normally not immediately written down to zero. Continued use indicates that the asset has service potential. However, depreciation estimates should be revised to account for the reduced service period.

- A noncurrent asset that is temporarily idled is not treated as abandoned.

Involuntary Conversion

An item of PPE is involuntarily converted when it is (1) lost through a casualty (flood, earthquake, fire, etc.), (2) expropriated (seized by a foreign government), or (3) condemned (through the governmental power of eminent domain).

- The accounting is the same as for other nonexchange dispositions.

- The **gain or loss** on an involuntary conversion is reported in income from continuing operations.

- A nonmonetary asset may be involuntarily converted to monetary assets (e.g., insurance proceeds).

- Gain or loss recognition is required even though the entity reinvests or is required to reinvest the proceeds in replacement nonmonetary assets.

  - Hence, the replacement property should be recorded at its cost. The involuntary conversion and replacement are not equivalent to a single exchange transaction between entities.

Example 7-13	Involuntary Conversion

A state government condemned Owner Co.'s parcel of real estate. Owner will receive $1,500,000 for this property, which has a carrying amount of $1,150,000. Owner incurred the following costs as a result of the condemnation:

Appraisal fees to support a $1,500,000 fair value	$5,000
Attorney fees for the closing with the state	7,000
Attorney fees to review contract to acquire replacement property	6,000
Title insurance on replacement property	8,000

Gain or loss must be recognized even if the entity reinvests or is required to reinvest the monetary assets in replacement nonmonetary assets. The gain equals the consideration received ($1,500,000) minus the sum of the carrying amount ($1,150,000) and the direct costs of condemnation ($7,000 attorney fees + $5,000 appraisal fees = $12,000). The gain is therefore $338,000 ($1,500,000 – $1,162,000). The costs of acquiring the replacement property (attorney fees and title insurance) are included in its carrying amount.

Exchanges

Accounting for exchanges of monetary assets (receivables, financial instruments, etc.) is straightforward because they are stated in terms of units of money.

- **Monetary exchanges** are measured at the fair value of the assets involved, with gain or loss recognized immediately.

- The **fair value of the assets given up** generally is used to measure the cost of the assets acquired unless the fair value of the assets received is more clearly evident.

A **nonmonetary exchange** of assets is treated as a monetary exchange when the fair value of both assets is determinable.

- The asset received is measured at the fair value of the asset given up, and any gain or loss is recognized immediately.

- This gain or loss is the difference between the fair value of the asset given up and its carrying amount.

    - If the fair value of the asset given up is greater (lower) than its carrying amount, a gain (loss) for the difference is recognized.

Stop & Review

You have completed the outline for this subunit.

Study multiple-choice questions 12 and 13 beginning on page 247.

7.7 Impairment of Long-Lived Assets

Two-Step Impairment Test

Testing for impairment occurs when events or changes in circumstances indicate that the carrying amount of the asset may not be recoverable, for example, when

- The market price has decreased significantly, or
- The use or physical condition of the asset has changed significantly and adversely.

The test for impairment has **two steps**.

- **Recoverability test.** The carrying amount of a long-lived asset to be held and used is not recoverable if it exceeds the sum of the **undiscounted** future cash flows expected from the use and disposition of the asset.

- If the carrying amount is not recoverable, an impairment loss may be recognized. It equals the excess of the carrying amount of the asset over its fair value.

  - An impairment loss is recognized in income from continuing operations.

The entry for an impairment of a depreciable asset is

Impairment loss	$XXX	
Accumulated depreciation		$XXX

Determination of an Impairment Loss
1. Events or changes in circumstances indicate a possible loss
2. Carrying amount > Sum of undiscounted cash flows
3. Loss = Carrying amount − Fair value

The carrying amount of a long-lived asset adjusted for an impairment loss is its new cost basis. A previously recognized impairment loss **must not be reversed**.

Example 7-14   Impairment Test for an Item of PPE

Lisa Co. purchased a machine with a 10-year estimated useful life for $200,000 on January 1, Year 1. On December 31, Year 2, as a result of low demand for Lisa's products, management concludes that the carrying amount of the machine may not be recoverable. Management estimates that the undiscounted future cash flows over the remaining useful life of the machine will be $150,000. On that date, the machine's estimated fair value is $136,000.

Annual straight-line depreciation expense is $20,000 ($200,000 depreciable base ÷ 10 years), and the machine's carrying amount on December 31, Year 2, is $160,000 ($200,000 historical cost – $20,000 Year 1 depreciation – $20,000 Year 2 depreciation). On December 31, Year 2, the carrying amount of the machine exceeds the undiscounted future cash flows expected from the machine ($160,000 > $150,000). Thus, the carrying amount is not recoverable. Accordingly, the amount of impairment loss recognized is the excess of the machine's carrying amount over its fair value ($160,000 – $136,000 = **$24,000**). The December 31, Year 2, journal entries are

Depreciation expense ($200,000 ÷ 10)	$20,000	
Accumulated depreciation		$20,000
Impairment loss	$24,000	
Accumulated depreciation		$24,000

The carrying amount of the machine reported in the financial statements on December 31, Year 2, is

Historical (initial) cost	$200,000
Accumulated depreciation	(40,000)
Impairment losses	(24,000)
Asset's carrying amount	$136,000

The carrying amount of an asset adjusted for an impairment loss is its new depreciation base.

Year 3 depreciation expense is $17,000 ($136,000 carrying amount ÷ 8 years remaining useful life). The carrying amount of the machine in Lisa's December 31, Year 3, financial statements is $119,000 ($136,000 – $17,000).

Stop & Review

You have completed the outline for this subunit.

Study multiple-choice questions 14 through 16 beginning on page 248.

7.8 Assets Classified as Held for Sale

Classification Criteria

An asset (disposal group) is classified as **held for sale** when six conditions are met:

- Management has committed to a **plan to sell**.
- The asset is **available for immediate sale** in its current condition on usual and customary terms.
- Actions (such as actively seeking a buyer) have begun to complete the plan.
- Completion of sale **within 1 year is probable**.
- The asset is **actively marketed** at a price reasonably related to current fair value.
- The likelihood is low of significant change in, or withdrawal of, the plan.

The **disposal group** consists of assets to be disposed of together in one transaction and directly associated liabilities to be transferred in the same transaction (for example, warranties associated with an acquired customer base).

Whenever the conditions are not met, the asset or disposal group must be reclassified as held and used.

If disposition is to be **other than by sale**, for example, by abandonment or exchange, the asset is classified as **held and used** until disposal. It will continue to be depreciated or amortized.

Measurement

Assets held for sale are measured at the **lower of carrying amount or fair value minus cost to sell**.

- An asset classified as held for sale is **not depreciated or amortized**, but expenses related to the liabilities of a disposal group are accrued.
- Costs to sell are the incremental direct costs. Examples are brokers' commissions, legal and title transfer fees, and closing costs (but not future operating losses expected to be incurred).
- A **loss** is recognized for a write-down to fair value minus cost to sell. A **gain** is recognized for any subsequent increase but only to the extent of previously recognized losses for write-downs.
- A gain or loss from the sale is recognized at the date of sale.

A plan of sale may change because of circumstances (previously unlikely) that result in a decision not to sell. The asset (disposal group) then must be reclassified as held and used.

- A reclassified long-lived asset is measured individually at the lower of
    - Carrying amount before the asset (disposal group) was classified as held for sale, minus any depreciation (amortization) that would have been recognized if it had always been classified as held and used, or
    - Fair value at the date of the decision not to sell.

Reporting

If a long-lived asset is held for sale, it is reported **separately**.

- If a disposal group is held for sale, its assets and liabilities are reported separately in the balance sheet and are not presented as one amount.

When a component of an entity is **reclassified** as held and used, its results of operations previously reported in discontinued operations are reclassified and included in income from continuing operations for all periods presented.

Stop & Review

You have completed the outline for this subunit. Study multiple-choice question 17 on page 250.

7.9 Depletion

Natural resources (wasting assets) are held for direct resale or consumption in other products. Examples are petroleum, gold, silver, timber, iron ore, gravel, and coal.

Natural resources differ from depreciable assets because they

- Lose their separate character during extraction and consumption
- Are produced only by natural processes
- Are recorded as inventory after extraction
    - The entry to record the inventory and the depletion of the natural resource is

        Inventory $XXX
            Accumulated depletion (a contra account) $XXX

    - But some entities credit the natural resource account directly.

Depletion is similar to depreciation. It is an accounting process of allocating the historical cost of a tangible asset to the periods benefited by its uses.

Components of the Depletion Base

- **Acquisition costs** of land (but not the costs of extractive machinery, which are depreciated and recognized as separate items of PPE)

- **Development costs** to prepare the site for extraction (added)

- **Restoration costs** required by law to return the land to its original condition (added)

- The **residual value** of the property (subtracted)

Calculating Periodic Depletion

Depletion is similar to usage-centered depreciation because it is most often determined by applying the units-of-output (production) method.

The per-unit depletion rate is determined by dividing the depletion base by the total number of units estimated to be economically recoverable during the property's useful life.

$$\text{Per-unit depletion rate} = \frac{\text{Depletion base}}{\text{Total estimated recoverable units}}$$

Units extracted times the depletion rate equals periodic depletion.

- To the extent that extracted units are sold, cost of goods sold is debited.
- Unsold units remain in inventory.

Example 7-15   Depletion

Mullinax Mining acquired a mine in Idaho for $3.2 million. The company estimates that the mine contains 1,125 recoverable grams of a particular rare earth. Mullinax further estimates that it will eventually be able to sell the mine for $600,000 after spending $200,000 on restoration. The company must spend $800,000 to prepare the site for mining. The depletion base for this mine is calculated as follows:

Purchase price	$3,200,000
Add: Preparation costs	800,000
Add: Restoration costs	200,000
Minus: Residual value	(600,000)
Depletion base	$3,600,000

The depletion charge for this mine will therefore be $3,200 per gram ($3,600,000 depletion base ÷ 1,125 total recoverable grams). During the first year of operations, the mine produced 200 grams of ore. The depletion charge for the first year was thus $640,000 (200 grams × $3,200 per gram).

Stop & Review

You have completed the outline for this subunit.

Study multiple-choice question 18 on page 250.

Questions

7.1 Initial Measurement of Property, Plant, and Equipment (PPE)

1. Merry Co. purchased a machine costing $125,000 for its manufacturing operations and paid shipping costs of $20,000. Merry spent an additional $10,000 testing and preparing the machine for use. What amount should Merry record as the cost of the machine?

A. $155,000

B. $145,000

C. $135,000

D. $125,000

✔ **Answer (A) is correct.**
Required: The amount to be recorded as the acquisition cost.
Discussion: The amount to be recorded as the acquisition cost of a machine includes all costs necessary to prepare it for its intended use. Thus, the cost of a machine used in the manufacturing operations of a company includes the cost of testing and preparing the machine for use and the shipping costs. The acquisition cost is $155,000 ($125,000 + $20,000 + $10,000).

✘ **Answer (B) is incorrect.** The amount of $145,000 does not include the $10,000 cost of testing and preparation.

✘ **Answer (C) is incorrect.** The amount of $135,000 does not include the shipping costs.

✘ **Answer (D) is incorrect.** The amount of $125,000 does not include the shipping, testing, and preparation costs.

2. During January, Yana Co. incurred landscaping costs of $120,000 to improve leased property. The estimated useful life of the landscaping is 15 years. The remaining term of the lease is 8 years, with an option to renew for an additional 4 years. However, Yana has not reached a decision with regard to the renewal option. In Yana's December 31 balance sheet, what should be the net carrying amount of landscaping costs?

A. $0

B. $105,000

C. $110,000

D. $112,000

✔ **Answer (B) is correct.**
Required: The net amount of leasehold improvements reported in the balance sheet.
Discussion: General improvements to leased property should be capitalized as leasehold improvements and amortized in accordance with the straight-line method over the shorter of their expected useful life or the lease term. However, if the useful life of the asset extends beyond the lease term and renewal of the lease is reasonably certain, the amortization period may include all or part of the renewal period. If renewal is uncertain, the useful life is the remaining term, and the salvage value is the amount, if any, to be paid by the lessor to the lessee at the expiration of the lease. Consequently, the amortization period is the 8-year lease term, and the net carrying amount at December 31 of the landscaping costs incurred in January is $105,000 [$120,000 × (7 years ÷ 8 years)].

✘ **Answer (A) is incorrect.** Land improvements with limited lives should be capitalized.

✘ **Answer (C) is incorrect.** The amount of $110,000 assumes that renewal for 4 years is likely.

✘ **Answer (D) is incorrect.** The amount of $112,000 assumes amortization over 15 years.

3. Star Co. leases a building for its product showroom. The 10-year nonrenewable lease will expire on December 31, Year 6. In January Year 1, Star redecorated its showroom and made leasehold improvements of $48,000. The estimated useful life of the improvements is 8 years. Star uses the straight-line method of amortization. What amount of leasehold improvements, net of amortization, should Star report in its June 30, Year 1, balance sheet?

A. $45,600

B. $45,000

C. $44,000

D. $43,200

✔ **Answer (C) is correct.**
Required: The net amount of leasehold improvements reported in the balance sheet.
Discussion: General improvements to leased property should be capitalized as leasehold improvements and amortized in accordance with the straight-line method over the shorter of their expected useful life or the lease term. Because the remaining lease term is less than the estimated life of the improvements, the cost should be amortized equally over 6 years. On 6/30/Year 1, $44,000 {$48,000 – [($48,000 ÷ 6 years) × 1/2 year]} should be reported for net leasehold improvements.

✘ **Answer (A) is incorrect.** The amount of $45,600 assumes the amortization period is 10 years.

✘ **Answer (B) is incorrect.** The amount of $45,000 assumes the amortization period is 8 years.

✘ **Answer (D) is incorrect.** The amount of $43,200 assumes that 1 year's amortization has been recorded and that the amortization period is 10 years.

7.2 Internally Constructed Assets (ICAs) -- Capitalization of Interest

4. A company is constructing an asset for its own use. Construction began in Year 3. The asset is being financed entirely with a specific new borrowing. Construction expenditures were made in Year 3 and Year 4 at the end of each quarter. The total amount of interest cost capitalized in Year 4 should be determined by applying the interest rate on the specific new borrowing to the

A. Total accumulated expenditures for the asset in Year 3 and Year 4.

B. Average accumulated expenditures for the asset in Year 3 and Year 4.

C. Average expenditures for the asset in Year 4.

D. Total expenditures for the asset in Year 4.

✔ **Answer (B) is correct.**
Required: The expenditures used in determining the capitalizable interest.
Discussion: An asset constructed for an entity's own use qualifies for capitalization of interest if (1) relevant expenditures have been made, (2) activities necessary to prepare the asset for its intended use are in progress, and (3) interest is being incurred. The capitalized amount is determined by applying an interest rate to the average qualifying expenditures accumulated during the period. These expenditures in any given period include those incurred in that period plus those incurred in the construction of the asset in all previous periods. Thus, the total interest cost capitalized in Year 4 equals the interest rate on the specific new borrowing times the average accumulated expenditures for the asset in Year 3 and Year 4.

✘ **Answer (A) is incorrect.** The basis is an average for Year 3 and Year 4, not the total.

✘ **Answer (C) is incorrect.** The basis includes expenditures during the entire construction period.

✘ **Answer (D) is incorrect.** The basis is an average for Year 3 and Year 4.

5. Clay Company started construction of a new office building on January 1, Year 8, and moved into the finished building on July 1, Year 9. Of the building's $2.5 million total cost, $2 million was incurred in Year 8 evenly throughout the year. Clay's incremental borrowing rate was 12% throughout Year 8, and the total amount of interest incurred by Clay during Year 8 was $102,000. What amount should Clay report as capitalized interest at December 31, Year 8?

A. $102,000

B. $120,000

C. $150,000

D. $240,000

✔ **Answer (A) is correct.**
Required: The amount of interest to be capitalized as a cost of an asset.
Discussion: The new office building qualifies for capitalization of interest cost because (1) the asset is being constructed for the entity's own use, (2) expenditures relative to the qualifying asset have been made, (3) activities necessary to prepare the asset for its intended use are in progress, and (4) interest cost is being incurred. The amount capitalized is determined by applying an interest rate to the average accumulated expenditures (AAE) for the period. The AAE equal the simple average of any cost that is incurred evenly throughout the year. Here, the AAE are $1,000,000 ($2,000,000 × .5). The amount of interest to be capitalized is the $1,000,000 AAE times the rate of interest paid during Year 8, which is given as 12%. Because the $120,000 result ($1,000,000 × 12%) exceeds the $102,000 total amount of interest incurred, $102,000 is the maximum amount of interest that can be capitalized during the period ending 12/31/Year 8.

7.3 Subsequent Expenditures for PPE

6. On June 18, Dell Printing Co. incurred the following costs for one of its printing presses:

Purchase of collating and stapling attachment	$84,000
Installation of attachment	36,000
Replacement parts for overhaul of press	26,000
Labor and overhead in connection with overhaul	14,000

The overhaul resulted in a significant increase in production. Neither the attachment nor the overhaul increased the estimated useful life of the press. What amount of the above costs should be capitalized?

A. $0

B. $84,000

C. $120,000

D. $160,000

✔ **Answer (D) is correct.**
Required: The amount of costs to be capitalized.
Discussion: Expenditures that increase the quality or quantity of a machine's output should be capitalized whether or not its useful life is extended. Thus, the amount of the cost to be capitalized equals $160,000 ($84,000 + $36,000 + $26,000 + $14,000).

✘ **Answer (A) is incorrect.** Zero omits all of the listed capital expenditures.

✘ **Answer (B) is incorrect.** The installation and overhaul costs are capitalized.

✘ **Answer (C) is incorrect.** The amount of $120,000 excludes the overhaul costs.

7. Tomson Co. installed new assembly line production equipment at a cost of $175,000. Tomson had to rearrange the assembly line and remove a wall to install the equipment. The rearrangement cost $12,000, and the wall removal cost $3,000. The rearrangement did not increase the life of the assembly line, but it did make it more efficient. What amount of these costs should be capitalized by Tomson?

A. $175,000

B. $178,000

C. $187,000

D. $190,000

✔ **Answer (D) is correct.**
Required: The capitalized cost of a new assembly line.
Discussion: The initial measurement equals the sum of the cost to acquire the equipment and the costs necessarily incurred to bring it to the condition and location necessary for its intended use. A rearrangement is the movement of existing assets to provide greater efficiency or to reduce production costs. If the rearrangement expenditure benefits future periods, it should be capitalized. If the wall removal costs likewise improve future service potential, they too should be capitalized. Thus, the capitalized cost is $190,000 ($175,000 + $12,000 + $3,000).

✖ **Answer (A) is incorrect.** The amount capitalized must include all costs incurred to bring the equipment to use.

✖ **Answer (B) is incorrect.** The rearrangement cost must be included in the amount capitalized. If this cost was incurred for the benefit of existing equipment, different rules apply.

✖ **Answer (C) is incorrect.** Cost of removal of the wall is capitalized.

7.4 Depreciation Methods -- Calculations

8. Ichor Co. reported equipment with an original cost of $379,000 and $344,000 and accumulated depreciation of $153,000 and $128,000, respectively, in its comparative financial statements for the years ended December 31, Year 2 and Year 1. During Year 2, Ichor purchased equipment costing $50,000 and sold equipment with a carrying amount of $9,000. What amount should Ichor report as depreciation expense for Year 2?

A. $19,000

B. $25,000

C. $31,000

D. $34,000

✔ **Answer (C) is correct.**
Required: The depreciation given comparative information and a purchase and a sale of equipment.
Discussion: The reported equipment cost increased by $35,000 ($379,000 – $344,000), and the reported accumulated depreciation increased by $25,000 ($153,000 – $128,000) from December 31, Year 1, to December 31, Year 2. Given that the equipment purchased had a cost of $50,000, the cost of the equipment sold must have been $15,000 ($50,000 – $35,000 increase in the equipment cost balance). Given also that the equipment sold had a carrying amount of $9,000, the accumulated depreciation removed from the books must have been $6,000 ($15,000 cost – $9,000). Accordingly, the depreciation expense for Year 2 must have been $31,000 ($25,000 net increase in accumulated depreciation + $6,000).

✖ **Answer (A) is incorrect.** The amount of $19,000 equals the $10,000 increase in the net equipment balance ($35,000 increase in cost – $25,000 increase in accumulated depreciation) plus $9,000.

✖ **Answer (B) is incorrect.** The amount of $25,000 is the increase in accumulated depreciation.

✖ **Answer (D) is incorrect.** The amount of $34,000 equals the increase in accumulated depreciation plus $9,000.

9. Rye Co. purchased a machine with a 4-year estimated useful life and an estimated 10% salvage value for $80,000 on January 1, Year 6. In its income statement, what should Rye report as the depreciation expense for Year 8 using the double-declining-balance (DDB) method?

A. $9,000

B. $10,000

C. $18,000

D. $20,000

✔ **Answer (B) is correct.**
Required: The DDB depreciation expense.
Discussion: Under the DDB method, a constant rate is applied to a declining carrying amount of an asset. Salvage value is ignored except that the asset is not depreciated below salvage value. Because the straight-line rate for this machine is 25% (100% ÷ 4 years), the DDB rate is 50% (25% × 2).

	Carrying Amount		DDB %		Depreciation Expense
Year 6:	$80,000	×	.50	=	$40,000
Year 7:	$40,000	×	.50	=	$20,000
Year 8:	$20,000	×	.50	=	$10,000

✘ **Answer (A) is incorrect.** The amount of $9,000 includes the $8,000 residual value in the calculation.

✘ **Answer (C) is incorrect.** The amount of $18,000 is the Year 7 depreciation expense if the residual value is included in the calculation.

✘ **Answer (D) is incorrect.** The amount of $20,000 is the depreciation expense for Year 7.

7.5 Depreciation Methods -- Changes and Comparison

10. On January 1, Year 5, Crater, Inc., purchased equipment having an estimated salvage value equal to 20% of its original cost at the end of a 10-year life. The equipment was sold December 31, Year 9, for 50% of its original cost. If the equipment's disposition resulted in a reported loss, which of the following depreciation methods did Crater use?

A. Double-declining balance.

B. Sum-of-the-years'-digits.

C. Straight-line.

D. Composite.

✔ **Answer (C) is correct.**
Required: The method that results in a reported loss upon disposition.
Discussion: The straight-line method of depreciation is the only one of the generally accepted methods that is not an accelerated method. It thus yields the lowest amount of depreciation for the early part of the depreciable life of the asset. Because only 50% of the original cost was received and straight-line accumulated depreciation equaled 40% of cost {[(100% − 20%) ÷ 10 years] × 5 years} at the time of sale, a 10% loss [50% − (100% − 40%)] results.

✘ **Answer (A) is incorrect.** The DDB method results in 5-year accumulated depreciation that is greater than 50% of cost.

✘ **Answer (B) is incorrect.** The SYD method results in 5-year accumulated depreciation that is greater than 50% of cost.

✘ **Answer (D) is incorrect.** The composite method of depreciation applies to the weighted average of multiple useful lives of assets, whereas only one asset is mentioned in this question. Moreover, it recognizes no gain or loss on disposition.

11. On January 2, Year 1, Union Co. purchased a machine for $264,000 and depreciated it by the straight-line method using an estimated useful life of 8 years with **no** salvage value. On January 2, Year 4, Union determined that the machine had a useful life of 6 years from the date of acquisition and will have a salvage value of $24,000. An accounting change was made in Year 4 to reflect the additional data. The accumulated depreciation for this machine should have a balance at December 31, Year 4, of

A. $179,000

B. $160,000

C. $154,000

D. $146,000

✔ **Answer (D) is correct.**
Required: The accumulated depreciation for a machine given changes in estimates.
Discussion: A change in the estimates for depreciation is accounted for prospectively. The new estimates are used in the year of the change, and no cumulative-effect adjustments are recorded. For Years 1 through 3, the amount of depreciation was $33,000 per year ($264,000 old depreciable base ÷ 8 years old estimate of useful life), resulting in a balance of accumulated depreciation at December 31, Year 3, of $99,000 ($33,000 × 3 years). On January 2, Year 4, Union estimates the machine's original depreciable base to be $240,000 ($264,000 historical cost – $24,000 revised salvage value). The remaining depreciable base at January 2, Year 4, is thus $141,000 ($240,000 revised depreciable base – $99,000 accumulated depreciation), resulting in a new annual depreciation expense of $47,000 ($141,000 ÷ 3 years revised estimated life remaining). Thus, accumulated depreciation at December 31, Year 4, is $146,000 ($99,000 + $47,000).

✘ **Answer (A) is incorrect.** The amount of $179,000 does not reflect subtraction of prior depreciation in calculating depreciation for Year 4.

✘ **Answer (B) is incorrect.** The amount of $160,000 would be the accumulated depreciation if the revised estimates had been used from the beginning.

✘ **Answer (C) is incorrect.** The amount of $154,000 does not reflect subtraction of the salvage value in calculating depreciation for Year 4.

7.6 Disposals of PPE

12. On July 1, one of Rudd Co.'s delivery vans was destroyed in an accident. On that date, the van's carrying value was $2,500. On July 15, Rudd received and recorded a $700 invoice for a new engine installed in the van in May and another $500 invoice for various repairs. In August, Rudd received $3,500 under its insurance policy on the van, which it plans to use to replace the van. What amount should Rudd report as gain (loss) on disposal of the van in its income statement for the year?

A. $1,000

B. $300

C. $0

D. $(200)

✔ **Answer (B) is correct.**
Required: The gain (loss) on disposal of the van.
Discussion: Gain (loss) is recognized on an involuntary conversion equal to the difference between the proceeds and the carrying amount. The carrying amount includes the carrying value at July 1 ($2,500) plus the capitalizable cost ($700) of the engine installed in May. This cost increased the carrying amount because it improved the future service potential of the asset. Ordinary repairs, however, are expensed. Consequently, the gain is $300 [$3,500 – ($2,500 + $700)].

✘ **Answer (A) is incorrect.** The amount of $1,000 results from expensing the cost of the engine.

✘ **Answer (C) is incorrect.** Gain (loss) is recognized on an involuntary conversion.

✘ **Answer (D) is incorrect.** The amount of $(200) assumes the cost of repairs increased the carrying amount.

13. A state government condemned Cory Co.'s parcel of real estate. Cory will receive $750,000 for this property, which has a carrying amount of $575,000. Cory incurred the following costs as a result of the condemnation:

Appraisal fees to support a $750,000 value	$2,500
Attorney fees for the closing with the state	3,500
Attorney fees to review contract to acquire replacement property	3,000
Title insurance on replacement property	4,000

What amount of cost should Cory use to determine the gain on the condemnation?

A. $581,000

B. $582,000

C. $584,000

D. $588,000

✔ **Answer (A) is correct.**
Required: The amount of cost used to determine the gain on the condemnation.
Discussion: A gain or loss must be recognized on an involuntary conversion. The determination of the gain is based on the carrying amount ($575,000) and the costs incurred as a direct result of the condemnation ($2,500 appraisal fees and $3,500 attorney fees), a total of $581,000. Because the recipient is not obligated to reinvest the condemnation proceeds in other nonmonetary assets, the costs associated with the acquisition of the replacement property (attorney fees and title insurance) should be treated as part of the consideration paid for that property.

✘ **Answer (B) is incorrect.** The amount of $582,000 includes the costs associated with the replacement property but not the costs incurred as a direct result of the condemnation.

✘ **Answer (C) is incorrect.** The amount of $584,000 includes the attorney fees associated with the replacement property.

✘ **Answer (D) is incorrect.** The amount of $588,000 includes the costs associated with the replacement property.

7.7 Impairment of Long-Lived Assets

14. Which of the following conditions must exist in order for an impairment loss to be recognized?

   I. The carrying amount of the long-lived asset is less than its fair value.

   II. The carrying amount of the long-lived asset is not recoverable.

A. I only.

B. II only.

C. Both I and II.

D. Neither I nor II.

✔ **Answer (B) is correct.**
Required: The condition(s), if any, for recognition of an impairment loss.
Discussion: A long-lived asset (or asset group) to which the guidance for impairment or disposal applies is tested for recoverability whenever events or changes in circumstances indicate that its carrying amount may not be recoverable. The carrying amount is not recoverable when it exceeds the sum of the undiscounted cash flows expected to result from the use and disposition of the asset (or asset group). If the carrying amount is not recoverable, an impairment loss is recognized equal to the excess of the carrying amount over the fair value.

15. On January 2, Year 1, Reed Co. purchased a machine for $800,000 and established an annual depreciation charge of $100,000 over an 8-year life. At the beginning of Year 4, after issuing its Year 3 financial statements, Reed concluded that $250,000 was a reasonable estimate of the sum of the undiscounted net cash inflows expected to be recovered through use of the machine for the period January 1, Year 4 through December 31, Year 8. The machine's fair value was $200,000 at the beginning of Year 4. In Reed's December 31, Year 4, balance sheet, the machine should be reported at a carrying amount of

A. $0

B. $100,000

C. $160,000

D. $400,000

✔ **Answer (C) is correct.**
Required: The carrying amount of an asset.
Discussion: The asset should be written down to fair value if the carrying amount is not recoverable. Because the carrying amount ($800,000 cost – $300,000 accumulated depreciation = $500,000) exceeded the recoverable amount ($250,000) at the beginning of Year 4, Reed should have recognized an impairment loss of $300,000 ($500,000 carrying amount – $200,000 fair value at the beginning of Year 4). Accordingly, the new carrying amount on January 1, Year 4, was $200,000, and the new annual depreciation expense for the remaining 5-year useful life (Year 4 - Year 8) was $40,000 ($200,000 ÷ 5 years). The machine should be reported at a carrying amount of $160,000 ($200,000 – $40,000 depreciation expense in Year 4) on December 31, Year 4.

✘ **Answer (A) is incorrect.** The machine still has a carrying amount.

✘ **Answer (B) is incorrect.** The figure of $100,000 results from subtracting the originally computed annual depreciation from the new carrying amount.

✘ **Answer (D) is incorrect.** The amount of $400,000 assumes no impairment.

16. A company has a long-lived asset with a carrying value of $120,000, expected future cash flows of $130,000, present value of expected future cash flows of $100,000, and a market value of $105,000. What amount of impairment loss should be reported?

A. $0

B. $5,000

C. $15,000

D. $20,000

✔ **Answer (A) is correct.**
Required: The impairment loss.
Discussion: An impairment loss is recognized when a long-lived asset's carrying amount exceeds the sum of its undiscounted cash flows. Because the sum of the undiscounted cash flows ($130,000) exceeds the carrying amount ($120,000), the carrying amount is recoverable. Thus, no impairment is recognized.

✘ **Answer (B) is incorrect.** The difference between the fair value of the asset and the present value of the expected future cash flows is $5,000.

✘ **Answer (C) is incorrect.** The excess of the carrying amount over the fair value of the asset is $15,000. This unrealized holding loss is not recognized because the recoverability test has not been met.

✘ **Answer (D) is incorrect.** The difference between the carrying amount and the present value of the future cash flows is $20,000.

7.8 Assets Classified as Held for Sale

17. If a long-lived asset satisfies the criteria for classification as held for sale,

A. Its carrying amount is the cost at the acquisition date if the asset is newly acquired.

B. It is not depreciated.

C. Interest attributable to liabilities of a disposal group to which the asset belongs is not accrued.

D. It is classified as held for sale even if the criteria are not met until after the balance sheet date but before issuance of the financial statements.

✔ **Answer (B) is correct.**
Required: The treatment of a long-lived asset that meets the criteria for classification as held for sale.
Discussion: A long-lived asset is not depreciated (amortized) while it is classified as held for sale and measured at the lower of carrying amount or fair value minus cost to sell. The reason is that depreciation (amortization) would reduce the carrying amount below fair value minus cost to sell. Furthermore, fair value minus cost to sell must be evaluated each period, so any future decline will be recognized in the period of decline.

✗ **Answer (A) is incorrect.** The carrying amount of a newly acquired long-lived asset classified as held for sale is its fair value minus cost to sell at the acquisition date.

✗ **Answer (C) is incorrect.** Interest and other expenses attributable to liabilities of a disposal group to which the asset belongs are accrued.

✗ **Answer (D) is incorrect.** If the criteria are not met until after the balance sheet date but before issuance of the financial statements, the long-lived asset continues to be classified as held and used in those statements.

7.9 Depletion

18. In January, Vorst Co. purchased a mineral mine with removable ore estimated at 1.2 million tons for $2,640,000. After it has extracted all the ore, Vorst will be required by law to restore the land to its original condition at an estimated cost of $180,000. Vorst believes it will be able to sell the property afterwards for $300,000. During the year, Vorst incurred $360,000 of development costs preparing the mine for production and removed and sold 60,000 tons of ore. In its income statement for the year, what amount should Vorst report as depletion?

A. $135,000

B. $144,000

C. $150,000

D. $159,000

✔ **Answer (B) is correct.**
Required: The amount of depletion to be reported.
Discussion: Vorst's per-ton depletion charge is calculated as follows:

Purchase price	$2,640,000
Add: Restoration costs	180,000
Minus: Residual value	(300,000)
Add: Preparation costs	360,000
Depletion base	$2,880,000
Divided by: Estimated removable tons	÷1,200,000
Depletion charge per ton	$ 2.40

Accordingly, Vorst should report $144,000 (60,000 tons sold × $2.40 per ton) as depletion in its income statement for the year.

✗ **Answer (A) is incorrect.** The amount of $135,000 does not include the $180,000 restoration costs.

✗ **Answer (C) is incorrect.** The amount of $150,000 does not consider the restoration costs and the residual value of the land.

✗ **Answer (D) is incorrect.** The amount of $159,000 adds the $180,000 restoration cost instead of deducting the $120,000 net residual value of the land.

Study Unit Eight

Finite-Lived Intangible Assets and Other Issues

(10 pages of outline)

8.1 Finite-Lived Intangible Assets -- Initial Recognition

Intangible assets can take many forms. The following are the common categories:

- Marketing-related (e.g., trademarks)
- Customer-related (e.g., customer lists)
- Artistic-related (e.g., copyrights)
- Contract-related (e.g., franchise rights)
- Technology-related (e.g., computer software)
- Goodwill (recognized only in business combinations)

Intangible assets **lack physical substance**.

- In general, they convey to the holder a contractual or legal right to receive future economic benefits.

- They are **not financial assets**.

  - Intangible assets thus do not include such items as cash, equity investments, accounts and notes receivable, bonds receivable, or prepaid expenses.

Initial Recognition

Externally acquired intangible assets are initially recorded at acquisition cost plus any incidentals, such as legal fees.

Internally developed intangible assets are most often initially recorded at the amount of the incidental costs only (e.g., legal fees).

- Most of the costs of an internally generated intangible asset are expensed as incurred and not capitalized (e.g., research and development costs and marketing costs).

Example 8-1	Internally Developed Intangible Asset

A company invested $200,000 and $300,000 in the research phase and development phase, respectively, for the internal development of a patent. In addition, the company paid $10,000 and $15,000 for patent registration fees and legal fees, respectively.

The patent is recorded at the amount of the incidental costs, or $25,000 ($10,000 patent registration fees + $15,000 legal fees). The amounts paid for research and development must be expensed as incurred and are never capitalized as part of the cost of the asset.

Organization and Start-up Costs

Organization costs are those incurred in the formation of a business entity. They include payments to promoters, legal and accounting fees, and state registration costs of incorporation.

For financial accounting purposes, nongovernmental entities **must expense** all start-up and organization costs as incurred.

Stop & Review

You have completed the outline for this subunit.

Study multiple-choice questions 1 through 4 beginning on page 261.

8.2 Finite-Lived Intangible Assets -- Accounting Subsequent to Initial Recognition

Useful Life and Amortization

The useful life of an asset is the period during which it is expected to contribute either directly or indirectly to the future cash flows of the reporting entity.

An intangible asset with a **finite useful life** to the reporting entity is **amortized** over that useful life.

- The useful life should be reevaluated each reporting period. A change in the estimate results in a prospective change in amortization.

Amortization is based on the pattern of consumption of economic benefits, if reliably determinable. Otherwise, the **straight-line method** must be used.

- The **amortizable amount** equals the amount initially assigned minus the residual value.

- The **residual value** is the estimated fair value to the entity at the end of the asset's useful life minus disposal costs. This amount is zero unless

  - A third party has committed to purchase the asset, or

  - It can be determined from an exchange transaction in an existing market for the asset that is expected to exist at the end of the useful life.

- An intangible asset with an **indefinite useful life** is **not amortized**.

- The carrying amount of an intangible asset is the amount at which it is reported in the financial statements.

  - The carrying amount of an intangible asset with a **finite useful life** equals its historical cost minus accumulated amortization and impairment losses.

Example 8-2	Amortization of Intangible Assets

An intangible asset was purchased on the first day of the fiscal year for $1,000,000. Its useful life is 5 years, and it has a residual value of $100,000. However, its pattern of consumption of economic benefits is not reliably determinable. The year-end amortization entry is

Amortization expense	$180,000	
Accumulated amortization/Intangible asset		$180,000

[($1,000,000 − $100,000) ÷ 5 years = $180,000 straight-line amortization]

The intangible asset is reported in the year-end financial statements at the amount of $820,000 ($1,000,000 historical cost − $180,000 accumulated amortization).

Testing for Impairment

An **intangible asset with a finite useful life** (an **amortized** intangible asset) is reviewed for impairment when events or changes in circumstances indicate that its carrying amount may not be recoverable.

- The test for impairment is the same as the test for long-lived tangible assets described in Study Unit 7, Subunit 7. It is a **two-step test**:

  - **Recoverability test.** The carrying amount is not recoverable if it exceeds the sum of the **undiscounted** future cash flows expected from the use and disposition of the asset.

  - If the carrying amount is **not** recoverable, an impairment loss may be recognized. It equals the excess of the carrying amount of the asset over its fair value.

    - An impairment loss is recognized in income from continuing operations.

Determination of an Impairment Loss
1. Events or changes in circumstances indicate a possible loss.
2. Carrying amount > Sum of undiscounted cash flows
3. Loss = Carrying amount − Fair value

- The carrying amount of an intangible asset adjusted for an impairment loss is its new cost basis. A previously recognized impairment loss **must not be reversed**.

Example 8-3   Impairment Test for Finite Useful Life of Intangible Assets

A patent was purchased on the first day of the fiscal year for $900,000. Its useful life is 5 years with no residual value. At the end of Year 3, an event occurred indicating that the asset may be impaired. The patent's fair value is $350,000, and its undiscounted future net cash inflows are $355,000.

Step 1 -- The carrying amount of the patent at the end of Year 3 of $360,000 {$900,000 historical cost − [($900,000 ÷ 5 years) × 3 years] accumulated amortization} exceeds its undiscounted future net cash flows of $355,000. Thus, the carrying amount is not recoverable.

Step 2 -- The impairment loss is $10,000 ($360,000 carrying amount − $350,000 fair value). The journal entry to record the impairment is

Impairment loss	$10,000	
Patent		$10,000

The patent is reported in the year-end financial statements at the amount of **$350,000** ($900,000 historical cost − $540,000 accumulated amortization − $10,000 impairment loss recognized).

Stop & Review

You have completed the outline for this subunit.

Study multiple-choice questions 5 through 8 beginning on page 263.

8.3 Patents

Initial Recognition

Patents may be purchased or developed internally.

- The initial capitalized cost of a **purchased patent** is normally the fair value of the consideration given, that is, its purchase price plus incidental costs, such as registration and attorneys' fees.

- **Internally developed patents** are less likely to be capitalized because related R&D costs must be expensed when incurred.

  - Thus, only relatively minor costs can be capitalized, e.g., patent registration fees and legal fees.

Subsequent Accounting

The **amortization period** for a patent is the **shorter** of (1) its useful life or (2) the legal life remaining after acquisition or the moment the application was filed.

- The useful life may be substantially shorter than the legal life because of (1) changes in consumer tastes, (2) delays in marketing the product or service, and (3) development of substitutes or improvements.

The accounting treatment of the costs of the **legal defense of a patent** depends upon the outcome of the litigation.

- The costs of **successful litigation** are **capitalized** because they will benefit future periods. They are amortized over the shorter of the remaining legal life or the estimated useful life of the patent.

- The costs of **unsuccessful litigation** (damages, attorneys' fees) are **expensed** as incurred. An unsuccessful suit also indicates that the unamortized cost of the patent has no value and should be recognized as a loss.

Example 8-4	Accounting for Patents

A company has two patents, patent A1 and patent B2, both with an estimated useful life of 10 years. Both patents have allegedly been infringed by competitors. On January 1, Year 1, the company incurred legal costs in its attempt to stop the infringement of $20,000 and $25,000 for patents A1 and B2, respectively. The rights to patent A1 were defended successfully for an additional 12 years. The rights to patent B2 were unsuccessfully defended.

The costs of successful litigation of $20,000 for patent A1 are capitalized and recognized as part of the intangible asset. These costs are amortized over its estimated useful life of 10 years because the estimated useful life (10 years) is shorter than the legal life (12 years). The costs of unsuccessful litigation must be expensed as incurred.

The company records the following journal entries:

1/1/Year 1
Patent -- Capitalized legal costs $20,000
     Cash $20,000

Legal expense $25,000
     Cash $25,000

12/31/Year 1
Amortization expense ($20,000 ÷ 10) $2,000
     Patent -- Capitalized legal costs $2,000

Patents may be sold or temporarily licensed. A **license of a patent** is considered a license of functional intellectual property (IP). Other common examples of functional IP are a software license, a drug formula, and completed media content (e.g., films or music).

- **Revenue from a license of the right to use the functional IP is recognized at the point in time** at which the license is granted (but not before the customer can benefit from the license).

Example 8-5   Revenue from a Licensed Patent

On 1/1/Year 1, GWG Co. licensed patent rights for an approved drug compound for a 5-year period. In exchange for the license, GWG received fixed consideration of $100,000 per year starting from 12/31/Year 1. Because the payments are over a 5-year period, GWG determines that the contract includes a significant financial component. The present value of the five annual payments of $100,000 at the interest rate implicit in the contract is $382,000.

Because the licensed patent is a license of functional IP, revenue is recognized at the point in time at which the license is granted. Thus, a revenue of $382,000 from patent license fee is recognized by GWG on 1/1/Year 1.

Royalties from Licensed Intellectual Property

Revenue for sales-based or usage-based royalties from licensed IP (both functional and symbolic IP) is recognized when (or as) the later of the following occurs:

- The subsequent sale or usage occurs.

- The entity satisfied the performance obligations to which the sales-based or usage-based royalty relates.

Stop & Review

You have completed the outline for this subunit.
Study multiple-choice questions 9 through 12 beginning on page 265.

8.4 Franchise Accounting

Franchises

A franchise is a contractual agreement by a **franchisor** (grantor of the franchise) to permit a **franchisee** (purchaser) to operate a certain business.

- Thus, an exclusive right may be granted to sell a specified product or service in a given geographical area and to use trademarks, patents, trade secrets, etc.

Franchisee Accounting

The franchisee should capitalize the costs of acquiring the franchise. The **capitalizable amount** includes the initial fees and other expenditures (e.g., legal fees) that are necessary to acquire the franchise and that will provide future benefits.

- If the initial fees are paid over a period longer than 1 year, the present value of the payments is capitalized as part of franchise costs and recognized as an intangible asset.

Franchise costs (the amounts capitalized) are **amortized** over their **estimated useful life** if such life is **finite**.

Future payments based on a percentage of revenues or for franchisor services are expensed as incurred. They benefit only the period of payment.

Franchisor Accounting

A franchise right is considered symbolic intellectual property (IP). Other common examples of symbolic IP are trade names, brands, and logos. **Revenue from a license of the right to access symbolic IP is recognized over time.** Thus, franchise fee revenue is recognized over the franchise license period (or over its remaining economic life, if shorter).

- Revenue from initial fixed fees received generally is recognized evenly over the entire franchise license period.

- Revenue from sales-based royalties typically is recognized when the sales occur.

Example 8-6   Revenue from Licensing a Franchise

Abik Corp. has a franchise for a restaurant business. On January 1, Year 1, Abik granted Mika a license for 10 years to operate as a franchisee of one of its restaurants for an initial fixed fee of $3 million and a royalty of 2% of Mika's restaurant sales. The sales-based royalty is paid at the end of each year. In Year 1, Mika's restaurant had $600,000 of sales.

The initial fixed fee of $3 million is initially recorded as contract liability (unearned revenue) and recognized evenly over the franchise license period of 10 years. Thus, in Year 1, Abik recognized franchise fee revenue of $312,000 [($3,000,000 ÷ 10 years) + ($600,000 × 2%)]. The following journal entries were recorded by Abik in Year 1:

1/1/Year 1

Cash	$3,000,000	
Contract liability		$3,000,000

12/31/Year 1

Cash ($600,000 × 2%)	$ 12,000	
Contract liability	300,000	
Franchise fee revenue		$312,000

Stop & Review

You have completed the outline for this subunit.
Study multiple-choice question 13 on page 267.

8.5 Prepayments and Other Issues

Prepayments

An asset provides future economic benefits. If a cash payment is made in one period and the recognition of the related expense (receipt of the benefit) is not appropriate until a later period, the **deferred cost** is recorded as an **asset**.

- Examples include prepaid insurance, rent, interest, and income taxes.

- The amount of the prepaid expense that will be used up within the longer of 1 year or the next operating cycle of the entity is classified as a current asset.

Adjusting entries are made as of the balance sheet date to record the effects on periodic revenue and expense of deferrals (prepaid expenses) and accruals. The adjusting journal entry recorded depends on how the original transaction was initially recorded.

- If the payment is initially recorded as an asset (prepaid expenses), the year-end adjusting entry credits the asset and debits an expense for the expired portion.

- If the payment is initially recorded as an expense, the year-end adjusting entry debits an asset (prepaid expenses) and credits (decreases) expense for the unexpired portion.

Example 8-7	Adjusting Entries for Prepayments

On January 1, Year 1, a calendar-year company made an advance payment of $120,000 for 3 years of insurance coverage. The company did not record any additional journal entries in Year 1 related to the payment.

Payment was initially recorded as insurance expense. The insurance expense account and prepaid insurance account are reported in the unadjusted trial balance at $120,000 and $0, respectively. Because only one-third of the amount paid is for current-year insurance, the balances that should be reported in the financial statements are $40,000 for insurance expense and $80,000 for prepaid insurance. Thus, the year-end adjusting entry is to decrease insurance expense by $80,000 and recognize prepaid insurance for $80,000.

Prepaid insurance	$80,000	
Insurance expense		$80,000

Payment was initially recorded as prepaid insurance. The insurance expense account and prepaid insurance account are reported in the unadjusted trial balance at $0 and $120,000, respectively. Thus, the year-end adjusting entry is to recognize insurance expense of $40,000 and decrease prepaid insurance by $40,000.

Insurance expense	$40,000	
Prepaid insurance		$40,000

Deferred Charges

Deferred charges (other assets) is a catchall category. It includes long-term prepayments and any noncurrent assets not classified elsewhere.

Such a classification has been criticized because many assets (e.g., PPE) are deferred charges. Thus, they are noncurrent prepayments that will be depreciated or amortized.

Cloud Computing Arrangements

A cloud computing arrangement (CCA) is a **hosting arrangement** in which the end user of the software does not take possession of the software. Instead, the software resides on a remote vendor's hardware.

- The customer accesses and uses the software on an as-needed basis over the Internet.

The accounting question is to determine whether the CCA includes (1) only a **hosting service contract** or (2) a **software license** in addition to the service contract.

The CCA includes a **software license** if both of the following criteria are met:

- The customer has a contract right to possession of the software at any time during the arrangement period without significant penalty.

- The customer can (1) run the software on its own hardware without the vendor or (2) contract with another party unrelated to the vendor to host the software.

If the CCA **includes a software license** for internal use software, the customer's accounting for the license should be consistent with the acquisition of other software licenses. Generally, the cost of the license is capitalized and subsequently amortized on a straight-line basis.

- If a contract includes multiple elements (e.g., software license, hosting services, and rights to future upgrades), the contract price is allocated to each element based on its relative standalone price.

- After allocation, the accounting for each element (e.g., capitalization of costs or expense) is based on the nature of the cost incurred.

If a CCA does **not** include a software license, the customer should account for the arrangement as a regular **service contract**.

- The fees paid to a vendor in a CCA for using the software are **expensed as incurred**.

Stop & Review

You have completed the outline for this subunit.
Study multiple-choice questions 14 and 15 on page 268.

Questions

8.1 Finite-Lived Intangible Assets -- Initial Recognition

1. An entity purchases a trademark and incurs the following costs in connection with the trademark:

One-time trademark purchase price	$100,000
Nonrefundable VAT taxes	5,000
Training sales personnel on the use of the new trademark	7,000
Research expenditures associated with the purchase of the new trademark	24,000
Legal costs incurred to register the trademark	10,500
Salaries of the administrative personnel	12,000

Assuming that the trademark meets all of the applicable initial asset recognition criteria, the entity should recognize an asset in the amount of

A. $100,000

B. $115,500

C. $146,500

D. $158,500

✔ **Answer (B) is correct.**
Required: The initial amount recognized for an intangible asset.
Discussion: Cost includes the purchase price (including purchase taxes and import duties) and any directly attributable costs to prepare the asset for its intended use, such as legal fees. Thus, the intangible asset is initially recognized at $115,500 ($100,000 price + $5,000 value-added taxes + $10,500 of legal costs).

✗ **Answer (A) is incorrect.** Purchase taxes and legal fees for registration also are capitalized.

✗ **Answer (C) is incorrect.** Training and research costs are expensed as incurred.

✗ **Answer (D) is incorrect.** Training and research costs and administrative salaries and other overhead costs are not directly attributable costs.

2. On June 30, Year 5, Finn, Inc., exchanged 2,000 shares of Edlow Corp. $30 par-value common stock for a patent owned by Bisk Co. The Edlow stock was acquired in Year 1 at a cost of $50,000. At the exchange date, Edlow common stock had a fair value of $40 per share, and the patent had a net carrying amount of $100,000 on Bisk's books. Finn should record the patent at

A. $50,000

B. $60,000

C. $80,000

D. $100,000

✔ **Answer (C) is correct.**
Required: The amount at which a patent should be recorded.
Discussion: When an intangible asset is acquired in an exchange transaction, initial recognition is at the fair value of the more clearly evident of the consideration given or the asset acquired. The fair value of the assets given in return for the patent was $80,000 (2,000 shares of stock × $40 per share fair value).

✗ **Answer (A) is incorrect.** The acquisition cost of the stock is $50,000.

✗ **Answer (B) is incorrect.** The par value of the stock is $60,000.

✗ **Answer (D) is incorrect.** The net carrying amount of the patent is $100,000.

3. Which of the following statements is correct concerning start-up costs?

    A. Costs of start-up activities, including organization costs, should be expensed as incurred.

    B. Costs of start-up activities, including organization costs, should be capitalized and expensed only if an impairment exists.

    C. Costs of start-up activities, including organization costs, should be capitalized and amortized on a straight-line basis over the lesser of the estimated economic life of the company or 60 months.

    D. Costs of start-up activities should be capitalized and amortized on a straight-line basis over the lesser of the estimated economic life of the company or 60 months, while organization cost should be expensed as incurred.

✔ **Answer (A) is correct.**
Required: The true statement about start-up costs.
Discussion: Start-up costs are expenses incurred to begin a business activity, e.g., costs of organization, opening a facility, or product introduction. Organization costs are those incurred in the formation of a business entity. Under the federal tax code, organization and start-up costs must be capitalized and amortized over a period of not less than 15 years. However, for financial accounting purposes, nongovernmental entities must expense all start-up and organization costs as incurred.

✘ **Answer (B) is incorrect.** The accounting for intangible assets is not applied to start-up costs. They must be expensed as incurred.

✘ **Answer (C) is incorrect.** Capitalization and amortization is permitted for federal income tax purposes, not for financial accounting purposes.

✘ **Answer (D) is incorrect.** For financial accounting purposes, all start-up costs, including organizational costs, are expensed immediately.

4. Which of the following types of assets would typically be reported on a company's balance sheet as an intangible asset?

    A. Derivative securities.

    B. Cost of research and development.

    C. Leasehold improvements.

    D. Cost of patent registrations.

✔ **Answer (D) is correct.**
Required: The types of intangible assets.
Discussion: Internally developed intangibles other than goodwill are most often initially recorded at the amount of the incidental costs only. Thus, cost of patent registration is capitalized as patent cost and reported in the financial statements as an intangible asset.

✘ **Answer (A) is incorrect.** By definition, intangible assets are nonfinancial assets without physical substance. Derivative securities can be financial assets.

✘ **Answer (B) is incorrect.** Research and development costs are expensed as incurred and must not be capitalized.

✘ **Answer (C) is incorrect.** Leasehold improvements and other modifications made to the leased property by a lessee are recognized as items of property, plant, and equipment.

8.2 Finite-Lived Intangible Assets -- Accounting Subsequent to Initial Recognition

5. Wall Company bought a trademark from Black Corporation on January 1 for $112,000. An independent consultant retained by Wall estimated that the remaining useful life is 50 years. Its unamortized cost on Black's accounting records was $56,000. Wall decided to write off the trademark over the maximum period allowed. However, the pattern of consumption of the economic benefits of the trademark is not reliably determinable. How much should be amortized for the year ended December 31?

A. $1,120

B. $1,400

C. $2,240

D. $2,800

✔ **Answer (C) is correct.**
Required: The amount of amortization of a trademark for the first year.
Discussion: If the consideration given is cash, an exchange transaction is measured by the amount of cash paid. If the consideration given is not cash, measurement is based on the more reliably measurable of the fair value of the consideration given or the fair value of the assets (or net assets) acquired. The foregoing guidance should be followed when initially measuring the "cost" of an intangible asset at its fair value. When the useful life of a recognized intangible asset to the reporting entity is finite, the asset is amortized over that useful life. The amortization method should reflect the pattern in which the economic benefits of the intangible asset are consumed. If the pattern is not reliably determinable, the straight-line method is used. Consequently, annual amortization is $2,240 ($112,000 ÷ 50 years).

✘ **Answer (A) is incorrect.** The amount of $1,120 results from amortizing the unamortized cost on Black's books over 50 years.

✘ **Answer (B) is incorrect.** The amount of $1,400 results from amortizing the unamortized cost on Black's books over 40 years.

✘ **Answer (D) is incorrect.** The amount of $2,800 is based on a 40-year useful life.

6. After an impairment loss is recognized, the adjusted carrying amount of the intangible asset shall be its new accounting basis. Which of the following statements about subsequent reversal of a previously recognized impairment loss is correct?

A. It is prohibited.

B. It is required when the reversal is considered permanent.

C. It must be disclosed in the notes to the financial statements.

D. It is encouraged but not required.

✔ **Answer (A) is correct.**
Required: The treatment of previously recognized impairment losses.
Discussion: When an impairment of an intangible asset is recognized, the previous carrying amount of the asset is reduced by the impairment loss. The adjusted carrying amount is the new accounting basis. Thus, it cannot be increased subsequently for a change in fair value. This rule applies whether the intangible asset has a finite or an indefinite useful life.

✘ **Answer (B) is incorrect.** Recognition of an impairment loss is required when it is considered permanent, that is, when the applicable impairment test is met. Any increase in the fair value of an intangible asset related to the previous impairment loss is not recognized.

✘ **Answer (C) is incorrect.** Reversal is prohibited, so disclosure is not necessary.

✘ **Answer (D) is incorrect.** It is not encouraged, required, or even permitted to make an adjustment to the accounting of an intangible asset for a reversal of a previously recognized impairment loss.

7. In accordance with generally accepted accounting principles, which of the following methods of amortization is required for amortizable intangible assets if the pattern of consumption of economic benefits is **not** reliably determinable?

    A. Sum-of-the-years'-digits.

    B. Straight-line.

    C. Units-of-production.

    D. Double-declining-balance.

✓ **Answer (B) is correct.**
Required: The method of amortization of intangible assets if the pattern of consumption of economic benefits is not reliably determinable.
Discussion: The default method of amortization of intangible assets is the straight-line method.

✗ **Answer (A) is incorrect.** Sum-of-the-years'-digits may be used only if it is reliably determined to reflect the pattern of consumption of the economic benefits of the intangible asset.

✗ **Answer (C) is incorrect.** Units-of-production may be used only if it is reliably determined to reflect the pattern of consumption of the economic benefits of the intangible asset.

✗ **Answer (D) is incorrect.** Double-declining-balance may be used only if it is reliably determined to reflect the pattern of consumption of the economic benefits of the intangible asset.

8. A company recently acquired a copyright that now has a remaining legal life of 30 years. The copyright initially had a 38-year useful life assigned to it. An analysis of market trends and consumer habits indicated that the copyrighted material will generate positive cash flows for approximately 25 years. What is the remaining useful life, if any, over which the company can amortize the copyright for accounting purposes?

    A. 0 years.

    B. 25 years.

    C. 30 years.

    D. 38 years.

✓ **Answer (B) is correct.**
Required: The remaining useful life, if any, over which an entity amortizes a copyright.
Discussion: An intangible asset distinct from goodwill with a finite useful life to the reporting entity is amortized over that useful life. Because the entity expects the copyrighted material to generate positive cash flows for approximately 25 years, the copyright is amortized over 25 years.

✗ **Answer (A) is incorrect.** An intangible asset is not amortized if it has an indefinite useful life. The copyright does not have an indefinite useful life.

✗ **Answer (C) is incorrect.** The remaining legal life is not the useful life of the copyright.

✗ **Answer (D) is incorrect.** The useful life should be reevaluated each reporting period. Thus, the initial useful life is subject to revision.

8.3 Patents

9. During the year just ended, Jase Co. incurred research and development costs of $136,000 in its laboratories relating to a patent that was granted on July 1. Costs of registering the patent equaled $34,000. The patent's legal life is 20 years, and its estimated economic life is 10 years. In its December 31 balance sheet, what amount should Jase report for the patent, net of accumulated amortization?

    A. $32,300

    B. $33,150

    C. $161,500

    D. $165,000

✔ **Answer (A) is correct.**
Required: The amount reported for the patent, net of accumulated amortization.
Discussion: R&D costs are expensed as incurred. However, legal work in connection with patent applications or litigation and the sale or licensing of patents are specifically excluded from the definition of R&D. Hence, the legal costs of filing a patent should be capitalized. The patent should be amortized over its estimated economic life of 10 years. Amortization for the year equals $1,700 [($34,000 ÷ 10) × (6 ÷ 12)]. Thus, the reported amount of the patent at year end equals $32,300 ($34,000 – $1,700).

✘ **Answer (B) is incorrect.** The amount of $33,150 results from using the 20-year legal life of the patent.

✘ **Answer (C) is incorrect.** The $136,000 of R&D costs should not be capitalized.

✘ **Answer (D) is incorrect.** The R&D costs should not be capitalized, and the useful life, not the legal life, should be used.

10. Gray Co. was granted a patent on January 2, Year 5, and appropriately capitalized $45,000 of related costs. Gray was amortizing the patent over its estimated useful life of 15 years. During Year 8, Gray paid $15,000 in legal costs in successfully defending an attempted infringement of the patent. After the legal action was completed, Gray sold the patent to the plaintiff for $75,000. Gray's policy is to take **no** amortization in the year of disposal. In its Year 8 income statement, what amount should Gray report as gain from sale of patent?

    A. $15,000

    B. $24,000

    C. $27,000

    D. $39,000

✔ **Answer (B) is correct.**
Required: The amount reported as gain from the sale of a patent.
Discussion: The patent was capitalized at $45,000 in Year 5. Annual amortization of $3,000 ($45,000 ÷ 15 years) for Year 5, Year 6, and Year 7 reduced the carrying amount to $36,000. The $15,000 in legal costs for successfully defending an attempted infringement may be capitalized, which increases the carrying amount of the patent to $51,000 ($36,000 + $15,000). Accordingly, the gain from the sale is $24,000 ($75,000 – $51,000).

✘ **Answer (A) is incorrect.** The amount of legal costs for defending the patent is $15,000.

✘ **Answer (C) is incorrect.** The amount of $27,000 assumes amortization in the year of disposal.

✘ **Answer (D) is incorrect.** The amount of $39,000 results from not capitalizing the $15,000 in legal costs.

11. Grayson Co. incurred significant costs in defending its patent rights. Which of the following is the appropriate treatment of the related litigation costs?

   A. Litigation costs would be capitalized regardless of the outcome of the litigation.

   B. Litigation costs would be expensed regardless of the outcome of the litigation.

   C. Litigation costs would be capitalized if the patent right is successfully defended.

   D. Litigation costs would be capitalized only if the patent was purchased rather than internally developed.

✔ **Answer (C) is correct.**
Required: The accounting for significant costs of defending patent rights.
Discussion: Subsequent to the grant of a patent, its owner may need to bring or defend a suit for patent infringement. The unrecovered costs of successful litigation are capitalized because they will benefit future periods. They are amortized over the shorter of the remaining legal life or the estimated useful life of the patent. The costs of unsuccessful litigation (damages, attorneys' fees) are expensed.
✘ **Answer (A) is incorrect.** The costs of unsuccessful litigation are expensed.
✘ **Answer (B) is incorrect.** The costs of successful litigation are capitalized.
✘ **Answer (D) is incorrect.** Whether the costs of litigation are capitalized does not depend on whether the patent was purchased or developed internally. This distinction is significant only for measurement at initial recognition. The costs of purchase but not internal development are capitalized under U.S. GAAP.

12. During Year 1, Fleet Co.'s trademark was licensed to Hitch Corp. for royalties of 10% of net sales of the trademarked items. Returns were estimated to be 1% of gross sales. On signing the licensing agreement, Hitch paid Fleet $75,000 as an advance against future royalty earnings. Gross sales of the trademarked items during the year were $600,000. What amount should Fleet report as royalty income for Year 1?

   A. $54,000

   B. $59,400

   C. $60,000

   D. $75,000

✔ **Answer (B) is correct.**
Required: The royalty income reported by the licensor of a trademark.
Discussion: Revenue for sales-based royalties from licensed intellectual property, such as a trademark, is recognized as the subsequent sales occur. Net sales for Year 1 equal $594,000 [$600,000 gross sales × (100% − 1%)]. Thus, royalty income is $59,400 ($594,000 × 10%). On the date the contract was signed, the $75,000 cash advance was recognized as deferred revenue (liability).
✘ **Answer (A) is incorrect.** The amount of $54,000 results from assuming that returns are 10% of gross sales.
✘ **Answer (C) is incorrect.** The amount of $60,000 is based on gross, not net, sales.
✘ **Answer (D) is incorrect.** The amount of $75,000 is the advance payment, part of which was not earned in Year 1.

8.4 Franchise Accounting

13. Helsing Co. bought a franchise from Anya Co. on January 1 for $204,000. An independent consultant retained by Helsing estimated that the remaining useful life of the franchise was a finite period of 50 years and that the pattern of consumption of benefits of the franchise is not reliably determinable. Its unamortized cost on Anya's books on January 1 was $68,000. What amount should be amortized for the year ended December 31, assuming **no** residual value?

A. $5,100

B. $4,080

C. $3,400

D. $1,700

✔ **Answer (B) is correct.**

Required: The first-year amortization expense of the cost of a franchise.

Discussion: A franchise is an intangible asset. The initial measurement of an intangible asset acquired other than in a business combination is at fair value. Thus, the "cost" to be amortized should be based on the more reliably measurable of the fair value of the consideration given or the fair value of the assets acquired. If the useful life is finite, the intangible asset is amortized over that period. Moreover, if the consumption pattern of benefits of the intangible asset is not reliably determinable, the straight-line method of amortization is used. Accordingly, given no residual value, the amortization expense is $4,080 ($204,000 consideration given ÷ 50-year finite useful life).

✘ **Answer (A) is incorrect.** The amount of $5,100 is based on a 40-year period.

✘ **Answer (C) is incorrect.** The amount of $3,400 is the difference between the $204,000 franchise price and Anya's $68,000 unamortized cost, divided by 40 years.

✘ **Answer (D) is incorrect.** The amount of $1,700 equals the unamortized cost on Anya's books amortized over 40 years.

8.5 Prepayments and Other Issues

14. An analysis of Thrift Corp.'s unadjusted prepaid expense account at December 31, Year 4, revealed the following:

- An opening balance at $1,500 for Thrift's comprehensive insurance policy. Thrift had paid an annual premium of $3,000 on July 1, Year 3.

- A $3,200 annual insurance premium payment made July 1, Year 4.

- A $2,000 advance rental payment for a warehouse Thrift leased for 1 year beginning January 1, Year 5.

In its December 31, Year 4, balance sheet, what amount should Thrift report as prepaid expenses?

A. $5,200

B. $3,600

C. $2,000

D. $1,600

✔ **Answer (B) is correct.**
Required: The amount reported for prepaid expenses.
Discussion: The $1,500 beginning balance of prepaid insurance expired on 6/30/Yr 4, leaving a $0 balance. The $3,200 annual insurance premium paid on 7/1/Yr 4 should be allocated equally to Year 4 and Year 5, leaving a $1,600 prepaid insurance balance. The $2,000 advance rental payment is an expense that is wholly deferred until Year 5. Consequently, the total of prepaid expenses at year end is $3,600 ($1,600 + $2,000).

✘ **Answer (A) is incorrect.** Half of the $3,200 of prepaid insurance should be expensed in Year 4.

✘ **Answer (C) is incorrect.** Only half of the $3,200 of prepaid insurance should be expensed in Year 4.

✘ **Answer (D) is incorrect.** The prepaid rent is deferred until Year 5.

15. Roro, Inc., paid $7,200 to renew its only insurance policy for 3 years on March 1, Year 4, the effective date of the policy. At March 31, Year 4, Roro's unadjusted trial balance showed a balance of $300 for prepaid insurance and $7,200 for insurance expense. What amounts should be reported for prepaid insurance and insurance expense in Roro's financial statements for the 3 months ended March 31, Year 4?

	Prepaid Insurance	Insurance Expense
A.	$7,000	$300
B.	$7,000	$500
C.	$7,200	$300
D.	$7,300	$200

✔ **Answer (B) is correct.**
Required: The amounts reported for prepaid insurance and insurance expense.
Discussion: The entry to record the insurance renewal included a debit to insurance expense for $7,200, and the balance in prepaid insurance has expired. At year end, the expense and prepaid insurance accounts should be adjusted to reflect the expired amounts. The 3-year prepayment is amortized at $200 per month ($7,200 ÷ 36 months). Consequently, insurance expense for the period should be $500 ($300 prepaid insurance balance + $200 amortization of the renewal amount). The $7,000 unexpired amount should be debited to prepaid insurance.

✘ **Answer (A) is incorrect.** The amount of $300 does not include the $200 expense for March.

✘ **Answer (C) is incorrect.** Neither the prepaid insurance nor the insurance expense amounts have been adjusted for the $200 expense for March.

✘ **Answer (D) is incorrect.** Prepaid insurance includes $300 that should be expensed.

Study Unit Nine

Payables and Taxes

(29 pages of outline)

9.1 Accounts Payable

Definition

Accounts payable (trade payables) are **liabilities**. They are obligations to sellers incurred when an entity purchases inventory, supplies, or services on credit.

Accounts payable are usually **noninterest-bearing** unless they are not settled when due or payable.

- They also are usually **not** secured by collateral.

Current Liabilities

A current liability is an obligation that will be either paid using current assets or replaced by another current liability. Thus, a liability is classified as current if it is expected to be paid within the entity's operating cycle or 1 year, whichever is longer.

Current liabilities (accounts payable) should be recorded at **net settlement value**. Thus, they are measured at the undiscounted amounts of cash expected to be paid to liquidate an obligation.

- Obligations that are callable by the creditor within 1 year because of a violation of a debt agreement also are classified as current liabilities.

Checks written before the end of the period but not mailed to creditors should not be accounted for as cash payments for the period. The amounts remain current liabilities until control of the checks has been surrendered.

Gross Method vs. Net Method

Cash discounts are offered to induce early payment. Purchases and related accounts payable may be recorded using the gross method or the net method.

The **gross method** ignores cash discounts. It accounts for payables at their face amount.

- **Purchase discounts taken** are credited to a contra purchases account and closed to cost of goods sold.

The **net method** records payables net of the cash (sales) discount for early payment.

- When the discount is taken (the payment is within the discount period), no additional adjustment is required.

- Purchase discounts lost is recognized (debited) when payment is not made within the discount period.

Shipping Terms

The timing of recognition of accounts payable may depend on the shipping terms.

When goods are shipped **FOB shipping point**, the buyer records inventory and a payable at the time of shipment.

When goods are shipped **FOB destination**, the buyer records inventory and a payable when the goods are tendered at the destination.

Example 9-1	Effect of Shipping Terms on Accounts Payable

Kew Co.'s accounts payable balance at December 31, Year 3, was $2.2 million before considering the following:

- Goods shipped to Kew **FOB shipping point** on December 22, Year 3, were lost in transit. The invoice cost of $40,000 was not recorded by Kew. On January 7, Year 4, Kew filed a $40,000 claim against the common carrier.

- On December 27, Year 3, a vendor authorized Kew to return, for full credit, goods shipped and billed at $70,000 on December 3, Year 3. The returned goods were shipped by Kew on December 28, Year 3. A $70,000 credit memo was received and recorded by Kew on January 5, Year 4.

- Goods shipped to Kew **FOB destination** on December 20, Year 3, were received on January 6, Year 4. The invoice cost was $50,000.

When goods are shipped FOB shipping point, inventory and a payable are recognized at the time of shipment. Hence, Kew should currently recognize a $40,000 payable for the goods lost in transit. The $70,000 purchase return should be recognized currently because the seller authorized the credit on December 27. However, the goods shipped FOB destination and not received until January should be excluded. Kew should not recognize inventory and a payable until the goods are tendered at the destination. Accordingly, the ending accounts payable balance is $2,170,000 ($2,200,000 + $40,000 − $70,000).

Stop & Review

You have completed the outline for this subunit.
Study multiple-choice question 1 on page 298.

9.2 Accrued Expenses

Accrual Entries

Ordinarily, accrued expenses meet **recognition criteria** in the current period but have **not been paid** as of year end. They are accounted for using basic accrual entries.

Accruals may be used to facilitate accounting for expenses incurred but not paid at the end of an accounting period.

- For example, the year-end **accrual entry** for wages payable is

Wages expense	$XXX	
Wages payable		$XXX

Reversing Entries

The reversing entry at the beginning of the next period is

Wages payable	$XXX	
Wages expense		$XXX

No allocation between the liability and wages expense is needed when wages are paid in the subsequent period. The full amount of expenses paid in the next period can be debited to expense.

- The entry is simply

Wages expense	$XXX	
Cash		$XXX

No Reversing Entries

If reversing entries are **not** made, payments during the year are recorded by **debiting expense** for the full amount.

- The entry is

Wages expense	$XXX	
Cash		$XXX

At year end, the **liability** is adjusted to the balance owed at that date.

- For example, if the liability for accrued wages has decreased, the adjusting entry is

Wages payable	$XXX	
Wages expense		$XXX

Example 9-2   Accrual with and without Reversing Entries

Mike Co.'s salaried employees are paid monthly. The payment is always on the fifth day of the next month. In Year 1, the total monthly salary was $100,000. In Year 2, the employees received a 5% raise to $105,000.

<u>On December 31, Year 1,</u> Mike must accrue a liability of $100,000 for December salaries expense that will be paid on January 5, Year 2.

Salaries expense	$100,000	
Salaries payable		$100,000

In Year 2, the journal entries recorded by Mike depend on its bookkeeping approach to expense accrual.

1) Reversing Journal Entries

<u>January 1, Year 2 – Reversal of December 31, Year 1, entry</u>

Salaries payable	$100,000	
Salaries expense		$100,000

<u>January 5, Year 2 – Payment of December Year 1 salaries</u>

Salaries expense	$100,000	
Cash		$100,000

<u>February 5, Year 2, through December 5, Year 2: Monthly entry</u>

Salaries expense	$105,000	
Cash		$105,000

<u>December 31, Year 2 – Accrual of a liability for December Year 2 salaries</u>

Salaries expense	$105,000	
Salaries payable		$105,000

NOTE: The annual salaries expense for Year 2 is $1,260,000 ($105,000 monthly salary × 12 months). The salaries payable balance on December 31, Year 2, is $105,000.

2) No Reversing Journal Entries

<u>January 5, Year 2 – Payment of December Year 1 salaries</u>

Salaries expense	$100,000	
Cash		$100,000

<u>February 5, Year 2, through December 5, Year 2: Monthly entry</u>

Salaries expense	$105,000	
Cash		$105,000

<u>December 31, Year 2</u> – The liability is adjusted to the balance owed. The credit is $5,000 ($105,000 amount owed for December Year 2 – $100,000 unadjusted balance).

Salaries expense	$5,000	
Salaries payable		$5,000

NOTE: The annual salaries expense for Year 2 is $1,260,000 [$100,000 on 1/5/Year 2 + ($105,000 × 11 months) + $5,000 on 12/31/Year 2]. The salaries payable balance on December 31, Year 2, is $105,000 ($100,000 beginning balance + $5,000 adjustment on 12/31/Year 2).

Effects of Nonaccrual

If an entity fails to accrue expenses at year end, **income** is overstated in that period and understated in the next period (when they are paid and presumably expensed).

- Moreover, expenses incurred but unpaid and not recorded result in understated **accrued liabilities** and possibly understated assets (for example, if the amounts should be inventoried).

    - In addition, working capital (current assets – current liabilities) will be overstated, but cash flows will not be affected.

Example 9-3	Year-End Accrued Liabilities

Windy Co. must determine the December 31, Year 2, year-end accruals for advertising and rent expenses. A $500 advertising bill was received January 7, Year 3. It related to costs of $375 for advertisements in December Year 2 and $125 for advertisements in January Year 3. A one-year lease, effective December 16, Year 2, calls for fixed rent of $1,200 per month, payable beginning 1 month from the effective date.

The $375 of advertising expense should be accrued in Year 2 because this amount can be directly related to events in that period. The $125 amount is related to events in Year 3 and should not be accrued in Year 2.

The fixed rental is due at mid-month. Thus, the fixed rental for the last half month of Year 2 ($1,200 ÷ 2 = $600) also should be accrued.

In its December 31, Year 2, balance sheet, Windy should report accrued liabilities of $975 ($375 + $600).

Accrued Liability for Employees' Vacations

The accounting for compensated absences applies to employees' rights to receive compensation for future absences, such as **vacations**. It requires an accrual of a liability when four criteria are met:

- The payment of compensation is **probable**.

- The amount can be **reasonably estimated**.

- The benefits either **vest** or **accumulate**.

    - Rights **vest** if they do not depend on employees' future service. The employer has an obligation to pay even if an employee provides no future service.

    - Rights **accumulate** if earned but, if unused, may be carried forward to subsequent periods.

- The compensation relates to employees' **services** that have **already** been **rendered**.

The common way to **measure the liability** for compensated absences at the end of the reporting period is to multiply current employees' daily average wage rate by the number of vacation days earned and expected to be used in subsequent periods.

- In future periods, the wage rate may change. Thus, the amount paid for compensated absences may differ from the liability recognized. The difference is accounted for as a change in estimate and recognized in the income statement.

- The liability should be classified as

  - A **current liability** for the amount expected to be paid within 12 months after the end of the fiscal year and

  - A **noncurrent liability** for the remaining amount.

Example 9-4   Accrued Liability for Employees' Vacations

Entity A provides each of its 500 employees 15 days of paid vacation each year. The unused annual leave may be rolled over for an unlimited time and is payable even upon termination. The employees' daily average wage rate is $150. During Year 1, each employee used an average of 12 vacation days. Entity A expects that 80% of unused accumulated vacation days will be used in Year 2 and the rest in Year 3.

On December 31, Year 1, Entity A must recognize a liability for paid vacation earned and not yet used by the employees. The amount of liability recognized is $225,000 [500 employees × (15 days accrued annually – 12 average days used annually) × $150 daily average wage]. The current portion is $180,000 ($225,000 × 80%), and the noncurrent portion is $45,000 ($225,000 – $180,000). The following is the journal entry:

Vacation pay expense	$225,000	
Vacation payable -- current liability		$180,000
Vacation payable -- noncurrent liability		45,000

Stop & Review

You have completed the outline for this subunit.

Study multiple-choice questions 2 and 3 on page 299.

9.3 Certain Taxes Payable

Federal

Federal unemployment tax and the employer's share of **FICA taxes** are expenses incurred as employees earn wages. But they are only paid on a periodic basis to the federal government.

- Accordingly, liabilities should be accrued by the employer for both expenses.

Payroll tax expense	$XXX	
Employer FICA taxes payable		$XXX
Federal unemployment taxes payable		XXX

Income taxes withheld and the employees' share of FICA taxes are accrued as **withholding taxes** (payroll deductions), not as employer payroll tax expense.

Example 9-5   Payroll Taxes and Deductions

Zalman Co.'s payroll information for the month ended on January 31 was as follows:

Total wages paid at the end of the month	$100,000
Federal income tax withheld	$ 12,000
FICA for employer and employee	7% each
Unemployment taxes	1%

Assume that all wages paid were subject to FICA and unemployment tax. The following journal entries were recorded by Zalman on January 31:

Employer's wages expense

Wages expense	$100,000	
Withholding -- federal income tax payable		$12,000
FICA tax payable -- employees' share ($100,000 × 7%)		7,000
Cash		81,000

Employer's payroll tax expense

Payroll tax expense	$8,000	
FICA taxes payable -- employer's share ($100,000 × 7%)		$7,000
Federal unemployment taxes payable ($100,000 × 1%)		1,000

State

Most states impose **sales taxes** on certain types of merchandise. Ordinarily, the tax is paid by the buyer but is collected by the seller, and only later remitted to the state tax agency by the seller.

Most states require quarterly or monthly filing of sales tax returns and remittance of taxes collected.

Example 9-6	State Sales Taxes Payable

Snow Co. sold a winter coat for $1,000. All sales are subject to a 9% state sales tax. The following journal entry was recorded:

Cash	$1,090	
Sales revenue		$1,000
State sales tax payable		90

Local

Property taxes are usually expensed by monthly accrual over the fiscal period of the taxing authority.

Stop & Review

You have completed the outline for this subunit.
Study multiple-choice questions 4 and 5 on page 300.

9.4 Deposits and Other Advances

Definition

A deposit or other advance is a **contract liability**. It does not qualify for revenue recognition.

A contract liability is an obligation to transfer goods or services to a customer for which the consideration already has been received from the customer.

Alternative descriptions of a contract liability, such as **deferred revenue**, may be used in the statement of financial position.

Accounting Treatment

Cash advances (such as sales of gift certificates) are recorded as follows:

Cash	$XXX	
Contract liability (deferred revenue)		$XXX

The entity should derecognize the contract liability and recognize revenue when the promised goods or services are transferred to the customer.

Contract liability	$XXX	
Revenue		$XXX

Cash received from customers for **magazine subscriptions** creates a liability for unearned subscription revenue.

Example 9-7	Advance Payments

Nepal Co. requires advance payments with special orders for machinery constructed to customer specifications. These advances are nonrefundable. Revenue is recognized when control of the machinery is transferred to the customer (e.g., when the order is shipped). Information for Year 2 is as follows:

Customer advances -- balance 12/31/Year 1	$236,000
Advances received with orders in Year 2	368,000
Advances applied to orders shipped in Year 2	328,000
Advances applicable to orders canceled in Year 2	100,000

In Nepal's December 31, Year 2, balance sheet, the amount reported as a current liability is $176,000 ($236,000 beginning balance + $368,000 advances received – $328,000 advances credited to revenue after shipment of orders – $100,000 for canceled orders) for customer advances. Deposits or other advance payments are contract liabilities because they were received before Nepal transferred machinery to customers. The nonrefundable advances applicable to canceled orders qualify for revenue recognition (debit the liability, credit revenue) because the entity's performance obligations have been satisfied.

If a customer option to acquire additional goods or services for free or at a discount provides a material right to the customer, the customer in effect pays the entity in advance for future goods or services. The following is the accounting for such an option:

- The total transaction price is allocated to performance obligations based on their relative standalone selling prices (discussed in Study Unit 2, Subunit 3).

- At contract inception, the consideration allocated to the option is recognized as a **contract liability** (e.g., deferred revenue).

- Revenue is recognized when (1) those goods or services are transferred to the customer or (2) the option expires.

Example 9-8   Customer's Material Right to Additional Goods

On October 1, Year 1, BGU Co. sold 50 computers for $940 each. The cost of each computer to BGU is $400. In the package of a computer, BGU includes a voucher for a $100 credit on future purchases of BGU products. The voucher expires on May 1, Year 2, and requires a minimum future purchase of $800. The transaction price is the same as the standalone selling price of the computer ($940). BGU determines that this voucher represents a material right. Based on its past experience, BGU estimates that 60% of customers will redeem vouchers. Thus, the estimated standalone selling price of the voucher is $60 ($100 × 60%). The total transaction price of $940 is allocated as follows:

Performance Obligation	Standalone Selling Price	Percent of Allocation	Allocated Transaction Price
Computer	$ 940	94% [$940 ÷ ($940 − $60)]	**$883.6** ($940 × 94%)
Voucher	60	6% [$ 60 ÷ ($940 − $60)]	**56.4** ($940 × 6%)
Total	$1,000	100%	**$940**

The following journal entries are recorded by BGU on October 1, Year 1:

Cash ($940 × 50)	$47,000		Cost of goods sold ($400 × 50)	$20,000	
Revenue ($883.6 × 50)		$44,180	Computer inventory		$20,000
Contract liability ($56.4 × 50)		2,820			

By the end of Year 1, 18 vouchers had been redeemed, and BGU still estimates that a total of 30 vouchers (50 × 60%) will be redeemed. By the end of Year 1, BGU recognizes revenue from redeemed vouchers of $1,692 [$2,820 × (18 ÷ 30)]. On the December 31, Year 1, balance sheet, the contract liability is reported at $1,128 ($2,820 − $1,692). The following journal entry records the redemption of 18 vouchers in Year 1.

Contract liability	$1,692	
Revenue		$1,692

Stop & Review

You have completed the outline for this subunit.

Study multiple-choice questions 6 through 8 beginning on page 301.

9.5 Income Tax Accounting -- Overview

Background 9-1   Divergence of Tax Code from GAAP

Until 1954, business income reported to the IRS and income reported on financial statements were essentially the same. In that year, accelerated depreciation for tax purposes was permitted for the first time. Since then, more and more provisions of the tax code have diverged from GAAP. The procedures necessary to calculate the amount owed for taxes and current-year tax expense are the subject of the next five subunits.

Objectives

The objectives of accounting for income taxes are to recognize

- The amount of taxes currently payable or refundable

- Deferred tax liabilities and assets for the future tax consequences of events that have been recognized in the financial statements or tax returns

To achieve these objectives, an entity uses the **asset-and-liability approach** to account for (1) income taxes currently payable or deductible and (2) deferred taxes.

Interperiod Tax Allocation

Amounts in the entity's income tax return for a year include the tax consequences of most items recognized in the financial statements for the same year. But significant exceptions may exist.

Revenues and expenses reported in financial statements prepared in accordance with GAAP are based on the **accrual method** of accounting. However, revenues and expenses reported in an income tax return are based on the **income tax basis** of accounting.

- The accrual basis of accounting reports the effects of transactions and other events and circumstances on the entity's resources and claims when they occur, not necessarily when the cash flows occur.

- Under the income tax basis of accounting, certain revenues and expenses are recognized when cash is received or paid, respectively. Recognition does **not** depend on when (1) goods are delivered or received or (2) services are rendered.

    ■ Accordingly, **tax consequences** of some items may be recognized in **tax returns** for a year different from that in which their **financial-statement effects** are recognized (temporary differences).

    ■ Moreover, some items may have tax consequences or financial-statement effects but never both (permanent differences).

When tax consequences and financial-statement effects differ, income taxes currently payable or refundable also **may differ from** income tax expense or benefit.

- The accounting for these differences is **interperiod tax allocation**.

Intraperiod Tax Allocation

Intraperiod tax allocation **is required**. Income tax expense (benefit) is allocated to

- Continuing operations,
- Discontinued operations,
- Other comprehensive income, and
- Items debited or credited directly to equity.

Basic Definitions

Income tax expense or benefit is the sum of (1) current tax expense or benefit and (2) deferred tax expense or benefit.

Current tax expense or benefit is the amount of **taxes paid or payable** (or refundable) for the year as determined by applying the enacted tax law to the taxable income or excess of deductions over revenues for that year.

Taxable income is the income calculated under the tax code. Taxable income equals pretax accounting income adjusted for permanent and temporary differences.

Deferred tax expense or benefit is the net change during the year in an entity's deferred tax amounts.

A **deferred tax liability** records the deferred tax consequences of taxable temporary differences. It is measured using the enacted tax rate and enacted tax law.

A **deferred tax asset** records the deferred tax consequences of deductible temporary differences and carryforwards. It is measured using the enacted tax rate and enacted tax law.

A **valuation allowance** is the portion of a deferred tax asset for which it is more likely than not that a tax benefit will not be realized.

A **temporary difference (TD)** results when the GAAP basis and the tax basis of an asset or liability differ.

- Differences in the two bases arise when items of income and expense are recognized in different periods under GAAP and under the tax code.
- The effect is that a taxable or deductible amount will occur in future years when the asset is recovered or the liability is settled.
  - But some TDs may not be related to an asset or liability for financial reporting.

A **permanent difference** is an event that is recognized either in pretax financial income or in taxable income **but never in both**. It does not result in a deferred tax amount.

Basic Principles of Income Tax Accounting

A **current tax liability or asset** is recognized for the estimated taxes payable or refundable on current-year tax returns.

A **deferred tax liability or asset** is recognized for the estimated future tax effects of temporary differences and carryforwards.

Measurement of tax liabilities and assets is based on **enacted tax law**. The effects of future changes in that law are not anticipated.

A deferred tax asset is reduced by a **valuation allowance**.

Stop & Review

You have completed the outline for this subunit.
Study multiple-choice question 9 on page 302.

9.6　Income Tax Accounting --
Temporary and Permanent Differences

Success Tip

The AICPA has frequently tested candidates' knowledge of the recognition and measurement of deferred income taxes. The AICPA has released CPA Exam questions that require calculations of deferred tax assets or deferred tax liabilities.

Asset-and-Liability Approach

Income reported under **GAAP** (accrual basis) differs from income reported for **tax purposes** (income tax basis).

- The asset-and-liability approach accounts for the resulting temporary (but not permanent) differences.

This approach recognizes the deferred tax consequences for balance sheet measurements and related income statement amounts.

- As a result of temporary differences, the tax bases of assets and liabilities differ from their carrying amounts reported on the financial statements. A deferred tax amount equals the tax rate times the difference between (1) the tax basis and (2) the carrying amount.

(Tax basis – Carrying amount) × Tax rate = Deferred tax asset (liability)

- A positive difference results in recognition of a deferred tax asset, and a negative difference results in recognition of a deferred tax liability.

- In the equation on the previous page, tax bases and carrying amounts of assets will be included as positive amounts (illustrated in Example 9-9 on the next page). However, tax bases and carrying amounts of liabilities will be included as negative amounts (illustrated in Example 9-11 beginning on page 286).

Taxable temporary differences result in future taxable amounts and deferred tax liabilities (DTL).

Figure 9-1

Deductible temporary differences result in future deductible amounts and deferred tax assets (DTA).

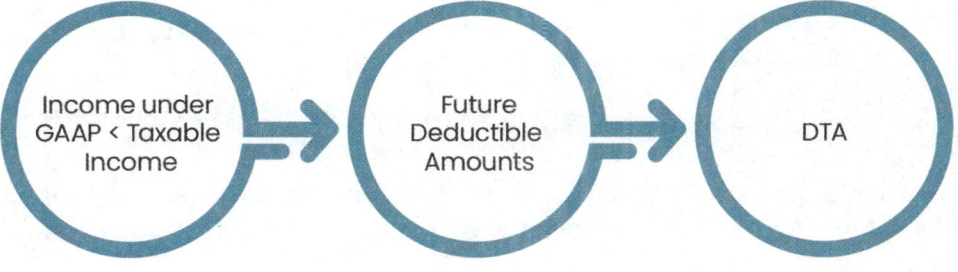

Figure 9-2

Deferred Tax Liabilities (DTLs) and Future Taxable Amounts

DTLs arise when **revenues or gains** are recognized under GAAP before they are included in taxable income. Examples include the following:

- Income recognized under the equity method for financial statement purposes and at the time of distribution in taxable income

- Sales revenue accrued for financial reporting and recognized on the installment basis for tax purposes

- Gains on involuntary conversion

DTL = Future taxable amount × Enacted tax rate

Example 9-9   DTL Due to Temporary Differences in Revenue

In Year 1, Luxor Corp. recognizes $800,000 of sales on credit. The cash will be collected in Years 2 through 5 in the amounts of $300,000, $200,000, $200,000, and $100,000, respectively. For tax purposes, these sales are recognized only when the cash is actually collected. The amounts collected are those by which taxable income in Years 2 through 5 will exceed GAAP income. Accordingly, they are future taxable amounts. The enacted tax rate for Year 1 through Year 5 is 40%.

Year 1 excess of GAAP income over taxable income	$800,000
Future taxable amount in Year 2	$300,000
Future taxable amount in Year 3	200,000
Future taxable amount in Year 4	200,000
Future taxable amount in Year 5	100,000
Total future taxable amount	$800,000
Enacted tax rate	× 40%
Deferred tax liability -- 12/31/Year 1	**$320,000**

The total future taxable amount, i.e., the amount that will reverse, equals the current-period difference between GAAP income and taxable income.

Tax basis of accounts receivable on 12/31/Year 1	$ 0
Carrying amount (GAAP basis) on 12/31/Year 1	− 800,000
Difference	$(800,000)
Tax rate	× 40%
Deferred tax liability -- 12/31/Year 1 balance	**$ 320,000**

DTLs also result when **expenses or losses** are deductible for tax purposes before they are recognized under GAAP. An example is accelerated tax depreciation of property.

Example 9-10   DTL Due to Temporary Differences in Expenses

On January 1, Year 1, Mika Co. purchased a machine for $100,000. The machine will be depreciated over its 4-year useful life on a straight-line basis for financial reporting (25% a year under GAAP). The following accelerated depreciation percentages are used for tax purposes: Year 1 – 60%, Year 2 – 20%, Year 3 – 10%, and Year 4 – 10%. The tax rate for these years is 40%.

The Year 1 excess of GAAP (financial statement) income over taxable income of $35,000 [$100,000 × (60% – 25%)] will be reversed in Years 2-4. The result will be future taxable amounts.

Future taxable amount in Year 2: $100,000 × (20% tax rate – 25% GAAP)	$ 5,000
Future taxable amount in Year 3: $100,000 × (10% tax rate – 25% GAAP)	15,000
Future taxable amount in Year 4: $100,000 × (10% tax rate – 25% GAAP)	15,000
Total future taxable amount	$35,000
Enacted tax rate	× 40%
Deferred tax liability 12/31/Year 1	**$14,000**

-- Continued on next page --

Example 9-10 -- Continued

Reported revenue was $90,000 in each of the Years 1-4. No expenses other than depreciation expense for the machine were incurred in Years 1-4.

Taxable Income		Income Tax Payable	
Year 1:	$30,000 ($90,000 – $60,000)	Year 1:	$12,000 ($30,000 × 40%)
Year 2:	$70,000 ($90,000 – $20,000)	Year 2:	$28,000 ($70,000 × 40%)
Year 3:	$80,000 ($90,000 – $10,000)	Year 3:	$32,000 ($80,000 × 40%)
Year 4:	$80,000 ($90,000 – $10,000)	Year 4:	$32,000 ($80,000 × 40%)

Tax basis of the machine on 12/31/Yr 1	$ 40,000	($100,000 cost – $60,000 accum. dep.)
Carrying amount (GAAP basis) on 12/31/Yr 1	– 75,000	($100,000 cost – $25,000 accum. dep.)
Difference	$(35,000)	
Tax rate	× 40%	
Deferred tax liability -- 12/31/Yr 1 balance	**$ 14,000**	
Tax basis of the machine on 12/31/Yr 2	$ 20,000	($100,000 cost – $80,000 accum. dep.)
Carrying amount (GAAP basis) on 12/31/Yr 2	– 50,000	($100,000 cost – $50,000 accum. dep.)
Difference	$(30,000)	
Tax rate	× 40%	
Deferred tax liability -- 12/31/Yr 2 balance	**$ 12,000**	
Tax basis of the machine on 12/31/Yr 3	$ 10,000	($100,000 cost – $90,000 accum. dep.)
Carrying amount (GAAP basis) on 12/31/Yr 3	– 25,000	($100,000 cost – $75,000 accum. dep.)
Difference	$(15,000)	
Tax rate	× 40%	
Deferred tax liability -- 12/31/Yr 3 balance	**$ 6,000**	
Tax basis of the machine on 12/31/Yr 4	$ 0	($100,000 cost – $100,000 accum. dep.)
Carrying amount (GAAP basis) on 12/31/Yr 4	– 0	($100,000 cost – $100,000 accum. dep.)
Difference	$ 0	
Tax rate	× 40%	
Deferred tax liability -- 12/31/Yr 4 balance	**$ 0**	

Journal entry -- 12/31/Yr 1			Journal entry -- 12/31/Yr 2		
Income tax expense -- current	$12,000		Income tax expense -- current	$28,000	
Income tax expense -- deferred	14,000		Deferred tax liability ($14,000 – $12,000)	2,000	
Income tax payable		$12,000	Income tax payable		$28,000
Deferred tax liability		14,000	Income tax expense -- deferred		2,000

Journal entry -- 12/31/Yr 3			Journal entry -- 12/31/Yr 4		
Income tax expense -- current	$32,000		Income tax expense -- current	$32,000	
Deferred tax liability ($12,000 – $6,000)	6,000		Deferred tax liability ($6,000 – $0)	6,000	
Income tax payable		$32,000	Income tax payable		$32,000
Income tax expense -- deferred		6,000	Income tax expense -- deferred		6,000

NOTE: Given no permanent differences, the total income tax expense recognized each year in the financial statements is $26,000. It equals income before taxes of $65,000 ($90,000 – $25,000) times the tax rate of 40%.

Deferred Tax Assets (DTAs) and Future Deductible Amounts

DTAs result when **revenues or gains** are included in taxable income before they are recognized under GAAP.

- Examples are unearned revenues such as rent and subscriptions received in advance.

DTA = Future deductible amount × Enacted tax rate

Example 9-11	DTA Due to Temporary Differences in Revenue

On January 1, Year 1, Shunia Co. sold 4-year subscriptions to its industry journal for $40,000 in cash. In its financial statements, it will recognize annual revenue of $10,000 from these subscriptions on the straight-line basis. For tax purposes, revenue is recognized when the payment is received. Thus, $40,000 of taxable revenue was recognized in Year 1. The tax rate for these years is 40%.

The Year 1 excess of taxable income over GAAP (financial statement) income of $30,000 ($40,000 – $10,000) will be reversed in Years 2-4. The result will be future deductible amounts.

Future deductible amount in Year 2: $10,000 GAAP – $0 taxes	$10,000
Future deductible amount in Year 3: $10,000 GAAP – $0 taxes	10,000
Future deductible amount in Year 4: $10,000 GAAP – $0 taxes	10,000
Total future deductible amount	$30,000
Enacted tax rate	× 40%
Deferred tax asset 12/31/Year 1	$12,000

-- Continued on next page --

Example 9-11 -- Continued

In addition to subscription revenue, reported annual revenue net of expenses from other activities was $100,000 for Years 1-4.

Taxable Income	Income Tax Payable
Year 1: $140,000 ($100,000 + $40,000)	Year 1: $56,000 ($-1140,000 × 40%)
Year 2: $100,000	Year 2: $40,000 ($100,000 × 40%)
Year 3: $100,000	Year 3: $40,000 ($100,000 × 40%)
Year 4: $100,000	Year 4: $40,000 ($100,000 × 40%)

Tax basis of unearned revenue (liability) on 12/31/Yr 1	$ 0	
Carrying amount of unearned revenue on 12/31/Yr 1	– (30,000)	($40,000 – $10,000)
Difference	$ 30,000	
Tax rate	× 40%	
Deferred tax asset -- 12/31/Yr 1 balance	**$ 12,000**	
Tax basis of unearned revenue (liability) on 12/31/Yr 2	$ 0	
Carrying amount of unearned revenue on 12/31/Yr 2	– (20,000)	($40,000 – $20,000)
Difference	$ 20,000	
Tax rate	× 40%	
Deferred tax asset -- 12/31/Yr 2 balance	**$ 8,000**	
Tax basis of unearned revenue (liability) on 12/31/Yr 3	$ 0	
Carrying amount of unearned revenue on 12/31/Yr 3	– (10,000)	($40,000 – $30,000)
Difference	$ 10,000	
Tax rate	× 40%	
Deferred tax asset -- 12/31/Yr 3 balance	**$ 4,000**	
Tax basis of unearned revenue (liability) on 12/31/Yr 4	$ 0	
Carrying amount of unearned revenue on 12/31/Yr 4	– 0	($40,000 – $40,000)
Difference	$ 0	
Tax rate	× 40%	
Deferred tax asset -- 12/31/Yr 4 balance	**$ 0**	

Journal entry -- 12/31/Yr 1
Income tax expense -- current	$56,000	
Deferred tax asset	12,000	
Income tax payable		$56,000
Income tax expense -- deferred		12,000

Journal entry -- 12/31/Yr 2
Income tax expense -- current	$40,000	
Income tax expense -- deferred	4,000	
Income tax payable		$40,000
Deferred tax asset ($12,000 – $8,000)		4,000

Journal entry -- 12/31/Yr 3
Income tax expense -- current	$40,000	
Income tax expense -- deferred	4,000	
Income tax payable		$40,000
Deferred tax asset ($8,000 – $4,000)		4,000

Journal entry -- 12/31/Yr 4
Income tax expense -- current	$40,000	
Income tax expense -- deferred	4,000	
Income tax payable		$40,000
Deferred tax asset ($4,000 – $0)		4,000

NOTE: Given no permanent differences, the total annual income tax expense recognized in the financial statements is $44,000. It equals income before taxes of $110,000 ($10,000 revenue from subscriptions + $100,000 other net revenue) times the tax rate of 40%.

DTAs also result when **expenses or losses** are recognized under GAAP before they are deductible for tax purposes. Examples include the following:

- Credit loss expense recognized under the allowance method
- Warranty costs
- Startup and organizational costs

Example 9-12   DTA Due to Temporary Differences in Expenses

In Year 1, Luxor accrued $70,000 of warranty costs for financial reporting purposes. From past experience, it expects these costs to be incurred in Years 2 through 5 as follows: $5,000, $15,000, $40,000, $10,000. For tax purposes, warranty costs are expensed as incurred.

Year 1 excess of taxable income over GAAP income	$ 70,000
Future deductible amount in Year 2	$ 5,000
Future deductible amount in Year 3	15,000
Future deductible amount in Year 4	40,000
Future deductible amount in Year 5	10,000
Total future deductible amount	$ 70,000
Enacted tax rate	× 40%
Deferred tax asset -- 12/31/Year 1	**$ 28,000**
Tax basis of warranty liability on 12/31/Year 1	$ 0
Carrying amount of warranty liability on 12/31/Year 1	– (70,000)
Difference	$ 70,000
Tax rate	× 40%
Deferred tax asset -- 12/31/Year 1 balance	**$ 28,000**

Permanent Differences -- No Deferred Tax Consequences

Permanent differences are never reversed. Therefore, they have no deferred tax consequences.

One category of permanent differences consists of income items included in **net income** but not taxable income. Examples include the following:

- State and municipal bond interest
- Proceeds from life insurance on key employees

Another category of permanent differences consists of items subtracted in calculating net income but **not taxable income**. Examples include the following:

- Premiums paid for life insurance on key employees
- Fines resulting from a violation of law

A third category of permanent differences consists of items subtracted in calculating taxable income but not net income. Examples include the following:

- Percentage depletion of natural resources
- The dividends-received deduction

Valuation Allowance

A valuation allowance reduces a **deferred tax asset**. It is recognized if it is **more likely than not** (probability > 50%) that some portion of the deferred tax asset will not be realized. The allowance should reduce the deferred tax asset to the amount that is more likely than not to be realized.

| Income tax expense | $XXX | |
| Deferred tax asset -- valuation allowance | | $XXX |

- A new judgment about realizability may require a change in the beginning balance. This revision ordinarily is an item of **income from continuing operations**.

Stop & Review

You have completed the outline for this subunit.
Study multiple-choice questions 10 and 11 on page 303.

9.7 Income Tax Accounting -- Applicable Tax Rate

Applicable Tax Rates

A deferred tax amount is measured using the **enacted tax rate(s)** expected to apply when the liability or asset is expected to be settled or realized. In the U.S., the **applicable tax rate** is the **regular rate**.

Example 9-13   Enacted Tax Rates

Using the data from Example 9-9 on page 284, assume that the enacted tax rates are 40% for Year 1, 35% for Year 2 through Year 4, and 30% for Year 5. Luxor Corp. calculates the December 31, Year 1, deferred tax liability (DTL) based on the enacted tax rates in effect when the temporary difference reverses.

	Future taxable amount		Enacted tax rate		
Year 2	$300,000	×	35%	=	$105,000
Year 3	200,000	×	35%	=	70,000
Year 4	200,000	×	35%	=	70,000
Year 5	100,000	×	30%	=	30,000
Year 1 DTL					$275,000

Enacted Changes in Law or Rates

Such changes require an adjustment of a deferred tax amount in the period of the enactment. The effect is included in the amount of income tax expense or benefit allocated to continuing operations.

Stop & Review

You have completed the outline for this subunit.
Study multiple-choice questions 12 and 13 on page 304.

9.8 Income Tax Accounting -- Recognition of Tax Expense

Calculating Taxable Income

Taxable income (or excess of deductions over revenue) equals pretax accounting income (or loss) adjusted for permanent and temporary differences.

Pretax accounting income		$XXX,XXX
Temporary differences:		
Subtract revenues recognized first under GAAP:		
Accrual sales (installment method for tax)	$(X,XXX)	
Equity method income	(X,XXX)	
Gain on involuntary conversion	(X,XXX)	(XX,XXX)
Subtract expenses recognized first on tax return:		
Excess tax depreciation	$(X,XXX)	(XX,XXX)
Add revenues recognized first on tax return:		
Unearned revenues (subscriptions, rent, etc.)	$ X,XXX	XX,XXX
Add expenses recognized first under GAAP:		
Excess financial statement depreciation	$ X,XXX	
Warranty costs	X,XXX	
Startup and organizational costs	X,XXX	
Credit loss expense using allowance method		
(direct write-off for tax)	X,XXX	XXX,XXX
Permanent differences:		
Subtract GAAP revenues that are not taxed:		
State and municipal bond interest	$(X,XXX)	
Proceeds from key officer life insurance	(X,XXX)	$(XX,XXX)
Subtract deductible expenses not recognized under GAAP:		
Percentage depletion of natural resources	$(X,XXX)	
Dividends-received deduction	(X,XXX)	(XX,XXX)
Add GAAP expenses that are not deductible:		
Premiums on key officer life insurance	$ X,XXX	
Fines resulting from violation of law	X,XXX	XX,XXX
Taxable income		$XXX,XXX

Calculating Tax Expense or Benefit

Income tax expense or benefit reported on the income statement is the sum of the current component and the deferred component.

- **Current tax expense or benefit** is the amount of taxes paid or payable (or refundable) for the year based on the enacted tax law.

  Current tax expense or benefit:

  Taxable income (or excess of deductions over revenue) × Tax rate

- **Deferred tax expense or benefit** is the net change during the year in an entity's deferred tax amounts.

  Deferred tax expense or benefit:

  Changes in DTL balances ± Changes in DTA balances

Basic Journal Entries

Current income tax expense is recorded as follows:

Income tax expense -- current	$XXX	
Income tax payable		$XXX

Deferred income tax expense or benefit is recognized for the net change during the year in the deferred tax amounts (DTL and DTA) and recorded as follows:

If the DTL balance increased during the year:			If the DTA balance increased during the year:		
Income tax expense -- deferred	$XXX		Deferred tax asset	$XXX	
Deferred tax liability		$XXX	Income tax expense -- deferred		$XXX
If the DTL balance decreased during the year:			**If the DTA balance decreased during the year:**		
Deferred tax liability	$XXX		Income tax expense -- deferred	$XXX	
Income tax expense -- deferred		$XXX	Deferred tax asset		$XXX

In the income statement, one line item is generally reported for the total amount of income tax expense or benefit (Current + Deferred) recognized for the period.

- The amounts of current income tax expense (or benefit) and deferred income tax expense (or benefit) are disclosed in the notes.

Example 9-14   Effects of Changes in Deferred Tax Amounts

Lucas Company had the following deferred tax balances for the year just ended. The deferred tax asset is fully realizable. The company's taxable income was $1,000,000 for the year. The enacted tax rate is 40%.

	Beginning Balance	Ending Balance
Deferred tax asset	$ 9,000	$17,000
Deferred tax liability	13,000	23,000

Lucas calculates income tax expense for the year as follows:

- Current tax expense is $400,000 ($1,000,000 × 40%).

- Deferred tax expense is the net change in the deferred tax liability and asset balances for the year. The DTL balance increased by $10,000 ($23,000 – $13,000) and the DTA balance increased by $8,000 ($17,000 – $9,000). Thus, the net DTL increase is $2,000 ($10,000 – $8,000).

Lucas records the following entry:

Income tax expense -- current	$400,000	
Income tax expense -- deferred	2,000	
Deferred tax asset	8,000	
Income tax payable		$400,000
Deferred tax liability		10,000

Stop & Review

You have completed the outline for this subunit.

Study multiple-choice questions 14 through 16 beginning on page 305.

9.9 Income Tax Accounting -- Other Issues

Net Operating Losses

Under the current tax laws, net operating loss (NOL) may be carried forward indefinitely. No carryback is allowed.

- The carryover is limited to 80% of the taxable income for the year to which it is carried. Any excess continues to carry over to future years until exhausted.

Initial Recognition of NOL Carryforward

Carryforwards are deductions or credits that may be carried forward to reduce taxable income or taxes payable in a future year.

A carryforward results in a **future deductible amount**, requiring recognition of a **deferred tax asset**.

The journal entry is

Deferred tax asset	$XXX	
Income tax benefit from loss carryforward		$XXX

Example 9-15   DTA Due to NOL Carryforward

Gaby Corp. incurred a $100,000 net operating loss in Year 1. The company determined that it is more likely than not that the full benefit of any loss carryforward will be realized. The tax rate is 21%, resulting in a tax benefit of $21,000 ($100,000 × 21%).

The company records the following journal entry:

Deferred tax asset	$21,000	
Income tax benefit from loss carryforward		$21,000

Realization of NOL Carryforward

The amount of the NOL carryforward is **realized** in future periods by reducing the taxable income for these periods.

Upon realization, the deferred tax asset reduces the amount of income tax payable in future periods and does not affect the total amount of income tax expense recognized.

Example 9-16   Realization of NOL

Using the data from Example 9-15, assume that Gaby's taxable income in Year 2 was $240,000. The entire NOL carryforward from Year 1 of $100,000 is realized in Year 2. Thus, the Year 2 taxable income after realization of the NOL carryforward is $140,000 ($240,000 – $100,000). Year 2 current income tax expense is $29,400 ($140,000 × 21%). Year 2 deferred income tax expense is $21,000 (realization of deferred tax asset).

The company records the following journal entry:

Income tax expense -- current	$29,400	
Income tax expense -- deferred	21,000	
Income tax payable		$29,400
Deferred tax asset		21,000

NOTE: The total income tax expense in Year 2 is $50,400 ($29,400 + $21,000). This amount equals taxable income before realization of the NOL carryforward times the tax rate ($240,000 × 21% = $50,400).

Financial Statement Presentation of Deferred Tax Amounts

In the statement of financial position, deferred tax liabilities and assets are classified as **noncurrent** amounts.

Deferred tax liabilities and assets and any related valuation allowance are **netted** and presented as a single noncurrent amount.

- However, deferred tax amounts attributable to different tax jurisdictions must not be netted.

Disclosures

The following are some of the required disclosures:

- Total deferred tax liabilities and total deferred tax assets
- Total DTA valuation allowance and the net annual change in it
- The significant components of income tax expense related to continuing operations

No disclosures about permanent differences are required.

The current income tax expense (or benefit) and deferred income tax expense (or benefit) recognized for the period must be disclosed in the financial statements or in the notes.

Accounting for Uncertainty in Income Taxes

A **tax position** is one taken or to be taken in a **tax return**. It is reflected in financial statement measurements of tax assets and liabilities, whether current or deferred.

- For example, tax positions may include

    - Decisions not to file,
    - Income exclusions,
    - Transaction exemptions,
    - Income characterizations, or
    - Shifts of income among jurisdictions.

The evaluation of a tax position is a two-stage procedure:

- **Recognition threshold.** The financial statement effects are initially recognized if it is **more likely than not** (probability > 50%) that the position will be sustained upon examination based on its technical merits. It also may be recognized if **effective settlement** has occurred.

- **Measurement.** The entity recognizes the largest benefit that is **more than 50% likely** to be realized.

Applying this guidance may result in recognition of a tax benefit different from the amount in the current tax return. Thus, **unrecognized tax benefits** are differences between a tax position in a tax return and the benefits recognized under GAAP.

- The result is a **contingent liability** (or reduction of a loss carryforward or refund). This result reflects the entity's possible future tax obligation because of a tax position not recognized in the financial statements.

- The entity ordinarily recognizes one or both of the following:

    - An increased liability for taxes payable or a reduced refund receivable
    - A decreased deferred tax asset or increased deferred tax liability

- A tax position recognized under this guidance may affect the **tax bases** of assets or liabilities and change (or create) **temporary differences**.

Example 9-17   Uncertain Tax Position

In Year 1, Luxor Corp. took a deduction on its tax return for $15,000. The effective tax rate was 40%, resulting in a tax benefit of $6,000. Luxor believes that it is more likely than not that this deduction will be sustained upon examination. However, Luxor prefers not to litigate the matter and would accept a settlement offer. Luxor has considered the amounts and probabilities of the possible estimated outcomes as follows:

Possible Estimated Outcome	Individual Probability of Occurring (%)	Cumulative Probability of Occurring (%)
$6,000	5	5
5,000	25	30
4,000	25	55
3,000	20	75
2,000	10	85
1,000	10	95
0	5	100

Because $4,000 is the largest benefit that is more likely than not (probability > 50%) to be realized upon settlement, the entity recognizes a tax benefit of $4,000 in the financial statements.

Stop & Review

You have completed the outline for this subunit.

Study multiple-choice questions 17 and 18 on page 307.

Questions

9.1 Accounts Payable

1. Lyle, Inc., is preparing its financial statements for the year ended December 31, Year 3. Accounts payable amounted to $360,000 before any necessary year-end adjustment related to the following:

- At December 31, Year 3, Lyle has a $50,000 debit balance in its accounts payable to Ross, a supplier, resulting from a $50,000 advance payment for goods to be manufactured to Lyle's specifications.

- Checks in the amount of $100,000 were written to vendors and recorded on December 29, Year 3. The checks were mailed on January 5, Year 4.

What amount should Lyle report as accounts payable in its December 31, Year 3, balance sheet?

- A. $510,000
- B. $410,000
- C. $310,000
- D. $210,000

✔ **Answer (A) is correct.**
Required: The amount of accounts payable reported after year-end adjustments.
Discussion: The ending accounts payable balance should include amounts owed as of December 31, Year 3, on trade payables. Although Lyle wrote checks for $100,000 to various vendors, that amount should still be included in the accounts payable balance because the company had not surrendered control of the checks at year end. The advance to the supplier was erroneously recorded as a reduction of (debit to) accounts payable. This amount should be recorded as a prepaid asset, and accounts payable should be credited (increased) by $50,000. Thus, accounts payable should be reported as $510,000 ($360,000 + $50,000 + $100,000).

✘ **Answer (B) is incorrect.** The amount of $410,000 does not include the $100,000 in checks not yet mailed at year end.

✘ **Answer (C) is incorrect.** The amount of $310,000 does not include the $100,000 in checks, and it reflects the subtraction, not the addition, of the $50,000 advance.

✘ **Answer (D) is incorrect.** The amount of $210,000 results from subtracting the advance payment and the checks.

9.2 Accrued Expenses

2. Ross Co. pays all salaried employees on a Monday for the 5-day workweek ended the previous Friday. The last payroll recorded for the year ended December 31, Year 4, was for the week ended December 25, Year 4. The payroll for the week ended January 1, Year 5, included regular weekly salaries of $80,000 and vacation pay of $25,000 for vacation time earned in Year 4 not taken by December 31, Year 4. Ross had accrued a liability of $20,000 for vacation pay at December 31, Year 3. In its December 31, Year 4, balance sheet, what amount should Ross report as accrued salary and vacation pay?

   A. $64,000

   B. $68,000

   C. $69,000

   D. $89,000

✔ **Answer (D) is correct.**
Required: The accrued salary and vacation pay.
Discussion: The salary accrual at December 31, Year 4, was for a 4-day period (December 28-31). Thus, the accrued salary (amount earned in Year 4 but not paid until Year 5) should be $64,000 [$80,000 in salaries for a 5-day week × (4 days ÷ 5 days)]. Vacation pay ($25,000) for time earned but not taken in Year 4 was not paid until Year 5. Hence, $25,000, not $20,000, should have been accrued at year end. The total accrual is $89,000 ($64,000 + $25,000).

✘ **Answer (A) is incorrect.** The amount of $64,000 does not include vacation pay.

✘ **Answer (B) is incorrect.** The amount of $68,000 equals the accrued Year 4 salary for a 3-day, rather than a 4-day, period, and the erroneous deduction of $20,000 for accrued Year 4 vacation time.

✘ **Answer (C) is incorrect.** The amount of $69,000 results from erroneously deducting $20,000.

3. In its Year 4 financial statements, Cris Co. reported interest expense of $85,000 in its income statement and cash paid for interest of $68,000 in its cash flow statement. There was **no** prepaid interest or interest capitalization at either the beginning or the end of Year 4. Accrued interest at December 31, Year 3, was $15,000. What amount should Cris report as accrued interest payable in its December 31, Year 4, balance sheet?

   A. $2,000

   B. $15,000

   C. $17,000

   D. $32,000

✔ **Answer (D) is correct.**
Required: The accrued interest payable at year end.
Discussion: The cash paid for interest was $68,000, including $15,000 of interest paid for Year 3. Consequently, $53,000 ($68,000 – $15,000) of the cash paid for interest related to Year 4. Interest payable is therefore $32,000 ($85,000 – $53,000).

✘ **Answer (A) is incorrect.** The amount of $2,000 results from adding the $15,000 to $68,000 and subtracting that sum from the $85,000 interest expense.

✘ **Answer (B) is incorrect.** The interest paid for Year 3 is $15,000.

✘ **Answer (C) is incorrect.** The difference between the interest expense and cash paid out is $17,000.

9.3 Certain Taxes Payable

4. Bloy Corp.'s payroll for the pay period ended October 31, Year 4, is summarized as follows:

Department Payroll	Total Wages	Federal Income Tax Withheld	Amount of Wages Subject to Payroll Taxes	
			FICA	Unemployment
Factory	$ 60,000	$ 7,000	$56,000	$18,000
Sales	22,000	3,000	16,000	2,000
Office	18,000	2,000	8,000	--
	$100,000	$12,000	$80,000	$20,000

Assume the following payroll tax rates:

FICA for employer and employee	7% each
Unemployment	3%

What amount should Bloy accrue as its share of payroll taxes in its October 31, Year 4, balance sheet?

- A. $18,200
- B. $12,600
- C. $11,800
- D. $6,200

✔ **Answer (D) is correct.**
Required: The amount to be accrued for payroll taxes.
Discussion: The amount of wages subject to payroll taxes for FICA purposes is $80,000. At a 7% rate, the employer's share of FICA taxes equals $5,600 ($80,000 × 7%). Wages subject to unemployment payroll taxes are $20,000. At a 3% rate, unemployment payroll taxes equal $600 ($20,000 × 3%). Consequently, the total of payroll taxes is $6,200 ($5,600 + $600). A 7% employee rate also applies to the wages subject to FICA taxes. This amount ($80,000 × 7% = $5,600) should be withheld from the employee's wages and remitted directly to the federal government by the employer, along with the $6,200 in employer payroll taxes. The employee's share, however, should be accrued as a withholding tax (an employee payroll deduction) and not as an employer payroll tax.

✘ **Answer (A) is incorrect.** The amount of $18,200 includes the federal income tax withheld.

✘ **Answer (B) is incorrect.** The amount of $12,600 is the sum of the federal income tax withheld and the unemployment tax.

✘ **Answer (C) is incorrect.** The amount of $11,800 includes the FICA employee taxes.

5. During the current year, Casual Wear Co. had total retail sales of $800,000 and collected a 5% state sales tax on all sales. At the end of the prior year, Casual Wear had $4,500 in sales taxes that had not been remitted to the state authorities. During the current year, Casual Wear remitted $39,500 in state sales tax. What amount should be recorded in Casual Wear's current-year financial statements?

- A. $5,000 in sales tax payable.
- B. $39,500 in sales tax expense.
- C. $40,000 in sales tax revenue.
- D. $840,000 in sales revenue.

✔ **Answer (A) is correct.**
Required: The current-year accounting for sales taxes collected and remitted to the state.
Discussion: During the current year, $40,000 ($800,000 × 5%) of state sales taxes were collected. The year-end amount of sales tax payable is $5,000 ($4,500 beginning balance of sales tax payable + $40,000 sales taxes collected during the year − $39,500 sales taxes remitted during the year).

9.4 Deposits and Other Advances

6. Barnel Corp. owns and manages 19 apartment complexes. On signing a lease, each tenant must pay the first and last months' rent and a $500 refundable security deposit. The security deposits are rarely refunded in total because cleaning costs of $150 per apartment are almost always deducted. About 30% of the time, the tenants are also charged for damages to the apartment, which typically cost $100 to repair. If a 1-year lease is signed on a $900 per month apartment, what amount would Barnel report as refundable security deposit?

A. $1,400

B. $500

C. $350

D. $320

✓ **Answer (B) is correct.**
Required: The amount of the refundable security deposit.
Discussion: The refundable security deposit is a liability. It involves a probable future sacrifice of economic benefits arising from a current obligation of a particular entity to transfer assets or provide services to another entity in the future as a result of a past transaction. The reported amount of the liability for the refundable security deposit ($500) is the probable future sacrifice of economic benefits. It may be in the form of (1) a $500 refund or (2) the sum of an estimated $320 refund, $150 of cleaning costs, and $30 of damages.

✗ **Answer (A) is incorrect.** The amount of $1,400 equals the deposit plus the last month's rent, an amount that is not refundable.

✗ **Answer (C) is incorrect.** The amount of $350 does not reflect the expected value of cleaning costs.

✗ **Answer (D) is incorrect.** The amount of $320 does not reflect the expected value of cleaning costs or damages.

7. Marr Co. sells its products in reusable containers. The customer is charged a deposit for each container delivered and receives a refund for each container returned within 2 years after the year of delivery. Marr accounts for the containers not returned within the time limit as being retired by sale at the deposit amount. The information for Year 4 is as follows:

Container deposits at December 31, Year 3, from deliveries in

Year 2	$150,000	
Year 3	430,000	$580,000

Deposits for containers delivered in Year 4 $780,000

Deposits for containers returned in Year 4 from deliveries in

Year 2	$ 90,000	
Year 3	250,000	
Year 4	286,000	$626,000

In Marr's December 31, Year 4, balance sheet, the liability for deposits on returnable containers should be

A. $494,000

B. $584,000

C. $674,000

D. $734,000

✓ **Answer (C) is correct.**
Required: The liability for deposits on returnable containers at year end.
Discussion: At the beginning of Year 4, the contract liability for deposits on returnable containers is given as $580,000. This liability is increased by the $780,000 attributable to containers delivered in Year 4. The liability is decreased by the $626,000 attributable to containers returned in Year 4. Moreover, the 2-year refund period for Year 2 deliveries has expired. Accordingly, the liability should also be decreased for $60,000 ($150,000 − $90,000) worth of containers deemed to be retired. As indicated below, the liability for returnable containers at December 31, Year 4, is $674,000.

Deposits on Returnable Containers

Containers		$580,000 12/31/Yr 3
returned	$626,000	780,000 Year 4 Containers
Year 2 retired	60,000	delivered
		$674,000 12/31/Yr 4

✗ **Answer (A) is incorrect.** The amount of $494,000 is the difference between total deposits for containers delivered in Year 4 and Year 4 deposits returned.

✗ **Answer (B) is incorrect.** The amount of $584,000 assumes that all Year 2 containers were retired.

✗ **Answer (D) is incorrect.** The amount of $734,000 omits the Year 2 containers retired by sale from the calculation.

8. Dunn Trading Stamp Company records stamp service revenue and provides for the cost of redemptions in the year stamps are sold to licensees. Dunn's past experience indicates that only 80% of the stamps sold to licensees will be redeemed. Dunn's liability for stamp redemptions was $6 million at December 31, Year 3. Additional information for Year 4 is as follows:

Stamp service revenue from
  stamps sold to licensees $4,000,000
Cost of redemptions
  (stamps sold prior to 1/1/Yr 4)   2,750,000

If all the stamps sold in Year 4 were presented for redemption in Year 5, the redemption cost would be $2,250,000. What amount should Dunn report as a liability for stamp redemptions at December 31, Year 4?

A. $7,250,000

B. $5,500,000

C. $5,050,000

D. $3,250,000

✔ **Answer (C) is correct.**
Required: The reported liability for stamp redemptions at year end.
Discussion: The liability for stamp redemptions at the beginning of Year 4 is given as $6 million. This liability would be increased in Year 4 by $2,250,000 if all stamps sold in Year 4 were presented for redemption. However, because only 80% are expected to be redeemed, the liability should be increased by $1,800,000 ($2,250,000 × 80%). The liability was decreased by the $2,750,000 attributable to the costs of redemptions. Thus, the liability for stamp redemptions at December 31, Year 4, is $5,050,000 ($6,000,000 + $1,800,000 − $2,750,000).

✘ **Answer (A) is incorrect.** The amount of $7,250,000 equals the beginning balance, plus stamp service revenue, minus redemptions of stamps sold before Year 4.

✘ **Answer (B) is incorrect.** The amount of $5,500,000 is based on an expected 100% redemption rate.

✘ **Answer (D) is incorrect.** The amount of $3,250,000 assumes that no stamps were sold in Year 4.

9.5 Income Tax Accounting -- Overview

9. Temporary differences arise when expenses are deductible for tax purposes

	After They Are Recognized in Financial Income	Before They Are Recognized in Financial Income
A.	No	No
B.	No	Yes
C.	Yes	Yes
D.	Yes	No

✔ **Answer (C) is correct.**
Required: The situations in which temporary differences arise.
Discussion: A temporary difference exists when (1) the reported amount of an asset or liability in the financial statements differs from the tax basis of that asset or liability, and (2) the difference will result in taxable or deductible amounts in future years when the asset is recovered or the liability is settled at its reported amount. A temporary difference may also exist although it cannot be identified with a specific asset or liability recognized for financial reporting purposes. Temporary differences most commonly arise when either expenses or revenues are recognized for tax purposes either earlier or later than in the determination of financial income.

9.6 Income Tax Accounting -- Temporary and Permanent Differences

10. Orlean Co., a cash-basis taxpayer, prepares accrual-basis financial statements. In its current-year balance sheet, Orlean's deferred income tax liabilities increased compared with those reported for the prior year. Assume that, for tax purposes, expenditures are deducted when actually paid. Which of the following changes would cause this increase in deferred income tax liabilities?

    I.   An increase in prepaid insurance
    II. An increase in rent receivable
    III. An increase in warranty obligations

    A. I only.

    B. I and II only.

    C. II and III only.

    D. III only.

✔ **Answer (B) is correct.**
Required: The change(s) causing an increase in deferred income tax liabilities.
Discussion: An increase in prepaid insurance signifies the recognition of a deduction on the tax return of a cash-basis taxpayer but not in the accrual-basis financial statements. The result is a temporary difference giving rise to taxable amounts in future years when the reported amount of the asset is recovered. An increase in rent receivable involves recognition of revenue in the accrual-basis financial statements but not in the tax return of a cash-basis taxpayer. This temporary difference also will result in future taxable amounts when the asset is recovered. A deferred tax liability records the tax consequences of taxable temporary differences. Hence, these transactions increase deferred tax liabilities. An increase in warranty obligations is a noncash expense recognized in accrual-basis financial statements but not on a modified-cash-basis tax return. The result is a deductible temporary difference and an increase in a deferred tax asset.

11. West Corp. leased a building and received the $36,000 annual rental payment on June 15, Year 4. The lease was classified as an operating lease. The beginning of the lease was July 1, Year 4. Rental income is taxable when received. West's tax rates are 30% for Year 4 and 40% thereafter. West had **no** other permanent or temporary differences. West determined that **no** valuation allowance was needed. What amount of deferred tax asset should West report in its December 31, Year 4, balance sheet?

    A. $5,400

    B. $7,200

    C. $10,800

    D. $14,400

✔ **Answer (B) is correct.**
Required: The amount of deferred tax asset reported at year end.
Discussion: The $36,000 rental payment is taxable in full when received in Year 4, but only $18,000 [$36,000 × (6 ÷ 12)] should be recognized in financial accounting income for the year. The result is a deductible temporary difference (deferred tax asset) arising from the difference between the tax basis ($0) of the liability for unearned rent and its reported amount in the year-end balance sheet ($36,000 – $18,000 = $18,000). The income tax payable for Year 4 based on the rental payment is $10,800 ($36,000 × 30% tax rate for Year 4), the deferred tax asset is $7,200 ($18,000 future deductible amount × 40% enacted tax rate applicable after Year 4 when the asset will be realized), and the income tax expense is $3,600 ($10,800 current tax expense – $7,200 deferred tax benefit). The deferred tax benefit equals the net change during the year in the entity's deferred tax liabilities and assets ($7,200 deferred tax asset recognized in Year 4 – $0).

✘ **Answer (A) is incorrect.** The amount of $5,400 is based on a 30% tax rate.

✘ **Answer (C) is incorrect.** The income tax payable is $10,800.

✘ **Answer (D) is incorrect.** The amount of $14,400 would be the income tax payable if the 40% tax rate applied in Year 4.

9.7 Income Tax Accounting -- Applicable Tax Rate

12. Scott Corp. received cash of $20,000 that was included in revenues in its Year 1 financial statements, of which $12,000 will not be taxable until Year 2. Scott's enacted tax rate is 30% for Year 1, and 25% for Year 2. What amount should Scott report in its Year 1 balance sheet for deferred income tax liability?

A. $2,000

B. $2,400

C. $3,000

D. $3,600

✓ Answer (C) is correct.
Required: The amount reported for deferred income tax liability.
Discussion: This transaction gives rise to a taxable temporary difference. The resulting deferred tax liability should be measured using the enacted rate expected to apply to taxable income in the period in which the deferred tax liability is expected to be settled. Hence, the deferred tax liability is $3,000 ($12,000 taxable amounts × 25% rate applicable in Year 2).

✗ Answer (A) is incorrect. The amount of $2,000 is 25% of $8,000, the amount taxable in Year 2.

✗ Answer (B) is incorrect. The amount of $2,400 is 30% of $8,000, the amount taxable in Year 1.

✗ Answer (D) is incorrect. The amount of $3,600 results from applying a 30% tax rate.

13. As a result of differences between depreciation for financial reporting purposes and tax purposes, the financial reporting basis of Noor Co.'s sole depreciable asset acquired in the current year exceeded its tax basis by $250,000 at December 31. This difference will reverse in future years. The enacted tax rate is 30% for the current year and 40% for future years. Noor has **no** other temporary differences. In its December 31 balance sheet, how should Noor report the deferred tax effect of this difference?

A. As an asset of $75,000.

B. As an asset of $100,000.

C. As a liability of $75,000.

D. As a liability of $100,000.

✓ Answer (D) is correct.
Required: The deferred tax effect of the difference between the financial reporting basis and the tax basis.
Discussion: The temporary difference arises because the excess of the reported amount of the depreciable asset over its tax basis will result in taxable amounts in future years when the reported amount is recovered. A taxable temporary difference results in a deferred tax liability. Because the enacted tax rate for future years is 40%, the deferred income tax liability is $100,000 ($250,000 × 40%).

✗ Answer (A) is incorrect. The deferred income tax effect should be calculated using the 40% rate, and it is a liability.

✗ Answer (B) is incorrect. The deferred income tax effect is a liability. The temporary difference results in taxable, not deductible, amounts.

✗ Answer (C) is incorrect. The amount of $75,000 is based on the current-year tax rate.

9.8 Income Tax Accounting -- Recognition of Tax Expense

14. In Year 2, Ajax, Inc., reported taxable income of $400,000 and pretax financial statement income of $300,000. The difference resulted from $60,000 of nondeductible premiums on Ajax's officers' life insurance and $40,000 of rental income received in advance. Rental income is taxable when received. Ajax's effective tax rate is 30%. In its Year 2 income statement, what amount should Ajax report as income tax expense -- current portion?

    A. $90,000

    B. $102,000

    C. $108,000

    D. $120,000

✔ **Answer (D) is correct.**
Required: The current income tax expense given nondeductible insurance premiums and taxable rent received in advance.
Discussion: Current income tax expense or benefit is the amount of taxes paid or payable (or refundable) for the year based on enacted tax law applied to taxable income (or excess of deductions over revenues). Thus, current income tax expense is $120,000 ($400,000 × 30%).

✘ **Answer (A) is incorrect.** The amount of $90,000 equals the effective tax rate times pretax financial statement income.

✘ **Answer (B) is incorrect.** The amount of $102,000 equals the effective tax rate times the excess of reported taxable income over the nondeductible insurance premiums.

✘ **Answer (C) is incorrect.** The amount of $108,000 equals the effective tax rate times the excess of reported taxable income over rent received in advance.

15. Quinn Co. reported a net deferred tax asset of $9,000 in its December 31, Year 1, balance sheet. For Year 2, Quinn reported pretax financial statement income of $300,000. Temporary differences of $100,000 resulted in taxable income of $200,000 for Year 2. At December 31, Year 2, Quinn had cumulative taxable temporary differences of $70,000. Quinn's effective income tax rate is 30%. In its December 31, Year 2, income statement, what should Quinn report as deferred income tax expense?

    A. $12,000

    B. $21,000

    C. $30,000

    D. $60,000

✔ **Answer (C) is correct.**
Required: The deferred income tax expense.
Discussion: Deferred tax expense or benefit is the net change during the year in the entity's deferred tax liabilities and assets. Quinn had a net deferred tax asset of $9,000 at the beginning of Year 2 and a net deferred tax liability of $21,000 ($70,000 × 30%) at the end of Year 2. The net change (a deferred tax expense in this case) is $30,000 ($9,000 reduction in the deferred tax asset + $21,000 increase in deferred tax liabilities).

✘ **Answer (A) is incorrect.** The amount of $12,000 results from offsetting the deferred tax liability and the deferred tax asset.

✘ **Answer (B) is incorrect.** The deferred tax liability is $21,000.

✘ **Answer (D) is incorrect.** The amount of $60,000 is the current income tax expense for the year ($200,000 × 30%).

16. In its Year 4 income statement, Cere Co. reported income before income taxes of $300,000. Cere estimated that, because of permanent differences, taxable income for Year 4 would be $280,000. During Year 4, Cere made estimated tax payments of $50,000, which were debited to income tax expense. Cere is subject to a 30% tax rate. What amount should Cere report as income tax expense?

A. $34,000

B. $50,000

C. $84,000

D. $90,000

✓ **Answer (C) is correct.**
Required: The amount to be reported for income tax expense.
Discussion: A permanent difference does not result in a change in a deferred tax asset or liability, that is, in a deferred tax expense or benefit. Thus, total income tax expense equals current income tax expense, which is the amount of taxes paid or payable for the year. Income taxes payable for Year 4 equal $84,000 ($280,000 taxable income × 30%).

✗ **Answer (A) is incorrect.** The amount of $34,000 equals the $84,000 of income taxes payable minus the $50,000 of income taxes paid.

✗ **Answer (B) is incorrect.** The amount of $50,000 equals income taxes paid, not the total current income tax expense.

✗ **Answer (D) is incorrect.** The amount of $90,000 is equal to the reported income of $300,000 times the tax rate.

9.9 Income Tax Accounting -- Other Issues

17. Brass Co. reported income before income tax expense of $60,000 for Year 2. Brass had **no** permanent or temporary differences for tax purposes. Brass has an effective tax rate of 30% and a $40,000 net operating loss carryforward from Year 1. What is the maximum income tax benefit that Brass can realize from the loss carryforward for Year 2?

A. $12,000

B. $18,000

C. $20,000

D. $40,000

✔ **Answer (A) is correct.**
Required: The maximum tax benefit from a loss carryforward.
Discussion: Under current tax law, net operating loss may be carried forward indefinitely. The carryover is limited to 80% of the taxable income for the year to which it is carried. Any excess continues to carry over to future years until exhausted. Thus, the maximum loss carryforward that can be realized in Year 2 is $48,000 ($60,000 × 80%). Moreover, the $60,000 reported taxable income from Year 2 can absorb the entire $40,000 loss carryforward from Year 1. The tax benefit is $12,000 ($40,000 × 30% tax rate).

✘ **Answer (B) is incorrect.** The tax liability before the net operating loss carryforward is $18,000 ($60,000 × 30%).

✘ **Answer (C) is incorrect.** Taxable income is $20,000 ($60,000 – $40,000 NOL).

✘ **Answer (D) is incorrect.** The available net operating loss carryforward is $40,000.

18. At the end of Year 4, the tax effects of Thorn Co.'s temporary differences were as follows:

	Deferred Tax Assets (Liabilities)
Accelerated tax depreciation	$(75,000)
Additional costs in inventory for tax purposes	25,000
	$(50,000)

A valuation allowance was not considered necessary. Thorn anticipates that $10,000 of the deferred tax liability will reverse in Year 5. In Thorn's December 31, Year 4, balance sheet, what amount should Thorn report as noncurrent deferred tax liability?

A. $40,000

B. $50,000

C. $65,000

D. $75,000

✔ **Answer (B) is correct.**
Required: The classification of deferred taxes on the balance sheet.
Discussion: In the statement of financial position, deferred tax liabilities and assets are classified as noncurrent amounts. In addition, deferred tax liabilities and assets and any related valuation allowance are netted and presented as a single noncurrent amount. Thus, in Thorn's balance sheet, the deferred tax liability of $50,000 ($75,000 – $25,000) must be classified as noncurrent.

Study Unit Ten

Noncurrent Liabilities

(24 pages of outline)

10.1 Types of Bond Liabilities

Classification of Bonds

A bond is a formal contract to pay an amount of money (face amount) at the maturity date plus interest at the stated rate at specific intervals.

- All of the terms of the agreement are stated in an **indenture**.

Bonds may be classified as follows:

- Nature of security
    - **Mortgage bonds** are backed by specific assets, usually real estate.
    - **Debentures** are backed only by the borrower's general credit.
    - **Collateral trust bonds** are backed by specific securities.
    - **Guaranty bonds** are guaranteed by a third party, e.g., the parent of the subsidiary that issued the bonds.
- Maturity pattern
    - A **term bond** has a single maturity date at the end of its term.
    - A **serial bond** matures in stated amounts at regular intervals.
- Ownership
    - **Registered bonds** are issued in the name of the owner, who receives interest payments directly.
        - When the owner sells the bonds, the certificates must be surrendered and new certificates must be issued.
    - **Bearer bonds** (coupon bonds) are bearer instruments.
        - Whoever presents the interest coupons is entitled to payment.
- Priority
    - **Subordinated debentures** and **second mortgage bonds** are junior securities with claims inferior to those of senior bonds.

- Repayment provisions

  - **Income bonds** pay interest contingent on the debtor's profitability.
  - **Revenue bonds** are issued by governments and are payable from specific revenue sources.
  - **Participating bonds** share in excess earnings of the debtor.

- Valuation

  - **Variable rate bonds** pay interest that is dependent on market conditions.

  - **Zero-coupon** or **deep-discount bonds** are noninterest-bearing.

    ‣ Because they are sold at less than their face amount, an interest rate is imputed.

  - **Commodity-backed bonds** are payable at prices related to a commodity, such as gold.

- Redemption provisions

  - **Callable bonds** may be repurchased by the issuer at a specified price before maturity.

    ‣ During a period of falling interest rates, the call provision allows the issuer to replace old high-interest debt with new low-interest debt.

    ‣ Because only the issuer can benefit from the call provision, callable bonds generally have a higher yield than comparable noncallable bonds.

  - **Convertible bonds** may be converted into equity securities of the issuer at the option of the holder (buyer) under specified conditions.

    ‣ The debt and equity elements of convertible debt are treated as inseparable and reported as a liability until conversion.

A bond indenture may require a **bond sinking fund** (a long-term investment).

- Payments into the fund plus the revenue earned on its investments provide the assets to settle bond liabilities.

Stop & Review

You have completed the outline for this subunit.
Study multiple-choice questions 1 and 2 on page 333.

10.2 Time Value of Money

Time value of money concepts are important in financial accounting. They affect the accounting for noncurrent receivables and payables (bonds and notes), leases, and certain employee benefits.

A quantity of money to be received or paid in the future is worth less than the same amount now. The difference is measured in terms of interest calculated using the appropriate **discount rate**. Interest is the payment received by an owner of money from the current consumer to forgo current consumption.

Standard tables have been developed to facilitate the calculation of present and future values. Each entry in one of these tables represents the factor by which any monetary amount can be modified to obtain its present or future value.

Present Value (PV) of a Single Amount

The present value of a single amount is the value today of some future payment.

It equals the future payment times the present value of 1 (a factor found in a standard table) for the given number of periods and interest rate.

Example 10-1	Present Value of a Single Amount	

	Present Value Factor of a Single Amount		
No. of Periods	6%	8%	10%
1	0.943	0.926	0.909
2	0.890	0.857	0.826
3	0.840	**0.794**	0.751
4	0.792	0.735	0.683
5	0.747	0.681	0.621

The present value of $1,000, to be received in 3 years and discounted at 8%, is $794 ($1,000 future value of a single amount × 0.794 present value factor).

This situation can be depicted as follows:

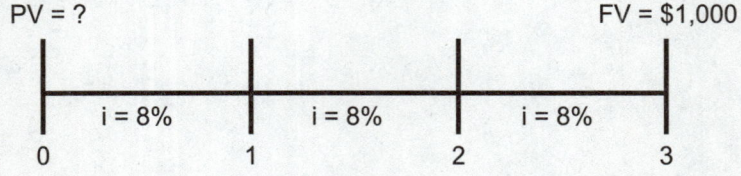

Figure 10-1

FV: Future value of a single amount (the amount to be paid or received in the future)
PV: Present value of a single amount
i: Interest rate

Future Value (FV) of a Single Amount

The future value of a single amount is the amount available at a specified time in the future based on a single investment (deposit) today. The FV is the amount to be computed if one knows the present value and the appropriate discount rate.

It equals the current payment times the future value of 1 (a factor found in a standard table) for the given number of periods and interest rate.

Example 10-2   Future Value of a Single Amount

	Future Value Factor of a Single Amount		
No. of Periods	6%	8%	**10%**
1	1.060	1.080	1.100
2	1.124	1.166	1.210
3	1.191	1.260	1.331
4	1.262	1.360	**1.464**
5	1.338	1.469	1.610

The future value of $1,000 invested today for 4 years at 10% interest will be $1,464 ($1,000 present value of a single amount × 1.464 future value factor).

This situation can be depicted as follows:

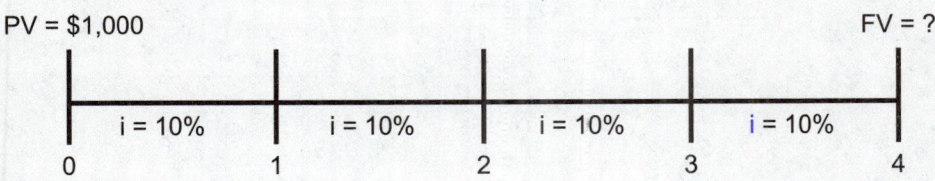

PV = $1,000   FV = ?

0 — i = 10% — 1 — i = 10% — 2 — i = 10% — 3 — i = 10% — 4

Figure 10-2

Annuities

An annuity is a series of equal payments at equal intervals of time, e.g., $1,000 at the end of every year for 10 years. The two types of annuities are ordinary annuities (annuity in arrears) and annuities due (annuity in advance).

- An **ordinary annuity (annuity in arrears)** is a series of payments occurring at the **end** of each period. In an **annuity due (annuity in advance)**, the payments are made (received) at the **beginning** of each period.

The **present value of an annuity** is the value today of a series of future equal payments at equal intervals discounted at a given rate.

- The first payment of an ordinary annuity is discounted, but the first payment of an annuity due is not discounted (since it was received today, it is worth its exact face amount, regardless of the discount rate).

- A typical present value table is for an ordinary annuity, but the present value factor for an annuity due can be easily derived. The present value factor of an annuity due is equal to the present value factor of an ordinary annuity multiplied by $(1 + i)$.

Example 10-3   Present Value of an Annuity

	Present Value Factor of an Ordinary Annuity		
No. of Periods	6%	**8%**	10%
1	0.943	0.926	0.909
2	1.833	1.783	1.736
3	2.673	2.577	2.487
4	3.465	3.312	3.170
5	4.212	**3.993**	3.791

To calculate the present value of an **ordinary annuity** of five payments of $1,000 each discounted at 8%, multiply $1,000 by the appropriate factor ($1,000 payment per period × 3.993 present value factor of an ordinary annuity = **$3,993**).

This situation can be depicted as follows:

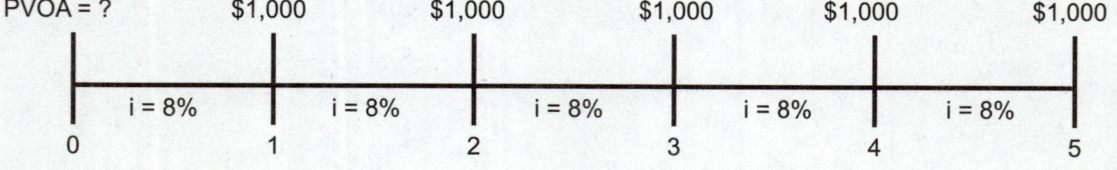

Figure 10-3

PVOA: Present value of an ordinary annuity
i: Interest rate

Using the same table, the present value of an **annuity due** of five payments of $1,000 each also may be calculated. It equals **$4,312** [$1,000 payment per period × 3.993 present value factor of an ordinary annuity × (1 + 0.08)]. The present value of the annuity due ($4,312) is greater than the present value of the ordinary annuity ($3,993) because the payments occur 1 year sooner.

The **future value of an annuity** is the value that a series of equal payments will have at a certain moment in the future if the interest is earned at a given rate.

- Interest is not earned for the first period of an ordinary annuity. Interest is earned on the first payment of an annuity due.

- A typical future value table is for an ordinary annuity, but the future value factor for an annuity due can be easily derived. The future value factor of annuity due is equal to the future value factor of an ordinary annuity multiplied by $(1 + i)$.

Example 10-4   Future Value of an Annuity

	Future Value		
No. of Periods	6%	8%	10%
1	1.000	1.000	1.000
2	2.060	2.080	2.100
3	**3.184**	3.246	3.310
4	4.375	4.506	4.641
5	5.637	5.867	6.105

To calculate the FV of a 3-year **ordinary annuity** with payments of $1,000 each at 6% interest, multiply $1,000 by the appropriate factor ($1,000 × 3.184 = $3,184).

The FV of an **annuity due** also may be determined from the same table. It equals $3,375 [$1,000 × 3.184 × (1 + 0.06)].

The future value of the annuity due ($3,375) is greater than the future value of an ordinary annuity ($3,184). The deposits are made earlier and therefore earn more interest.

Stop & Review

You have completed the outline for this subunit.

Study multiple-choice questions 3 and 4 on page 334.

10.3 Bonds Payable -- Initial Measurement

Calculation of Proceeds

Of primary concern to an entity issuing bonds is the amount of cash that it will receive from investors on the day the bonds are sold.

- This amount is equal to the sum of the **present value of the cash flows** associated with the bonds discounted at the interest rate prevailing in the market at the time (called the market rate or effective rate).

  - The cash flows associated with bonds are

    - **Face amount** (present value of a single amount)
    - **Interest payments** (present value of an annuity)

- Using the effective rate as the discount rate ensures that the bonds' **yield to maturity** (that is, their ultimate rate of return to the investor) is equal to the rate of return prevailing in the market at the time of the sale.

This present value calculation can result in cash proceeds equal to, less than, or greater than the face amount of the bonds, depending on the relationship of the bonds' stated rate of interest to the market rate.

- If the bonds' stated rate equals the market rate at the time of sale, the present value of the bonds will exactly equal their face amount, and the bonds are said to be sold **at par.**

Issuance at a Premium

If the bonds' stated rate is greater than the current market rate, the cash proceeds are greater than the face amount, and the bonds are sold at a premium.

Premium on bonds = Cash proceeds − Bonds' face amount

- Sometimes the issue price is an exact percentage of the face amount. In these cases, the bonds are said to be sold, for example, "at 101" or "at 102."

   - Bonds issued "at 101" are issued at a price equal to 101% of the face amount.

Example 10-5   Bonds Issued at a Premium

On January 1, Year 1, Pritzker, Inc., issues 200 8%, 5-year, $5,000 bonds when the prevailing interest rate in the market is 6%. The total face amount of bonds issued is therefore $1,000,000 ($5,000 face amount × 200 bonds). Annual cash interest payments of $80,000 ($1,000,000 face amount × 8% stated rate) will be made at the end of each year. The present value of the cash flows associated with this bond issue, discounted at the market rate of 6%, is calculated as follows:

Present value of face amount ($1,000,000 × 0.74726)	$ 747,260
Present value of cash interest ($80,000 × 4.21236)	336,987 (rounded)
Cash proceeds from bond issue	$1,084,247

Because the bonds are issued at a premium, the cash proceeds exceed the face amount. Pritzker records the following entry:

Cash (present value of cash flows)	$1,084,247	
Bonds payable (face amount)		$1,000,000
Premium on bonds payable (difference)		84,247

Issuance at a Discount

If the bonds' stated rate is less than the current market rate, the cash proceeds are less than the face amount, and the bonds are sold at a discount.

$$\text{Discount on bonds} = \text{Bonds' face amount} - \text{Cash proceeds}$$

- Sometimes the issue price is an exact percentage of the face amount. In these cases, the bonds are said to be sold, for example, "at 97" or "at 98."

  - Bonds issued "at 99" are issued at a price equal to 99% of the face amount.

Example 10-6   Bonds Issued at a Discount

On January 1, Year 1, Disler Co. issues 200 6%, 5-year, $5,000 bonds when the prevailing interest rate in the market is 8%. The total face amount of bonds issued is therefore $1,000,000 ($5,000 face amount × 200 bonds). Annual cash interest payments of $60,000 ($1,000,000 face amount × 6% stated rate) will be made at the end of each year. The present value of the cash flows associated with this bond issue, discounted at the market rate of 8%, is calculated as follows:

Present value of face amount ($1,000,000 × 0.68058)	$680,580
Present value of cash interest ($60,000 × 3.99271)	239,566 (rounded)
Cash proceeds from bond issue	$920,146

Because the bonds are issued at a discount, the cash proceeds are less than the face amount. Disler records the following entry:

Cash (present value of cash flows)	$920,146	
Discount on bonds payable (difference)	79,854	
Bonds payable (face amount)		$1,000,000

Success Tip

Stated Rate of Bonds	Cash Proceeds from Bonds	Bonds Issued at
Equals the market (effective) rate	Equals face amount	Par
Greater than the market (effective) rate	Greater than face amount	Premium
Lower than the market (effective) rate	Lower than face amount	Discount

Bonds Sold between Interest Dates

When bonds are sold between interest payment dates, the buyer pays the issuer the amount of interest that has accrued since the last payment date.

Example 10-7   Bonds Sold between Interest Dates

On November 1, Year 1, Bland Co. issues, at par, a 15-year bond with a face amount of $100,000. It has a stated rate of 9%, and interest is payable annually on July 1.

Annual interest on the bond is $9,000 ($100,000 face amount × 9% stated rate). On the next payment date (July 1, Year 2), Bland will pay the full annual interest of $9,000 to the buyer. The buyer therefore must pay Bland for the time during the most recent period that the buyer does not hold the bond (July 1– November 1, Year 1). The buyer includes accrued interest of $3,000 [$9,000 × (4 ÷ 12)] in the purchase price of the bond. The following entries will be recorded by Bland Co. and the buyer.

Bland Co.			Buyer		
November 1, Year 1:					
Cash	$103,000		Investment in bond	$100,000	
Bond payable		$100,000	Interest receivable	3,000	
Interest payable		3,000	Cash		$103,000
December 31, Year 1:					
Interest expense [$9,000 × (2 ÷ 12)]	$1,500		Interest receivable	$1,500	
Interest payable		$1,500	Interest income		$1,500
July 1, Year 2:					
Interest expense	$4,500		Cash	$9,000	
Interest payable	4,500		Interest receivable		$4,500
Cash		$9,000	Interest income		4,500

Stop & Review

You have completed the outline for this subunit.

Study multiple-choice questions 5 through 7 beginning on page 335.

10.4 Bonds Payable -- Subsequent Measurement

Balance Sheet Presentation

Bonds payable are reported in the balance sheet at their face amount (1) minus (plus) any unamortized discount (premium) and (2) minus any unamortized debt issuance costs.

$$\text{Carrying amount of bonds payable} = \text{Face amount} \pm \text{Unamortized premium (discount)} - \text{Unamortized debt issuance costs}$$

Effective Interest Method of Amortization

Success Tip

CPA candidates should understand the effective interest method and expect to see a question asking for the calculation of interest expense. Remembering the associated journal entries will allow you to handle any question regarding the effective interest method with confidence.

Bond discount or premium must be amortized using the effective interest method (unless the results of another method are not materially different).

- Under this method, interest expense changes every period, but the effective interest rate remains constant.

$$\text{Annual interest expense} = \text{Carrying amount} \times \text{Effective interest rate}$$

- The cash paid for periodic interest also remains constant over the life of the bonds.

$$\text{Cash interest paid} = \text{Face amount} \times \text{Stated rate}$$

The difference between interest expense and cash interest paid is the discount or premium amortization.

- At the maturity date, the discount or premium is fully amortized, and the carrying amount of the bonds equals the face amount.

Amortization Schedules

Premium amortized, total interest expense, and the carrying amount of the bonds **decrease** each period when amortizing a premium. The entry is

Interest expense	$XXX	
Premium on bonds payable	XXX	
Cash		$XXX

Example 10-8   Bonds Amortization Schedule -- Premium

Pritzker, which issued bonds at a premium, uses the following amortization schedule:

Year	Beginning Carrying Amount	Times: Effective Rate	Equals: Interest Expense	Minus: Cash Paid	Equals: Premium Amortized	Ending Carrying Amount
1	$1,084,247	6%	$65,055	$80,000	$(14,945)	$1,069,302
2	1,069,302	6%	64,158	80,000	(15,842)	1,053,460
3	1,053,460	6%	63,208	80,000	(16,792)	1,036,668
4	1,036,668	6%	62,200	80,000	(17,800)	1,018,868
5	1,018,868	6%	61,132	80,000	(18,868)	1,000,000
					$(84,247)	

December 31, Year 1			December 31, Year 2		
Interest expense	$65,055		Interest expense	$64,158	
Premium on bonds payable	14,945		Premium on bonds payable	15,842	
Cash		$80,000	Cash		$80,000

The bonds payable are reported on the December 31, Year 1, balance sheet at their carrying amount of $1,069,302.

Discount amortized, total interest expense, and the carrying amount of the bonds **increase** each period when amortizing a discount. The entry is

Interest expense	$XXX	
Discount on bonds payable		$XXX
Cash		XXX

Example 10-9   Bonds Amortization Schedule -- Discount

Disler, which issued bonds at a discount, uses the following amortization schedule:

Year	Beginning Carrying Amount	Times: Effective Rate	Equals: Interest Expense	Minus: Cash Paid	Equals: Discount Amortized	Ending Carrying Amount
1	$920,146	8%	$73,612	$60,000	$13,612	$ 933,758
2	933,758	8%	74,701	60,000	14,701	948,458
3	948,458	8%	75,877	60,000	15,877	964,335
4	964,335	8%	77,147	60,000	17,147	981,482
5	981,482	8%	78,519	60,000	18,519	1,000,000
					$79,854	

December 31, Year 1			December 31, Year 2		
Interest expense	$73,612		Interest expense	$74,701	
Discount on bonds payable		$13,612	Discount on bonds payable		$14,701
Cash		60,000	Cash		60,000

The bonds payable are reported on the December 31, Year 1, balance sheet at their carrying amount of $933,758.

Interest on Bonds Paid More Often than Annually

Some bonds may pay interest more often than annually, e.g., semiannually. The accounting for these bonds is based on the number of periods in which interest is paid.

- The interest rates on bonds are provided on an annual basis. For the sake of simplicity, the stated rate and the market (effective) interest rate that apply to each period can be calculated as follows:

$$\frac{\text{Interest rate on an annual basis}}{\text{Number of times interest is paid per year}}$$

Example 10-10   Interest on Bonds Paid Twice a Year

On January 1, Year 1, Eva Co. issued 5-year, 6%, $100,000 bonds. The bonds pay interest semiannually on July 1 and December 31. The bonds were issued to yield 10%. Thus, the market rate on the day of issuance was 10%. Because interest is paid twice a year, the interest is paid over 10 (5 years × 2) semiannual periods. The stated and effective interest rates on each period are 3% (6% ÷ 2) and 5% (10% ÷ 2), respectively.

The proceeds from the bonds equal the present value of the cash flows associated with the bond issue. These proceeds are calculated based on the following information: 10 periods, stated rate of 3%, cash interest payment each period of $3,000 ($100,000 × 3%), and market (effective) rate of 5%.

Bonds' face amount ($100,000) multiplied by the present value of $1 at 5% for 10 periods (0.614)	$61,400
Semiannual cash interest ($3,000) multiplied by the present value of an ordinary annuity of $1 at 5% for 10 periods (7.722)	23,166
Cash proceeds from bond issue	$84,566

January 1, Year 1

Cash	$84,566	
Discount on bonds payable	15,434	
Bonds payable		$100,000

July 1, Year 1

Interest expense ($84,566 × 5%)	$4,228	
Discount on bonds payable		$1,228
Cash		3,000

Success Tip

- When bonds are issued at a **premium**, interest expense for the period equals (1) cash interest paid during the period **minus** (2) premium amortized during the period.
- When bonds are issued at a **discount**, interest expense for the period equals (1) cash interest paid during the period **plus** (2) discount amortized during the period.

Stop & Review

You have completed the outline for this subunit.

Study multiple-choice questions 8 through 10 beginning on page 336.

10.5 Debt Issue Costs

Costs Included

Issue costs are incurred to bring debt to market. They include

- Printing and engraving costs,
- Legal fees,
- Accountants' fees,
- Underwriters' commissions,
- Registration fees, and
- Promotion costs.

Accounting Treatment

Costs to issue debt securities must be reported in the balance sheet as a **direct deduction** from the **face amount of the debt**.

Example 10-11   Bond Issuance Costs

Ron Co. issued, at 98, 50 of its 10%, $1,000 bonds. Ron paid legal and registration fees of $2,000 to issue the bonds. On the issuance date, Ron records the following journal entries:

Cash (50 × $1,000 × 98%)	$49,000		Debt issue costs	$2,000	
Discount on bonds	1,000		Cash		$2,000
Bond payable (face amount)		$50,000			

On the face of the balance sheet, the bonds payable are reported at $47,000 ($50,000 face amount – $1,000 bond discount – $2,000 debt issue costs).

Debt issue costs should be amortized over the term of the debt using the **effective interest method**. But the straight-line amortization method may be applied if the results are not materially different.

Stop & Review

You have completed the outline for this subunit.
Study multiple-choice questions 11 and 12 on page 338.

10.6 Extinguishment of Debt

Early Extinguishment

Issuers sometimes retire debt before maturity, for example, to eliminate high-interest debt when rates are declining or to improve debt ratios.

All extinguishments of debt before scheduled maturities are fundamentally alike and should be accounted for similarly.

The carrying amount is the amount due at maturity, adjusted for unamortized premium or discount and unamortized issue costs.

The reacquisition price is the amount paid on extinguishment, including any call premium and miscellaneous costs of reacquisition.

- An extinguishment may be done by exchanging new securities for the old (a refunding). The reacquisition price equals the total present value of the new securities.

Gains or Losses

Gains or losses are recognized in earnings in the period of extinguishment.

- The gain or loss is measured by the difference between the reacquisition price and the carrying amount of the debt, which includes any unamortized debt issue cost.

Example 10-12   Extinguishment of Debt

Debtor has a noncurrent note payable outstanding with a face amount of $1,000,000. When Debtor decides to extinguish the note at a cost of $1,050,000, the unamortized premium and debt issue costs are $20,000 and $12,500, respectively. Thus, the carrying amount of the note payable on that date is $1,007,500 ($1,000,000 face amount + $20,000 unamortized premium – $12,500 unamortized debt issue costs). Accordingly, the loss on extinguishment is $42,500 ($1,050,000 cost – $1,007,500).

Noncurrent note payable	$1,007,500	
Loss on extinguishment	42,500	
Cash		$1,050,000

Derecognition

A debtor derecognizes a liability only if it has been extinguished. Extinguishment results only if the debtor

- Pays the creditor and is relieved of its obligation with respect to the liability or
- Is legally released from being the primary obligor, either judicially or by the creditor.

Stop & Review

You have completed the outline for this subunit.
Study multiple-choice questions 13 and 14 on page 339.

10.7 Noncurrent Notes Payable

Notes payable are essentially accounted for the same as bonds. However,

- A note is payable to a single creditor, while bonds are payable to many creditors.
- Notes are usually of shorter duration than bonds.
- A loan agreement may require the debtor to pay principal and interest at specified intervals.

Any material premium or discount is amortized using the effective-interest method, as described in Subunit 10.4.

- Discount or premium, loan origination fees, etc., are amortized in accordance with the effective-interest method.
- Discount or premium is not an asset or liability separable from the related note.
  - A discount or premium is therefore reported in the balance sheet as a direct subtraction from, or addition to, the face amount of the note.

Noncurrent notes that are payable in installments are classified as current to the extent of any principal payments due in the coming year.

- Payments not due in the current year are classified as noncurrent.

Different Patterns of Repayments

Some notes require one principal payment at the end of the note's term plus periodic interest payments during the note's term (like a term bond).

Example 10-13   Annual Interest Payments and Term-End Principal Payment

An entity agrees to give, in return for merchandise, a 3-year, $100,000 note bearing 8% interest paid annually. The effective interest rate is 6%. Because the note's stated rate exceeds the effective rate, the note will be issued at a premium.

The entity records the note at the present value of (1) a single payment of $100,000 in 3 years and (2) three interest payments of $8,000 each. These payments are discounted at the effective rate (five decimal places are used for increased accuracy).

Present value of principal ($100,000 × 0.83962)	$ 83,962
Present value of interest ($8,000 × 2.67301)	21,384
Present value of note	$105,346

The entry to record the note is

Inventory	$105,346	
Premium on note payable		$ 5,346
Note payable		100,000

Other notes require equal periodic principal payments plus interest. Each periodic payment includes an equal amount of return of principal and an amount of interest accrued on the beginning carrying amount.

Example 10-14   Equal Periodic Payments Plus Interest

On January 1, Year 1, Shark Co. borrowed $120,000 on a 10% note payable to Bank. Three equal annual principal payments of $40,000 plus interest are paid beginning December 31, Year 1.

Year	Beginning Carrying Amount (a)	Interest Rate	Interest Payment/ Expense (b)	Principal Payment (c)	Total Payment (b) + (c)	Ending Carrying Amount (a) − (c)
1	$120,000	10%	$12,000	$40,000	$52,000	$80,000
2	80,000	10%	8,000	40,000	48,000	40,000
3	40,000	10%	4,000	40,000	44,000	0

A third type of note requires equal periodic cash payments. Each payment includes a principal component (i.e., return of principal) and an interest component.

Example 10-15 Equal Periodic Cash Payments

On January 1, Year 1, Star Co. borrowed $120,000 on a 10% note payable to Bank. Three equal annual payments of $48,254 are paid beginning December 31, Year 1.

Year	Beginning Carrying Amount (a)	Interest Rate	Interest Payment/ Expense (b)	Total Payment (c)	Principal Payment (c) – (b) = (d)	Ending Carrying Amount (a) – (d)
1	$120,000	10%	$12,000	$43,254	$36,254	$83,746
2	83,746	10%	8,375	48,254	39,879	43,867
3	43,867	10%	4,387	48,254	43,867	0

NOTE: The proceeds from the note are equal to the present value of the cash payments associated with the note. The equal annual payment ($48,254) multiplied by the present value of an ordinary annuity of $1 at 10% for three periods (2.48685) equals the proceeds from the note of $120,000.

Stop & Review

You have completed the outline for this subunit.

Study multiple-choice questions 15 and 16 on page 340.

10.8 Troubled Debt Restructurings -- Debtors

A troubled debt restructuring (TDR) occurs when the creditor for economic or legal reasons related to the debtor's financial difficulties grants a concession to the debtor that it would not otherwise consider.

A TDR can consist of either a settlement of the debt in full or a continuation of the debt with a modification in terms.

Settlement in Full with a Transfer of Assets

A **gain on restructuring** is recognized by the debtor when the carrying amount of the debt exceeds the fair value of the asset(s) given.

The debtor also recognizes a **gain or loss on disposition** of the asset equal to the difference between the fair value of the assets given and their carrying amount.

- The total gain (loss) on the restructuring transaction is recognized by the debtor when the carrying amount of the debt is greater (lower) than the carrying amount of the assets given.

Example 10-16   TDR Settled with Assets

Due to financial difficulties, a Debtor enters a troubled debt restructuring agreement for its mortgage with Creditor. Debtor transfers a building to Creditor in full settlement of the mortgage. The carrying amount of Debtor's mortgage is $5,000,000. The building's fair value is $4,500,000 and its carrying amount is $6,000,000.

Debtor's entry:

Mortgage payable (carrying amount)	$5,000,000	
Loss on disposition of building (Carrying amount – Fair value)	1,500,000	
Building (carrying amount)		$6,000,000
Gain on restructuring (Debt settled – Fair value of building)		500,000

NOTE: The total loss recognized by Debtor of $1,000,000 ($1,500,000 loss on disposition – $500,000 gain on restructuring) equals the excess of the carrying amount of the asset given ($6,000,000) over the carrying amount of the debt ($5,000,000).

Settlement in Full with a Transfer of an Equity Interest

A debtor issues an equity interest to a creditor to fully settle the debt.

The debtor recognizes a **gain** on the restructuring for the excess of the carrying amount of the debt over the fair value of the equity interest granted.

Example 10-17   TDR Settled with Equity Securities

Using the information from Example 10-16, assume that Debtor issued 100,000 shares of common stock ($10 par value) to Creditor to fully settle the mortgage. The fair value per share was $48.

Because the carrying amount of the mortgage payable of $5,000,000 is greater than the fair value of the equity securities transferred of $4,800,000 (100,000 × $48), a gain on restructuring is recognized by the Debtor.

Debtor's entry:

Mortgage payable (carrying amount)	$5,000,000	
Common stock (100,000 shares at $10 par)		$1,000,000
Additional paid-in capital (Fair value of stock – Total par value)		3,800,000
Gain on restructuring (Debt settled – Fair value of stock)		200,000

Modification of Terms

Three changes in the terms of the debt are common:

- A reduction in the principal
- An extension of the maturity date
- A lowering of the interest rate

The debtor accounts for the modification of terms based on the **undiscounted cash flows** (UCF) associated with the modified terms.

When the UCF associated with the modified terms are **greater** than the **carrying amount** of the troubled debt:

UCF > Carrying amount of the debt

- **No gain** is recognized by the debtor.
- The carrying amount of the debt is unchanged.

Example 10-18   Modified Terms -- UCF > Carrying Amount of Debt

Instead of a full settlement as illustrated in Examples 10-16 and 10-17, Creditor agrees that (1) the mortgage principal will be reduced from $5,000,000 to $4,000,000, (2) the final maturity will be extended from 1 year to 5 years, and (3) the interest rate on the mortgage will be reduced from 8% to 6%. Interest continues to be paid at year end.

The new principal of $4,000,000 plus interest of $1,200,000 ($4,000,000 × 6% × 5 years) yields a UCF of $5,200,000. Because the UCF exceeds the carrying amount of the debt ($5,200,000 > $5,000,000), Debtor recognizes no gain. It continues making journal entries to record periodic interest payments and retirement of debt.

When the UCF associated with the modified terms are **less** than the **carrying amount** of the troubled debt:

$$\text{UCF} < \text{Carrying amount of the debt}$$

- A **gain** is recognized by the debtor for the difference.

- The carrying amount of the debt is reduced to the undiscounted cash flows specified by the new term.

Example 10-19   Modified Terms -- UCF < Carrying Amount of Debt

Instead of reducing the principal to $4,000,000, Creditor agrees to reduce the principal to $3,000,000. The principal of $3,000,000 plus interest of $900,000 ($3,000,000 × 6% × 5 years) yields UCF of $3,900,000.

Because the UCF are less than the carrying amount of the debt ($3,900,000 < $5,000,000), Debtor recognizes a gain equal to the difference and reduces the carrying amount of the mortgage payable to the UCF of $3,900,000.

Debtor's entry:

Mortgage payable	$1,100,000	
Gain on restructuring		$1,100,000

Stop & Review

You have completed the outline for this subunit.
Study multiple-choice question 17 on page 341.

10.9 Asset Retirement Obligations

Certain long-lived tangible assets, such as mines or nuclear power plants, incur significant costs after the end of their productive lives.

An asset retirement obligation (ARO) reflects a legal obligation arising from acquisition, construction, development, or normal operation of an asset.

- A legal obligation is one arising from an existing or enacted law, statute, ordinance, or contract.

Initial Recognition and Measurement

An entity must recognize the fair value of a liability for an ARO. Upon initial recognition of such a liability, an entity must **capitalize** an **asset retirement cost (ARC)** by increasing the carrying amount of the related asset by the same amount as the liability recognized.

- The journal entry is

Asset	$XXX	
Liability for asset retirement obligation		$XXX

If an item of property, plant, and equipment with an existing ARO is acquired, the entity credits a liability for that obligation and debits the carrying amount of the item for the same amount (the ARC) at the acquisition date. The effect is the same as if that obligation were incurred on that date.

The fair value of the liability is **initially measured** by using an **expected present value technique**. The liability recognized equals the present value of the future cash flows expected to be paid to settle the obligation discounted at the **credit-adjusted risk-free rate**.

Example 10-20   Initial Recognition and Measurement of ARO

On January 1, Year 1, Akula Co. acquired a plant for $200,000. The estimated useful life of the plant is 5 years with no salvage value. Akula is required by law to remove the plant and restore the land at the end of the plant's useful life. Akula estimates that the total cost to settle the liability for retirement of the plant is $50,000. Akula's credit-adjusted risk-free rate is 6%. The present value of $1 for a 5-year period at 6% is 0.7473. The present value of the future cash flows expected to be paid to settle the liability is $37,365 ($50,000 × 0.7473).

On January 1, Year 1, Akula recorded the following journal entry:

Plant ($200,000 + $37,365)	$237,365	
Cash		$200,000
Liability for plant retirement obligation		37,365

Accounting Subsequent to Initial Recognition

After initial recognition, the ARC should be depreciated over the asset's useful life.

In addition, the liability recognized must be adjusted periodically for (1) the passage of time (accretion expense) and (2) revisions in the original estimate.

Example 10-21   Subsequent Accounting for ARO

By using the effective interest method, Akula Co. recognized the following accretion expenses in Years 1 through 5:

Year	Liability at Beginning of Year	Discount Rate	Accretion Expense	Liability at Year End
1	$37,365	6%	$2,242	$39,607
2	39,607	6%	2,375	41,982
3	41,982	6%	2,519	44,501
4	44,501	6%	2,670	47,171
5	47,171	6%	2,829	50,000

Akula recorded the following journal entries on December 31, Year 1:

Depreciation expense ($237,365 ÷ 5)	$47,473	
Accumulated depreciation		$47,473
Accretion expense	$2,242	
Liability for plant retirement obligation		$2,242

The plant and related liability are reported on the December 31, Year 1, balance sheet as follows:

Noncurrent assets:		Noncurrent liabilities:	
Plant	$237,365	Liability for plant retirement obligation	$39,607
Accumulated depreciation	(47,473)		
Carrying amount	$189,892		

At the end of the asset's useful life, the actual costs incurred to settle the liability may differ from the carrying amount of the liability on that date. The difference between the amount paid and the carrying amount of the liability for an ARO is recognized as a gain or loss on settlement of the ARO.

Example 10-22   Settlement of ARO

At the end of the plant's service life, Akula Co. incurred costs of $55,000 for restoring the land. The journal entry is

Asset retirement obligation	$50,000	
Loss on settlement of ARO	5,000	
Cash		$55,000

Stop & Review

You have completed the outline for this subunit.
Study multiple-choice question 18 on page 341.

Questions

10.1 Types of Bond Liabilities

1. Blue Corp.'s December 31, Year 4, balance sheet contained the following items in the long-term liabilities section:

9.75% registered debentures, callable in Year 15, due in Year 20	$700,000
9.50% collateral trust bonds, convertible into common stock beginning in Year 13, due in Year 23	600,000
10% subordinated debentures ($30,000 maturing annually beginning in Year 10)	300,000

What is the total amount of Blue's term bonds?

A. $600,000

B. $700,000

C. $1,000,000

D. $1,300,000

✔ **Answer (D) is correct.**
Required: The total amount of term bonds.
Discussion: Term bonds mature on a single date. Thus, the registered bonds and the collateral trust bonds are term bonds, a total of $1,300,000 ($700,000 + $600,000).

✗ **Answer (A) is incorrect.** The registered bonds are also term bonds.

✗ **Answer (B) is incorrect.** The collateral trust bonds are also term bonds.

✗ **Answer (C) is incorrect.** The collateral trust bonds, not the subordinated debentures, are term bonds.

2. Bonds payable issued with scheduled maturities at various dates are called

	Serial Bonds	Term Bonds
A.	No	Yes
B.	No	No
C.	Yes	No
D.	Yes	Yes

✔ **Answer (C) is correct.**
Required: The name(s) for bonds issued with scheduled maturities at various dates.
Discussion: Serial bonds are bond issues that mature in installments at various dates. Term bonds mature on a single date.

10.2 Time Value of Money

3. On December 30, Chang Co. sold a machine to Door Co. in exchange for a noninterest-bearing note requiring 10 annual payments of $10,000. Door made the first payment on December 30. The market interest rate for similar notes at date of issuance was 8%. Information on present value factors is as follows:

Number of Periods	Present Value of $1 at 8%	Present Value of Ordinary Annuity of $1 at 8%
9	0.50	6.25
10	0.46	6.71

In its December 31 balance sheet, what amount should Chang report as note receivable?

A. $45,000

B. $46,000

C. $62,500

D. $67,100

✔ **Answer (C) is correct.**
Required: The carrying amount of a noninterest-bearing note receivable at the date of issuance.
Discussion: The purchase agreement calls for a $10,000 initial payment and equal payments of $10,000 to be received at the end of each of the next 9 years. The amount reported for the receivable should consist of the present value of the nine future payments. The present value factor to be used is the present value of an ordinary annuity for nine periods at 8%, or 6.25. The note receivable should be recorded at $62,500 ($10,000 × 6.25).

✘ **Answer (A) is incorrect.** The amount of $45,000 results from multiplying $90,000 ($10,000 payments × 9 years) by 0.50.

✘ **Answer (B) is incorrect.** The amount of $46,000 results from multiplying the $100,000 total by 0.46.

✘ **Answer (D) is incorrect.** The amount of $67,100 results from using the present value of an ordinary annuity of $1 at 8% for 10 years instead of 9 years.

4. For which of the following transactions would the use of the present value of an annuity due concept be appropriate in calculating the present value of the asset obtained or liability owed at the date of incurrence?

A. A finance lease is entered into with the initial lease payment due 1 month subsequent to the signing of the lease agreement.

B. A finance lease is entered into with the initial lease payment due upon the signing of the lease agreement.

C. A 10-year, 8% bond is issued on January 2 with interest payable semiannually on July 1 and January 1, yielding 7%.

D. A 10-year, 8% bond is issued on January 2 with interest payable semiannually on July 1 and January 1, yielding 9%.

✔ **Answer (B) is correct.**
Required: The transaction for which the present value of an annuity due concept would be appropriate.
Discussion: In an annuity due, the first payment is made at the beginning of the first period and is therefore not discounted. In an ordinary annuity, the first payment is made at the end of the first period and therefore is discounted. For annuities due, the first payment is included in the computation at its face value.

✘ **Answer (A) is incorrect.** Given that the first payment is due 1 month from signing and not on the day of signing, an ordinary annuity, not an annuity due, is the relevant model.

✘ **Answer (C) is incorrect.** The bonds have just passed an interest payment (coupon) date. The next one is not for another 6 months. Given no immediate payment, the annuity is ordinary. Furthermore, the yield percentage is irrelevant to annuity.

✘ **Answer (D) is incorrect.** The initial payment is not due immediately.

10.3 Bonds Payable -- Initial Measurement

5. On November 1, Mason Corp. issued $800,000 of its 10-year, 8% term bonds dated October 1. The bonds were sold to yield 10%, with total proceeds of $700,000 plus accrued interest. Interest is paid every April 1 and October 1. What amount should Mason report for interest payable in its December 31 balance sheet?

   A. $17,500

   B. $16,000

   C. $11,667

   D. $10,667

✓ **Answer (B) is correct.**
Required: The interest payable reported in the balance sheet.
Discussion: Interest payable equals the face amount of the bonds, times the nominal (stated) interest rate, times the portion of the interest period included in the accounting period. The yield rate and sale between interest periods for an amount including accrued interest do not affect interest payable. Accordingly, interest payable equals $16,000 [($800,000 × 8%) × (3 ÷ 12 months)].

✗ **Answer (A) is incorrect.** The amount of $17,500 equals 3 months of interest based on the yield rate and the sale proceeds (exclusive of accrued interest).

✗ **Answer (C) is incorrect.** The amount of $11,667 equals 2 months of interest based on the yield rate and the sale proceeds (exclusive of accrued interest).

✗ **Answer (D) is incorrect.** The amount of $10,667 equals the interest for 2 months.

6. The following information pertains to Camp Corp.'s issuance of bonds on July 1, Year 4:

Face amount	$800,000
Term	10 years
Stated interest rate	6%
Interest payment dates	Annually on July 1
Yield	9%

	At 6%	At 9%
Present value of 1 for 10 periods	0.558	0.422
Future value of 1 for 10 periods	1.791	2.367
Present value of ordinary annuity of 1 for 10 periods	7.360	6.418

What should the issue price be for each $1,000 bond?

   A. $1,000

   B. $943

   C. $864

   D. $807

✓ **Answer (D) is correct.**
Required: The issue price for each bond.
Discussion: The issue price of a bond equals the sum of the present values of the future cash flows (Principal + Interest). This amount is $807 [($1,000 face amount × .422 PV of 1 for 10 periods at 9%) principal + ($1,000 face amount × 6% stated rate × 6.418 PV of an ordinary annuity for 10 periods at 9%) interest].

✗ **Answer (A) is incorrect.** The face amount is $1,000.

✗ **Answer (B) is incorrect.** The amount of $943 is the result of discounting the interest payments at 9% and the face amount at 6%.

✗ **Answer (C) is incorrect.** The amount of $864 is the result of discounting the interest payments at 6% and the face amount at 9%.

7. Album Co. issued 10-year $200,000 debenture bonds on January 2. The bonds pay interest semiannually. Album uses the effective interest method to amortize bond premiums and discounts. The carrying amount of the bonds on January 2 was $185,953. A journal entry was recorded for the first interest payment on June 30, debiting interest expense for $13,016 and crediting cash for $12,000. What is the annual stated interest rate for the debenture bonds?

A. 6%

B. 7%

C. 12%

D. 14%

Answer (C) is correct.
Required: The annual stated interest rate for bonds.
Discussion: The cash disbursed for semiannual interest was $12,000, so interest for an entire year is $24,000 ($12,000 × 2). Dividing this amount by the face amount of the bonds results in a stated rate of 12% ($24,000 ÷ $200,000). The other data are irrelevant.
Answer (A) is incorrect. This percentage is half of the annual stated rate. The first interest payment is one of two semiannual payments.
Answer (B) is incorrect. This percentage is half of the annual effective rate.
Answer (D) is incorrect. This percentage is the annual effective rate [2 × ($13,016 ÷ $185,953)].

10.4 Bonds Payable -- Subsequent Measurement

8. How is the carrying amount of a bond payable affected by amortization of the following?

	Discount	Premium
A.	Increase	Increase
B.	Decrease	Decrease
C.	Increase	Decrease
D.	Decrease	Increase

Answer (C) is correct.
Required: The effect of discount and premium amortization on the carrying value of a bond payable.
Discussion: The carrying amount of a bond payable is equal to its maturity (face) amount plus any unamortized premium or minus any unamortized discount. Amortization results in a reduction of the discount or premium. Consequently, the carrying amount of a bond is increased when discount is amortized and decreased when premium is amortized.

9. On January 1, Year 2, Oak Co. issued 400 of its 8%, $1,000 bonds at 97 plus accrued interest. The bonds are dated October 1, Year 1, and mature on October 1, Year 11. Interest is payable semiannually on April 1 and October 1. Accrued interest for the period October 1, Year 1, to January 1, Year 2, amounted to $8,000. On January 1, Year 2, what amount should Oak report as bonds payable, net of discount?

A. $380,300

B. $388,000

C. $388,300

D. $392,000

Answer (B) is correct.
Required: The bonds payable, net of discount.
Discussion: A bond issued "at 97" is issued at a price equal to 97% of its face amount (400 bonds × $1,000 face amount × .97 = $388,000). At the issue date, no time has passed, so no amortization has occurred, and the accrued interest is credited to either interest payable or interest expense. The reported amount is therefore $388,000 ($400,000 − $12,000).
Answer (A) is incorrect. The amount of $380,300 deducts the accrued interest from the net bonds payable and adds 3 months of discount amortization.
Answer (C) is incorrect. The amount of $388,300 includes 3 months of discount amortization.
Answer (D) is incorrect. The amount of $392,000 equals face amount minus accrued interest.

10. On December 31, Year 1, Arnold, Inc., issued $200,000, 8% serial bonds, to be repaid in the amount of $40,000 each year. Interest is payable annually on December 31. The bonds were issued to yield 10% per year. The bond proceeds were $190,280 based on the present values at December 31, Year 1, of the five annual payments:

Due Date	Amounts Due Principal	Amounts Due Interest	Present Value at 12/31/Yr 1
12/31/Yr 2	$40,000	$16,000	$ 50,900
12/31/Yr 3	40,000	12,800	43,610
12/31/Yr 4	40,000	9,600	37,250
12/31/Yr 5	40,000	6,400	31,690
12/31/Yr 6	40,000	3,200	26,830
			$190,280

Arnold amortizes the bond discount by the interest method. In its December 31, Year 2, balance sheet, at what amount should Arnold report the carrying amount of the bonds?

A. $139,380

B. $149,100

C. $150,280

D. $153,308

✔ **Answer (D) is correct.**

Required: The carrying amount after year one of bonds issued at a discount.

Discussion: The carrying amount of the bonds at the end of Year 1 equals the proceeds of $190,280. Interest expense for Year 2 at the 10% effective rate is thus $19,028. Actual interest paid is $16,000, discount amortization is $3,028 ($19,028 – $16,000), and the discount remaining at year end is $6,692 [($200,000 face amount – $190,280 issue proceeds) – $3,028 discount amortization]. Given that $40,000 in principal is paid at year end, the December 31, Year 2, carrying amount is $153,308 ($160,000 face amount – $6,692 unamortized discount).

✘ **Answer (A) is incorrect.** The amount of $139,380 is the carrying amount of the bonds at December 31, Year 2, less the total amount due in Year 3.

✘ **Answer (B) is incorrect.** The amount of $149,100 is the difference between the face amount of the bonds and the total payment in Year 3.

✘ **Answer (C) is incorrect.** The amount of $150,280 results from reducing the carrying amount at December 31, Year 2, by the payment of principal during Year 3.

10.5 Debt Issue Costs

11. On March 1, Year 1, Cain Corp. issued, at 103 plus accrued interest, 200 of its 9%, $1,000 bonds. The bonds are dated January 1, Year 1, and mature on January 1, Year 11. Interest is payable semiannually on January 1 and July 1. Cain paid bond issue costs of $10,000. Cain should realize net cash receipts from the bond issuance of

   A. $216,000

   B. $209,000

   C. $206,000

   D. $199,000

✔ **Answer (D) is correct.**
Required: The cash received from the issuance of a bond at a premium plus accrued interest.
Discussion: The face amount of the bonds is $200,000 (200 bonds × $1,000 face amount). Excluding interest, the proceeds from the issuance of the bonds were $206,000 ($200,000 × 103%). Accrued interest for 2 months (January 1 through March 1) was $3,000 ($200,000 face amount × 9% coupon rate × 2/12). The net cash receipts from the issuance of the bonds were therefore equal to $199,000 ($206,000 bond proceeds + $3,000 accrued interest – $10,000 bond issue costs).

✘ **Answer (A) is incorrect.** The amount of $216,000 equals the sum of the bond proceeds (excluding accrued interest) and the bond issue costs.

✘ **Answer (B) is incorrect.** The amount of $209,000 is the sum of the bond proceeds and the accrued interest.

✘ **Answer (C) is incorrect.** The amount of $206,000 is the sum of the bond proceeds (excluding accrued interest).

12. Lake Co. issued 3,000 of its 9%, $1,000 face amount bonds at 101 1/2. In connection with the sale of these bonds, Lake paid the following expenses:

Promotion costs	$ 20,000
Engraving and printing	25,000
Underwriters' commissions	200,000

What amount should Lake record as bond issue costs to be amortized over the term of the bonds?

   A. $0

   B. $220,000

   C. $225,000

   D. $245,000

✔ **Answer (D) is correct.**
Required: The amount to be recorded as debt issue costs.
Discussion: Debt issue costs include (1) printing costs, (2) underwriters' commissions, (3) attorney's fees, and (4) promotion costs (including preparation of a prospectus). The issue costs to be amortized equal $245,000 ($20,000 promotion costs + $25,000 printing costs + $200,000 underwriters' commissions). Debt issue costs are presented as a direct deduction from the related debt liability.

✘ **Answer (A) is incorrect.** An amount of debt issue costs should be amortized.

✘ **Answer (B) is incorrect.** The $25,000 of printing costs also are debt issue costs that should be amortized.

✘ **Answer (C) is incorrect.** The $20,000 of promotion costs also are debt issue costs that should be amortized.

10.6 Extinguishment of Debt

13. On June 30, Year 7, King Co. had outstanding 9%, $5,000,000 face value bonds maturing on June 30, Year 9. Interest was payable semiannually every June 30 and December 31. On June 30, Year 7, after amortization was recorded for the period, the unamortized bond premium and bond issue costs were $30,000 and $50,000, respectively. On that date, King acquired all its outstanding bonds on the open market at 98 and retired them. At June 30, Year 7, what amount should King recognize as gain before income taxes on redemption of bonds?

   A. $20,000

   B. $80,000

   C. $120,000

   D. $180,000

✔ **Answer (B) is correct.**
Required: The amount of gain from the redemption of bonds.
Discussion: The amount of gain or loss on the redemption of bonds is equal to the difference between the proceeds paid and the carrying amount of the debt. The carrying amount of the bonds is equal to the face amount, plus unamortized bond premium, minus unamortized bond issue costs. Thus, the carrying amount of the bonds is $4,980,000 ($5,000,000 + $30,000 – $50,000). The $80,000 gain is the difference between the carrying amount ($4,980,000) and the amount paid $4,900,000 ($5,000,000 × 98%).

✘ **Answer (A) is incorrect.** The amount of $20,000 results from subtracting the unamortized bond premium and bond issue costs from the face amount of the bond.

✘ **Answer (C) is incorrect.** The amount of $120,000 results from adding the unamortized bond issue costs and subtracting the issue costs to find the carrying amount.

✘ **Answer (D) is incorrect.** The amount of $180,000 results from adding the unamortized bond issue costs and bond premium to find the carrying amount of the bond.

14. Ray Finance, Inc., issued a 10-year, $100,000, 9% note on January 1, Year 1. The note was issued to yield 10% for proceeds of $93,770. Interest is payable semiannually. The note is callable after 2 years at a price of $96,000. Due to a decline in the market rate to 8%, Ray retired the note on December 31, Year 3. On that date, the carrying amount of the note was $94,582, and the discounted amount of its cash flows based on the market rate was $105,280. What amount should Ray report as gain (loss) from retirement of the note for the year ended December 31, Year 3?

   A. $9,280

   B. $4,000

   C. $(2,230)

   D. $(1,418)

✔ **Answer (D) is correct.**
Required: The amount of gain (loss) from the extinguishment of a note.
Discussion: The amount of gain or loss resulting from the extinguishment of debt is the difference between the amount paid and the carrying amount of the note. Thus, a loss of $1,418 ($94,582 carrying amount – $96,000 amount paid) results from the extinguishment.

✘ **Answer (A) is incorrect.** The difference between the discounted amount, based on the market rate, and the call price is $9,280.

✘ **Answer (B) is incorrect.** The difference between the face amount of the note and the call price is $4,000.

✘ **Answer (C) is incorrect.** The difference between the original amount received and the call price is $(2,230).

10.7 Noncurrent Notes Payable

Questions 15 and 16 are based on the following information.

House Publishers offered a contest in which the winner would receive $1 million, payable over 20 years. On December 31, Year 4, House announced the winner of the contest and signed a note payable to the winner for $1 million, payable in $50,000 installments every January 2. Also on December 31, Year 4, House purchased an annuity for $418,250 to provide the $950,000 prize monies remaining after the first $50,000 installment, which was paid on January 2, Year 5.

15. In its Year 4 income statement, what should House report as contest prize expense?

    A. $0

    B. $418,250

    C. $468,250

    D. $1,000,000

✔ **Answer (C) is correct.**
Required: The contest prize expense.
Discussion: The contest prize expense equals $468,250 ($418,250 cost of the annuity + $50,000 first installment).

✘ **Answer (A) is incorrect.** The sum of the cost of the annuity and the first installment must be recognized as an expense in Year 4.

✘ **Answer (B) is incorrect.** The amount of $418,250 does not include the $50,000 installment due in Year 5.

✘ **Answer (D) is incorrect.** The face amount of the note is $1,000,000.

16. In its December 31, Year 4, balance sheet, at what amount should House measure the note payable, net of current portion?

    A. $368,250

    B. $418,250

    C. $900,000

    D. $950,000

✔ **Answer (B) is correct.**
Required: The amount at which the note payable should be measured.
Discussion: Noninterest-bearing notes payable should be measured at their present value rather than their face amount. Thus, the measure of the note payable, net of the current portion, which has a nominal amount equal to its present value at December 31, Year 4, of $50,000, is its present value of $418,250 (debit annuity cost $418,250, debit discount $531,750, credit note payable $950,000). The present value of the noncurrent portion of the note is assumed to be the cash given for the annuity ($418,250) because no other right or privilege was exchanged.

✘ **Answer (A) is incorrect.** The amount of $368,250 includes a reduction of $50,000 for the first installment.

✘ **Answer (C) is incorrect.** The amount of $900,000 equals the face amount of the note payable minus two installments.

✘ **Answer (D) is incorrect.** The amount of $950,000 equals the face amount of the note payable minus the first installment.

10.8 Troubled Debt Restructurings -- Debtors

17. For a troubled debt restructuring involving only a modification of terms, which of the following items specified by the new terms would be compared with the carrying amount of the debt to determine whether the debtor should report a gain on restructuring?

A. The total future cash payments.

B. The present value of the debt at the original interest rate.

C. The present value of the debt at the modified interest rate.

D. The amount of future cash payments designated as principal repayments.

✔ **Answer (A) is correct.**
Required: The item used to determine the debtor's gain on a troubled debt restructuring.
Discussion: When a troubled debt restructuring includes a modification of terms that results in future undiscounted cash flows less than the carrying amount of the debt, the debtor recognizes a gain equal to the difference. No gain is recognized if the future undiscounted cash flows are greater than the carrying amount of the debt.

10.9 Asset Retirement Obligations

18. On January 1, 10 years ago, Andrew Co. created a subsidiary for the purpose of buying an oil tanker depot at a cost of $1,500,000. Andrew expected to operate the depot for 10 years, at which time it is legally required to dismantle the depot and remove underground storage tanks. It was estimated that it would cost $150,000 to dismantle the depot and remove the tanks at the end of the depot's useful life. However, the actual cost to demolish and dismantle the depot and remove the tanks in the 10th year is $155,000. What amount of loss should Andrew recognize in its financial statements in Year 10?

A. None.

B. $5,000.

C. $150,000.

D. $155,000.

✔ **Answer (B) is correct.**
Required: The settlement loss for an ARO.
Discussion: The asset retirement obligation (ARO) is recognized at fair value when incurred. An expected present value technique ordinarily is used to estimate the fair value. An amount equal to the ARO is the associated asset retirement cost (ARC). It is debited to the long-lived asset when the ARO is credited. The ARC is allocated to expense using the straight-line method over the life of the underlying asset (debit depreciation expense, credit accumulated depreciation). Furthermore, the entity recognizes accretion expense as an allocation of the difference between the maturity amount and the carrying amount of the ARO. Accretion expense for a period equals the beginning carrying amount of the ARO times the credit-adjusted risk-free interest rate. This amount is debited to accretion expense and credited to the ARO. At the end of the useful life of the underlying asset (the depot), the ARO should equal its maturity amount ($150,000). Moreover, the carrying amount of the ARC is zero. The total credits to accumulated depreciation equal the initial debit to record the ARC. Accordingly, given that the ARO liability after 10 years is $150,000, and the settlement cost is $155,000, the entry to record the settlement is to debit the ARO for $150,000, debit a loss for $5,000, and credit cash (or other accounts) for $155,000.

✘ **Answer (A) is incorrect.** The actual settlement cost exceeded the ARO.

✘ **Answer (C) is incorrect.** The amount of $150,000 is the maturity amount of the ARO.

✘ **Answer (D) is incorrect.** The actual settlement cost equals $155,000.

Study Unit Eleven

Lessee Accounting, Contingencies, and Warranties

(21 pages of outline)

11.1 Lease Classification

Basic Definitions

A **lease** is a contractual agreement in which the **lessor** (owner) conveys to the **lessee** the right to control the use of specific **property, plant, or equipment** for a stated period in exchange for a stated payment. The lease standard does not apply to leases of intangible assets or inventory.

The **commencement date of the lease** is the date on which a lessor makes a leased asset available for use by a lessee.

The **lease term** is the noncancelable period for which the lessee has the right to use the leased asset. Periods covered by an option to extend the lease are **included** in the lease term if (1) the lessee is reasonably certain to exercise that option or (2) the option is controlled by the lessor.

- The periods covered by the option to terminate the lease are included in the lease term only if the lessee is reasonably certain not to exercise that option.

A **right-of-use asset** represents a **lessee's** right to use a leased asset for the lease term.

Lease payments at the lease commencement date consist of the following:

- **Rental payments** are the periodic amounts owed by the lessee minus any incentives paid or payable to the lessee.

- A **purchase option** is the exercise price of an option to purchase the leased asset if the lessee is reasonably certain to exercise the option.

- **Penalties for terminating the lease** (nonrenewal penalties) are included if the lessee is expected to exercise the option to terminate the lease.

  - For a lessee, the lease payments also include the amounts probable of being owed by the lessee under **residual value guarantees**.

The **guaranteed residual value** is a guarantee made to a lessor that the value of a leased asset returned to the lessor at the end of a lease term will be at least a specified amount. This residual value can be guaranteed by the lessee or any other third party unrelated to the lessor.

The **discount rate** for the lease is the **rate implicit in the lease**. If the lessee cannot determine the rate implicit in the lease, the lessee uses its **incremental borrowing rate**.

- The **rate implicit in the lease** is the interest rate that on the lease commencement date causes (1) the fair value of the leased asset to equal (2) the present value of the lease payments plus the present value of the amount that the lessor expects to derive from the leased asset following the end of the lease term.

$$
\begin{array}{ccc}
\textbf{Fair value of the} & = & \textbf{PV of the lease} \\
\textbf{leased asset} & & \textbf{payments}
\end{array}
\quad + \quad
\begin{array}{c}
\textbf{PV of the amount that the lessor} \\
\textbf{expects to derive from the leased asset} \\
\textbf{following the end of the lease term}
\end{array}
$$

  - The amount that a lessor expects to derive from the asset following the end of the lease term includes

    - The guaranteed residual value and
    - The unguaranteed residual value of the leased asset.

- A lessee that is not a public business entity can use a risk-free discount rate for the lease instead of its incremental borrowing rate.

Lease Classification

A lease is classified as a **finance lease by the lessee** if, at lease commencement, **at least one** of the **five criteria** below is met:

1. The lease **transfers ownership** of the leased asset to the lessee by the end of the lease term.

2. The lease includes an **option to purchase** the leased asset that the lessee is reasonably certain to exercise.

3. The lease term is for the major part of the remaining **economic life** of the leased asset.

    - A lease term of **75%** or more of the remaining economic life of the leased asset generally is considered to be a major part of its remaining economic life.

    - This criterion is inapplicable if the beginning of the lease term is at or near the end of the economic life of the leased asset. This period generally is considered to be the last 25% of the leased asset's total economic life.

4. The **present value** of the sum of (a) the **lease payments** and (b) any **residual value guaranteed by the lessee** equals or exceeds substantially all of the **fair value** of the leased asset.

    - A present value of **90%** or more of the fair value of the leased asset generally is considered to be substantially all of its fair value.

5. The leased asset is so specialized that it is expected to have **no alternative use** to the lessor at the end of the lease term.

When none of the five classification criteria described above are met, the lease is classified as an **operating lease** by the **lessee**.

A **short-term lease** is a lease that, at the commencement date, has a lease term of **12 months or less** and does not include a purchase option that the lessee is reasonably certain to exercise.

- As an accounting policy for **short-term leases**, a **lessee** may elect **not** to recognize the **right-of-use asset** and **lease liability**.

- Under this short-term lease exception, the lessee recognizes lease payments as rent expense on the straight-line basis over the full lease term.

    - The lessee records the following journal entry:

Rent expense	$XXX	
Cash or rent payable		$XXX

Example 11-1   Short-Term Lease -- Lessee

On October 1, Year 1, Gulf Co. entered into a 1-year lease contract for its warehouse. It elected not to recognize the right-of-use asset and lease liability for its short-term lease. The following are the lease terms:

- The first 2 months' rent are free.
- Monthly rent from December of Year 1 through September of Year 2 is $3,600.

The total rent expense over the lease term of $36,000 ($3,600 × 10 months) is recognized on a straight-line basis over the entire lease term of 12 months. Accordingly, from October of Year 1, monthly rent expense recognized is $3,000 ($36,000 total rent expense over the lease term ÷ 12-month lease term). Rent expense recognized is $9,000 ($3,000 × 3 months) in Year 1 and $27,000 ($3,000 × 9 months) in Year 2.

Decision Tree: Classification of the Lease by the Lessee

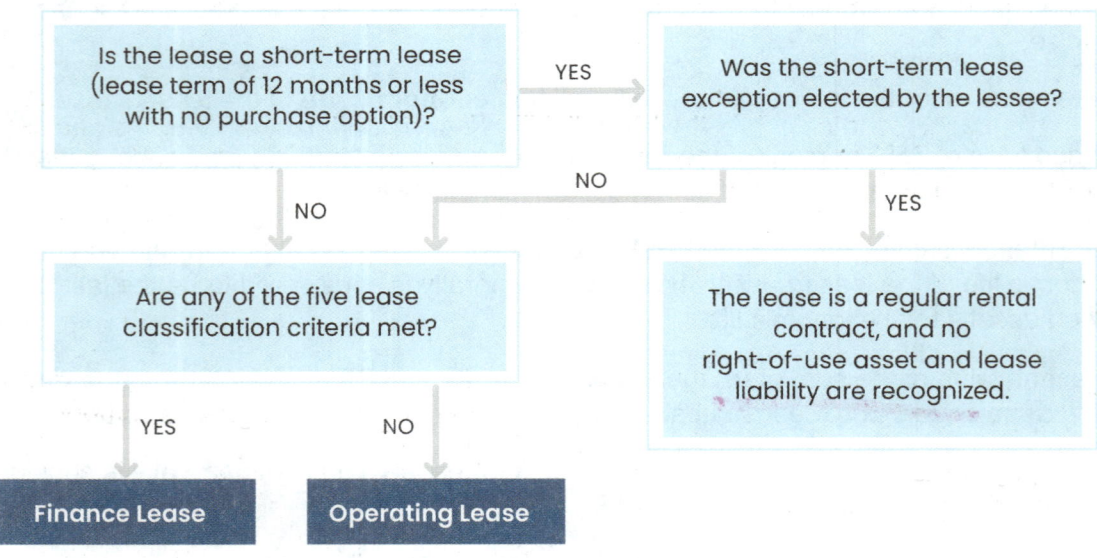

Figure 11-1

Stop & Review

You have completed the outline for this subunit.

Study multiple-choice questions 1 and 2 beginning on page 365.

11.2 Lessee Accounting -- Initial Measurement

General Rule

For **finance and operating leases**, a **lessee** must recognize a **lease liability** and a **right-of-use asset** at the lease commencement date.

Finance and operating leases result in the **same accounting** for

- Initial recognition and measurement of the lease liability,
- Initial recognition and measurement of the right-of-use asset, and
- Subsequent measurement of the lease liability.

The accounting for subsequent measurement of a right-of-use asset differs under finance and operating leases.

Lease Liability

At the lease commencement date, a **lease liability** is measured at the **present value of the lease payments** to be made over the lease term.

The lease payments are discounted using the discount rate for the lease.

- It is the rate implicit in the lease, if known to the lessee.
- If not, it is the lessee's incremental borrowing rate.

The lease payments used to calculate the lease liability depend on the specific terms of each lease contract.

- If the lease includes a purchase option that the lessee is reasonably certain to exercise, the lease payments consist of the

  - Rental payments
  - Exercise price of the purchase option

- If no purchase option exists, the lease payments may have the following three components:

  1. Rental payments
  2. Any penalties for terminating the lease (nonrenewal penalties)
  3. Amounts probable of being owed by the lessee under residual value guarantees

Author's Note | For the **"substantially all of the fair value"** lease classification criterion, the present value of the **full amount** of the residual value guaranteed by the lessee is included in the test. However, in measuring the lease liability, only the amounts **probable of being owed** by the lessee under residual value guarantees are included.

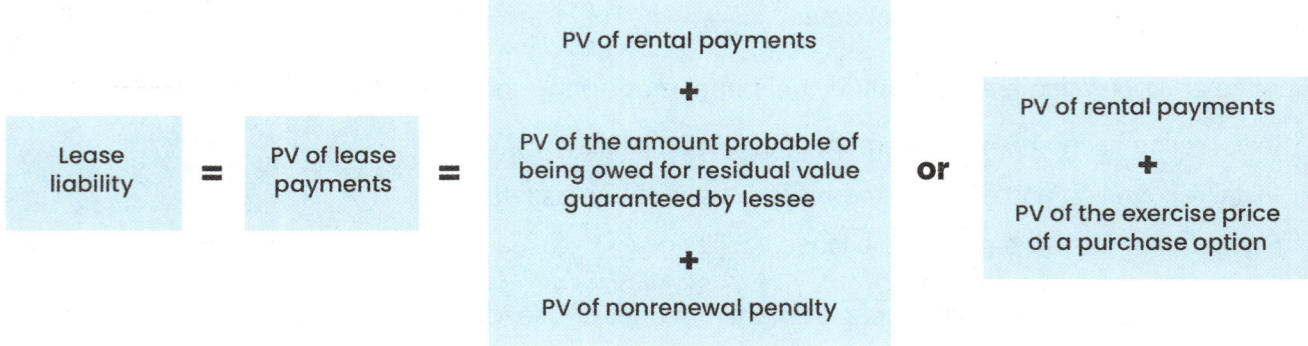

Figure 11-2

Example 11-2   Residual Value Guaranteed by the Lessee

In a lease contract, a lessee guarantees that the residual value of the leased property at the end of the lease term is at least $50,000. At the lease commencement date, the lessee estimates that the value of the property at the end of the lease term will be only $40,000. Thus, it is probable that the lessee will owe $10,000 to the lessor under the residual value guarantee.

- To test the "substantially all of the fair value" lease classification criterion, the present value of the full amount of the $50,000 residual value guaranteed by the lessee is included.

- In the measurement of the lease liability, only the present value of the amount that is probable of being owed by the lessee under the residual value guarantee of $10,000 is included.

In a balance sheet, the total lease liability is allocated between current and noncurrent portions. The current portion at a balance sheet date is the reduction of the lease liability in the forthcoming year.

Right-of-Use Asset

At the lease commencement date, a right-of-use asset is measured at the amount at which the lease liability was recognized plus initial direct costs incurred by the lessee.

When no initial direct costs were incurred by the lessee, a **right-of-use asset equals the lease liability** recognized.

- The following journal entry is recorded by the lessee:

Right-of-use asset	$XXX	
Lease liability		$XXX

Subsequent to initial recognition, the right-of-use asset is reported in the balance sheet at cost minus accumulated amortization and any impairment losses.

Example 11-3   Finance Lease

On January 1, Year 1, Cottle, Inc., entered into a 3-year lease of a machine from Crimson, LLC. Cottle must pay Crimson three annual payments of $100,000 starting on December 31, Year 1. The machine's useful life from the lease commencement date is 5 years. The lease allows Cottle the option to purchase the machine at the end of the lease term for $15,000. Cottle is reasonably certain to exercise this purchase option. Cottle's incremental borrowing rate is 15%, but the rate implicit in the lease is 10%, which is known to Cottle.

- The present value factor for an ordinary annuity at 10% for 3 periods is 2.48685, and the present value of $1 at 10% for 3 periods is 0.7513.

- The present value factor for an ordinary annuity at 15% for 3 periods is 2.28323, and the present value of $1 at 15% for 3 periods is 0.65752.

The lease is a **finance lease** because it meets the lease classification criterion of including a purchase option that the lessee is reasonably certain to exercise. The rate implicit in the lease of 10% is used to calculate the present value of the lease payments because Cottle knows this rate.

PV of rental payments ($100,000 × 2.48685)	$248,685
PV of purchase option ($15,000 × 0.7513)	11,270
PV of lease payments	$259,955

Right-of-use asset	$259,955	
Lease liability		$259,955

Example 11-4   Operating Lease -- Lessee

Using the scenario presented in Example 11-3, assume that (1) Cottle concludes that the contract is an **operating lease**, (2) the lease does not include a purchase option, (3) the rental payments are $100,000 at the end of Years 1 and 2 and $160,000 at the end of Year 3, and (4) the rate implicit in the lease is not known to Cottle.

Because Cottle does not know the rate implicit in the lease, it uses its **incremental borrowing rate** of 15% to calculate the present value of lease payments.

The PV of the rental payments is $267,774 [($100,000 × 2.28323) + ($60,000 × 0.65752)].

Right-of-use asset	$267,774	
Lease liability		$267,774

Stop & Review

You have completed the outline for this subunit.

Study multiple-choice questions 3 through 5 beginning on page 366.

11.3   Lessee Accounting for Finance Leases -- Subsequent Measurement

Interest Expense and Amortization of a Lease Liability

Each periodic lease payment made by the lessee has two components: **interest expense** and the **reduction of the lease liability**.

- If the first periodic lease payment is made at the **commencement date** of the lease, its only component is the reduction of the lease liability. No interest expense is recognized for the first payment because no time has elapsed between the lease commencement date and the payment.

Interest expense is calculated using the effective interest method (also known as the effective-rate method or the interest method).

- It is calculated as the carrying amount of the lease liability at the beginning of the period times the discount rate of the lease.

> **Interest expense = Lease liability at the beginning of the period × Discount rate**

The **reduction of the lease liability** is the excess of the periodic lease payment over the interest expense recognized during the period.

> **Reduction of lease liability = Periodic lease payment − Interest expense**

Example 11-5   Interest Expense and Amortization of Lease Liability

In Example 11-3, the lease was classified as a **finance lease**. Cottle prepares the following amortization schedule and records the following journal entries:

Date	Period Beginning Lease Liability		Effective Interest Rate		Interest Expense		Cash Payment		Reduction of Lease Liability	Period Ending Lease Liability
1/1/Yr 1	$259,955	×	10%	=	$25,995	−	$100,000	=	$ 74,005	$185,950
1/1/Yr 2	185,950	×	10%	=	18,595	−	100,000	=	81,405	104,545
1/1/Yr 3	104,545	×	10%	=	10,455	−	115,000	=	104,545	0

The last payment on 12/31/Yr 3 is $115,000 ($100,000 annual rental payment + $15,000 exercise price of the option to purchase the machine).

12/31/Yr 1

Interest expense	$25,995	
Lease liability	74,005	
Cash		$100,000

On December 31, Year 1, the carrying amount of the lease liability is **$185,950**. In its 12/31/Yr 1 balance sheet, Cottle reports a current lease liability of $81,405 and a noncurrent lease liability of $104,545.

12/31/Yr 2

Interest expense	$18,595	
Lease liability	81,405	
Cash		$100,000

-- Continued on next page --

Example 11-5 -- Continued

On December 31, Year 2, the carrying amount of the lease liability is **$104,545**. This entire amount is reported as a current liability in the 12/31/Yr 2 balance sheet because Cottle expects to pay the entire amount in Year 3.

12/31/Yr 3		
Interest expense	$ 10,455	
Lease liability	104,545	
Cash		$115,000 ($100,000 annual payment + $15,000 option price)

Amortization of a Right-of-Use Asset

A lessee amortizes the right-of-use (ROU) asset on a **straight-line basis**.

The right-of-use asset is amortized over the shorter of (1) its **useful life** or (2) the **lease term**.

- However, if, at the end of the lease term, (1) the ownership of the leased asset is transferred to the lessee or (2) the lessee is reasonably certain to exercise the purchase option, the amortization period is the **useful life of the leased asset**.

Lease Classification Criterion Satisfied	Amortization Period of the ROU Asset
Criterion 1 - Transfer of ownership	Useful life of the leased asset
Criterion 2 - Exercise of purchase option	Useful life of the leased asset
Criterion 3 - Major part of the remaining economic life	Shorter of ROU asset's useful life or lease term
Criterion 4 - Substantially all of the fair value	Shorter of ROU asset's useful life or lease term
Criterion 5 - No alternative use to the lessor	Shorter of ROU asset's useful life or lease term

---

Example 11-6   Amortization of Right-of-Use Asset over Useful Life

In Example 11-5, Cottle is reasonably certain to exercise the option to purchase the machine. The right-of-use asset therefore is amortized over the useful life of the machine of 5 years. Annual amortization expense of $51,991 ($259,955 ÷ 5 years) is recognized by Cottle. The journal entry is

Amortization expense	$51,991	
Right-of-use asset		$51,991

In its 12/31/Yr 1 balance sheet, Cottle reports the right-of-use asset at **$207,964** ($259,955 initial cost − $51,991 accumulated amortization).

Amortization of Leasehold Improvements

Leasehold improvements are amortized over the shorter of (1) their **useful life** or (2) the **remaining lease term**.

- If, at the end of the lease term, (1) the ownership of the leased asset is transferred to the lessee or (2) the lessee is reasonably certain to exercise a purchase option, the amortization period is the **useful life of the leasehold improvements**.

Financial Statement Presentation

In the **income statement**, interest expense on a lease liability and amortization of a right-of-use asset must be **reported separately**.

In the **statement of cash flows**, repayment of the principal portion of a finance lease liability is classified as a cash outflow from **financing activities**.

- Payment of **interest** on a lease liability is classified as a cash outflow **from operating activities**.

In the footnotes to the financial statements, the lessee must disclose the **total finance lease cost** for the period. The total finance lease cost should be segregated between the amortization of the right-of-use assets and interest expense on the lease liabilities.

Stop & Review

You have completed the outline for this subunit.
Study multiple-choice questions 6 through 8 beginning on page 368.

11.4 Lessee Accounting for Operating Leases -- Subsequent Measurement

Finance Leases vs. Operating Leases

As noted in Subunit 11.2, accounting for finance leases and operating leases is **the same** for

- Initial recognition and measurement of the lease liability,
- Initial recognition and measurement of the right-of-use asset, and
- Subsequent measurement of the lease liability.

The following are the **differences** in accounting for finance and operating leases:

- Subsequent accounting for (amortization of) the right-of-use asset
- Income statement presentation of interest expense and amortization of the right-of-use asset
- Statement of cash flow classification of cash lease payments

Recognition of Lease Expense in Operating Leases

A **single (equal) lease expense** is recognized in each period. It is calculated so that the total undiscounted lease payments are allocated over the lease term on a **straight-line basis**.

Single periodic lease expense = Total undiscounted lease payments ($) ÷ Lease term (years)

- Initial direct costs incurred by the lessee are included in the total undiscounted lease payments. Thus, they are recognized in the single periodic lease expense on a straight-line basis over the lease term.

The single periodic lease expense has two components, (1) interest expense on the lease liability and (2) amortization of the right-of-use asset.

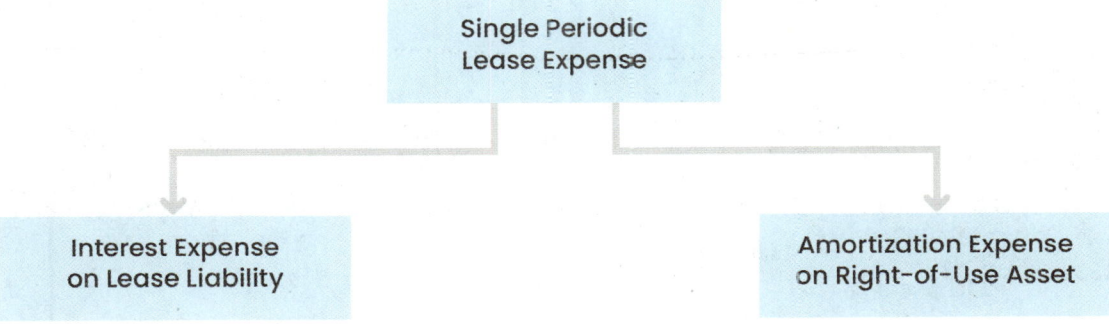

Figure 11-3

In the **income statement**, a single amount for the total lease expense for the period is reported in income from continuing operations.

- Thus, interest expense for the lease liability and amortization expense for the right-of-use asset are **not reported separately**.

Amortization of the Right-of-Use Asset

Amortization of the right-of-use asset is the difference between the (1) single periodic lease expense and (2) interest expense on the lease liability recognized for the period.

$$\text{Amortization expense on right-of-use asset} = \text{Single periodic lease expense} - \text{Interest expense on lease liability}$$

Interest expense equals the carrying amount of the lease liability at the beginning of the period times the discount rate of the lease.

Example 11-7   Lessee's Operating Lease -- Amortization of the ROU Asset

On January 1, Year 1, Lor, Inc., entered into a 3-year lease for a building and determined that this contract is an **operating lease**. Based on the contract terms, Lor is required to pay three annual payments of $20,000 starting on December 31, Year 1. The building's remaining useful life is 30 years. The rate implicit in the lease is not known to Lor. Thus, Lor uses its incremental borrowing rate of 8% to measure the lease liability and right-of-use asset. The present value factor for an ordinary annuity at 8% for 3 periods is 2.5771.

- The lease liability and right-of-use (ROU) asset are recognized at the present value of the lease payments of **$51,542** ($20,000 × 2.5771).

- The single amount of annual lease expense is **$20,000** [($20,000 × 3) total undiscounted lease payments ÷ 3 years].

January 1, Year 1

ROU asset	$51,542	
Lease liability		$51,542

December 31, Year 1

The interest expense component of Year 1 lease expense is $4,124 ($51,542 × 8%). The amortization of the ROU asset component of Year 1 lease expense is $15,876 ($20,000 annual lease expense – $4,124 interest expense).

Lease liability	$15,876 ($20,000 lease payment – $4,124 interest expense)	
Lease expense	20,000	
Cash		$20,000
ROU asset		15,876

Lease expense of **$20,000** is recognized in the Year 1 income statement. The carrying amount of the lease liability and ROU asset on 12/31/Year 1 is **$35,666** ($51,542 – $15,876).

December 31, Year 2

The interest expense component of Year 2 lease expense is $2,853 ($35,666 × 8%). The amortization of the ROU asset component of Year 2 lease expense is $17,147 ($20,000 annual lease expense – $2,853 interest expense).

Lease liability	$17,147 ($20,000 lease payment – $2,853 interest expense)	
Lease expense	20,000	
Cash		$20,000
ROU asset		17,147

Lease expense of **$20,000** is recognized in the Year 2 income statement. The carrying amount of the lease liability and ROU asset on 12/31/Year 2 is **$18,519** ($35,666 – $17,147).

December 31, Year 3

The interest expense component of Year 3 lease expense is $1,481 ($18,519 × 8%). The amortization of the ROU asset component of Year 3 lease expense is $18,519 ($20,000 annual lease expense – $1,481 interest expense).

Lease liability	$18,519 ($20,000 lease payment – $1,481 interest expense)	
Lease expense	20,000	
Cash		$20,000
ROU asset		18,519

Lease expense of **$20,000** is recognized in the Year 3 income statement. The balance of the lease liability and ROU asset on 12/31/Year 3 is **$0** ($18,519 – $18,519).

NOTE: (1) When annual lease payments are paid in arrears and in equal amounts (annuity in arrears), the carrying amounts of the lease liability and right-of-use asset are the same throughout the entire lease term. (2) In the balance sheet, the lease liability should be allocated between current and noncurrent portions.

Example 11-8   Lessee's Operating Lease -- Amortization of the ROU Asset

Using the data from Example 11-4, in which the lease was classified as an operating lease, the following is Cottle's accounting for the lease of a machine from Crimson:

- Total amount of undiscounted lease payments is **$360,000** ($100,000 + $100,000 + $160,000).

- The single amount of annual lease expense is **$120,000** ($360,000 ÷ 3 years).

- The amount of the lease liability and right-of-use (ROU) asset is initially recognized at the present value of lease payments of **$267,774** [($100,000 × 2.28323) + ($60,000 × 0.65752)].

January 1, Year 1

ROU asset	$267,774	
Lease liability		$267,774

December 31, Year 1
The interest expense component of Year 1 lease expense is $40,166 ($267,774 × 15%). The amortization of the ROU asset component of Year 1 lease expense is $79,834 ($120,000 annual lease expense – $40,166 interest expense).

Lease liability	$ 59,834 ($100,000 lease payment – $40,166 interest expense)	
Lease expense	120,000	
Cash		$100,000
ROU asset		79,834

Lease expense of **$120,000** is recognized in the Year 1 income statement. On December 31, Year 1, the carrying amount of the lease liability is **$207,940** ($267,774 – $59,834), and the carrying amount of the ROU asset is **$187,940** ($267,774 – $79,834).

December 31, Year 2
The interest expense component of Year 2 lease expense is $31,191 ($207,940 × 15%). The amortization of the ROU asset component of Year 2 lease expense is $88,809 ($120,000 annual lease expense – $31,191 interest expense).

Lease liability	$ 68,809 ($100,000 lease payment – $31,191 interest expense)	
Lease expense	120,000	
Cash		$100,000
ROU asset		88,809

Lease expense of **$120,000** is recognized in the Year 2 income statement. On December 31, Year 2, the carrying amount of the lease liability is **$139,131** ($207,940 – $68,809), and the carrying amount of the ROU asset is **$99,131** ($187,940 – $88,809).

December 31, Year 3
The interest expense component of Year 3 lease expense is $20,869 ($139,131 × 15%). The amortization of the ROU asset component of Year 3 lease expense is $99,131 ($120,000 annual lease expense – $20,869 interest expense).

Lease liability	$139,131 ($160,000 lease payment – $20,869 interest expense)	
Lease expense	120,000	
Cash		$160,000
ROU asset		99,131

Lease expense of $120,000 is recognized in the Year 3 income statement. On December 31, Year 3, the carrying amount of the lease liability is $0 ($139,131 – $139,131), and the carrying amount of the ROU asset is $0 ($99,131 – $99,131).

Financial Statement Presentation

In the **balance sheet**, **finance lease liabilities** and **operating lease liabilities** must **not** be presented together in the same line item.

- They are presented in the balance sheet or disclosed in the notes, separately from each other and separately from other liabilities.

In the **balance sheet**, **finance lease right-of-use assets** and **operating lease right-of-use assets** must **not** be presented together in the same line item.

- They are presented in the balance sheet or disclosed in the notes, separately from each other and separately from other assets.

In the **statement of cash flows**, payments for operating leases (repayment of the lease liability and interest expense on the lease liability) are cash outflows from **operating activities**.

- Payments for leases classified as **short-term leases** are cash outflows from **operating activities**.

Modifications of the Lease Contract

A lease contract may be modified by (1) extending or reducing the lease term or (2) changing the consideration in the contract.

On the lease modification date, a lessee must

- Remeasure and reallocate the remaining consideration in the contract,

- Remeasure the lease liability using the discount rate determined at the effective date of the modification,

- Adjust the corresponding right-of-use asset for the same amount the lease liability was adjusted, and

- Check whether lease classification has changed.

Lease modifications does not affect profit or loss

Example 11-9   Modifications of the Lease Contract

Using the data from Example 11-7, assume that at the beginning of Year 3 the lease contract was modified as follows:

- The lease term increased from 3 years to 6 years.
- The annual lease payments increased to $25,000 for the remaining 4 years after the modification.

Lor's (lessee's) incremental borrowing rate on 1/1/Year 3 was 10%. The present value factor for an ordinary annuity at 10% for 4 periods is 3.17.

On 1/1/Year 3, the carrying amount of the lease liability and ROU asset was $18,519 (see Example 11-7).

The modified lease liability is calculated based on a 4-year remaining lease term, four remaining annual payments of $25,000, and Lor's incremental borrowing rate on 1/1/Year 3 of 10%. Consequently, the modified lease liability is $79,250 ($25,000 × 3.17). The increase in lease liability of $60,731 ($79,250 modified lease liability – $18,519 lease liability before lease modification) is recognized as an adjustment of the ROU asset. The profit or loss is not affected.

The following journal entry is recorded by Lor on 1/1/Year 3

ROU asset	$60,731	
Lease liability		$60,731

These lease modifications did not change the classification of the lease, and Lor will continue to account for the lease as an operating lease. However, if the lease contract were modified by increasing the lease term from 3 years to 25 years, Lor would classify the modified lease as a finance lease. The remaining lease term of 23 years is for a major part of the 28-year (30-year remaining useful life on 1/1Year 1 – 2 years) remaining useful life of the building.

Stop & Review

You have completed the outline for this subunit.

Study multiple-choice questions 9 through 11 beginning on page 369.

11.5 Contingencies

Definition

A contingency is "an existing condition, situation, or set of circumstances **involving uncertainty** as to possible gain (a gain contingency) or loss (a loss contingency) to an entity that will ultimately be resolved when one or more future events occur or fail to occur."

A contingency may be

- **Probable.** Future events are likely to occur.
- **Reasonably possible.** The chance of occurrence is more than remote but less than probable.
- **Remote.** The chance of occurrence is slight.

Probable Loss Contingencies

<u>Criteria for accrual.</u> A **contingent loss** must be accrued (debit loss and credit liability) when **two conditions are met**. Based on information available prior to the issuance of the financial statements, accrual is required if

- It is **probable** that, at a balance sheet date, an asset has been impaired or a liability has been incurred, and
- The amount of the loss can be **reasonably estimated**.

<u>Measurement of the loss.</u> When the assessment of a **range of probable losses** is provided, the amount that appears to be a better estimate than any other within this range must be accrued.

- If no amount within that range appears to be a better estimate than any other, the **minimum** of the range should be accrued.

<u>Disclosures.</u> Disclosure in the financial statements of the nature of the accrual and the amount or the range of loss is required.

Reasonably Possible Loss Contingencies

Disclosure must be made if any condition to accrue a loss contingency is not met, but the probability of the loss is at least **reasonably possible**. The following should be disclosed:

- The nature of the contingency

- An estimate of the possible loss or range of loss or a statement that such an estimate cannot be made

Example 11-10 Contingent Liability

1. During Year 1, Crab Co. was sued by Apple Co. for patent infringement. At the end of Year 1, Crab's legal counsel believes that (a) an unfavorable outcome is probable, (b) an estimated amount of loss is in the range of $100,000 to $500,000, and (c) all amounts in the range are equally likely. In its December 31, Year 1, financial statements Crab Co. must

   - Accrue a liability and recognize a loss of $100,000 (the minimum of the range).

   - Disclose the nature of the contingency, the range of loss, and the exposure to an additional amount of loss of up to $400,000.

2. Now assume that Crab's legal counsel believes that a loss of $200,000 is a better estimate than any other amount in the range of probable losses. In its December 31, Year 1, financial statements Crab Co. must

   - Accrue a liability and recognize a loss of $200,000 (the better estimate within the range).

   - Disclose the nature of the contingency, the range of loss, and the exposure to an additional amount of loss of up to $300,000.

3. Now assume that Crab's legal counsel believes that an unfavorable verdict is only reasonably possible (but not probable). No liability is accrued and no loss is recognized. Disclosure of the nature of the contingency and the range of loss is required.

Remote Loss Contingencies

These loss contingencies ordinarily are **not disclosed**.

However, a **guarantee** (e.g., of the indebtedness of another or to repurchase receivables) must be disclosed even if the probability of loss is remote. The disclosure should include the nature and amount of the guarantee.

- A guarantee is a **noncontingent obligation** to perform after the occurrence of a triggering event or condition. It is coupled with a **contingent** obligation to make payments if such an event or condition occurs.

    - Thus, **recognition of a liability** at the inception of a guarantee is required even when it is not probable that payments will be made.

- The **initial measurement** of a noncontingent obligation ordinarily is at **fair value**. If a contingent loss and liability also are required to be recognized, the liability recognized by the guarantor is the greater of the fair value measurement or the contingent liability amount.

No accrual is permitted for general or unspecified business risks, for example, those related to national and international economic conditions. No disclosure is required.

Unasserted Claims

With respect to unasserted claims, an entity must determine the degree of probability that a suit may be filed and the possibility of an unfavorable outcome.

If it is probable that a suit will be filed against an entity and the two conditions to accrue a contingent liability are met (i.e., the loss is probable and can be reasonably estimated), a contingent loss must be accrued.

Gain Contingencies

Gain contingencies are **recognized only when realized**.

- For example, an award of damages in a lawsuit is not realized if it is being appealed.

A gain contingency must be adequately disclosed in the notes to the financial statements.

Stop & Review

You have completed the outline for this subunit.
Study multiple-choice questions 12 through 16 beginning on page 371.

11.6 Warranties

A warranty is a written guarantee of the integrity of a product or service. The seller may also agree to repair or replace a product or provide additional service.

- A warranty customarily is offered for a limited time, such as 2 years.
- It may or may not be sold separately from the product or service.

A warranty that provides a customer assurance that a product will function as expected in accordance with agreed-upon specifications is an **assurance-type warranty**.

- A standard one-year computer warranty against manufacturing defects is an example of an assurance-type warranty.

A warranty that provides a customer with a service in addition to the assurance that the product complies with agreed-upon specifications is a **service-type warranty**.

- A warranty against customer-inflicted damages, such as dropping the computer on the floor or into water, is an example of a service-type warranty.
- A service-type warranty is accounted for as a **separate** performance obligation in the contract.

Classification of a Warranty as an Assurance- or Service-Type Warranty

A warranty that can be **purchased separately** by the customer is a **service-type warranty**.

- If a customer does **not** have the option to purchase a warranty separately, the warranty is an **assurance-type warranty**.

A warranty required by law is an assurance-type warranty.

The length of the warranty coverage period may indicate the type of warranty. A service-type warranty is more likely to have a longer coverage period. A longer warranty is more likely to provide service in addition to the assurance that the product complies with agreed-upon specifications.

If an assurance-type warranty and a service-type warranty provided in the contract cannot be separated, the warranties are accounted for as a single performance obligation in a contract (that is, as a service-type warranty).

Accounting for an Assurance-Type Warranty

An assurance-type warranty is **not** a separate performance obligation in a contract. Thus, no transaction price is allocated to the warranty.

An assurance-type warranty creates a **loss contingency**. **Accrual accounting** should be used if

- Incurrence of warranty expense is probable,
- The amount can be reasonably estimated, and
- The amount is material.

A liability for warranty costs is recognized when the related revenue is recognized, i.e., on the day the product is sold.

- Even if the warranty covers a period longer than the period in which the product is sold, the **entire liability** (expense) for the expected warranty costs must be recognized on the day the product is sold. The warranty liability (expense) must not be prorated over the annual periods covered by the warranty.

Beginning warranty liability	$XXX
Warranty expense recognized in the current period	XXX
Warranty payments in the current period	(XXX)
Ending warranty liability	$XXX

- Actual payments for warranty costs reduce the amount of warranty liability recognized and do not affect warranty expense.

    - If the warranty payments for the period are greater than the amount of warranty liability recognized, the excess is recognized as warranty expense.

The following are **accrual-basis** entries for warranty expense estimated as a percentage of sales when the **warranty is not separable**:

- To record a sale of product

Cash or accounts receivable	$XXX	
Sales revenue		$XXX

- To record related warranty expense recognized on the day of sale

Warranty expense	$XXX	
Estimated warranty liability		$XXX

- To record actual warranty expenditures paid in the current period

Estimated warranty liability	$XXX	
Cash		$XXX

Example 11-11   Assurance-Type Warranty

In Year 1, a company began selling a product under a standard 2-year warranty. The estimated warranty costs are 3% of sales in the year of sale and 5% in the following year. Sales and actual warranty payments for Year 1 and Year 2 are as follows:

	Sales	Warranty Payments
Year 1	$300,000	$ 5,000
Year 2	500,000	37,000

In Year 1, warranty expense of $24,000 [$300,000 × (3% + 5%)] is recognized. The warranty liability of $19,000 ($24,000 – $5,000) is reported on the December 31, Year 1, balance sheet.

In Year 2, warranty expense of $40,000 [$500,000 × (3% + 5%)] is recognized. The warranty liability of $22,000 is reported on the December 31, Year 2, balance sheet.

Beginning warranty liability (1/1/Year 2)	$ 19,000
Warranty expense recognized in the current period	40,000
Warranty payments in the current period	(37,000)
Ending warranty liability (12/31/Year 2)	$ 22,000

Accounting for a Service-Type Warranty

A service-type warranty is a **separate performance obligation in a contract**. Thus, a portion of the total transaction price is allocated to the service-type warranty.

- The total transaction price is allocated to the service-type warranty and the related product sold based on their estimated standalone selling prices.

At contract inception, the consideration received for the service-type warranty is accounted for as an advance payment and a contract liability is recognized. The following entry is recorded on a sale of a product with a service-type warranty:

Cash	$XXX (total transaction price)	
Revenue		$XXX (transaction price allocated to the product)
Contract liability		XXX (transaction price allocated to the service-type warranty)

Revenue from a service-type warranty is recognized over time (i.e., over the coverage period). The pattern of revenue recognized from a service-type warranty depends on the way the warranty performance obligation is satisfied.

- If warranty service is provided continuously over the warranty period, revenue is recognized on the **straight-line basis** over the coverage period.

- If warranty service costs are **not incurred on a straight-line basis**, revenue recognition over the contract's term should be proportionate to the estimated service costs.

- The following entry is recorded when revenue from a service-type warranty is recognized:

Contract liability	$XXX	
Revenue		$XXX

- The following entry is recorded when an entity pays for the costs related to the claims under the warranty:

Warranty expense	$XXX	
Cash		$XXX

Stop & Review

You have completed the outline for this subunit.
Study multiple-choice questions 17 and 18 on page 373.

Questions

11.1 Lease Classification

1. Lease M does not contain a purchase option, but the present value of the lease payments is equal to 91% of the fair value of the leased asset. Lease P does not transfer ownership to the lessee by the end of the lease term, but the lease term is equal to 77% of the estimated economic life of the leased asset. How should the lessee classify these leases?

Lease M	Lease P
A. Finance lease	Operating lease
B. Finance lease	Finance lease
C. Operating lease	Finance lease
D. Operating lease	Operating lease

✔ **Answer (B) is correct.**
Required: The proper classification of leases.
Discussion: A lease is classified as a finance lease by the lessee and as a sales-type lease by the lessor if, at lease commencement, at least one of the following five criteria is met: (1) The ownership of the leased asset is transferred to the lessee by the end of the lease term, (2) the lease includes an option to purchase the leased asset that the lessee is reasonably certain to exercise, (3) the lease term is for the major part (generally considered as 75%) of the remaining economic life of the leased asset, (4) the present value of the sum of the lease payments and any residual value guaranteed by the lessee equals or exceeds substantially all of the fair value (generally considered as 90%) of the leased asset, and (5) the leased asset is so specialized that it is expected to have no alternative use to the lessor at the end of the lease term. When no classification criterion is met, the lease is classified as an operating lease by the lessee. Thus, both lease M (91% of the fair value of the leased asset) and lease P (77% of the economic life of the leased asset) are classified as finance leases.

✘ **Answer (A) is incorrect.** Lease P meets the 75% of the economic life of the leased asset classification criterion.

✘ **Answer (C) is incorrect.** Lease M meets the 90% of the fair value of the leased asset classification criterion.

✘ **Answer (D) is incorrect.** Lease P meets the 75% of the economic life of the leased asset classification criterion. Lease M meets the 90% of the fair value of the leased asset classification criterion.

2. Beal, Inc., intends to lease a machine from Paul Corp. Beal's incremental borrowing rate is 14%. The prime rate of interest is 8%. Paul's implicit rate in the lease is 10%, which is known to Beal. Beal computes the present value of the lease payments using

A. 8%

B. 10%

C. 12%

D. 14%

✔ **Answer (B) is correct.**
Required: The discount rate used by the lessee to determine the present value of lease payments if the incremental borrowing rate and implicit rate are known.
Discussion: The discount rate for the lease is the rate implicit in the lease. If the lessee cannot determine the rate implicit in the lease, the lessee uses its incremental borrowing rate. Because the implicit rate of 10% is known to Beal, it is used as the discount rate of the lease.

✘ **Answer (A) is incorrect.** The prime rate (8%) is irrelevant.

✘ **Answer (C) is incorrect.** The rate of 12% is the average of the implicit rate and the incremental rate.

✘ **Answer (D) is incorrect.** The implicit rate is known to Beal. Thus, it must be used as the discount rate for the lease.

11.2 Lessee Accounting -- Initial Measurement

3. Robbin, Inc., leased a machine from Ready Leasing Co. The lease requires 10 annual payments of $10,000 beginning immediately. The lease contract specifies the rate implicit in the lease of 12% and a purchase option of $10,000 at the end of the tenth year, even though the machine's estimated value on that date is $20,000. Robbin is reasonably certain to exercise the purchase option. Robbin's incremental borrowing rate is 14%.

The present value of an annuity due of 1 at:
    12% for 10 years is 6.328
    14% for 10 years is 5.946

The present value of 1 at:
    12% for 10 years is .322
    14% for 10 years is .270

What amount should Robbin record as lease liability at the beginning of the lease term?

A. $62,160

B. $64,860

C. $66,500

D. $69,720

✔ **Answer (C) is correct.**
Required: The amount that should be reported as a finance lease liability.
Discussion: For a finance or an operating lease, a lessee initially must recognize a lease liability and a right-of-use asset. At the lease commencement date, a lease liability is measured at the present value of the lease payments to be made over the lease term. When the lease includes a purchase option that the lessee is reasonably certain to exercise, the lease is a finance lease. The lease payments therefore consist of rental payments and the exercise price of the purchase option. The discount rate for the lease is the rate implicit in the lease of 12% because it is known by Robbin. Thus, the lease liability is equal to $66,500 [($10,000 × 6.328) + ($10,000 × .322)].

✘ **Answer (A) is incorrect.** The present value of the payment required by the purchase option and the annual lease payments should be discounted at 12% instead of 14%.

✘ **Answer (B) is incorrect.** The amount of the purchase option is $10,000, not the estimated value at that date. Also, the discount rate for both the option amount and the annual payments should be 12% instead of 14%.

✘ **Answer (D) is incorrect.** The payment required by the purchase option should be included in the present value of minimum lease payments, not the estimated value of the asset at the end of the lease.

4. Koby Co. entered into a lease with a vendor for equipment on January 2 for 7 years. The equipment has **no** guaranteed residual value. The lease required Koby to pay $500,000 annually on January 2, beginning with the current year. The present value of an annuity due for seven years was 5.35 at the inception of the lease. What amount should Koby recognize for the lease asset?

A. $500,000
B. $825,000
C. $2,675,000
D. $3,500,000

✔ **Answer (C) is correct.**
Required: The amount recognized for the leased asset
Discussion: For finance and operating leases, a lessee must recognize a lease liability and a right-of-use asset at the lease commencement date. A right-of-use asset initially is measured at the amount at which the lease liability was recognized (i.e., present value of lease payments) plus initial direct costs incurred by the lessee. These payments include the initial payment at the inception of the lease. Thus, the annual payments constitute an annuity due. In the absence of a purchase option, guaranteed residual value, or nonrenewal penalty, the amount recognized as leased asset (right-of-use asset) is $2,675,000 ($500,000 annual payment × 5.35 present value of an annuity due for 7 years).

✘ **Answer (A) is incorrect.** The annual payment is $500,000.

✘ **Answer (B) is incorrect.** The amount of $825,000 is the discount (nominal amount of the payments – their present value).

✘ **Answer (D) is incorrect.** The nominal amount (undiscounted sum) of the payments is $3,500,000.

5. On January 1, Emerald Co. entered into a 10-year noncancelable lease requiring year-end payments of $90,000. Emerald's incremental borrowing rate is 12%, while the lessor's implicit interest rate, known to Emerald, is 10%. Present value factors for an ordinary annuity for 10 periods are 6.145 at 10% and 5.650 at 12%. Ownership of the property remains with the lessor at expiration of the lease. There is **no** option to purchase the leased property. The leased property has an estimated economic life of 15 years. The fair value of the leased property is $1.2 million. What amount should Emerald recognize for the right-of-use asset on January 1?

A. $900,000
B. $553,050
C. $508,500
D. $0

✔ **Answer (B) is correct.**
Required: The amount of right-of-use asset recognized at lease commencement date.
Discussion: Under both finance and operating leases, at the lease commencement date, a lessee must recognize a lease liability and a right-of-use asset. At the lease commencement date, a right-of-use asset is measured at the amount at which the lease liability was recognized (i.e., the present value of the lease payments to be made over the lease term) plus initial direct costs incurred by the lessee. The rate implicit in the lease, if it is known to the lessee, of 10% is the discount rate for the lease. Thus, on January 1, the right-of-use asset recognized by Emerald is $553,050 ($90,000 × 6.145).

✘ **Answer (A) is incorrect.** At the lease commencement date, a right-of-use asset is measured at the present value of the lease payments to be made over the lease term.

✘ **Answer (C) is incorrect.** If the rate implicit in the lease is known to the lessee, it must be used as the discount rate of the lease.

✘ **Answer (D) is incorrect.** Under both finance and operating leases, at the lease commencement date, a lessee must recognize a lease liability and a right-of-use asset.

11.3 Lessee Accounting for Finance Leases -- Subsequent Measurement

6. On January 1 of the current year, Tell Co. leased equipment from Swill Co. under a 9-year lease. The equipment had a cost of $400,000 and an estimated useful life of 15 years. Semiannual lease payments of $44,000 are due every January 1 and July 1. The present value of lease payments at the discount rate of the lease of 12% was $505,000, which equals the fair value of the equipment. What amount should Tell recognize as amortization expense on the right-of-use asset in the current year?

 A. $26,667

 B. $33,667

 C. $44,444

 D. $56,111

✔ **Answer (D) is correct.**
Required: The amortization expense for a lease.
Discussion: Tell Co. classifies the lease as a finance lease because the present value of the lease payments equals the fair value of the leased equipment. The right-of-use asset is initially measured at the present value of lease payments of $505,000. Under a finance lease when (1) the ownership of the leased asset is not transferred to the lessee, and (2) the lease does not include a purchase option that the lessee is reasonably certain to exercise, the right-of-use asset is amortized on a straight-line basis over the shorter of its useful life or lease term. Thus, annual amortization of the right-of-use asset is $56,111 ($505,000 ÷ 9 years).

✘ **Answer (A) is incorrect.** The amount of $26,667 is based on the equipment's cost and estimated useful life.

✘ **Answer (B) is incorrect.** The amount of $33,667 is based on the estimated useful life, not the lease term.

✘ **Answer (C) is incorrect.** The amount of $44,444 is based on the equipment's cost.

7. On January 1, Year 4, Harrow Co., as lessee, signed a 5-year noncancelable equipment lease with annual payments of $100,000 beginning December 31, Year 4. Harrow treated this transaction as a finance lease. The five lease payments have a present value of $379,000 at January 1, Year 4, based on interest of 10%. What amount should Harrow report as interest expense for the year ended December 31, Year 4?

 A. $37,900

 B. $27,900

 C. $24,200

 D. $0

✔ **Answer (A) is correct.**
Required: The interest to be recognized in the first year of a finance lease.
Discussion: Under the effective-interest method, interest expense for the first year is $37,900 ($379,000 lease liability × 10% effective interest rate).

✘ **Answer (B) is incorrect.** The amount of $27,900 assumes the initial payment was made immediately.

✘ **Answer (C) is incorrect.** The amount of $24,200 is one-fifth of the total interest ($500,000 – $379,000 PV).

✘ **Answer (D) is incorrect.** Interest must be accrued.

8. In the long-term liabilities section of its balance sheet at December 31, Year 3, Mene Co. reported a finance lease liability of $75,000, net of current portion of $1,364. Payments of $9,000 were made on both January 2, Year 4, and January 2, Year 5. Mene's incremental borrowing rate on the date of the lease was 11%, and the lessor's implicit rate, which was known to Mene, was 10%. In its December 31, Year 4, long-term liabilities section of the balance sheet, what amount should Mene report as a finance lease liability, net of current portion?

A. $66,000

B. $73,500

C. $73,636

D. $74,250

✔ **Answer (B) is correct.**
Required: The finance lease liability, net of current portion.
Discussion: The total lease liability on 12/31/Yr 3 was $76,364 ($75,000 noncurrent portion + $1,364 current portion). Each periodic lease payment made by the lessee has two components: interest expense and reduction of lease liability. After the Year 4 payment, which included the current portion, the lease liability was $75,000. Consequently, the Year 5 payment included interest of $7,500 ($75,000 carrying amount during Year 4 × 10% lessor's implicit rate, which is known to the lessee and a principal component of $1,500 ($9,000 cash – $7,500 interest). The latter is the current portion of the lease liability on 12/31/Year 4. The finance lease liability at December 31, Year 4, net of current portion, is therefore $73,500 ($75,000 – $1,500).

✘ **Answer (A) is incorrect.** The amount of $66,000 results from treating the full $9,000 payment made in Year 5 as principal.

✘ **Answer (C) is incorrect.** The amount of $73,636 assumes the current portion is the same as the previous years'.

✘ **Answer (D) is incorrect.** The amount of $74,250 is based on an 11% rate.

11.4 Lessee Accounting for Operating Leases -- Subsequent Measurement

9. On June 1, Oren Co. entered into a 5-year nonrenewable operating lease, commencing on that date, for office space and made the following payments to Rose Properties:

Bonus to obtain lease	$30,000
First month's rent	10,000
Last month's rent	10,000

The lease term requires monthly rent payments of $10,000. In its income statement for the year ended June 30, what amount should Oren report as lease expense?

A. $10,000

B. $10,500

C. $40,000

D. $50,000

✔ **Answer (B) is correct.**
Required: The amount to be reported as lease expense for an operating lease.
Discussion: In an operating lease, a single lease expense is recognized in each period. It is calculated so that the total undiscounted lease payments are allocated over the lease term on a straight-line basis. The rent expense in June is $10,000, the amount to be paid each month. The bonus to obtain the lease is an initial direct cost incurred by Oren. Initial direct costs incurred by the lessee are included in the total undiscounted lease payments. Thus, they are recognized in the single periodic lease expense on a straight-line basis over the lease term. Lease expense for June is $10,500 {$10,000 for the month's rent + [($30,000 ÷ 5) ÷ 12 amortization of the bonus]}.

✘ **Answer (A) is incorrect.** The expense should include amortization of the bonus.

✘ **Answer (C) is incorrect.** The bonus should be amortized over the lease term benefited.

✘ **Answer (D) is incorrect.** The last month's rent payment should be deferred and expensed in the period it benefits. Also, the bonus should be amortized over the lease term.

10. Oak Co. leased equipment for 9 years, agreeing to pay $50,000 at the start of the lease term on December 31, Year 4, and $50,000 annually on each December 31 for the next 8 years. The present value on December 31, Year 4, of the nine lease payments over the lease term, using the rate implicit in the lease, was $316,500. Oak knows that this rate is 10%. The December 31, Year 4, present value of the lease payments using Oak's incremental borrowing rate of 12% was $298,500. Oak made a timely second lease payment. The lease was classified as an operating lease by Oak. What amount should Oak report as a lease liability in its December 31, Year 5, balance sheet?

A. $350,000

B. $243,150

C. $228,320

D. $0

✓ **Answer (B) is correct.**
Required: The amount to be reported as a lease liability for an operating lease.
Discussion: For a finance or operating lease, a lessee initially must recognize a lease liability and a right-of-use asset. At the lease commencement date, a lease liability is measured at the present value of the lease payments to be made over the lease term. Subsequent to initial recognition, the lease liability is reduced for the excess of the periodic lease payment over the interest expense recognized during the period. Oak knows the implicit rate. Thus, the present value of the lease payments of this lease is $316,500, the amount based on the lessor's implicit rate. After the initial payment of $50,000, which contains no interest component, is deducted, the carrying amount during Year 5 is $266,500. Accordingly, the interest component of the next payment is $26,650 ($266,500 × 10% implicit rate), and the lease liability on December 31, Year 5, is $243,150 [$266,500 − ($50,000 − $26,650)].

✗ **Answer (A) is incorrect.** The sum of the nine lease payments is $350,000.

✗ **Answer (C) is incorrect.** The amount of $228,320 is based on a 12% rate.

✗ **Answer (D) is incorrect.** Both finance and operating leases result in recognition of a lease liability at the lease commencement date.

11. On December 30, Year 1, Rafferty Corp. leased equipment under an operating lease. Annual lease payments of $20,000 are due December 31 for 10 years. The equipment's useful life is 10 years, and the interest rate implicit in the lease of 10% is known to Rafferty. The operating lease obligation was recorded on December 30 at $135,000, and the first lease payment was made on that date. What amount should Rafferty include in current liabilities for this lease in its December 31, Year 1, balance sheet?

A. $6,500

B. $8,500

C. $11,500

D. $20,000

✓ **Answer (B) is correct.**
Required: The current liability for the operating lease.
Discussion: In a classified balance sheet, a lease liability must be allocated between the current and noncurrent portions. The current portion at a balance sheet date is the reduction of the lease liability in the forthcoming year. The portion of the lease payment that exceeds the amount of interest expense is the reduction of the liability in the forthcoming year. At the beginning of the following year, the lease liability is $115,000 ($135,000 opening balance − $20,000 initial payment), and the following year's interest expense will be $11,500 ($115,000 lease liability × 10% effective rate). The reduction of the liability when the next payment is made will be $8,500 ($20,000 cash − $11,500 interest).

✗ **Answer (A) is incorrect.** The amount of $6,500 results from assuming that the carrying amount of the lease liability in the following year will be $135,000.

✗ **Answer (C) is incorrect.** The interest expense component of the single periodic lease expense recognized for an operating lease is $11,500.

✗ **Answer (D) is incorrect.** The full payment due in the following year is $20,000.

11.5 Contingencies

12. Invern, Inc., has a self-insurance plan. Each year, retained earnings is appropriated for contingencies in an amount equal to insurance premiums saved less recognized losses from lawsuits and other claims. As a result of a Year 4 accident, Invern is a defendant in a lawsuit in which it will probably have to pay damages of $190,000. What are the effects of this lawsuit's probable outcome on Invern's Year 4 financial statements?

A. An increase in expenses and **no** effect on liabilities.

B. An increase in both expenses and liabilities.

C. **No** effect on expenses and an increase in liabilities.

D. **No** effect on either expenses or liabilities.

Answer (B) is correct.
Required: The effect on the financial statements of litigation with a probable unfavorable outcome.
Discussion: A loss contingency is an existing condition, situation, or set of circumstances involving uncertainty as to the impairment of an asset's value or the incurrence of a liability as of the balance sheet date. Resolution of the uncertainty depends on the occurrence or nonoccurence of one or more future events. A loss should be debited and either an asset valuation allowance or a liability credited when the loss contingency is both probable and reasonably estimable. Thus, the company should accrue a loss and a liability.

13. Wyatt Co. has a probable loss that can only be reasonably estimated within a range of outcomes. **No** single amount within the range is a better estimate than any other amount. The loss accrual should be

A. Zero.

B. The maximum of the range.

C. The mean of the range.

D. The minimum of the range.

Answer (D) is correct.
Required: The contingent loss that should be accrued when a range of estimates is provided.
Discussion: Because the loss is probable and can be reasonably estimated, it should be accrued if the amount is material. If the estimate is stated within a given range and no amount within that range appears to be a better estimate than any other, the minimum of the range should be accrued.

14. Bell Co. is a defendant in a lawsuit that could result in a large payment to the plaintiff. Bell's attorney believes that there is a 90% chance that Bell will lose the suit and estimates that the loss will be anywhere from $5,000,000 to $20,000,000 and possibly as much as $30,000,000. None of the estimates are better than the others. What amount of liability should Bell report on its balance sheet related to the lawsuit?

A. $0

B. $5,000,000

C. $20,000,000

D. $30,000,000

Answer (B) is correct.
Required: The liability of a defendant in a lawsuit.
Discussion: A loss contingency is accrued by a debit to expense and a credit to a liability if it is probable that a loss will occur and the loss can be reasonably estimated. The $5,000,000 estimated loss is reported on the balance sheet, and the range of the contingent loss is disclosed in the notes. The loss is probable (likely to occur) given expert opinion that the chance of loss is 90%. When no amount within a reasonable estimated range is a better estimate than any other, the minimum is accrued.

15. In Year 4, hail damaged several of Toncan Co.'s vans. Hailstorms had frequently inflicted similar damage to Toncan's vans. Over the years, Toncan had saved money by not buying hail insurance and either paying for repairs or selling damaged vans and then replacing them. In Year 4, the damaged vans were sold for less than their carrying amount. How should the hail damage cost be reported in Toncan's Year 4 financial statements?

A. The actual Year 4 hail damage loss as a discontinued operation, net of income taxes.

B. The actual Year 4 hail damage loss in continuing operations, with **no** separate disclosure.

C. The expected average hail damage loss in continuing operations, with **no** separate disclosure.

D. The expected average hail damage loss in continuing operations, with separate disclosure.

✔ **Answer (B) is correct.**
Required: The reporting of hail damage costs when a company is uninsured and sells the damaged item for a loss.
Discussion: Because Toncan sold its damaged vans for less than their carrying amount, the company suffered a loss. The actual loss should be reported even though the company is uninsured against future hail damage and a contingency exists. With respect to future hailstorms, no asset has been impaired and no contingent loss should be recorded. Furthermore, this occurrence is not unusual or infrequent, and a separate disclosure is not needed.

✗ **Answer (A) is incorrect.** Hail damage does not meet the definition of a discontinued operation.

✗ **Answer (C) is incorrect.** Toncan should report the actual loss incurred in Year 4.

✗ **Answer (D) is incorrect.** Toncan should report the actual loss, and a separate disclosure is not needed because this occurrence is not unusual or infrequent.

16. On February 5, Year 2, an employee filed a $2 million lawsuit against Steel Co. for damages suffered when one of Steel's plants exploded on December 29, Year 1. Steel's legal counsel expects the company will lose the lawsuit and estimates the loss to be between $500,000 and $1 million. The employee has offered to settle the lawsuit out of court for $900,000, but Steel will not agree to the settlement. In its December 31, Year 1, balance sheet, what amount should Steel report as liability from lawsuit?

A. $2,000,000

B. $1,000,000

C. $900,000

D. $500,000

✔ **Answer (D) is correct.**
Required: The contingent loss that should be accrued when a range of estimates is provided.
Discussion: Because the loss is probable and can be reasonably estimated, it should be accrued if the amount is material. If the estimate is stated within a given range, and no amount within that range appears to be a better estimate than any other, the minimum of the range should be accrued. Thus, Steel should report a $500,000 contingent liability.

✗ **Answer (A) is incorrect.** The minimum of the range should be accrued.

✗ **Answer (B) is incorrect.** The minimum of the range should be accrued.

✗ **Answer (C) is incorrect.** The amount of $900,000 is the proposed settlement amount.

11.6 Warranties

17. Vadis Co. sells appliances that include a standard 3-year assurance-type warranty. Service calls under the warranty are performed by an independent mechanic under a contract with Vadis. Based on experience, warranty costs are estimated at $30 for each machine sold. When should Vadis recognize these warranty costs?

A. Evenly over the life of the warranty.

B. When the service calls are performed.

C. When payments are made to the mechanic.

D. When the machines are sold.

✔ **Answer (D) is correct.**
Required: The recording of warranty costs.
Discussion: An assurance-type warranty creates a loss contingency. Under the accrual method, a provision for warranty costs is made when the related revenue is recognized.

✘ **Answer (A) is incorrect.** The accrual method matches the costs and the related revenues.

✘ **Answer (B) is incorrect.** When the warranty costs can be reasonably estimated, the accrual method should be used. Recognizing the costs when the service calls are performed is the cash basis.

✘ **Answer (C) is incorrect.** Recognizing costs when paid is the cash basis.

18. During Year 3, Rex Co. introduced a new product carrying a 2-year warranty against defects. The estimated warranty costs related to dollar sales are 2% within 12 months following sale and 4% in the second 12 months following sale. Sales and actual warranty expenditures for the years ended December 31, Year 3 and Year 4, are as follows:

	Sales	Actual Warranty Expenditures
Year 3	$ 600,000	$ 9,000
Year 4	1,000,000	30,000
	$1,600,000	$39,000

At December 31, Year 4, Rex should report an estimated warranty liability of

A. $0

B. $39,000

C. $57,000

D. $96,000

✔ **Answer (C) is correct.**
Required: The estimated warranty liability at the end of the second year.
Discussion: An assurance-type warranty creates a loss contingency. Because this product is new, the beginning balance in the estimated warranty liability account at the beginning of Year 3 is $0. For Year 3, the estimated warranty costs related to dollar sales are 6% (2% + 4%) of sales or $36,000 ($600,000 × 6%). For Year 4, the estimated warranty costs are $60,000 ($1,000,000 sales × 6%). These amounts are charged to warranty expense and credited to the estimated warranty liability account. This liability account is debited for expenditures of $9,000 and $30,000 in Year 3 and Year 4, respectively. Thus, the estimated warranty liability at 12/31/Yr 4 is $57,000.

Estimated Warranty Liability			
		$ 0	1/1/Yr 3
Yr 3 expenditures	$ 9,000	36,000	Yr 3 expense
Yr 4 expenditures	30,000	60,000	Yr 4 expense
		$57,000	12/31/Yr 4

✘ **Answer (A) is incorrect.** All warranties have not expired.

✘ **Answer (B) is incorrect.** The total warranty expenditures to date equals $39,000.

✘ **Answer (D) is incorrect.** The total warranty expense to date equals $96,000.

GLEIM
Go to Online Course

Access the **Gleim CPA Premium Review System** featuring our SmartAdapt technology from your Gleim Personal Classroom to continue your studies.

You will experience a personalized study environment with exam-emulating multiple-choice questions.

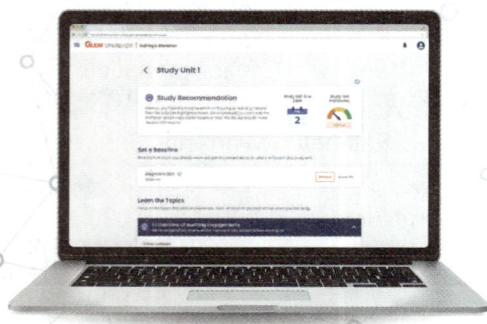

Study Unit Twelve

Equity

(20 pages of outline)

12.1   Classes of Equity

Reporting

Equity is reported on the face of the balance sheet.

Example 12-1   Presentation of Equity

Capital stock:		
Preferred stock, $50 par value, 6% cumulative, 10,000 shares authorized, issued, and outstanding	$ 500,000	
Preferred stock, $40 par value, 7% cumulative, 5,000 shares authorized, issued, and outstanding, each convertible to 1 share of common stock	200,000	
Common stock, stated value $1 per share, 60,000 shares authorized, issued, and outstanding	60,000	
Common stock dividend distributable, 4,500 shares	4,500	
Stock warrants outstanding	1,500	
Total capital stock		$ 766,000
Additional paid-in capital:		
Excess over par -- preferred	$ 464,000	
Excess over par -- common	800,000	1,264,000
Total paid-in capital		$2,030,000
Retained earnings:		
Retained earnings -- unappropriated	$5,800,000	
Retained earnings -- appropriated for expansion	1,520,000	
Total retained earnings		7,320,000
Total paid-in capital and retained earnings		$9,350,000
Accumulated other comprehensive income		527,000
Minus: Cost of treasury stock (5,000 common shares)		(100,000)
Total shareholders' equity		$9,777,000

Stock Authorized, Issued, and Outstanding

Stock authorized is the maximum amount of stock that a corporation is legally allowed to issue.

- The charter (articles of incorporation) filed with the secretary of state of the state of incorporation indicates the classes of stock that may be issued and their authorized amounts in terms of shares or total dollar value.

Stock issued is the amount of stock authorized that was actually issued by the corporation.

Stock outstanding is the amount of stock issued that was purchased and is held by shareholders.

- Stock outstanding may be lower than stock issued as a result of the entity's repurchases of its own stock (treasury stock).

Common Stock

The most widely used classes of stock are common and preferred. Common shareholders are entitled to receive **liquidating distributions** only after all other claims have been satisfied, including those of preferred shareholders.

Common shareholders are not entitled to **dividends**.

- A corporation may choose not to declare dividends. Among the reasons are insufficient retained earnings to meet a legal requirement or the need to use cash for some other purpose.

State statutes typically permit different classes of common stock with different rights or privileges, e.g., class A common with voting rights and class B common with no voting rights.

If only one class of stock is issued, it is treated as common, and each shareholder must be treated equally.

Common shareholders elect directors to the board.

Preferred Stock

Preferred shareholders have the right to receive (1) dividends at a specified rate (before common shareholders may receive any) and (2) distributions before common shareholders (but after creditors) upon liquidation. But they tend not to have voting rights or to enjoy the same capital gains as the common shareholders.

Background 12-1   Presentation of Preferred Stock

In the equity section, preferred stock is generally reported before common stock because it is a hybrid of debt and equity. This position reminds readers that, in liquidation, the claims of the preferred shareholders must be satisfied before the common shareholders can be paid.

If a board issues preferred stock, it may establish different classes or series. Each may be assigned independent rights, dividend rates, and redemption prices.

Holders of **convertible preferred stock** have the right to convert the stock into shares of another class (usually common stock) at a predetermined ratio set forth in the articles or bylaws.

Callable preferred stock is issued with the condition that it may be called (redeemed or repurchased) by the issuer at a stated price and time. Issuers may establish a sinking fund for this purpose.

Mandatorily redeemable financial instruments (MRFIs) are redeemable shares that embody an unconditional obligation to transfer assets at a fixed or determinable time or upon an event certain to occur.

- MRFIs must be accounted for as **liabilities** unless the redemption is required only upon the liquidation or termination of the entity.

Equity Accounts

Contributed capital (paid-in capital) represents amounts invested by owners in exchange for stock (common or preferred).

- **Capital stock** (stated capital) is the **par value** (or stated value) of all shares issued and outstanding.

    - Amounts for common and preferred stock are separately listed. Absent treasury stock, the number of shares may be determined by dividing these amounts by the related par value per share.

- **Additional paid-in capital** (paid-in capital in excess of par value) consists of amounts in excess of stated capital.

Retained earnings is increased by net income and decreased by (1) net losses, (2) cash or property dividends, (3) stock dividends, (4) split-ups effected in the form of a dividend, and (5) certain treasury stock transactions.

- Prior-period adjustments (error corrections) also are made to retained earnings.

- A change in accounting principle is applied retrospectively. The cumulative effect on all prior periods is reflected in the opening balances of assets, liabilities, and retained earnings (or other appropriate components of equity) for the first period presented.

Retained earnings amounts may be **appropriated** (restricted) at management's discretion to disclose that earnings are to be used for purposes other than dividends. An appropriation must be clearly displayed within equity.

- Purposes include (1) compliance with a bond indenture (bond contract), (2) retention of assets for internally financed expansion, (3) anticipation of losses, or (4) adherence to legal restrictions. For example, a state law may restrict retained earnings by an amount equal to the cost of treasury stock.

- The appropriation **does not set aside assets**. It limits the availability of dividends. A formal entry (debit retained earnings, credit retained earnings appropriated) or disclosure in a note may be made.

- Transfers to and from an appropriation do not affect net income.

  - Costs and losses are not debited to an appropriation, and no amount is transferred to income.

Treasury stock is the entity's own stock that was repurchased by the entity subsequent to its initial issuance to shareholders.

- Treasury stock reduces the shares outstanding, not the shares authorized.
- It is commonly accounted for at cost (discussed later in this study unit).
- Treasury stock is not an asset, and dividends are never paid to these shares.

Accumulated other comprehensive income is a separate component of equity that includes items excluded from net income. Items in that component should be classified according to their nature. A list of items reported as other comprehensive income is in Study Unit 1, Subunit 3.

Stop & Review

You have completed the outline for this subunit.
Study multiple-choice questions 1 and 2 on page 396.

12.2 Issuance of Stock

Par Value

The par value of stock is an arbitrary amount assigned by the issuer. Most states treat par value as **legal capital**, an amount unavailable for dividends.

- Common and preferred stock are reported in the financial statements at par value.
- When no-par stock is issued, most states require it to have a stated value equivalent to par value.

Issuance of Stock

Cash is debited, the appropriate stock account is credited for the total par value, and additional paid-in capital (paid-in capital in excess of par) is credited for the difference.

Example 12-2   Issuance of Stock

Parvenu Corp. issued 50,000 shares of its $1 par-value common stock. The market price of the stock was $17 per share on the day of issue.

Cash (50,000 shares × $17 market price)	$850,000	
Common stock (50,000 shares × $1 par value)		$ 50,000
Additional paid-in capital -- common (difference)		800,000

Parvenu also issued 10,000 shares of $50 par-value, 6% preferred stock. The market price at the time was $62 per share.

Cash (10,000 shares × $62 market price)	$620,000	
6% preferred stock (10,000 shares × $50 par value)		$500,000
Additional paid-in capital -- preferred (difference)		120,000

Costs of Issuance

Direct costs of issuing stock (underwriting, legal, accounting, tax, registration, etc.) reduce the net proceeds received and additional paid-in capital. Equity interests and the issue costs inherent to them are permanent. Thus, they are not expensed.

Example 12-3	Direct Costs of Issuing Stock

In the common stock issue illustrated in Example 12-2, Parvenu incurred direct issue costs of $10,000. The entry is the following:

Additional paid-in capital -- common	$10,000	
Cash		$10,000

- In contrast, **debt issue costs** reduce the carrying amount of the debt and are amortized. They benefit the entity only for the life of the debt, and the cost therefore must be systematically and rationally allocated over that life.

Share-Based Payment for Goods or Services

Occasionally, stock is issued for goods received or services rendered.

- The transaction should be recorded at the **grant-date fair value** of the stock issued.

- The grant date is the date at which a mutual understanding of the key terms and conditions of the share-based payment award was reached.

Example 12-4	Share-Based Payment for Services

Consultant agreed to perform an internal control study in return for 500 shares of Parvenu common stock. On the day the contract was signed, Parvenu common stock was trading at $12.50 per share. Consultant spent 39 hours on the study, and its normal billing rate is $160 per hour. At the time Consultant submitted the completed study to Parvenu's management, the stock was trading at $13.50 per share.

Parvenu records the transaction at the stock market price on the date the contract was signed.

Consulting expense (500 shares × $12.50 price at time of contract)	$6,250	
Common stock (500 shares × $1 par value)		$ 500
Additional paid-in capital -- common (difference)		5,750

Donated Capital

In general, contributions received must be recognized as revenues or gains in the period of receipt. They should be measured at fair value.

The receipt of a contribution of an **entity's own stock** is recorded at fair value as increases in both contributed capital and treasury stock.

- Because these accounts offset, the transaction has no net effect on equity. Also, transactions in an entity's own stock cannot result in a gain or loss.

Conversion of Convertible Preferred Stock

When conversion occurs, all related amounts are removed from the books and replaced with amounts related to the new security.

- Transactions in an entity's own stock may not result in a gain or loss. Thus, the conversion is reported using the **book value method**. The new shares are recorded at the carrying amount of the converted shares.

Example 12-5   Conversion of Preferred Stock

Parvenu issued 5,000 shares of $40 par-value, 7% preferred stock, each share convertible into 5 shares of its $1 par-value common stock beginning 6 months after issue. The market price on the day of issue was $68 per share.

Cash (5,000 shares × $68 market price)	$340,000	
7% convertible preferred stock (5,000 shares × $40 par value)		$200,000
Additional paid-in capital -- preferred (difference)		140,000

Six months after the convertible preferred stock was issued, all the shareholders exercised their conversion privilege.

7% convertible preferred stock (balance)	$200,000	
Additional paid-in capital -- preferred (balance)	140,000	
Common stock (5,000 shares × 5 × $1 par value)		$ 25,000
Additional paid-in capital -- common (difference)		315,000

Combined Issuance

The proceeds of the combined issuance of different classes of securities are allocated based on the relative fair values of the securities.

Example 12-6   Combined Issuance of Common Stock and Preferred Stock

Parvenu issued 2,000 shares of its $1 par-value common stock and 1,000 shares of its $50 par-value, 6% preferred stock for a lump sum of $99,000. At the time, the common stock was trading at $15 per share, and the preferred stock was trading at $60 per share.

Fair value of common stock (2,000 shares × $15 market price)	$30,000
Fair value of preferred stock (1,000 shares × $60 market price)	60,000
Total fair value issued	$90,000

Common stock is 33.3333% of the total ($30,000 ÷ $90,000), and preferred stock is 66.6667% ($60,000 ÷ $90,000). The proceeds are therefore assigned as $33,000 to common stock ($99,000 × 33.3333%) and $66,000 to preferred stock ($99,000 × 66.6667%). The sale is recorded as follows:

Cash (lump sum)	$99,000	
Common stock (2,000 shares × $1 par value)		$ 2,000
Additional paid-in capital -- common ($33,000 – $2,000)		31,000
6% preferred stock (1,000 shares × $50 par value)		50,000
Additional paid-in capital -- preferred ($66,000 – $50,000)		16,000

If the fair value of one class of securities is not known, the **incremental method** is used. The other securities are recorded at their fair values. The remaining proceeds are credited to the securities for which fair value is not determinable.

Example 12-7   Combined Issuance -- Incremental Method

Simdyne, Inc., a closely held corporation, issued 5,000 shares of $2 par-value common stock and 8% bonds with a face amount of $100,000 for a lump sum of $120,000. Because no active market exists for Simdyne's stock, its fair value cannot be determined. If the bonds had been issued separately, they would have resulted in proceeds of $80,000.

Lump sum received	$120,000
Fair value of bonds	(80,000)
Remainder assigned to common stock	$ 40,000

The sale is recorded as follows:

Cash (lump sum)	$120,000	
Discount on bonds payable (difference)	20,000	
Bonds payable (face amount)		$100,000
Common stock (5,000 shares × $2 par value)		10,000
Additional paid-in capital -- common ($40,000 – $10,000)		30,000

Stop & Review

You have completed the outline for this subunit.

Study multiple-choice questions 3 through 5 beginning on page 397.

12.3   Stock Warrants and Stock Rights

Stock Warrants

A warrant is a certificate representing **a right to purchase shares** at a specified price within a specified period. Thus, it is an equity security. Warrants are usually attached to other securities.

Preemptive Right

The preemptive right safeguards a shareholder's proportionate ownership. It is the **right to purchase a pro rata amount** of a new issuance of the same class of stock.

Issuer's Accounting

In a rights offering, each shareholder is issued a warrant that is an option to buy a certain number of shares at a fixed price.

- When rights are issued for no consideration, the issuer makes only a memorandum entry.

- If rights previously issued without consideration are allowed to lapse, contributed capital is unaffected.

If the **rights are exercised** and stock is issued, the issuer will reflect the proceeds received as a credit to (an increase in) common (preferred) stock at par value, with any remainder credited to additional paid-in capital.

Transaction costs associated with the redemption of stock rights reduce equity.

Recipient's Accounting

The recipient of stock rights must **allocate the carrying amount of the shares owned** between the shares and rights based on their relative fair values at the time the rights are received. The recipient then has three options:

1. If the rights are exercised, the amount allocated to them becomes part of the carrying amount of the acquired shares.

2. If the rights are sold, their carrying amount is credited, cash is debited, and a gain (loss) is credited (debited).

3. If the rights expire, a loss is recorded.

Stop & Review

You have completed the outline for this subunit.
Study multiple-choice question 6 on page 398.

12.4 Treasury Stock -- Acquisition

Success Tip

The AICPA has released multiple CPA questions involving treasury stock calculations under both the cost and par-value methods. Successful candidates need to know the journal entries used by each method to be able to identify the correct debits and credits.

Cost Method vs. Par-Value Method

Under the **cost method**, treasury shares are reported at their reacquisition price, and the journal entry is a debit to treasury stock and a credit to cash.

- On the balance sheet, treasury stock is reported separately as a reduction of total shareholders' equity.

- The cost method is much more common in practice.

Under the **par-value method**, the acquisition is treated as a constructive retirement. All related amounts are removed from the books.

Acquisition Price > Original Issue Price

Under the par-value method, if the acquisition price is greater than the original issue price, the difference is a reduction of retained earnings or a credit balance in additional paid-in capital (APiC) from treasury stock transactions.

Example 12-8	Treasury Stock -- Cost Method vs. Par-Value Method

Parvenu reacquired 5,000 shares of its $1 par-value common stock for $20 per share. This stock had originally been issued at $17 per share. Parvenu had no prior treasury stock transactions.

Cost Method:

Treasury stock (5,000 shares × $20 market price)	$100,000	
Cash (payment)		$100,000

Par-Value Method:

Treasury stock (5,000 shares × $1 par value)	$ 5,000	
Additional paid-in capital -- common (5,000 shares × $16 original issue excess)	80,000	
Retained earnings (difference)	15,000	
Cash (payment)		$100,000

Acquisition Price < Original Issue Price

Under the par-value method, if the acquisition price is less than the original issue price, additional paid-in capital is decreased (debited) for the difference between the acquisition price and the par value of the stock reacquired.

Example 12-9	Treasury Stock -- Acquisition Price < Issue Price

Parvenu reacquired 5,000 shares of its $1 par-value common stock for $10 per share.

Cost Method:

Treasury stock (5,000 shares × $10 market price)	$50,000	
Cash (payment)		$50,000

Par-Value Method:

Treasury stock (5,000 shares × $1 par value)	$ 5,000	
Additional paid-in capital -- common (difference)	45,000	
Cash (payment)		$50,000

However, if the acquisition price is less than the par value of stock reacquired, the difference is an increase in PiC from treasury stock transactions. (Gains and losses are not recognized on transactions in an entity's own stock.)

Presentation

Treasury stock is not an asset. It is reported as a contra-equity account and decreases the total number of shares outstanding.

Stop & Review

You have completed the outline for this subunit.
Study multiple-choice questions 7 and 8 on page 399.

12.5 Treasury Stock -- Reissue

Reissue Price > Cost

The excess is credited to paid-in capital from treasury stock transactions.

Example 12-10	Treasury Stock -- Reissue Price > Cost

Parvenu reissued 1,000 shares of its treasury stock that had been acquired for $20 per share. At the time of reissue, the market price was $22 per share.

Cost Method:

Cash (1,000 shares × $22 market price)	$22,000	
Treasury stock (1,000 shares × $20 cost)		$20,000
PiC from treasury stock transactions (difference)		2,000

Par-Value Method:

Cash (1,000 shares × $22 market price)	$22,000	
Treasury stock (1,000 shares × $1 par value)		$ 1,000
PiC from treasury stock transactions (difference)		21,000

Reissue Price < Cost

Under the cost method, the difference is debited to paid-in capital from treasury stock transactions to the extent of any credit balance. Otherwise, the debit is to retained earnings.

Under the par-value method, the difference is credited to paid-in capital from treasury stock transactions.

Example 12-11   Treasury Stock -- Reissue Price < Cost

Parvenu reissued 1,000 shares of its treasury stock that had been acquired for $20 per share. At the time of reissue, the market price was $18 per share. Parvenu had no prior reissuance of treasury stock. Thus, the accounting under the cost method includes a debit to retained earnings for the entire difference between the cost and the price of the reissued shares.

Cost Method:

Cash (1,000 shares × $18 market price)	$18,000	
Retained earnings (difference)	2,000	
Treasury stock (1,000 shares × $20 cost)		$20,000

Par-Value Method:

Cash (1,000 shares × $18 market price)	$18,000	
Treasury stock (1,000 shares × $1 par value)		$ 1,000
PiC from treasury stock transactions (difference)		17,000

Success Tip

The AICPA has also released a number of CPA questions addressing the reissue price and associated journal entries used when a corporation reissues previously purchased treasury stock.

Stop & Review

You have completed the outline for this subunit.
Study multiple-choice questions 9 and 10 beginning on page 400.

12.6 Retirement of Stock

Occasionally, a company decides to retire its own stock. The company may retire treasury stock it already owns or non-treasury stock it purchases. The journal entry to record this retirement includes the following:

- When treasury stock is retired, the treasury stock account is credited. When non-treasury stock is retired, cash or other consideration given is credited.

- The stock account is debited for the par or stated value.

- Additional paid-in capital is debited to the extent it exists from the original issuance.

- Any remainder is debited to retained earnings or credited to paid-in capital from stock retirement.

Example 12-12   Acquisition and Retirement of Stock

Mainecat Co. reacquired 10,000 shares of its only class of common stock (par value $1 per share) for $50,000. The shares were issued at $10 per share. Mainecat uses the cost method to account for treasury stock transactions but has no current balances related to them. The following are the entries to record the acquisition and retirement of the shares:

Treasury stock	$50,000	
Cash		$50,000
Common stock	$10,000	
Additional paid-in capital -- common	90,000	
Treasury stock		$50,000
PiC from retirement of treasury stock		50,000

No gain or loss is reported on transactions involving an entity's own stock.

A retirement of treasury stock does not change the number of shares authorized.

Stop & Review

You have completed the outline for this subunit.
Study multiple-choice question 11 on page 401.

12.7 Cash Dividends

Dividends may be distributed in the form of cash or property. (Stock dividends, discussed later in this study unit, are not a form of return on investment.)

- Dividends are paid on outstanding shares only, not on treasury stock.

Relevant Dates

On the **date of declaration**, the board of directors formally approves a dividend.

- Unlike a stock dividend, a cash or property dividend cannot be withdrawn once declared. Thus, a cash or property dividend becomes a legal liability of the corporation on the date of declaration.

- The dividend is recorded by reclassifying a portion of retained earnings as a payable.

  - In most states, a corporation may not declare a dividend in excess of its balance of retained earnings.

All holders of the stock on the **date of record** are legally entitled to receive the dividend.

The **date of payment** is the date on which the dividend is paid.

Example 12-13	Dividend Declaration and Payment

On September 12, Parvenu's board of directors declared a $4 per-share dividend to be paid on October 15 to all holders of common stock as of October 1. On the date of declaration, Parvenu held 5,000 of its common shares in the treasury, and 45,000 shares were outstanding.

September 12:

Retained earnings (45,000 shares outstanding × $4 per share)	$180,000	
Dividend payable		$180,000

October 15:

Dividend payable	$180,000	
Cash		$180,000

Dividends on Preferred Stock

Most preferred shares are issued with a **stated dividend rate**.

- The dividends on preferred stock equal the par value of the stock times its stated dividend rate.

Unlike interest on debt, dividends on preferred stock are not a legal obligation of the corporation until the board chooses to declare them. Common shareholders may not receive a dividend unless the current-year preferred dividend has been paid.

When a corporation has outstanding **cumulative preferred stock**, common shareholders may not receive a dividend until all preferred dividends in arrears have been paid.

- **Dividends in arrears** are preferred dividends that were not declared in prior years.

- Although they are not legal liabilities of the corporation, dividends in arrears must be disclosed either on the face of the balance sheet or in the notes both in the aggregate and per share.

Example 12-14	Dividends on Preferred Stock

On January 10 of the current year, Parvenu's board declared a $3 per-share dividend to all holders of common stock. Parvenu has not paid dividends on its 10,000 outstanding shares of $50 par-value, 6% cumulative preferred stock for the previous 2 years. Parvenu had 45,000 shares of common stock outstanding. On the date of declaration, Parvenu makes the following calculation:

Preferred dividends -- arrears (10,000 shares × $50 par value × 6% × 2 years)	$ 60,000
Preferred dividends -- current (10,000 shares × $50 par value × 6%)	30,000
Common dividends (45,000 shares × $3 per share)	135,000
Debit to retained earnings	$225,000

Stop & Review

You have completed the outline for this subunit.

Study multiple-choice questions 12 and 13 on page 402.

12.8   Property Dividends and Liquidating Dividends

Property Dividends

When a corporation declares a dividend consisting of tangible property, the property is first remeasured to fair value as of the date of declaration. The remeasurement to fair value is recognized in the income statement.

Example 12-15   Property Dividend

Parvenu's board of directors resolved to distribute obsolete inventory from its warehouse to holders of common stock. The inventory had a carrying amount of $40,000 and a fair value of $10,000.

Date of declaration:		
Loss on inventory revaluation (Carrying amount – Fair value)	$30,000	
Inventory		$30,000
Retained earnings (fair value)	$10,000	
Property dividend payable		$10,000
Date of distribution:		
Property dividend payable	$10,000	
Inventory		$10,000

The distribution of a property dividend affects retained earnings in two ways:

1. Remeasurement of the property to fair value affects net income for the period.
2. The decrease for the fair value of the property distributed.

- Thus, the total decrease in retained earnings as a result of a property dividend declaration equals the carrying amount of the property distributed.

Liquidating Dividends

Dividends in excess of a corporation's retained earnings are liquidating dividends. They are not considered dividends but are treated as a return of capital.

- The effect of a liquidating dividend is to decrease contributed capital.

- Additional paid-in capital is debited first to the extent available before other contributed capital accounts are charged.

Stop & Review

You have completed the outline for this subunit.
Study multiple-choice questions 14 and 15 beginning on page 402.

12.9   Stock Dividends and Stock Splits

Definitions

Stock dividends and stock splits are distributions of stock to current shareholders in return for no consideration.

- In a **stock dividend**, a portion of retained earnings is capitalized as part of paid-in capital.

  - The **par value** of the shares is unchanged.

  - An issuance of shares **less than 20% to 25%** of the previously outstanding common shares should be recognized as a **stock dividend**.

    - The **SEC requires** an issuance of less than 25% by a public entity to be treated as a stock dividend.

  - An issuance of **more than 20% to 25%** of the previously outstanding common shares (25% or more for public entities) more closely resembles a **stock split** than a dividend.

    - An entity may be legally required to capitalize the par value of the additional shares issued. In this case, the term **stock split in the form of a dividend** should be used.

- In a **stock split**, no journal entry is made other than a memorandum entry.

  - The **par value** of the shares is reduced.

Stock dividends and stock splits do not affect the fair value of a shareholder's interest or the proportionate amount of that interest. Thus, the effect is simply a reclassification of equity.

- However, because more shares are outstanding, the fair value (and market price) per share is reduced.

Stock Dividends

In accounting for a stock dividend, the fair value of the additional shares issued is reclassified from retained earnings to capital stock (at par value) and the difference to additional paid-in capital.

Example 12-16   Stock Dividend

Parvenu's board of directors declared a 10% stock dividend on the 45,000 shares of common stock outstanding ($1 par value). The stock was trading for $15 per share at the declaration date.

Date of declaration:

Retained earnings [(45,000 shares × 10%) × $15 market price]	$67,500	
Common stock dividend distributable [(45,000 shares × 10%) × $1 par value]		$ 4,500
Additional paid-in capital -- common (difference)		63,000

Date of distribution:

Common stock dividend distributable	$4,500	
Common stock		$4,500

Stock Split in the Form of a Dividend

The state of incorporation may require capitalization of retained earnings for a **stock split in the form of a dividend**, usually in an amount based on **par value**.

Example 12-17   Stock Split in the Form of a Dividend

Use the information in Example 12-16, but assume that a 40% stock split in the form of a dividend was declared.

Date of declaration:

Retained earnings [(45,000 shares × 40%) × $1 par value]	$18,000	
Common stock dividend distributable [(45,000 shares × 40%) × $1]		$18,000

Date of distribution:

Common stock dividend distributable	$18,000	
Common stock		$18,000

Stock Splits

The **primary purpose of** a stock split is to improve the stock's marketability by reducing its market price and proportionally increasing the number of shares outstanding.

A stock split does not require an adjustment to retained earnings or paid-in capital and **does not affect total equity**.

Example 12-18   Stock Split

Parvenu's board of directors declared a 2-for-1 common stock split. Prior to the stock split, Parvenu had 45,000 shares of $1 par-value common stock outstanding and 5,000 treasury shares. The laws of Parvenu's state of incorporation protect treasury stock from dilution. Thus, Parvenu reduces the par value of its common stock to $0.50 per share and issues 100,000 new shares: 90,000 to shareholders (45,000 × 2) and 10,000 to the treasury (5,000 × 2). Total equity is unchanged.

$$100,000 \text{ shares} \times \$0.50 \text{ (new)} = 50,000 \text{ shares} \times \$1 \text{ (old)}$$

A **reverse stock split** reduces the number of shares outstanding, which serves to increase the fair value per share of those shares still outstanding.

Other Issues

The **recipient** of a stock dividend or stock split should **not recognize income**. After receipt, the shareholder has the same proportionate interest in the corporation and the same total carrying amount as before the declaration.

Treasury stock may be adjusted for stock dividends and splits to protect it from dilution. However, **some states prohibit** the payment of stock dividends on treasury stock.

Stop & Review

You have completed the outline for this subunit.
Study multiple-choice questions 16 through 18 beginning on page 403.

Questions

12.1 Classes of Equity

1. Munn Corp.'s records included the following equity accounts:

Preferred stock, par value $15, authorized 20,000 shares	$255,000
Additional paid-in capital, preferred stock	15,000
Common stock, **no** par, $5 stated value, 100,000 shares authorized	300,000

In Munn's statement of equity, the number of issued and outstanding shares for each class of stock is

	Common Stock	Preferred Stock
A.	60,000	17,000
B.	60,000	18,000
C.	63,000	17,000
D.	63,000	18,000

✔ **Answer (A) is correct.**
Required: The number of issued and outstanding shares of common and preferred stock.
Discussion: If an entity does not hold any stock as treasury stock, the number of shares of each type of stock may be determined by dividing the amount allocated to each stock account by the related par value. The number of shares of preferred stock issued and outstanding is therefore 17,000 ($255,000 ÷ $15 par value), and the number of shares of common stock issued and outstanding is 60,000 ($300,000 ÷ $5 stated value).

✘ **Answer (B) is incorrect.** The 18,000 shares of preferred would have a par value of $270,000.

✘ **Answer (C) is incorrect.** The 63,000 shares of common would have a stated value of $315,000.

✘ **Answer (D) is incorrect.** The 18,000 shares of preferred would have a par value of $270,000, and 63,000 shares of common would have a stated value of $315,000.

2. Which of the following financial instruments issued by a public company should be reported on the issuer's books as a liability on the date of issuance?

A. Cumulative preferred stock.

B. Preferred stock that is convertible to common stock 5 years from the issue date.

C. Common stock that contains an unconditional redemption feature.

D. Common stock that is issued at a 5% discount as part of an employee share purchase plan.

✔ **Answer (C) is correct.**
Required: The financial instrument reported as a liability.
Discussion: Mandatorily redeemable financial instruments (MRFIs) are redeemable shares that embody an unconditional obligation to transfer assets at a fixed or determinable time or upon an event certain to occur. MRFIs must be accounted for as liabilities.

✘ **Answer (A) is incorrect.** Cumulative preferred stock is reported as equity, not a liability. Both common stock and preferred stock that is not unconditionally redeemable are treated as equity.

✘ **Answer (B) is incorrect.** Convertible preferred stock is reported as equity.

✘ **Answer (D) is incorrect.** Common stock that is issued at a 5% discount as part of an employee share purchase plan is still classified as equity. Both common stock and preferred stock that is not redeemable are treated as equity.

12.2 Issuance of Stock

3. On February 1, Hyde Corp., a newly formed company, had the following stock issued and outstanding:

- Common stock, **no** par, $1 stated value, 10,000 shares originally issued for $15 per share

- Preferred stock, $10 par value, 3,000 shares originally issued for $25 per share

Hyde's February 1 statement of equity should report

	Common Stock	Preferred Stock	Additional Paid-in Capital
A.	$150,000	$30,000	$45,000
B.	$150,000	$75,000	$0
C.	$10,000	$75,000	$140,000
D.	$10,000	$30,000	$185,000

✔ **Answer (D) is correct.**
Required: The amounts of common stock, preferred stock, and additional paid-in capital to be reported in the statement of equity.
Discussion: The common stock was issued for a total of $150,000 (10,000 shares × $15). Of this amount, $10,000 (10,000 shares × $1 stated value) should be allocated to the common stock, with the remaining $140,000 ($150,000 – $10,000) credited to additional paid-in capital. The preferred stock was issued for $75,000 (3,000 shares × $25), of which $30,000 (3,000 shares × $10 par value) should be allocated to the preferred stock and $45,000 ($75,000 – $30,000) should be allocated to additional paid-in capital. In the statement of equity, Hyde therefore should report $10,000 in the common stock account, $30,000 in the preferred stock account, and $185,000 ($140,000 + $45,000) as additional paid-in capital.

4. During the prior year, Brad Co. issued 5,000 shares of $100 par-value convertible preferred stock for $110 per share. One share of preferred stock can be converted into three shares of Brad's $25 par-value common stock at the option of the preferred shareholder. On December 31 of the current year, when the market value of the common stock was $40 per share, all of the preferred stock was converted. What amount should Brad credit to common stock and to additional paid-in capital -- common stock as a result of the conversion?

	Common Stock	Additional Paid-in Capital
A.	$375,000	$175,000
B.	$375,000	$225,000
C.	$500,000	$50,000
D.	$600,000	$0

✔ **Answer (A) is correct.**
Required: The amounts credited to common stock and additional paid-in capital.
Discussion: Brad recorded the issue of the convertible preferred stock with this entry:

Cash (5,000 shares × $110 market value)	$550,000	
Preferred stock (5,000 shares × $100 par value)		$500,000
Additional paid-in capital -- preferred (difference)		50,000

Brad recorded the conversion as follows:

Preferred stock (balance)	$500,000	
Additional paid-in capital -- preferred (balance)	50,000	
Common stock (5,000 shares × 3 × $25 par value)		$375,000
Additional paid-in capital -- common (difference)		175,000

✘ **Answer (B) is incorrect.** The amount of $175,000 is credited to additional paid-in capital ($550,000 – $375,000).

✘ **Answer (C) is incorrect.** The amount of $500,000 is the par value of the preferred stock, not the common stock.

✘ **Answer (D) is incorrect.** The amount of $600,000 equals the fair value of the common stock at the date of conversion.

5. East Co. issued 1,000 shares of its $5 par-value common stock to Howe as compensation for 1,000 hours of legal services performed. Howe usually bills $160 per hour for legal services. On the date of issuance, the stock was trading on a public exchange at $140 per share. By what amount should the additional paid-in capital account increase as a result of this transaction?

A. $135,000

B. $140,000

C. $155,000

D. $160,000

✓ **Answer (A) is correct.**
Required: The increase in additional paid-in capital.
Discussion: When stock is issued in exchange for goods or services, the transaction is recorded at the grant-date fair value of the stock issued. The quoted price of the stock is used to measure the services received. The entry is to debit legal expense for $140,000 (1,000 shares × $140 market price), credit common stock for $5,000 (1,000 shares × $5 par value), and credit additional paid-in capital for the difference ($135,000).

✗ **Answer (B) is incorrect.** The amount of $5,000 should be allocated to common stock.

✗ **Answer (C) is incorrect.** The fair value of the stock should be used to record the transaction.

✗ **Answer (D) is incorrect.** The amount of $5,000 should be allocated to common stock, and the fair value of the stock should be used to record the transaction.

12.3 Stock Warrants and Stock Rights

6. An entity issued rights to its existing shareholders without consideration. The rights allowed the recipients to purchase unissued common stock for an amount in excess of par value. When the rights are issued, which of the following accounts will be increased?

	Common Stock	Additional Paid-in Capital
A.	Yes	Yes
B.	Yes	No
C.	No	No
D.	No	Yes

✓ **Answer (C) is correct.**
Required: The effect on common stock and additional paid-in capital when rights are issued without consideration.
Discussion: When rights are issued without consideration, only a memorandum entry is made. Common stock and additional paid-in capital are affected only if the rights are exercised.

12.4 Treasury Stock -- Acquisition

7. Ten thousand shares of $10 par value common stock were issued initially at $15 per share. Subsequently, 1,000 of these shares were purchased as treasury stock at $13 per share. The cost method of accounting for treasury stock is used. What is the effect of the purchase of the treasury stock on the amount reported in the balance sheet on each of the following?

	Additional Paid-in Capital	Total Equity
A.	No effect	No effect
B.	No effect	Decrease
C.	Decrease	No effect
D.	Decrease	Decrease

✔ **Answer (B) is correct.**
Required: The effect of the purchase of the treasury stock on additional paid-in capital and total shareholders' equity.
Discussion: Under the cost method, the acquisition of treasury stock is recorded as a debit to treasury stock and a credit to cash equal to the amount of the purchase price. This transaction results in a decrease in both total assets and total equity. Additional paid-in capital is unaffected by the treasury stock purchase.

8. Lem Co., which accounts for treasury stock under the par-value method, acquired 100 shares of its $6 par value common stock for $10 per share. The shares had originally been issued by Lem for $7 per share. By what amount would Lem's additional paid-in capital from common stock decrease as a result of the acquisition?

A. $0

B. $100

C. $300

D. $400

✔ **Answer (B) is correct.**
Required: The decrease in additional paid-in capital from an acquisition of treasury stock accounted for under the par-value method.
Discussion: The entry for issuance of the stock was

Cash	$700	
Common stock ($6 per share)		$600
Additional paid-in capital		100

The par-value method treats a treasury stock purchase as a constructive retirement. Assuming no balance in paid-in capital from treasury stock transactions, the entry for the treasury stock purchase using the par-value method is

Treasury stock	$600	
Additional paid-in capital	100	
Retained earnings	300	
Cash		$1,000

✘ **Answer (A) is incorrect.** Under the par-value method, the acquisition of treasury stock is accounted for by reducing additional paid-in capital by the amount recorded when the shares were originally issued.

✘ **Answer (C) is incorrect.** The amount of $300 is the debit to retained earnings.

✘ **Answer (D) is incorrect.** The amount of $400 is the sum of the debit to additional paid-in capital and the debit to retained earnings.

12.5 Treasury Stock -- Reissue

Pugh Co. reported the following in its statement of equity on January 1:

Common stock, $5 par value, authorized 200,000 shares, issued 100,000 shares	$ 500,000
Additional paid-in capital	1,500,000
Retained earnings	516,000
	$2,516,000
Minus: Treasury stock, at cost, 5,000 shares	(40,000)
Total equity	$2,476,000

The following events occurred during the year:

May 1 -- 1,000 shares of treasury stock were sold for $10,000.
July 9 -- 10,000 shares of previously unissued common stock sold for $12 per share.
October 1 -- The distribution of a 2-for-1 stock split resulted in the common stock's per-share par value being halved.

Pugh accounts for treasury stock under the cost method. Laws in the state of Pugh's incorporation protect shares held in treasury from dilution when stock dividends or stock splits are declared.

9. In Pugh's December 31 statement of equity, the par value of the issued common stock should be

A. $550,000

B. $530,000

C. $275,000

D. $265,000

✓ **Answer (A) is correct.**
Required: The par value of the issued common stock.
Discussion: At the beginning of the year, 100,000 shares with a par value of $500,000 had been issued. These shares included the treasury stock (issued but not outstanding) accounted for at cost. Under the cost method, the par value recorded in the common stock account is unaffected by purchases and sales of treasury stock. On July 9, 10,000 shares of previously unissued common stock were sold. This transaction increased the aggregate par value to $550,000 (110,000 shares issued × $5). The 2-for-1 stock split reduced the par value per share by 50% but did not affect the aggregate par value of the issued stock. Thus, state law presumably did not require capitalization of retained earnings as a result of the stock split.

✗ **Answer (B) is incorrect.** The par value of the issued and outstanding shares is $530,000.

✗ **Answer (C) is incorrect.** Half the par value of the issued stock is $275,000.

✗ **Answer (D) is incorrect.** Half the par value of the issued and outstanding stock is $265,000.

10. Selected information from the accounts of Row Co. at December 31, Year 4, follows:

Total income since incorporation	$420,000
Total cash dividends paid	130,000
Total value of property dividends distributed	30,000
Excess of proceeds over cost of treasury stock sold, accounted for using the cost method	110,000

In its December 31, Year 4, financial statements, what amount should Row report as retained earnings?

A. $260,000

B. $290,000

C. $370,000

D. $400,000

✔ **Answer (A) is correct.**
Required: The amount to be reported as retained earnings.
Discussion: Retained earnings is increased by net income and decreased by net losses, dividends, and certain treasury stock transactions. Thus, retained earnings is $260,000 ($420,000 – $130,000 – $30,000). Because Row uses the cost method to account for treasury stock, the $110,000 excess of proceeds over the cost of treasury stock sold does not affect retained earnings. Under the cost method, the excess should be credited to additional paid-in capital.

✘ **Answer (B) is incorrect.** The amount of $290,000 fails to subtract the $30,000 in property dividends.

✘ **Answer (C) is incorrect.** The amount of $370,000 includes the $110,000 excess of proceeds over cost of treasury stock.

✘ **Answer (D) is incorrect.** The amount of $400,000 includes the $110,000 excess of proceeds over cost of treasury stock and does not subtract the $30,000 value of property dividends distributed.

12.6 Retirement of Stock

11. Cross Corp. had 2,000 outstanding shares of 11% preferred stock, $50 par. These shares were not mandatorily redeemable. On August 8, Cross redeemed and retired 25% of these shares for $22,500. On that date, Cross's additional paid-in capital from preferred stock totaled $30,000. To record this transaction, Cross should debit (credit) its capital accounts as follows:

	Preferred Stock	Additional Paid-in Capital	Retained Earnings
A.	$25,000	$7,500	$(10,000)
B.	$25,000	--	$(2,500)
C.	$25,000	$(2,500)	--
D.	$22,500	--	--

✔ **Answer (C) is correct.**
Required: The accounting for redemption and retirement of preferred stock.
Discussion: Under the cost method, the entry to record a treasury stock purchase is to debit treasury stock at cost ($22,500) and credit cash. The entry to retire this stock is to debit preferred stock at par [(2,000 shares × 25%) × $50 = $25,000], debit additional paid-in capital from the original issuance ($30,000 × 25% = $7,500), credit treasury stock at cost ($22,500), and credit additional paid-in capital from stock retirement ($10,000). Thus, the net effect on additional paid-in capital is a $2,500 credit ($10,000 credit – $7,500 debit). No entry to retained earnings is necessary.

✘ **Answer (A) is incorrect.** If the reacquisition price is less than the issuance price, a credit is made to additional paid-in capital, not retained earnings.

✘ **Answer (B) is incorrect.** Additional paid-in capital is debited to the extent it exists from the original issuance ($30,000 × 25% = $7,500), and a credit is made to additional paid-in capital for the stock retirement ($10,000). Retained earnings is not affected by this transaction.

✘ **Answer (D) is incorrect.** Preferred stock must be debited for the par value of the retired shares.

12.7 Cash Dividends

12. On January 15, Year 5, Rico Co. declared its annual cash dividend on common stock for the year ended January 31, Year 5. The dividend was paid on February 9, Year 5, to shareholders of record as of January 28, Year 5. On what date should Rico decrease retained earnings by the amount of the dividend?

A. January 15, Year 5.

B. January 31, Year 5.

C. January 28, Year 5.

D. February 9, Year 5.

Answer (A) is correct.
Required: The date to decrease retained earnings by the amount of the dividend.
Discussion: On the date of declaration, a cash dividend becomes a legal liability of the corporation (unlike stock dividends, cash dividends cannot be rescinded). Thus, on January 15, a portion of retained earnings was reclassified as dividends payable.

13. At December 31, Year 3 and Year 4, Apex Co. had 3,000 shares of $100 par, 5% cumulative preferred stock outstanding. **No** dividends were in arrears as of December 31, Year 2. Apex did not declare a dividend during Year 3. During Year 4, Apex paid a cash dividend of $10,000 on its preferred stock. Apex should report dividends in arrears in its Year 4 financial statements as a(n)

A. Accrued liability of $15,000.

B. Disclosure of $15,000.

C. Accrued liability of $20,000.

D. Disclosure of $20,000.

Answer (D) is correct.
Required: The accounting for preferred dividends in arrears.
Discussion: Dividends in arrears on preferred stock are not obligations of the company and are not recognized in the financial statements. However, the aggregate and per-share amounts of arrearages in cumulative preferred dividends should be disclosed on the face of the balance sheet or in the notes. The aggregate amount in arrears is $20,000 [(3,000 shares × $100 par × 5% × 2 years) – $10,000 paid in Year 4].

Answer (A) is incorrect. Dividends in arrears do not meet recognition criteria.
Answer (B) is incorrect. The amount of $15,000 is the arrearage for 1 year.
Answer (C) is incorrect. Dividends in arrears should be disclosed on the face of the balance sheet or in the notes, not accrued.

12.8 Property Dividends and Liquidating Dividends

14. On December 1, Year 4, Pott Co. declared and distributed a property dividend when the fair value exceeded the carrying amount. As a consequence of the dividend declaration and distribution, what are the accounting effects?

	Property Dividends Recorded at	Retained Earnings
A.	Fair value	Decreased
B.	Fair value	Increased
C.	Cost	Increased
D.	Cost	Decreased

Answer (A) is correct.
Required: The effects of a property dividend.
Discussion: When a corporation declares a dividend consisting of tangible property, the property is first remeasured to fair value as of the date of declaration. The dividend should then be recognized as a decrease in (debit to) retained earnings and a corresponding increase in (credit to) a dividend payable. The distribution of the property dividend is recognized by a debit to property dividend payable and a credit to the property account.

Answer (B) is incorrect. Retained earnings is decreased.
Answer (C) is incorrect. Retained earnings is decreased and the dividends are recorded at fair value.
Answer (D) is incorrect. Property dividends are recorded at fair value.

15. A corporation declared a dividend, a portion of which was liquidating. How does this declaration affect each of the following?

	Additional Paid-in Capital	Retained Earnings
A.	Decrease	No effect
B.	Decrease	Decrease
C.	No effect	Decrease
D.	No effect	No effect

✔ **Answer (B) is correct.**
Required: The effect of a dividend, a portion of which was liquidating, on additional paid-in capital and retained earnings.
Discussion: The portion of a dividend that is liquidating results in a distribution in excess of the corporation's retained earnings. The effect of a liquidating dividend is to decrease contributed capital. Additional paid-in capital is debited first to the extent available before other contributed capital accounts are charged. Thus, declaration of a cash dividend, a portion of which is liquidating, decreases both additional paid-in capital and retained earnings.

✘ **Answer (A) is incorrect.** Retained earnings is also decreased.

✘ **Answer (C) is incorrect.** Additional paid-in capital is also decreased.

✘ **Answer (D) is incorrect.** Both additional paid-in capital and retained earnings are decreased.

12.9 Stock Dividends and Stock Splits

16. Nest Co. issued 100,000 shares of common stock. Of these, 5,000 were held as treasury stock at December 31, Year 3. During Year 4, transactions involving Nest's common stock were as follows:

May 3: 1,000 shares of treasury stock were sold.
August 6: 10,000 shares of previously unissued stock were sold.
November 18: A 2-for-1 stock split took effect.

Laws in Nest's state of incorporation protect treasury stock from dilution. At December 31, Year 4, how many shares of Nest's common stock were issued and outstanding?

	Shares Issued	Outstanding
A.	220,000	212,000
B.	220,000	216,000
C.	222,000	214,000
D.	222,000	218,000

✔ **Answer (A) is correct.**
Required: The number of shares of common stock issued and outstanding.
Discussion: In Nest's state, stock splits and dividends apply to treasury stock. Accordingly, the number of shares issued is 220,000 [(100,000 + 10,000) × 2]. The number of shares outstanding is 212,000 [(95,000 + 1,000 + 10,000) × 2].

✘ **Answer (B) is incorrect.** The figure 216,000 does not properly account for the stock split on the treasury stock.

✘ **Answer (C) is incorrect.** The figure 222,000 includes 1,000 shares of treasury stock sold on May 3 twice [(100,000 + 1,000 + 10,000) × 2].

✘ **Answer (D) is incorrect.** The figure 222,000 includes 1,000 shares of treasury stock sold on May 3 twice [(100,000 + 1,000 + 10,000) × 2]. Moreover, 218,000 shares outstanding includes 4,000 treasury stock shares that are not outstanding [(95,000 + 4,000 + 10,000) × 2].

17. Universe Co. issued 500,000 shares of common stock in the current year. Universe declared a 30% stock dividend. The market value was $50 per share, the par value was $10, and the average issue price was $30 per share. By what amount will Universe decrease shareholders' equity for the dividend?

   A. $0

   B. $1,500,000

   C. $4,500,000

   D. $7,500,000

✓ **Answer (A) is correct.**
Required: The decrease in equity after declaration of a stock dividend.
Discussion: When a stock dividend is declared, a portion of retained earnings is reclassified as contributed capital. The net effect on total equity is thus $0.

18. A company whose stock is trading at $10 per share has 1,000 shares of $1 par common stock outstanding when the board of directors declares a 30% common stock dividend. Which of the following adjustments should be made when recording the stock dividend?

   A. Treasury stock is debited for $300.

   B. Additional paid-in capital is credited for $2,700.

   C. Retained earnings is debited for $300.

   D. Common stock is debited for $3,000.

✓ **Answer (C) is correct.**
Required: The recording of a stock dividend.
Discussion: The board of directors declared a 30% common stock dividend. As this issuance is more than 25% of the previously outstanding common shares, it should be accounted for as a stock split in the form of a dividend. Generally (depending on the state of incorporation), the company will capitalize retained earnings in an amount based on the par value. Thus, the journal entry at the date of declaration will be:

Retained earnings (1,000 shares × 30%) $300
   Common stock dividend distributable $300

✗ **Answer (A) is incorrect.** In a stock dividend, or stock split in the form of a dividend, a portion of retained earnings is capitalized as part of paid-in capital. In this case, the treasury stock account is unaffected.

✗ **Answer (B) is incorrect.** This issuance is not accounted for as a regular stock dividend. Because the issuance is more than 25% of the previously outstanding common shares, it should be accounted for as a stock split in the form of a dividend.

✗ **Answer (D) is incorrect.** In a stock dividend, or stock split in the form of a dividend, the common stock account is increased (credited), not decreased (debited).

Study Unit Thirteen

Consolidated Financial Reporting and Financial Statement Analysis

(26 pages of outline)

13.1 Accounting for Business Combinations

Definitions

A **business combination** (hereafter called a combination) is "a transaction or other event in which an acquirer obtains control of one or more businesses."

Control is a controlling financial interest. It is the direct or indirect ability to determine the direction of management and policies of the investee. This usually means one entity's direct or indirect ownership of **more than 50%** of the outstanding voting interests of another entity.

A **parent** is an entity that has a controlling financial interest in one or more **subsidiaries**.

A **business** consists of an integrated set of activities and assets that can be conducted to provide a return of economic benefits directly to investors or others.

Differences between Accounting for Asset Acquisitions and Business Combinations

	Business Combinations	Asset Acquisitions
Direct acquisition costs	Expensed as incurred	Capitalized to assets' cost
Goodwill	May be recognized	Never recognized
Initial recognition of assets acquired	Acquisition date fair value	Allocation of cost based on relative fair values

Consolidated Reporting

When one entity controls another, consolidated financial statements must be issued by a parent company regardless of the percentage of ownership.

- **Consolidated statements** present amounts for the parent and subsidiary(ies) as if they were a single economic entity.

A parent and subsidiary may exist separately for an indefinite period, but consolidated financial statements must be issued that report them as a single economic entity.

Required consolidated reporting is an example of substance over form. Even if the two entities remain legally separate, the financial statements are more meaningful to users if they see the effects of control by one over the other.

Costs Associated with Business Combinations

Acquisition-related costs, such as finder's fees, professional and consulting fees, and general administrative costs, are expensed as incurred.

Issue costs for securities are accounted for as follows:

- **Direct issue costs of equity** (underwriting, legal, accounting, tax, registration, etc.) reduce additional paid-in capital.

  - Indirect costs of issue, records maintenance, and ownership transfers (e.g., a stock transfer agent's fees) are expensed.

- **Debt issue costs** are reported in the balance sheet as a direct deduction from the carrying amount of the debt.

Example 13-1   Costs Associated with Business Combinations

On January 1, Year 1, Lipp Co. issued 100,000 shares of its $1 par-value common stock and transferred $300,000 in cash in exchange for all of Rahm Co.'s outstanding common stock. To finance the acquisition, Lipp issued bonds with a par value of $300,000. The following costs in relation to the acquisition were incurred by Lipp:

- Bond issue costs of $15,000
- Printer's fee of $10,000 for stock certificates
- Finder's and consulting fees of $40,000

Bond issue costs (debt issue costs) are reported in the balance sheet as a direct deduction from the carrying amount of the debt. The journal entry is

Debt issue costs	$15,000	
Cash		$15,000

A printer's fee for stock certificates is a direct issue cost of equity that reduces additional paid-in capital. The journal entry is

Additional paid-in capital	$10,000	
Cash		$10,000

Finder's and consulting fees are acquisition-related costs that must be expensed as incurred. The journal entry is

Business combination expense	$40,000	
Cash		$40,000

Acquisition Method

A business combination must be accounted for using the **acquisition method**. It

- Determines the acquirer and the acquisition date.

- Recognizes and **measures at acquisition-date fair value** the

  - Identifiable assets acquired,
  - Liabilities assumed, and
  - Any noncontrolling interest in the acquiree.

- Recognizes goodwill or a gain from a bargain purchase and measures it using the goodwill equation.

The consideration transferred in a business combination must be measured at **acquisition-date fair value**.

Calculation of Goodwill or Gain from a Bargain Purchase

Goodwill is an intangible asset reflecting the future economic benefits arising from other assets acquired in a business combination that are not individually identified and separately recognized.

At the acquisition date, the acquirer recognizes and measures goodwill or a gain from a bargain purchase using the **goodwill equation**.

- A **positive outcome** of the equation results in recognition of **goodwill** in the consolidated balance sheet.

- A **negative outcome** of the equation results in recognition of a **gain from a bargain purchase** in the consolidated income statement.

- All components of the goodwill equation are measured at **acquisition-date fair value**.

- The identifiable net assets acquired equal the identifiable assets acquired minus liabilities assumed.

- Below is the **goodwill equation**:

  Fair value of the consideration transferred
  + Fair value of any noncontrolling interest in the acquiree
  + Fair value of any previously held equity interest in the acquiree
  – Fair value of identifiable net assets acquired
  _____
  Positive outcome = Goodwill; Negative outcome = Gain from a bargain purchase

- A noncontrolling interest exists when less than 100% of the acquiree was acquired.

- A previously held equity interest exists when control of the acquiree was achieved in several transactions.

Example 13-2   Goodwill

Platonic issued stock with a fair value of $120,000 to acquire all the outstanding stock of Socratic Corp. The carrying amount of Socratic's net assets is $100,000. This carrying amount equals the fair value of Socratic's net assets except that the fair values of inventory and property, plant, and equipment exceed their carrying amounts by $4,000 and $10,000, respectively. The acquisition-date fair value of the identifiable net assets acquired is $114,000 ($100,000 carrying amount of net assets acquired + $4,000 excess fair value of inventory + $10,000 excess fair value of PPE). Given no noncontrolling interest or prior equity interest, goodwill is calculated as follows:

Acquisition-date fair value of the consideration transferred	$120,000
Acquisition-date fair value of identifiable net assets acquired	(114,000)
Goodwill	**$ 6,000**

Stop & Review

You have completed the outline for this subunit.

Study multiple-choice questions 1 and 2 beginning on page 432.

13.2 Consolidated Financial Reporting -- Acquisition-Date Balance Sheet

Acquisition-Date Balance Sheet

A balance sheet should be prepared that reports the financial position of the consolidated entity at the acquisition date.

- Step 1 -- Determine the amount of goodwill or gain from bargain purchase recognized on the business combination.

Example 13-3   Goodwill

On December 31, Year 0, Platonic and Socratic have the following condensed balance sheets:

	Platonic	Socratic		Platonic	Socratic
Current assets	$140,000	$ 40,000	Current liabilities	$ 60,000	$ 20,000
Noncurrent assets	180,000	80,000	Noncurrent liabilities	100,000	0
			Equity	160,000	100,000
Total assets	$320,000	$120,000	Total liabilities and equity	$320,000	$120,000

On January 1, Year 1, Platonic borrowed $120,000 on a 5-year balloon note and used the proceeds to purchase 80% of the outstanding common shares of Socratic. Platonic had no prior equity interest in Socratic. Assume that the carrying amounts of Socratic's assets and liabilities equal their fair values except that the fair value of land exceeds its carrying amount by $25,000. Also assume that the fair value of the noncontrolling interest (NCI) was $30,000.

Platonic performs the following calculation:

Consideration transferred		$120,000
Noncontrolling interest		30,000
Acquisition-date fair value of net assets acquired:		
Carrying amount	$(100,000)	
Excess fair value -- land	(25,000)	(125,000)
Goodwill		$ 25,000

- Step 2 -- Prepare the assets section of the consolidated balance sheet. Assets and liabilities are reported at 100% of their fair value even though an NCI exists.

Example 13-4   Assets Section of the Balance Sheet

Consolidated assets are calculated as follows:

Current assets of parent	$140,000	Noncurrent assets of parent	$180,000
Current assets of subsidiary	40,000	Noncurrent assets of subsidiary	80,000
Consolidated current assets	$180,000	Excess fair value -- land	25,000
		Goodwill	25,000
		Consolidated noncurrent assets	$310,000

- Step 3 -- Prepare the liabilities section of the consolidated balance sheet.

Example 13-5   Liabilities Section of the Balance Sheet

The new debt issued will be paid in one amount at the end of Year 5. Thus, it is classified as noncurrent debt.

Consolidated liabilities are calculated as follows:

Current liabilities of parent	$60,000	Noncurrent liabilities of parent	$100,000
Current liabilities of subsidiary	20,000	Noncurrent liabilities of subsidiary	0
Consolidated current liabilities	$80,000	New noncurrent debt	120,000
		Consolidated noncurrent liabilities	$220,000

- Step 4 -- Determine the NCI. An NCI is not reported for every asset and liability. The entire NCI is reported as a single component of consolidated equity. (The fair value of the NCI was given in Example 13-3 as $30,000.)

- Step 5 -- Because a combination is an acquisition of net assets, the subsidiary's equity accounts are eliminated. Thus, in the absence of a bargain purchase, the equity of the consolidated entity immediately after acquisition is the equity of the parent just prior to acquisition plus the fair value of the noncontrolling interest.

Example 13-6   Consolidated Total Equity

Consolidated equity is calculated as follows:

Platonic's shareholders' equity	$160,000
Noncontrolling interest	30,000
Consolidated total equity	$190,000

- Step 6 -- Prepare the acquisition-date balance sheet.

Example 13-7   Acquisition-Date Balance Sheet

Platonic's condensed consolidated balance sheet at the acquisition date is as follows:

Consolidated current assets	$180,000	Consolidated current liabilities	$ 80,000
Consolidated noncurrent assets	310,000	Consolidated noncurrent liabilities	220,000
		Platonic's shareholders' equity	160,000
		Noncontrolling interest	30,000
Consolidated total assets	$490,000	Consolidated total liabilities and equity	$490,000

- If the subsidiary holds shares of the common stock of the parent, this reciprocal investment must be eliminated. Subsidiary shareholdings in a parent are treated as treasury stock of the consolidated entity. Because no gain or loss on treasury stock transactions is recognized, reciprocal investments have no effect on the net income or retained earnings of the consolidated entity.

Example 13-8   Reciprocal Investment

Assume that, on the date of acquisition, Socratic held 1,000 shares of Platonic common stock. In preparing the consolidated balance sheet, this holding is eliminated by a debit to treasury stock and a credit to investment in Platonic.

Stop & Review

You have completed the outline for this subunit.

Study multiple-choice questions 3 through 7 beginning on page 434.

13.3 Consolidated Financial Reporting -- Subsequent to the Acquisition Date

Consolidation Process

After the close of the fiscal year in which the combination occurred, the consolidated entity prepares its first full set of consolidated financial statements.

The following steps must be performed when preparing consolidated financial statements:

- All line items of assets, liabilities, revenues, expenses, gains, losses, and OCI of a subsidiary are added item by item to those of the parent. These items are reported at the consolidated amounts.

- No investment in the subsidiary account is presented in the consolidated financial statements. Consolidated statements report the assets and liabilities of the subsidiary and the parent as if they are a single economic entity.

- All the equity accounts of the subsidiary are eliminated (not presented in the consolidated financial statements).

- The periodic net income or loss and OCI of a consolidated subsidiary attributable to NCIs are presented separately from the periodic net income or loss and OCI attributable to the shareholders of the parent.

- Goodwill from the acquisition of a subsidiary is presented separately in the noncurrent assets section of the consolidated balance sheet.

- Intraentity balances, transactions, income, and expenses must be eliminated in full (discussed in Subunit 13.4).

- NCI is reported separately in one line item in the equity section. The NCI must be adjusted for its proportionate share of

  - The subsidiary's net income (an increase) or net loss (a decrease),
  - Dividends declared by the subsidiary (a decrease) and
  - Items of OCI recognized by the subsidiary.

- Adjustments should be made to report the subsidiary's assets and liabilities at amounts based on their acquisition-date fair values.

Example 13-9   Reporting Based on Acquisition-Date Fair Value

On January 1, Year 1, Parent Co. acquired all of the outstanding shares of common stock of Son Co. On the acquisition date, the carrying amount of a building in Son's financial statements was $100,000, and its fair value was $120,000. Son depreciates this building using the straight-line depreciation method over 10 years with no salvage value.

In its December 31, Year 1, separate financial statements, Son reports the following for the building:

> December 31, Year 1, Son's separate financial statements
> Depreciation expense: $10,000 = $100,000 ÷ 10 years
> Building's carrying amount: $90,000 = $100,000 – $10,000

However, the building and the related depreciation expense in the consolidated financial statements must be reported based on the $120,000 acquisition-date fair value of the building.

> December 31, Year 1, consolidated financial statements
> Depreciation expense: $12,000 = $120,000 ÷ 10 years
> Building's carrying amount: $108,000 = $120,000 – $12,000

When preparing the December 31, Year 1, consolidated financial statements, the first step of the consolidation process combines all assets, liabilities, and income statement items of the subsidiary with those of the parent. Thus, the following adjustments must be made by the parent to report the building and related depreciation expense in the December 31, Year 1, consolidated financial statements:

> Increase depreciation expense by $2,000 ($12,000 – $10,000)
> Increase the carrying amount of the building by $18,000 ($108,000 – $90,000)

Consolidated Net Income

The consolidated income statement must present separate amounts for the following:

- Total consolidated net income
- Net income attributable to the NCI
- Net income attributable to the shareholders of the parent

Example 13-10   Net Income Attributable to Shareholders of Parent and Subsidiary

The following are the separate statements of income of Platonic and Socratic, excluding Platonic's share of income from Socratic, for the year ended December 31, Year 1:

	Platonic	Socratic
Sales	$250,000	$120,000
Cost of goods sold	(120,000)	(70,000)
Selling and administrative expenses	(50,000)	(10,000)
Interest costs	(20,000)	0
Income tax expense	(21,000)	(14,000)
Net income	$ 39,000	$ 26,000

-- Continued on next page --

Example 13-10 -- Continued

Assume that (1) the ownership percentages were the same as at the acquisition date (80%), (2) no items of other comprehensive income were recognized in Year 1, and (3) no intraentity transactions occurred during Year 1. Platonic's Year 1 consolidated statement of income is presented as follows:

Sales	$370,000
Cost of goods sold	(190,000)
Selling and administrative expenses	(60,000)
Interest costs	(20,000)
Income tax expense	(35,000)
Net income	$ 65,000
Net income attributable to NCI ($26,000 net income reported by Socratic × 20%)	(5,200)
Net income attributable to Platonic's shareholders [$39,000 + ($26,000 × 80%)]	$ 59,800

If an acquisition occurs after the first business day of the year, revenues, expenses, gains, losses, and OCI of the subsidiary are included in the financial statements of the consolidated entity only from the date of the acquisition.

Dividends Paid

Consolidated dividends are those paid to parties outside the consolidated entity by the parent and the subsidiary.

- Dividends declared by the parent decreases the amount of consolidated retained earnings.

- The NCI's share of the subsidiary's dividends decreases the balance of the NCI.

- The parent's share of a subsidiary's dividends is not reported in the consolidated financial statements. No cash was paid outside of the consolidated entity.

Example 13-11　　Consolidated Dividends

Platonic and Socratic declared and paid $40,000 and $20,000 of dividends, respectively, during the year. Consolidated dividends paid are calculated as follows:

Dividends paid by parent	$40,000
Dividends paid by subsidiary	20,000
Parent's proportionate share of subsidiary's dividends ($20,000 × 80%)	(16,000)
Consolidated dividends paid	$44,000
NCI's share of subsidiary's dividends ($20,000 × 20%)	(4,000)
Decrease in consolidated retained earnings	$40,000

Retained Earnings

Retained earnings of the consolidated entity **at the acquisition date** consist solely of the retained earnings of the parent. Equity amounts of the subsidiary are eliminated.

Retained earnings of the consolidated entity at a subsequent reporting date consist of (1) acquisition-date retained earnings, plus (2) the net income (loss) for the subsequent period(s) attributable to the shareholders of the parent, minus (3) dividends paid by the parent to entities outside the consolidated entity.

Example 13-12	Consolidated Retained Earnings

Platonic's equity balance of $160,000 just prior to acquisition consisted of common stock of $10,000, additional paid-in capital of $100,000, and retained earnings of $50,000. Consolidated retained earnings is calculated on December 31, Year 1, as follows:

Acquisition-date retained earnings of parent	$50,000
Consolidated net income attributable to parent's shareholders	59,800
Parent's dividends paid since acquisition date	(40,000)
Consolidated retained earnings at reporting date	$69,800

Noncontrolling Interest

The NCI must be adjusted for its proportionate share of (1) the net income of the subsidiary included in consolidated net income, (2) items of consolidated other comprehensive income attributable to the subsidiary, and (3) dividends paid by the subsidiary.

Example 13-13	NCI

Platonic owns 80% of Socratic. At the acquisition date, Platonic recognized $30,000 for the fair value of the NCI. During the current year, the subsidiary's net income and dividends paid were $26,000 and $20,000, respectively. The NCI at the reporting date is calculated as follows:

NCI at acquisition date	$30,000
Net income attributable to NCI ($26,000 × 20%)	5,200
NCI share in dividends paid by subsidiary ($20,000 × 20%)	(4,000)
Total NCI at reporting date	$31,200

Consolidated Statement of Changes in Equity

This statement satisfies the requirement for a presentation of a reconciliation of the beginning and ending balances of (1) total equity, (2) equity attributable to the parent, and (3) equity attributable to the NCI.

Example 13-14   Consolidated Statement of Changes in Equity

The following is Platonic's Year 1 consolidated statement of changes in equity:

			Platonic's Shareholders' Equity			
	Total	Retained Earnings	Accumulated OCI	Common Stock	APIC	NCI
Beginning balance	$190,000	$50,000	–	$10,000	$100,000	$30,000
Net income (loss)	65,000	59,800				5,200
Dividends paid	(44,000)	(40,000)	–	–	–	(4,000)
Ending balance	$211,000	$69,800	–	$10,000	$100,000	$31,200

Stop & Review

You have completed the outline for this subunit.

Study multiple-choice questions 8 and 9 beginning on page 436.

13.4 Consolidated Financial Reporting -- Intraentity Eliminations

Year-End Consolidated Financial Statements

Consolidating entities routinely conduct business with each other. The effects of these intraentity transactions must be eliminated in full during the preparation of the consolidated financial statements.

Consolidated financial statements report the financial position, results of operations, and cash flows as if the consolidated entities were a single economic entity.

- Thus, all line items in the consolidated financial statements must be presented at the amounts that would have been reported **if the intraentity transactions had never occurred**.

After adding together all the assets, liabilities, and income statement items of a parent and a subsidiary, **eliminating journal entries** for intraentity transactions must be recorded for proper presentation of the consolidated financial statements.

Reciprocal Balances

In a consolidated balance sheet, reciprocal balances, such as receivables and payables, between a parent and a subsidiary are eliminated in their entirety, regardless of the portion of the subsidiary's stock held by the parent.

Example 13-15   Intraentity Eliminations -- Reciprocal Balances
Platonic's separate balance sheet reports a $12,600 receivable from and an $8,500 payable to Socratic. Socratic's separate balance sheet reports an $8,500 receivable from and a $12,600 payable to Platonic. These balances are not reported on the consolidated balance sheet.

Intraentity Inventory Transactions -- Gross Profit

Intraentity transactions that give rise to gross profit require more complex treatment.

- Profit from the sale of inventory between consolidating entities is a component of the net income of the entity that sold the inventory.

- However, the consolidated entity recognizes profit on this exchange only in proportion to the inventory that is sold to nonaffiliated parties. Accordingly, the gross profit included in the inventory remaining on the purchaser's books must be eliminated from consolidated net income.

- The year-end eliminating journal entry eliminates the gross profit recognized for the inventory remaining on the purchaser's books and reduces the inventory account to the balance it would have had if the intraentity transactions had never occurred.

  - The **sales** account is debited (decreased) for the amount recognized by the seller on the intraentity sale.

  - The **inventory** account is credited (decreased) for the amount equal to the unrealized intraentity gross profit (Seller's gross profit percentage × Inventory remaining on purchaser's books).

  - The **cost of goods sold** account is credited (decreased) for the difference between sales and inventory. The total decrease in both the sales account and cost of goods sold account is exactly equal to the amount of gross profit eliminated.

  Gross Profit Eliminated:

  Inventory remaining on purchaser's books × Seller's gross profit percentage

---

Example 13-16   Intraentity Eliminations -- Inventory Transaction

During the year, Platonic sold $100,000 of goods to Socratic on the same terms as sales made to third parties. Socratic sold 90% of this inventory to others. Socratic's cost of goods sold in connection with these outside sales was $90,000. Platonic had total sales of $800,000 and total cost of goods sold of $650,000 for the year.

Seller's gross profit percentage: [($800,000 − $650,000) ÷ $800,000] = 18.75%

Unsold inventory on purchaser's books	$ 10,000
Seller's gross profit percentage	× 18.75%
Unrealized intraentity gross profit	$ 1,875

The eliminating journal entry is as follows:

Sales	$100,000	
Inventory		$ 1,875
Cost of goods sold		98,125

If no inventory from an intraentity transaction remains on the purchaser's books at the end of the reporting period, no adjustment is necessary for unrealized gross profit in ending inventory. The only adjustment for the intraentity sale is to eliminate (1) the sale recognized by the seller and (2) the cost of goods sold recognized by the purchaser.

Example 13-17   Intraentity Inventory Transaction -- None Retained

Using the data from Example 13-16, assume that Socratic (subsidiary) sold all of the inventory that was purchased from Platonic (parent) to third parties.

The year-end eliminating journal entry is as follows:

Sales	$100,000	
Cost of goods sold		$100,000

Intraentity Noncurrent Assets Transactions

Transfers of noncurrent assets require elimination of any **gain or loss on sale** recognized on the intraentity transaction.

All the accounts related to the asset transferred must be reported in the consolidated financial statements at the amounts that would have been reported if the intraentity transactions had never occurred.

- Thus, the **depreciation expense** recognized in the consolidated financial statements must be the depreciation expense as it would have been recognized in the seller's separate financial statements.

- If the original useful life and the depreciation method remain the same, the depreciation expense eliminated (added) is equal to the amount of gain (loss) on sale of equipment divided by the years of useful life remaining.

Example 13-18 Intraentity Sale of Equipment

On the first day of its fiscal year, Platonic sold equipment to Socratic for $99,000. The equipment was originally purchased by Platonic 3 years ago for $120,000. Platonic depreciated the equipment using the straight-line method over 8 years with no salvage value. Socratic depreciates the equipment using the straight-line method over 5 years with no salvage value. The following steps must be performed to record the eliminating journal entry for proper presentation of the equipment in the year-end consolidated financial statements:

- Eliminate the gain or loss on sale of the equipment that was recognized. Platonic recognized depreciation expense each year of $15,000 ($120,000 historical cost ÷ 8 years). Thus, the carrying amount of the equipment on the sale date in Platonic's separate financial statements was $75,000 ($120,000 historical cost – $45,000 accumulated depreciation). In its separate financial statements, Platonic recognized a gain on sale of **$24,000** ($99,000 transfer price – $75,000 seller's carrying amount). This gain must be eliminated (debited) in the eliminating journal entry.

- The depreciation expense must be equal to the depreciation expense that would have been recognized by Platonic ($15,000) as if the intraentity transaction had never occurred. Because the equipment is on Socratic's books, the depreciation expense before the eliminating journal entry is $19,800 ($99,000 transfer price ÷ 5 years). Thus, the depreciation expense must be decreased (credited) in the eliminating journal entry by **$4,800** ($15,000 – $19,800). This amount is equal to the gain on sale recognized divided by the years of useful life remaining ($24,000 ÷ 5 = $4,800).

- The cost of the equipment in the consolidated financial statements must be $120,000 (the amount that would have been reported if the intraentity transaction had never occurred). Thus, the equipment account must be increased (debited) in the eliminating journal entry by **$21,000** ($120,000 historical cost – $99,000 transfer price).

- The accumulated depreciation balance in the consolidated financial statements must be $60,000 ($15,000 × 4). This amount would have been reported if the intraentity transaction had never occurred. Thus, the accumulated depreciation account must be increased (credited) in the eliminating journal entry by **$40,200** ($60,000 – $19,800).

- The eliminating journal entry is as follows:

Equipment	$21,000	
Gain on sale of equipment	24,000	
Accumulated depreciation		$40,200
Depreciation expense		4,800

Debt

When one entity holds the debt securities of another entity with which it is consolidated, the elimination is treated as an extinguishment of debt, with recognition of any resulting gain or loss.

- All accounts related to the debt, such as the maturity amount, interest receivable (payable), and interest income (expense), must be eliminated.

Example 13-19   Intraentity Debt

Wagner, a holder of a $1 million Palmer, Inc., bond, collected the interest due on March 31 and then sold the bond to Seal, Inc., for $975,000. On that date, Palmer, a 75% owner of Seal, had a $1,075,000 carrying amount for this bond. The purchase was in substance a retirement of debt by the consolidated group for less than its carrying amount. The transaction resulted in a gain of $100,000 ($1,075,000 carrying amount – $975,000 price).

The premium or discount on the debtor's and creditor's books, and any related amortization, is eliminated and recognized as a gain or loss on extinguishment in the period of purchase.

Reciprocal Dividends

When consolidated entities hold reciprocal equity stakes, the portion of dividends paid to each other must be eliminated from the consolidated financial statements.

- The portion of the parent's dividends paid to outside parties reduces consolidated retained earnings.
- The portion of the subsidiary's dividends paid to outside parties reduces any noncontrolling interest.

Dividends	Consolidated Treatment
Parent's dividends to subsidiary	Eliminated
Subsidiary's dividends to parent	Eliminated
Parent's dividends to third parties	Reduces retained earnings
Subsidiary's dividends to third parties	Reduces NCI

Success Tip

The AICPA has released exam questions asking for the amount of a line item shown on the consolidated financial statements. When intraentity transactions are involved, determining the consolidated amount involves calculating the amount that must be eliminated for any intraentity transactions. Testable items include inventory; receivables; payables; property, plant, and equipment; accumulated depreciation; etc.

Stop & Review

You have completed the outline for this subunit.

Study multiple-choice questions 10 through 14 beginning on page 438.

13.5 Financial Statement Analysis -- Liquidity

The most common form of financial statement analysis is ratio analysis, in which two financial statement measures are compared.

Liquidity

Liquidity is a firm's ability to pay its current obligations as they come due and thus remain in business in the short run. Liquidity measures the ease with which assets can be converted to cash.

Liquidity ratios measure this ability by relating a firm's liquid assets to its current liabilities.

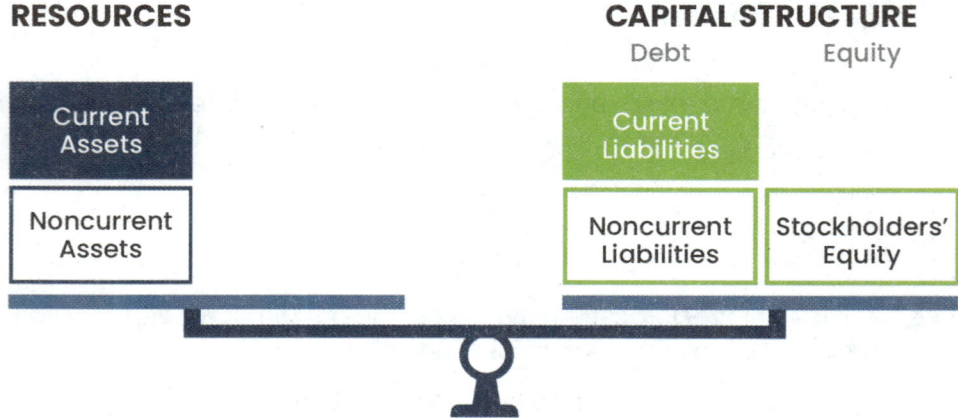

Figure 13-1

Example 13-20   Balance Sheet

RESOURCES			FINANCING		
CURRENT ASSETS:	**Current Year End**	**Prior Year End**	**CURRENT LIABILITIES:**	**Current Year End**	**Prior Year End**
Cash and equivalents	$ 325,000	$ 275,000	Accounts payable	$ 150,000	$ 75,000
Available-for-sale securities	165,000	145,000	Notes payable	50,000	50,000
Accounts receivable	120,000	115,000	Accrued interest on note	5,000	5,000
Notes receivable	55,000	40,000	Current maturities of L.T. debt	100,000	100,000
Inventories	85,000	55,000	Accrued salaries and wages	15,000	10,000
Prepaid expenses	10,000	5,000	Income taxes payable	70,000	35,000
Total current assets	**$ 760,000**	**$ 635,000**	**Total current liabilities**	**$ 390,000**	**$ 275,000**
NONCURRENT ASSETS:			**NONCURRENT LIABILITIES:**		
Equity-method investments	$ 120,000	$ 115,000	Bonds payable	$ 500,000	$ 600,000
Property, plant, and equip.	1,000,000	900,000	Long-term notes payable	90,000	60,000
Minus: Accum. depreciation	(85,000)	(55,000)	Employee-related obligations	15,000	10,000
Goodwill	5,000	5,000	Deferred income taxes	5,000	5,000
Total noncurrent assets	**$1,040,000**	**$ 965,000**	**Total noncurrent liabilities**	**$ 610,000**	**$ 675,000**
			Total liabilities	**$1,000,000**	**$ 950,000**
			SHAREHOLDERS' EQUITY:		
			Preferred stock, $50 par	$ 120,000	$ 0
			Common stock, $1 par	500,000	500,000
			Additional paid-in capital	110,000	100,000
			Retained earnings	70,000	50,000
			Total shareholders' equity	**$ 800,000**	**$ 650,000**
Total assets	**$1,800,000**	**$1,600,000**	**Total liabilities and shareholders' equity**	**$1,800,000**	**$1,600,000**

Success Tip

A candidate should know the formulas used to calculate the various financial ratios and be able to analyze the results. Certain ratios that may have more than one commonly agreed upon definition will be provided or defined by the AICPA, but you are expected to know simple ratios, such as the current ratio. Similarly, the numbers necessary to calculate a ratio often are not given directly. As a future CPA, you will be expected to determine these numbers using information given in the question and then calculate the ratio.

Liquidity Ratios

The **current ratio** (also called the working capital ratio) is the most common measure of liquidity.

$$\frac{\text{Current assets}}{\text{Current liabilities}}$$

Example 13-21   Current Ratio

Current year: $760,000 ÷ $390,000 = 1.95
Prior year: $635,000 ÷ $275,000 = 2.31

Although working capital increased in absolute terms ($10,000), current assets now provide less proportional coverage of current liabilities than in the prior year.

The **quick (acid-test) ratio** excludes inventories and prepaids from the numerator, recognizing that those assets are difficult to liquidate at their stated values. The quick ratio is thus a more conservative measure than the basic current ratio.

$$\frac{\text{Cash and equivalents + Marketable securities + Net receivables}}{\text{Current liabilities}}$$

Example 13-22   Quick (Acid-Test) Ratio

Current year: ($325,000 + $165,000 + $120,000 + $55,000) ÷ $390,000 = 1.71
Prior year: ($275,000 + $145,000 + $115,000 + $40,000) ÷ $275,000 = 2.09

In spite of its increase in total working capital, the company's position in its most liquid assets deteriorated significantly.

Effects of Transactions

If a ratio is less than 1.0, the numerator is lower than the denominator.

- A transaction that causes equal changes in the numerator and denominator will thus have a proportionally greater effect on the numerator, resulting in a change in the ratio in the same direction.

If a ratio is equal to 1.0, the numerator and denominator are the same.

- A transaction that causes equal changes in the numerator and denominator results in no change in the ratio.

If a ratio is greater than 1.0, the numerator is higher than the denominator.

- A transaction that causes equal changes in the numerator and denominator will thus have a proportionally greater effect on the denominator, resulting in a change in the ratio in the opposite direction.

Ratio range	Effect on ratio of equal increase to numerator and denominator	Effect on ratio of equal decrease to numerator and denominator
< 1.0	Increase	Decrease
= 1.0	No effect	No effect
> 1.0	Decrease	Increase

Stop & Review

You have completed the outline for this subunit.

Study multiple-choice questions 15 through 17 beginning on page 440.

13.6 Financial Statement Analysis -- Activity

Receivables Ratios

Example 13-23   Excerpt from an Income Statement

	Current Year	Prior Year
Net sales	$1,800,000	$1,400,000
Cost of goods sold	(1,650,000)	(1,330,000)
Gross profit	$ 150,000	$ 70,000

The **accounts receivable turnover ratio** is the number of times in a year the total balance of receivables is converted to cash.

$$\text{Accounts receivable turnover} = \frac{\text{Net credit sales}}{\text{Average balance in receivables}}$$

Example 13-24   Accounts Receivable Turnover Ratio

All of the company's sales are on credit (see Example 13-20 on page 423). Net trade receivables at the balance sheet date of the second prior year were $105,000.

Current year: $1,800,000 ÷ [($120,000 + $115,000) ÷ 2] = 15.3 times
Prior year: $1,400,000 ÷ [($115,000 + $105,000) ÷ 2] = 12.7 times

The company turned over its trade receivables balance 2.6 more times during the current year, even as receivables were growing in absolute terms. Thus, the company's effectiveness at collecting accounts receivable has improved noticeably.

The **average collection period** (also called the **days' sales in receivables**) measures the average number of days that pass between the time of a sale and receipt of the invoice amount.

$$\text{Days' sales in receivables} = \frac{\text{Days in year}}{\text{Accounts receivable turnover ratio}}$$

Example 13-25   Average Collection Period

Current year: 365 days ÷ 15.3 times = 23.9 days
Prior year: 365 days ÷ 12.7 times = 28.7 days

The denominator (calculated in Example 13-24 above) increased and the numerator is a constant. Consequently, days' sales must decrease. In addition to improving its collection practices, the company also may have become better at assessing the creditworthiness of its customers.

Inventory Ratios

Inventory turnover measures the number of times in a year the total balance of inventory is converted to cash or receivables.

- Generally, the higher the inventory turnover rate, the more efficient the inventory management of the firm. A high rate may imply that the firm is not carrying excess levels of inventory or inventory that is obsolete.

$$\text{Inventory turnover} = \frac{\text{Cost of goods sold}}{\text{Average balance in inventory}}$$

Example 13-26   Inventory Turnover

The balance in inventories at the balance sheet date of the second prior year was $45,000.

Current year: $1,650,000 ÷ [($85,000 + $55,000) ÷ 2] = 23.6 times
Prior year: $1,330,000 ÷ [($55,000 + $45,000) ÷ 2] = 26.6 times

The company did not turn over its inventories as many times during the current year. This is to be expected during a period of growing sales (and building inventory level) and so is not necessarily a sign of poor inventory management.

Days' sales in inventory measures the average number of days that pass between the acquisition of inventory and its sale.

$$\text{Days' sales in inventory} = \frac{\text{Days in year}}{\text{Inventory turnover ratio}}$$

Example 13-27   Day's Sales in Inventory

Current year: 365 days ÷ 23.6 times = 15.5 days
Prior year: 365 days ÷ 26.6 times = 13.7 days

The numerator is a constant, so the decreased inventory turnover means that days' sales in inventory increase. This common phenomenon occurs during a period of increasing sales.

Operating Cycle

A firm's operating cycle is the amount of time that passes between the acquisition of inventory and the collection of cash on the sale of that inventory.

Operating cycle = Days' sales in receivables + Days' sales in inventory

Example 13-28   Operating Cycle

Current year: 23.9 days + 15.5 days = 39.4 days
Prior year: 28.7 days + 13.7 days = 42.4 days

The company has managed to slightly reduce its operating cycle, even while increasing sales and inventories.

Cash Conversion Cycle

A firm's cash conversion cycle is the amount of time that passes between the actual outlay of cash for inventory purchases and the collection of cash from the sale of that inventory.

$$\begin{array}{rl} & \text{Average collection period} \\ + & \text{Days' sales in inventory} \\ - & \underline{\text{Average payables period}} \\ = & \text{Cash conversion cycle} \end{array}$$

- The accounts payable turnover ratio is the number of times during a period that the firm pays its accounts payable.

$$\text{Accounts payable turnover} = \frac{\text{Cost of goods sold}}{\text{Average balance in accounts payable}}$$

- The average payables period (also called payables turnover in days, or payables deferral period) is the average time between the purchase of inventories and the payment of cash.

$$\text{Average payable period} = \frac{\text{Days in year}}{\text{Accounts payable turnover}}$$

A difference between the operating cycle and the cash conversion cycle exists because the firm's purchases of inventory are made on credit. Thus, the cash conversion cycle is equal to the operating cycle minus the average payables period.

Other Turnover Ratios

The total assets turnover and fixed assets turnover are broader-based ratios that measure the efficiency with which assets are used to generate revenue.

- Both cash and credit sales are included in the numerator.

$$\text{Total assets turnover} = \frac{\text{Net total sales}}{\text{Average total assets}}$$

$$\text{Fixed assets turnover} = \frac{\text{Net total sales}}{\text{Average net fixed assets}}$$

Example 13-29   Other Turnover Ratios

Current year total assets turnover: $1,800,000 ÷ [($1,800,000 + $1,600,000) ÷ 2] = 1.06 times
Current year fixed assets turnover: $1,800,000 ÷ [($915,000 + $845,000) ÷ 2]   = 2.04 times

NOTE: The current- and prior-year net carrying amounts of fixed assets are $915,000 ($1,000,000 – $85,000) and $845,000 ($900,000 – $55,000), respectively.

Stop & Review

You have completed the outline for this subunit.

Study multiple-choice questions 18 through 22 beginning on page 442.

13.7 Financial Statement Analysis -- Solvency, Performance, and Comparative Analysis

Solvency and Leverage

Solvency is a firm's ability to pay its noncurrent obligations as they come due and thus remain in business in the long run (contrast with liquidity).

- Leverage in this context refers to the use of a high level of debt relative to equity in the firm's capital structure.

- An overleveraged firm risks insolvency.

$$\text{Debt-to-equity ratio} = \frac{\text{Total liabilities}}{\text{Total equity}}$$

The total debt ratio reports the total debt burden carried by the firm per dollar of assets.

$$\text{Total debt ratio} = \frac{\text{Total debt}}{\text{Total assets}}$$

The ability to service debt out of current earnings is a key aspect of the successful use of leverage.

$$\text{Times-interest-earned ratio} = \frac{\text{Earnings before interest and taxes}}{\text{Interest expense}}$$

Profitability Ratios

Profitability ratios measure how effectively the firm is using its resource base to generate a return.

$$\text{Gross profit margin} = \frac{\text{Gross profit}}{\text{Sales}}$$

$$\text{Net profit margin} = \frac{\text{Net income}}{\text{Sales}}$$

$$\text{Return on assets} = \frac{\text{Net income}}{\text{Average total assets}}$$

$$\text{Return on equity} = \frac{\text{Net income}}{\text{Average total equity}}$$

$$\text{Operating profit margin} = \frac{\text{Operating income}}{\text{Sales}}$$

- Operating profit margin is known as return on sales. This ratio may also be defined as earnings before interest and taxes (EBIT) divided by sales.

Corporate Valuation and Performance Measures

These ratios reflect and shape the stock market's assessment of a firm's current standing and future prospects.

$$\text{Book value per common share} = \frac{\text{Net assets available to common shareholders}}{\text{Ending common shares outstanding}}$$

$$\text{Price-to-earnings ratio} = \frac{\text{Price per common share}}{\text{Basic EPS}}$$

The dividend payout ratio measures what portion of net income was actually paid out to common shareholders in the form of dividends.

$$\text{Dividend payout ratio} = \frac{\text{Dividend paid per share}}{\text{Earnings per share (EPS)}} = \frac{\text{Cash dividend}}{\text{Net income}}$$

Success Tip

The AICPA has traditionally tested financial ratios. Gleim materials contain CPA questions dating back to the mid 1980s that test candidates' knowledge of financial ratios, and the AICPA continues to release new questions on this topic. Successful CPA candidates have memorized the various ratios and are able to correctly answer the majority of financial ratio questions in the Gleim materials.

Comparative Analysis

Comparative analysis involves both horizontal and vertical analysis. Horizontal (trend) analysis compares analytical data over a period of time. Vertical analysis makes comparisons among a single year's data.

Common-size financial statements are used to compare entities of different sizes. Items on common-size financial statements are expressed as percentages of corresponding base amounts. A base amount is assigned the value of 100%.

- The **horizontal** form of common-size analysis is useful for evaluating trends. Each amount for subsequent years is stated as a percentage of a **base-year amount**.

- **Vertical** common-size analysis presents amounts for a single year expressed as percentages of a base amount on the **balance sheet** (e.g., total assets) and on the **income statement** (e.g., sales). Common-size analysis permits management to compare individual expenses or asset categories with those of other entities and with industry averages.

Comparing an entity's performance with respect to its industry may identify strengths and weaknesses. Horizontal analysis of the industry may identify industry-wide trends and practices.

Stop & Review

You have completed the outline for this subunit.

Study multiple-choice questions 23 and 24 on page 444.

Questions

13.1 Accounting for Business Combinations

1. Alton Corporation purchased 100% of the shares of Jones Corporation for $600,000. Financial information for Jones Corporation is provided below.

	Jones Corp. ($000)	
	Carrying Amount	Fair Value
Cash	$ 50	$ 50
Accounts receivable	100	100
Inventory	150	100
Total current assets	$300	$250
Property, plant, and equipment (net)	500	600
Total assets	$800	$850
Current liabilities	$150	$150
Long-term debt	200	200
Total liabilities	$350	$350
Common stock	150	150
Paid-in capital	80	80
Retained earnings	220	
Total shareholders' equity	$450	
Total liabilities and shareholders' equity	$800	

The amount of goodwill resulting from this purchase, if any, would be

A. $200,000

B. $150,000

C. $100,000

D. $0

✔ **Answer (C) is correct.**

Required: The amount of goodwill resulting from a purchase of an entity.

Discussion: Goodwill is the excess of (1) the sum of the acquisition-date fair values of (a) the consideration transferred ($600,000), (b) any noncontrolling interest in the acquiree ($0), and (c) the acquirer's previously held equity interest in the acquiree ($0) over (2) the net of the acquisition-date fair values of the identifiable assets acquired ($850,000) and liabilities assumed ($350,000). The amount of goodwill is calculated as follows:

Consideration transferred	$600,000
Acquisition-date fair value of net assets acquired ($850,000 − $350,000)	(500,000)
Goodwill	$100,000

✘ **Answer (A) is incorrect.** The amount of $200,000 is the goodwill that would have been recognized if the consideration transferred was $700,000.

✘ **Answer (B) is incorrect.** The amount of $150,000 is based on the carrying amount of the net assets acquired instead of their fair value.

✘ **Answer (D) is incorrect.** The consideration transferred is greater than the fair value of the net assets acquired.

2. Acquirer Corporation acquired for cash at $10 per share 100,000 shares of the outstanding common stock of Acquiree Company. The total fair value of the identifiable assets acquired minus liabilities assumed of Acquiree was $1.4 million on the acquisition date, including the fair value of its property, plant, and equipment (its only noncurrent asset) of $250,000. The consolidated financial statements of Acquirer Corporation and its wholly owned subsidiary must reflect

A. A deferred credit of $150,000.

B. Goodwill of $150,000.

C. A gain of $150,000.

D. A gain of $400,000.

✔ **Answer (D) is correct.**
Required: The accounting for a bargain purchase.
Discussion: When (1) the net of the acquisition-date fair values of the identifiable assets acquired and liabilities assumed exceeds (2) the sum of the acquisition-date fair values of (a) the consideration transferred, (b) any noncontrolling interest in the acquiree, and (c) the acquirer's previously held equity interest in the acquiree, the acquirer recognizes the excess as a gain from bargain purchase.

Acquisition-date fair value of consideration transferred (100,000 shares × $10)	$ 1,000,000
Acquisition-date fair value of identifiable net assets acquired	(1,400,000)
Gain from a bargain purchase	$ (400,000)

✘ **Answer (A) is incorrect.** A deferred credit is never recognized for a bargain purchase.

✘ **Answer (B) is incorrect.** This acquisition results in a gain from bargain purchase, not goodwill.

✘ **Answer (C) is incorrect.** A gain of $150,000 results from reducing the fair value of the PPE to zero.

13.2 Consolidated Financial Reporting -- Acquisition-Date Balance Sheet

Questions 3 through 7 are based on the following information.

On January 2, Parma borrowed $60,000 and used the proceeds to purchase 90% of the outstanding common shares of Seville. Parma had no prior equity interest in Seville. Ten equal principal and interest payments begin December 30. The excess of the implied fair value of Seville over the carrying amount of its identifiable net assets should be assigned 60% to inventory and 40% to goodwill. Moreover, the fair value of the noncontrolling interest (NCI) is 10% of the implied fair value of the acquiree. The following are the balance sheets of Parma and Seville on January 1:

	Parma	Seville
Current assets	$ 70,000	$20,000
Noncurrent assets	90,000	40,000
Total assets	$160,000	$60,000
Current liabilities	$ 30,000	$10,000
Noncurrent liabilities	50,000	--
Equity	80,000	50,000
Total liabilities and equity	$160,000	$60,000

3. On Parma's January 2 consolidated balance sheet, Parma's shareholders' equity should be

A. $80,000

B. $86,667

C. $90,000

D. $130,000

✔ **Answer (A) is correct.**
Required: The equity in the consolidated balance sheet.
Discussion: In the absence of a bargain purchase, the total equity immediately after acquisition is the parent's equity just prior to acquisition plus the fair value of the NCI. An NCI is the equity in a subsidiary not attributable to the parent. Thus, the portion of total consolidated equity attributable to the shareholders of the parent (Parma) equals the parent's (Parma's) equity just prior to the acquisition of $80,000.

✘ **Answer (B) is incorrect.** Parma's equity at 1/1 plus the fair value of the noncontrolling interest is $86,667.

✘ **Answer (C) is incorrect.** The total liabilities of the two entities at 1/1 equal $90,000.

✘ **Answer (D) is incorrect.** The sum of the equity amounts for Parma and Seville at 1/1 is $130,000.

4. On Parma's January 2 consolidated balance sheet, current liabilities equal

A. $50,000

B. $46,000

C. $40,000

D. $30,000

✔ **Answer (B) is correct.**
Required: The consolidated current liabilities.
Discussion: Consolidated current liabilities are the current portion of debt issued by Parma to finance the acquisition ($60,000 ÷ 10 equal principal payments = $6,000). Reported current liabilities equal $46,000.

Current liabilities of Parma	$30,000
Current liabilities of Seville	10,000
Current component of new debt	6,000
Consolidated current liabilities	$46,000

✘ **Answer (A) is incorrect.** The pre-existing noncurrent debt is $50,000.

✘ **Answer (C) is incorrect.** The amount of $40,000 ignores the new borrowing.

✘ **Answer (D) is incorrect.** The amount of Parma's pre-existing current liabilities is $30,000.

5. On Parma's January 2 consolidated balance sheet, current assets equal

A. $100,000

B. $96,000

C. $90,000

D. $80,000

✔ **Answer (A) is correct.**
Required: The consolidated current assets.
Discussion: The implied fair value of the subsidiary is $66,667 ($60,000 cash paid by the parent ÷ 90%). The excess of this amount over the carrying amount of the subsidiary's identifiable net assets is $16,667 ($66,667 – $50,000). This amount is allocated $10,000 to inventory ($16,667 × 60%) and $6,667 to goodwill ($16,667 × 40%). Thus, the reported amount of the current assets is $100,000.

Current assets of Parma	$ 70,000
Current assets of Seville	20,000
Undervaluation of inventory	10,000
Consolidated current assets	$100,000

✘ **Answer (B) is incorrect.** The amount of $96,000 assumes an assignment of $6,000 to inventory.

✘ **Answer (C) is incorrect.** The amount of $90,000 ignores the $10,000 excess of the fair value of inventory over its carrying amount.

✘ **Answer (D) is incorrect.** The amount of $80,000 excludes the carrying amount of Seville's current assets.

6. On Parma's January 2 consolidated balance sheet, noncurrent assets equal

A. $130,000

B. $134,000

C. $136,667

D. $140,000

✔ **Answer (C) is correct.**
Required: The consolidated noncurrent assets.
Discussion: The implied fair value of the subsidiary is $66,667 ($60,000 cash paid by the parent ÷ 90%). The excess of this amount over the carrying amount of the subsidiary's identifiable net assets is $16,667 ($66,667 – $50,000). This amount is allocated $10,000 to inventory ($16,667 × 60%) and $6,667 to goodwill ($16,667 × 40%). Thus, reported noncurrent assets equal $136,667.

Noncurrent assets of Parma	$ 90,000
Noncurrent assets of Seville	40,000
Goodwill	6,667
Consolidated noncurrent assets	$136,667

✘ **Answer (A) is incorrect.** The amount of $130,000 ignores goodwill.

✘ **Answer (B) is incorrect.** The amount of $134,000 assumes that a 100% interest was acquired and that goodwill was therefore $4,000 [($60,000 – $50,000) × 40%].

✘ **Answer (D) is incorrect.** The amount of $140,000 assumes that a 100% interest was acquired and that goodwill was $10,000.

7. Refer to the information on the preceding page(s). On Parma's January 2 consolidated balance sheet, the sum of the noncurrent liabilities and the NCI equal

A. $116,667

B. $110,667

C. $104,000

D. $50,000

✓ **Answer (B) is correct.**

Required: The sum of the noncurrent liabilities and the NCI.

Discussion: Consolidated noncurrent liabilities include the noncurrent portion of the debt issued by Parma to finance the acquisition ($60,000 – $6,000 = $54,000). Thus, reported noncurrent liabilities equal $104,000.

Noncurrent liabilities of Parma	$ 50,000
Noncurrent component of new debt	54,000
Consolidated noncurrent liabilities	$104,000

The subsidiary's implied fair value is $66,667 ($60,000 cash paid by the parent ÷ 90%), and the NCI is $6,667 ($66,667 × 10%). The sum of the noncurrent liabilities and NCI is therefore $110,667 ($104,000 + $6,667).

✗ **Answer (A) is incorrect.** The amount of $116,667 is the sum of noncurrent liabilities (excluding the new borrowing) and the implied fair value of the subsidiary.

✗ **Answer (C) is incorrect.** The amount of $104,000 omits the NCI.

✗ **Answer (D) is incorrect.** The amount of $50,000 ignores the new borrowing and the NCI.

13.3 Consolidated Financial Reporting -- Subsequent to the Acquisition Date

8. On January 2 of the current year, Peace Co. paid $310,000 to purchase 75% of the voting shares of Surge Co. Surge held **no** shares in Peace. Peace reported retained earnings of $80,000, and Surge reported contributed capital of $300,000 and retained earnings of $100,000. The purchase differential was attributed to depreciable assets with a remaining useful life of 10 years. Peace used the equity method in accounting for its investment in Surge. Surge reported net income of $20,000 and paid dividends of $8,000 during the current year. Peace reported income, exclusive of its income from Surge, of $30,000 and paid dividends of $15,000 during the current year. What amount will Peace report as dividends declared and paid in its current year's consolidated statement of changes in equity?

A. $8,000

B. $15,000

C. $17,000

D. $23,000

✓ **Answer (C) is correct.**

Required: The consolidated dividends declared and paid.

Discussion: Peace acquired a greater than 50% share of the voting interests in Surge. Accordingly, Peace must consolidate Surge unless it does not have control. Moreover, the equity method is not appropriate except in parent-only statements. The consolidated statements should report only dividends paid to parties outside the consolidated entity. Because Peace acquired only 75% of the voting shares of Surge, a 25% noncontrolling interest exists. Thus, 25% of Surge's dividends were paid to parties outside the consolidated entity. Furthermore, all of Peace's dividends were paid to parties outside of the consolidated entity. Accordingly, consolidated dividends paid are calculated as follows:

Dividends paid by parent	$15,000
Dividends paid by subsidiary	8,000
Parent's proportionate share of sub's dividends ($8,000 × 75%)	(6,000)
Consolidated dividends paid	$17,000

✗ **Answer (A) is incorrect.** The amount of $8,000 equals the dividends declared by Surge.

✗ **Answer (B) is incorrect.** The amount of $15,000 equals the dividends paid by Peace.

✗ **Answer (D) is incorrect.** The amount of $23,000 includes $6,000 of intraentity dividends.

9. On January 1, Year 4, Pane Corp. exchanged 150,000 shares of its $20 par value common stock for all of Sky Corp.'s common stock. At that date, the fair value of Pane's common stock issued was equal to the fair value of the identifiable assets acquired and liabilities assumed. Both corporations continued to operate as separate businesses, maintaining accounting records with years ending December 31. In its separate statements, Pane accounts for the investment using the equity method. Information from separate company operations follows:

	Pane	Sky
Retained earnings -- 12/31/Yr 3	$3,200,000	$925,000
Dividends paid -- 3/25/Yr 4	750,000	200,000

If consolidated net income was $800,000, what amount of retained earnings should Pane report in its December 31, Year 4, consolidated balance sheet?

A. $4,925,000

B. $4,125,000

C. $3,050,000

D. $3,250,000

✓ **Answer (D) is correct.**

Required: The consolidated retained earnings.

Discussion: Retained earnings of the consolidated entity at the acquisition date consist solely of the retained earnings of the parent. The consolidated entity does not report any equity amounts of the subsidiary. Retained earnings of the consolidated entity at the reporting date consist of acquisition-date retained earnings, plus consolidated net income (no NCI exists), minus consolidated dividends paid. Sky's dividends, if any, are paid solely to Pane. Thus, consolidated dividends (those paid outside the entity) consist entirely of those paid by Pane.

Acquisition-date retained earnings (Pane)	$3,200,000
Consolidated net income since acquisition date	800,000
Consolidated dividends paid since acquisition date	(750,000)
Consolidated retained earnings at reporting date	$3,250,000

✗ **Answer (A) is incorrect.** The amount of $4,925,000 includes Sky's retained earnings at 12/31/Yr 3 and does not reflect an adjustment for the dividends paid.

✗ **Answer (B) is incorrect.** The amount of $4,125,000 is the sum of the retained earnings of Pane and Sky at 12/31/Yr 3.

✗ **Answer (C) is incorrect.** The amount of $3,050,000 results from treating Sky's dividends as consolidated dividends.

13.4 Consolidated Financial Reporting -- Intraentity Eliminations

10. Wright Corp. has several subsidiaries that are included in its consolidated financial statements. In its December 31 trial balance, Wright had the following intraentity balances before eliminations:

	Debit	Credit
Current receivable due from Main Co.	$ 32,000	
Noncurrent receivable from Main Co.	114,000	
Cash advance to Corn Corp.	6,000	
Cash advance from King Co.		$ 15,000
Payable to King Co.		101,000

In its December 31 consolidated balance sheet, what amount should Wright report as intraentity receivables?

A. $152,000

B. $146,000

C. $36,000

D. $0

✔ **Answer (D) is correct.**
Required: The amount reported as intraentity receivables.
Discussion: In a consolidated balance sheet, reciprocal balances, such as receivables and payables, between a parent and a consolidated subsidiary are eliminated in their entirety, regardless of the portion of the subsidiary's stock held by the parent. Thus, Wright should report $0 as intraentity receivables.
✘ **Answer (A) is incorrect.** The amount of $152,000 includes intraentity transactions in the consolidated financial statements.
✘ **Answer (B) is incorrect.** The effects of intraentity transactions should be completely eliminated in consolidated financial statements.
✘ **Answer (C) is incorrect.** Intraentity transactions should not be netted out in the consolidated financial statements.

11. Dunn Corp. owns 100% of Grey Corp.'s common stock. On January 2, Year 3, Dunn sold to Grey for $40,000 machinery with a carrying amount of $30,000. Grey is depreciating the acquired machinery over a 5-year life by the straight-line method. The net adjustments to compute Year 3 and Year 4 consolidated income before income tax are an increase (decrease) of

	Year 3	Year 4
A.	$(8,000)	$2,000
B.	$(8,000)	$0
C.	$(10,000)	$2,000
D.	$(10,000)	$0

✔ **Answer (A) is correct.**
Required: The net adjustments to pretax comparative consolidated income resulting from an intraentity transaction.
Discussion: In consolidated financial statements, intraentity transactions should be eliminated. Transfers of plant assets require elimination of any gain or loss on sale recognized. If the original useful life and depreciation method remain the same, the depreciation expense eliminated is equal to the amount of gain on sale of equipment divided by the years of useful life remaining. Thus, in Year 3 the $10,000 ($40,000 selling price – $30,000 carrying amount) gain and the $2,000 excess depreciation ($10,000 ÷ 5 years) should be eliminated. The $2,000 of excess depreciation should also be eliminated in Year 4. The net adjustment to Year 3 pretax consolidated income is an $8,000 decrease ($2,000 excess depreciation added back – $10,000 gain subtracted). In Year 4, the adjustment is a $2,000 increase resulting from adding back the excess depreciation.
✘ **Answer (B) is incorrect.** The amount of $2,000 of excess depreciation should be added back in Year 4.
✘ **Answer (C) is incorrect.** The $8,000 net gain should be subtracted in Year 3.
✘ **Answer (D) is incorrect.** The $8,000 net gain should be subtracted in Year 3, and $2,000 of excess depreciation should be added back in Year 4.

12. Wagner, a holder of a $1 million Palmer, Inc., bond, collected the interest due on March 31, and then sold the bond to Seal, Inc., for $975,000. On that date, Palmer, a 75% owner of Seal, had a $1,075,000 carrying amount for this bond. What was the effect of Seal's purchase of Palmer's bond on the retained earnings and noncontrolling interest amounts reported in Palmer's March 31 consolidated balance sheet?

	Retained Earnings	Noncontrolling Interest
A.	$100,000 increase	$0
B.	$75,000 increase	$25,000 increase
C.	$0	$25,000 increase
D.	$0	$100,000 increase

✔ **Answer (A) is correct.**
Required: The effect of the purchase by the subsidiary of the parent's debt.
Discussion: The purchase was in substance a retirement of debt by the consolidated entity for less than its carrying amount. The transaction resulted in a constructive gain of $100,000 ($1,075,000 carrying amount – $975,000 price) and therefore a $100,000 increase in consolidated retained earnings. The noncontrolling interest was unaffected. The noncontrolling interest is based on the subsidiary's carrying amounts adjusted for subsidiary income and dividends. This transaction did not result in gain or loss for Seal.

✘ **Answer (B) is incorrect.** The gain is not allocated.

✘ **Answer (C) is incorrect.** The noncontrolling interest is not affected.

✘ **Answer (D) is incorrect.** Retained earnings is increased by $100,000.

13. Zest Co. owns 100% of Cinn, Inc. On January 2, Zest sold equipment with an original cost of $80,000 and a carrying amount of $48,000 to Cinn for $72,000. Zest had been depreciating the equipment over a 5-year period using straight-line depreciation with **no** residual value. Cinn is using straight-line depreciation over 3 years with **no** residual value. In Zest's December 31 consolidating worksheet, by what amount should depreciation expense be decreased?

A. $0

B. $8,000

C. $16,000

D. $24,000

✔ **Answer (B) is correct.**
Required: The decrease in depreciation expense on the consolidating worksheet.
Discussion: Annual depreciation taken by the purchaser-subsidiary is $24,000 ($72,000 ÷ 3 years). Annual depreciation taken by the seller-parent was $16,000 ($80,000 ÷ 5 years). The $8,000 difference should be eliminated in the eliminating journal entry. Note that this amount is exactly equal to the gain on sale recognized of $24,000 ($72,000 – $48,000) divided by the years of useful life remaining (3 years).

✘ **Answer (A) is incorrect.** The difference in depreciation arising from a sale within the consolidated entity must be eliminated.

✘ **Answer (C) is incorrect.** The annual depreciation recognized by the parent is $16,000.

✘ **Answer (D) is incorrect.** The annual depreciation recognized by the subsidiary is $24,000.

14. Jane Co. owns 90% of the common stock of Dun Corp. and 100% of the common stock of Beech Corp. On December 30, Dun and Beech each declared a cash dividend of $100,000 for the current year. What is the total amount of dividends that should be reported in the December 31 consolidated financial statements of Jane and its subsidiaries, Dun and Beech?

A. $10,000

B. $100,000

C. $190,000

D. $200,000

✔ **Answer (A) is correct.**
Required: The total dividends reported in the consolidated financial statements.
Discussion: The only dividends declared by the subsidiaries that are reported are those paid to noncontrolling interests. Beech has no NCIs because the parent (Jane) owns 100% of its shares. Accordingly, the dividends reported equal $10,000 ($100,000 declared by Dun × 10% noncontrolling ownership interest in Dun). The amount of dividends declared attributable to the noncontrolling interest is reported in the consolidated financial statements as a reduction in the NCI account.

✘ **Answer (B) is incorrect.** The amount of $100,000 is the amount declared by Dun or Beech.

✘ **Answer (C) is incorrect.** The amount of $190,000 is the amount eliminated in the consolidation.

✘ **Answer (D) is incorrect.** The amount of $200,000 is the total declared by Dun and Beech.

13.5 Financial Statement Analysis -- Liquidity

15. Zenk Co. wrote off obsolete inventory of $100,000 during the year. What was the effect of this write-off on Zenk's ratio analysis?

A. Decrease in current ratio but not in quick ratio.

B. Decrease in quick ratio but not in current ratio.

C. Increase in current ratio but not in quick ratio.

D. Increase in quick ratio but not in current ratio.

✔ **Answer (A) is correct.**
Required: The effect of writing off obsolete inventory.
Discussion: Inventory is included in the numerator of the current ratio but not the quick ratio. Consequently, an inventory write-off decreases the current ratio but not the quick ratio.

16. North Bank is analyzing Belle Corp.'s financial statements for a possible extension of credit. Belle's quick ratio is significantly better than the industry average. Which of the following factors should North consider as a possible limitation of using this ratio when evaluating Belle's creditworthiness?

   A. Fluctuating market prices of short-term investments may adversely affect the ratio.

   B. Increasing market prices for Belle's inventory may adversely affect the ratio.

   C. Belle may need to sell its available-for-sale investments to meet its current obligations.

   D. Belle may need to liquidate its inventory to meet its long-term obligations.

✔ **Answer (A) is correct.**
Required: The possible limitation of using the quick ratio to evaluate creditworthiness.
Discussion: The quick ratio equals cash plus short-term investment securities plus net receivables, divided by current liabilities. Because short-term investment securities are included in the numerator, fluctuating market prices of these investments may adversely affect the ratio if Belle holds a substantial amount of such current assets.

✘ **Answer (B) is incorrect.** Inventory is excluded from the calculation of the quick ratio.

✘ **Answer (C) is incorrect.** If the available-for-sale securities are not current, they are not included in the calculation of the ratio. If they are classified as current, their sale to meet current obligations is consistent with normal current assets management practices.

✘ **Answer (D) is incorrect.** Inventory and noncurrent obligations are excluded from the calculation of the quick ratio.

17. A company's year-end balance sheet is shown below:

Assets

Cash	$ 300,000
Accounts receivable	350,000
Inventory	600,000
Property, plant, and equipment (net)	2,000,000
	$3,250,000

Liabilities and Shareholder Equity

Current liabilities	$ 700,000
Long-term liabilities	600,000
Common stock	800,000
Retained earnings	1,150,000
	$3,250,000

What is the current ratio as of December 31?

   A. 1.79

   B. 0.93

   C. 0.67

   D. 0.43

✔ **Answer (A) is correct.**
Required: The current ratio.
Discussion: The current ratio equals current assets divided by current liabilities [($300,000 + $350,000 + $600,000) ÷ $700,000 = 1.79].

✘ **Answer (B) is incorrect.** Inventory is included in current assets.

✘ **Answer (C) is incorrect.** Retained earnings is not included in current liabilities.

✘ **Answer (D) is incorrect.** Accounts receivable and inventory are included in current assets.

13.6 Financial Statement Analysis -- Activity

18. Selected information for Clay Corp. for the year ended December 31 follows:

Ave. days' sales in inventories   124
Ave. days' sales in accounts receivable   48

The average number of days in the operating cycle for the year was

A. 172

B. 124

C. 86

D. 76

✔ Answer (A) is correct.
Required: The number of days in the operating cycle.
Discussion: The operating cycle is the time needed to turn cash into inventory, inventory into receivables, and receivables back into cash. It is equal to the sum of the number of days' sales in inventory and the number of days' sales in receivables. The number of days in Clay's operating cycle is thus 172 (124 + 48).

✘ Answer (B) is incorrect. The average days' sales in inventories is 124.

✘ Answer (C) is incorrect. The amount of 86 days equals the sum of the average days' sales in inventories and the average days' sales in receivables, divided by 2.

✘ Answer (D) is incorrect. The amount of 76 days is the average days' sales in inventories minus the average days' sales in receivables.

19. The following financial ratios and calculations were based on information from Kale Co.'s financial statements for the current year:

Accounts receivable turnover
Ten times during the year

Total assets turnover
Two times during the year

Average receivables during the year
$200,000

What was Kale's average total assets for the year?

A. $2,000,000

B. $1,000,000

C. $400,000

D. $200,000

✔ Answer (B) is correct.
Required: The average total assets.
Discussion: The total assets turnover ratio (given as 2.0) equals net sales divided by average total assets. The accounts receivable turnover ratio (given as 10.0) equals net sales divided by average accounts receivable (it must be assumed that all sales are on credit). Given $200,000 of average accounts receivable, net sales must equal $2,000,000 ($200,000 × 10.0). Accordingly, average total assets equals $1,000,000 ($2,000,000 net revenue ÷ 2.0 total assets turnover).

✘ Answer (A) is incorrect. The amount of $2,000,000 equals net revenue.

✘ Answer (C) is incorrect. The amount of $400,000 equals average accounts receivable times total assets turnover.

✘ Answer (D) is incorrect. The amount of $200,000 equals average receivables during the year.

Questions 20 through 22 are based on the following information.

Selected data pertaining to Lore Co. for the Year 4 calendar year is as follows:

Net cash sales	$ 3,000
Cost of goods sold	18,000
Inventory at beginning of year	6,000
Purchases	24,000
Accounts receivable at beginning of year	20,000
Accounts receivable at end of year	22,000

20. The accounts receivable turnover for Year 4 was 5.0 times. What were Lore's Year 4 net credit sales?

A. $105,000

B. $107,000

C. $110,000

D. $210,000

✔ **Answer (A) is correct.**
Required: The net credit sales.
Discussion: Credit sales may be determined from the accounts receivable turnover formula (Credit sales ÷ Average accounts receivable). Credit sales are equal to 5.0 times average receivables [($20,000 + $22,000) ÷ 2], or $105,000.

✘ **Answer (B) is incorrect.** The amount of $107,000 equals ending accounts receivable multiplied by the accounts receivable turnover ratio, minus cash sales.

✘ **Answer (C) is incorrect.** The amount of $110,000 equals ending accounts receivable multiplied by the accounts receivable turnover ratio.

✘ **Answer (D) is incorrect.** The amount of $210,000 equals beginning accounts receivable plus ending accounts receivable, multiplied by the accounts receivable turnover ratio.

21. What was Lore's inventory turnover for Year 4?

A. 1.2 times.

B. 1.5 times.

C. 2.0 times.

D. 3.0 times.

✔ **Answer (C) is correct.**
Required: The inventory turnover ratio.
Discussion: Inventory turnover is equal to cost of goods sold divided by average inventory. Ending inventory equals beginning inventory, plus purchases, minus cost of goods sold, or $12,000 ($6,000 + $24,000 − $18,000). Average inventory is $9,000 [($6,000 + $12,000) ÷ 2]. Inventory turnover is 2.0 times ($18,000 cost of goods sold ÷ $9,000 average inventory).

✘ **Answer (A) is incorrect.** The amount of 1.2 times uses the average of beginning inventory and purchases.

✘ **Answer (B) is incorrect.** The amount of 1.5 times uses ending inventory instead of average inventory.

✘ **Answer (D) is incorrect.** The amount of 3.0 times uses beginning inventory instead of average inventory.

22. Lore would use which of the following to determine the average days' sales in inventory?

	Numerator	Denominator
A.	365	Average inventory
B.	365	Inventory turnover
C.	Average inventory	Sales divided by 365
D.	Sales divided by 365	Inventory turnover

✔ **Answer (B) is correct.**
Required: The formula to calculate average days' sales in inventory.
Discussion: The average days' sales in inventory is calculated by dividing the number of days in the year by the inventory turnover.

13.7 Financial Statement Analysis -- Solvency, Performance, and Comparative Analysis

23. The following data pertain to Cowl, Inc., for the year ended December 31, Year 4:

Net sales	$ 600,000
Net income	150,000
Total assets, Jan. 1, Year 4	2,000,000
Total assets, Dec. 31, Year 4	3,000,000

What was Cowl's rate of return on assets for Year 4?

A. 5%

B. 6%

C. 20%

D. 24%

✔ **Answer (B) is correct.**
Required: The rate of return on assets.
Discussion: Return on assets equals net income ($150,000) divided by average total assets [($2,000,000 + $3,000,000) ÷ 2 = $2,500,000], or 6%.

✘ **Answer (A) is incorrect.** A return of 5% results from using ending total assets instead of the average total assets.

✘ **Answer (C) is incorrect.** A return of 20% results from dividing net sales by ending total assets.

✘ **Answer (D) is incorrect.** A return of 24% results from using net sales rather than net income in the numerator.

24. The following is the equity section of Harbor Co.'s balance sheet at December 31:

Common stock $10 par, 100,000 shares authorized, 50,000 shares issued, of which 5,000 have been reacquired and are held in treasury	$ 450,000
Additional paid-in capital- common stock	1,100,000
Retained earnings	800,000
Subtotal	$2,350,000
Minus: Treasury stock (at cost)	(150,000)
Total stockholders' equity	$2,200,000

Harbor has insignificant amounts of convertible securities, stock warrants, and stock options. What is the book value per share of Harbor's common stock?

A. $31

B. $44

C. $46

D. $49

✔ **Answer (D) is correct.**
Required: The book value per share of common stock.
Discussion: The book value per share of common stock equals net assets available to common shareholders divided by ending common shares outstanding. Net assets available to common shareholders can also be stated as total equity minus liquidation value of preferred stock. Given no preferred shares, the numerator equals equity (assets minus liabilities). Thus, the book value per share of common stock is $49 [$2,200,000 equity ÷ (50,000 shares issued − 5,000 shares held in treasury)].

✘ **Answer (A) is incorrect.** The amount of $31 results from not including retained earnings in the numerator.

✘ **Answer (B) is incorrect.** The amount of $44 results from including treasury shares in the denominator.

✘ **Answer (C) is incorrect.** The amount of $46 results from measuring the treasury shares at $10 per share and including those shares in the denominator.

Study Unit Fourteen

Statement of Cash Flows

(12 pages of outline)

14.1 Statement of Cash Flows -- Classifications

The **primary purpose** of a statement of cash flows is to provide information about the cash receipts and payments of an entity during a period. To achieve its primary purpose, the statement should provide information about cash inflows and outflows from **operating, investing, and financing activities** of an entity. This is the accepted order of presentation.

- The format reconciles the cash and cash equivalents balance at the beginning of the period with the balance at the end of the period.

Example 14-1   Summary Statement of Cash Flows

The following is an example of the summarized format of the statement of cash flows (headings only). The amounts of cash and cash equivalents at the beginning and end of the year are taken from the balance sheet.

Entity A's Statement of Cash Flows for the Year Ended December 31, Year 1

Net cash provided by (used in) operating activities	$XXX
Net cash provided by (used in) investing activities	XXX
Net cash provided by (used in) financing activities	XXX
Net increase (decrease) in cash, cash equivalents, and restricted cash	$XXX
Cash, cash equivalents, and restricted cash at beginning of year (January 1, Year 1)	XXX
Cash, cash equivalents, and restricted cash at end of year (December 31, Year 1)	$XXX

A statement of cash flows is required as part of a full set of financial statements of most business and not-for-profit entities.

- If an entity reports financial position and results of operations, it must present a statement of cash flows for any period for which results of operations are presented.

- Cash flow per share is not reported.

The two ways of presenting the statement of cash flows are the direct method and the **indirect method**.

- On the CPA Exam, only the indirect method is tested.

Treatment of Cash and Cash Equivalents

If an entity invests its cash in cash equivalents, it should use the descriptive term "cash and cash equivalents." Otherwise, the term "cash" is acceptable.

Cash equivalents are readily convertible to known amounts of cash and are so near maturity that they present insignificant risk of changes in value because of changes in interest rates.

- Usually, investments with **original maturities of 3 months or less** qualify. Thus, a 3-year Treasury note meets the definition if purchased 3 months from maturity. However, if the note was purchased 3 years ago, it does not meet the definition when its remaining maturity is 3 months.

    - Other examples of cash equivalents are Treasury bills, commercial paper, and money market funds.

    - The statement of cash flows explains the change in cash, cash equivalents, and restricted cash during the period. However, exchanges of items within the category of cash, cash equivalents, and restricted cash need not be reported in the statement of cash flows.

Not all qualifying investments must be classified as cash equivalents. An entity should **consistently apply a policy** for classifying cash equivalents.

- For example, an entity with operations that primarily involve investing in short-term, highly liquid investments may choose not to treat them as cash equivalents.

- Any change in policy is a change in accounting principle that requires retrospective application.

- The policy for determining which items are cash equivalents must be disclosed.

Operating Activities

Operating activities are all transactions and other events that are **not financing or investing activities**. Cash flows from operating activities are primarily derived from the principal revenue-producing activities of the entity. They generally result from transactions and other events that enter into the determination of net income.

The following are examples of **cash inflows** from operating activities:

- Cash receipts from the sale of goods and services (including collections of accounts receivable)

- Cash receipts from royalties, fees, commissions, and other revenue

- Cash received in the form of **interest** or **dividends**

- Cash receipts from certain loans and other debt and equity instruments of other entities that are **acquired specifically for resale in the short term**

The following are examples of **cash outflows** from operating activities:

- Cash payments to suppliers for goods and services
- Cash payments to employees
- Cash payments to government for taxes, duties, fines, and other fees or penalties
- Payments of **interest on debt**

Investing Activities

Cash flows from investing activities represent the extent to which expenditures have been made for resources intended to generate future income and cash flows.

The following are examples of **cash outflows (and inflows)** from investing activities:

- Cash payments to acquire (cash receipts from sale of) property, plant and equipment; intangible assets; and other long lived assets

- Cash payments to acquire (cash receipts from sale and maturity of) equity and debt instruments of other entities for investing purposes

  - Cash flows from purchases, sales, and maturities of available-for-sale debt securities and held-to-maturity debt securities are from investing activities.

- Cash advances and loans made to other parties (cash receipts from repayment of advances and loans made to other parties)

Investing activities **exclude** transactions in cash equivalents and certain loans or other debt or equity instruments acquired specifically for resale in the short-term. These transactions are classified as operating activities.

Financing Activities

Cash flows from financing activities generally involve the cash effects of transactions and other events that relate to the issuance, settlement, or reacquisition of the entity's debt and equity instruments.

The following are examples of **cash inflows** from financing activities:

- Cash proceeds from issuing shares and other equity instruments (obtaining resources from owners)

- Cash proceeds from issuing loans, notes, bonds, and other short-term or long-term borrowings

The following are examples of **cash outflows** from financing activities:

- Cash repayments of amounts borrowed
- Payments of **cash dividends**
- Cash payments to acquire or redeem the entity's own shares
- Cash payments by a lessee for a reduction of the outstanding liability relating to a finance lease

Noncash Investing and Financing Activities

Information about all **investing and financing activities** that affect recognized assets or liabilities **but not cash flows** must be disclosed. Given only a few transactions, disclosure may be on the same page as the statement of cash flows. Otherwise, they may be reported elsewhere in the statements with a clear reference to the statement of cash flows.

The following are examples of noncash investing and financing activities:

- Conversion of debt to equity
- Acquisition of assets either by assuming directly related liabilities or by means of a finance lease
- Exchange of a noncash asset or liability for another
- Obtaining a building or investment asset by gift

Stop & Review

You have completed the outline for this subunit.
Study multiple-choice questions 1 through 3 beginning on page 458.

14.2   Statement of Cash Flows -- Calculations

Many questions about the statement of cash flows ask for the calculation of the appropriate amount. This subunit consists entirely of such questions. Please review Subunit 14.1 before answering the questions.

Stop & Review

You have completed the outline for this subunit.
Study multiple-choice questions 4 through 9 beginning on page 459.

14.3   Presentation of Operating Cash Flows

The Indirect Method

The CPA Exam tests only the indirect method.

Under the indirect method (also called the reconciliation method), the net cash flow from operating activities is determined by adjusting the net income of a business (or the change in the net assets of a not-for-profit entity) for the effect of the following:

- **Noncash revenue and expenses** that were **included in net income**, such as depreciation and amortization expenses, impairment losses, undistributed earnings of equity method investments, and amortization of discount and premium on bonds

- Items **included in net income** whose cash effects relate to **investing or financing cash flows**, such as gains or losses on sales of PPE items (related to investing activities) and gains or losses on extinguishment of debt (related to financing activities)

- All **deferrals** of past operating cash flows, such as changes during the period in inventory and deferred income

- All **accruals** of expected future operating cash flows, such as changes during the period in accounts receivable and accounts payable

The reconciliation of net income to net cash flow from operating activities must disclose all **major classes** of reconciling items. For example, major classes of deferrals or accruals of operating cash flows must be separately disclosed. At a minimum, this disclosure reports changes in (1) accounts receivable and accounts payable related to operating activities and (2) inventories.

Under the indirect method, an entity must provide a supplemental disclosure of the following amounts paid during the period:

- Interest paid (net of amounts capitalized)
- Income taxes paid

Example 14-2   Indirect Method -- Adjustments for Changes in Current Assets and Liabilities

During Year 2, Bishop Corp. had the following transactions:

- Inventory (cost $9,000) was sold for $14,000, with $13,000 on credit and $1,000 in cash.
- Cash collected on credit sales to customers was $12,000.
- Inventory was purchased for $6,500.
- Bishop paid $8,500 to suppliers.

The following is Bishop's income statement for the year ended on December 31, Year 2:

Sales	$14,000
Cost of goods sold	(9,000)
Net income	**$ 5,000**

The following are Bishop's balance sheet accounts on December 31, Year 1, and December 31, Year 2:

	December 31			December 31	
Current assets	Year 1	Year 2	Current liabilities	Year 1	Year 2
Cash	$10,000	$14,500	Acc. payable	$ 5,000	$ 3,000
Net acc. receivable	6,000	7,000	Equity		
Inventory	14,000	11,500	Common stock	21,000	21,000
			Retained earnings	4,000	9,000
Total assets	$30,000	$33,000	Total liability and equity	$30,000	$33,000

Under the indirect method, the net cash flow from operating activities is determined by adjusting net income for the period.

Bishop's Statement of Cash Flows for the Year Ended on December 31, Year 2

Cash flows from operating activities:			
Net income		$ 5,000	
Increase in accounts receivable ($6,000 – $7,000)	$(1,000)		(1)
Decrease in inventory ($11,500 – $14,000)	2,500		(2)
Decrease in accounts payable ($3,000 – $5,000)	(2,000)		(3)
Total adjustments		(500)	
Net cash provided by operating activities		**$ 4,500**	
Cash at beginning of year		10,000	
Cash at end of year		**$14,500**	

Explanation:

(1) The amount of accounts receivable increased during the year by $1,000, implying that cash collections were less than credit sales. The net income for the period is an accrual accounting amount. Thus, the increase in accounts receivable during the period must be subtracted from net income to determine the cash flow from operating activities.

(2) Inventory decreased by $2,500, implying that purchases were less than the amount of cost of goods sold. Thus, it must be added to net income to determine the cash flow from operating activities.

(3) Accounts payable decreased by $2,000, implying that cash paid to suppliers was greater than purchases. Thus, it must be subtracted from net income.

Success Tip

The following rules will help you to reconcile the net income to net cash flow from operating activities:

Increase in current operating liabilities	Added to net income
Decrease in current operating assets	Added to net income
Increase in current operating assets	Subtracted from net income
Decrease in current operating liabilities	Subtracted from net income

---

Example 14-3   Indirect Method

During Year 2, Knight Corp. had the following transactions:

- On December 31, Year 2, a machine was sold for $47,000 in cash. The machine was acquired by Knight on January 1, Year 1, for $50,000. Its useful life is 10 years with no salvage value, and it is depreciated using the straight-line method.

- On December 31, Year 2, the $31,500 due on a loan (Principal + Accumulated interest) was repaid. The term of the loan was 1 year from December 31, Year 1. The annual interest rate was 5%.

- During Year 2, Knight received $14,000 in cash for services provided to customers.

The following is Knight's income statement for the year ended on December 31, Year 2:

Revenue	$14,000
Depreciation expense ($50,000 ÷ 10)	(5,000)
Interest expense ($30,000 × 5%)	(1,500)
Gain on machine disposal [$47,000 – ($50,000 – $10,000)]	7,000
Net income	**$14,500**

The following are Knight's balance sheets on December 31, Year 1, and December 31, Year 2:

	December 31			December 31	
Current assets	Year 1	Year 2	Current liabilities	Year 1	Year 2
Cash	$10,000	$39,500	Loan	$30,000	$ 0
Fixed assets			Equity		
Machine at cost	50,000	0	Common stock	21,000	21,000
Accumulated depreciation	(5,000)	0	Retained earnings	4,000	18,500
Net fixed assets	$45,000	$ 0			
Total assets	$55,000	$39,500	Total liability and equity	$55,000	$39,500

-- Continued on next page --

Example 14-3 -- Continued

Under the indirect method, the net cash flow from operating activities is determined by adjusting net income for the period.

Knight's Statement of Cash Flows for the Year Ended on December 31, Year 2

Cash flows from operating activities:		
Net income		$ 14,500
Depreciation expense	$ 5,000	(1)
Gain on sale of machine	(7,000)	(2)
Total adjustments		(2,000)
Net cash provided by operating activities		**$ 12,500**
Cash flows from investing activities:		
Proceeds from sale of machine	47,000	
Net cash provided by investing activities		**$ 47,000**
Cash flows from financing activities:		
Repayment of loan	(30,000)	
Net cash used in financing activities		**$(30,000)**
Net increase in cash		**$ 29,500**
Cash at beginning of year		10,000
Cash at end of year		**$ 39,500**

Explanation:

(1) **Depreciation expense** is a noncash expense included in net income. Thus, it must be added to net income to determine the net cash flow from operating activities.

(2) **Gain on sale of machine** is an item included in net income. Its cash effect is related to investing activities. Thus, it must be subtracted from net income to determine the net cash flow from operating activities.

Success Tip

The following rules will help you to reconcile net income to net cash flow from operating activities:

Noncash losses and expenses included in net income	Added to net income
Losses and expenses whose cash effects are related to investing or financing cash flows	Added to net income
Noncash gains and revenues included in net income	Subtracted from net income
Gains and revenues whose cash effects are related to investing or financing cash flows	Subtracted from net income

Stop & Review

You have completed the outline for this subunit.

Study multiple-choice questions 10 through 12 on page 462.

14.4 Comprehensive Example

Example 14-4   Indirect Presentation

Dice Corp's consolidated balance sheet accounts as of December 31, Year 6 and Year 5, are presented below. Information relating to Year 6 activities is to the left.

Information Relating to Year 6 Activities

- Cash dividends of $240,000 were declared and paid by Dice in Year 6.

- The accounts receivable balances at the beginning and end of Year 6 were net of allowances for credit losses of $50,000 and $60,000, respectively. Dice wrote off $40,000 of accounts receivable during Year 6.

- Current investments consist of Treasury bills maturing on 6/30/Year 7. They were acquired for cash on December 31, Year 6.

- Equipment costing $400,000 and having a carrying amount of $140,000 was sold on January 1, Year 6, for $150,000 in cash. Additional plant assets were purchased in Year 6 for cash.

- Dice accounts for its interest in Thrice Corp. under the equity method. Its equity in Thrice's Year 6 earnings was $25,000. During Year 6, Dice received a $10,000 cash dividend from Thrice. At the end of Year 6, Dice sold part of its investment in Thrice for $135,000 in cash. Significant influence over Thrice was not lost as a result of the sale.

- The provision for Year 6 income taxes was $210,000.

- 10,000 shares of common stock were issued in Year 6 for $22 a share.

	December 31	
Assets	Year 6	Year 5
Cash	$ 195,000	$ 100,000
Current investments	300,000	0
Accounts receivable (net)	480,000	510,000
Inventory	680,000	600,000
Prepaid expenses	15,000	20,000
Equity method investment	215,000	300,000
Plant assets	1,730,000	1,000,000
Accumulated depreciation	(480,000)	(450,000)
Goodwill	90,000	100,000
Total assets	$3,225,000	$2,180,000
Liabilities and Equity		
Accounts payable	$ 825,000	$ 720,000
Interest payable	15,000	10,000
Income tax payable	20,000	30,000
Current debt	325,000	0
Deferred taxes	250,000	300,000
Common stock, $10 par	800,000	700,000
Additional paid-in capital	370,000	250,000
Retained earnings	620,000	170,000
Total liabilities and equity	$3,225,000	$2,180,000

The following computations are necessary to determine the net cash flows from operating, investing, and financing activities:

- **Net income.** The starting point for presenting the net cash flow from operating activities is net income (loss) for the period. Net income can be calculated as follows:

Ending retained earnings	$620,000
Dividends declared	240,000
Beginning retained earnings	(170,000)
Year 6, net income	**$690,000**

- The $240,000 of cash dividends paid in Year 6 are a cash outflow from financing activities.

-- Continued on next page --

Example 14-4 -- Continued

- **Accounts receivable.** The easiest way to determine the reconciling adjustment for accounts receivable is to calculate the change in their net amount (Accounts receivable – Allowance for credit losses). Net accounts receivable are current operating assets. A decrease in net accounts receivable of **$30,000** ($510,000 – $480,000) is **added** to net income to determine the net cash flow from operating activities.

- **Plant assets.** The items that affect the presentation of cash flow from operating activities are depreciation expense, gain or loss on disposal, and impairment loss.

   - **Depreciation expense** for Year 6 can be calculated as follows:

Ending accumulated depreciation	$480,000
Accumulated depreciation on items sold	260,000
Beginning accumulated depreciation	(450,000)
Depreciation expense	**$290,000**

     Depreciation expense is a noncash expense included in net income. Thus, $290,000 is added to net income in determining the net cash flows from operating activities.

   - The **gain on disposal** of the equipment is **$10,000** ($150,000 cash received – $140,000 carrying amount). The cash effect is related to investing activities. Thus, it is **subtracted** from net income to determine the net cash flow from operating activities.

   - The $150,000 of cash proceeds from sale of equipment is a cash inflow from investing activities.

   - Plant assets purchased in Year 6 (cash outflow from investing activities) can be calculated as follows:

Ending plant assets at cost	$1,730,000
Plant assets sold at cost	400,000
Beginning plant assets at cost	(1,000,000)
Plant assets purchased	**$1,130,000**

NOTE: The following equation may be useful for deriving the required information if the data given in the question are for the carrying amount (Cost – Accumulated depreciation) of the PPE item.

Beginning carrying amount	$XXX
Purchases during the period	XXX
Depreciation expense	(XXX)
Disposals during the period	(XXX)
Ending carrying amount	**$XXX**

-- Continued on next page --

Example 14-4 -- Continued

- **Equity-method investment.** The carrying amount of the equity-method investment sold can be calculated as follows:

Beginning carrying amount	$300,000
Equity in Thrice's current year earnings	25,000
Dividends received from Thrice	(10,000)
Ending carrying amount	(215,000)
Carrying amount of investment sold	**$100,000**

  - **The gain on sale of the investment is $35,000** ($135,000 cash received – $100,000 carrying amount). The cash effect is related to investing activities. Thus, it is **subtracted** from net income in determining the net cash flows from operating activities.

  - **Undistributed earnings on equity-method investment.** Under the equity method, the investor's share of the investee's earnings is debited to the investment account and credited to income. A cash dividend from the investee is a return of an investment that results in a debit to cash and a credit to the investment. The undistributed earnings on the equity-method investments equal **$15,000** ($25,000 share in earnings – $10,000 dividends received). This amount is a noncash revenue included in net income. Thus, it is **subtracted** from net income in determining the net cash flow from operating activities.

  - The cash received on the sale of the $135,000 investment is a cash inflow from investing activities.

- **Goodwill.** Goodwill is not amortized. Thus, the **$10,000** decrease in the amount of goodwill ($100,000 beginning balance – $90,000 ending balance) must be a result of impairment. A loss on impairment of goodwill is a noncash loss included in net income. Thus, it is **added** to net income in determining the net cash flow from operating activities.

- **Current investments.** The purchase of current investments for $300,000 is a cash outflow from investing activities.

- **Common stock.** The proceeds from issuing common stock were $220,000 (10,000 × $22). This cash inflow from financing activities equals the sum of the increases in the common stock and additional paid-in capital accounts.

- **Inventory** is a current operating asset. Inventory increased by **$80,000** ($680,000 – $600,000). This amount is **subtracted** from net income in determining the net cash flow from operating activities.

- **Prepaid expenses** are current operating assets. Prepaid expenses decreased by **$5,000** ($15,000 – $20,000). This amount is **added** to net income in determining the net cash flow from operating activities.

- **Accounts payable** is a current operating liability. Accounts payable increased by **$105,000** ($825,000 – $720,000). This amount is **added** to net income in determining the net cash flow from operating activities.

- **Interest payable** is a current operating liability. Interest payable increased by **$5,000** ($15,000 – $10,000). This amount is **added** to net income in determining the net cash flow from operating activities.

- **Income tax payable** is a current operating liability. Income tax payable decreased by **$10,000** ($20,000 – $30,000). This amount is **subtracted** from net income in determining the net cash flow from operating activities.

- **Current debt.** The issuance of $325,000 of current debt ($325,000 – $0) is a cash inflow from financing activities.

- The **deferred tax liability** decreased by **$50,000** ($250,000 – $300,000). The decrease in the deferred tax liability increases net income by decreasing income tax expense. This decrease is a noncash item included in net income. Thus, it is **subtracted** from net income in determining the net cash flow from operating activities.

-- Continued on next page --

Example 14-4 -- Continued

Dice Corp.
Consolidated Statement of Cash Flows
for the Year Ended December 31, Year 6

Cash flows from operating activities:

Net income for Year 6	$ 690,000	a.
Decrease in accounts receivable	30,000	b.
Depreciation expense	290,000	c1.
Gain on disposal of equipment	(10,000)	c2.
Gain on sale of investment	(35,000)	d1.
Undistributed earnings of equity-method investment	(15,000)	d2.
Loss on impairment of goodwill	10,000	e.
Increase in inventories	(80,000)	h.
Decrease in prepaid expenses	5,000	i.
Increase in accounts payable	105,000	j.
Increase in interest payable	5,000	k.
Decrease in income tax payable	(10,000)	l.
Decrease in deferred tax liability	(50,000)	n.
Net cash provided by operating activities		**$ 935,000**

Cash flows from investing activities:

Proceeds from sale of equipment	$ 150,000	c3.
Purchases of plant assets	(1,130,000)	c4.
Proceeds from sale of equity-method investment	135,000	d3.
Purchases of current investments	(300,000)	f.
Net cash used in investing activities		**$(1,145,000)**

Cash flows from financing activities:

Dividends paid	$ (240,000)	a1.
Proceeds from issuing common stock	220,000	g.
Proceeds from current debt	325,000	m.
Net cash provided by financing activities		**$ 305,000**
Net increase in cash		**$ 95,000**
Cash, beginning of year		100,000
Cash, end of year		**$ 195,000**

Stop & Review

You have completed the outline for this subunit.

Study multiple-choice questions 13 through 16 beginning on page 463.

Questions

14.1 Statement of Cash Flows -- Classifications

1. In a statement of cash flows, interest payments to lenders and other creditors should be classified as cash outflows for

A. Operating activities.

B. Borrowing activities.

C. Lending activities.

D. Financing activities.

✔ **Answer (A) is correct.**
Required: The classification of interest payments to lenders and other creditors.
Discussion: Cash receipts from sales of goods and services, interest on loans, and dividends on equity securities are from operating activities. Cash payments to (1) suppliers for inventory; (2) employees for services; (3) other suppliers for other goods and services; (4) governments for taxes, duties, fines, and fees; and (5) lenders for interest are also from operating activities.

✘ **Answer (B) is incorrect.** Borrowing is not among the three categories of cash flows.

✘ **Answer (C) is incorrect.** Lending is not among the three categories of cash flows.

✘ **Answer (D) is incorrect.** Financing activities include (1) issuance of stock, (2) payment of distributions to owners, (3) treasury stock transactions, (4) issuance of debt, (5) repayment or other settlement of debt obligations, and (6) receipt of resources donor-restricted for long-term purposes.

2. In a statement of cash flows, payments to acquire debt instruments of other entities (other than cash equivalents and debt instruments acquired specifically for resale) should be classified as cash outflows for

A. Operating activities.

B. Investing activities.

C. Financing activities.

D. Lending activities.

✔ **Answer (B) is correct.**
Required: The proper classification of payments.
Discussion: Investing activities include the lending of money; the collection of those loans; and the acquisition, sale, or other disposal of (1) loans and other securities that are not cash equivalents and that have not been acquired specifically for resale and (2) property, plant, equipment, and other productive assets.

✘ **Answer (A) is incorrect.** Operating activities are transactions and other events not classified as investing and financing activities. In general, the cash effects of operating activities (other than gains and losses) enter into the determination of income from continuing operations.

✘ **Answer (C) is incorrect.** Financing activities include the issuance of stock, the payment of dividends and other distributions to owners, treasury stock transactions, the issuance of debt, and the repayment or other settlement of debt obligations. It also includes receiving restricted resources that by donor stipulation must be used for long-term purposes.

✘ **Answer (D) is incorrect.** Cash flows result from investing, financing, or operating activities.

3. The primary purpose of a statement of cash flows is to provide relevant information about

   A. Differences between net income and associated cash receipts and disbursements.

   B. An entity's ability to generate future positive net cash flows.

   C. The cash receipts and cash disbursements of an entity during a period.

   D. An entity's ability to meet cash operating needs.

✔ **Answer (C) is correct.**
Required: The primary purpose of a statement of cash flows.
Discussion: The primary purpose is to provide information about the cash receipts and cash payments of a business entity during a period. This information helps investors, creditors, and other users to assess the entity's ability to generate net cash inflows, meet its obligations, pay dividends, and secure external financing. It also helps assess reasons for the differences between net income and net cash flow and the effects of cash and noncash financing and investing activities.

14.2 Statement of Cash Flows -- Calculations

4. New England Co. had net cash provided by operating activities of $351,000, net cash used by investing activities of $420,000, and cash provided by financing activities of $250,000. New England's cash balance was $27,000 on January 1. During the year, there was a sale of land that resulted in a gain of $25,000, and proceeds of $40,000 were received from the sale. What was New England's cash balance at the end of the year?

   A. $27,000

   B. $40,000

   C. $208,000

   D. $248,000

✔ **Answer (C) is correct.**
Required: The cash balance at year end.
Discussion: The cash balance at year end is $208,000 ($27,000 on January 1 + $351,000 provided by operations – $420,000 used by investing activities + $250,000 provided by financing activities). The proceeds from the land sale are included in the calculation of the cash used by investing activities.

✘ **Answer (A) is incorrect.** The amount of $27,000 represents the cash balance on January 1.

✘ **Answer (B) is incorrect.** The amount of $40,000 equals the proceeds from the sale of land.

✘ **Answer (D) is incorrect.** The amount of $248,000 results from double-counting the land sale proceeds.

5. Fara Co. reported bonds payable of $47,000 on December 31, Year 1, and $50,000 on December 31, Year 2. During Year 2, Fara issued $20,000 of bonds payable in exchange for equipment. There was **no** amortization of bond premium or discount during the year. What amount should Fara report in its Year 2 statement of cash flows for redemption of bonds payable?

   A. $3,000

   B. $17,000

   C. $20,000

   D. $23,000

✔ **Answer (B) is correct.**
Required: The amount reported in the statement of cash flows for redemption of bonds payable.
Discussion: Assuming no amortization of premium or discount, the net amount of bonds payable reported was affected solely by the issuance of bonds for equipment and the redemption of bonds. Given that $20,000 of bonds were issued and that the amount reported increased by only $3,000, $17,000 of bonds must have been redeemed. This amount should be reported in the statement of cash flows as a cash outflow from a financing activity.

✘ **Answer (A) is incorrect.** The amount of $3,000 equals the increase in bonds payable.

✘ **Answer (C) is incorrect.** The amount of bonds issued is $20,000.

✘ **Answer (D) is incorrect.** The amount of $23,000 is the sum of the bonds issued and the increase in bonds payable.

6. Paper Co. had net income of $70,000 during the year. Dividend payment was $10,000. The following information is available:

Mortgage repayment	$20,000
Available-for-sale securities purchased	10,000 increase
Bonds payable-issued	50,000 increase
Inventory	40,000 increase
Accounts payable	30,000 decrease

What amount should Paper report as net cash provided by operating activities in its statement of cash flows for the year?

A. $0

B. $10,000

C. $20,000

D. $30,000

✓ **Answer (A) is correct.**
Required: The net cash provided by operating activities.
Discussion: The payment of dividends, the repayment of debt (the mortgage), and the issuance of debt (the bonds) are financing activities. The purchase of debt or equity instruments the (available-for-sale securities) is an investing activity. Operating cash flows exclude these financing and investing cash flows. Moreover, these items do not affect net income. Consequently, net cash provided by operating activities can be determined by adjusting net income for the changes in inventory and accounts payable. To account for the difference between cost of goods sold (a deduction from income) and cash paid to suppliers, a two-step adjustment is necessary. The difference between cost of goods sold and purchases is the change in inventory. The difference between purchases and the amount paid to suppliers is the change in accounts payable. Accordingly, the conversion of cost of goods sold to cash paid to suppliers requires subtracting the inventory increase and the accounts payable decrease. The net cash provided by operating activities is therefore $0 ($70,000 net income – $40,000 inventory increase – $30,000 accounts payable decrease).

✗ **Answer (B) is incorrect.** The amount of $10,000 is the difference between the bond proceeds and the sum of the cash outflows for dividends paid, the mortgage repayment, and the securities purchase.

✗ **Answer (C) is incorrect.** The amount of $20,000 equals net income minus the bond proceeds.

✗ **Answer (D) is incorrect.** The amount of $30,000 equals net income minus the inventory increase.

7. Green Co. had the following transactions at December 31:

Cash proceeds from sale of investment in bonds of Blue Co. classified as available-for-sale (carrying amount = $60,000)	$75,000
Dividends received on Grey Co. stock	10,500
Common stock purchased from Brown Co.	38,000

What amount should Green recognize as net cash from investing activities in its statement of cash flows at December 31?

A. $37,000

B. $47,500

C. $75,000

D. $85,500

✓ **Answer (A) is correct.**
Required: The amount of net cash flows from investing activities.
Discussion: The sale proceeds of available-for-sale debt securities ($75,000) are a cash inflow from an investing activity. Cash outflows from acquiring equity instruments ($38,000) also are from an investing activity. But cash inflows from operating activities include cash receipts in the form of dividends ($10,500). Thus, the net cash flow from investing activities is $37,000 ($75,000 – $38,000).

✗ **Answer (B) is incorrect.** Cash inflows from operating activities include cash receipts in the form of dividends ($10,500).

✗ **Answer (C) is incorrect.** The purchase of common stock, a cash outflow of $38,000, is an investing activity.

✗ **Answer (D) is incorrect.** The purchase of common stock, a cash outflow of $38,000, is an investing activity. Cash inflows from operating activities include cash receipts in the form of dividends ($10,500).

Questions 8 and 9 are based on the following information.

Kollar Corp.'s transactions for the year ended December 31, Year 6, included the following:

- Purchased real estate for $550,000 cash borrowed from a bank
- Sold available-for-sale debt securities for $500,000
- Paid dividends of $600,000
- Issued 500 shares of common stock for $250,000
- Purchased machinery and equipment for $125,000 cash
- Paid $450,000 toward a bank loan
- Reduced accounts receivable by $100,000
- Increased accounts payable by $200,000

8. Kollar's net cash used in investing activities for Year 6 was

   A. $675,000
   B. $375,000
   C. $175,000
   D. $50,000

✔ **Answer (C) is correct.**
Required: The net cash used in investing activities.
Discussion: The purchases of real estate and of machinery and equipment were uses of cash in investing activities. The sale of available-for-sale debt securities provided cash from an investing activity. Consequently, the net cash used in investing activities was $175,000 ($550,000 – $500,000 + $125,000). The reduction in accounts receivable and the increase in accounts payable were operating activities.

✘ **Answer (A) is incorrect.** The amount of $675,000 omits the sale of securities.

✘ **Answer (B) is incorrect.** The amount of $375,000 results from either (1) improperly including the increase in accounts payable, a noncash transaction, as a use of cash in an investing activity ($550,000 cash borrowed – $500,000 sale of securities + $125,000 purchase of machinery + $200,000 increase in accounts payable) or (2) improperly calculating the net cash used in investing activities as the difference between the $500,000 sale of securities and the $125,000 purchase of machinery.

✘ **Answer (D) is incorrect.** The amount of $50,000 does not include the purchase of machinery and equipment.

9. Kollar's net cash used in financing activities for Year 6 was

   A. $50,000
   B. $250,000
   C. $450,000
   D. $500,000

✔ **Answer (B) is correct.**
Required: The net cash used in financing activities.
Discussion: The dividend payment and the payment of the bank loan were uses of cash in financing activities. The borrowing from the bank and the issuance of stock provided cash from financing activities. Thus, the net cash used in financing activities was $250,000 ($600,000 – $550,000 – $250,000 + $450,000).

✘ **Answer (A) is incorrect.** The amount of $50,000 omits the issuance of stock and the repayment of the bank loan.

✘ **Answer (C) is incorrect.** The amount of $450,000 results from including the increase in accounts payable, a noncash transaction, as a use of cash in a financing activity.

✘ **Answer (D) is incorrect.** The amount of $500,000 excludes the issuance of stock.

14.3 Presentation of Operating Cash Flows

10. Payne Co. prepares its statement of cash flows using the indirect method. Payne's unamortized bond discount account decreased by $25,000 during the year. How should Payne report the change in unamortized bond discount in its statement of cash flows?

   A. As a financing cash inflow.

   B. As a financing cash outflow.

   C. As an addition to net income in the operating activities section.

   D. As a subtraction from net income in the operating activities section.

✔ **Answer (C) is correct.**
Required: The reporting of a change in unamortized bond discount in a statement of cash flows.
Discussion: Bond discount (debit interest expense, credit discount) amortization is a noncash item that reduces net income. Under the indirect method, net operating cash flow is determined by adjusting net income. The indirect method begins with net income and then removes the effects of (1) deferrals of past operating cash receipts and payments, (2) accruals of estimated future operating cash receipts and payments, and (3) net income items not affecting operating cash flows. Thus, bond discount amortization is added to net income in the reconciliation to net operating cash flow.

✘ **Answer (A) is incorrect.** Amortization of bond discount is not a cash flow.

✘ **Answer (B) is incorrect.** Amortization of bond discount is not a cash flow.

✘ **Answer (D) is incorrect.** The amortization of bond discount is added to net income.

11. Dee's inventory and accounts payable balances at December 31, Year 2, increased over their December 31, Year 1, balances. Should these increases be added to or deducted from cash payments to suppliers to arrive at Year 2 cost of goods sold?

	Increase in Inventory	Increase in Accounts Payable
A.	Added to	Deducted from
B.	Added to	Added to
C.	Deducted from	Deducted from
D.	Deducted from	Added to

✔ **Answer (D) is correct.**
Required: The effect of increases in inventory and accounts payable on the reconciliation of cash payments to suppliers to cost of goods sold.
Discussion: A two-step adjustment is needed. The first step is to adjust for the difference between cash paid to suppliers and purchases. Because accounts payable increased, purchases must have been greater than cash paid to suppliers. Thus, the increase in accounts payable is an addition. The second step adjusts for the difference between purchases and cost of goods sold. Given that inventory increased, purchases must have exceeded cost of goods sold. Hence, the increase in inventories is a subtraction.

12. How should the amortization of bond discount on long-term debt be reported in a statement of cash flows prepared using the indirect method?

   A. As a financing activities inflow.

   B. As a financing activities outflow.

   C. In operating activities as a deduction from income.

   D. In operating activities as an addition to income.

✔ **Answer (D) is correct.**
Required: The reporting of bond discount amortization in a statement of cash flows.
Discussion: Amortization of bond discount on long-term debt is presented in the operating activities section as an addition to net income. It is a noncash expense.

✘ **Answer (A) is incorrect.** Amortization of bond discount is a noncash item presented in operating activities as an addition to income.

✘ **Answer (B) is incorrect.** Amortization of bond discount is a noncash item presented in operating activities as an addition to income.

✘ **Answer (C) is incorrect.** Amortization of bond discount is an addition to income. It is a noncash expense.

14.4 Comprehensive Example

Royce Company had the following transactions during the fiscal year ended December 31, Year 2:

- Accounts receivable decreased from $115,000 on December 31, Year 1, to $100,000 on December 31, Year 2.
- Royce's board of directors declared dividends on December 31, Year 2, of $.05 per share on the 2.8 million shares outstanding, payable to shareholders of record on January 31, Year 3. The company did not declare or pay dividends for fiscal Year 1.

- Sold a truck with a net carrying amount of $7,000 for $5,000 cash, reporting a loss of $2,000.
- Paid interest to bondholders of $780,000.
- The cash balance was $106,000 on December 31, Year 1, and $284,000 on December 31, Year 2.

---

13. Royce Company uses the indirect method to prepare its Year 2 statement of cash flows. It reports a(n)

   A. Source or inflow of funds of $5,000 from the sale of the truck in the financing section.

   B. Use or outflow of funds of $140,000 in the financing section, representing dividends.

   C. Deduction of $15,000 in the operating section, representing the decrease in year-end accounts receivable.

   D. Addition of $2,000 in the operating section for the $2,000 loss on the sale of the truck.

✔ **Answer (D) is correct.**
Required: The correct presentation of an item on a statement of cash flows prepared under the indirect method.
Discussion: The indirect method determines net operating cash flow by adjusting net income for items that did not affect cash. Under the indirect method, the $5,000 cash inflow from the sale of the truck is shown in the investing section. A $2,000 loss was recognized and properly subtracted to determine net income. This loss, however, did not require the use of cash and should be added to net income in the operating section.

✘ **Answer (A) is incorrect.** The $5,000 inflow is reported in the investing section.

✘ **Answer (B) is incorrect.** No outflow of cash dividends occurred in Year 2.

✘ **Answer (C) is incorrect.** The decrease in receivables should be added to net income.

---

14. The total of cash provided (used) by operating activities plus cash provided (used) by investing activities plus cash provided (used) by financing activities is

   A. Cash provided of $284,000.

   B. Cash provided of $178,000.

   C. Cash used of $582,000.

   D. Equal to net income reported for fiscal year ended December 31, Year 2.

✔ **Answer (B) is correct.**
Required: The net total of cash provided and used.
Discussion: The total of cash provided (used) by the three activities (operating, investing, and financing) should equal the increase or decrease in cash for the year. During Year 2, the cash balance increased from $106,000 to $284,000. Thus, the sources of cash must have exceeded the uses by $178,000.

✘ **Answer (A) is incorrect.** The amount of $284,000 is the ending cash balance, not the change in the cash balance. It ignores the beginning balance.

✘ **Answer (C) is incorrect.** The cash balance increased during the year.

✘ **Answer (D) is incorrect.** Net income must be adjusted for noncash expenses and other accruals and deferrals.

15. Metro, Inc., reported net income of $150,000 for the current year. Changes occurred in several balance sheet accounts during the current year as follows:

Investment in Videogold, Inc., stock, all of which was acquired in the previous year, carried on the equity basis	$5,500 increase
Accumulated depreciation, caused by major repair to projection equipment	2,100 decrease
Premium on bonds payable	1,400 decrease
Deferred income tax liability (long-term)	1,800 increase

In Metro's current-year cash flow statement, the reported net cash provided by operating activities should be

A. $150,400

B. $148,300

C. $144,900

D. $142,800

✔ **Answer (C) is correct.**
Required: The net cash provided by operating activities.
Discussion: The increase in the equity-based investment reflects the investor's share of the investee's net income after adjustment for dividends received. Thus, it is a noncash revenue and should be subtracted in the reconciliation of net income to net operating cash inflow. A major repair provides benefits to more than one period and therefore should not be expensed. One method of accounting for a major repair is to charge accumulated depreciation if the useful life of the asset has been extended, with the offsetting credit to cash, a payable, etc. However, the cash outflow, if any, is from an investing activity. The item has no effect on net income and no adjustment is necessary. Amortization of bond premium is a noncash income statement item that reduces accrual-basis expenses and therefore must be subtracted from net income to arrive at net cash flow from operating activities. The increase in the deferred tax liability is a noncash item that reduces net income and should be added in the reconciliation. Accordingly, net cash provided by operations is $144,900 ($150,000 – $5,500 – $1,400 + $1,800).

✘ **Answer (A) is incorrect.** The amount of $150,400 results from omitting the adjustment for the equity-based investment.

✘ **Answer (B) is incorrect.** The amount of $148,300 results from omitting the adjustment for the equity-based investment and improperly subtracting the decrease in accumulated depreciation.

✘ **Answer (D) is incorrect.** The amount of $142,800 results from improperly subtracting the decrease in accumulated depreciation.

16. Tam Co. reported the following items in its year-end financial statements:

Capital expenditures	$1,000,000
Finance lease payments	125,000
Income taxes paid	325,000
Dividends paid	200,000
Net interest payments	220,000

What amount should Tam report as supplemental disclosures in its statement of cash flows prepared using the indirect method?

A. $545,000

B. $745,000

C. $1,125,000

D. $1,870,000

✔ **Answer (A) is correct.**
Required: The amount of supplemental disclosures in a statement of cash flows prepared using the indirect method.
Discussion: If an entity uses the indirect method to present its statement of cash flows, the interest paid (excluding amounts capitalized) and income taxes paid must be disclosed. The sum of these amounts is $545,000 ($220,000 + $325,000).

✘ **Answer (B) is incorrect.** Dividends paid ($200,000) are not required to be included in the supplemental disclosures when the indirect method is used.

✘ **Answer (C) is incorrect.** The total of capital expenditures and finance lease payments is $1,125,000.

✘ **Answer (D) is incorrect.** The sum of all listed items is $1,870,000.

Study Unit Fifteen

Governmental Accounting Basics and Not-for-Profit Accounting

(23 pages of outline)

The first subunit of this study unit relates to the state and local governments content area. It is an overview of the basic accounting system used by state and local governments.

The subsequent subunits address accounting and reporting by **nongovernmental not-for-profit entities (NFPs)** in accordance with GAAP established by the FASB. Among the many kinds of NFPs are (1) educational institutions, (2) healthcare entities, (3) cultural organizations, (4) voluntary health and welfare entities, (5) federated fundraising organizations, (6) unions, (7) political parties, and (8) public broadcasting stations.

15.1 Governmental Accounting --
Basis of Accounting and Funds

Basis of Accounting -- Financial Statements of Governmental Funds

The basis of accounting is the timing of recognition in the financial records of economic events or transactions.

- The basis of accounting of a fund depends on its measurement focus. This **measurement focus** is what is being measured or tracked by information in the financial statements.

The **modified accrual** basis of accounting is used in the governmental funds.

- The measurement focus is on **current financial resources**, that is, on determining financial position and changes in it.

- The reporting elements are sources, uses, and balances.

Revenues, interfund transfers (one-way asset flows with no repayment required), and debt issue proceeds increase fund financial resources. Increases in financial resources are recognized when they are **susceptible to accrual**.

- **Revenue** (net of uncollectibles) is accrued when measurable and available.

  - **Available** means collectible within the current period or **soon enough thereafter** to be used to pay current liabilities.

  - Material revenues ordinarily are not recorded until received. However, they are accrued if receipt is delayed beyond the normal time.

- **Expenditures** decrease in fund financial resources.

  - They usually are measurable and recognizable when goods or services are acquired, i.e., when the related **liability is incurred**.

    - But expenditures for principal and interest on **general long-term debt** usually are recognized only when those amounts are **due**.

- **Expenses** are **not** recognized under the modified accrual basis of accounting.

Basis of Accounting -- Other Financial Statements

The **accrual basis of accounting** is used in (1) government-wide, (2) proprietary fund, and (3) fiduciary fund statements. Thus, revenues and expenses are measured in the same way as in for-profit accounting.

- The measurement focus is on **economic resource**. The emphasis is on (1) a longer-term measure of operating results and (2) the cost of services.

- An **expense** is recognized when goods or services are used or consumed.

- Acquired but unused goods and services are assets.

- Components of financial statements that result from **exchange** or exchange-like transactions are accrued when the exchange occurs.

- Except for revenues, recognition of **nonexchange** transactions is **not** affected by the basis of accounting.

- **Transfers** are recognized when the interfund receivable and payable are recognized.

Funds

The diversity of governmental activities and the need for legal compliance require multiple accounting entities.

A **fund** is an independent, distinct fiscal and accounting entity with a self-balancing set of accounts. Items are segregated because they relate to activities or objectives that are subject to special regulations or limitations. A fund records

- Financial resources (including cash).
- Deferred outflows of resources.
- Liabilities.
- Deferred inflows of resources.
- Residual equities or balances.
- Changes in them.

No more than the funds required by law and efficient financial administration should be created.

Funds are classified as governmental, proprietary, or fiduciary. Below are summaries of funds.

- **Governmental funds** emphasize fiscal accountability. They account for the nonbusiness activities of a government and are most often financed by taxes. Accordingly, they use the **modified accrual basis of accounting** with a current financial resources measurement focus. Thus, they do **not** report capital assets and long-term liabilities.

  - Governmental funds, unlike proprietary and fiduciary funds, use encumbrances (budgetary cost estimates), but only for internal purposes.

  - The **general fund** accounts for all financial resources not accounted for in another fund. Only one general fund is reported.

  - **Special revenue funds** account for **restricted or committed** inflows from specific revenue sources. Expenditure must be for a specified purpose (but not debt service or a capital project). Examples of resources accounted for are grants and gas taxes.

    ▸ These funds are required only if (1) legally mandated or (2) resources will be used for future payments of principal and interest.

    ▸ A special revenue fund is **not** used for resources of a fiduciary activity.

- ■ **Capital projects funds** account for financial resources **restricted, committed, or assigned** to be expended for capital purposes, e.g., general obligation bond proceeds for construction of major capital facilities, such as schools or bridges.

  - ▸ These funds do **not** account for capital assets.
  - ▸ Other capital facilities may be financed through proprietary funds or certain trust funds.

- ■ **Debt service funds** account for resources **restricted, committed, or assigned** to paying principal and interest. But these funds do not account for the debt.

- ■ **Permanent funds** account for resources **restricted** to the use of earnings (not principal) for the benefit of the government or its citizens.

  - ▸ An example is a perpetual-care fund for a public cemetery.

- ● **Proprietary funds** account for the business-type activities of a government. They use the **accrual basis** of accounting with an economic resources measurement focus. They generally are financed through fees. Related capital assets and long-term liabilities are reported in the funds and in the government-wide statements.

  - ■ **Enterprise funds** account for activities (e.g., utilities) that primarily benefit outside parties who are willing to pay for them.

  - ■ **Internal service funds** account for activities performed primarily for the benefit of other agencies, such as an IT department.

  - ■ Unless an enterprise fund is the predominant participant in an internal service fund, the activities it accounts for generally are governmental.

- ● **Fiduciary funds** account for the **fiduciary activities** of a government. They use the **accrual basis** of accounting and have an economic resources measurement focus. They report (1) capital assets, (2) long-term liabilities, and (3) deferred flows of resources.

  - ■ **Pension (and other employee benefit)** trust funds report activities for pensions, other postemployment benefit plans, and certain other employee benefit programs.

  - ■ **Investment trust funds** report activities involving (1) the external portion of investment pools and (2) individual investment accounts held in a trust meeting certain criteria.

  - ■ **Private-purpose trust funds** report all fiduciary activities (1) not reported in the other fiduciary trust funds and (2) accounted for in a trust meeting certain criteria.

  - ■ **Custodial funds** report fiduciary activities not required to be reported in the other fiduciary funds, such as collection of sales taxes for other governments.

Stop & Review

You have completed the outline for this subunit.
Study multiple-choice questions 1 through 3 on page 488.

15.2 Not-for-Profit Accounting -- Financial Statements

Objectives of Financial Reporting by NFPs

Nongovernmental not-for-profit entities (NFPs) have **characteristics** that differentiate them from businesses.

- NFPs receive significant resources from providers who do not expect to receive repayment or proportionate economic benefits (nonreciprocal transactions).

    - They have transactions that are infrequent in businesses, such as grants and contributions, and no transactions with owners, such as dividend payments.

- NFPs have operating purposes other than to provide goods or services at a profit.

- NFPs lack defined ownership interests that (1) can be sold, transferred, or redeemed or (2) entitle an owner to distributions upon liquidation of the entity.

However, the operating environments of NFPs and business entities are similar. For example, both operating environments

- Obtain scarce resources in exchange transactions in markets.
- Produce and distribute goods and services.
- Pay for labor, materials, and facilities now or promise to pay in the future.
- Borrow funds (1) using direct loans or (2) issuing debt and securities.
- Should provide information to creditors about risks and returns of securities.

Financial reporting should provide information useful to **resource providers** (e.g., the members, donors, and guarantors of NFPs) in making resource allocation decisions.

- Whatever the reason for giving resources, all providers seek information about (1) economic resources, (2) liabilities, (3) net resources, (4) changes in resources and liabilities, and (5) factors affecting liquidity (source and uses of liquid assets, borrowing, and repayment).

- All providers also focus on indicators of performance and management stewardship. For example, donors want to know whether managers (1) comply with restrictions and (2) act consistently with the entity's objectives.

    - But NFPs often do **not** have a single indicator of performance comparable to net income.

Users of information about an NFP are interested in how effectively and efficiently it performs services. This information, e.g., about **service efforts** relevant to the mission, helps to evaluate

- The NFP's ability to continue performing those services.
- How well objectives are met.
- Whether to continue support.

Financial Reporting Model

The primary purpose of financial statements of NFPs is to provide relevant information serving the common interests of donors, creditors, and other external resource providers. This information should be provided about the following:

- Assets, liabilities, and net assets
- Changes in net assets
- Flows of economic resources
- Cash flows, borrowing and repayment of borrowing, and other factors affecting liquidity
- Service efforts

Reporting is based on a **net assets model**. Net assets equals the excess or deficiency of assets over liabilities. Net assets is classified as

- With donor restrictions or
- Without donor restrictions.

The following are an NFP's general-purpose financial statements:

- A **statement of financial position** is equivalent to a for-profit entity's balance sheet.

  - The **elements** are assets, liabilities, and net assets. The statement presents information about the elements and their relationships at a moment in time.

  - The statement must be for the entity as a whole and present five amounts: total assets, total liabilities, total net assets with donor restrictions, total net assets without donor restrictions, and total net assets.

- A **statement of activities** is an operating statement equivalent to a for-profit entity's income statement.

  - Its **elements** are revenues, expenses, gains, and losses. Comprehensive income is **not** an element of an NFP's statement of activities. The statement provides information about

    - The effects of transactions and other events and circumstances that change the amount and nature of net assets.

    - The relationships among those transactions, etc.

    - How resources are used to provide programs and services.

- A **statement of cash flows** is similar to the statement reported by for-profit entities.

Fund terminology is **not** used because the emphasis is on net assets and changes in net assets taken as a whole.

- Reporting by **fund groups** therefore is **not** required for external reporting. But disaggregating information by fund groups is allowed.

Statement of Financial Position

The items bolded in the example below must be presented.

Example 15-1	Consolidated Statement of Financial Position

The American National Red Cross
Consolidated Statement of Financial Position
June 30, 20X2 (with comparative information as of June 30, 20X1)
(in thousands)

Assets	20X2	20X1
Current assets:		
Cash and cash equivalents	$ 52,905	$ 372,662
Investments	626,872	695,856
Trade receivables, including grants, net of allowance for credit losses of $5,657 in 20X2 and $3,818 in 20X1	216,517	222,430
Contributions receivable	70,011	66,977
Inventories, net of allowance for obsolescence of $4,105 in 20X2 and $1,382 in 20X1	113,876	126,382
Collateral under securities loaned agreements	--	110,943
Other current assets	24,922	28,901
Total current assets	$1,105,103	$1,624,151
Investments	1,356,851	1,309,580
Contributions receivable	16,030	14,134
Land, buildings, and other property, net	1,050,793	1,077,945
Other assets	249,184	227,771
Total assets	**$3,777,961**	**$4,253,581**
Liabilities and net assets		
Current liabilities:		
Accounts payable and accrued expenses	$ 281,012	$ 333,223
Current portion of debt	14,400	14,418
Postretirement benefits	3,991	4,147
Payables under securities loaned agreements	--	110,943
Other current liabilities	164,121	185,134
Total current liabilities	$ 463,524	$ 647,865
Debt	538,958	558,963
Pension and postretirement benefits	1,001,636	667,987
Other liabilities	178,620	186,843
Total liabilities	**$2,182,738**	**$2,061,658**
Net assets:		
Net assets without donor restrictions	**$ 133,687**	**$ 655,029**
Net assets with donor restrictions	**1,461,536**	**1,536,894**
Total net assets	**$1,595,223**	**$2,191,923**
Commitments and contingencies		
Total liabilities and net assets	**$3,777,961**	**$4,253,581**

The **minimum** required classes of net assets are (1) those with donor restrictions and (2) those without donor restrictions.

- Amounts are reported for (1) each of the two classes (even if disaggregated) and (2) total net assets.

- **Donor restricted support** consists of contribution revenues or gains that increase net assets with donor restrictions. A **restriction** is a stipulation that is more specific than the limits resulting from (1) the nature of the entity, (2) its environment, or (3) its organizational objectives (e.g., those stated in bylaws).

  - Some restrictions are **temporary**. For example, a stipulation may require resources to be used (1) in a later period or after a specific date (**time** restriction), (2) for a specific purpose (**purpose** restriction), or (3) both.

  - Other restrictions are **perpetual**. For example, the stipulation may require resources to be maintained in perpetuity.

  - A law may extend donor-imposed restrictions, for example, to investment returns.

- A governing board of an NFP may limit use of part of its net assets **without donor restrictions** by

  - Establishing a quasi-endowment **(a board-designated endowment fund)** or

  - Self-imposing specific earmarks **(board-designated net assets)**, e.g., for investment, contingencies, or construction of fixed assets.

- Information about the nature and amounts of **restrictions** must be provided on the face of the statement or in the notes. Also, to report different types of restrictions, separate line items may be included in (1) net assets with donor restrictions or (2) the notes.

Example 15-2   Temporary Restriction

A disease-fighting charity may receive a grant specifying that the amount must be used for vaccinations in Africa for 5 years. Any balance remaining at the end of that time may be used for any purpose the board deems appropriate.

Example 15-3   Perpetual Restriction

In Example 15-2, the entity may receive a grant that must be invested in AAA-grade bonds in perpetuity, with the income being spent on vaccinations in Africa (a donor-restricted perpetual endowment).

- **Assets liabilities** must be combined into reasonably homogeneous groups.

  - Assets (including cash) that are donor-restricted to long-term use must **not** be classified with assets without donor restrictions that are currently available.

  - The nature and amount of limitations on the use of **cash and cash equivalents** should be disclosed in the notes or on the statement of financial position.

- An NFP must recognize a liability for (1) its **unconditional promise to give** or (2) an amount received in an agency transaction.

- The guidance for reporting current and noncurrent assets and liabilities applies to for-profit entities and NFPs.

- **Property, plant, and equipment (PPE)** consist of long-lived tangible assets.

  - The amount initially recognized for contributed PPE includes all costs incurred to place the assets in use, e.g., freight and installation costs.

  - NFPs recognize depreciation on most items of PPE.

    - **Depreciation** expense decreases net assets without donor restrictions. A donor's time restriction on a depreciable asset therefore expires as the economic benefits are used.

  - Land used as a building site and certain individual works of art and historical treasures with very long useful lives are **not** depreciated.

    - A **work of art** or **historical treasure** is nondepreciable only if verifiable evidence supports the conclusions that

      - It has cultural, aesthetic, or historical value worth preserving perpetually.
      - The holder has the means of, and is, preserving its full service potential.

    - However, the capitalized costs of major preservation or restoration efforts should be depreciated.

- Contributions of **works of art, historical treasures, and similar items** are recognized as assets and as revenues or gains if they are **not** collection items.

  - **Collections** are works of art, historical treasures, and similar items that are

    - Held for public exhibition, education, or research to further public service rather than for financial gain.

    - Protected, kept unencumbered, cared for, and preserved.

    - Subject to a policy that requires the proceeds of items sold to be used for acquisitions of new collection items, the direct care of existing items, or both.

  - An NFP may choose to (1) capitalize its collections, (2) capitalize prospectively items acquired after a certain date, or (3) not capitalize collections.

    - Capitalization of part of the collections is **not** permitted.

  - If collections are **not capitalized**, no assets or contribution revenues or gains are recognized.

    - The NFP may purchase or sell collection items or receive insurance proceeds. Separate recognition is in the appropriate class of net assets. The entry for purchase with net assets without donor restrictions is

Net assets without donor restrictions	$XXX	
Cash		$XXX

    - Cash flows of uncapitalized collection items are reported in the investing activities section of the statement of cash flows.

Statement of Activities

The statement of activities reports the **changes** in (1) net assets and (2) the categories of net assets for the reporting period.

- Revenues, expenses, gains, and losses must be combined into reasonably homogeneous groups.

  - They also must be reported as increases or decreases in (1) net assets with donor restrictions or (2) net assets without donor restrictions.

- Other events, e.g., expirations of donor-imposed time or purpose restrictions, result in **reclassifications of net assets**. They are reported separately as **net assets released from restrictions**.

  - A reclassification of net assets is displayed as an increase in one net assets class and a decrease in the other. The reclassification entry does not include cash flows.

Example 15-4   Net Assets Released from Restrictions

A patron gave an art museum $100,000 to award fellowships to graduate art students. When the NFP received the contribution, it should have been classified as net assets with donor restrictions because it was to be used for a specified purpose. When the purpose is fulfilled by awarding fellowships, the restriction expires. The amount then should be reclassified as a decrease in net assets with donor restrictions and an increase in net assets without donor restrictions. The reduction of net assets (the expense incurred by awarding fellowships) is reflected by decreasing net assets without donor restrictions.

Example 15-5   Consolidated Statement of Activities

The American National Red Cross
Consolidated Statement of Activities
Year Ended June 30, 20X2
(with summarized information for the year ended June 30, 20X1)
(in thousands)

	Without Donor Restrictions	With Donor Restrictions	Totals 20X2	Totals 20X1
Operating revenues and gains				
Contributions:				
Corporate, foundation, and individual giving	$ 224,373	$ 213,395	$ 437,768	$ 685,947
United Way and other federated	31,024	69,203	100,227	111,273
Legacies and bequests	51,359	43,270	94,629	81,548
Services and materials	18,537	18,887	37,424	35,272
Products and services:				
Biomedical	2,153,870	--	2,153,870	2,189,663
Program materials	136,876	--	136,876	139,222
Contracts, including federal government	82,552	--	82,552	112,804
Investment income	27,098	31,002	58,100	49,584
Other revenues	63,628	5,443	69,071	65,222
Net assets released from restrictions	438,468	(438,468)	--	--
Total operating revenues and gains	**$3,227,785**	**$ (57,268)**	**$3,170,517**	**$3,470,535**
Operating expenses				
Program services:				
(1) Services to the Armed Forces	$ 53,045	$ --	$ 53,045	$ 57,403
(2) Biomedical services	2,239,784	--	2,239,784	2,195,108
(3) Community services	77,538	--	77,538	90,558
(4) Domestic disaster services	279,190	--	279,190	282,974
(5) Health and safety services	195,596	--	195,596	203,735
(6) International relief and development services	186,726	–	186,726	340,106
Total program services	**$3,031,879**	**$ –**	**$3,031,879**	**$3,169,884**
Supporting activities:				
(7) Fundraising	172,407	--	172,407	127,019
(8) Management and general	140,847	--	140,847	142,682
Total supporting services	**$ 313,254**	**$ --**	**$ 313,254**	**$ 269,701**
Total operating expenses	**$3,345,133**	**$ --**	**$3,345,133**	**$3,439,585**
Change in net assets from operations	(117,348)	(57,268)	(174,616)	30,950
Nonoperating gains (losses)	(18,424)	(18,090)	(36,514)	193,157
Pension-related changes other than net periodic benefit cost	(385,570)	--	(385,570)	8,929
Change in net assets	**$ (521,342)**	**$ (75,358)**	**$ (596,700)**	**$ 233,036**
Net assets, beginning of year	655,029	1,536,894	2,191,923	1,958,887
Net assets, end of year	**$ 133,687**	**$1,461,536**	**$1,595,223**	**$2,191,923**

NOTE: Items (1)-(8) are functional expenses.

- **Revenues** are reported as increases in net assets without donor restrictions unless the use of the assets received is restricted by the donor.

Example 15-6   Classification of Revenues

Fees for services and investment income ordinarily are without donor restrictions.

Income from a perpetual or term endowment ordinarily increases net assets with donor restrictions.

  - The **gross** amounts of revenues and expenses from the entity's **ongoing major or central operations** are reported.
  - The accounting for **contributions** is described in Subunit 15.3.
- **Exchange transactions** must be accounted for in accordance with the guidance for **revenue from contracts with customers** in Study Unit 2, Subunit 3.
  - Resources received in exchange transactions must be classified as revenues in net assets without donor restrictions even if the provider (e.g., a government) limits their use.
- **Gains and losses** on assets or liabilities are changes in net assets without donor restrictions unless their use is restricted explicitly by the donor or by law.
  - Gains and losses may be reported as **net** amounts if they result from
    - Peripheral or incidental transactions or
    - Other events and circumstances largely beyond the NFP's control.
- Most **expenses** are reported as decreases in net assets without donor restrictions.
  - An exception is **investment expense**. It must be netted against investment return (not related to program services) and reported in the same net asset category.
  - A statement of activities or the notes must provide information about expenses by **functional** classification (program services and supporting activities).
    - All NFPs must report information about **all** expenses in one place: (1) the statement of activities, (2) a schedule in the notes, or (3) a separate statement.
    - An analysis must be presented that disaggregates functional expense classifications by **natural** expense classifications (e.g., salaries, rent, interest, electricity, awards and grants to others, supplies, professional fees, and depreciation).
- Certain other categories of changes in net assets may be useful.
  - The following are examples:
    - Operating and nonoperating
    - Recurring and nonrecurring
    - Recognized and unrecognized
    - Expendable or nonexpendable
  - If an intermediate operating measure (e.g., operating profit or operating income) is used, it must be in a financial statement that at a minimum reports the change in net assets without donor restrictions.

Functional Classification of Expenses

Program services distribute goods and services to beneficiaries, customers, or members to fulfill the purposes of the entity.

- Those services are the major purpose and output of the entity and often relate to several major programs.

Supporting activities of an NFP are **not** program services. They usually include the following:

- Management and General

    - Oversight and business management
    - Budgeting, financing, and related activities
    - Recordkeeping
    - Most management and administrative activities

- Fundraising

    - Publicity and conducting campaigns
    - Maintenance of donor lists
    - Special events
    - Preparing and distributing related materials
    - Other solicitation activities

- Membership Development

    - Soliciting for members and dues
    - Member relations

Some expenses relate to more than one major program or supporting activity.

- **Direct** identification (assignment) of specific expenses (direct expenses) with programs, services, or support activities is preferable when feasible. Otherwise, **allocation** (indirect expenses) must be rational and systematic, and the result must be reasonable.

    - For example, the cost of a direct-mail solicitation may need to be allocated between fundraising (a supporting activity) and the NFP's educational mission (a program service).

Statement of Cash Flows

The FASB's guidance for reporting a statement of cash flows applies to **all NFPs** and business entities. For example, the term **"income statement"** includes a statement of activities, and the term **"net income"** includes the change in net assets. The outline in this section includes the guidance specific to NFPs.

Example 15-7	Consolidated Statement of Cash Flows

The American National Red Cross
Consolidated Statement of Cash Flows
Year Ended June 30, 20X2 (with comparative
information for the year ended June 30, 20X1)
(in thousands)

	20X2	20X1
Cash flows from operating activities:		
Change in net assets	$(596,700)	$ 233,036
Adjustments to reconcile change in net assets to net cash used in operating activities:		
Depreciation and amortization	78,925	83,331
Provision for credit losses on accounts receivable	2,954	1,252
Provision for obsolete inventory	2,930	(495)
Net gain on sales of property	(938)	(2,699)
Net investment and derivative gain (loss)	24,784	(192,075)
Pension-related changes other than net periodic benefit cost	385,570	(8,929)
Perpetually restricted contributions	(34,748)	(22,032)
Changes in operating assets and liabilities:		
Receivables	(1,971)	(123,257)
Inventories	9,576	3,869
Other assets	(17,434)	(78,999)
Accounts payable and accrued expenses	(52,211)	(37,821)
Other liabilities	(35,949)	192,930
Pension and postretirement benefits	(52,077)	(81,229)
Net cash used in operating activities	**$(287,289)**	**$ (33,118)**
Cash flows from investing activities:		
Purchases of property	$ (55,299)	$ (74,452)
Proceeds from sales of property	4,464	6,407
Purchases of investments	(277,416)	(158,583)
Proceeds from sales of investments	281,058	222,948
Net cash used in investing activities	**$ (47,193)**	**$ (3,680)**
Cash flows from financing activities:		
Contributions with donor restrictions	$ 34,748	$ 20,932
Proceeds from borrowings	--	20,109
Repayments of debt	(20,023)	(38,785)
Net cash provided by financing activities	**$ 14,725**	**$ 2,256**
Net decrease in cash and cash equivalents	$(319,757)	$ (34,542)
Cash and cash equivalents, beginning of year	372,662	407,204
Cash and cash equivalents, end of year	**$ 52,905**	**$ 372,662**
Supplemental disclosures of cash flow information:		
Cash paid during the year for interest	$ 18,590	$ 21,342
Noncash investing and financing transactions:		
Donated stock and beneficial interest in perpetual trust	4,267	1,499

Cash inflows from operating activities include receipts of contributions without donor restrictions.

- NFPs and for-profit entities also treat **interest** and **dividends** on investments without donor restrictions as operating cash flows.

- Either the direct or indirect method of presenting cash flows from operating activities may be used.

    - If the direct method is used, a reconciliation to the indirect method is permitted but **not** required.

- Operating activities may include **agency transactions** in which the NFP receives assets in voluntary transfers but has little discretion in their use.

Cash inflows from financing activities include receipts of resources that are donor-restricted for long-term purposes.

- Accordingly, cash donor-restricted to (1) acquiring, constructing, or improving long-lived assets (e.g., a building or equipment) or (2) establishing or increasing a donor-restricted endowment fund is a cash inflow from a financing activity. Moreover, it is also reported as a cash **outflow** from an **investing** activity.

    - Receipts of investment income (cash interest and dividends) that are donor-restricted for such purposes also are financing cash inflows.

- Financing cash outflows include payments on the principal of indebtedness (but not payments of interest, an operating activity).

Investing activities include cash flows from purchases, sales, and insurance recoveries of unrecognized, noncapitalized **collection items**.

Noncash investing and financing activities, e.g., issuance of a note payable and receipt of a contribution of a building, securities, or recognized collection items, are separately **disclosed**.

Stop & Review

You have completed the outline for this subunit.
Study multiple-choice questions 4 through 14 beginning on page 489.

15.3 Not-for-Profit Accounting -- Contributions

NOTE: The accounting for contributions applies to NFPs and businesses (but not transfers from governments to businesses).

A **contribution** is an unconditional, voluntary, and nonreciprocal transfer of assets (or a reduction, cancellation, or settlement of liabilities). It also may be an unconditional promise to give or consist of nonfinancial assets.

- A contribution is **not**

  - An investment by, or a distribution to, an owner.

  - An involuntary nonreciprocal transfer (e.g., taxes).

  - An **exchange transaction**, a reciprocal transfer in which each party receives and sacrifices **approximately commensurate value**.

- A **promise to give** is an oral or written agreement to contribute assets to another entity. It is **unconditional** if it depends only upon the passage of time or a demand by the promisee for performance.

  - Sufficient verifiable **documentation** must exist.

  - An ambiguous promise is unconditional if it is unconditional and legally enforceable.

- Contributed **nonfinancial assets** (gifts-in-kind) may, for example, be land, buildings, intangible assets, or recognized contributed services.

Donor-Imposed Conditions

A donor-imposed condition is a **barrier** that must be overcome before the recipient is entitled to the assets. If it is not overcome, the contributor must have a **right of return** of the assets or the promisor a **right of release** from its obligation.

- A conditional promise to give is **not** recognized until the condition is substantially met (i.e., the barrier is overcome).

  - A transfer of assets before the condition is met is a **conditional contribution**. It is accounted for as a refundable advance until the condition is (1) substantially met or (2) explicitly waived by the donor.

Assets	$XXX	
Liability-refundable advances		$XXX

- Whether a contribution is conditional must be determinable from an **agreement**. It should be sufficiently clear that the recipient has an entitlement **only** if it has overcome the barrier.

- The following **indicators** may be useful in determining whether a barrier exists:

  - A **measurable performance-related** barrier may consist of a specified service level, output, or outcome.

  - An **other measurable** barrier may be an identified event, e.g., a matching requirement.

- The recipient's **limited discretion** over the conduct of an activity may extend to (1) guidelines about qualifying expenses or (2) a protocol that must be followed.

- A stipulation related to the **purpose of the agreement** may be a barrier, e.g., a homeless shelter's serving a specified number of meals. But administrative and trivial stipulations (e.g., routine reporting) are not barriers.

Accounting for Contributions

Contributions **received** ordinarily are accounted for when received at **fair value**.

- Debits are to

  - **Assets** (e.g., cash, pledge receivables, securities, or other assets),
  - **Liabilities** (e.g., for payment of an NFP's debt), or
  - **Expenses** (e.g., services when the contribution is received and used at the same time).

- Credits are to income, specifically to

  - **Contribution revenues** if the transactions are part of the NFP's ongoing major or central operations, e.g., soliciting contributions.

  - **Contribution gains** if the transactions are peripheral or incidental.

Present value may be used to measure the fair value of an unconditional promise to give cash.

- Interest accruals are recognized using the interest method as

  - Contribution revenue by donees and
  - Contribution expense by donors.

Contributions (pledges) receivable	$20,000,000	
Contribution revenue -- net assets with donor restrictions		$16,454,000
Discount		3,546,000

- However, unconditional promises to give expected to be collected in less than 1 year may be recognized at **net realizable value** (that is, minus an estimated uncollectible amount).

- The recipient of an unconditional promise to give must disclose the allowance for **uncollectible promises receivable**. But the allowance excludes amounts determined to be uncollectible when the receivable was measured initially.

Example 15-8	Uncollectible Promises Receivable

On December 31, Year 1, the end of NFP's fiscal year, it received unconditional promises to give in the amount of $100,000. NFP determines that (1) the estimated future cash inflows are $80,000 and (2) their present value is $60,000. The entry is

Contributions receivable	$80,000	
Contribution revenue -- net assets with donor restrictions		$60,000
Discount		20,000

Contributions of services are recognized if they either

- Create or enhance **nonfinancial assets** (e.g., buildings) or

- Require special skills, are provided by those having such skills, and usually would be purchased if not donated.

Example 15-9　　Contributions of Services

An animal shelter is an NFP that receives contributed services from the following individuals measured at their normal billing rates:

Veterinarian provides volunteer animal care	$8,000
A board member who is a CPA volunteers to prepare books for audit	4,500
Registered nurse volunteers as receptionist	3,000
Teacher provides volunteer dog walking	2,000

What amount should the shelter record as contribution revenue?

The services provided by the veterinarian and the CPA are recognized as contribution revenue. The services provided by the registered nurse and the teacher are not. Veterinary services and bookkeeping (1) require special skills, (2) are provided by persons with such skills, and (3) otherwise would be paid for by an animal shelter. Thus, the animal shelter should record $12,500 ($8,000 + $4,500) as contribution revenue.

Expenses	$12,500	
Contribution revenue -- net assets without donor restrictions		$12,500

A contribution of **utilities**, such as electricity, is a contribution of other assets, not services. A simultaneous receipt and use of utilities should be recognized in the period of receipt and use.

Expense	$XXX	
Revenue -- net assets without donor restrictions		$XXX

Contributions made are recognized at fair value when made as (1) expenses and (2) decreases of assets or increases in liabilities.

Reporting Contributions

- An NFP distinguishes between (1) contributions received with donor purpose or time restrictions and (2) those without such restrictions.

  - **Donor-restricted support** consists of contribution revenues or gains that increase net assets with donor restrictions.

  - Contribution revenues or gains **without** donor restrictions increase net assets without donor restrictions in the statement of financial position.

  - An NFP must recognize the **expiration** of a donor restriction on a contribution in the period when it expires. **Expiration** occurs when (1) the time stipulated has lapsed, (2) the purpose stipulated has been fulfilled, or (3) both.

  - Donor restrictions may expire in the period that the contributions are made. An NFP may **elect** to report such contributions as support within net assets without donor restrictions. The NFP must

    - Have a similar policy for investment gains and income,
    - Report consistently, and
    - Disclose the policy.

- **Unconditional promises to give**, with payments due in **future** periods, are reported as donor-restricted support unless the donor clearly intended support for current activities.

  - Unconditional promises to give cash in future years usually increase net assets with donor restrictions.

- Contributions restricted to acquisition of long-term assets are reported initially as donor-restricted support.

  - Unless a donor has stipulated a time restriction on the use of such assets, donor restrictions expire when the assets are placed in service.

  - An NFP must **not** imply a time restriction that expires over the term of a long-lived asset.

Example 15-10   Contribution of Long-Term Assets to Support Donee's Mission

On June 30, Year 4, Donee, an NFP, received a building and the land on which it was constructed as a gift from Donor. The building is intended to support the entity's education and training mission or any other purpose consistent with the entity's mission. Immediately prior to the contribution, the fair values of the building and land were appraised at $350,000 and $150,000, respectively. Donor's carrying amounts on June 30, Year 4, were $290,000 and $75,000, respectively.

The terms of this gift allow the long-lived assets to be used for any purpose consistent with the NFP's mission. A policy implying time restrictions on gifts of long-lived assets is not permitted. Thus, the contribution increased net assets without donor restrictions.

- **Dues** from members may have elements of a contribution and an exchange if members receive tangible or intangible benefits from membership. Dues and **nonrefundable fees** received in exchange transactions are recognized as revenues in accordance with the guidance for revenue from contracts with customers.

Example 15-11   Nonrefundable Fees

In Year 3, a not-for-profit trade association enrolled five new member companies, each of which was obligated to pay nonrefundable initiation fees of $1,000. These fees were receivable by the association in Year 4. Three of the new members paid the initiation fees in Year 3, and the other two new members paid their initiation fees in Year 4. Annual dues (excluding initiation fees) received by the association from all of its members always have covered the organization's costs of services provided to members. The reasonable expectation is that future dues will cover all costs of the organization's future services to members. Average membership duration is 10 years because of mergers, attrition, and economic factors. What amount of initiation fees from these five new members should the association recognize as revenue in Year 4?

Membership dues received or receivable in exchange transactions that relate to several accounting periods should be allocated and recognized as revenue in those periods as the performance obligation is satisfied. The entity applies the input method based on time elapsed. The nonrefundable initiation and life membership fees are recognized as revenue when they are receivable because the entity has no performance obligations to satisfy. Thus, the $5,000 in nonrefundable initiation fees should be recognized as revenue when assessed and reported as such in the Year 4 statement of activities.

Deferred revenue -- fees paid in advance	$3,000	
Cash	2,000	
Fee revenue		$5,000

A **donation on behalf of a beneficiary** is a contribution of cash or other financial assets to an NFP that agrees to use it on behalf of a third party.

- If the donor explicitly grants **variance power**, the NFP records the asset and contribution revenue at fair value. Variance power is the **unilateral** power to redirect the use of the assets to another beneficiary.

- If the donor does **not** grant variance power, the NFP recognizes an asset and a **liability** to the beneficiary, which also recognizes an asset.

Common stock -- X Corp.	$XXX	
Liability -- beneficiary Y		$XXX

- If the assets are **nonfinancial**, such as materials or supplies, the recipient is **not** required to recognize the assets and the liability. The NFP must disclose this accounting policy and apply it consistently.

Example 15-12   Donation without Variance Power for Beneficiary

A family lost its home in a fire. In December Year 3, a donor sent money to NFP to purchase furniture for the family. The donor did not explicitly grant NFP the unilateral power to redirect the use of the assets. During January Year 4, NFP purchased this furniture. How should NFP report the receipt of the money in its Year 3 financial statements?

The recipient and beneficiary presumably are **not** financially interrelated. Furthermore, the donor explicitly does **not** grant the recipient variance power. Accordingly, the donation is an agency transaction, and the NFP is a pass-through entity. Because NFP was not explicitly granted variance power, it is an agent or trustee acting on behalf of the third-party donee and has little or no discretion in use of the cash. Thus, NFP should account for the transfer as a liability, not a contribution.

A **split-interest** arrangement is an agreement in which a donor enters into a trust or other arrangement under which the not-for-profit entity receives benefits that are shared with other beneficiaries.

- For example, a charitable remainder trust is part of a split-interest agreement in which the donor (or a third-party beneficiary) receives distributions during its term.

  - After trust termination, an NFP receives the remaining trust assets.

Stop & Review

You have completed the outline for this subunit.
Study multiple-choice questions 15 and 16 on page 494.

15.4 Not-for-Profit Accounting -- Investments

Success Tip

Laws address the use of the investment return on donor-restricted endowment funds. The majority of jurisdictions follow a statutory version of the relevant uniform act (Uniform Prudent Management of Institutional Funds Act of 2006, or UPMIFA). Others follow trust law. One issue is whether the investment return is available to be spent.

The outline and questions in this subunit assume that UPMIFA applies. However, if the endowment is subject to trust law, the original gift and net appreciation generally are unavailable to be spent. But ordinary income (interest, dividends, etc.) generally may be spent assuming no purpose or other donor restriction.

Debt and Equity Securities

Purchased debt and equity securities initially are measured at acquisition **cost** (excluding transaction costs). Subsequent measurement is at fair value for (1) debt (quoted market prices) and (2) equity securities with readily determinable fair value.

- Debt and equity securities received as contributions or through agency transactions initially are measured at **fair value**.

  - If a debt or equity security is acquired by contribution, it is recognized as an asset and as a revenue or gain when received.

Gains and losses, dividends, interest, and other investment income are reported in the statement of activities as changes in net assets without donor restrictions. But, if they are **donor-restricted** (or if they are subject to a **law** that extends donor restrictions), they are reported as changes in net assets with donor restrictions.

- Donor-restricted gains and investment income may be reported as increases in net assets without donor restrictions if the **restrictions expire** in the period the gains and income are recognized. The NFP must

  - Have a similar policy for contributions received,
  - Report consistently, and
  - Disclose the policy.

- Investment return not related to program services must be reported net of related external, and direct internal, investment expenses.

Study Unit 4, Subunit 3, outlines the guidance for subsequent measurement of **equity securities**.

Donor-Restricted Endowment Funds

A donor-restricted endowment fund is created by a donor stipulation requiring a gift to be invested for a specified period or in perpetuity.

- This definition excludes **board-designated** endowment funds.

- Classifying a donor-restricted endowment fund within net assets with donor restrictions or net assets without donor restrictions depends on (1) the donor's specific stipulation and (2) the applicable law.

  - Without a donor or legal restriction, **investment return** (income and appreciation) generally is free of donor restrictions. But most donor-restricted endowment funds are subject to a statute that **extends** a donor restriction to use of the assets, including the return, until **appropriation for expenditure** by the governing board.

    ▸ Thus, without contrary language in the gift instrument, the assets in the fund (including the return) are net assets with donor restrictions until appropriation.

    ▸ An appropriation reduces net assets with donor restrictions if all time and purpose restrictions have been met. The result is a reclassification to net assets without donor restrictions.

      - Appropriation occurs upon **approval** for expenditure unless a legal interpretation states otherwise.

Example 15-13   Perpetual Endowment Fund Subject to Majority Legal Rules

A nongovernmental not-for-profit entity received a $2 million gift from a donor who specified that it be used to create an endowment fund to be invested in perpetuity. The income from the fund is to be used to support a specific program in the second year and beyond. Income from investments purchased with the gift was $40,000 during the first year. At the end of the first year, the fair value of the investments was $2,010,000. What is the net effect on net assets with donor restrictions at year end?

The applicable state law follows the majority rule, and the donor gave no instruction on use of the appreciation of the fund investments. In these circumstances, the income increases net assets with donor restrictions because the time and purpose restrictions have not been met. Also, (1) the jurisdiction follows the majority legal rule that extends donor restrictions to use of the investment return, and (2) no amount was appropriated for expenditure by the governing board. Accordingly, the $10,000 gain on the perpetual endowment and the $40,000 of income increase net assets with donor restrictions by $50,000.

Stop & Review

You have completed the outline for this subunit.
Study multiple-choice questions 17 through 20 beginning on page 495.

Questions

15.1 Governmental Accounting -- Basis of Accounting and Funds

1. Kew City received a $15,000,000 federal grant to finance the construction of a center for rehabilitation of drug addicts. The proceeds of this grant should be accounted for in the

    A. Special revenue funds.

    B. General fund.

    C. Capital projects funds.

    D. Trust funds.

✔ **Answer (C) is correct.**
Required: The fund used to account for a federal grant to finance the construction of a center for rehabilitation of drug addicts.
Discussion: A capital projects fund is used to account for the receipt and disbursement of resources restricted to the acquisition of major capital facilities (other than those financed by proprietary and trust funds) through purchase or construction.

✖ **Answer (A) is incorrect.** Special revenue funds do not record resources to be used for major capital facilities.

✖ **Answer (B) is incorrect.** The general fund does not record resources to be used for major capital facilities.

✖ **Answer (D) is incorrect.** A grant for a drug rehabilitation center is not accounted for in a trust fund. A trust fund accounts for assets held as a fiduciary activity.

2. A local governmental unit could use which of the following types of funds?

	Fiduciary	Proprietary
A.	Yes	No
B.	Yes	Yes
C.	No	Yes
D.	No	No

✔ **Answer (B) is correct.**
Required: The types of funds that could be used by a local government.
Discussion: The three categories of fund types that can be used by a state or local government are (1) governmental (general, special revenue, debt service, capital projects, and permanent funds), (2) proprietary (internal service and enterprise funds), and (3) fiduciary (pension and other employee benefit trust, investment trust, private-purpose trust, and custodial funds).

3. In the fund financial statements of which of the following fund types of a city government are revenues and expenditures recognized on the same basis of accounting as the general fund?

    A. Private-purpose trust.

    B. Internal service.

    C. Enterprise.

    D. Debt service.

✔ **Answer (D) is correct.**
Required: The fund that recognizes revenues and expenditures in the same manner as the general fund.
Discussion: A debt service fund is the only type of fund listed that is classified as a governmental fund. The other funds are proprietary or fiduciary. The modified accrual basis is used to prepare the financial statements for governmental funds. Proprietary and fiduciary funds are reported on the accrual basis.

✖ **Answer (A) is incorrect.** A private-purpose trust fund is a fiduciary fund. Its financial statements are prepared on the same basis as those of proprietary funds.

✖ **Answer (B) is incorrect.** An internal service fund is a proprietary fund. Its financial statements are prepared using the accrual basis of accounting.

✖ **Answer (C) is incorrect.** An enterprise fund is a proprietary fund. Its financial statements are prepared using the accrual basis of accounting.

15.2 Not-for-Profit Accounting -- Financial Statements

4. Forkin Manor, a nongovernmental not-for-profit entity (NFP), wants to reformat its financial statements using terminology that is more readily associated with for-profit entities. The director believes that the term "operating profit" and the practice of segregating recurring and nonrecurring items more accurately depict the NFP's activities. Under what condition will Forkin be allowed to use "operating profit" and to segregate its recurring items from its nonrecurring items in its statement of activities?

A. The NFP reports the change in net assets without donor restrictions for the period.

B. A parenthetical disclosure in the notes implies that the NFP is seeking for-profit entity status.

C. Forkin receives special authorization from the Internal Revenue Service that this wording is appropriate.

D. At a minimum, the NFP reports the change in net assets with donor restrictions for the period.

✔ **Answer (A) is correct.**
Required: The condition allowing an NFP to use the term "operating profit" and to segregate recurring and nonrecurring items in its statement of activities.
Discussion: In its statement of activities, an NFP may use such classifications as (1) operating and nonoperating, (2) expendable and nonexpendable, (3) recognized and unrecognized, and (4) recurring and nonrecurring. Furthermore, if an intermediate operating measure (e.g., operating income or operating profit) is used, it must be in a financial statement that at a minimum reports the change in net assets without donor restrictions.

✘ **Answer (B) is incorrect.** The NFP need not seek for-profit status to report in the described manner.

✘ **Answer (C) is incorrect.** The NFP need not obtain IRS authorization to report in the described manner.

✘ **Answer (D) is incorrect.** The NFP must report the changes in the two classes of net assets regardless of whether additional classifications are included in the statement of activities.

5. A complete set of general-purpose external financial statements issued by a nongovernmental not-for-profit entity must include

A. Statements of financial position as of the beginning and end of the reporting period, a statement of cash flows, and a statement of activities.

B. A statement of financial position as of the end of the reporting period and a statement of revenues, expenditures, and changes in fund balances.

C. A statement of financial position as of the end of the reporting period, a statement of cash flows, and a statement of activities.

D. Statements of financial position as of the beginning and end of the reporting period, comparative statements of cash flows, and comparative statements of activities.

✔ **Answer (C) is correct.**
Required: The statements included in a complete set of financial statements of NFPs.
Discussion: A complete set of financial statements of an NFP must include (1) a statement of financial position as of the end of the reporting period, (2) a statement of activities and a statement of cash flows for the reporting period, and (3) accompanying notes.

✘ **Answer (A) is incorrect.** The statement of financial position must be as of the end of the reporting period.

✘ **Answer (B) is incorrect.** A statement of revenues, expenditures, and changes in fund balances is reported for the governmental funds of a state or local governmental entity.

✘ **Answer (D) is incorrect.** The statement of financial position must be as of the end of the reporting period, and comparative statements are not required.

6. Net assets is an element of the financial statements of nongovernmental not-for-profit entities (NFPs). It

   A. Is the residual interest in the assets of an NFP after subtracting its liabilities.

   B. Is the change in equity during a period from transactions and other events and circumstances not involving resource providers.

   C. Differs from equity in businesses because it is not a residual interest.

   D. Consists of the probable future economic benefits obtained or controlled by a particular entity as a result of past transactions or events.

✔ **Answer (A) is correct.**
Required: The definition of the net assets element of the financial statements of NFPs.
Discussion: Net assets equals the residual interest in the assets of an entity that remains after subtracting its liabilities. In an NFP, which has no ownership interest, net assets is classified at a minimum as net assets without donor restrictions and net assets with donor restrictions.

✘ **Answer (B) is incorrect.** Comprehensive income is the change in equity of a business during a period from transactions and other events and circumstances from nonowner sources.

✘ **Answer (C) is incorrect.** Equity and net assets are residuals.

✘ **Answer (D) is incorrect.** Assets, not net assets, are probable future economic benefits obtained or controlled by a particular entity as a result of past transactions or events.

7. At the beginning of the year, the Baker Fund, a nongovernmental not-for-profit corporation, received a $125,000 contribution restricted to youth activity programs. During the year, youth activities generated revenues of $89,000 and had program expenses of $95,000. What amount should Baker report as net assets released from restrictions for the current year?

   A. $0

   B. $6,000

   C. $95,000

   D. $125,000

✔ **Answer (C) is correct.**
Required: The net assets released from restrictions for the current year.
Discussion: At the time the contribution was made, net assets with donor restrictions increased by $125,000. The restriction stated that the funds were to be used for youth activity programs. The amount of actual program expenses for the year ($95,000) is reported under net assets released from restrictions.

✘ **Answer (A) is incorrect.** The incurrence of program expenses reduced net assets with donor restrictions by fulfilling the purpose of the restriction to the extent the resources were used.

✘ **Answer (B) is incorrect.** The amount of $6,000 is the excess of program expenses over revenues generated by youth activities.

✘ **Answer (D) is incorrect.** The purpose of the restriction was fulfilled only to the extent the contribution was used for the stated purpose.

8. A nongovernmental not-for-profit entity borrowed $5,000, which it used to purchase a truck. In which section of the entity's statement of cash flows should the transaction be reported?

   A. In cash inflow and cash outflow from investing activities.

   B. In cash inflow and cash outflow from financing activities.

   C. In cash inflow from financing activities and cash outflow from investing activities.

   D. In cash inflow from operating activities and cash outflow from investing activities.

✔ **Answer (C) is correct.**
Required: The section of the statement of cash flows in which the purchase of a truck is reported by an NFP.
Discussion: The borrowing is a cash inflow from a financing activity because it results from issuing debt. The purchase of the truck is a cash outflow from an investing activity because it involves the acquisition of property, plant, or equipment or other productive assets.

9. A nongovernmental not-for-profit entity has the following current information to be reflected in its statement of cash flows:

	Jan. 1	Dec. 31
Accounts receivable	$9,500	$16,000
Allowance for credit losses	300	700
Prepaid rent expense	7,200	4,400
Accounts payable	8,700	10,700

The current-year change in net assets is $55,000. Net cash provided by operating activities in the statement of cash flows should be

A. $49,600

B. $56,200

C. $53,000

D. $53,700

✔ **Answer (D) is correct.**
Required: The net cash provided by operating activities.
Discussion: The change in net assets should be adjusted for the effects of items properly included in its determination but having either a different effect or no effect on net operating cash flow. The increase in gross accounts receivable should be subtracted. The increase indicates that revenues exceeded cash received. The increase in the allowance for credit losses should be added. This amount is a noncash expense. The decrease in prepaid rent expense should be added. The cash was paid in a prior period, but the expense is recognized currently as a noncash item. The increase in accounts payable should be added. It indicates that liabilities and related expenses were recognized without cash outflows. The net cash provided by operating activities is therefore $53,700.

$55,000	Change in net assets
(6,500)	Increase in gross AR
400	Increase in allowance for credit losses
2,800	Decrease in prepaid rent
2,000	Increase in accounts payable
$53,700	Net cash provided by operating activities

✘ **Answer (A) is incorrect.** The amount of $49,600 results from subtracting the increase in accounts payable.

✘ **Answer (B) is incorrect.** The amount of $56,200 results from adding the change in accounts receivable and subtracting the changes in the other balances.

✘ **Answer (C) is incorrect.** The amount of $53,000 results from subtracting the change in the allowance for credit losses.

10. Functional expenses recorded in the general ledger of ABC, a nongovernmental not-for-profit entity, are as follows:

Soliciting prospective members	$45,000
Printing membership benefits brochures	30,000
Soliciting membership dues	25,000
Maintaining donor list	10,000

What amount should ABC report as fundraising expenses?

A. $10,000

B. $35,000

C. $70,000

D. $110,000

✔ **Answer (A) is correct.**
Required: The fundraising expenses.
Discussion: The major functional classes of expenses for an NFP are program services and supporting activities. An analysis also must be presented that disaggregates functional expense classifications by natural expense classifications (e.g., salaries, interest, rent, and depreciation). Supporting activities include (1) management and general, (2) fundraising, and (3) membership-development activities. Fundraising expenses include maintaining donor lists ($10,000). Soliciting members and dues and printing membership benefits brochures are membership-development activities.

✘ **Answer (B) is incorrect.** The amount of $35,000 includes the cost of soliciting dues, a membership-development activity.

✘ **Answer (C) is incorrect.** The amount of $70,000 is the cost of soliciting members and dues.

✘ **Answer (D) is incorrect.** Only the cost of the donor list is an expense of fundraising.

Question 11 is based on the following information.

NFP, a nongovernmental not-for-profit entity, reported a change in net assets of $300,000 for the current year. Changes occurred in several balance sheet accounts as follows:

Equipment $25,000 increase
Accumulated depreciation   40,000 increase
Note payable   30,000 increase

Additional Information:

- During the current year, NFP sold equipment costing $25,000, with accumulated depreciation of $12,000, for a gain of $5,000.
- In December of the current year, NFP purchased equipment costing $50,000 with $20,000 cash and a 12% note payable of $30,000.
- Depreciation expense for the year was $52,000.

11. In NFP's current-year statement of cash flows, net cash provided by operating activities should be

   A. $340,000

   B. $347,000

   C. $352,000

   D. $357,000

✔ **Answer (B) is correct.**
Required: The net cash provided by operating activities in the statement of cash flows.
Discussion: The FASB's guidance for presenting a statement of cash flows applies to a nongovernmental not-for-profit entity. For example, "net income" includes the change in net assets. An NFP should adjust the change in net assets for the effects of items that have no effect on net cash provided by operating activities. Depreciation is included in the determination of the change in net assets but has no cash effect. Thus, depreciation should be added. The sale of equipment resulted in a gain included in the determination of the change in net assets, but the cash effect is classified as an inflow from an investing activity. Thus, the gain should be subtracted. The cash outflow for the purchase of equipment is from an investing activity and has no effect on the change in net assets. It requires no adjustment. The net cash provided by operating activities is $347,000 ($300,000 change in net assets + $52,000 depreciation – $5,000 gain).

✘ **Answer (A) is incorrect.** The amount of $340,000 reflects addition of the accumulated depreciation.

✘ **Answer (C) is incorrect.** The amount of $352,000 results from not subtracting the gain.

✘ **Answer (D) is incorrect.** The amount of $357,000 results from adding the gain.

12. In its fiscal year ended June 30, Year 4, Barr College, a large nongovernmental not-for-profit entity, received $100,000 designated by the donor for scholarships for superior students. On July 26, Year 4, Barr selected the students and awarded the scholarships. How should the July 26 transaction be reported in Barr's statement of activities for the year ended June 30, Year 5?

A. As both an increase and a decrease of $100,000 in net assets without donor restrictions.

B. As a decrease only in net assets without donor restrictions.

C. By footnote disclosure only.

D. Not reported.

✔ **Answer (A) is correct.**
Required: The treatment by a private not-for-profit entity of funds received and used for a designated purpose.
Discussion: When the NFP received the contribution, it should have been classified as net assets with donor restrictions because it was to be used for a specified purpose. When the purpose is fulfilled, the restriction expires. The amount then should be reclassified as a decrease in net assets with donor restrictions and an increase in net assets without donor restrictions. When the scholarships are awarded, net assets without donor restrictions is decreased.

✘ **Answer (B) is incorrect.** Net assets without donor restrictions also must be increased.

✘ **Answer (C) is incorrect.** A donation must be reported on the face of the statement of activities.

✘ **Answer (D) is incorrect.** This donation must be reported as (1) an increase and a decrease in net assets without donor restrictions and (2) a decrease in net assets with donor restrictions when its purpose is fulfilled and the scholarships are awarded.

13. On January 1, Year 4, a nongovernmental not-for-profit botanical society received a gift of an exhaustible fixed asset with an estimated useful life of 10 years and **no** salvage value. The donor's cost of this asset was $20,000, and its fair value at the date of the gift was $30,000. What amount of depreciation of this asset should the society recognize in its Year 4 financial statements?

A. $3,000

B. $2,500

C. $2,000

D. $0

✔ **Answer (A) is correct.**
Required: The amount of depreciation to be recognized in the financial statements.
Discussion: NFPs must recognize depreciation. Moreover, contributions are recorded at their fair value when received. Assuming the straight-line method is used, the amount of depreciation that the NFP should recognize is $3,000 [($30,000 fair value − $0 salvage value) ÷ 10 years].

✘ **Answer (B) is incorrect.** Annual straight-line depreciation for this asset is $3,000.

✘ **Answer (C) is incorrect.** The amount of $2,000 results from using cost as the depreciable basis of the asset.

✘ **Answer (D) is incorrect.** NFPs recognize depreciation on most property and equipment.

14. During the current year, Mill Foundation, a nongovernmental not-for-profit entity, received $100,000 in unrestricted contributions from the general public. Mill's board of directors stipulated that $75,000 of these contributions would be used to create an endowment. At the end of the current year, how should Mill report the $75,000 in the net assets section of the statement of financial position?

A. Permanently restricted.

B. Net assets without donor restrictions.

C. Temporarily restricted.

D. Donor restricted.

✔ **Answer (B) is correct.**
Required: The reporting of unrestricted contributions designated as an endowment.
Discussion: An internal decision to designate a portion of net assets without donor restrictions as an endowment (a board-designated endowment fund) is not a restriction. If the contributions had been restricted by the donor, the classification of the assets would have been net assets with donor restrictions.

✘ **Answer (A) is incorrect.** The contributions were not restricted by the donors.

✘ **Answer (C) is incorrect.** The contributions were unrestricted because the endowment was designated by the board.

✘ **Answer (D) is incorrect.** The board of directors, not the donors, designated a portion of the contributions as an endowment.

15.3 Not-for-Profit Accounting -- Contributions

15. NFP has received a $2,000,000 research grant from a government. NFP may retain the rights to the research and is permitted to publish the findings. However, NFP must (1) follow a certain protocol (regulations established by the government), (2) incur specified qualifying expenses, (3) forfeit unspent money, and (4) report the research findings to the government. This transfer of assets to NFP from a government is

   A. An unconditional contribution.

   B. An exchange transaction.

   C. A conditional contribution.

   D. A conditional exchange transaction.

✔ **Answer (C) is correct.**
Required: The nature of a governmental grant.
Discussion: An exchange transaction is a reciprocal transfer in which each party receives and sacrifices approximately commensurate value. But the government (resource provider) does not receive commensurate value. NFP retains the rights to the research, and the government receives only an indirect benefit. NFP and the public receive the direct (primary) benefit. The transaction is a conditional contribution to the extent the assets are received before the condition is met. The agreement (donor stipulation) states a barrier that must be overcome before the recipient is entitled to the assets. This condition is deemed to exist because of certain indicators (e.g., a protocol to be followed and incurrence of qualifying expenses). They established that a barrier exists in the form of limits on the recipient's discretion over the conduct of the research activity. Before the condition is substantially met (or explicitly waived), NFP recognizes a refundable advance (liability). After the condition is substantially met, NFP recognizes contribution revenue. The transfer of assets is then unconditional as well as voluntary and nonreciprocal.

✘ **Answer (A) is incorrect.** The agreement contains indicators of the existence of a barrier (a condition) that must be overcome before the recipient is entitled to the assets.

✘ **Answer (B) is incorrect.** The government did not receive commensurate value.

✘ **Answer (D) is incorrect.** The guidance regarding conditions applies to contributions, not exchange transactions.

16. During the current year, a voluntary health and welfare entity received $300,000 in pledges without donor-imposed restrictions. Of this amount, $100,000 has been designated by donors for use next year to support operations. If 15% of the pledges without donor-imposed restrictions are expected to be uncollectible, what amount of support that increases net assets without donor restrictions should the entity recognize in its current-year financial statements?

   A. $300,000

   B. $270,000

   C. $200,000

   D. $170,000

✔ **Answer (D) is correct.**
Required: The current-year support that increases net assets without donor restrictions to be recognized.
Discussion: Only $200,000 of the pledged total constitutes support that increases net assets without donor restrictions. These pledges may be recognized at net realizable value (NRV) if their collection is expected in less than 1 year. The NRV of these pledges is $170,000 [$200,000 × (1.0 − .15 estimated uncollectible)].

✘ **Answer (A) is incorrect.** The amount of $300,000 is the total amount of pledges.

✘ **Answer (B) is incorrect.** The amount of $100,000 of the pledges is restricted until the next year.

✘ **Answer (C) is incorrect.** The amount of $200,000 does not reflect the estimated uncollectible pledges.

15.4 Not-for-Profit Accounting -- Investments

17. A voluntary health and welfare entity received a $500,000 perpetual endowment at the beginning of the year. The donor stipulated that the income be used for a mental health program. Also, **no** reporting date fair value was stipulated by the donor or required by law. The endowment fund reported a $60,000 net decrease in fair value and $30,000 of investment income. The entity spent $45,000 on the mental health program during the year. What amount of change in net assets with donor restrictions should the entity report?

A. $75,000 decrease.

B. $15,000 decrease.

C. $440,000 increase.

D. $470,000 increase.

✔ **Answer (C) is correct.**

Required: The change in net assets with donor restrictions from receipt of a perpetual endowment with a purpose restriction on income.

Discussion: The $500,000 contribution to a perpetual endowment is an increase in net assets with donor restrictions. The income is subject to a donor-imposed purpose restriction. However, if the restriction is met in the period the income is recognized, it may be reported as an increase in net assets without donor restrictions if the entity (1) has a similar policy for reporting contributions received, (2) reports consistently, and (3) discloses the policy. Assuming these criteria were satisfied, the restriction on the $30,000 of investment income expired when it was spent (with an additional $15,000, presumably from other sources). The endowment fund is underwater because its reporting date fair value ($500,000 gift – $60,000 = $440,000) is less than the amount of the gift. (No reporting date fair value was stipulated by the donor or required by law.) The loss is included with the fund in net assets with donor restrictions. The effect on net assets with donor restrictions of (1) creation of the endowment (an increase of $500,000 in net assets with donor restrictions), (2) the receipt and expenditure in the same period of income (an increase of $30,000 in net assets without donor restrictions), and (3) the loss on the principal of the endowment (a decrease of $60,000 in net assets with donor restrictions) is $440,000.

✘ **Answer (A) is incorrect.** The amount of $75,000 is the sum of the fair value decrease and the excess of spending over income.

✘ **Answer (B) is incorrect.** The amount of $15,000 is the excess of the amount spent over the income.

✘ **Answer (D) is incorrect.** The amount of $470,000 equals the contribution (perpetual endowment) minus the excess of the fair value decrease over the income.

18. A voluntary health and welfare entity received a $700,000 perpetual endowment during the year. The donor stipulated that the income and investment appreciation be used to maintain its senior center. The endowment fund reported a net investment appreciation of $80,000 and investment income of $50,000. The entity spent $60,000 to maintain its senior center during the year. What amount of change in net assets with donor restrictions should the entity report?

    A. $50,000

    B. $770,000

    C. $130,000

    D. $70,000

✔ **Answer (B) is correct.**
Required: The NFP's change in net assets after receiving a perpetual endowment with a purpose restriction on appreciation and income.
Discussion: The $700,000 contribution to a perpetual endowment is an increase in net assets with donor restrictions. Income or appreciation from donor-restricted perpetual endowments is an increase in donor-restricted support if the donor restricts its use. However, if the restriction expires in the period the income and appreciation are recognized, it may be reported as net assets without donor restrictions if the entity (1) has a similar policy for reporting contributions received, (2) reports consistently, and (3) discloses its accounting policy. If these criteria are met, the restriction on the income and gains is deemed to have expired to the extent it was expended during the year. Accordingly, the change in net assets with donor restrictions was $70,000 ($80,000 gain + $50,000 income – $60,000 spent). The total change in net assets with donor restrictions is $770,000 ($700,000 contribution to a permanent endowment + $70,000 unexpended gain and income).

✖ **Answer (A) is incorrect.** The amount of $50,000 is the VHWE's investment income.

✖ **Answer (C) is incorrect.** The amount of $130,000 is the sum of the appreciation and income.

✖ **Answer (D) is incorrect.** The amount of $70,000 equals the sum of the unexpended gain and income.

19. On December 31 of the current year, Communities Organized for Social Improvement (COSI), a not-for-profit entity, holds an investment in common stock of one publicly traded entity and an investment in debt securities of another. The not-for-profit entity holds the common stock as a long-term investment and has the intent and the ability to hold the debt securities until maturity.

	Investment in Common Stock	Investment in Debt Securities
Original cost	$50,000	$35,000
Amortized cost		28,000
Fair value	63,000	40,000

In the December 31 statement of financial position for the current year, COSI should value these investments as

	Investment in Common Stock	Investment in Debt Securities
A.	$50,000	$28,000
B.	$50,000	$40,000
C.	$63,000	$28,000
D.	$63,000	$40,000

✔ **Answer (D) is correct.**
Required: The amount to be recorded by an NFP for investments in equity and debt securities.
Discussion: GAAP applying to accounting for certain investments held by NFPs require them to measure investments in equity securities with readily determinable fair values and all investments in debt securities at fair value in the statement of financial position.

✖ **Answer (A) is incorrect.** The investment in common stock should not be measured at original cost. The investment in debt securities should not be measured at amortized cost.

✖ **Answer (B) is incorrect.** The investment in common stock should not be measured at original cost.

✖ **Answer (C) is incorrect.** The investment in debt securities should not be measured at amortized cost.

20. Lane Foundation, a voluntary health and welfare entity, received a perpetual endowment of $500,000 in Year 3 from Gant Enterprises. The endowment assets were invested in publicly traded securities, and Gant did not specify how gains and losses from dispositions of endowment assets were to be treated. **No** donor-imposed restrictions were placed on the use of dividends received and interest earned on fund resources. In Year 4, Lane realized gains of $50,000 on sales of fund investments and received total interest and dividends of $40,000 on fund securities. Lane's governing board has not appropriated any part of the investment return. If the Uniform Prudent Management of Institutional Funds Act (UPMIFA) applies, what amount of these capital gains, interest, and dividends increases net assets without donor restrictions?

A. $0
B. $40,000
C. $50,000
D. $90,000

✔ **Answer (A) is correct.**
Required: The amount of capital gains, interest, and dividends that increases net assets without donor restrictions.
Discussion: The donor did not specify how income (interest and dividends), gains, and losses were to be treated. Nevertheless, the NFP is subject to statute (UPMIFA) that extends a donor restriction (i.e., on the endowment held in perpetuity). It applies to use of the assets, including the return, until appropriation for expenditure by the governing board. Thus, without other language in the gift instrument, the assets in the fund (including the return) are net assets with donor restrictions until appropriation. An appropriation reduces net assets with donor restrictions if all time and purpose restrictions have been met. The result is a reclassification to net assets without donor restrictions. Without a contrary legal interpretation, appropriation occurs upon approval for expenditure. In the absence of an appropriation by the governing board, the NFP's capital gain, interest, and dividends therefore increase net assets with donor restrictions, not net assets without donor restrictions.

✘ **Answer (B) is incorrect.** The amount of $40,000 (interest and dividends) increases net assets with donor restrictions.

✘ **Answer (C) is incorrect.** The amount of $50,000 (capital gains) increases net assets with donor restrictions.

✘ **Answer (D) is incorrect.** The amount of $90,000 (capital gains, interest, and dividends) increases net assets with donor restrictions.

Go to Online Course

Access the **Gleim CPA Premium Review System** featuring our SmartAdapt technology from your Gleim Personal Classroom to continue your studies.

You will experience a personalized study environment with exam-emulating multiple-choice questions.

Appendix A
AICPA Uniform CPA Examination
FAR Blueprint with Gleim Cross-References

The AICPA has indicated that the Blueprints have several purposes, including to

✓ *Document the minimum level of knowledge and skills necessary for initial licensure.*

✓ *Assist candidates in preparing for the Exam by outlining the knowledge and skills that may be tested.*

✓ *Apprise educators about the knowledge and skills candidates will need to function as newly licensed CPAs.*

✓ *Guide the development of Exam questions.*

For your convenience, we have reproduced the AICPA's Financial Blueprint. We also have provided cross-references to the study units in this book that correspond to the Blueprint's coverage.

Area I – Financial Reporting (30–40%)

A. General-Purpose Financial Reporting: For-Profit Business Entities

Gleim Study Unit	Content group/topic	Remembering & Understanding	Application	Analysis	Evaluation	Representative Task
SU 1	1. Balance sheet/Statement of financial position		✓			Prepare a classified balance sheet from a trial balance and supporting documentation.
			✓			Adjust the balance sheet to correct identified errors.
				✓		Detect, investigate and correct discrepancies while agreeing the balance sheet amounts to supporting documentation, including the source data.
SU 1	2. Income statement/Statement of profit or loss		✓			Prepare a single-step or multi-step income statement (e.g., operating, nonoperating, discontinued operations) from a trial balance and supporting documentation.
			✓			Adjust the income statement to correct identified errors.
			✓			Calculate transaction gains or losses recognized from monetary transactions denominated in a foreign currency.
				✓		Detect, investigate and correct discrepancies while agreeing the income statement amounts to supporting documentation, including the source data.
SU 1	3. Statement of comprehensive income	✓				Recall the purpose, objectives and structure of the statement of comprehensive income.
		✓				Identify items classified as other comprehensive income.
SU 1	4. Statement of changes in equity		✓			Prepare a statement of changes in equity from a trial balance and supporting documentation.
			✓			Adjust the statement of changes in equity to correct identified errors.
				✓		Detect, investigate and correct discrepancies while agreeing the statement of changes in equity amounts to supporting documentation, including the source data.

Area I – Financial Reporting (30–40%) (continued)

Gleim Study Unit	Content group/topic	Remembering & Understanding	Application	Analysis	Evaluation	Representative Task
	A. General-Purpose Financial Reporting: For-Profit Business Entities (continued)					
SU 14	5. Statement of cash flows		✓			Prepare a statement of cash flow using the indirect method and required disclosures from supporting documentation.
			✓			Adjust a statement of cash flows to correct identified errors.
				✓		Detect, investigate and correct discrepancies while agreeing the statement of cash flows amounts to supporting documentation, including the source data.
				✓		Derive the impact of transactions on the statement of cash flows.
SU 13	6. Consolidated financial statements (including wholly-owned subsidiaries and noncontrolling interests)		✓			Prepare consolidated financial statements (adjustments, and/or eliminations) from supporting documentation.
			✓			Adjust consolidated financial statements to correct identified errors.
				✓		Detect, investigate and correct discrepancies identified while agreeing the consolidated financial statement amounts to supporting documentation, including the source data.
SU 3	7. Notes to financial statements		✓			Adjust the notes to the financial statements to correct identified errors and omissions.
				✓		Compare the notes to the financial statements to the financial statements and supporting documentation, including the source data, to identify inconsistencies and investigate those inconsistencies.
	B. General-Purpose Financial Reporting: Nongovernmental Not-for-Profit Entities					
SU 15	1. Statement of financial position	✓				Recall the purpose and objectives of the statement of financial position for a nongovernmental, not-for-profit entity.

Area I – Financial Reporting (30–40%) (continued)

Gleim Study Unit	Content group/topic	Skill				Representative Task
		Remembering & Understanding	Application	Analysis	Evaluation	
SU 15	**B. General-Purpose Financial Reporting: Nongovernmental Not-for-Profit Entities (continued)**					
	1. Statement of financial position (continued)		✓			Prepare a statement of financial position for a nongovernmental, not-for-profit entity from a trial balance and supporting documentation.
			✓			Adjust the statement of financial position for a nongovernmental, not-for-profit entity to correct identified errors.
	2. Statement of activities	✓				Recall the purpose and objectives of the statement of activities for a nongovernmental, not-for-profit entity.
			✓			Prepare a statement of activities for a nongovernmental, not-for-profit entity, including donor restrictions and releases from donor restrictions, from a trial balance and supporting documentation.
			✓			Adjust the statement of activities for a nongovernmental, not-for-profit entity to correct identified errors.
			✓			Report expenses by nature and function in either the statement of activities, the notes to the financial statements or a statement of functional expenses for a nongovernmental, not-for-profit entity.
	3. Statement of cash flows	✓				Recall the purpose and objectives of the statement of cash flows for a nongovernmental, not-for-profit entity.
			✓			Prepare a statement of cash flows and required disclosures using the direct method or indirect method for a nongovernmental, not-for-profit entity.
			✓			Adjust the statement of cash flows for a nongovernmental, not-for-profit entity to correct identified errors.
	4. Notes to the financial statements		✓			Adjust the notes to the financial statements to correct identified errors and omissions.

Area I – Financial Reporting (30–40%) (continued)

Gleim Study Unit	Content group/topic	Remembering & Understanding	Application	Analysis	Evaluation	Representative Task
SU 15	C. State and Local Government Concepts					
	1. Measurement focus and basis of accounting	✓				Recall the measurement focus and basis of accounting used by state and local governments for fund and government-wide financial reporting.
	2. Purpose of funds		✓			Determine the appropriate fund(s) that a state or local government should use to record its activities.
	D. Public Company Reporting Topics					
SU 3		✓				Recall the purpose of forms 10-Q, 10-K and 8-K that a U.S. registrant is required to file with the U.S. Securities and Exchange Commission under the Securities Exchange Act of 1934.
SU 3		✓				Identify the items of Form 10-Q (Part I Items 1 through 3) and Form 10-K (Part II Items 7, 7A and 8) filed with the U.S. Securities and Exchange Commission.
SU 2			✓			Calculate basic earnings per share and diluted earnings per share considering the impact of stock options, preferred stock, convertible preferred stock and/or convertible debt.
Subunit 1.5	E. Special Purpose Frameworks	✓				Recall appropriate financial statement titles to be used for the financial statements prepared under a special purpose framework.
			✓			Perform calculations to convert cash basis or modified cash basis financial statements to accrual basis financial statements.
			✓			Prepare financial statements using the cash basis or modified cash basis of accounting.
			✓			Prepare financial statements using the income tax basis of accounting.

Area I – Financial Reporting (30–40%) (continued)

Gleim Study Unit	Content group/topic	Skill				Representative Task
		Remembering & Understanding	Application	Analysis	Evaluation	
SU 13	F. Financial Statement Ratios and Performance Metrics	✓				Identify the appropriate financial statement ratio or performance metric to perform a specified type of analysis.
			✓			Calculate profitability ratios (e.g., gross profit margin, return on sales, return on assets, return on equity).
			✓			Calculate liquidity ratios (e.g., current, quick, accounts receivable turnover, inventory turnover, accounts payable turnover).
			✓			Calculate solvency ratios (e.g., debt-to-equity, total debt, times interest earned).
			✓			Calculate performance metrics (e.g., EBITDA, price-to-earnings, dividend payout, asset turnover).
			✓			Calculate variances between budget and actual results.

Area II – Select Balance Sheet Accounts (30–40%)

Gleim Study Unit	Content group/topic	Skill: Remembering & Understanding	Skill: Application	Skill: Analysis	Skill: Evaluation	Representative Task
SU 4	A. Cash and cash equivalents	✓				Calculate cash and cash equivalents balances to be reported in the financial statements.
			✓			Reconcile the cash balance per the bank statement to the general ledger.
			✓			Investigate unreconciled cash balances to determine whether an adjustment to the general ledger is necessary.
SU 5	B. Trade receivables	✓				Calculate trade receivables and allowances (e.g., credit losses, sales returns) and prepare journal entries.
			✓			Prepare any required journal entries to record the transfer of trade receivables (secured borrowings, factoring, assignment, pledging).
				✓		Prepare a rollforward of the trade receivables account balance using various sources of data and information.
				✓		Reconcile and investigate differences between the subledger and general ledger for trade receivables to determine whether an adjustment is necessary.
SU 6	C. Inventory	✓				Calculate the carrying amount of inventory and prepare journal entries using various costing methods.
			✓			Use the lower of cost and net realizable value or the lower of cost or market approach to calculate the carrying amount of inventory.
				✓		Prepare a rollforward of the inventory account balance using various sources of data and information.
				✓		Reconcile and investigate differences between the subledger and general ledger for inventory to determine whether an adjustment is necessary.

Area II – Select Balance Sheet Accounts (30–40%) (continued)

Gleim Study Unit	Content group/topic	Remembering & Understanding	Application	Analysis	Evaluation	Representative Task
				Skill		
SU7	D. Property, plant and equipment					
			✓			Calculate the gross and net property, plant and equipment balances and prepare journal entries.
			✓			Calculate gains or losses on the disposal of long-lived assets to be recognized in the financial statements.
			✓			Calculate impairment losses on long-lived assets to be recognized in the financial statements.
			✓			Determine whether an asset qualifies to be reported as held for sale in the financial statements.
			✓			Adjust the carrying amount of assets held for sale and calculate the loss to be recognized in the financial statements.
				✓		Prepare a rollforward of the property, plant and equipment account balance using various sources of data and information.
				✓		Reconcile and investigate differences between the subledger and general ledger for property, plant and equipment to determine whether an adjustment is necessary.
SU4	E. Investments					
	1. Financial assets at fair value					
		✓				Identify investments that are eligible or required to be reported at fair value in the financial statements.
			✓			Calculate the carrying amount of investments measured at fair value (excluding impairment).
			✓			Calculate investment income to be recognized in net income for investments measured at fair value and prepare journal entries.
			✓			Calculate impairment losses to be recognized on applicable investments reported at fair value in the financial statements.

Area II – Select Balance Sheet Accounts (30–40%) (continued)

Gleim Study Unit	Content group/topic	Skill — Remembering & Understanding	Skill — Application	Skill — Analysis	Skill — Evaluation	Representative Task
SU 4	E. Investments (continued)					
	2. Financial assets at amortized cost	✓				Identify investments that are eligible to be reported at amortized cost in the financial statements.
			✓			Calculate the carrying amount of investments measured at amortized cost and prepare journal entries (excluding impairment).
			✓			Calculate impairment losses to be recognized on investments reported at amortized cost in the financial statements.
	3. Equity method investments	✓				Identify when the equity method of accounting can be applied to an investment.
			✓			Calculate the carrying amount of equity method investments and prepare journal entries (excluding impairment).
SU 8	F. Intangible assets	✓				Identify the criteria for recognizing intangible assets in the statement of financial position and classify intangible assets as either finite-lived or indefinite-lived.
			✓			Calculate the carrying amount of finite-lived intangible assets reported in the financial statements (initial measurement, amortization and impairment) and prepare journal entries.
			✓			Calculate the carrying amount of purchased software and cloud computing arrangements reported in the financial statements (initial measurement, amortization and impairment) and prepare journal entries.

Area II – Select Balance Sheet Accounts (30–40%) (continued)

Gleim Study Unit	Content group/topic	Remembering & Understanding	Application	Analysis	Evaluation	Representative Task
SU9	G. Payables and accrued liabilities	✓				Recall the recognition and measurement requirements for asset retirement obligations.
			✓			Calculate the carrying amount of payables (e.g., accounts payable, dividends payable) and accrued liabilities (e.g., accrued wages, accrued vacation, accrued bonuses, self-insurance liabilities) and prepare journal entries.
			✓			Identify and calculate liabilities arising from exit or disposal activities (e.g., one-time termination benefits, severance arrangements) and determine the timing of recognition in the financial statements.
				✓		Reconcile and investigate differences between the subledger and general ledger for accounts payable and accrued liabilities to determine whether an adjustment is necessary.
SU10	H. Debt (financial liabilities)					
	1. Notes and bonds payable	✓				Recall the criteria to classify a change to a debt instrument as either a modification of terms or an extinguishment of debt.
		✓				Understand when a change to the terms of a debt instrument qualifies as a troubled debt restructuring.
			✓			Calculate the interest expense attributable to notes and bonds payable reported in the financial statements (e.g., discounts, premiums, debt issuance costs).
			✓			Calculate the carrying amount of notes and bonds payable and prepare journal entries.
	2. Debt covenant compliance		✓			Perform debt covenant calculations as stipulated in a debt agreement to ascertain compliance.
SU12	I. Equity		✓			Prepare journal entries to recognize equity transactions in the financial statements (e.g., equity issuance, stock dividends, stock splits, treasury stock, capital account activity in pass-through entities).

Area III – Select Transactions (25–35%)

Gleim Study Unit	Content group/topic	Skill					Representative Task
		Remembering & Understanding	Application	Analysis	Evaluation		
SU3	A. Accounting changes and error corrections		✓				Calculate a required adjustment to the financial statements due to an accounting change (change in accounting principle or change in accounting estimate) or error correction and determine whether it requires prospective or retrospective application.
				✓			Derive the impact to the financial statements and related note disclosures of an identified accounting change or an error correction.
SU11	B. Contingencies and commitments	✓					Recall the recognition and disclosure criteria used to identify commitments and contingencies.
			✓				Calculate amounts of contingencies and prepare journal entries.
				✓			Review supporting documentation to determine whether a commitment or contingency requires recognition and/or disclosure in the financial statements.
SU2	C. Revenue recognition	✓					Recall concepts of accounting for revenue using the five-step model.
		✓					Recall the recognition requirements associated with conditional and unconditional promises to give (pledges) for a nongovernmental, not-for-profit entity.
		✓					Identify transfers to a nongovernmental, not-for-profit entity acting as an agent or intermediary that are not recognized as contributions.
			✓				Determine the amount and timing of revenue to be recognized using the five-step model and prepare journal entries.
			✓				Determine the recognition and subsequent measurement requirements for contract costs and prepare journal entries.

Area III – Select Transactions (25–35%) (continued)

Gleim Study Unit	Content group/topic	Skill				Representative Task
		Remembering & Understanding	Application	Analysis	Evaluation	
	C. Revenue recognition (continued)					
SU 15			✓			Determine the amount and timing of revenue to be recognized by a nongovernmental, not-for-profit entity for contributed services received and prepare journal entries.
			✓			Calculate the amount to be recognized for contributions (financial assets and nonfinancial assets) to a nongovernmental, not-for-profit entity.
	D. Accounting for income taxes					
SU 9		✓				Recall the accounting treatment for uncertainty in income taxes.
		✓				Recall the criteria for recognizing or adjusting a valuation allowance for a deferred tax asset.
			✓			Calculate the income tax expense and current taxes payable/receivable.
			✓			Calculate deferred tax assets/liabilities resulting from book to tax basis differences (e.g., allowance for credit losses, inventory costing methods, property, plant and equipment).
			✓			Prepare journal entries to record the tax provision.
	E. Fair value measurements					
SU 3		✓				Identify the valuation techniques used to measure fair value.
		✓				Recall assumptions (e.g., highest and best use, market participant assumptions, unit of account) and approaches (cost, income, market) used to measure fair value.
			✓			Use the fair value hierarchy to determine the classification of a fair value measurement.

Area III – Select Transactions (25–35%) (continued)

Gleim Study Unit	Content group/topic	Skill					Representative Task
		Remembering & Understanding	Application	Analysis	Evaluation		
SU 11	F. Lessee accounting	✓					Recall the appropriate accounting treatment for residual value guarantees, purchase options and variable lease payments included in leasing arrangements for a lessee.
		✓					Identify the criteria for classifying a lease arrangement for a lessee.
			✓				Calculate the carrying amount of lease-related assets and liabilities and prepare journal entries that a lessee should record.
			✓				Calculate the lease costs that a lessee should recognize in the income statement.
SU 3	G. Subsequent events	✓					Identify a subsequent event and recall its appropriate accounting treatment.
			✓				Calculate required adjustments to financial statements and/or note disclosures based on identified subsequent events.
				✓			Derive the impact to the financial statements and required note disclosures due to identified subsequent events.

INDEX